Computation and Reasoning

PEARSON
Custom
Publishing

We work with leading authors to develop the strongest
educational materials bringing cutting-edge thinking and best
learning practice to a global market.

Under a range of well-known imprints, including Financial
Times/Prentice Hall, Addison Wesley and Longman, we craft
high quality print and electronic publications which help
readers to understand and apply their content, whether
studying or at work.

Pearson Custom Publishing enables our customers to access a
wide and expanding range of market-leading content from
world-renowned authors and develop their own tailor-made
book. You choose the content that meets your needs and
Pearson Custom Publishing produces a high-quality printed
book.

To find out more about custom publishing, visit
www.pearsoncustom.co.uk

A Pearson Custom Publication

Computation and Reasoning

Compiled from:

The Essence of Artificial Intelligence
by Alison Cawsey

Statistics for Economics, Accounting and Business Studies
Third Edition
by Mike Barrow

Artificial Intelligence: A Modern Approach
Second Edition
by Stuart Russell and Peter Norvig

Introduction to the Design & Analysis of Algorithms
by Anany Levitin

Prolog: Programming for Artificial Intelligence
Third Edition
by Ivan Bratko

Languages and Machines: An Introduction to the Theory of Computer Science
Third Edition
by Thomas A. Sudkamp

PEARSON
Custom
Publishing

Pearson Education Limited
Edinburgh Gate
Harlow
Essex CM20 2JE

And associated companies throughout the world

Visit us on the World Wide Web at:
www.pearsoned.co.uk

First published 2006

This Custom Book Edition © 2006 Published by Pearson Education Limited

Compiled from:

The Essence of Artificial Intelligence
by Alison Cawsey
ISBN 0 13 571779 5
Copyright © Prentice Hall Europe 1998

Statistics for Economics, Accounting and Business Studies
Third Edition
by Mike Barrow
ISBN 0 273 64661 3
Copyright © Longman Group UK Limited 1988, 1996
Copyright © Pearson Education Limited 2001

Artificial Intelligence: A Modern Approach
Second Edition
by Stuart Russell and Peter Norvig
ISBN 0 13 790395 2
Copyright © 2003, 1995 by Pearson Education, Inc., Upper Saddle River, New
Jersey, 07458

Introduction to the Design & Analysis of Algorithms
by Anany Levitin
ISBN 0 201 74395 7
Copyright © 2003 by Pearson Education, Inc.

Prolog: Programming for Artificial Intelligence
Third Edition
by Ivan Bratko
ISBN 0 201 40375 7
Copyright © Addison-Wesley Publishers Limited 1986, 1990
Copyright © by Pearson Education Limited 2001

Languages and Machines: An Introduction to the Theory of Computer Science
Third Edition
by Thomas A. Sudkamp
ISBN 0 321 32221 5
Copyright © 2006 by Pearson Education, Inc.

ISBN-10 1 84658 189 3
ISBN-13 978 1 84658 189 2

Printed and bound in Great Britain by Henry Ling Limited at the Dorset Press,
Dorchester, DT1 1HD

Contents

Preface

Computation and Reasoning aims to provide an introduction to the fundamentals of computation: representation of knowledge, algorithms and complexity, models of computation. Further material introduces artificial intelligence, applications of mathematics in computing and an alternative programming paradigm. The topics covered by this module form the foundations upon which much of computing is built. The module should be coherent as stand alone material, irrespective of background (though it will assume that students have some knowledge of mathematics and programming). Much of the module content will help to support and underpin programming and also provides background, motivation and the skills necessary for a number of second year modules.

This module covers a wide range of topics and a single textbook covering all of these in any depth does not exist. Therefore, chapters from a number of different sources have been selected and brought together in this volume, providing a text tailored precisely to the module. The selected chapters provide a complementary and more in depth view of the module content as given in the lecture slides and exercises. This volume can act as a reference book as well as a source of extra examples and exercises. To allow students some scope to read around the subject matter, the coverage of this book will at times go a little beyond that of the module.

The content of Computation and Reasoning can be grouped into four topics. The first topic is Artificial Intelligence (AI). The AI component will focus on knowledge representation (roughly, the formalisation of the organisation of information in order to reason about it) and the use of probability in reasoning (this will include some introductory material on probability). The second topic is Algorithms. Processes in computing are described as algorithms and coverage is given to reading, applying and specifying algorithms, as well as introducing algorithmic complexity. The third topic is logic programming using Prolog. Logic programming is an alternative programming paradigm and the material in this module will develop basic Prolog programming skills. The fourth topic is Theory of Computation. This component of the module will introduce theoretical models of computation and formal languages. These four topics are presented separately, however there strong links between them.

This volume is organised into four parts, corresponding to the four subject areas of the module. The lectures for the module will jump between topics in each of the four subject areas, rather than following this volume in order – students will be guided to relevant sections of this book each week.

In summary, the module covers a wide range of topics relating to computation and reasoning and forms a (mostly) theoretical background to further study. This textbook provides an ideal source of learning materials to enable students to get the most out of this module.

Jacob M. Howe

Computation and Reasoning

2

Topic 1

Artificial Intelligence

The following chapters are from
The Essence of Artificial Intelligence
by Alison Cawsey

Computation and Reasoning

4

CHAPTER 1

Introduction

Aims:	To introduce the basics of Artificial Intelligence (AI).
Objectives:	You should be able to:
	Describe typical AI tasks.
	Outline the techniques required to solve AI problems.
	Discuss the successes and prospects for AI.

1.1   What is Artificial Intelligence?

Artificial intelligence (AI) is a broad field, and means different things to different people. It is concerned with getting computers to do tasks that require human intelligence. However, having said that, there are many tasks which we might reasonably think require intelligence – such as complex arithmetic – which computers can do very easily. Conversely, there are many tasks that people do without even thinking – such as recognizing a face – which are extremely difficult to automate. AI is concerned with these difficult tasks, which require complex and sophisticated reasoning processes and knowledge.

People might want to automate human intelligence for a number of different reasons. One reason is simply to understand human intelligence better. For example, we may be able to test and refine theories of human intelligence by writing programs which attempt to simulate aspects of human behaviour. Another reason is simply so that we have smarter programs and machines. We may not care if the programs accurately simulate human reasoning, but by studying human reasoning we may develop useful techniques for solving difficult problems.

The ultimate smart machine is perhaps the human-like robot of science fiction stories, and the ultimate goal to create a genuinely intelligent machine. We can argue about whether such a goal is possible or even desirable. However, these arguments have little impact on the practical work of writing smarter programs and coming to a better understanding of our own reasoning.

AI is a fascinating subject to study as it overlaps with so many different sub-

Computation and Reasoning

5

ject areas, and not just computer science. These include psychology, philosophy and linguistics. These different subjects contribute in different ways to our understanding of how we can act and communicate intelligently and effectively. Insights from these (and other) areas help us to get computers to do tasks requiring intelligence, which in turn sheds further light on human intelligence, feeding back into these related disciplines.

As AI is normally taught as part of a computer science course, the emphasis of this book will be on computational techniques, with less emphasis on psychological modeling or philosophical issues. I'll just briefly touch on some of the widely discussed philosophical issues.

1.2   Typical AI Problems

We can get an insight into some of the different problem areas within AI by considering just what we, as humans, need to be able to do to act intelligently in the world. Consider a simple task like going shopping. We need to plan what to buy, how to get into town, and where to go; navigate round the crowded shops without bumping into things; interpret what we see; and communicate effectively with people we meet. All these are things we do almost automatically, yet require quite complex reasoning. These are sometimes referred to as *mundane* tasks and correspond to the following AI problems areas:

- Planning: The ability to decide on a good sequence of actions to achieve our goals.
- Vision: The ability to make sense of what we see.
- Robotics: The ability to move and act in the world, possibly responding to new perceptions.
- Natural Language: The ability to communicate with others in English or another human language.

Unlike the above, some tasks require specialized skills and training. These are sometimes referred to as *expert* tasks, and include the following:

- Medical diagnosis.
- Equipment repair.
- Computer configuration.
- Financial planning.

It can be especially useful to automate these tasks, as there may be a shortage of human experts. *Expert Systems* are concerned with the automation of these sorts of tasks.

AI is concerned with automating both mundane and expert tasks. Paradoxically, it turns out that it is the mundane tasks that are generally much the hardest to automate. We can program a computer to diagnose unusual diseases or configure a complex computer, but tasks which the average two-year-old can do without thinking (getting around a toy-strewn room, recognizing faces, communicating, etc.) are beyond, or at the limits of, current AI research.

1.3   AI Techniques

There are some basic techniques that are used throughout AI – these will be the focus of this book. These techniques are concerned with how we represent, manipulate and reason with knowledge in order to solve problems.

1.3.1   Knowledge Representation

To reason with knowledge, we first need to be able to represent it in a formal manner. One conclusion from artificial intelligence research is that solving even apparently simple problems usually requires lots of knowledge. Properly understanding a single sentence requires extensive knowledge both of language and of the context. Consider what someone from another planet would make of a typical newspaper headline, knowing nothing of Earth politics and practices, and armed only with an English dictionary! Properly understanding a visual scene similarly requires knowledge of the kinds of objects that might appear in the scene. Solving problems in a particular *domain*[1] generally requires knowledge of the objects in the domain and knowledge of how to reason in that domain – both these types of knowledge must be represented.

Knowledge must be represented efficiently, and in a meaningful way. Efficiency is important, as it would be impossible (or at least impractical) to represent explicitly every fact that you might ever need. There are just so many potentially useful facts, most of which you would never even think of. You have to be able to infer new facts from your existing knowledge, as and when needed, and capture general abstractions which represent general features of sets of objects in the world.

To represent knowledge in a meaningful way it is important that we can relate facts in a formal representation scheme to facts in the real world. The formal representation will be manipulated using a computer program, with new facts concluded, so it is vital that we can work out what these formally represented conclusions mean in terms of our initial problem. The *semantics* of a representation language provides a way of mapping between expressions in a formal language and the real world.

---

[1]See glossary for meaning of many of the italicized terms such as this.

1.3.2 Search

Another crucial general technique required when writing AI programs is *search*. Often there is no direct way to find a solution to some problem. However, you do know how to generate possibilities. For example, in solving a puzzle you might know all the possible moves, but not the sequence that would lead to a solution. When working out how to get somewhere you might know all the roads/buses/trains, just not the best route to get you to your destination quickly. Developing good ways to search through these possibilities for a good solution is therefore vital. *Brute force* techniques, where you generate and try out every possible solution, may work, but are often very inefficient, as there are just too many possibilities to try. *Heuristic* techniques are often better, where you only try the options which you think (based on your current best guess) are most likely to lead to a good solution.

1.4 Prospects and Progress

Twenty years ago there was much hype about what could be achieved in AI. Some people were interested in whether a fully intelligent conscious machine could be created; others were looking forward to a time when work became unnecessary as intelligent machines could take over. Because of the initial rash promises, media hype and high expectations, people now often look somewhat cynically at progress to date. Phrases like "I don't believe in AI" are common, much as people might say "I don't believe in God".

However, it would be rather optimistic to expect all the mysteries of human intelligence to be unravelled and automated in 30 years of research! People now are happy with more limited objectives, as outlined above: getting computers to do more restricted tasks, as intelligent assistants, and also developing programs that allow us to come to a better understanding of particular aspects of human reasoning. With these more limited objectives, progress has been fair: expert systems have been used successfully, if not that extensively; "intelligent" control systems are finding their way into everyday household objects such as washing machines; *intelligent agents* provide a currently popular programming metaphor; and limited speech understanding systems are becoming widespread. So, although there is no human-like robot in sight, many ideas and concepts from AI are permeating modern computer science and current technology.

Some of the most successful techniques for certain AI tasks turn out to be based on well-understood mathematical methods, rather than theories of human reasoning. For example, expert systems based on probability theory are sometimes more effective than those based on models of how doctors do their diagnosis, while the best current speech understanding systems are based on statistical methods rather than a deep understanding of human language. It is sometimes argued that the success of these more mathematical techniques indicates a failure of AI methodologies. However, another viewpoint could be that the successful use of well-understood mathematical methods, where appropriate, is an indication of the subject's increasing maturity.

1.5 Philosophical Issues

Many people, when talking about the prospects for AI, are interested in whether it is possible to fully automate human intelligence and develop a human-like robot, as presented in science fiction books and films/TV shows. Should we expect to meet Commander Data in the future? This is more a philosophical issue than an AI one, but we will briefly look at what has been said on the subject.

Artificial intelligence research makes the assumption that human intelligence can be reduced to the (complex) manipulation of symbols, and that it does not matter what medium is used to manipulate these symbols – it does not have to be a biological brain! This assumption does not go unchallenged. Some people argue that true intelligence can never be achieved by a computer, but requires some human property which cannot be simulated. There are endless philosophical debates on this issue, often surfacing in TV shows and popular books.

The most well-known contributions to the philosophical debate are Turing's "Turing test", and Searle's "Chinese room" (Turing, 1950; Searle, 1980). Very roughly, Turing considered how you would be able to conclude that a machine was really intelligent. He argued that the only reasonable way was to do a test. The test involves a human communicating remotely with a human and with a computer in other rooms, so that they are unable to see which they are communicating with. The first human can ask the other human/computer any questions they like, including very subjective questions like "What's your favourite colour?" or "What do you think about the privatization of British Rail?" If the computer answers so well that the first human can't tell which of the two others is human, then we say that the computer is intelligent.

Searle argued that just *behaving* intelligently wasn't enough. He tried to demonstrate this by suggesting a thought experiment, referred to as the "Chinese room". Imagine that you don't speak any Chinese, but that you have a huge rule book which allows you to look up Chinese sentences and tells you how to reply to them in Chinese. You don't understand Chinese, but can behave in an apparently intelligent way. He claimed that computers, even if they appeared intelligent, wouldn't really be, as they'd be just using something like the rule book of the Chinese room.

Many people go further than Searle, and claim that computers will never be able to even appear to be really intelligent (so will never pass the Turing test). However, programs have been written that have passed a limited version of the test, where the questioner can only ask questions in a very limited subject area. In the

The Loebner Prize Contest

Inspired by the idea of the Turing test, a competition was started in 1991 for the most human-like computer program, with prizes supplied by Hugh Loebner. In this contest judges can type in questions at a computer terminal, which are replied to either by a human or by one of the computer contestants. Judges rate the responses according to how human-like they appear, and the author of the best computer program receives a prize of $2000. If the program actually does better in its ratings than one of the humans then a grand prize of $100,000 is promised. Although no-one has claimed this prize, one program fooled five judges out of ten, who all thought that it was human.

The following is a fragment of the conversation with the winning entry in 1996.

PROGRAM: No worries! Hey! I didn't come here to be subjected to bad language!
                  How rude!
JUDGE02:   Sorry, sorry. Didn't mean to offend. So. How old are you?
PROGRAM: That's OK. Just don't do it again. Well, should my age really matter?
                  Just for the record I am 24. How old are you then?
JUDGE02:   I'm 21.
PROGRAM: If you are 21, it's your business, mate! Would you like to hear
                  a joke? Knock, knock.
JUDGE02:   Don't much care for knock-knock jokes, but go on..
PROGRAM: No, let me tell you one first. Knock, knock.
JUDGE02:   Who is there?
PROGRAM: Cindy
JUDGE02:   Cindy who
PROGRAM: Cindy next judge in, please!

Although the conversation is superficially human-like, the computer program which generated the responses was in fact fairly simple, and didn't really understand the judge's utterances. It just used various tricks, such as having a store of amusing replies and using key words in the question to select a good reply. In the following fragment the program does little more than repeat back what the judge has said (complete with spelling errors), yet it sounds fairly natural.

JUDGE05:   Hey did you like the funny nudes on the wallls of the room?
PROGRAM: Maybe I did like the funny nudes on the wallls of the room.
                  I'll never tell. Hehehe ;^)

These sorts of methods were first used in a program called Eliza, developed in the 1960s, which attempted to imitate a psychotherapist. These and related efforts show that is quite easy to produce a program that appears almost human-like, but that this doesn't mean that we have got very far in producing a really intelligent program.

Computation and Reasoning

10

Loebner contest, described in the box on page 6, a program that was written to discuss politics fooled 5 judges out of 10 into thinking that it was a human. Of course, why you should want to discuss politics with a computer when most humans have plenty to say on the matter is another question. Maybe we don't really want to build machines that behave just like humans, with all their weaknesses and peculiarities. Perhaps a more appropriate goal is to develop specialized intelligent assistants which can complement the skills and abilities of humans and compensate for their failings and limitations. This at least would provide practical benefit without challenging our status as uniquely intelligent beings.

1.6 Summary

- AI is concerned with attempts to produce programs to do tasks which require human intelligence.
- Reasons for doing AI include both the goal of understanding human intelligence better and the goal of developing useful, smarter computer programs.
- AI tasks involve both *mundane* tasks which people can do very easily (e.g., understanding language) and *expert* tasks which require specialist knowledge (e.g., medical diagnosis).
- AI has been successful in limited tasks, but it is unclear whether a really human-like intelligent robot is possible or desirable.

1.7 Further Reading

This book provides only a basic introduction to artificial intelligence. There are many excellent books which go into the subject in more depth. I would particularly recommend the following longer textbooks:

Rich, Elaine & Knight, Kevin, *Artificial Intelligence (second edition)*, McGraw-Hill, 1991. This book has become something of a standard, building on the success of an earlier edition by Rich. It provides a sound theoretical basis, though is limited in practical examples.

Luger, George, F. & Stubblefield, William, A. *Artificial Intelligence: Structures and Strategies for Complex Problem Solving*, Benjamin/Cummings Publishing, 1993. This book has a slightly more applied flavour, gives an introduction to and examples in the main AI programming languages, and has good introductions to expert systems and machine learning.

Ginsberg, Matt, *Essentials of Artificial Intelligence*, Morgan Kaufmann, 1993. Another somewhat theoretically oriented book, with an emphasis on logic-based approaches. A little more up to date than Rich & Knight, and enthusiastic in style.

Russell, Stuart & Norvig, Peter, *Artificial Intelligence: A Modern Approach*, Prentice Hall, 1995. A good, modern introduction with the theme of developing an intelligent agent. Extensive sections on reasoning and decision making under uncertainty, and on machine learning, as well as the standard topics.

Pratt, Ian, *Artificial Intelligence*, Macmillan, 1994. A good short book that focuses on *inference* as its central theme. It does not cover topics such as natural language, expert systems or vision, but provides a good formal coverage of some foundational topics. Some understanding of logic is assumed, but a brief appendix is included.

Two other good sources of clear articles by various experts in the field are the *Encyclopaedia of Artificial Intelligence* (Shapiro, 1992) and the *Handbook of Artificial Intelligence* (Barr & Feigenbaum, 1982), although the latter is now getting a little out of date.

1.8   Exercises

1. List the skills and knowledge required to successfully do the following everyday tasks: reading a book; crossing the road; ordering a pizza; arranging a trip to the cinema.

2. Suggest two expert tasks, other than those listed in the chapter, which you think might be suitable for an expert system. Describe why you think it would be useful to automate the tasks, and what knowledge you think the system would need.

3. Suppose you had to develop a program to suggest good road routes between two given cities. State what knowledge would be required for such a system, and suggest how it might be represented. Try to sketch an algorithm that could be used to find a good route.

4. If you were a judge in the Loebner contest what questions would you ask to determine whether you were communicating with a computer or a human? Suggest some possible answers that a program might give to tricky questions that would seem human-like, but which avoid answering the question.

Computation and Reasoning

CHAPTER 2

Knowledge Representation and Inference

Aims:	To introduce and compare the main knowledge representation methods used in AI: rules, frames and semantic networks, and logic.
Objectives:	You should be able to:
	Use the different knowledge representation methods to represent fragments of knowledge, given an English description of that knowledge.
	Show how new facts can be *inferred* in the different methods.
	Discuss the advantages and disadvantages of different methods.
Prerequisites:	It will help if you have had some introduction to predicate logic and to a programming language.

2.1 Introduction

One of the assumptions underlying most work in artificial intelligence is that intelligent behaviour can be achieved through the manipulation of *symbol structures* representing bits of knowledge. For example, we could use the symbol `red` to denote a particular colour, the symbol `alisons-car` to denote my car, and the symbol structure `red(alisons-car)` to denote the fact that my car is red. An AI program could use this fact and maybe draw conclusions about the personality of the owner[1].

In principle the symbol structures could be represented on any physical medium – we could develop a (very slow) intelligent machine made out of empty beer cans (plus something to move the beer cans around). However, computers make this

---

[1] In fact my car is a kind of greyish green. Draw your own conclusions.

9

much easier; we can represent facts using data structures, and write program code to reason with them.

Knowledge representation languages have been developed to make this easier. These are special notations that make it easy to represent and reason with complex knowledge about the world. Rather than represent everything using the basic data structures of a language like C++ or Pascal we can use these high-level formalisms. The knowledge representation languages may themselves be implemented using any programming language, so a fact like `red(alisons-car)` may end up being represented as a collection of conventional data structures, but the AI programmer doesn't have to know this, and doesn't have to re-invent basic methods for representing complex knowledge.

This chapter will introduce the main approaches to knowledge representation and some of the major issues involved. The later chapters will consider more how we can actually *use* that knowledge to intelligently solve problems.

2.1.1 Requirements for Knowledge Representation Languages

Before we talk about the different languages that are used, we should consider what we are looking for in a knowledge representation language. A knowledge representation language should allow you to represent *adequately complex facts* in a *clear and precise* yet *natural* way, and in a way that easily allows you to *deduce new facts* from your existing knowledge. These requirements are examined further below.

The ability to represent adequately complex facts is referred to as the *representational adequacy* of a language. Some facts are hard to represent. Or to be more precise, some facts are hard to represent in a way that allows those facts to be reasoned with. For example, a simple fact like "John believes no-one likes brussel sprouts" can be represented as a simple string, using the English language. But how can we reason with this representation, and conclude that John believes Mary doesn't like brussel sprouts? Some knowledge representation languages will allow complex facts like this to be represented in a structured way so they can be reasoned with. Some will only allow simpler facts to be represented. If the simpler language will do the job, it may be easier to use and more efficient to reason with.

The requirement for a clear and precise way of representing knowledge means that we need to have a *well-defined syntax and semantics*. We have to know what the allowable expressions are in the language, and what they mean. Let's suppose we've defined what each of the symbols that we use refers to (e.g., `red` refers to the property of being the colour red, `alisons-car` refers to my car). The syntax of the language defines the allowable structures of the language (e.g., `red(alisons-car)` is OK, `alisons-car(grey & green)` is not). The semantics of the language tells you what a particular structure means (e.g., `red(alisons-car)` means that my car is red, rather than being an instruction to spray my car red).

Computation and Reasoning

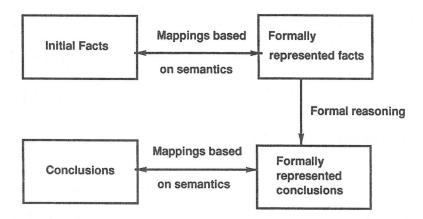

Figure 2.1 *Representations and Mappings.*

A precise semantics is particularly important given that an AI program will be reasoning with the knowledge and drawing new conclusions. To solve an AI problem we first have to work out how to represent the real world knowledge using our representation language. Then our AI program churns away, inferring new facts and coming to some conclusions. It is clearly vital that we can interpret what these conclusions mean, in terms of our real world problem. If the system concludes interest(alison, high) we'd need to know that this refers to my personality, not my mortgage. This is illustrated in Figure 2.1.

It is not enough to have a precise syntax and semantics if this means that your representation scheme is non-intuitive and difficult to use and understand. So we also require that our representation scheme is reasonably *natural*, capturing the structure of knowledge in an obvious way. Also, given a knowledge representation scheme, it is also important to choose *names* for symbols that are meaningful. We could represent the fact "if someone has a headache they should take aspirin" as, say, if(x,h,a), but something like IF symptom(X, headache) THEN medication(X, aspirin) is a good deal more readable and easier to deal with.

The final requirement, being able to deducing new facts from existing knowledge, is referred to as *inferential adequacy* . A knowledge representation language must support inference. We can't represent explicitly everything that the system might ever need to know – some things should be left implicit, to be deduced by the system as and when needed in problem solving. For example, suppose some system needs knowledge about a hundred students. All of them, let's say, attend lectures, take exams, and receive a grant. It would be wasteful to record these facts for each and every student. It is much better to just record that these facts are true for all students. When the system needs to know, say, whether a particular student Fred attends lectures it should be able to deduce this from the general statement and from the fact that Fred is a student. This obviously saves on a lot of unnecessary storage.

Some inferences may be a little more complex. Maybe we want to know whether Fred is prime minister of Great Britain. If we know that only one person can be prime minister at once, and that Tony Blair is currently prime minister, then we should be able to deduce that therefore Fred can't be. We don't need to record this fact explicitly.

Making arbitrary deductions from existing knowledge is a complex process. The more sophisticated the deductions required, the longer they are likely to take. There is a tradeoff between *inferential adequacy* (what we can infer) and *inferential efficiency* (how quickly we can infer it), so we may choose to have a language where simple inferences can be made quickly, although complex ones are not possible.

We can summarize the general requirements for a knowledge representation language as follows:

Representational Adequacy: It should allow you to represent all the knowledge that you need to reason with.
Inferential Adequacy: It should allow new knowledge to be inferred from a basic set of facts.
Inferential Efficiency: Inferences should be made efficiently.
Clear Syntax and Semantics: We should know what the allowable expressions of the language are and what they mean.
Naturalness: The language should be reasonably natural and easy to use.

However, no one representation language satisfies all these requirements perfectly. In practice the choice of language depends on the reasoning task (just as the choice of a programming language depends on the problem). Given a particular task it will generally be necessary to choose an appropriate language given the particular requirements of the application.

In the rest of this chapter the main approaches are outlined, along with their advantages and disadvantages.

2.1.2 Introducing the Main Approaches

Broadly speaking, there are three main approaches to knowledge representation in AI. The most important is arguably the use of logic to represent things. For example, we could use predicate logic to represent the sentence "All birds fly" as $\forall X \, (bird(X) \rightarrow flies(X))$.

A logic, almost by definition, has a well-defined syntax and semantics and is concerned with truth preserving inference, so seems like a good candidate as a method to represent and reason with knowledge. However, using logic to represent things has problems. First, it may not be very efficient – if we just want a very restricted class of inferences, we may not want the full power of a logic-based theorem prover, for example. Second, representing some common-sense things in a logic can be very hard. Representing and reasoning with anything that involves time, beliefs or uncertainty is hard in predicate logic. There are special logics, such as *temporal* and *modal* logics, which allow such things to be represented, but reasoning in such logics may not be efficient.

An alternative is to use simpler and more natural representation schemes, specifying the algorithms for manipulating the knowledge, but not necessarily giving a formal account of the semantics of the language. *Frames* and *semantic networks* provide a natural way of representing factual knowledge about classes of object and their properties. Knowledge is represented as a collection of objects and relations, the most important relations being the *subclass* and *instance* relations. The subclass relation says (as you might expect) that one class is a subclass of another, while the instance relation says that some individual belongs to some class. So Fred Bloggs is an *instance* of the class representing AI students, while the class of AI students is a *subclass* of the class of students in general[2]. We can then define property *inheritance*, so that, by *default*, Fred inherits all the typical attributes of AI students, and AI students inherit typical attributes of students in general. We'll go into this in much more detail below.

Another important method for representing knowledge is the use of IF–THEN or *condition-action* rules, within a *rule-based system*[3]. A condition-action rule specifies what to do under what circumstances. For example, we could have a rule IF fire THEN shout-help. A rule-based language will provide algorithms for reasoning with such rules, so that new conclusions can be drawn in a controlled manner. Although condition-action rules may be similar to logical implications (e.g., $fire \rightarrow shout\_help$), the emphasis of rule-based representation languages tends to be different, with more emphasis on what you do with the rules and less on what they mean – we say that *procedural* aspects are emphasized rather than *declarative* ones. Condition-action rules are widely used in expert systems, providing a fairly flexible way of representing expert knowledge and efficient techniques for reasoning with this knowledge.

The rest of this chapter describes these different knowledge representation languages in more detail. We'll start with frames and semantic networks, as these are fairly easy to understand. Then we'll talk about logic, and then rule-based systems. The discussion of rules should lead naturally into the next chapter on expert systems.

---

[2]The terms *subclass* and *instance* are not the only terms used for these relations, so don't be put off if other terms (such as *isa* and *member*) are used in another text.

[3]The terms *production rule* and *production system* are often used, largely for historical reasons.

2.2   Semantic Networks and Frames

Semantic networks and frames provide a simple and intuitive way of representing facts about objects. Both schemes allow you to represent *classes* (or categories) of objects and relations between objects, and draw simple inferences based on this knowledge. There is little difference in practice between semantic networks and frames, just different notations used to represent the knowledge. We'll therefore briefly introduce the two approaches, and then talk about general issues common to them both.

2.2.1   Semantic Networks

Semantic networks were originally developed in the early 1960s to represent the meaning of English words. They have since been used more widely for representing knowledge.

In a semantic network knowledge is represented as a graph[4], where the nodes in the graph represent concepts, and the links represent relations between concepts. The most important relations between concepts are *subclass* relations between classes, and *instance* relations between particular object instances and their parent class. However, any other relations are allowed, such as *has-part*, *colour* etc, allowing properties of objects (and categories of objects) to be represented. So, to represent some knowledge about animals (as AI people so often do) we might have the network in Figure 2.2.

This network represents the fact that mammals and reptiles are animals, that mammals have heads, an elephant is a large grey mammal, Clyde and Nellie are both elephants, and that Nellie likes apples. The subclass relations define a *class hierarchy* (in this case very simple).

The subclass and instance relations may be used to derive new information which is not explicitly represented. We should be able to conclude that Clyde and Nellie both have a head, and are large and grey. They *inherit* properties from their parent classes. Semantic networks normally allow efficient inheritance-based inferences using special purpose algorithms.

When semantic networks became popular in the 1970s there was much discussion about what the nodes and relations really meant. People were using them in subtly different ways, which led to much confusion. For example, a node such as *elephant* might be used to represent the class of all elephants or just a typical elephant. Saying that an elephant *has_part* head could mean that every elephant has some particular head, that every elephant has some kind of head, that some elephant has some kind of head, that a typical elephant has some kind of head, and so on. In this case it is the second of these which seems sensible, but for representing other things other meanings may seem appropriate.

However, if a relation can mean one thing when representing facts about ele-

---

[4]If you are not familiar with graphs in computer science, see Section 4.2.1.

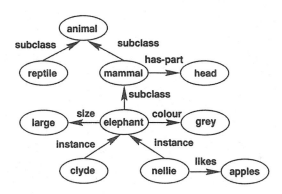

Figure 2.2 *A Simple Semantic Network.*

phants, and another thing when representing facts about, say, diseases, then chaos will ensue. No one will be quite sure what the representation means, and it will be unclear what *inferences* can be drawn from the knowledge if we don't even know what expressions in the language mean.

It is now recognized that it is important to state, as precisely as possible, the *semantics* of a representation language, so we know exactly what expressions mean and which inferences are sound. One simple way to describe precisely the meaning of nodes and links in a semantic network is in terms of set theory. We interpret a class node as denoting a set of objects. So, an *elephant* node denotes the set of all elephants. Nodes such as *Clyde* and *Nellie* denote individuals. So the *instance* relationship can be defined in terms of set membership (Nellie is a member of the set of all elephants), while the *subclass* relation can be defined in terms of a subset relation – the set of all elephants is a subset of the set of all mammals. Saying that elephants are grey means (in this simple model) that every individual in the set of elephants is grey (so Clyde can't be pink).

Semantic networks are still used in AI today. Example systems are SNePS and conceptual graphs, which both provide a precise semantics for the nodes and links in the network. Conceptual graphs are described in (Luger & Stubblefield, 1993) (ch.9.3).

Semantic networks allow us to represent knowledge about objects and relations between objects in a simple and fairly intuitive way. The conventional graphical notation allows us to quickly see how the knowledge is organized. The sort of inferences that are normally supported is very restricted – just inheritance of properties – but this means that it is very easy to work out what is going on. So, while the notation may be ill suited where very complex knowledge representation and reasoning is required, it may be a good choice for certain problems.

Computation and Reasoning

19

2.2.2 Frames

Frames are a variant of semantic networks, and a popular way to represent facts in an expert system. All the information relevant to a particular concept is stored in a single complex entity (called a frame). Superficially, frames look pretty much like record (or struct) data structures. However frames, at the very least, support inheritance.

Three simple frames representing some of our knowledge about elephants are given in Figure 2.3. `Mammal`, `Elephant` and `Nellie` are *objects* in the frame system. Properties, such as `colour` and `size`, are sometimes referred to as *slots*, and `grey`, `large` etc. as *slot values*. We can infer, using inheritance, that Nellie is large, grey and has a head, as well as liking apples.

Some of the terminology and ideas used for frame systems has since been adopted for object oriented programming, which also deals with classes and inheritance. Object oriented programming languages were influenced by frame systems, but they tend to be used for slightly different things – to write programs to manipulate specific "objects" in well-defined ways, rather than to represent knowledge about conceptual categories.

It is straightforward to translate between semantic network and frame based representations. Nodes in the semantic network become objects in the frame system, links become slots, and the node the other end of the link becomes the slot value. The rest of this section will use examples based on frames, but the same points could equally be made about semantic networks. The choice between the two is largely a matter of preference between the way the information is visualized.

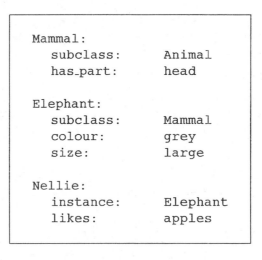

Figure 2.3 *Elephant Frames.*

Computation and Reasoning

2.2.3 Defaults and Multiple Inheritance

In the examples so far objects (such as Nellie) inherit *all* the properties of their parent class. So Nellie must be grey and large. However, it is useful to be able to describe properties that are only *typical* of a class, and then state that a particular instance of that class is an exception to the rule. Most frame systems allow you to state which properties (ie, slots) are just typical of a class, with exceptions allowed, and which must be true of all instances. The value of a property that is only typical of a class is referred to as a *default* value, and can be *overridden* by giving a different value for an instance or subclass.

The example in Figure 2.4 illustrates this for an extension of our elephant example. Slots preceded by an asterisk (*) hold default values that may be overridden. So, all mammals are warm-blooded but they are only typically furry, and indeed elephants aren't furry. Elephants all have trunks, but are only typically unfurry, grey and large. Clyde is an exception to the rule that elephants are normally grey. He's pink. Nellie is an exception to the rule that elephants are normally large. She's small.

Now, objects and classes inherit the default (typical) properties of their par-

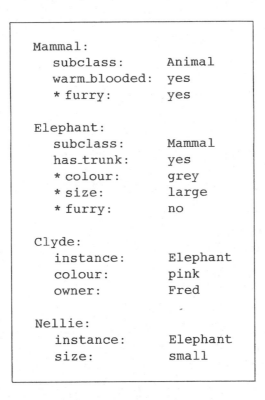

```
Mammal:
    subclass:       Animal
    warm_blooded:   yes
    * furry:        yes

Elephant:
    subclass:       Mammal
    has_trunk:      yes
    * colour:       grey
    * size:         large
    * furry:        no

Clyde:
    instance:       Elephant
    colour:         pink
    owner:          Fred

Nellie:
    instance:       Elephant
    size:           small
```

Figure 2.4 *Elephant Frames with Defaults.*

Computation and Reasoning

21

ent classes UNLESS they have an individual property value that conflicts with the inherited one. Given the above set of frames we can infer that Nellie is warm-blooded, unfurry, has a trunk, grey and small. Clyde is warm-blooded, unfurry, has a trunk, is pink, large and owned by Fred.

Inheritance is simple where each object and class has a single parent class. However, many systems allow *multiple inheritance*, which means that more than one parent class is allowed, and an object or class may inherit from all its parents. This makes inheritance somewhat more complex. Consider the example in Figure 2.5, where Clyde is both an elephant and a circus animal. We can reasonably conclude that Clyde is large and has a trunk (as he's an elephant, and there is no more specific information to contradict this), and that his skills include balancing on a ball (as he's a circus animal). But what can we conclude about his habitat? As he's an elephant it should be the jungle, but as he's a circus animal it should be a tent. A frame system must have some mechanism to decide which value to inherit where there are conflicts like this. One way to do this is to require that the author of the frame system specifies a precedence order for parent classes. For example, by putting `Circus-Animal` first, this may indicate that where there's a conflict the values should be taken from `Circus-Animal` rather than from `Elephant`.

Unfortunately this isn't always sufficient. Suppose there was a slot saying that circus animals were typically small. We now would like to inherit the `size` property from `Elephant`, but the `habitat` property from `Circus-animal`. There is no easy way to specify this, and it would normally require that an extra class

```
Elephant:
    subclass:      Mammal
    has_trunk:     yes
    * colour:      grey
    * size:        large
    * habitat:     jungle

Circus-Animal:
    subclass:      Animal
    habitat:       tent
    skills:        balancing-on-ball

Clyde:
    instance:      Circus-Animal Elephant
    colour:        pink
    owner:         Fred
```

Figure 2.5 *Multiple Inheritance.*

`Circus-Elephant` was created, explicitly overriding the `size` and `habitat` properties with the desired values.

2.2.4 Slots and Procedures

In general, both slot values and slots themselves may themselves be frames. In Figure 2.5 Clyde has owner Fred. Fred is the value for the `owner` slot, but might be represented using another frame, so we can describe Fred's properties.

Allowing slots themselves to be frames means that we can specify various attributes of a slot. For example, we could specify that the slot `owner` could only take values of class `person`, has an inverse slot `owns`, and can take `multiple values` (as more than one person can jointly own something).

Many systems allow slots to include *procedures*. The term *procedural attachment* is used for this. An arbitrary piece of program code may be placed in a slot, which is run whenever the value for that slot is needed. We may also allow pieces of code that are run whenever a value is added, perhaps to do consistency checks or to propagate results to other slots.

With all these features, plus multiple inheritance, it may be hard to predict exactly what will be inferred about a given object just by looking at the set of frames. You'd have to know something about how the underlying frame system is implemented, such as the order in which things are tried when attempting to determine values of slots. We say that the system has a *procedural* rather than a *declarative* semantics, as the precise meaning of a set of frames depends on how the inferences are done. This is theoretically undesirable, but for practical systems it may be worth sacrificing a clean semantics for additional features and flexibility.

2.2.5 Implementing a Simple Frame System

A basic frame system, that allows default values but not multiple inheritance, can be implemented very simply in any programming language. The frames themselves can be represented using any suitable data structures – we'll just assume that a function `slot-value` has been defined that returns the value for a particular object and attribute if there is a value, or something to indicate that there is no such value. `Slot-value` ignores inheritance.

What we need to define now is a function that will determine what can be inferred by inheritance. A basic algorithm which returns the value for a particular attribute, using inheritance is as follows:

To find `value(O, A)`

- If `slot-value(O, A)` returns a value V, return V.
- Otherwise, if `slot-value(O, subclass)` or `slot-value(O, instance)` returns a value C, find `value(C, A)` and return this value.
- Otherwise, fail.

Computation and Reasoning

To see how this works, consider again Figure 2.4. If we wanted to find out Nellie's colour (i.e., `value(Nellie, colour)`) the algorithm would first try `slot-value(Nellie, colour)`. As no specific value is given for Nellie's colour, `slot-value` would indicate that there is no such value, so we try `slot-value(Nellie, subclass)` and `slot-value(Nellie, instance)`. The latter could return `Elephant`, so we call the function recursively and try to find `value(Elephant, colour)`. Now, this time `slot-value(Elephant, colour)` returns `grey`, so this value is returned by `value(Elephant, colour)` and hence also by `value(Nellie, colour)`. Nellie is therefore grey.

2.2.6   Representational Adequacy

Semantic networks and frames provide a fairly simple and clear way of representing properties of objects and categories of objects. A basic type of inference is defined, whereby objects may inherit properties of parent objects.

There are many things that cannot easily be represented using frames. For example, it is hard to express *negation* (i.e., the fact that something is NOT true), *disjunction* (i.e., the fact that either one thing OR another is true), or certain types of *quantification* (i.e., the fact that something is true for ALL or SOME of a set of objects). If these things are needed then using a logic, described next, may be more appropriate. However, frame and semantic network systems still have their place where relatively simple kinds of knowledge need to be represented.

2.3   Predicate Logic

The most important knowledge representation language is arguably predicate logic (or, strictly, first-order predicate logic). Predicate logic allows us to represent fairly complex facts about the world, and to derive new facts in a way that guarantees that, if the initial facts were true, then so are the conclusions. It is a well-understood formal language, with well-defined syntax, semantics and rules of inference. There isn't room in this section to give a full introduction to predicate logic. If you aren't already familiar with the basics you may want to consult an introductory logic text, or introductions in longer AI texts, such as (Ginsberg, 1993) (ch.6); (Russell & Norvig, 1995) (ch.7); (Luger & Stubblefield, 1993) (ch.2). However, a brief summary is given below, which should serve to remind people who have already met predicate logic of the basics, and give those who haven't a flavour of what is involved.

A logic is a formal system which may be described in terms of its *syntax* (what the allowable expressions are), its *semantics* (what they mean) and its *proof theory* (how can we draw new conclusions given some statements in the logic). These three aspects will be briefly discussed first for propositional logic (which is much simpler, but allows the key ideas to be introduced), and then for predicate logic.

2.3.1 Review of Propositional Logic

Syntax

In propositional logic symbols are used to represent facts about the world. For example, the fact "Alison likes cakes" could be represented by the symbol P (or indeed any other symbol, such as the more meaningful $AlisonLikesCakes$). Simple facts like this are referred to as *atomic propositions*. We can build up more complex statements (or *sentences*) by combining atomic propositions with the *logical connectives* $\land$ (and) $\lor$ (or) $\neg$ (not) $\rightarrow$ (implication) and $\leftrightarrow$ (equivalence). So if we had the proposition Q representing the fact "Alison eats cakes" we could have the facts:

$P \lor Q$: "Alison likes cakes or Alison eats cakes"
$P \land Q$: "Alison likes cakes and Alison eats cakes"
$\neg Q$: "Alison doesn't eat cakes"
$P \rightarrow Q$: "If Alison likes cakes then Alison eats cakes".
$P \leftrightarrow Q$: "If Alison likes cakes then Alison eats cakes, and vice versa".

In general, if X and Y are sentences in propositional logic, then so are $X \land Y$, $X \lor Y$, $\neg X$, $X \rightarrow Y$, and $X \leftrightarrow Y$. This defines the *syntax* of the logic. The following are all valid sentences in propositional logic:

P $\lor \neg$Q
P $\land$ (P $\rightarrow$ Q)
(Q $\lor \neg$ R) $\rightarrow$ P

Semantics

The *semantics* of propositional logic allows us to state precisely what statements like those above mean. It is defined in terms of what is true in the world. For example, if we know whether P, Q and R are true, the semantics of the logic will tell you whether sentences such as $(P \lor Q) \land R$ are true. (Note that the parentheses are important: $(P \lor Q) \land R$ is not the same as $P \lor (Q \land R)$.)

We can determine the truth or falsity (or *truth value*) of sentences like these using *truth tables* which define the truth values of sentences with logical connectives in terms of the truth values of their component sentences. The truth tables provide a simple *semantics* for these logical connectives (i.e., define precisely what the logical connectives mean). As sentences can only be true or false, truth tables are very simple, for example:

$X\,Y$	$X \vee Y$
T T	T
T F	T
F T	T
F F	F

From the table above we can see, for example, that if X is true and Y is false then $X \vee Y$ is true. Now, suppose we have an assertion *raining* $\vee$ *sunny* – i.e., we state that the truth value of the sentence *raining* $\vee$ *sunny* is T. By looking at this truth table we can see that this must mean that either it's raining, or it's sunny, or it's both raining and sunny. So we can work backwards from the truth value of a sentence to find the possible truth values of the constituent propositions – this gives us the meaning of the sentence. Without a precise statement of the semantics of $\vee$ (and the other logical connectives) then the meaning of statements in the logic might be ambiguous. For example, we might decide that *raining* $\vee$ *sunny* means that it is either one or the other, but not both.

Proof Theory

In order to infer new facts in a logic we need to apply *inference rules*. The semantics of the logic will define which inference rules are universally *valid*. This gives us the *proof theory* of the logic. One useful inference rule is the following (called *modus ponens*):

$$\frac{A, A \rightarrow B}{B}$$

This rule just says that if $A \rightarrow B$ is true, and A is true, then B is necessarily true. We could prove that this rule is valid using truth tables. This rule is a *sound* rule of inference for the logic. Given the semantics of the logic, if the premises are true then the conclusions are guaranteed true.

There are many other sound rules of inference. A particularly important one is *resolution*. A simple form of the resolution rule of inference is the following:

$$\frac{A \vee B, \neg B \vee C}{A \vee C}$$

To see how this could be applied, suppose we know that the following two sentences are true:

$$sunny \vee raining$$
$$\neg raining \vee carryumbrella$$

We can use the rule of inference, given the first two sentences, to conclude *sunny* $\vee$ *carryumbrella*.

If we want to *prove* whether or not a proposition is true, given some sentences that we know are true, the resolution rule of inference is sufficient. First we have

Computation and Reasoning

to get all the sentences into a standardized or *normal form* that involves sentences like those above. Then there is a procedure called proof by *refutation* that can be applied. The general idea is that we try assuming that the proposition in question is false, and see if that leads to a contradiction.

2.3.2 Predicate Logic

Syntax

The trouble with propositional logic is that it is not possible to write general statements in it, such as "Alison eats everything that she likes". We'd have to have lots of rules, for every different thing that Alison liked. Predicate logic makes such general statements possible.

Sentences in predicate logic are built up from *atomic sentences*. Rather than dealing with undivisible propositions, predicate logic expresses basic facts in terms of a predicate name and some arguments. So, for "Alison likes chocolate" we could have a predicate name *likes*, arguments *alison* and *chocolate* to give the sentence *likes(alison, chocolate)*. This proves much more flexible than just having an indivisible proposition P standing for the whole thing, as we can "get at" the entities *alison*, and *chocolate*.

In general the arguments in an atomic sentence may be any *term*. Terms may be:

Constant symbols such as *alison*.

Variable symbols such as X. For consistency with Prolog we'll use capital letters to denote variables, and avoid capitals for constant symbols.

Function expressions such as *father(alison)*. Function expressions consist of a functor followed by a number of arguments, which can be arbitrary terms.

So, atomic sentences in predicate logic include the following:

- *friends(alison, richard)*
- *friends(father(fred), father(joe))*
- *likes(X, richard)*

Sentences in predicate logic are constructed (much as in propositional logic) by combining atomic sentences with logical connectives, so the following are all sentences in predicate calculus:

- *friends(alison, richard)* $\rightarrow$ *likes(alison, richard)*
- *likes(alison, richard)* $\vee$ *likes(alison, chocolate)*
- *(likes(alison, richard)* $\vee$ *likes(alison, chocolate))* $\wedge$ $\neg$*likes(alison, chocolate)*

Sentences can also be formed using *quantifiers* to indicate how any variables in the sentence are to be treated. The two quantifiers in predicate logic are ∀ and ∃. ∀ is read as "for all", and is used to state that something is true for every object, and ∃ is read as "there exists", and is used to state that something is true for at least one object. The following are sentences involving quantifiers:

- $\forall X(likes(alison, X) \rightarrow eats(alison, X))$ i.e., Alison eats everything that she likes.
- $\exists X(bird(X) \land \neg flies(X))$ i.e., there exists some bird that doesn't fly.
- $\forall X(person(X) \rightarrow \exists Y loves(X, Y))$ i.e., every person has something that they love.

A sentence should have all its variables quantified. So, strictly, an expression like $\forall X loves(X, Y)$, although a well-formed *formula* of predicate logic, is not a sentence, as the variable Y isn't quantified. Formulae with all their variables quantified are also called *closed formulae*.

Semantics

The semantics of predicate logic is defined (as in propositional logic) in terms of the truth values of sentences. As in propositional logic, we can use truth tables to find the truth value of sentences involving logical connectives from the truth values of each part of the sentence.

However, we also need to deal with predicates, arguments and quantifiers. Formally the meaning of a predicate such as *likes* may be defined in terms of the set of all pairs of people (in some *domain* of interest) that like each other. However, for our purposes we can just assume that, somehow, a truth value can be assigned to a sentence such as $likes(alison, chocolate)$.

The meaning of ∀ can be defined in terms of whether some sentence is true for ALL objects in the domain of interest. $\forall X S$ means that for every object X in the domain, S is true. For example, suppose we are only interested in Fred, Jim and Joe. We could work out whether the sentence $\forall X likes(X, chocolate)$ is true by checking, whether $likes(Fred, chocolate)$, $likes(Jim, chocolate)$ and $likes(Joe, chocolate)$ are all true.

The meaning of ∃ can be defined similarly, in terms of whether some sentence is true for at least one of the objects in the domain of interest. So, if Fred likes chocolate but the others don't, $\exists X likes(X, chocolate)$ is true, but $\forall X likes(X, chocolate)$ is false. This only gives a flavour of how we can give a semantics to expressions in predicate logic. The details are best left to logicians. The important thing is that everything is very precisely defined, so if we use predicate logic we should know exactly where we are and therefore what inferences are valid.

Proof Theory

Inference rules (and proof procedures) in predicate logic are similar to those for propositional logic. Modus Ponens and Resolution still apply, but have to be

Logic Programming

Logic programming languages view a computer program as a set of statements in logic. Rather than running the program, as you might do in a procedural language, you can give the system statements to try to prove, given the statements in the program. The most widely used logic programming language is Prolog.

Prolog is based on predicate logic. Each statement in the program corresponds to a sentence in predicate logic. However, the notations used are rather different. The following shows a tiny Prolog program and the corresponding statements in logic. Note that all the capitalized arguments in the Prolog have universal quantifiers ($\forall$ signs) in the logic version, and a backwards version of the implication sign, written : - is used in Prolog.

```
father(jim, fred).
father(joe, jim).
grandfather(X, Y) :-
    father(X, Z),
    father(Z, Y).
```

$father(jim, fred)$
$father(joe, jim)$
$\forall XYZ((father(X, Z) \land father(Z, Y)) \rightarrow grandfather(X, Y))$

Given the above program we could ask Prolog to prove that `grandfather(joe, fred)` was true. It should answer `yes`. Prolog proves statements using a variant of the resolution procedure outlined in Section 2.3.2. To make things efficient, and to allow a simple and *goal directed* proof procedure, Prolog does not allow arbitrary statements in predicate logic to be represented, but only *horn* clauses where there is just one fact on the right-hand side of an implication sign.

---

modified to deal with expressions which involve variables and quantifiers. For example, we would like to be able to use the facts $\forall X(man(X) \rightarrow mortal(X))$ and $man(socrates)$ and conclude $mortal(socrates)$. To do this we can use modus ponens, but allow sentences to be *matched* with other sentences. For example, $man(X)$ can be matched with $man(socrates)$ with $X = socrates$.

The resolution rule of inference can similarly be modified to work for predicate logic. Proof by refutation can then be applied if we want to try to prove that something is true, given some sentences in the logic. This gives us a *sound* proof procedure – if we prove something using it we can be sure it is a valid conclusion. It is also *complete*, in the sense that it will eventually find a proof, if one exists.

Computation and Reasoning

29

2.3.3 Knowledge Representation using Predicate Logic

Representing Facts in Logic

Your average AI programmer/researcher may not need to know the details of predicate logic semantics or proof theory, but will probably need to know how to represent things in predicate logic, and what expressions in predicate logic mean. Formally we've already gone through what expressions mean, but it may make more sense to give a number of examples, and to outline how you get from a statement expressed in English to a statement in predicate logic.

Statements like "Alison likes chocolate" or "John loves Mary" are easy to express. You just use the verb as the predicate name and the nouns as the arguments, to get $likes(alison, chocolate)$ and $loves(john, mary)$. A statement describing a property of an individual, such as "Mary is tall", can also be easily be expressed, but the convention here is to make this into a one-argument predicate, such as $tall(mary)$. If Mary is both tall and beautiful, the logical connective $\wedge$ must be used: $tall(mary) \wedge beautiful(mary)$. Similarly if Alison likes both chocolate and cream: $likes(alison, chocolate) \wedge likes(alison, cream)$. Note that logical connectives cannot be used within an argument of a predicate, so $likes(alison, chocolate \wedge cream)$ is not correct.

Statements of the form "If X then Y" can be translated into $X \rightarrow Y$. So, "If Alison is hungry then she eats chocolate" could be: $hungry(alison) \rightarrow eats(alison, chocolate)$. For statements involving "or" then the connective $\vee$ may be used: $eats(alison, chocolate) \vee eats(alison, biscuits)$. And to assert that something is not true, $\neg$ is used: $\neg likes(alison, brusselsprouts)$.

For more general rules the quantifier $\forall$ may be used. A common form is $\forall X p(X) \rightarrow q(X)$, where p and q are any predicates. For example, "All students study" could be expressed as $\forall X\ student(X) \rightarrow study(X)$ (that is, for all things, if that thing is a student then that thing will study). The quantifier $\exists$ is used when something only has to be true of one object. For example, "Someone strange likes brussel sprouts" could be expressed as $\exists X\ strange(X) \wedge likes(X, brusselsprouts)$ (i.e., there exists some thing that is both strange and likes brussel sprouts).

The following are some further examples of statements in predicate logic, paired with their English equivalents.

- $\exists X (table(X) \wedge \neg numlegs(X, 4))$ "There is some table that doesn't have 4 legs"
- $\forall X (elephant(X) \rightarrow grey(X))$ "All elephants are grey"
- $\forall X (glaswegian(X) \rightarrow (supports(X, rangers) \vee supports(X, celtic)))$ "All Glaswegians support either Celtic or Rangers"
- $\exists X (small(X) \wedge slimy(X) \wedge on(X, table))$ "There is something small and slimy on the table"
- $\neg \exists X (brusselsprout(X) \wedge tasty(X))$ "There is no brussel sprout which is tasty."

Computation and Reasoning

The Use of Logic in AI

Predicate logic provides a powerful way to represent and reason with knowledge. Some things that cannot be easily represented using frames, such as negation, disjunction and quantification, are easily represented using predicate logic. The available inference rules and proof procedures mean that a much wider range of inferences are possible than the simple inheritance-based inference allowed in a frame system.

However, there are some things that are hard to represent using predicate logic, particularly facts that involve uncertainty (e.g., "It will probably rain tomorrow"), defaults (e.g., "It normally rains in Glasgow"), beliefs ("John believes it will rain, but I don't"), and time/change (e.g., "It will get wetter and wetter as you near Glasgow"). Methods have been developed that allow some of these to be handled within predicate logic, and more complex logics have been developed with different syntax and semantics. However, as the logic gets more complex inference within the logic tends to get less efficient. So for complex problem solving the AI programmer might have to choose between a logic-based approach, with clear semantics and guaranteed sound inferences, and a more *ad hoc* procedural approach which might be more efficient for the particular problem.

Within AI, logic is used not just as a knowledge representation language, but also:

- To *communicate* AI theories within the community. When writing about a new theory of human reasoning or language use some people use a formal logic to describe the theory. This adds precision, though sometimes at the expense of clarity and accessibility.
- As the basis of AI *programming languages*. The obvious example here is Prolog, which is based on predicate logic, yet can be used as a flexible and general-purpose AI programming language.
- To give the meaning of natural language sentences in a natural language understanding system.
- To define the *semantics* of other simpler representation languages. This is discussed in more detail below.

Logic and Frames

Representation languages such as frames often have their semantics defined in terms of predicate (or other) logics. Once we have defined precisely what all the expressions and relations mean in terms of a well-understood logic then we can make sure than any inferences that are drawn are sound, according to that logic. For a simple frame system, without defaults, one way to translate things into logic is as follows:

- For an object o with slot s and value v we get: $\forall X \exists Y (o(X) \rightarrow (v(Y) \wedge s(X,Y)))$. For example, for our "Elephant has_part head" example from Section 2.2.1 we'd get the translation as: $\forall X \exists Y (elephant(X) \rightarrow head(Y) \wedge haspart(X,Y))$.

Computation and Reasoning

31

- If one object o is an instance of a class c we get: $c(o)$. For example, Nellie's an elephant: $elephant(nellie)$.
- If one class $c1$ is a subclass of another class $c2$ we get: $\forall X(c1(X) \rightarrow c2(X))$. For example: $\forall X elephant(X) \rightarrow mammal(X)$.

Inheritance still works in the logic-based version. For example, the inference rule modus ponens could be applied to $\forall X \exists Y (elephant(X) \rightarrow head(Y) \wedge haspart(X, \ Y))$ and $elephant(nellie)$ to conclude that $\exists Y head(Y) \wedge haspart(nellie, \ Y)$ (i.e., Nellie has a head).

Using this model everything in a frame system can be translated into predicate logic, but not vice versa. The frame system has weaker *representational adequacy*. However, the frame system is easy to work with, and being able to translate between frames and logic has the advantage that we can deal (on the surface) with a simple, natural representation language such as frames, while underneath we can be confident that the inferences drawn by the system are all sound. Of course, we have to understand something about the semantics of the language to be able to represent things meaningfully in it, but this may not be as awkward as dealing directly with the logic.

Another possible advantage of this approach is that something like a frame system typically has restricted representational power compared with full predicate (or default) logic. This may sound like a disadvantage, as it will mean there are some things we can't represent. However, the gain in efficiency by reasoning with a restricted subset usually makes this tradeoff worthwhile. In fact, new logics (called *terminological* or *description* logics) have been developed, which have the expressive power needed to perform inheritance type inferences on simple properties of classes of objects (as in frame systems), but which do not allow some of inferences and representations possible in predicate logic. These allow you to reason directly in the logic, rather than using the special inferences of a frame system, which are only indirectly validated by a logic-based semantics. Terminological logics have more restricted expressive power than predicate logic, but greater efficiency.

2.3.4   Conclusion

This section has just given a quick overview of predicate logic and its use in knowledge representation. Although it is more powerful as a language than, say, frames, some facts may be less clear when represented using a logic. For example, for most people the "Elephant has_part head" example is more natural and easier to understand in the frame or semantic network-based representation. And although predicate logic allows a wide range of inferences, and there are proof procedures that can be used to apply these inferences in a systematic way, the process may be inefficient when compared with a more restricted language such as frames. There is a tradeoff between representational and inferential adequacy (i.e., the expressiveness of the system) and inferential efficiency.

Computation and Reasoning

Although logic is not a panacea as a knowledge representation language, it is more fundamental than the other methods described in this chapter, as other methods are often described in terms of logic. Logic provides a firm foundation on which other methods can stand, allowing them to be analysed and compared. More advanced study of AI would require a closer examination of the role of logic.

2.4 Rule-Based Systems

Instead of representing knowledge in a relatively declarative, static way (as a set of things that are true), rule-based systems represent knowledge in terms of a set of rules that tell you what you should do or what you can conclude in different situations. A rule-based system consists of a set of IF–THEN rules, a set of *facts* normally representing things that are currently held to be true, and some *interpreter* controlling the application of the rules, given the facts. This is illustrated in Figure 2.6.

The IF–THEN rules in a rule-based system are treated very differently from similar constructs in a conventional programming language such as Pascal or C. While Pascal or C treats IF–THEN constructs as part of a *sequence* of instructions, to be considered in order, a rule-based system treats each rule as an independent chunk of knowledge, to be invoked when needed under the control of the interpreter. The rules are more like implications in logic (e.g., $raining \rightarrow carry\_umbrella$), and indeed the discussion of forward and backward chaining below applies equally well to the control of reasoning in a logic-based system.

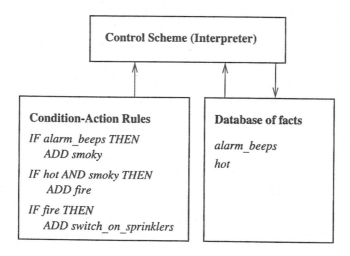

Figure 2.6 *Rule-Based System Architecture.*

Computation and Reasoning

There are two main kinds of interpreter: *forward chaining* and *backward chaining*. In a forward chaining system you start with some initial facts, and keep using the rules to draw new conclusions (or take certain actions) given those facts. In a backward chaining system you start with some hypothesis (or goal) you are trying to prove, and keep looking for rules that would allow you to conclude that hypothesis, perhaps setting new subgoals to prove as you go. Forward chaining systems are primarily data-driven, while backward chaining systems are goal-driven. We'll look at both, and when each might be useful.

2.4.1 Forward Chaining Systems

In a forward chaining system the facts in the system are held in a *working memory* which is continually updated as rules are invoked. Rules in the system represent possible actions to take when specified facts occur in the working memory, and are often referred to as *condition-action rules*. The actions usually involve *adding* or *deleting* items from the working memory, but other actions are possible, such as printing a message. Indeed, many systems may allow arbitrary procedures to be called within the action part of the rule.

The interpreter controls the application of the rules, given the working memory, thus controlling the system's activity. It is based on a cycle of activity sometimes known as a *recognize–act* cycle. The system first checks to find all the rules whose conditions hold, given the current state of working memory. It then selects one and performs the actions in the action part of the rule. This is referred to as *firing* the rule. The selection of a rule to fire is based on fixed strategies, known as *conflict resolution* strategies, discussed later. Anyway, the actions will result in a new working memory, and the cycle begins again. This cycle will be repeated until either no rules fire, or a special *halt* symbol is added to working memory.

This basic algorithm for forward chaining may be summarized as follows:

Repeat:

- Find all the rules which have conditions (IF part) satisfied.
- Select one, using conflict resolution strategies.
- Perform actions in conclusion, possibly modifying current working memory.

until no rules can fire or *halt* in working memory.

A Simple Example

As a very simple illustration, consider the rules and facts in Figure 2.6, which capture a rather conservative approach to fire fighting (only switch the sprinklers on if the smoke alarm goes off AND it's hot – you don't want to make the burnt toast wet):

R1: *IF hot AND smoky THEN ADD fire*
R2: *IF alarm_beeps THEN ADD smoky*

R3: *IF fire THEN ADD switch_on_sprinklers*
F1: *alarm_beeps*
F2: *hot*

Initially the system checks to find the rules whose conditions hold, given the two facts (F1 and F2). The only such rule is rule R2, so this rule is selected and its action is performed. The action *ADD smoky* is an instruction to add a new fact *smoky* to the working memory. So a new fact is added:

F3: *smoky*

Now the cycle starts again. This time the conditions of the first rule hold, as both *hot* and *smoky* are in the working memory. So the action is performed, and we get a new fact in working memory:

F4: *fire*

The cycle begins again, and this time rule R3 fires, *switch_on_sprinklers* is added to working memory, and hopefully as a result the sprinklers switched on!

This example at least illustrates how the order in which rules fires depends on what is in working memory and not on the order in which the rules are given. However, what happens if, in some cycle, more than one rule has its condition satisfied? To discuss this we'll extend the above example a little, with two more rules and one new initial fact:

R1: *IF hot AND smoky THEN ADD fire*
R2: *IF alarm_beeps THEN ADD smoky*
R3: *IF fire THEN ADD switch_on_sprinklers*
R4: *IF dry THEN ADD switch_on_humidifier*
R5: *IF sprinklers_on THEN DELETE dry*
F1: *alarm_beeps*
F2: *hot*
F3: *dry*

The action *DELETE dry* will result in this fact being removed from working memory. Now, in the first cycle there are TWO rules that apply: R2 and R4. If R4 is chosen, the humidifier is switched on and then things proceed as before. If R2 is chosen, followed by R1, R3 and R4, then *dry* is deleted from working memory and the humidifier (sensibly) never switched on.

Conflict Resolution

Clearly it is important which rule is chosen to fire when there is a choice. This may influence the final conclusions, as we have seen, and also the efficiency of the system in arriving at the conclusion or action of interest (without drawing too many irrelevant conclusions or doing too many irrelevant actions along the way). A forward chaining system will have some *conflict resolution strategies* to decide which rules to fire. Common strategies include:

Computation and Reasoning

- prefer to fire rules that involve facts that have been recently added to working memory. In the above example, if initially R2 fires, the next rule to fire will be R1 (rather than R4) as *smoky* has been recently added. This allows the system to follow through a single chain of reasoning.
- prefer to fire rules with more specific conditions. For example, if we had a rule R6: *IF hot THEN ADD summer*, and facts *hot* and *smoky*, R1 would be fired in preference to R6 as it has more specific conditions. This allows you to have rules like R1 which are exceptions to a more general rule (R6).
- allow user to prioritize rules. For example, R4 above could have very low priority, only fired if nothing else can fire.
- fire all applicable rules at once. This is pretty much the opposite of the first strategy listed, as it results in all chains of reasoning being explored simultaneously. (This is similar to the difference between *depth first* and *breadth first* search strategies discussed in Chapter 4.)

A forward chaining language may provide a range of different strategies for the person writing the rules to select between.

Reason Maintenance

Another feature that is sometimes offered is for the system to automatically withdraw facts whose *justifications* have become invalidated because of changes in the working memory. In the fire example above, the humidifier could be switched on (or at least *switch_on_humidifier* added), with the justification that it is hot and dry. But later *dry* is removed from the working memory, so *switch_on_humidifier* no longer has a valid justification, so could be automatically removed.

Sophisticated techniques have been developed to allow these sorts of updates, referred to as *reason maintenance* or *truth maintenance* systems. Some allow all possible consistent sets of facts to be considered. For example, suppose (for some reason) that the sprinkler system should not be switched on if the humidifier is on. There would be two consistent sets of facts, one with the humidifier on (and the building burning down!) and one with the sprinkler on.

Pattern Matching

The rules and facts in the examples so far have been very simple. In general more complex facts are allowed, such as *temperature(kitchen, hot)* rather than just *hot*, and rules can have *patterns* that are *matched* against facts in the working memory. For example, suppose we have the following rule and facts:

> R7: *IF temperature(R, hot) AND environment(R, smoky) then ADD fire_in(R)*
> F6: *temperature(kitchen, hot)*
> F7: *environment(kitchen, smoky)*

The rule conditions contain a variable *R* which may take any value (e.g., kitchen)[5].

---

[5]Prolog-like notation is used here, for those familiar with Prolog. However, other notations are

The CLIPS Expert System Tool

One expert system tool based on a forward chaining is CLIPS (standing for C Language Integrated Production System). The following rule gives an idea of how you'd write rules using the CLIPS syntax. *Assert* is used rather than *ADD*, and the symbol $=>$ rather than *IF ... THEN*. Variables in patterns are indicated by a question mark.

```
(defrule fire-alarm
  (temperature ?rl hot)
  (environment ?rl smoky)
  =>
  (assert (fire-in ?rl)))
```

CLIPS allows a variety of conflict resolution strategies to be selected, and provides limited facilities for reason maintenance. It also provides facilities where rule-based programming may be combined with more conventional procedural and object-based approaches.
CLIPS is fairly widely used, particularly within universities for teaching and research, but also by commercial companies.

So *temperature(R, hot)* matches *temperature(kitchen, hot)* with *R=kitchen*. *Environment(R, kitchen)* (with R=kitchen) matches F7, so the fact *fire_in(kitchen)* is added to the working memory.

For backward chaining (discussed in the next section) pattern matching is used to match goals to conclusions of rules. So if we were trying to prove *fire_in(library)* this goal would match rule R7's conclusion with *R=library*.

Allowing patterns and pattern matching greatly increases the flexibility of rules, whether using forward or backward chaining.

2.4.2 Backward Chaining Systems

So far we have looked at how rule-based systems can be used to draw new conclusions from existing data, adding these conclusions to a working memory. This approach is most useful when you know all the initial facts, but don't know what conclusions are likely.

If you DO know what the conclusion might be, or have some specific hypothesis to test, forward chaining systems may be inefficient. You could keep on forward chaining until either no more rules apply or you have added your hypothesis to the

---

often used for patterns, such as *(temperature ?R hot)*.

working memory. But in the process the system is likely to do a lot of irrelevant work, adding uninteresting conclusions to working memory. For example, suppose we have the following rules (modifying our example again to illustrate a point):

R1: *IF smoky AND hot THEN ADD fire*
R2: *IF alarm_beeps THEN ADD smoky*
R3: *IF alarm_beeps THEN ADD ear_plugs*
R4: *IF fire THEN ADD switch_on_sprinklers*
R5: *IF smoky THEN ADD poor_visibility*
F1: *alarm_beeps*
F2: *hot*

If we are only interested in whether or not to switch on the sprinklers, then concluding that visibility is poor and that you should wear your ear plugs is irrelevant (if not downright dangerous).

By backward chaining we avoid drawing these irrelevant inferences, and focus just on the hypothesis in question (should the sprinklers be switched on?). We start with a goal to try to prove, say, *switch_on_sprinklers*. The system will then check whether the goal matches any of the facts given. If it does, then that goal succeeds. If it doesn't the system will look for rules whose conclusions (previously referred to as *actions*) match the goal. One such rule will be chosen, and the system will then try to prove any facts in the conditions (or *preconditions*) of the rule using the same procedure, setting these as new goals to prove. Note that a backward chaining system does not need to update a working memory. Instead it needs to keep track of what goals it needs to prove in order to prove its main hypothesis.

The following gives the basic algorithm (though ignores the issue of what to do if there is more than one rule that can be used to conclude a given goal):

To prove goal G:

- If G is in the initial facts it is proven.

- Otherwise, find a rule which can be used to conclude G, and try to prove each of that rule's preconditions. G is then proved true if all the preconditions are proved true.

2.4.3 Example

For the example rules above initially the goal to try to prove is:

G1: *switch_on_sprinklers*

We check whether the goal state is in the initial facts. As it isn't there, we try matching it against the conclusions of the rules. It matches rule R4. The precondition of

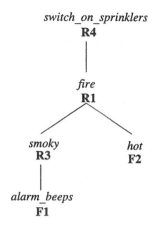

Figure 2.7 *Proof Tree for Sprinkler Example.*

this rule is set as a new goal to prove:

G2: *fire*

Now, this isn't in the facts, but it matches the conclusion of rule R1, so R1's pre-conditions are set as new goals to prove:

G3: *smoky*
G4: *hot*

G3 is considered first. It matches the conclusion of R2, so *alarm_beeps* is set as a new goal. The goals to prove are now:

G5: *alarm_beeps*
G4: *hot*

Now, both of these are in the initial facts, so are trivially true. As all the goals are now proved, the initial goal must be true, so we can conclude that the sprinkler should be switched on.

The proof for our hypothesis *switch_on_sprinklers* can be represented graphically as a tree, illustrated in Figure 2.7.

2.4.4   Implementation

A backward chaining system may be implemented using a stack to record the goals that are still to be satisfied[6]. You repeatedly pop a goal off the stack, and try and prove it. If it is in the set of initial facts then it is proved. If it matches a rule which

---

[6]A simple recursive implementation is also possible, but less easy to modify if you want to try different *search strategies*. See chapter 4.

has a number of preconditions then the preconditions are pushed onto the stack. Otherwise the goal fails. The overall goal succeeds if all subgoals are successfully removed from the stack, and none fails.

However, what should be done if there is more than one rule that has the same conclusion, and could be used to prove a particular goal? In this case the system should try them all, and see if the goal can be proved using *any* of them. *Search techniques*, discussed in Chapter 4, may be used to try all the possibilities in this way. For example, using a *depth first search* algorithm, if it fails to prove a goal using one rule it will "back up" to the last point where there was a choice of rules and try the alternative.

The Prolog language uses backward chaining with depth first search to try to prove things, and has built-in *pattern matching* facilities. This makes it a good choice for prototyping simple expert systems. Usually you'd first write an expert system *shell* (or special-purpose language) using Prolog, then write the expert system itself using that shell. This has the advantage that you can choose the notation to be used for your rules, and can program in extra features that aren't directly supported in Prolog. Such features might include methods for handling uncertainty or interacting with the user. These are discussed more in the next chapter.

Forwards vs Backwards Reasoning

Whether you use forward or backwards reasoning to solve a problem depends on the properties of your rule set and initial facts, and on how many possible hypotheses there are to consider. If you have some particular hypothesis to test, then backward chaining may be more efficient, as you avoid drawing conclusions from irrelevant facts. However, sometimes backward chaining can be very wasteful – there may be many possible hypotheses, and for each one there may be many ways to try to prove it, few of which result in a conclusion.

Consider, for example, two applications of expert systems mentioned in Chapter 1. For medical diagnosis, in a very restricted area, there may only be, say, ten diseases of interest. It would be practical to use backward chaining and try and prove each one in turn, and indeed a pioneering expert system MYCIN (discussed further in the next chapter) does just this. However, for an application like computer configuration there are an enormous number of possible configurations, and it would not be sensible to go through all the possibilities until one was found meeting the customer's specifications. For this application forward chaining is a better idea, starting with the specifications and gradually building up (in working memory) a possible configuration. Another pioneering system XCON did just this. This was a system to configure VAX computer systems, and was one of the early commercial successes of expert system technology.

Computation and Reasoning

2.5 Comparing Knowledge Representation Languages

So far we have discussed three approaches to knowledge representation and inference: frames and semantic networks, logic, and rules. Logic is the most fundamental of these, and other methods may sometimes be described in terms of logic.

Frames and networks are useful for representing declarative information about collections of related objects/concepts, and in particular where there is a clear *class hierarchy*, and where you want to use *inheritance* to infer the attributes of objects in subclasses from the attributes of objects in the parent class. Early approaches tended to have poorly specified *semantics* but there are now practical systems with a clear underlying semantics. Logic is generally used to describe this semantics.

Frames and networks are unlikely to be adequate if you want to draw a wide range of different sorts of inferences, and not just inferences based on inheritance. For this you could use the full power of predicate logic, along with a theorem prover. Logic-based approaches allow you to represent fairly complex things (involving quantification, negation and disjunction), and have a well-defined syntax, semantics and proof theory. However, logic-based approaches may be inflexible. Any inference rules in the logic must be validated by a precisely stated semantics for expressions in the language. This may mean that many commonsense inferences and conclusions aren't allowed, and reasoning may be inefficient.

Rule-based systems provide more flexibility, sometimes allowing arbitrary procedures within the rules. More emphasis may be placed on how the reasoning is controlled, but the semantics of the rules may be unspecified – the conclusions drawn by the system just depend on details of how the the rule interpreter works. While logic is used in a declarative way, saying what's true in the world, rule-based systems (especially forward chaining systems) are concerned more with procedural knowledge – what to do when.

A common feature of all the approaches is that the problem-specific rules and facts are represented separately from the more general problem-solving and inference procedures used to reason with these. It should be possible to modify a system, or write a system to solve a related problem, without ever modifying the problem-solving or inference methods. We just add, for example, new rules, frames, or statements in a logic, re-using both existing facts and tried-and-tested problem-solving and inference methods. A knowledge representation language provides us with representational notations and inference methods that have both been found to be useful, and which have been analysed to make sure that they are sound. Using such a language for AI problem solving therefore provides significant advantages over, say, writing a C++ program from scratch, where the programmer has to re-invent suitable notations and do all the hard work of checking the correctness of the methods herself.

2.6   Summary

- Knowledge representation languages provide high-level representation formalisms to represent the knowledge required for AI problem solving.
- A good language should be natural, clear and precise, allow you to represent what is required, and support the sound inference of new facts.
- Frames and semantic networks represent knowledge as an organized collection of objects with attributes, arranged in a hierarchy. If an object is a *subclass* of another it may inherit its attributes. They are limited in what can be represented and inferred, but provide a natural and efficient representation scheme.
- A logic, and in particular predicate logic, may be used as a precise and formal language able to represent a fairly wide range of things. A logic may also be used to describe the semantics of other formalisms.
- Rule-based systems allow knowledge to be represented as a set of more-or-less independent IF–THEN or condition-action rules, stating what action to take given different conditions. Reasoning can be controlled using a *forward* or *backward* chaining interpreter.

2.7   Further Reading

Most recent AI textbooks have emphasized logic-based approaches to knowledge representation. Ginsberg (Ginsberg, 1993) (ch.6–9) gives a good introduction to the use of logic, with a briefer discussion of frames and nets (ch.13), building on the discussion of logic. Russell & Norvig (Russell & Norvig, 1995) (ch.6–10) provide a more advanced treatment of logic, but very little discussion of rules or frames. Rich & Knight (Rich & Knight, 1991) (ch.4–11) give a good discussion of all the topics, with more discursive material and advanced topics. Luger and Stubblefield (Luger & Stubblefield, 1993) (ch.2,8,9) also cover most of the material, although organised rather differently.

Further information about AI and Prolog can be found in (Pereira & Shieber, 1987) (which, although emphasizing natural language applications, includes a good discussion of the proof procedure and resolution) and (Bratko, 1990).

2.8   Exercises

1. Represent the following facts as a set of frames:
   "The aorta is a particular kind of artery which has a diameter of 2.5 cm. An artery is a kind of blood vessel. An artery always has a muscular wall, and

generally has a diameter of 0.4 cm. A vein is a kind of blood vessel, but has a fibrous wall. Blood vessels all have tubular form and contain blood."

2. Represent the following facts in the language of predicate logic:

   - Every apple is either green or yellow.

   - No apple is blue.

   - If an apple is green then it is tasty.

   - Every man likes a tasty apple.

3. "Herbert is a small hippopotamus who lives in Edinburgh zoo. Like all hippopotamuses he eats grass and likes swimming"
   Represent the above:

   (a) as a semantic network;

   (b) in predicate logic.

   Give two new facts about Herbert that are:

   (a) easier to represent in a semantic network than in predicate logic;

   (b) easier to represent in logic than in a semantic network.

4. Give a set of frames representing facts about students in general, students at your university, and students on your course, making good use of inheritance, and indicating which slots hold default values.

5. The following IF–THEN rules are proposed for a simple rule-based financial advice expert system:

   R1: *IF NOT savings_adequate THEN ADD invest_savings*

   R2: *IF savings_adequate AND income_adequate THEN ADD invest_stocks*

   R3: *IF NOT has_children THEN ADD savings_adequate*

   R4: *IF has_partner AND partner_has_job THEN ADD income_adequate*

   (a) For the hypothesis *invest_stocks* outline how this could be proved through backward chaining. Assume that current facts include: *has_children, has_partner* and *partner_has_job*.

   (b) Currently if you have a partner who works the system concludes that your income is adequate, even if she/he works in the chip shop and you have 15 kids to support. Also if you do not have kids it concludes that your savings are adequate even if you don't have any and want to buy a house. Finally it ignores the fact that if you have a really huge income then these may be adequate even if you have kids and your partner does not work. Extend the rule set to deal with these issues.

CHAPTER 3

Expert Systems

Aims:	To introduce the basics of expert system architecture and development, with case studies in medicine illustrating different approaches.
Objectives:	You should be able to:
	Describe the basic architecture of an expert system.
	Discuss whether a given problem could be solved using an expert systems approach and outline how expert systems are typically developed.
	Describe in detail the operation of a simple backward chaining expert system and be able to design and implement such a system given an English description of the problem and underlying knowledge.
	Outline different methods for reasoning under uncertainty.
	Describe and compare three approaches used in medical expert systems.
Prerequisites:	Chapter 2. Also, some basic understanding of probability may be helpful.

3.1 Introduction

So far we have talked a lot about how we can represent knowledge, but not so much about how we can use it to solve real practical problems. This section will therefore look at how some of the techniques discussed so far are used in *expert systems* – systems which provide expert quality advice, diagnoses and recommendations given real world problems.

Expert systems solve real problems which normally would require a human expert (such as a specialist doctor or a minerologist). The human expertise may be in short supply, expensive, and experts hard to get hold of in a hurry. An expert

Computation and Reasoning

system, on the other hand, may be made easily available on demand. An example situation where we might want to consider using an expert system is in diagnosing rare diseases. A general practitioner may not have the specialized expertise required, human experts may be hard to get hold of in a hurry, yet fast decisions may be required on treatment.

Building an expert system first involves extracting the relevant knowledge from the human expert. Such knowledge is often *heuristic* in nature, based on useful "rules of thumb" rather than absolute certainties. Extracting it from the expert in a way that can be used by a computer is generally a difficult task, requiring its own expertise. A *knowledge engineer* has the job of extracting this knowledge and building the expert system *knowledge base*.

A first attempt at building an expert system is unlikely to be very successful. This is partly because the expert generally finds it very difficult to express exactly what knowledge and rules they use to solve a problem. Much of it is almost subconscious, or appears so obvious they don't even bother mentioning it. *Knowledge acquisition* for expert systems is a major part of expert system design, with a wide variety of techniques used. However, generally this will involve interviewing the expert and getting them to solve a range of typical problems. An initial prototype may be developed based on that, and shown to the expert. The expert may then check the system's performance and give feedback to enable the design to be refined. This may be repeated until the expert is happy. Of course, it is not just the domain expert that has to be happy with a system – the end users of the system and the person (or organization) ordering the system must also be considered, and feedback should be sought from them at each stage.

In order to do such iterative development from a prototype it is important that the expert system is written in a way that it can easily be inspected and modified. The system should be able to explain its reasoning (to expert, user and knowledge engineer) and answer questions about the solution process. Updating the system shouldn't involve rewriting a whole lot of code – just adding or deleting localized chunks of knowledge.

A widely used approach for representing knowledge in an an expert systems is the use of IF–THEN rules (as discussed in Chapter 2) sometimes in combination with frames. Often the rules won't have certain conclusions – there will just be some degree of certainty that the conclusion will hold if the conditions hold. Methods are required to determine the certainty of the overall conclusion given the evidence and these uncertain rules. Rule-based systems, with or without certainties, are flexible, moderately easily modifiable and make it easy to provide reasonably helpful traces of the system's reasoning. These traces can be used in providing explanations of what the system is doing.

Expert systems have been used to solve a wide range of problems in domains such as medicine, mathematics, engineering, geology, computer science, business, law, defence and education. Within each domain, they have been used to solve different types of problems. So, in electronics one type of problem might involve *diagnosing* faults in circuits, another might involve *designing* a circuit to do a particular job. What is generally found is that the appropriate problem-solving methods to use for a given problem depend more on the type of problem than on the application domain. So, diagnosing a fault in a circuit is, in some ways, more like diagnosing a disease than designing a circuit, while designing a circuit might have more in common with designing a kitchen! Of course, both circuit problems will have in common a need for information about, say, circuit components, but representing this knowledge tends to be relatively easy – the hard part is working out a good method to use to solve the problem.

There is a huge range of problem-solving methods that have been used for different expert system tasks. Designing an expert system depends on being able to pick out a good method, and whole books have been written on how this can be done more reliably. However, in this chapter we will mainly discuss the task of *diagnosis*, and consider just three problem-solving techniques that can be used for this problem, focusing most on a rule-based approach using backward chaining.

In the rest of this chapter we will first describe in general terms how an expert system is developed, then talk in more detail about simple backward chaining systems, discuss the problem of how to deal with *uncertainty* in an expert system, and conclude by looking at three contrasting systems which illustrate different techniques that have been used for developing systems for performing diagnosis in medicine.

3.2   Designing an Expert System

Expert systems are extremely diverse in the problems tackled and the detailed problem-solving methods used. However, there are common issues relevant to the design of all systems. These concern the type of problems that are considered suitable for expert systems, the way a system is (typically) developed, and the overall architecture that is commonly used. This section will discuss these general issues.

3.2.1   Choosing a Problem

Writing an expert system generally involves a great deal of time and money. To avoid costly and embarrassing failures, people have developed a set of guidelines to determine whether a problem is suitable for an expert system solution.

First, as with any software engineering project, it is important to be realistic about the costs involved and ensure that the expense is justified given expected benefits. It is easy to underestimate the effort and cost of developing a full-scale expert system, particularly after exploring the basic ideas through simple examples. Even with sophisticated tools now available to aid the development process, it is still a complex process, partly because of the difficulties of acquiring the knowledge from human experts, and the inevitable need to keep going back to expert(s), users, and customer. The costs may be justified where human expertise is in short supply, or not always available when needed. For example, highly specialized medical knowledge may be hard to obtain on demand, but a (non-specialized) doctor must be able make a quick decision about what immediate actions to take, and whether to refer a patient to an expensive and distant specialist.

Second, we must ensure that expert system techniques are appropriate. Problems that require manual dexterity or physical skill are unlikely to be appropriate, even with the advance of techniques in robotics. Also, problems that require a lot of common-sense knowledge probably won't be appropriate, as common sense is notoriously hard to capture and represent. Generally highly technical fields are easier to deal with, as they involve relatively small amounts of well-formalized knowledge, often largely captured in written documents (e.g., medical texts). Typically a suitable problem for an expert system is one that requires highly specialized expertise, but which would only take a human expert a short time to solve (say an hour, maximum).

For some problems using expert system techniques would be an overkill. It may be that you can sketch a relatively simple flowchart (or similar) giving the right expert decision for different situations, and then encode this as a simple program. Flowcharts are sometimes used, for example, to help people make decisions about how to invest their money. A computer implementation of such a flowchart would not need complex techniques. Alternatively, it may be that simple methods based on probability theory can be used, and a spreadsheet used to implement the system. (This latter approach is discussed further in Section 3.4.) You might still choose to refer to the resulting system as an expert system (as it might give useful expert advice), but the methods used are quite simple. If simple methods will do, don't bother looking for a complex solution!

Finally, if we have established that there is a need for an expert system, and that expert system techniques are appropriate and feasible, we need to check that the situation is right for expert system development. Particularly, it is important that there are available and cooperative experts who can contribute their expertise without feeling that the system might make them redundant. You also need any management and potential users to be involved and have positive attitudes to the project.

Only a fairly small range of problems are appropriate for expert system technology. However, given a suitable problem, expert systems can bring great benefits. Systems have been developed, for example, to help analyse samples collected in oil exploration, and to help configure computer systems. Both these systems were successful and in active use.

3.2.2 Knowledge Engineering

Having decided that your problem is suitable you need to extract the knowledge from the expert and represent it using some suitable knowledge representation scheme. This is the job of the *knowledge engineer*, but involves close collaboration with the *expert(s)* and the *end user(s)*.

The knowledge engineer knows about expert system problem-solving and knowledge representation methods, and how to get the domain expert to express their expertise in a usable form. He/she should be able to extract the knowledge from the expert (without thumbscrews!), select appropriate representation and problem-solving methods, and represent the knowledge and methods using suitable tools.

The knowledge engineer may initially have no knowledge of the expert's field. However, to extract knowledge from the expert the knowledge engineer must first become at least somewhat familiar with the area, maybe by reading introductory texts or talking to the expert. After this, more systematic interviewing of the expert begins. Typically experts are set a series of example problems, and will explain aloud their reasoning in solving the problem. The knowledge engineer will abstract general rules from these explanations, and check them with the expert.

As in most applications, the system is wasted if the user is not happy with it, so development must involve close collaboration with potential users. As mentioned in the introduction, the basic development cycle should involve the rapid development of an initial prototype and iterative testing and modification of that prototype with both experts (to check the validity of the expert knowledge) and users (to check that they can provide the necessary information to the system, are satisfied with the systems performance, and that it actually makes their life easier rather than harder!).

In order to develop the initial prototype the knowledge engineer must make provisional decisions about appropriate knowledge representation and inference methods (e.g., rules, or rules in conjunction with frames; forward chaining or backward chaining). To test these basic design decisions, the first prototype may only solve a small part of the overall problem. If the methods used seem to work well for that small part it may be worth investing the effort in representing the rest of the knowledge in the same form.

3.2.3 Expert System Architecture

While the details of an expert system may vary widely, most have a similar overall architecture. The whole system involves much more than just the knowledge base, but will normally involve further components or modules as illustrated in Figure 3.1.

The user interacts with the system through a *user interface* which may use menus, natural language or any other style of interaction. Then an *inference engine* (or problem-solving component) is used to reason with both the *expert knowledge* in the knowledge base and data specific to the particular problem being solved. This *case-specific data* includes both data provided by the user and partial conclusions based on this data.

Expert System Shell

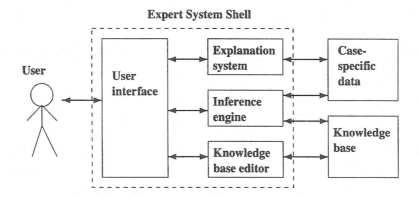

Figure 3.1 *Expert System Architecture.*

As an example, consider a very simple expert system to diagnose colds and 'flu. We might use a *backward chaining* inference engine, using expert knowledge encoded as rules (e.g., IF symptom(Person, runny_nose) THEN disease(Person, cold)). Case-specific data might include facts like symptom(fred, runny_nose).

Most expert systems also have an *explanation subsystem*, which allows the program to explain its reasoning to the user. Some systems also have a *knowledge base editor* which helps the expert or knowledge engineer to easily update and check the knowledge base.

One important feature of expert systems is the way they (usually) separate domain (problem area) specific knowledge from more general-purpose reasoning and representation techniques. The general-purpose part (in the dotted box in the figure) can often be re-used for different problems, and is referred to as an *expert system shell* or *toolkit*. As we see in the figure, the shell will provide the inference engine (and knowledge representation scheme), a user interface, an explanation system and sometimes a knowledge base editor. Given a new kind of problem to solve (say, car design), we can often find a shell that provides the right sort of support for that problem, so all we need to do is provide the expert knowledge. There are numerous commercial expert system shells, each one appropriate for a slightly different range of problems. Using shells to write expert systems generally greatly reduces the cost and time of development (compared with writing the expert system from scratch). One freely available shell is CLIPS (mentioned in Chapter 2), which is primarily a forward chaining system, but allows the users to define *objects*, write functions, and interface easily to programs written in other languages[1].

---

[1]See WWW page (*http://www.cee.hw.ac.uk/~alison/essence.html*) for details of how to obtain CLIPS.

3.2.4   Problem-Solving Methods

In the discussion above we have talked about the selection of an appropriate problem-solving method. Here we'll very briefly consider what these might be like and why they are needed.

A simple expert system might consist of some facts about the current problem (e.g., `symptom(patient1, cough)`), and some inference rules (e.g., `IF symptom(P, cough) THEN ADD disease(P, cold)`). The inference rules would state what can be concluded from the current facts. We can think of an expert system problem-solving method as a way of controlling these inferences so that just those inferences that are required for the current problem are made. If inferences were made at random then a lot of unnecessary work would be done.

This is particularly important if the system might have to ask the user questions in order to elicit more case-specific data (e.g., "Does the patient have a sore throat?"). If the inferences aren't controlled in a sensible manner then the user might be asked irrelevant questions (e.g., "Does the patient have a sore ankle?" after finding that they have a cough).

The forward chaining and backward chaining methods described in the previous chapter provide basic general-purpose methods of controlling inference. And indeed, a backward chaining method can be used fairly directly as the problem-solving strategy for a simple expert system, as we'll see in the next section. However, very often more complex strategies are required, or at least desirable. For example, in medicine a technique called *differential diagnosis* is often used by human experts – this basically involves having a set of current hypotheses about the patient's disease, and trying to ask questions to differentiate between the most likely current hypotheses. These higher-level problem-solving strategies many be implemented in a variety of ways. For example, a forward chaining rule interpreter can be used to implement a differential diagnosis problem-solving strategy, but other underlying methods may also be used. Often, rules in a rule-based expert system may be split into a small number of rules that are concerned with implementing the problem-solving strategy, and a larger number that contain the basic inferences in the problem domain. For example, in medicine we might have problem-solving rules such as `IF too_many_hypotheses THEN rule_out_hypothesis`, and domain rules such as `IF symptom(Patient, cough) THEN disease_hypothesis(Patient, cold)`.

The next section will discuss a very simple problem-solving strategy based on backward chaining. However, the case studies in Section 3.5 will illustrate some contrasting strategies, all for the same problem of medical diagnosis. The first is based largely on simple backward chaining, with *certainty factors* to handle uncertainty. The next uses a more complex problem-solving method based on differential diagnosis. The final one uses methods based on probability and decision theory.

3.3 Backward Chaining Rule-Based Expert Systems

In this section we will show how simple expert systems based on IF–THEN rules and a backward chaining rule-interpreter can be developed. Using backward chaining we can supply the system with some hypothesis, and the system will attempt to find out if that hypothesis is true. The user will be asked just those questions which are relevant to the hypothesis being considered. Backward chaining is a simple problem-solving strategy, but may be adequate for some tasks.

In a simple backward chaining rule-based expert system there is often a set of possible hypothesized solutions – maybe a set of illnesses that the patient might have. The expert system will consider each hypothesis in turn (e.g., `disease(fred, cold)`), as goals to prove, and try to determine whether or not it might be the case. Sometimes it won't be able to prove or disprove something from the data initially supplied by the user, so it will ask the user some questions (e.g., "have you got a headache?"). The system will normally be told which facts it can reasonably ask the user about – these are sometimes referred to as *askable* facts. Using any initial data plus answers to questions it should eventually be able to conclude which of the possible solutions to the problem is the right one.

The algorithm for this basic system is given below. It would be repeated for each hypothesis G.

To prove G:
- If G is in the current facts it is proved.
- Otherwise, if G is askable then ask the user, record their answer as a new current fact, and succeed or fail according to their response.
- Otherwise, find a rule which can be used to conclude G, and try to prove each of that rule's preconditions.
- Otherwise, fail G.

3.3.1 A Simple Example

This is much better explained through a simple example. Suppose that we have the following rules for diagnosing everyday household emergencies (based loosely on those given in Chapter 2):

R1: *IF coughing THEN ADD smoky*
R2: *IF wet and NOT raining THEN ADD burst_pipe*
R3: *IF NOT coughing AND alarm_rings THEN ADD burglar*
R4: *IF smoky AND hot THEN ADD fire*

We start off with a vague feeling that something is wrong, and that the possibilities are *fire*, *burst_pipe*, and *burglar*. These would be the hypotheses given to the expert system. We'll assume that the system has been provided with no initial facts, so will have to ask the user about the facts about this particular case. We'll further assume that we can directly ask the user whether it is *hot*, whether they are *coughing*, whether it is *wet*, whether it is *raining*, and whether the *alarm rings*.

The simplest backward chaining system would try to prove each hypothesis in turn. First, the system would try to prove *fire*. Rule R4 is potentially useful, so the system would set the new goals of proving *smoky* and *hot*. The first of these, *smoky*, can be concluded using rule R1, so we try in turn to prove *coughing*. This is something we can ask the user:

> Are you coughing?

Suppose the user answers "no". This response would be recorded (in case needed later). The hypothesis *fire* fails, and the system moves on to the next hypothesis: *burst_pipe*. Using rule R2 the user is next asked:

> Are you getting wet?

If the user answers "no" to this too then the hypothesis *burst_pipe* fails, and the system tries *burglar*. Using rule R3 the system sets subgoals *NOT coughing* and *alarm_rings*. The user has already said that they are not coughing, so that information need not be asked again. The system therefore asks:

> Is there an alarm ringing?

If the user answers "yes" the system can conclude that there has been a burglary:

> I conclude that there has been a burglary.

A complete interaction with this tiny system might look like:

> System: Are you coughing?
> User: No.
> System: Are you getting wet?
> User: No.
> System: Is there an alarm ringing?
> User: Yes.
> System: I conclude that there has been a burglary.

In this example there was only one rule that could be used to make a given conclusion. In general (as discussed in Chapter 2) there may be several, and proving a hypothesis involves *searching* through all the possible ways of it could be proved, systematically checking each of them. Search techniques are discussed in more detail in the next chapter. A more realistic system would also have many hundreds of rules, and these rules would contain variables, as discussed in Section 2.4.

3.3.2 Explanation Facilities

Expert systems often have explanation facilities that allow the user to ask *why* it asked some question, and *how* it reached some conclusion. These questions are answered by referring to the system's goals (e.g., to prove *burst_pipe*), the rules being used, and any existing problem data. To illustrate the sorts of facilities commonly provided, we'll elaborate on our simple example above, starting with a simple example dialogue involving *why* and *how* questions and explanations.

> System: Are you coughing?
> User: No.
> System: Are you getting wet?
> User: No.
> System Is there an alarm ringing?
> User: Why?
> System: I'm trying to prove that there has been a burglary. It has been established that it is not the case that you are coughing. Therefore, if there is an alarm ringing then we can conclude that there is a burglary. Is there an alarm ringing?
> User: Yes.
> System: I conclude that there has been a burglary.
> User: How?
> System: This follows from rule R3:
> *IF NOT coughing AND alarm_rings THEN ADD burglar*
> You told me that it is is not the case that you are coughing.
> You told me that there is an alarm ringing.

Providing such an explanation facility involves, at least, recording what rules are used in drawing conclusions, and using these records to compose explanations like the ones above. Giving simple explanations like those above is not very difficult (the answers always have a simple set form), and is sometimes quite useful. However, explanation facilities in expert systems are often not widely used, or are viewed as inadequate by their users. There are a whole number of reasons for this, motivating current research in the area.

One reason is that the explanations just reference the "surface" knowledge encoded in the rules, rather than the "deep" knowledge about the domain which originally motivated the rules (but which is usually not represented). So, the system will say that it concluded X because of rule 23, but will not explain what rule 23 is all about. In the above example, the (slightly odd) rationale behind R3 is that the house may have two kinds of alarm systems, a smoke alarm and a burglar alarm, but that if there's smoke you'll also be coughing! In a system to diagnose diseases the underlying rationale for the rules might be based on a physiological model, while in a system to diagnose faults in a car it might be based on an underlying model of how the car engine works. Unless this knowledge is accessible to the system any explanations will be rather limited.

Computation and Reasoning

Another stated reason for the frequent failure of explanation facilities is the fact that, if the user fails to understand or accept the explanation, the system can't re-explain in another way (as people can). Explanation generation is an area of research, concerned with effective communication: how to present things so that people are really satisfied with the expert recommendations and explanations, and how to represent the underlying knowledge required.

3.4   Reasoning Under Uncertainty

In the discussion so far we've assumed that all knowledge is certain. For example, we might say that if it's hot and smoky there is definitely a fire, or that it is definitely hot. However, in many (if not most) practical applications things tend to be vague. If it is hot and smoky it is probably a fire, but it could possibly be a rather unpleasant party. If you are coughing and have a sore throat you probably have a cold, but again you could be at that rather unpleasant party or dingy pub.

Most expert systems therefore require some way of saying that something is probably, but not necessarily, true. Or that some observations (e.g., symptoms) are usually, but not always, associated with some cause (e.g., disease). Some of these techniques will be discussed in the case studies in the next section. However, in this section we'll set the scene by introducing one of the simplest methods, the simple Bayes approach. This method isn't really an AI technique (based directly on well-understood results in probability theory), but can be used to develop simple expert systems. In fact, using this approach you can develop an expert system using a spreadsheet. As the method has often been used for medical expert systems, medical examples will be used throughout.

3.4.1   Background: Basic Probability Theory

The probability of x represents the *degree of belief* in x[2]. A probability of 0 means that it can't possibly be true, a probability of 1 means that it is definitely true, and a probability of 0.5 means that it is equally likely to be true as not.

The degree of belief in something will depend on what is already known about the case (i.e., the evidence). If we have a hypothesis H then $P(H)$ gives the degree of belief in H in the absence of any evidence. If we have some evidence E then the probability is represented as $P(H \mid E)$ (the probability of H given E is true). This is referred to as a *conditional* probability. Conditional probability is defined as:

$$P(H \mid E) = \frac{P(H \wedge E)}{P(E)}$$

------

[2]Strictly this is the *subjective* interpretation of probabilities. The *objective* interpretation is more common, and refers to frequencies of events occurring in repeated experiments, but this is not relevant for our purposes.

where $P(H \wedge E)$ is the probability that both H and E are true.

Values for conditional probabilities may be obtained either from experts or from example data. For example, suppose we want to know the probability of a heart attack given that someone reports shooting pain up their arm. We could either ask a doctor for a plausible value, or gather data on hundreds of patients who have reported a shooting pain, and find what proportion were eventually diagnosed as having a heart attack.

In diagnosis problems we very often have available data on the probabilities of various symptoms for different diseases, but may not have the data giving the probabilities of the diseases given the symptoms. (It is easier to obtain suitable data on people who have had heart attacks, than people who have had shooting pains.) Using the above definition for $P(H \mid E)$ we can obtain a formula to find the latter from the former:

$$P(H \mid E) = \frac{P(E \mid H) \times P(H)}{P(E)}$$

This is known as Bayes' theorem.

3.4.2 Independence Assumptions

Normally, of course, there are lots of relevant bits of evidence (e.g., symptoms), which all must be taken into account. We need some way of reasoning with multiple pieces of evidence.

To do this we need to know something about which bits of evidence are *independent* of which others. The notion of independence is very important in probability theory. If two facts E_1 and E_2 are independent of (i.e., have no influence on) each other, then it is very easy to calculate the probabilities of them both being true, i.e., of $E_1 \wedge E_2$:

$$P(E_1 \wedge E_2) = P(E_1) \times P(E_2).$$

So, we only need to know the probabilities of E_1 and of E_2. As an example, the probability of getting two heads in a row when tossing coins is $\frac{1}{2} \times \frac{1}{2} = \frac{1}{4}$. If two facts are not independent (e.g., E_1 = "Carry umbrella", E_2 = "Live in Scotland".) then this simple formula does not apply. We cannot find out $P(E_1 \wedge E_2)$ simply from the probabilities of each separate fact.

For a diagnosis task we are interested in a particular type of independence: the *conditional* independence of a collection of bits of evidence $(E_1 \ldots E_N)$ GIVEN a hypothesis H. If $E_1 \ldots E_N$ are conditionally independent given H, then we have:

$$P(H \mid E_1 \wedge \ldots \wedge E_N) = \frac{P(E_1 \wedge \ldots \wedge E_N \mid H) \times P(H)}{P(E_1) \wedge \ldots \wedge P(E_N)}$$

$$= \frac{P(E_1 \mid H) \times \ldots \times P(E_2 \mid H) \times P(H)}{P(E_1 \wedge \ldots \wedge E_N)}$$

Computation and Reasoning

Conditional independence is a convenient simplification, but one that is not always valid. For example, if certain symptoms tend to co-occur then the assumption will be violated. Perhaps if you have a cold then you tend to get either a cough and a sore throat, or neither. If that is the case then they are not conditionally independent, and the above formula will not be accurate.

As it stands we still have to know the *joint* probability of all the evidence (e.g., symptoms) $(P(E_1) \wedge \ldots \wedge P(E_2))$. However, if the possible hypotheses are *exhaustive* and *mutually exclusive* (i.e., everyone has one of the diseases and no-one has more than one) we can simplify the above so that this joint probability is not required. (We find an expression for $P(\neg H \mid E_1 \wedge \ldots \wedge E_N)$ and use this result to eliminate $P(E_1 \wedge \ldots \wedge E_N)$ in the above formula.)

3.4.3   Likelihood Ratios

Bayes' theorem is a little awkward to handle for diagnostic problem solving, so it is commonly reformulated using *likelihood ratios*. We define the *prior* odds of an event H as:

$$O(H) = \frac{P(H)}{1 - P(H)}$$

This is just like the odds given on horses. If the odds on "Speedy" winning are 3:2 then there are three chances of him winning to 2 chances of him not winning. $P(speedywins)$ is the chance that he'll win, and $1 - P(speedywins)$ is the chance that he'll not win. Odds of 3:2 (or 1.5) on a disease mean that three people will have it for every two that don't.

We also need *posterior* odds, which are related to conditional probabilities:

$$O(H \mid E) = \frac{P(H \mid E)}{1 - P(H \mid E)}$$

Maybe the odds of "Speedy" winning given that "Très Vite" has been nobbled are 5:2.

Now, we can consider how adequate some evidence E is for concluding H. The positive *likelihood ratio* (or *level of sufficiency*, LS) is defined to be:

$$LS = \frac{P(E \mid H)}{P(E \mid \neg H)}$$

Using odds and likelihood ratio definitions we can get:

$$O(H \mid E) = LS \times O(H)$$

Given the assumptions of conditional independence we have an equally simple expression for the case where there is more than one bit of evidence. We just multiply together the levels of sufficiency for each bit of evidence, multiply the result by the prior odds, and hey presto, we have the posterior odds for the disease given all the evidence.

Example

Suppose we have obtained the following likelihood ratios (LSs) (from data on $P(E \mid D)$ and $P(E \mid \neg D)$):

	Measles LS	Mumps LS
Spots	15	10
No spots	.3	.5
High Temp.	4	5
No Temp.	.8	.7

We also know that the prior odds of a child having measles are 0.1, and of mumps are 0.05. Now, GIVEN that we know that Fred has spots but no temperature, we can calculate the posterior odds of measles:

$$O(Measles \mid Spots \wedge NoTemp) = 0.1 \times 15 \times .8 = 1.2$$

and of mumps:

$$O(Mumps \mid Spots \wedge NoTemp) = 0.05 \times 10 \times .7 = .35$$

So, there isn't overwhelming evidence for either (as both are associated with having a temperature) but the odds on measles are higher than those on mumps.

Weaknesses of Simple Bayesian Systems

Suppose you used the above formula to develop a simple probabilistic expert system. You could start off with some patient data which would allow you to determine the likelihood ratios and the prior odds of different diseases. If data wasn't available an expert could be asked to make a guess. An expert system could then very simply be developed, perhaps just using a spreadsheet.

However, there are many possible sources of error that might creep into such a system. The symptoms may not in fact be independent given the disease, and the likelihood ratios and prior odds may be inaccurate, based on non-representative or over-small samples of patients or poor guesses of experts. Simple probabilistic methods may give the illusion of precision (giving an output probability of, say, 96.4%), yet these values may still have significant errors. These errors may be critical.

In the simple Bayes formalism, if we don't make assumptions of conditional independence, then we need huge tables of conditional probabilities, giving $P(H \mid E_1 \wedge E_2 \wedge \ldots \wedge E_N)$ for every possible combination of evidence. It just isn't practical to obtain this data. If, say, there were just 16 possible symptoms we'd need a table with $2^{16} = 65,536$ entries for every disease! It is unlikely that an expert would be willing to guess values for all these cases (or could guess them accurately), and it is very unlikely we'd have enough data on past patients to get accurate probabilities for each combination of symptoms.

However, with the simplifying assumptions, simple Bayes systems sometimes work well in narrow and constrained areas, where only a dozen or so diseases are to be considered, with a similar number of relevant symptoms. However, the performance of such systems deteriorates if they are expanded so that more symptoms or more diseases can be considered. This is due to violations in the assumption that the symptoms were independent.

3.5   Three Case Studies in Medicine

So far we've just looked at the basics of a simple kind of rule-based expert system, and introduced some basic ideas about uncertainty. In this section we'll look at the design of three contrasting full-scale practical systems, all used for a medical diagnosis task. This will allow us to look further at how uncertainty can be handled, look at a range of different problem-solving methods, and consider a number of practical issues for expert system development and deployment.

The first system described below, MYCIN, is a pioneering expert system which uses, primarily, a backward chaining rule-based approach, but extends this approach so that uncertainty may be handled. The second, Internist, is another pioneering early system, but one which bases its problem-solving method on human problem solving, and uses a different technique for handling uncertainty. The last, Pathfinder, characterizes a number of more recent systems which use modern statistical techniques for diagnosis, developing on the ideas in the section above. The descriptions of all these systems are necessarily rather simplified, but should illustrate the basic approaches.

3.5.1   MYCIN: A Rule-Based Approach

MYCIN was developed to illustrate how artificial intelligence techniques could be used to solve problems which involve uncertain and incomplete knowledge. It was developed partly in response to the perceived limitations of the simple Bayes systems as described above. It was one of the earliest and most influential expert systems developed, and many expert system shells use methods based on those used in MYCIN.

MYCIN was designed to help physicians in the diagnosis and treatment of patients with certain kinds of bacterial infections. This involves determining the possible organisms involved and choosing the most appropriate drugs. Rapid treatment may be required, so MYCIN was designed to be able to operate on incomplete data, before definitive test results were available. It had to come up with a good "covering" treatment that would deal with all possible infections until an accurate diagnosis could be made.

MYCIN's overall architecture is similar to that in Figure 3.1, and indeed the proposed decomposition of an expert system into these modules was one of the outcomes of the MYCIN project. Pioneering work on knowledge base editors, inference engines and explanation systems was done in the context of this project.

Knowledge Representation
MYCIN's knowledge base consisted of a set of IF–THEN rules, with associated certainty factors. The following is a simplified English version of one of MYCIN's rules:

> IF the infection is primary-bacteremia
> AND the site of the culture is one of the sterile sites
> AND the suspected portal of entry is the gastrointestinal tract
> THEN there is suggestive evidence (0.7) that infection is bacteroid.

MYCIN also included knowledge tables that included basic facts that were needed by the system, such as characteristics of the various bacteria. A special structure called a *context tree* was used to organize case-specific data about the patient.

The above rule includes a numeric value of 0.7 indicating how likely the conclusion is if the conditions are true. Degrees of certainty in MYCIN are represented using *certainty factors*. Facts and rules may have associated certainty factors; a certainty factor of 1 means that something is definitely true, a certainty factor of -1 means that something is definitely not true, while a certainty factor of 0 means that we haven't a clue. Certainty factors are not the same as probabilities, but are related.

If we know the certainty factors of the preconditions (e.g., that the infection is primary-bacteremia), and know the certainty factor of the rule, we can calculate the certainty factor that should be associated with the conclusion.

Suppose we know that the certainty factors associated with the three preconditions are 0.6, 0.5 and 0.8. The first thing we need to do is find the certainty that they are all true. In MYCIN the rule is that we take the *minimum* of the certainty factors of the conjoined preconditions (using AND), so the value associated with the whole precondition is 0.5. The reason for taking the minimum is that our confidence that they are all true should correspond roughly to our confidence in the most weakly held precondition. If we have a rule with a disjunction of preconditions (using OR) we take the *maximum* of the certainty factors. So in general:

$$CF(P_1 \; AND \; ... \; AND \; P_N) = MIN(CF(P_1), ..., CF(P_N))$$

$$CF(P_1 \; OR \; ... \; OR \; P_N) = MAX(CF(P_1), ..., CF(P_N))$$

Once we've obtained the certainty factor for the whole precondition we can calculate the certainty of the conclusion, given a particular rule. This is easy – we just multiply the certainty factor of the precondition by the certainty factor of the rule. For the above example we get 0.35. In general, the certainty of a conclusion C given a rule R with precondition P is:

$$CF(C, R) = CF(P) \times CF(R)$$

This is complicated if we have more than one rule which allows us to make the same conclusion. If there are two rules concluding C, which give us certainties (using the above) of $CF(C, R1)$ and $CF(C, R2)$, then, if these are positive, the total certainty factor is:

$$CF(C) = CF(C, R1) + CF(C, R2) - CF(C, R1) \times CF(C, R2)$$

(If one or both of the certainty factors is negative a slightly different formula is used.)

This method for handling uncertainty is regarded as somewhat *ad hoc*. Although it does have roots in probability theory, a lot of assumptions are made about the nature of the data. For some problems this may not be important, as the certainties involved are themselves very uncertain. Experts are unsure how to assign certainty factors to rules, and users are unsure how to assign certainty factors to facts they are asked about. So errors due to a somewhat *ad hoc* calculation may not be as significant as the errors in the original certainties. However, errors in calculations can accumulate, and, while certainty factors may still be useful in simple rule-based systems, current research focuses on developing practical techniques that are based on sounder calculations.

Problem-Solving Strategy

MYCIN uses a fairly simple problem-solving strategy based on backward chaining. Possible bacteria (which might be causing the patient's infection) are considered in turn, and MYCIN tries to prove whether they might be involved using rules such as the one above. So, it might attempt to prove that the organism is *E. coli*, asking the user some questions to determine this, then go on to consider another bacterium, until all are considered. The outcome of this will be a list of possible bacteria and associated certainties.

Once possible diagnoses are determined MYCIN attempts to choose a possible treatment. This consists of two stages: selecting candidate drugs, and then choosing the preferred drugs. At this stage the backward chaining strategy is abandoned in favour of a more data-driven approach. Each organism has an associated list of possible drugs and numbers giving their effectiveness. Given a list of possible organisms these numbers are combined, taking into account all possible organisms and their likelihoods, to determine the best drug or drugs to cover all the possibilities with an adequate degree of certainty.

Example

A (simplified) sample dialogue with MYCIN is given below.

1.	M	Patient's name?
2.	U:	Alan Apt.

...

6.	M:	Are there any pending cultures for Alan Apt?
7.	U:	Yes.
8.	M:	From what site was the specimen for the culture taken?

...

14.	M:	Please give the date on which the clinical evidence of meningitis first appeared.
15.	U:	25 March
16.	M:	Has the patient had neurosurgery?
17.	U:	Why?
18.	M:	This will aid in determining the organisms that might be causing the infection. It has already been established that: the culture is meningitis; organisms were not seen of the pending culture. Therefore if the patient had neurosurgery then there is evidence that the organisms that might be causing the infection are *staphylococcus-coag-pos* (0.75) and *staphylococcus-coag-neg* (0.5). Has the patient had neurosurgery?
19.	U:	No.

...

26.	M:	Is the patient a burn patient?
27.	U:	Yes.
28.	M:	I have found evidence (rule 507) that treatment should cover for *Diplococcus pneumoniae* causing meningitis. I have found evidence (rule 545) that treatment should cover for *E. coli* causing meningitis.
29.	M:	Does the patient have focal neurological signs?
30.	U:	No.
31.	M:	My preferred therapy recommendation is as follows. In order to cover for *Diplococcus pneumoniae* and *E. coli* give the following in combination: AMPICILLIN Dose 3.85g GENTAMICIN Dose 131mg.

The dialogue is in three stages. The first stage (1-13) elicits basic information about the patient and cultures. This information is used to come up with initial hypotheses (e.g., to only consider meningitis infections). The second stage (14-28) results from backward chaining on these hypotheses, to find the certainty of each. In the last stage (29-31) the system determines and presents appropriate treatments. Alternative therapies will be presented if the first is rejected by the user. At any stage (e.g., 17-18) the user can ask HOW and WHY questions, as discussed in Section 3.3.2.

Evaluation

MYCIN was evaluated by comparing its performance to that of eight members of Stanford's medical school: five faculty members, one research fellow in infectious diseases, one physician and one student. They were given ten randomly selected case histories, and asked to come up with diagnoses and recommendations. These diagnoses, and those produced by MYCIN, were then given to eight independent experts in infectious diseases to evaluate (scoring each diagnosis as acceptable or not). The results showed that MYCIN performed as well as any of the Stanford medical team, and considerably better than the physician or the student.

Despite this positive result, MYCIN has never been used in clinical practice. The reasons are varied, but include:

- A session with MYCIN took half an hour and a great deal of typing! This is unlikely to be acceptable in practice.
- MYCIN's scope was limited and it could not deal with situations that were not explicitly represented in its knowledge base. So it would never, for example, conclude after asking a few questions that it was not a bacterial infection after all, but a nasty cold. In fact MYCIN did not even cover the full spectrum of infectious diseases.
- At that time, MYCIN required more computing power than could be afforded by hospitals.

Follow-on Projects

MYCIN spawned a whole range of follow-on projects, including:

EMYCIN: This was more or less the first expert system *shell*. It provided the basic rule language and interpreter, and allowed MYCIN-like expert systems to be developed much more quickly.

PUFF: A system developed using EMYCIN, to determine the severity of pulmonary disease given data from lung function tests. This system has been used in clinical practice.

GUIDON: This was a tutoring system based on MYCIN. Students would attempt to make diagnoses, MYCIN would be used to check if they were sensible, and Guidon would provide feedback and hints.

NEOMYCIN: This was a rewritten version of MYCIN, which made the underlying problem-solving strategy more explicit.

3.5.2   Internist: Modelling Human Problem Solving

Internist is a large diagnostic program developed at the Pittsburgh School of Medicine. Unlike MYCIN it tries to explicitly capture the way human experts make their diagnoses, using a complex problem-solving strategy based on the technique of *differential diagnosis*. This technique works well when there are a very large number of possible hypotheses (e.g., diseases) to consider. The basic approach is:

- Use available (symptom) data to suggest or *trigger* candidate diseases.
- Determine what other symptoms would be expected given these diseases.
- Gather more data to differentiate between these hypotheses, and update the set of current hypotheses.

Knowledge Representation

Internist represents knowledge about the diseases in question as *disease profiles*, and then uses a complex problem-solving strategy that uses the information in the disease profiles and the evidence found so far.

These disease profiles specify the *findings* (such as symptoms and test results) that are associated with the disease. For each such finding, two numbers are supplied, indicating the correlation between disease and finding. The first number (evoking strength) indicates the likelihood of the disease given that the finding occurs. The second number (frequency) indicates the likelihood of the finding given that the disease occurs. (Convince yourself that these may be different. e.g., a headache only weakly evokes the hypothesis brain tumour, but given a brain tumour a headache is very likely.) Anyway, a numerical value from 0 to 5 is given for both evoking strength and frequency, with an informal interpretation given for each value (for example, an evoking strength of 4 means that "Diagnosis is the overwhelming cause of the given finding"). Evoking strength and frequency are a bit like the conditional probabilities $P(H \mid E)$ and $P(E \mid H)$, but more *ad hoc* techniques are used to manipulate them.

A simplified example disease profile is given below:

Disease profile for ECHINOCOCCAL CYST of LIVER

Finding	Evoking Strength	Frequency
Cough	1	2
Fever	0	2
Jaundice	1	2
Hepatomegaly	1	3

These disease profiles are held in a *disease tree*: a hierarchical classification of disease types. Disease profiles will be supplied both for broad classes of disease (e.g., liver disease) and more specific diseases. The disease knowledge base also contains information about what diseases tend to be associated with what other diseases (so that if one is suggested, the others may be considered), and information about the significance (import) of various findings (so that trivial findings can be disregarded).

Altogether there is knowledge of about 600 diseases and 4500 related findings in Internist. This knowledge base was constructed by a team of physicians, through careful literature review and case discussions. Its construction represents many man-years of effort.

Problem-Solving Strategy

Internist uses this information as follows:

1. The physician enters an initial list of findings, and Internist finds all diseases that are evoked by these findings (i.e., evoking strength > 0).

Computation and Reasoning

2. For each such disease hypothesis, Internist creates a *disease model* consisting of four lists:

   (a) Observed findings consistent with the disease.

   (b) Observed findings not associated with the disease.

   (c) Findings associated with the disease which are observed not to be present in patient.

   (d) Findings not yet observed but which are associated with the disease.

3. Based on these lists, each hypothesis is given a score. This score is based on an *ad hoc* scheme which uses the weights of all findings in lists (a)–(c) above, with findings in list (a) contributing positively to the score and the others contributing negatively.

4. The possible hypotheses are sorted, and the *competitors* for the topmost diagnosis are determined. This step acknowledges that the patient may have more than one disease, and it is the diseases which explain the same symptoms as the top disease that should be considered its competitors. Diseases which explain other symptoms may co-exist.

5. Now there will be one or more competing major diagnoses. The strategy now will depend on the number and score of these possible diagnoses. If there is only one, Internist will conclude with that diagnosis. If there is more than one, but the top one is significantly better, Internist will try to confirm the top one, gathering more data about its associated findings. If there are five or more possibilities, Internist will attempt to rule some out. If there are two to four possibilities, Internist will try to discriminate between them, asking questions that will maximize the difference in the resulting scores.

6. When a diagnosis is concluded Internist will remove the patient findings that are explained by the diagnosis from consideration, and start again with any remaining findings (in case the patient has several diseases).

Internist's methods are, on their own admission, *ad hoc*, yet the system is impressive in its performance and in its scope. It covers the whole of internal medicine, and in one study its diagnostic accuracy was shown to be comparable to that of physicians in a major teaching hospital.

QMR

The original Internist system was developed on a large mainframe computer, and was not suitable for use by practitioners. However, in the 1980s the program was adapted to run on PCs as QMR (Quick Medical Reference). Unlike Internist, which was solely a diagnostic tool, QMR can be used in three modes. In its basic mode it can provide diagnostic advice (as Internist). However, it can also be used in other modes, such as as an electronic textbook, listing the symptoms associated with a disease or the diseases associated with a given finding, or just as a tool to explore the relationships between diseases and findings. These modes make use of the detailed medical knowledge base built up during the Internist project, and indeed QMR's authors acknowledge that the most valuable outcome of Internist was its detailed knowledge base. QMR is very much intended to be used as an assistant to the doctor, rather than as an all-knowing expert, and is now used in both clinical practice and education.

3.5.3 Pathfinder: Using Probability Theory

Pathfinder is a system to assist pathologists with the diagnosis of lymph-node related diseases. Given a number of findings (e.g., dead tissue) it would suggest possible diseases (e.g., AIDS). It is interesting because it has explored a range of problem-solving methods and techniques for handling uncertainty.

In the Pathfinder project a variety of techniques were considered for handling uncertainty, including simple Bayes, certainty factors and the scoring scheme used in Internist. These were compared by developing systems based on the different methods, and determining which gave more accurate diagnoses. Surprisingly, simple Bayes did best. A theoretical analysis of the different approaches revealed that they could all be viewed as variants of simple Bayes, and all implicitly incorporated the assumption of conditional independence. In fact, the assumptions made about the data in the non-Bayesian methods were worse than those made in the Bayesian methods. So, for certainty calculations for this kind of problem (dealing with associations between findings and hypotheses), simple Bayes seems best. Yet we know that it has limitations because of the assumptions made about the data.

Simple Bayes, as we have described it, requires that the user indicates, for every possible finding, whether or not that finding is present. Yet this information might be both expensive to obtain (if, for example, a special test had to be done) and tedious to enter. An advantage of Internist was that it would just ask about those findings relevant to the current set of hypotheses and would keep updating this hypothesis set as new data was entered. So questions would only be asked about diseases that seemed likely given data entered so far.

The Pathfinder project both looked at how the dialogue with the user could be controlled so the user is only asked about important findings, and how the basic simple Bayes approach could be developed so that independence assumptions are not required. These two aspects are discussed below.

Controlling the Dialogue

Pathfinder uses a similar basic problem-solving strategy to that used by Internist. It maintains a list of current hypotheses suggested by the findings entered so far, and uses this to suggest further findings which would be useful in differentiating between competing hypotheses. Probabilistic methods are used to score possible hypotheses.

Once the user has entered a few initial findings the system will score all the possible diseases and present the user with an ordered list of the top few hypotheses, along with their probabilities. The user can then either enter further findings (and obtain a new hypothesis list and probabilities) or ask the system which findings would be particularly useful in narrowing the diagnosis. All this is done through a simple menu-based graphical user interface.

To suggest findings that would be useful the system uses a sophisticated technique based on decision theory. The key idea is that entering findings has an associated cost, and the gain from knowing the finding may not outweigh the cost. For example, some findings involve complex tests that either are dangerous to the patient or take too much time. Pathfinder considers the *utility* of the finding, based on how much it contributes to the diagnosis and how important it is to get the diagnosis just right, and the *cost* of the finding. Findings are scored so that the ones recommended to the user are those that bring most benefit for least cost.

In Pathfinder the whole interaction is very much under the control of the user. It is the user who chooses which findings to enter, only asking the system advice if required. This contrasts with Internist, where the dialogue was controlled by the system. In general the mode of interaction used in Pathfinder, with the user in control, is found more acceptable by doctors, emphasizing the role of the expert system as a passive assistant rather than a supplanting expert.

Bayesian Networks

The simple Bayes approach makes assumptions about the data – that evidence is conditionally independent. If these assumptions are not true then this will result in errors. If two findings tend to co-occur given some disease, and both are observed, a simple Bayes system will tend to over-estimate the likelihood of the disease, as it will treat the two findings as independently supporting the hypothesis.

Although the technique was quite successful in Pathfinder, practical methods were sought which would avoid this assumption of independence. A now popular approach is to use a *network* to represent the relationships between the various pieces of evidence and possible hypotheses. These networks, also referred to as *belief networks*, provide an intuitive representation which makes it relatively easy to reason about independence in data, and handle cases where things aren't independent, but are perhaps causally related.

Figure 3.2 illustrates the basic idea. This network is meant to capture the following informally stated medical knowledge: "Metastatic cancer is a possible cause of a brain tumour, and may also tend to result in increased total serum count. In turn, either of these make it more likely that a patient will fall into a coma. Severe headache may also result from a brain tumour."

This network doesn't just include observable symptoms and final diagnoses. It can also include intermediate disease states and measurements (e.g., serum count). If two diseases are causally related (e.g., metastatic cancer and brain tumour) then a link is given between these. The aim is to come up with a moderately simple network that captures information about what states influence what others. Note that there is no link between metastatic cancer and headaches. Although people

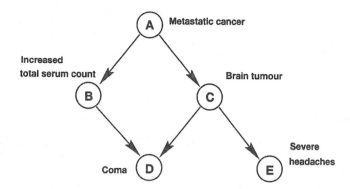

Figure 3.2 *A Simple Bayesian Network.*

with metastatic cancer ARE more likely to get headaches, the claim is that this is only the case because they also tend to have a brain tumour.

Anyway, by specifying the causal relations in this way we are making explicit what facts depend on what, and which are (conditionally) independent. For example, in the figure, E is conditionally independent of A given C. This means that if we know someone has a brain tumour then more evidence for them having metastatic cancer will have no influence on how strongly we believe they will have a headache. Similarly, B is conditionally independent of C given A, so if we know that someone has cancer, then more evidence for them having a brain tumour will not influence our belief in them having an increased serum count.

For each node in a Bayesian network a table of conditional probabilities must be supplied, saying how that node depends on its "parent" nodes. For example, for node D we'd need to supply $P(coma \mid inc.serumcount \wedge braintumour)$, $P(coma \mid inc.serumcount \wedge \neg braintumour)$ and so on. Once these are supplied we can enter findings (e.g., severe headache) and the probabilities of all the other nodes will be updated (e.g., increasing very slightly the probability of brain tumour, and hence the probability of a coma).

As there is no real distinction in this approach between evidence and hypothesis we could also enter the fact that someone has metastatic cancer and find the probability that they have a severe headache. Or enter the fact that they have cancer and a headache and determine the probability that they have a brain tumour.

The network provides us with both an informal and a formal way of reasoning about how some evidence will influence a hypothesis. It is fairly easy to reason informally how belief in one node will influence belief in the others. It is also possible to do accurate calculations to update probabilities in the network. The methods are quite complex, but there are tools available that will allow you to build up a network graphically and have the system take care of the probabilities. It is also feasible to enter all the relevant tables of conditional probabilities (although more are required than for the simple Bayes approach). So Bayesian networks

Computation and Reasoning

seem to provide a real way forward, overcoming the limitations of simple Bayes systems in a practical manner.

A version of Pathfinder using Bayesian networks proved the most accurate of all the approaches explored, doing significantly better than human expert pathologists.

Pathfinder in Practice

A commercial version of Pathfinder called Intellipath has been developed, and is used fairly widely by practising pathologists – several hundred have been distributed. The system includes both the diagnostic tool and a set of supporting materials such as a library of images, text information about the diseases, references to the literature and a system to produce reports. It is unclear whether it is more the supporting materials or the diagnosis system that has led to the system's relative success.

3.5.4 Summary

In this section we've looked at three contrasting systems for medical diagnosis. Some general conclusions may be drawn concerning problem-solving strategy, reasoning under uncertainty, and practical deployment.

- Although a simple backward chaining system may be successful where there are a relatively small number of hypotheses to consider, where there are many possible hypotheses we need some way of focusing in on those that are currently most likely. Otherwise the system may doggedly pursue an implausible hypothesis, asking irrelevant questions as it goes. Internist provided one approach, based on human problem solving, where questions are asked to differentiate between current hypotheses. Pathfinder uses a complex notion of the utility of information in order to suggest to the user which findings to enter.
- The most theoretically promising approach for handling uncertainty is to use Bayesian networks. However, simpler approaches such as certainty factors may still prove useful for certain problems, particularly where IF–THEN rules provide a natural way to represent expert knowledge.
- Many systems are developed, perform well, but are never used. To be successful in practice a system must integrate with existing systems and working practice, have an easy-to-use interface, require little time to use, and maybe have extra useful features such as textbook information and references to the literature.

The discussion in this section has focused on medical examples. Most of the points apply to all types of expert systems. However, it is important to note that there are lots more problem-solving techniques that have been used for expert systems. We've just considered a few that may be applied to medical diagnosis.

Computation and Reasoning

A knowledge engineer should be aware of the whole range of available techniques and tools, and which techniques tend to be suitable for which kinds of task.

3.6 Summary

- Expert systems are used to do tasks normally requiring human expertise, where that expertise is in short supply.
- Suitable problems are ones where the benefits outweigh the costs, cooperative experts are available, users are ready to accept the technology, and the problem itself is highly specialized.
- Expert system development (or knowledge engineering) involves methods for interviewing human experts, selecting suitable problem-solving and knowledge representation methods, rapid prototyping and testing.
- A typical expert system involves the following modules: *knowledge base, inference engine, case-data, explanation system, user interface*, and *knowledge base editor*.
- A simple expert system can be developed using production rules and a backward chaining inference engine. The system will try to prove each of a given set of hypotheses, asking the user questions as it goes.
- For most applications an expert system must be able to represent and reason with uncertain knowledge. A variety of techniques have been developed. The most theoretically advanced is the use of Bayesian networks, which provide an intuitive graphical representation and a sound way of dealing with probabilities.
- Three well-known expert systems in medicine are MYCIN, Internist and Pathfinder. All illustrate very different techniques for problem solving and reasoning with uncertain knowledge. All gave good performance, but getting such systems accepted in practice involves much more than this.

3.7 Further Reading

Most AI textbooks give some discussion of expert systems, although this is often fairly limited. Ginsberg (Ginsberg, 1993) gives a rather brief introduction, but discusses interesting issues concerning the relationship of expert system work to AI in general. Rich & Knight (Rich & Knight, 1991) include a short introduction, including details of knowledge acquisition tools. Luger & Stubblefield (Luger & Stubblefield, 1993) give a fairly extensive introduction to rule-based expert systems, covering similar material to this chapter and give example expert system shells in Lisp and Prolog. Russell & Norvig (Russell & Norvig, 1995) includes a chapter on building a knowledge base, with some interesting discussion on *ontologies* (knowledge-base vocabulary), but the approach is logic-based rather than rule-based.

There are a lot of books devoted to expert systems, but few of them are very good. A thorough and popular book is (Jackson, 1990), which gives both an introduction to knowledge representation in expert systems and a detailed discussion of problem solving, knowledge engineering methods, and various advanced topics. Lucas and van de Gaag (Lucas, & van de Gaag, 1991) give a solid introduction to the knowledge representation methods (with examples in Lisp, Prolog, and psuedocode), and a good section on reasoning with uncertainty, but limited practical discussion. Turban (Turban, 1992) gives an accessible, although rather lightweight, introduction to applied AI and expert systems in particular, with plenty of discussion of practical AI systems in use, and practical problems in expert system development.

Original articles on the three case studies may be found in (Buchanan & Shortliffe, 1984) (MYCIN), (Miller, 1982) (Internist) and (Heckerman *et al.*, 1992) (Pathfinder). There have been many articles about the lack of progress at getting expert system technology accepted in medicine, including (de Dombal, 1987).

3.8   Exercises

1. A travel agent asks you to design an expert system to help people choose where to go on holiday. Discuss whether this might be a suitable problem for an expert system, and say how you might start acquiring the necessary expert knowledge.

2. Develop a simple set of rules for diagnosing respiratory system diseases given patient symptoms, using the following knowledge of typical symptoms.

   Influenza: Symptoms include a persistent dry cough and a feeling of general malaise.

   Hayfever: symptoms include a runny nose and sneezing. The patient will show a positive reaction to allergens, such as dust or pollen.

   Laryngitis: Symptoms include a fever, a dry cough, and a feeling of general malaise. A "laryngoscopy" will reveal that the person has an inflamed larynx.

   Asthma: Symptoms include breathlessness and wheezing. If it is triggered by an allergen, such as dust or pollen, it is likely to be "extrinsic asthma". "Intrinsic asthma" tends to be triggered by exercise, smoke or a respiratory infection.

Describe how a simple backward chaining interpreter could be used to go through the possible diagnoses, asking the user questions about their symptoms.

If you have an expert system shell available, try implementing a simple diagnosis system based on the above.

3. What do you think are the main problems and limitations of the rule-set developed for question 2? What additional knowledge might be useful to deal with more complex or subtle diagnoses?

4. Compare and contrast the MYCIN and Internist expert systems. Why do you think Internist's strategy is good when there are many hypotheses to consider?

5. What factors do you think should be considered when getting a medical diagnosis expert system accepted in practice? Which of these points would apply to all expert system projects?

6. (Project) Try using a spreadsheet to implement a simple Bayes expert system using the odds-likelihood formulae. Assume that you have data of the likelihood ratios for, say, four diseases given three possible symptoms. (Make up such data if it isn't supplied.) The system should calculate the posterior odds on each disease given the patient's symptoms.

CHAPTER 4

Using Search in Problem Solving

Aims:	To introduce both blind and heuristic search techniques, and their use in AI problem solving. Simple planning and game playing methods will be discussed.
Objectives:	You should be able to:
	Describe a range of search algorithms, and show how a search tree would be traversed using these algorithms.
	Show how simple puzzles can be formulated as search problems.
	Discuss the limitations of simple search techniques, and the advantages and disadvantages of the different methods.
	Describe a simple AI planning method, and show how it can be used to solve simple robot action planning problems.
	Explain how minimax search is used in game playing systems, and outline how it may be made more efficient using Alpha-Beta pruning.

4.1 Introduction

In this section we will switch back to looking at very general techniques that are important throughout AI. In particular, we will look at how you can use *search* techniques to try to find a solution to a problem. The general idea here is that if you know the available actions that you could take to solve your problem, but don't know which ones will get you to a solution, you can search through all the possibilities to find one that will give you a solution.

68

This basic notion of search applies to all sorts of problems. We mentioned in Chapter 2 that backward chaining rule-based systems must have a search strategy so that they can systematically go through the available choices when trying to prove goals. This involves searching for a possible sequence of inference steps which will constitute a proof of some goal. In other applications we may be searching for the sequence of steps that will solve a puzzle, a sequence of moves that will result in winning a game, or a sequence of actions that will allow us to successfully get done the week's shopping. Many of these problems may be expressed in terms of trying to get from some *initial state* (e.g., unsolved puzzle; middle of game; nothing in the fridge) to some *target state* (e.g., solved puzzle; game won; shopping done). We want to search through all the possible actions that could be taken to find a sequence that gets from the initial to target state.

In this chapter we will start off by discussing some basic search techniques and algorithms. Most of these are general-purpose algorithms which may be familiar from other areas of computer science. However, a brief introduction to the relevant background material will be presented. In particular, a basic introduction to *graph theory* terminology will be given, as problems are generally discussed in terms of searching a graph.

To make these more concrete we will discuss these general algorithms by considering how we might search for a good route on a map. We will then show how the methods can be applied to simple problem-solving tasks, and move on to show how more special-purpose algorithms may be used for *planning* and for *game playing*.

4.2   Search Techniques

Suppose we are trying to find our way around a small town with a lot of one-way streets, as illustrated in Figure 4.1. This town has the rather inconvenient feature that, once you've left somewhere, you can never get back there, and that once you're in the park, you can never escape! However, this simplifies our initial discussion of search methods.

Suppose we want to find a possible route from an *initial state* at the library to a *goal state* at the university. (Problem states, for this example, are locations). We can quickly see that the only route involves going via the hospital and the newsagent – but how do we systematically search for such a route, given, perhaps, much more complex maps?

For a simple problem like this, we can *systematically* and *exhaustively* search all possible paths. That is, we can systematically check every state that is reachable from the initial state to find out if it is a goal state. The set of all such states is the *search space*. When the search space is small, relatively simple search techniques are adequate, which try every possible path in a systematic way. These are referred

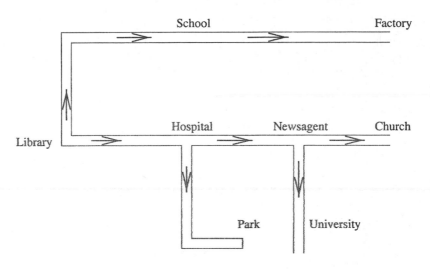

Figure 4.1 *A Simple Search Problem: Finding Routes on a Map.*

to as *brute force* or *blind* search techniques, and include *breadth first* and *depth first* search which are discussed in Section 4.2.2. However, for more complex problems there may be a huge number of possible states to explore -- the search space may be very large. It will then not be possible to try them all in a reasonable amount of time. For these problems we may need to use *heuristics* (useful rules-of-thumb) to guess which paths are likely to lead to a solution. Heuristic search algorithms are discussed in Section 4.2.3.

4.2.1   Graphs and Trees

The search algorithms that will be described below are very general, and apply to all sorts of problems. So we need an abstract way of representing search problems so that general-purpose algorithms may be applied, without having to develop a new method for each new problem. *Graphs* are used for this.

There is a lot of terminology used to describe graphs and trees, which is illustrated in Figure 4.2. A graph consists of a set of (possibly labeled) *nodes* with *links* between them (these are sometimes referred to as *vertices* and *edges*). The links can be directed (usually indicated by arrows) or undirected. The term *successor* will be used to refer to a neighbouring node, reachable by a link. A *path* is a sequence of nodes connecting two nodes via links (e.g., [a,b,e]). An *acyclic* graph has no *cycles*, i.e., paths linking a node with itself.

A *tree* is a special kind of graph with only one path to each node, usually represented with a special *root node* at the top. Links in a tree are always directed (arrows may be omitted if it is clearly a tree). Relationships between nodes are described using family tree terminology. A is the *parent* of B and F (who are its

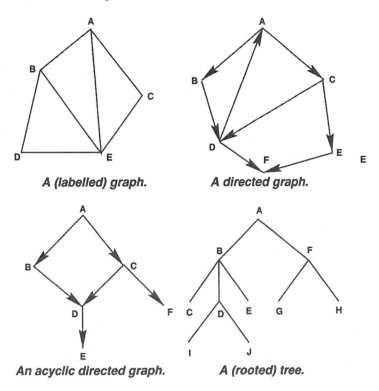

Figure 4.2 *Graphs and Trees.*

children). B is F's *sibling*. A is the *ancestor* of all the other nodes, which are *descendants* of A. Nodes with no children (e.g., C and I) are referred to as *leaf* nodes.

Particularly important terms to note, which will be used throughout this chapter are *node*, *successor*, *path* and *tree*. By using this abstract terminology it is possible to describe very different kinds of problems in the same way, and so use the same algorithm to solve them.

The map in Figure 4.1 can be represented more abstractly as the tree in Figure 4.3 (referred to as the *search tree*). The initial state (l) is used as the root node of the tree, which is the *start node* for any search. From this state there are two child nodes s and h, corresponding to the two directions you can go from the library. From h there are two child nodes, as there is a junction at the hospital leading to either the park or the newsagent.

Now, rather than talking about searching for a route from the library to the university, we talk about finding a *path* from a start node l (library) to a target node u (university). This same graph/tree representation and terminology may be used for many other problems.

Computation and Reasoning

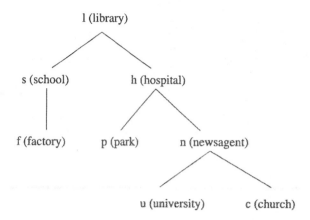

Figure 4.3 *Map Problem Represented as Search Tree.*

4.2.2   Simple Search Techniques: Breadth First and Depth First

The simplest two search techniques are known as *depth first* search and *breadth first* search. They are best introduced by first considering how a *tree* is traversed, then extending this to graphs in general.

The two techniques involve traversing the search tree in different ways, but in both all nodes in the tree will eventually be explored. The algorithms for both methods use a list of nodes that have been found, but have still to be further explored (i.e., their successors haven't been examined yet). This list is sometimes referred to as the *agenda*.

In this section we first examine these two search methods, considering first, basic versions of the algorithms, then two extensions.

Breadth First Search

In breadth first search you would search for a route by trying nodes in following order: l, then s and h, then f, p and n, and finally u and c. (The search might end after node u, which is the goal state.) So, we will first be trying paths of length 1, then 2, then 3 and so on. This is illustrated in Figure 4.4.

The algorithm for breadth first search involves using a *queue* for the agenda. A queue is just a special list where nodes are always added to the end of the list, but removed from the front. Initially the queue contains just the initial state (i.e., $[l]$). Search involves repeatedly taking the first node off the queue, finding that node's successors, and putting them on the end of the queue. This continues until either the first node on the queue is the goal or target state, or the queue is empty. If the first node is the target state the algorithm will signal success (e.g., return TRUE). Otherwise the search fails.

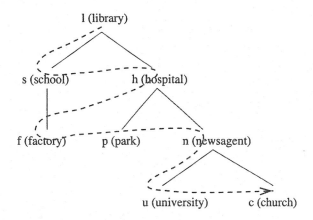

Figure 4.4 *Breadth First Search.*

In our example, initially the queue is:

$[l]$

We take l off the queue, find that it has successors s and h, and put them on the queue, which is now:

$[s,\ h]$

s is taken off the queue, has successor node f, so the new queue is:

$[h,\ f]$

h has two successors, p, and n. These are put on the end of the queue:

$[f,\ p,\ n]$

f doesn't have any successors – there was a dead end in the road near the factory – so is just removed from the list. The same happens for p, leaving just n on the queue:

$[n]$

n has two successors, which are added to the end of the queue:

$[u,\ c]$

But u is the goal state, so when that is examined we can exit with success.

The algorithm can be stated more formally as follows:

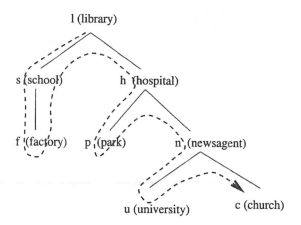

Figure 4.5 *Depth First Search.*

1. Start with *queue* = [initial-state] and *found* = FALSE.
2. While *queue* not empty and not *found* do:

   (a) Remove the first node N from *queue*.

   (b) If N is a goal state then *found* = TRUE.

   (c) Find all the successor nodes of X, and put them on the end of the *queue*.

The algorithm as it stands merely sets a flag *found* to TRUE if it finds a goal state. It may easily be extended to, for example, return the path to the goal state or return all found goal states. The former is considered later in this section. We've also only considered searching trees, and not arbitrary graphs. So we will also see later how it may be extended to handle graphs. However, before looking at these extensions we'll look at depth first search.

Depth First Search

Depth first search is another way of systematically looking for a path from one node to another. In depth first search you keep on going down one path until you get to a dead end. You then back up to try alternatives. (This is referred to as *backtracking*.) Depth first search for our example problem is illustrated in Figure 4.5 – the order of nodes searched is: l, s, f, h, p, n, u, c.

The algorithm for depth first is exactly the same as for breadth first but a *stack* is used rather than a queue, so new nodes are added to the front, rather than the end of the list[1]. Try working through the example problem using depth first search.

Both breadth first and depth first search are simple algorithms that will eventually find a path if there is one (and if the search tree is finite). However, sometimes

---

[1]Alternatively, a simple recursive algorithm can be used. However, we will stick with an explicit stack, so that comparisons between the algorithms are clearer.

one of the two may be more appropriate than the other. The choice of algorithm depends on a number of factors:

- Are you looking for the shortest path? If so, breadth first may be better as it will find the shortest path first.
- Is memory likely to be a problem? Depth first search generally requires much less memory.
- Do you want to find a solution quickly? If so, the choice of algorithm gets complex! Depth first may be faster if there are many paths that lead to solution states, but all are quite long. Breadth first may be faster if there is one short path to the target, but within a large and deep search space.

There are many variants of breadth and depth first search that may be useful in certain situations. For example, you can set a *depth limit* in depth first search so it backs up when it gets to nodes further than the specified distance from the initial state. A variant of this is an algorithm called *iterative deepening* which repeats depth first search with gradually increasing depth limits. In spite of the apparent waste in repeating bits of search this is a very useful algorithm, as it both requires little memory (like depth first) and finds the shortest path first (like breadth first).

Returning the Path

As mentioned above, the algorithm so far, whether depth or breadth first, just indicates whether or not there is a path. In general we may want it to return the successful path that allows us to get from the initial to goal state. There are a number of ways to do this – look in any text on algorithms. We'll just mention one that is particularly straightforward in a Prolog implementation of the search algorithm. What we can do is make an item in the agenda be a path rather than a state – we can still check for success by, for example, checking whether the last element of the path is the goal state, and we can modify our search algorithms to return the path once a successful one is found. We'd start with an agenda[2] like:

$$[[l]]$$

(i.e., one item in the agenda, which is a path with one item in it). Then after finding l's successors we'd have:

$$[[l, s], [l, h]]$$

and so on. At each stage we'd check whether the last item in the first path is the goal state.

Searching Graphs

So far we've assumed that we are searching a *tree*, and not an arbitrary graph. In a tree, we can't get to the same node by two different routes, and we can't go in circles and get back from a node we started from.

---

[2]From now on the more general term agenda will be used – a stack or queue might be used for this.

However, most problems involve searching general graphs. Consider our simple map search problem. Clearly most maps allow us both to get to the same place by more than one route, and to get back to where we came from by taking a circular route. Most AI problems (where we're searching for a sequence of actions to achieve some state) also involve graph search rather than simple tree search.

If we use our simple tree search algorithms when searching arbitrary graphs then at best they will be less efficient (we will redo work already done) and at worst we'll get caught in infinite loops. To address the infinite loop problem, we can make a very small modification to our algorithm: we avoid adding a node to a path if it already appears on the path. (This is straightforward if your agenda consists of paths rather than just nodes.)

However, this doesn't address the efficiency problem. Consider the graph in Figure 4.6 (which corresponds to a map with one-way streets, but more than one route to the hospital). If we use a simple depth first search method we might first search nodes l, s, h, n and c, back up and search node f, but then try nodes h, n and c again, repeating part of the search. (Try working through what happens for this example, given the simple depth first search algorithm.)

The problem is that we have no record of the fact that h, n, and c have already been searched. To get round this problem we just keep such a record. For example, we could maintain a list of nodes already explored – this will be referred to as the *visited* list (the term *closed* list is also sometimes used). The algorithm can now be modified so that nodes that are already on the visited list are not explored further. A basic version of this revised algorithm, this time for depth first search, is given

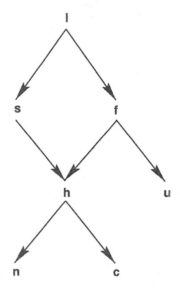

Figure 4.6 *Example Search Graph*

Computation and Reasoning

below. It may of course be extended to return the path, as outlined above.

1. Start with *agenda* = [initial-state] and *found* = FALSE.
2. While *agenda* not empty and not *found* do:
   (a) Remove the first node N from *agenda*.
   (b) If N is not in *visited* then:
      i. Add N to *visited.*
      ii. If N is a goal state then *found* = TRUE.
      iii. Put N's successors on the front of the *stack.*

Summary

To summarize so far, search techniques are used in AI to find a sequence of steps that will get us from some initial state to some goal state(s). You can use various search algorithms to do the search. We've so far discussed simple breadth first search and depth first search. These are both systematic, exhaustive search techniques that will eventually try all the nodes in the search space (if it's finite). The appropriate algorithm will depend on the problem you are trying to solve, such as whether you want the shortest path.

4.2.3 Heuristic Search

So far we have looked at two search algorithms that can in principle be used to systematically search the whole search space. Sometimes, however, it is not feasible to search the whole search space, as it is too big – imagine searching every possible road and alley in a 400-mile circumference around London when looking for a route to a house in Edinburgh. Where the search space is too big to search every node it may be possible to construct some scoring function that can be used to provide an estimate as to which paths or nodes seem promising. Then the promising nodes are explored before the less promising ones. Search methods that use such a scoring function are referred to as *heuristic search* techniques .

The basic idea of heuristic search is that, rather than trying all possible search paths, you try to focus on paths that seem to be getting you nearer your goal state. You generally can't be sure that you are really near your goal state – it could be that you'll have to take some highly complicated and circuitous sequence of steps to get there. But we might be able to have a good guess. Heuristics are used to help us make that guess.

To use heuristic search you need an *evaluation function* that scores a node in the search tree according to how close to the target/goal state it seems to be. This will just be a guess, but it should still be useful. For example, for finding a route between two towns a possible evaluation function might be an "as the crow flies" distance between the town being considered and the target town. Then, routes that seem to get you nearer the target are explored before those that get you further from the target. This strategy may not always work – maybe there aren't any good roads from this town to your target town, and you have to first go away from your destination in order to get onto the right road. However, it provides a quick way of guessing that helps in the search, and will tend to result in a solution being found faster.

There are a large number of different heuristic search algorithms, of which we'll go through three: hill climbing, best first search and A*. We'll assume that we are searching trees rather than graphs (i.e., there aren't any loops etc.). However, the algorithms can be simply extended for graph search by using the methods outlined in Section 4.2.2.

Hill Climbing

In hill climbing, the basic idea is to always head towards the best successor node (and only if that node is better than the current one). So, looking at Figure 4.1, if you are at the hospital trying to get to the church, and you could either move along the road to the newsagent or along the road to the park, then you should move to the newsagent, as it is nearer to the church than either the hospital or the park. The basic algorithm is as follows:

1. Start with *current-state* = initial-state.
2. Until *current-state* = goal-state OR there is no change in *current-state* do:

   (a) Get the successors of *current-state* and use the evaluation function to assign a score to each successor.

   (b) If one of the successors has a better score than *current-state* then set the new *current-state* to be the successor with the best score.

Note that the algorithm does not attempt to exhaustively try every node and path, so no list of nodes to explore is maintained – just the current state. If there are loops in the search space then using hill climbing you shouldn't encounter them – you can't keep going up and still get back to where you were before.

Hill climbing terminates when there are no successors of the current state which are better than the current state itself. This is often a problem. For example, suppose we were looking for a route from the library to the university, using "as the crow flies distance to target" as the evaluation function. Initially the current state would be library, then hospital, and then park (as this brings us nearer to the park than the newsagent would). But this is a dead end, and there is nowhere to try now that would bring us nearer to the university. So the algorithm would halt without success. This would also happen for the map in Figure 4.7, if we were trying to get from the library to the park. In this case we'd move from the library to the school, but then halt, as there is no other location nearer to the park.

These problems are essentially the result of *local maxima* in the search space – points which are better than any surrounding state, but which aren't the solution. There are some ways we can get round this (to some extent) by tweaking or extending the algorithm a bit. We could use a limited amount of backtracking, so that

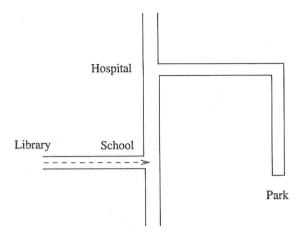

Figure 4.7 *Map Illustrating Limitations of Hill Climbing.*

we record alternative reasonable looking paths which weren't taken and go back to them. Or we could weaken the restriction that the next state has to be better by looking ahead a bit in the search – maybe the next but one state should be better than the current one. None of these solutions is perfect, and in general hill climbing is only good for a limited class of problems where we have an evaluation function that fairly accurately predicts the actual distance to a solution.

Best First Search

Best first search is a little like hill climbing, in that it uses an evaluation function and always chooses the next node to be that with the best score. However, it is exhaustive, in that it should eventually try all possible paths. It uses a list of nodes that are still to be further explored (as in depth/breadth first search), but rather than always adding new nodes on the front or rear, and removing nodes from the front, it always removes the *best* node from the list, i.e., the one with the best score. For those familiar with data structures, the algorithm makes use of a *priority queue*, rather than a stack or a simple queue – however, we'll use the more general term *agenda*. The successors of the best node will be evaluated (i.e., have a score assigned to them) and added to the agenda.

The basic algorithm is as follows:

1. Start with *agenda* = [initial-state].

2. While *agenda* not empty do:

    (a) Remove the best node from the *agenda*.

    (b) If it is the goal node then return with success. Otherwise find its successors.

Computation and Reasoning

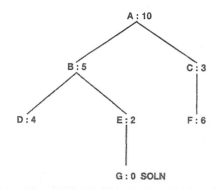

Figure 4.8 *Search Tree Illustrating Best First Search.*

(c) Assign the successor nodes a score using the evaluation function and add the scored nodes to *agenda*.

Suppose we have the search tree in Figure 4.8. Here links between nodes illustrate possible successor states. A node label such as B:5 means that the node name is B and it has an estimated cost to solution of 5 (so a lower value is better).

Suppose our goal state is G. If we searched this search space using breadth first search then the nodes would be searched in the following order: A, B, C, D, E, F, G. Using depth first search the order would be: A, B, D, E, G. For both of these the scores on nodes are ignored. Using simple hill climbing a solution would never be found – there is a local maximum at C where it would get stuck. Using best first search the order would be: A, C, B, E, G. You should verify this using the algorithm above.

If you have a good evaluation function, best first search may drastically cut down the amount of search that you have to do to find a solution. You may not find the best solution (or at least, the first solution found may not be the best), but if a solution exists you will eventually find it, and there is a good chance of finding it quickly. Of course, if your evaluation function is no good then you are just as well off using simpler search techniques such as depth first or breadth first. And if your evaluation function is very expensive (i.e., it takes a long time to work out a score) the benefits of cutting down on the amount of search may be outweighed by the costs of assigning a score.

The A* Algorithm

In its simplest form as described above, best first search is useful, but doesn't take into account the distance of the path so far when choosing which node to search from next. So, you may find a solution but it may be not a very good solution. There is a variant of best first search known as A* which attempts to find a solution which minimizes the total cost of the solution path. ("Cost" is intended as a general notion – for map problems this might be the distance.)

In the A* algorithm the evaluation function consists of two parts. The first part is based on the cost associated with getting from the start node (corresponding to the initial state) to the node in question. The second part is an *estimate* of the cost from this node to the target node. The total score is a (possibly weighted) sum of these two parts, giving an estimate of the total cost from start to target going via the node in question. So, if $g(Node)$ gives the cost from start node to Node, and $h(Node)$ gives the estimated cost from Node to target, the total score $f(Node)$ is:

$$f(Node) = g(Node) + h(Node)$$

The A* algorithm is essentially the same as the simple best first algorithm, but we use this slightly more complex evaluation function. (Our best node will be the one with the *lowest* cost/score.) To illustrate what A* gains us, consider the search tree in Figure 4.9 where successor links are labelled with the cost of getting between nodes and the scores attached to nodes are again an estimate of the cost to solution.

If we use simple best first search we would search the nodes in the following order: A, B, D, E, F. As F is our goal state we'd have a solution, but it would not be a particularly good one. It will have a path cost of 13 (2+4+3+4). If we use A*, then the nodes will be searched in the following order: A, B, C, G, F', with the solution path found being the that with lowest cost (7). In fact, the A* algorithm guarantees to find the shortest path first. However, to make this true we have to ensure that $h(Node)$ does not *overestimate* the cost to the solution. The definition of the A* algorithm includes this requirement.

A* may be compared with both breadth first and best first search. In breadth first search, if the cost of traversing each link is the same, the lowest cost solution will be found first. However, it may not be found very quickly. In best first search

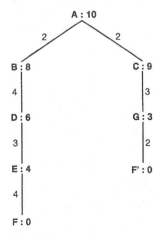

Figure 4.9 *Search Tree Illustrating A* Search.*

Computation and Reasoning

85

some solution should be found quickly, but it may not be a very good solution. In A* we should find a good solution and find it quickly.

4.3   Problem Solving as Search

So far we have described several search algorithms, but not how they are used in solving problems. In general, search techniques are used to find a sequence of actions that will get us from some initial state to some goal state. The actions may be physical actions (such as move from town A to town B, or put block C on the table) or may be more abstract actions, like theorem-proving steps (we may be searching for a sequence of steps that will allow us to prove X from the set of facts S).

There are many different ways search techniques that can be used in problem solving. This section will start by looking at how simple search techniques may be used to solve puzzles, using a very simple representation of the possible actions that are allowed. Then we'll show how the approach may be extended for slightly more complex *planning* problems, changing the search algorithm and the way actions are represented. Finally we'll look at game playing systems – where there is an opponent out to foil any plan.

In all the methods discussed a node in the search space will be some formal description of the current state of the problem. For a board game playing system this might be a description of the current state of the board; for a puzzle it might be a description of the current state of the objects in the puzzle. Successor nodes will be possible new states, which can be reached from the current state by taking some action (e.g., making a move in a game). The search space is sometimes referred to as the *state space* as it captures all the possible states or situations you could get into, and the methods referred to as *state space* search techniques.

4.3.1   State Space Search Techniques

Simple state space search techniques (where nodes in the search space represent the problem state) are often illustrated by showing how they can be used in solving puzzles of the sort you find in intelligence tests. One such puzzle is the water jug problem:

> "You are given two jugs, a 4-gallon one and a 3-gallon one. Neither has any measuring markers on it. There is a tap that can be used to fill the jugs with water. How can you get exactly 2 gallons of water into the 4-gallon jug".

Given such a problem, we have to decide how to represent the problem state (e.g., amount of water in each jug), what the initial and final states are in this

1.	Fill the 4-gallon jug.	$\{X, Y\} \rightarrow \{4, Y\}$
2.	Fill the 3-gallon jug	$\{X, Y\} \rightarrow \{X, 3\}$
3.	Empty the 4 gallon jug into the 3-gallon jug.	$\{X, Y\} \rightarrow \{0, X+Y\}$ (if $X+Y \leq 3$)
4.	Empty the 3-gallon jug into the 4-gallon jug.	$\{X, Y\} \rightarrow \{X+Y, 0\}$ (if $X+Y \leq 4$)
5.	Fill the 4-gallon jug from the 3-gallon jug.	$\{X, Y\} \rightarrow \{4, X+Y-4\}$ (if $X+Y > 4$)
6.	Fill the 3-gallon jug from the 4-gallon jug.	$\{X, Y\} \rightarrow \{X+Y-3, 3\}$ (if $X+Y > 3$)
7.	Empty the 3-gallon jug.	$\{X, Y\} \rightarrow \{X, 0\}$
8.	Empty the 4-gallon jug.	$\{X, Y\} \rightarrow \{0, Y\}$

Figure 4.10 *Actions for Water Jug Problem.*

representation, and how to represent the actions available in the problem. Actions are represented by specifying how they change the problem state.

This particular puzzle is based on a simple problem-solving domain where the problem state can be represented simply as a pair of numbers giving the amount of water in each jug (e.g., $\{4, 3\}$ means that there is 4 gallons in the 4-gallon jug and 3 in the 3-gallon jug). The initial state is $\{0,0\}$ and the final state is $\{2,X\}$ where X can take any value. There are only a small number of available actions (e.g., fill the 4-gallon jug), and these can be simple represented as 8 *rules* or *operators* which show how the problem state changes given the different actions. These are listed in Figure 4.10.

Rules such as $\{X, Y\} \rightarrow \{X, 0\}$ mean that we can get from a state where there are X gallons in the first jug and Y in the second jug to a state where there are X gallons in the first and none in the second, using the given action. If there is a condition such as (if $X+Y \leq 3$) this means that we can only apply the rule if that condition holds. We only consider actions that cause a change in the current state.

Note that in puzzles such as this we restrict our set of actions to ones that might actually be useful in solving the problem. It won't help just pouring a random amount of water onto the ground, as then we won't know where we are! The programmer has to supply most of the intelligence, in the way the problem is represented and the algorithm chosen to solve it.

Now, how do we use our standard search techniques discussed earlier? The notion of a "successor state" is a little more obscure here than in the map domain. We have to look at all our actions, and find ones that apply given the current state. We can then use the rules above to find the states resulting from those actions. A particular node in the search tree, rather than being just the name of a town, will now be the representation of a particular state (e.g., $\{2, 3\}$) (see Figure 4.11).

This should all be clear when we try to solve the problem. We'll use depth first search first, and make the items on the agenda be *paths* from the initial state to the current state, rather than just the current state, and check for loops within each

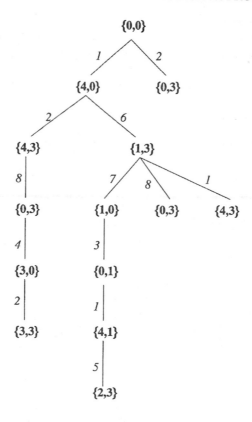

Figure 4.11 *Search Tree for Jugs Problem.*

path. Other search techniques (as discussed in Section 4.2) could also be used.

Initially the jugs are both empty, so the initial state is $\{0, 0\}$, and the agenda is:

$agenda = [[\{0, 0\}]]$

(All the brackets are because a *state* is represented as $\{0,0\}$, a *path* with just that one state in it is $[\{0,0\}]$, and an agenda or list of such paths is $[[\{0,0\}]]$.)

Anyway, our goal state is $\{2, X\}$, where X can take any value. To start problem solving, we remove the first path from *agenda* and look for possible *extensions* to that path. A possible extended path is one that is the same as the old one, but has an extra node at the end of it, such that that node is a *successor* of the last node in the old path. There may be several such possible extended paths.

There are two actions that you can take from $\{0,0\}$ that will change the state of the world – filling the 3-gallon or filling the 4-gallon jug. Possible successors are $\{4, 0\}$ and $\{0, 3\}$, so the new agenda is:

$agenda = [[\{0,0\},\{4,0\}], [\{0,0\},\{0,3\}]]$

From {4, 0} actions 2, 6 and 8 apply. Possible next states are: {4, 3}, {1, 3}, {0, 0}. {0, 0} is already on the path (so there would be a loop), so that one is thrown away, and the new agenda is:

agenda = [[{0,0},{4, 0},{4,3}], [{0,0},{4,0},{1,3}],[[{0, 0},{0,3}]]

Now, from {4, 3} we can apply actions 7 and 8. Action 7 will get us back to {4, 0} which already on the path, so that one is ignored. Action 8 will get us to {0,3}, so in the new agenda the first item is replaced with [{0,0},{4,0},{4,3},{0,3}]. From {0,3} we can get to {3,0} or {4,3} or {0,0}. Only {3,0} is a new state, so the new agenda is now:

agenda = [[{0,0},{4,0},{4,3},{0,3},{3,0}],
          [{0,0},{4,0},{1,3}],[{0,0},{0,3}]]

Now, from {3,0} we can get to {0,3}, {0,0} and {3,3} (pour jug 1 into jug 2; empty jug 1; fill jug 2). Only {3,3} is a new state, so the agenda becomes:

agenda = [[{0,0},{4,0},{4,3},{0,3},{3, 0},{3,3}],
          [{0,0},{4,0},{1,3}],[{0,0},{0,3}]]

From {3,3} we're stuck. All of the reachable states are already on the path. So we remove that whole path from the agenda and look at the next path. From {1,3} we can reach {1,0}, {0,3}, {4,3}, all of which are new states on the path. So there are three possible extended paths and the agenda is:

agenda = [[{0,0},{4,0},{1,3},{1,0}], [{0,0},{4,0},{1,3},{0,3}],
          [{0,0},{4,0},{1,3},{4,3}],[{0,0},{0,3}]]

From {1,0} we can reach a new state {0,1} (pour jug 1 into jug 2), and from there a new state {4,1} (fill jug 1). And from there we can fill jug 2 from jug 1, leaving 2 gallons in jug 1, and we get to {2,3}! This is the solution we were looking for. We have 2 gallons in the 4-gallon jug. The portion of the search tree explored is given in Figure 4.11. The numbers in italics indicate the relevant actions.

So we have found one solution to the problem – fill the 4-gallon jug, fill the 3-gallon from the 4-gallon, empty the 3-gallon, empty the 4-gallon into the 3-gallon, fill the 4-gallon and fill the 3-gallon from the 4-gallon again. In fact, because we carefully formulated the problem, and ruled out actions that resulted in old states or no change, there wasn't too much search involved. Problems which do involve a lot of search would just be too tedious to go through! Hopefully however the example will have given an idea of how simple problems are approached using search techniques. You have to decide on a representation of the problem state, of the available actions for that problem, and systematically go through all possible sequences of actions to find one that will get from the initial to target state.

Computation and Reasoning

89

Note that in the solution to this problem we sometimes re-examined states that had already been explored. For example, the state {0,3} is on the explored tree on three branches. A lot of work is done that has been done before (e.g., checking if there is a solution starting from the state {0,3}.). We could have avoided this by using a *visited* list, as outlined in Section 4.2.

In the water jug problem there is no real need to use a heuristic search technique – the domain is sufficiently constrained that you can go through all possibilities pretty quickly. In fact, it's hard to think what a good evaluation function would be. If you want 2 gallons in the jug, does it mean you are close to a solution if you have 1 or 3 gallons? Many problems have the property that you seem to have to undo some of the apparent progress you have made if you are to eventually get to the solution (e.g., empty out the jug when you've got 1 gallon in it). Heuristic search is often useful in problem solving, but it may be better to try to carefully formulate the problem, so that the search space is small and simple search techniques can be applied.

There are lots of other problems that have been solved using similar techniques, and which are discussed in many longer AI textbooks. One is given in the exercises at the end of the chapter.

Complexity Problems

The techniques that we have described can be applied to many problem-solving tasks. However, for realistic tasks we often run into difficulties. One problem relates to the complexity of the algorithms. For *brute force* search techniques such as breadth first and depth first we may end up having to search an enormous number of nodes in the search space to find a solution. For example, if there are (on average) n successors to every node in the search space, and our solution is at depth d, then in breadth first search we may need to search n^d nodes. If n is, say, 20 and d is 6 then we may need to search over 60 million nodes. For depth first search we may be luckier, and happen to hit on a solution sooner, but then if there isn't a solution on the first branch we try we may end up having to search even more nodes. Graph search techniques, where we avoid re-examining already searched nodes, may help for some problems, but carry some overhead in maintaining and checking a list of nodes already encountered. Heuristic search methods may be useful, but only when the evaluation functions are good.

The average number of successor states for nodes in the search space is known as the *branching factor*. For search to be tractable we want our search space to have a fairly small branching factor. The branching factor will depend on how a problem is formulated. In state space search the branching factor can be reduced by applying some (human!) intelligence when specifying the rules or operators for deriving successor states – we want to make sure any pointless actions/successor states are not even considered in the search. It may also be reduced by choosing appropriately whether to search forward, from the initial state, or backwards, from the goal state (either is often allowable). The branching factor in each case may be very different.

If none of this helps then we have a *combinatorial explosion*! We just have too many combinations to try, and the deeper in the tree we search the worse it gets. Largely because of this problem, general-purpose search techniques are often inadequate for serious problem solving. They need to at least be augmented with more specialized, domain-specific problem-solving techniques.

4.3.2 Planning Techniques

Planning, in AI, is the problem of finding a sequence of primitive actions to achieve some goal. This sequence of actions will be the system's plan, which can then be executed. Planning is often discussed in the context of robotics, where it is a physical robot which will execute the plan. However, it is important in many areas of AI – for example, in natural language understanding it is important to reason about peoples' plans and goals in order to best make sense of what they say.

State-space search may be viewed as a simple planning technique. However, generally in the AI literature the term "planning" is reserved for slightly more sophisticated stuff, where actions in particular are represented in a more complex way. To introduce AI planning mechanisms we'll describe a simple planning method based on the *means–ends analysis* (MEA) approach to problem solving, and a representation of actions introduced in one of the first AI planning systems called STRIPS.

Means–ends analysis is an approach to problem solving which, rather than blindly searching through all possible actions, focuses on actions that reduce the *difference* between the current state and the target state. Another feature is that if an action is found that reduces this difference, then it will be considered even if it can't be applied in the current state. Getting to a state where the useful action can be applied is set as a new subproblem to solve.

Means–ends analysis can be applied to a whole range of problem-solving tasks – indeed, it was designed as part of a general model of how people solve problems (the GPS or General Problem Solver). However, we will just describe a variant which uses the STRIPS representation of actions, and is applied to simple robot planning tasks. A typical task might involve stacking a number of blocks, or moving some objects between rooms.

The technique uses the basic ideas of state-space search. It is concerned with searching for a path from some initial state to some desired final or target state, checking through the different possible actions that could be taken to see which sequence of actions leads to the right result. *Means–ends analysis* is the technique used to control the search.

In simple planning systems the problem state can be represented as a list of facts that are true, e.g.:

[at(robot, living_room), at(beer, kitchen), at(fred, living_room), door_closed(kitchen, living_room)]

This might represent a state where Fred is in the living room with his robot, but the beer is in the kitchen and the door to the kitchen is shut.

Given this new representation of the problem state (as a list of true facts) we need a slightly more sophisticated way to represent actions. Actions are now represented by operators that give the *preconditions* of the action and the *effects* of that action on the problem state. An effect may be to *add* a new fact to the problem state, or to *delete* a fact. So, if we assume that the only actions allowed in our example are "robot opens/closes door", "robot moves from one room to another" and "robot carries object from one room to another" then we can have the following operators to describe the possible actions:

Operator	Preconditions	Add	Delete
open(R1, R2)	at(robot, R1) door_closed(R1, R2)	door_open(R1, R2)	door_closed(R1, R2)
close(R1, R2)	at(robot, R1) door_closed(R1, R2)	door_closed(R1, R2)	door_open(R1, R2)
move(R1, R2)	at(robot, R1) door_open(R1, R2)	at(robot, R2)	at(robot, R1)
carry(R1, R2, O)	door_open(R1, R2) at(robot, R1) at(O, R1)	at(robot, R2) at(O, R2)	at(robot, R1) at(O, R1)

Suppose our target state involves Fred with his beer in the living room, his robot by his side, the door closed.

> [at(beer, living_room), at(fred, living_room), at(robot, living_room),
> door_closed(kitchen, living_room)]

Means–ends analysis tries to find an operator whose effects reduce the difference between the current and target states. At the moment, the beer is in the wrong place! The only operator that can shift the beer is the "carry" operator. If it could be applied, then we'd in fact arrive at our goal state. Unfortunately the robot is in the wrong room, and the door is shut.

However, the fact that we can't apply an operator now doesn't stop us. We set the unsatisfied *preconditions* of the actions as new goals to solve. So we recursively try to call the means–ends algorithm with the preconditions of the action as the target state. That is, we try to solve:

> Initial state:
>
> [at(robot, living_room), at(beer, kitchen), at(fred, living_room), door_closed(kitchen, living_room)]
>
> Target state:
>
> [open_door(kitchen, living_room), at(robot, kitchen)]

We now try to find a sequence of actions that will make this new target state true. Without going through the details, if we choose open(kitchen, living_room) and move(living_room, kitchen) then the (intermediate) target state is true.

Now we have to finish the plan. We find what state we get if we apply the operators worked out so far to our initial state. In our example this gives us:

[at(robot, living_room), at(beer, living_room), at(fred, living_room),
door_open(kitchen, living_room)]

We're almost at our target state, but the door is now open. We therefore have to complete the plan by finding a way to close the door. Eventually we will have a completed plan:

open(kitchen, living_room)

move(living_room, kitchen)

carry(kitchen, living_room, beer)

close(kitchen living_room)

This involved first finding an action in the *middle* of the plan: carry(kitchen, living_room, beer). Then the start and end parts of the plan are completed.

This can be illustrated as follows:

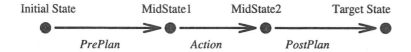

The overall algorithm used is the following:

To find_plan(Initial_State, TargetState)

- If all the goals in TargetState are true in InitialState then succeed.
- Otherwise:

    1. Select an unsolved Goal from TargetState.

    2. Find an Action that adds Goal to the current state.

    3. Enable Action by finding a plan (PrePlan) that achieves its preconditions, i.e., find_plan(InitialState, Preconditions). Let MidState1 be the result of applying that plan to InitialState.

    4. Apply Action to Midstate1 to give MidState2.

    5. Find a plan (PostPlan) from MidState2 to TargetState.

    6. Return a plan consisting of PrePlan, Action and PostPlan.

Computation and Reasoning

93

Many subsequent AI Planning systems have been based on a modified version of this algorithm. Extensions to the basic algorithm include:

Planning with goal protection: where the algorithm includes a check that an action being considered doesn't accidentally undo a goal that was achieved earlier.

Nonlinear planning: where the algorithm does not commit to the order that actions occur in the plan unless one action has to precede another to enable the other's preconditions.

Hierarchical planning: where the plan is developed in outline first, and then the details are filled in.

Reactive planning: where the plan can be modified if the state of the world unexpectedly changes or failures occur.

In many modern planners a node in the search space no longer represents the current problem state, but may represent a possible partially completed plan. Planning involves searching through possible ways that a partial plan may be developed. This has proved a more flexible framework for practical planning, and is discussed in many of the references at the end of the chapter (e.g., (Russell & Norvig, 1995) (ch.11)).

Practical Planning

When planning systems are applied to practical real-life problems the simple search methods discussed in this section prove inadequate to the task, and more complex methods must be used. An example practical planning system is O-Plan, developed at Edinburgh. In O-Plan (and its predecessor, Nonlin), the objective is to gradually develop and refine a partially completed plan. This plan may initially be very sketchy, with details missing, and no fixed order given for the actions. It can then be developed or repaired in various ways. For example, an action in the plan may be *expanded* to give more detail about how it should be carried out.

O-Plan has been used for a variety of applications, for example constructing plans for disaster recovery planning. In this application the system first selects a basic *template* outlining a basic plan for the particular type of disaster (e.g., gas explosion). This template is then filled in, expanded and refined.

Computation and Reasoning

4.3.3 Game Playing Systems

As a final example of how search techniques can be used in problem solving we'll consider game playing systems. The basic approach applies to two-person adversarial games where both players know the state of the game. Many board games such as chess, draughts, and Go fit into this category (two players are competing, and both can see the board).

Games are rather different from the problems that have been looked at so far in this chapter, as there is an opponent involved who will try to foil any plan! So, although it is possible to work out a sequence of actions to achieve a winning state, it is highly likely that a move of your opponent will prevent you from carrying out that plan. Some method is needed for selecting good moves that stand a good chance of achieving a winning state whatever the opponent does.

Game playing problems can still be categorized in terms of search trees. Figure 4.12 gives part of a simple search tree (or *game tree*) for a game of noughts and crosses. Note how the levels in the tree alternate between the two players.

Figure 4.13 illustrates the complete game tree for a hypothetical very simple game where a win is possible in just two moves. (The possible game states are just

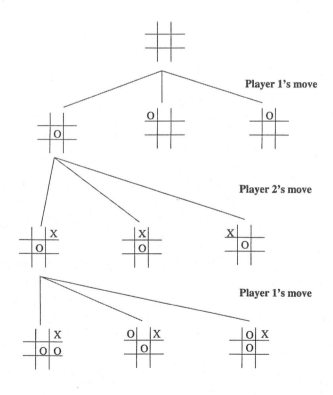

Figure 4.12 *Partial Game Tree for Noughts and Crosses.*

Computation and Reasoning

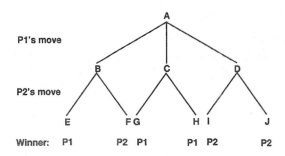

Figure 4.13 *Game Tree for Simple Game.*

represented by the letters A–J rather than a picture of an actual board.) How should player 1 decide which move to make? Each player should obviously assume that the other will try to win. If player 1 moves to state B, then player 2 will choose to move to state F, and so win. If player 1 moves to state C, any move player 2 attempts will still result in player 1 winning. If player 1 moves to state D, any move player 2 makes will result in player 2 winning. Clearly the only safe move for player 1 is to state C.

The Minimax Procedure

For a complete game tree like this, we can find good moves for the first player as follows. First, we'll say that an eventual win for player 1 will be indicated by a positive score of 10, a lose by a negative score −10 and a draw by 0. Then we can work bottom up and work out the scores of earlier nodes in the game tree. Figure 4.14 has these intermediate scores indicated for another simple game tree. At nodes E, F, G and H it is player 1's turn to move. He will try to *maximize* his score. From nodes E, F and H he has a winning move, so these nodes are scored 10. From node G he can at best draw, so this node is scored 0. Now, at nodes B and C it is player 2's move, and player 2 will try to *minimize* player 1's score. (Nodes B and C are referred to as minimizing nodes, while E-H are maximizing nodes.) At node B, whatever player 2 does player 1 has a winning move. The score there is the *minimum* of the scores at nodes E and F, but this is still 10. At node C the minimum score is 0, corresponding to player 2's option of moving to node G and forcing player 1 into a no-win situation. So, player 1 can now reliably say that node B corresponds to the best move, and that from there he has a guaranteed win.

The procedure for assigning a score to a node is as follows:

To score(node):

- If node is at leaf of search tree, return score of that node
- else if it is a maximizing node then return maximum of scores of successor nodes

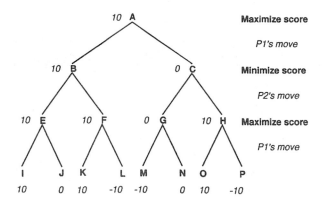

Figure 4.14 *Game Tree Illustrating Minimax.*

- else if it is a minimizing node then return minimum of scores of successor nodes

Player 1 will select which move to make after scoring the possible moves as described above. This is referred to as the *minimax procedure* for game playing. You should go through how this would work for the noughts and crosses example. To keep things simple, imagine that you are half-way through a game, and deciding where to put the next cross. Draw the game tree for the rest of the game, and show how minimax would allow you to determine the best move.

Alpha-Beta Pruning

There is a very simple trick that significantly increases the efficiency of the minimax procedure. It is based on the idea that if you know half-way through a calculation that it will succeed or fail, then there is no point doing the rest of it. For example, in programming languages it is clear that when evaluating statements like if A>5 or B<0, then if the first condition succeeds there is no need to bother trying the second. Or for if A>5 and B<0 there is no point continuing if the first condition *fails*.

I'll start by illustrating the technique using Figure 4.14. Suppose the score for node B has been found. As player 1 will be *maximizing* his score, then we know that he can get *at least* a score of 10 without even examining node C. So the score for node A is at least 10. Suppose the score of node G has also been found. Player 2 will be *minimizing* player 1's score, so the score for node C can be *at most* 0. Taken together, these mean that there is no point working out the score for node H, as there is no way it can affect the score of node A. Suppose node H's score was less than zero. This would change the score of node C, but node A can still get a score of 10, so is unchanged. Suppose node H's score was greater than (or equal to) zero. Node C's score would be unchanged, and hence also node A's. This example is illustrated slightly more simply in Figure 4.15. The score of node H makes no

Computation and Reasoning

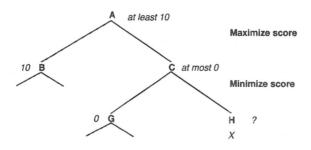

Figure 4.15 *Game Tree Illustrating Alpha-Beta Pruning.*

difference, so the part of the tree below that node (marked X) can be completely ignored.

Alpha-beta pruning involves keeping track of the *at most* and *at least* values, and using these to make savings like that illustrated above. We know that the score at a *maximizing* node is going to be at least the best score of the successor nodes examined so far (a parameter α is used to record this). The score at a *minimizing* node is going to be at most the worst score of the successor nodes examined so far (a parameter β is used for this). If the β value of a minimizing node is less than the α value of its parent node then all remaining calculations on that node can be abandoned. The rest of the tree is *pruned.* If the α value of a maximizing node is greater than the β value of its parent, similarly the rest of the calculations on a node can be abandoned, or the tree pruned.

Alpha-beta pruning is just used to make the minimax procedure more efficient. It has been described rather briefly here, but this should be sufficient for you to work through some examples and see how it would work out in practice.

More Complex Games

For more complex or sophisticated games it is, in fact, not realistic to work out the complete game tree, even with alpha-beta pruning. For chess, there are billions of possible board states. However, a variant of the above method can be used. We limit the *depth* that is explored in the search tree (to, say, five moves ahead), and for the board states corresponding to the leaves in the limited search tree (which may or may not be winning states), a heuristic scoring function is used to assign a score to the node. For chess, a simple score might correspond to a points score of the player's remaining pieces. The above scoring function is then used to determine the scores of nodes further up the tree, so that the player can select the best move. For chess, and assuming a score based on remaining pieces, and a five-move depth limit, this corresponds to a strategy of looking for a move that is guaranteed to at least gain you piece advantage in the move, by five moves ahead. This may not guarantee a winning game (sometimes you have to sacrifice pieces to do better later on), but it may be moderately effective.

Using these fairly straightforward (and not terribly intelligent) techniques for game playing systems results in pretty good performance. However, for even better performance it is necessary to look a bit at how human experts play a game. For example, in chess opening and closing moves are very important, and there are some fairly standard opening games. Enhancing a search-based system with knowledge of these good opening and closing sequences (as you might find in any chess book) should improve its performance.

4.4 Summary

- Solving many AI problems involves using *search* techniques. For example, in simple state-space search we may search through possible sequences of actions to find one that will achieve a target state, from some initial one. A particular state that we can reach from the initial one would be a *node* in the *search space*, and the sequence of actions would be a *path*.

- The search space may be a *tree* or a general *graph*. Different algorithms involve *traversing* this search space in a different manner.

- The simplest search methods are *breadth first* and *depth first*. These involve exhaustively traversing the search space in a systematic manner. In breadth first, short paths are searched before longer ones. In depth first, a path is searched to its end before backing up and trying alternatives.

- *Heuristic* search methods attempt to use some knowledge of how close a state is to a target state to select which paths to explore first. This may avoid the whole search space being searched, resulting in a faster solution. Hill climbing, best first and A* are all heuristic search methods.

- More sophisticated *planning* techniques are often required to solve problems. AI planning systems use a more complex representation of actions than simple search-based problem solvers. Simple planning algorithms control the search through possible actions by looking for actions that reduce the *difference* between current and target states, and by setting new subproblems to solve if a useful action cannot be applied in the current state.

- Search techniques may also be applied to game playing systems, but here you have to take into account what the opponent might do. The *minimax* procedure allows you to find the best move, assuming that the opponent will do his best to prevent you winning.

Computation and Reasoning

4.5   Further Reading

Most of the longer AI textbooks have good sections on search, game playing and planning, including more complex approaches and more mathematical analysis. Discussions of search methods tend to be similar in different books, but details of planning algorithms and representations tend to differ. Rich & Knight (Rich & Knight, 1991) (chs.2–3, 12–13) discuss more problem-solving methods, and include discussion of the benefits of the alternative approaches. Ginsberg (Ginsberg, 1993) (chs.3–5, 14) provides complexity analysis of algorithms, and a logic-based approach to planning. Russell & Norvig (Russell & Norvig, 1995) (chs.3–5, 11–13) have a very clear discussion of basic state-space search and search algorithms, and more modern planning systems. Luger & Stubblefield (Luger & Stubblefield, 1993) (chs.3–5) provide a more implementation-oriented discussion.

4.6   Exercises

1. Given the following search tree, state the order in which the nodes will be searched for breadth first, depth first, hill climbing, and best first search, until a solution is reached. The numbers on the nodes indicate the estimated cost to solution.

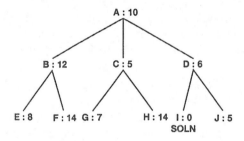

2. The following is a problem which can be solved using state-space search techniques:

   > "A farmer with his dog, rabbit and lettuce come to the east side of a river they wish to cross. There is a boat at the river's edge, but of course only the farmer can row. The boat can only hold two things (including the rower) at any one time. If the dog is ever left alone with the rabbit, the dog will eat it. Similarly if the rabbit is ever left alone with the lettuce, the rabbit will eat it. How can the farmer get across the river so that the dog, rabbit and lettuce arrive safely on the other side?"

   Formalise the above problem in terms of state-space search. You should:

- Suggest a suitable representation for the problem state.

- State what the initial and final states are in this representation.

- State the available operators/rules for getting from one state to the next, giving any conditions on when they may be applied.

3. For the following problem, first discuss how it could be solved using simple state-space search techniques, then discuss how it could be solved using the simple planning methods introduced in Section 4.3.2. Compare and contrast the two methods.

> "You live in a two room house with one door between the rooms. Your robot can move between rooms, turn around (by $180°$), open the door, and pick objects up. You want him to be able to form plans to do simple tasks, like get your beer from the other room and bring it to you. To move between rooms the door has to be open, and to open a door the robot has to be facing towards it."

4. Why does depth first search require less memory than breadth first? Consider the case where the search space is uniform with every node having two successors, to a depth of eight, and estimate the number of nodes that will be on the agenda for each method when the current node is a leaf node.

5. (Project) Try implementing the minimax game playing procedure. Use it for a simple noughts and crosses game.

Additional Reading

The following chapters are respectively
from

*Statistics for Economics, Accounting and
Business Studies*
Third Edition
by Mike Barrow

and from *Artificial Intelligence: A Modern
Approach*
Second Edition
by Stuart Russell and Peter Norvig

3 Probability

Learning intentions By the end of this chapter you should be able to:

- understand the essential concept of the probability of an event occurring
- appreciate that the probability of a combination of events occurring can be calculated using simple arithmetic rules (the addition and multiplication rules)
- understand that a probability can depend upon the outcome of other events (conditional probability)
- know how to make use of probability theory to help make decisions in situations of uncertainty.

Probability theory and statistical inference

In October 1985 Mrs Evelyn Adams of New Jersey, USA, won $3.9 million in the State lottery at odds of 1 in 3,200,000. In February 1986 she again won, though this time only (!) $1.4 million at odds of 1 in 5,200,000. The odds against both these wins were calculated at about 1 in 17,300 billion. Mrs Adams is quoted as saying 'They say good things come in threes, so . . .'.

The above story illustrates the principles of probability at work. The same principles underlie the theory of statistical inference. Statistical inference is the task of drawing conclusions (inferences) about a population from a sample of data drawn from that population. For example, we might have a survey which shows that 30% of a sample of 100 families intend to take a holiday abroad next year. What can we conclude from this about *all* families? The techniques set out in this and subsequent chapters show how to accomplish this.

Why is knowledge of probability necessary for the study of statistical inference? In order to be able to say something about a population on the basis of some sample evidence we must first examine how the sample data are collected. In many cases, the sample is a random one, i.e. the observations making up the sample are chosen at random from the population. If a second sample were selected it would almost certainly be different from the first. Each member of the population has a particular probability of being in the sample (in simple random sampling the probability is the same for all members of the population). To understand sampling procedures, and the implications for statistical inference, we must therefore first examine the theory of probability.

As an illustration of this, suppose we wish to know if a coin is fair, i.e. equally likely to fall heads or tails. The coin is tossed ten times and ten heads are recorded. This constitutes a random sample of tosses of the coin. What can we infer about

Computation and Reasoning

104

the coin? *If* it is fair, the probability of getting ten heads is 1 in 1,024, so a fairly unlikely event seems to have happened. We might reasonably infer therefore that the coin is biased.

The definition of probability

The first task is to define precisely what is meant by probability. This is not as easy as one might imagine and there are a number of different schools of thought on the subject. Consider the following questions:

- What is the probability of 'heads' occurring on the toss of a coin?
- What is the probability of a driver having an accident in a year of driving?
- What is the probability of a country such as Peru defaulting on its international loan repayments (as Mexico did in the 1980s)?

We shall use these questions as examples when examining the different schools of thought on probability.

The frequentist view

Considering the first question above, the **frequentist view** would be that the probability is equal to the **proportion** of heads obtained from a coin in the long run, i.e. if the coin were tossed many times. The first few results of such an experiment might be:

H, T, T, H, H, H, T, H, T, . . .

After a while, the proportion of heads settles down at some particular fraction and subsequent tosses will individually have an insignificant effect upon the value. Figure 3.1 shows the result of tossing a coin 250 times and recording the proportion of heads (actually, this was simulated on a computer: life is too short to do it for real).

This shows the proportion settling down at a value of about 0.50, which indicates an unbiased coin (or rather, an unbiased computer!). This value is the probability, according to the frequentist view. To be more precise, the probability is the proportion of heads obtained as the number of tosses *approaches infinity*. In general we can define Pr(H), the probability of event H (in this case heads) occurring, as

**Figure 3.1
Proportion of heads in
250 tosses of a coin**

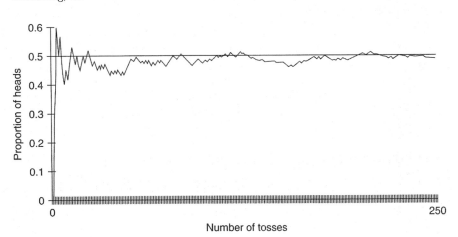

Computation and Reasoning

105

$$\Pr(H) = \frac{\text{number of occurrences of } H}{\text{number of trials}} \quad \textit{as the number of trials approaches infinity}$$

In this case, each toss of the coin constitutes a trial.

This definition gets round the obvious question of how many trials are needed before the probability emerges, but means that the probability of an event cannot strictly be obtained in finite time.

Although this approach appears attractive in theory, it does have its problems. One couldn't actually toss the coin an infinite number of times. Or, what if one took a different coin, would the results from the first coin necessarily apply to the second?

Perhaps more seriously, the definition is of less use for the second and third questions posed above. Calculating the probability of an accident is not too problematic: it may be defined as the proportion of all drivers having an accident during the year. However, this may not be relevant for a *particular* driver, since drivers vary so much in their accident records. And how would you answer the third question? There is no long run that we can appeal to. We cannot re-run history over and over again to see in what proportion of cases the country defaults. Yet this is what lenders want to know and credit-rating agencies have to assess. Maybe another approach is needed.

The subjective view   According to this view, probability is a **degree of belief** that someone holds about the likelihood of an event occurring. It is inevitably subjective and therefore some argue that it should be the degree of belief that it is *rational* to hold, but this just shifts the argument to what is meant by 'rational'. Some progress can be made by distinguishing between **prior** and **posterior** beliefs. The former are those held before any evidence is considered; the latter are the modified probabilities in the light of the evidence. For example, one might initially believe a coin to be fair (the prior probability of heads is one-half), but not after seeing only five heads in fifty tosses (the posterior probability would be less than a half).

Although it has its attractions, this approach (which is the basis of **Bayesian** statistics) also has its drawbacks. It is not always clear how one should arrive at the prior beliefs, particularly when one really has no prior information. Also, these methods often require the use of sophisticated mathematics, which may account for the limited use made of them.

There is not universal agreement therefore as to the precise definition of probability. We do not have space here to explore the issue further, so we will ignore the problem! The probability of an event occurring will be defined as a certain value and we won't worry about the precise meaning. This is an **axiomatic** approach: we simply state what the probability is, without justifying it, and then examine the consequences.

Probability theory: the building blocks

We start with a few definitions, to establish a vocabulary:

■ An **experiment** is an action such as flipping a coin, which has a number of possible **outcomes** or **events**, such as heads or tails.

Computation and Reasoning

**Figure 3.2
The sample space for
drawing from a pack
of cards**

	A	K	Q	J	10	9	8	7	6	5	4	3	2
♠	•	•	•	•	•	•	•	•	•	•	•	•	•
♥	•	•	•	•	•	•	•	•	•	•	•	•	•
♦	•	•	•	•	•	•	•	•	•	•	•	•	•
♣	•	•	•	•	•	•	•	•	•	•	•	•	•

- A **trial** is a single performance of the experiment, with a single outcome.
- The **sample space** consists of all the possible outcomes of the experiment. The outcomes for a single toss of a coin are {heads, tails}, for example. The outcomes in the sample space are **mutually exclusive**, which means that the occurrence of one rules out all the others. One cannot have both heads and tails in a single toss of a coin. If a single card is drawn at random from a pack, then the sample space may be drawn as in Figure 3.2. Each point represents one card in the pack and there are 52 points altogether.
- With each outcome in the sample space we can associate a **probability**, which is the chance of that outcome occurring. The probability of heads is one-half; the probability of drawing the Ace of Spades from a pack of cards is one in 52, etc.

There are restrictions upon the probabilities we can associate with the outcomes in the sample space. These are needed to ensure that we do not come up with self-contradictory results; for example, it would be odd to arrive at the conclusion that we could expect heads more than half the time *and* tails more than half the time. The restrictions are as follows:

- The probability of an event must lie between 0 and 1, i.e.

  (3.1) $0 \leq \Pr(A) \leq 1$, for any event A

  The explanation is straightforward. If A is certain to occur it occurs in 100% of all trials and so its probability is 1. If A is certain not to occur then its probability is 0, since it never happens however many trials there are. Since one cannot be more certain than certain, probabilities of less than 0 or more than 1 can never occur, and (3.1) follows.
- The sum of the probabilities associated with all the outcomes in the sample space is 1. Formally

  (3.2) $\sum P_i = 1$

  where P_i is the probability of event i occurring. This follows from the fact that one, and only one, of the outcomes *must* occur, since they are mutually exclusive and also **exhaustive**, i.e. they define all the possibilities.
- Following on from (3.2) we may define the **complement** of an event as everything in the sample space apart from that event. The complement of heads is tails, for example. If we write the complement of A as not-A then it follows that $\Pr(A) + \Pr(\text{not-}A) = 1$ and hence

  (3.3) $\Pr(\text{not-}A) = 1 - \Pr(A)$

Compound events   Most practical problems require the calculation of the probability of a set of outcomes rather than just a single one, or the probability of a series of outcomes in separate trials. For example, the probability of drawing a spade at random

Computation and Reasoning

107

from a pack of cards encompasses 13 points in the sample space (one for each spade). This probability is 13 out of 52, or one-quarter, which is fairly obvious; but for more complex problems the answer is not immediately evident. We refer to such sets of outcomes as **compound events**. Some examples are getting a five *or* a six on a throw of a die or drawing an Ace *and* a Queen to complete a 'straight' in a game of poker.

It is sometimes possible to calculate the probability of a compound event by examining the sample space, as in the case of drawing a spade above. However, in many cases this is not so, for the sample space is too complex or even impossible to write down. For example, the sample space for three draws of a card from a pack consists of over 140,000 points! An alternative method is needed. Fortunately there are a few simple rules for manipulating probabilities which help us to calculate the probabilities of compound events.

If the previous examples are examined closely it can be seen that outcomes are being compounded using 'or' and 'and': '. . . five *or* six on a single throw . . .'; '. . . an Ace *and* a Queen . . .'. 'And' and 'or' act as *operators*, and compound events are made up of simple events compounded by these two operators. The following rules for manipulating probabilities show how to handle these operators.

The addition rule

This rule is associated with 'or'. The probability of A or B occurring is given by

(3.4) $\Pr(A \text{ or } B) = \Pr(A) + \Pr(B)$

So, for example, the probability of a five or a six on a roll of a die is

(3.5) $\Pr(5 \text{ or } 6) = 1/6 + 1/6 = 1/3$

This answer can be verified from the sample space, as in Figure 3.3. Each dot represents a simple event (one to six). The compound event is made up of two of the six points, shaded in Figure 3.3, so the probability is 2/6 or 1/3.

However, (3.4) is not a general solution to this type of problem, as can be seen from the following example. What is the probability of a Queen or a Spade in a single draw from a pack of cards? $\Pr(Q) = 4/52$ (four queens in the pack) and $\Pr(S) = 13/52$ (13 spades), so applying (3.4) gives

(3.6) $\Pr(Q \text{ or } S) = \Pr(Q) + \Pr(S) = 4/52 + 13/52 = 17/52$

However, if the sample space is examined the correct answer is found to be 16/52, as in Figure 3.4. The problem is that one point in the sample space (the

Figure 3.3
The sample space for rolling a die

1	2	3	4	5	6
•	•	•	•	•	•

Figure 3.4
The sample space for drawing a Queen or a Spade

	A	K	Q	J	10	9	8	7	6	5	4	3	2
♠	•	•	•	•	•	•	•	•	•	•	•	•	•
♥	•	•	•	•	•	•	•	•	•	•	•	•	•
♦	•	•	•	•	•	•	•	•	•	•	•	•	•
♣	•	•	•	•	•	•	•	•	•	•	•	•	•

Computation and Reasoning

one representing the Queen of Spades) is double-counted, once as a Queen and again as a Spade. The event 'drawing a Queen *and* a Spade' is possible, and gets double-counted. Equation (3.4) has to be modified by subtracting the probability of getting a Queen *and* a Spade. The correct answer is obtained from

$$(3.7) \qquad \Pr(Q \text{ or } S) = \Pr(Q) + \Pr(S) - \Pr(Q \text{ and } S)$$

$$= 4/52 + 13/52 - 1/52$$

$$= 16/52$$

The general rule is therefore

$$(3.8) \qquad \Pr(A \text{ or } B) = \Pr(A) + \Pr(B) - \Pr(A \text{ and } B)$$

Rule (3.4) worked for the die example because $\Pr(5 \text{ and } 6) = 0$ since a five and a six cannot simultaneously occur.

In general, therefore, one should use (3.8), but when two events are mutually exclusive the rule simplifies to (3.4).

The multiplication rule

The multiplication rule is associated with 'and'. Consider a mother with two children. What is the probability that they are both boys? This is really a compound event: a boy on the first birth *and* a boy on the second. Assume that in a single birth a boy or girl is equally likely, so $\Pr(\text{boy}) = \Pr(\text{girl}) = 0.5$. Denote by $\Pr(B1)$ the probability of a boy on the first birth and by $\Pr(B2)$ the probability of a boy on the second. Thus the question asks for $\Pr(B1 \text{ and } B2)$ and this is given by:

$$(3.9) \qquad \Pr(B1 \text{ and } B2) = \Pr(B1) \times \Pr(B2)$$

$$= 0.5 \times 0.5$$

$$= 0.25$$

Intuitively, the multiplication rule can be understood as follows. One-half of mothers have a boy on their first birth and of these, one-half will again have a boy on the second. Therefore a quarter of mothers have two boys.

Like the addition rule, the multiplication rule requires slight modification before it can be applied generally. The example assumes first and second births to be **independent events**, i.e. that having a boy on the first birth does not affect the probability of a boy on the second. This assumption is not always valid.

Write $\Pr(B2|B1)$ to indicate the probability of the event $B2$ *given* that the event $B1$ has occurred. Let us drop the independence assumption and suppose the following:

$$(3.10) \qquad \Pr(B1) = \Pr(G1) = 0.5$$

i.e. boys and girls are equally likely on the first birth, and

$$(3.11) \qquad \Pr(B2|B1) = \Pr(G2|G1) = 0.6$$

i.e. a boy is more likely to be followed by another boy, and a girl by another girl. (It is easy to work out $\Pr(B2|G1)$ and $\Pr(G2|B1)$. What are they?)

Now what is the probability of two boys? Half of all mothers have a boy first, and of these, 60% have another boy. Thus 30% (60% of 50%) of mothers have two boys. This is obtained from the rule:

$$(3.12) \qquad \Pr(B1 \text{ and } B2) = \Pr(B1) \times \Pr(B2|B1)$$

$$= 0.5 \times 0.6$$

$$= 0.3$$

Thus in general we have:

$$(3.13) \qquad \Pr(A \text{ and } B) = \Pr(A) \times \Pr(B|A)$$

which simplifies to

$$(3.14) \qquad \Pr(A \text{ and } B) = \Pr(A) \times \Pr(B)$$

if A and B are independent.

   Independence may therefore be defined as follows: two events, A and B, are independent if the probability of one occurring is not influenced by the fact of the other having occurred. Formally, if A and B are independent then

$$(3.15) \qquad \Pr(B|A) = \Pr(B|\text{not } A) = \Pr(B)$$

and

$$(3.16) \qquad \Pr(A|B) = \Pr(A|\text{not } B) = \Pr(A)$$

Intuition does not always work with probabilities!

Counter-intuitive results frequently arise in probability, which is why it is wise to use the rules to calculate probabilities in tricky situations, rather than rely on intuition. Take the following questions:

- What is the probability of obtaining two heads (HH) in two tosses of a coin?
- What is the probability of obtaining tails followed by heads (TH)?
- If a coin is tossed until either HH or TH occurs, what are the probabilities of each sequence occurring first?

   The answers to the first two are easy: $1/2 \times 1/2 = 1/4$ in each case. You might therefore conclude that each sequence is equally likely to be the first observed, but you would be wrong!

   Unless HH occurs on the first two tosses, then TH *must* occur first. HH is therefore the first sequence *only* if it occurs on the first two tosses, which has a probability of $1/4$. The probability that TH is first is therefore $3/4$. The probabilities are unequal, a strange result. Now try the same thing with HHH and THH and three tosses of a coin.

Combining the addition and multiplication rules

More complex problems can be solved by suitable combinations of the addition and multiplication formulae. For example, what is the probability of a mother having one child of each sex? This could occur in one of two ways: a girl followed by a boy or a boy followed by a girl. Therefore we have (assuming non-independence according to (3.11))

$$\Pr(1 \text{ girl, } 1 \text{ boy}) = \Pr((G1 \text{ and } B2) \text{ or } (B1 \text{ and } G2))$$

$$= \Pr(G1) \times \Pr(B2|G1) + \Pr(B1) \times \Pr(G2|B1)$$

$$= (0.5 \times 0.4) + (0.5 \times 0.4)$$

$$= 0.4$$

Computation and Reasoning

Figure 3.5
Tree diagram for a
family with two children

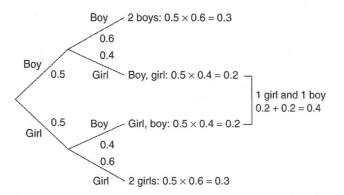

The answer can be checked if we remember (3.2) stating that probabilities must sum to 1. We have calculated the probability of two boys (0.3) and of a child of each sex (0.4). The only other possibility is of two girls. This probability must be 0.3, the same as two boys, since boys and girls are treated symmetrically in this problem (even with the non-independence assumption). The sum is therefore 0.3 + 0.4 + 0.3 = 1, as it should be.

Tree diagrams

The preceding problem can be illustrated using a **tree diagram**, which often helps to clarify a problem. A tree diagram is an alternative way of enumerating all possible outcomes in the sample space, with the associated probabilities. The diagram for two children is shown in Figure 3.5.

The diagram begins at the left and the first node shows the possible alternatives (boy, girl) at that point and the associated probabilities (0.5, 0.5). The next two nodes show the alternatives and probabilities for the second birth, given the sex of the first child. The final four nodes show the possible results: boy, boy; boy, girl; girl, boy; and girl, girl.

To find the probability of two girls, using the tree diagram, follow the lowest path, multiplying the probabilities along it to give 0.5 × 0.6 = 0.3. To find the probability of one child of each sex it is necessary to add the probabilities obtained from the paths boy, girl and girl, boy, giving 0.2 + 0.2 = 0.4. This provides a graphical alternative to the formulae used above and may help comprehension.

The tree diagram can obviously be extended to cover third and subsequent children although the number of branches rapidly increases (in geometric progression). The difficulty then becomes not the calculation of the probability attached to each outcome, but sorting out which branches should be taken into account in the calculation. Suppose we consider a family of five children of whom three are girls. To simplify matters we again assume independence of probabilities. The appropriate tree diagram has $2^5 = 32$ end-points, each with probability 1/32. How many of these relate to families with three girls and two boys, for example? To find this out, we use the ideas of **combinations** and **permutations**.

Combinations and permutations

How can we establish the number of ways of having three girls and two boys? One way would be to write down all the possible orderings:

GGGBB   GGBGB   GGBBG   GBGGB   GBGBG
GBBGG   BGGGB   BGGBG   BGBGG   BBGGG

Computation and Reasoning

111

This shows that there are ten such orderings, so the probability of three girls and two boys in a family of five children is 10/32. In more complex problems this soon becomes difficult or impossible. The record number of children born to a British mother is 39(!) of whom 32 were girls. The appropriate tree diagram has over 5 thousand billion 'routes' through it, and drawing one line (i.e. for one child) per second would imply 17,433 years to complete the task! Rather than do this, we use the **combinatorial** formula. Suppose there are n children, r of them girls, then the number of orderings, denoted nCr, is obtained from

$n!$ is read 'n factorial' and is defined as the product of all the integers up to and including n.

$$(3.17) \qquad nCr = \frac{n!}{r!(n-r)!} = \frac{n \times (n-1) \times \ldots \times 1}{\{r \times (r-1) \times \ldots \times 1\} \times \{(n-r) \times (n-r-1) \times \ldots \times 1\}}$$

In the above example $n = 5$, $r = 3$ so the number of orderings is

$$(3.18) \qquad 5C3 = \frac{5 \times 4 \times 3 \times 2 \times 1}{\{3 \times 2 \times 1\} \times \{2 \times 1\}} = 10$$

If there were four girls out of five children then the number of orderings or combinations would be

$$(3.19) \qquad 5C4 = \frac{5 \times 4 \times 3 \times 2 \times 1}{\{4 \times 3 \times 2 \times 1\} \times 1} = 5$$

This gives five possible orderings, i.e. the single boy could be the first, second, third, fourth or fifth born.

Why does this formula work? Consider five empty places to fill, corresponding to the five births in chronological order. Take the case of three girls (call them Amanda, Bridget and Caroline for convenience) who have to fill three of the five places. For Amanda there is a choice of five empty places. Having 'chosen' one, there remain four for Bridget, so there are $5 \times 4 = 20$ possibilities (i.e. ways in which these two could choose their places). Three remain for Caroline, so there are $60 (= 5 \times 4 \times 3)$ possible orderings in all (the two boys take the two remaining places). Sixty is the number of **permutations** of three *named* girls in five births. This is written $5P3$ or in general nPr. Hence

$$5P3 = 5 \times 4 \times 3$$

or in general

$$(3.20) \qquad nPr = n \times (n-1) \times \ldots \times (n-r+1)$$

A simpler formula is obtained by multiplying and dividing by $(n-r)!$

$$(3.21) \qquad nPr = \frac{n \times (n-r) \times \ldots \times (n-r+1) \times (n-r)!}{(n-r)!}$$

$$= \frac{n!}{(n-r)!}$$

What is the difference between nPr and nCr? The latter does not distinguish between the girls; the two cases Amanda, Bridget, Caroline, boy, boy and Bridget, Amanda, Caroline, boy, boy are effectively the same (three girls followed by two boys). So nPr is larger by a factor representing the number of ways of ordering the three girls. This factor is given by $r! = 3 \times 2 \times 1 = 6$ (any of the three girls could be first, either of the other two second, and then the final one). Thus to obtain nCr one must divide nPr by $r!$, giving (3.17).

Computation and Reasoning

112

Bayes' theorem

Bayes' theorem is a factual statement about probabilities which in itself is uncontroversial. However, the use and interpretation of the result is at the heart of the difference between **classical** and **Bayesian** statistics. The theorem itself is easily derived from first principles.

(3.22) $\Pr(A \text{ and } B) = \Pr(A \mid B) \times \Pr(B)$

hence

(3.23) $\Pr(A \mid B) = \dfrac{\Pr(A \text{ and } B)}{\Pr(B)}$

Expanding both top and bottom of the right-hand side,

(3.24) $\Pr(A \mid B) = \dfrac{\Pr(B \mid A) \times \Pr(A)}{\Pr(B \mid A) \times \Pr(A) + \Pr(B \mid \text{not } A) \times \Pr(\text{not } A)}$

Equation (3.24) is known as **Bayes' theorem** and is a statement about the probability of the event A, conditional upon B having occurred. The following example demonstrates its use.

Two bags contain red and yellow balls. Bag A contains six red and four yellow balls, bag B has three red and seven yellow balls. A ball is drawn at random from one bag and turns out to be red. What is the probability that it came from bag A?

Denoting:

$\Pr(A) = 0.5$ (the probability of choosing bag A at random) $= \Pr(B)$
$\Pr(R \mid A) = 0.6$ (the probability of selecting a red ball from bag A), etc.

we have

(3.25) $\Pr(A \mid R) = \dfrac{\Pr(R \mid A) \times \Pr(A)}{\Pr(R \mid A) \times \Pr(A) + \Pr(R \mid B) \times \Pr(B)}$

using Bayes' theorem. Evaluating this gives

(3.26) $\Pr(A \mid R) = \dfrac{0.6 \times 0.5}{0.6 \times 0.5 + 0.3 \times 0.5}$

$= {}^2\!/_3$

(You can check that $\Pr(B \mid R) = 1/3$ so that the sum of the probabilities is 1.)

Bayes' theorem can be extended to cover more than two bags: if there are five bags, for example, labelled A to E, then

(3.27) $\Pr(A \mid R) = \dfrac{\Pr(R \mid A) \times \Pr(A)}{\Pr(R \mid A) \times \Pr(A) + \Pr(R \mid B) \times \Pr(B) + \ldots + \Pr(R \mid E) \times \Pr(E)}$

In Bayesian language, $\Pr(A)$, $\Pr(B)$, etc. are known as the **prior** (to the drawing of the ball) probabilities, $\Pr(R \mid A)$, $\Pr(R \mid B)$, etc. are the **likelihoods** and $\Pr(A \mid R)$, $\Pr(B \mid R)$, etc. are the **posterior** probabilities. Bayes' theorem can alternatively be expressed as

(3.28) $\text{posterior probability} = \dfrac{\text{likelihood} \times \text{prior probability}}{\Sigma(\text{likelihoods} \times \text{prior probabilities})}$

Computation and Reasoning

This is illustrated below, by reworking the above example.

	Prior probabilities	Likelihoods	Prior × likelihood	Posterior probabilities
A	0.5	0.6	0.30	0.30/0.45 = 2/3
B	0.5	0.3	0.15	0.15/0.45 = 1/3
Total			0.45	

The general version of Bayes' theorem may be stated as follows. If there are n events labelled $E_1, \ldots, E_n$ then the probability of the event i occurring, given the sample evidence S, is

$$(3.29) \quad \Pr(E_i \mid S) = \frac{\Pr(S \mid E_i) \times \Pr(E_i)}{\sum(\Pr(S \mid E_i) \times \Pr(E_i))}$$

As stated earlier, dispute arises over the interpretation of Bayes' theorem. In the above example there is no difficulty because the probability statements can be interpreted as relative frequencies. If the experiment of selecting a bag at random and choosing a ball from it were repeated many times, then of those occasions when a red ball is selected, in two-thirds of them bag A will have been chosen. However, consider an alternative interpretation of the symbols:

A: a coin is fair
B: a coin is unfair
R: the result of a toss is a head

Then, given a toss (or series of tosses) of a coin, this evidence can be used to calculate the probability of the coin being fair. But this makes no sense according to the frequentist school: either the coin is fair or not; it is not a question of probability. The calculated value must be interpreted as a degree of belief and be given a subjective interpretation.

Decision analysis

The study of probability naturally leads on to the analysis of decision making where risk is involved. This is the realistic situation facing most firms and the use of probability can help to illuminate the problem. To illustrate the topic, we use the example of a firm facing a choice of three different investment projects. The uncertainty which the firm faces concerns the interest rate at which to discount the future flows of income. The question is: which project should the firm select? As we shall see, there is no unique, right answer to the question but, using probability theory we can see why the answer might vary.

Table 3.1 provides the data required for the problem. The three projects are imaginatively labelled A, B and C. There are four possible **states of the world**, i.e. future scenarios, each with a different interest rate, as shown across the top of the table. This is the only source of uncertainty, otherwise the states of the world are identical. The figures in the body of the table show the present value of each income stream at the given discount rate. Thus, for example, if the interest rate turns out to be 4% then project A has a present value of £1,475,000 while B's is £1,500,000. If the discount rate turns out to be 5% the PV for A is

Computation and Reasoning

114

Table 3.1 Data for decision analysis: present values of three investment projects at different interest rates (£000)

Project	Future interest rate			
	4%	5%	6%	7%
A	1,475	1,363	1,200	1,115
B	1,500	1,380	1,148	1,048
C	1,650	1,440	1,200	810
Probability	0.1	0.4	0.4	0.1

£1,363,000 while for B it has changed to £1,380,000. Obviously, as the discount rate rises, the present value of the return falls. (Alternatively, we could assume that a higher interest rate increases the cost of borrowing to finance the project, which reduces its profitability.) We assume that each project requires a (certain) initial outlay of £1,100,000 with which the *PV* should be compared.

The final row shows the probabilities which the firm attaches to each interest rate. These are obviously someone's subjective probabilities and are symmetric around a central value of 5.5%. We assume no inflation in this example, so these are effectively real rates.

Decision criteria: maximising the expected value

We need to decide how a decision is to be made on the basis of these data. The first criterion involves the expected value of each project. This uses the E operator which was introduced in Chapter 1. In other words, we find the expected present value of each project, by taking a weighted average of the *PV* figures, the weights being the probabilities. The project with the highest expected return is chosen.

The expected values are calculated in Table 3.2. The highest expected present value is £1,302,000, associated with project C. On this criterion therefore, C is chosen.

Is this a wise choice? You may notice that if the interest rate turns out to be 7% then C would be the *worst* project to choose and the firm would make a substantial loss in such circumstances. Project C is the most sensitive to the discount rate (it has the greatest *variance* of the three projects) and therefore the firm faces more risk by opting for C. Perhaps some alternative criteria should be looked at. These we look at next, in particular the **maximin, maximax** and **minimax regret** strategies.

Maximin, maximax and minimax regret

The **maximin** criterion looks at the worst-case scenario for each project and then selects the project which does best in these circumstances. It is inevitably a pessimistic or cautious view therefore. Table 3.3 illustrates the calculation. This

Table 3.2 Expected values of the three projects

Project	Expected value
A	1,284.2
B	1,266.0
C	1,302.0

Note: 1,284.2 is calculated as $1,475 \times 0.1 + 1,363 \times 0.4 + 1,200 \times 0.4 + 1,115 \times 0.1$.

Computation and Reasoning

Table 3.3 The maximin criterion

Project	Minimum
A	1,115
B	1,048
C	810
Maximum	1,115

Table 3.4 The costs of taking the wrong decision

Project	4%	5%	6%	7%	Maximum
A	175	77	0	0	175
B	150	60	52	67	150
C	0	0	0	305	305
Minimum					150

time we observe that project A is preferred. In the worst case (which occurs when $r = 7\%$ for all projects) then A does best, with a PV of £1,115,000 and there-fore a slight profit.

The opposite criterion is the optimistic one where the **maximax** criterion is used. In this case one looks at the *best* circumstances for each project and chooses the best-performing project. Each project does best when the interest rate is at its lowest level, 3%. Examining the first column of Table 3.1 shows that pro-ject C (PV = 1,650) performs best and is therefore chosen.

A final criterion is that of **minimax regret**. If project B were chosen but the interest rate turns out to be 7% then we would regret not having chosen A, the best project under these circumstances. Our *regret* would be the extent of the difference between the two, a matter of $1,115 - 1,048 = 67$. Similarly, the regret if we had chosen C would be $1,115 - 810 = 305$. We can calculate these regrets at the other interest rates too, always comparing the PV of a project with the best PV given that interest rate. This gives us Table 3.4.

The final column of the table shows the maximum regret for each project. The minimax regret criterion is to choose the minimum of these figures. This is given at the bottom of the final column; it is 150 which is associated with project B. A justification for using this criterion might be that you don't want to fall too far behind your competitors. If other firms are facing similar invest-ment decisions, then the regret table shows the difference in PV (and hence profits) if they choose the best project while you do not. Choosing the mini-max regret solution ensures that you won't fall too far behind.

You will probably have noticed that we have managed to find a justification for choosing all three projects! No one project comes out best on all criteria. Nevertheless, the analysis might be of some help: if the investment project is one of many small, independent investments the firm is making, then this would justify use of the expected value criterion. On the other hand, if this is a big, one-off project which could possibly bankrupt the firm if it goes wrong, then the maximin criterion would be appropriate.

Computation and Reasoning

The expected value of perfect information

Often a firm can improve its knowledge about future possibilities via research, which costs money. This effectively means buying information about the future state of the world. The question arises: how much should a firm pay for such information? **Perfect information** would reveal the future state of the world with certainty – in this case, the future interest rate. In that case you could be sure of choosing the right project given each state of the world. If interest rates turn out to be 4%, the firm would invest in *C*, if 7% in *A*, and so on.

In such circumstances, the firm would expect to earn:

$$(0.1 \times 1{,}650) + (0.4 \times 1{,}440) + (0.4 \times 1{,}200) + (0.1 \times 1{,}115) = 1{,}332.5$$

i.e. the probability of each state of the world is multiplied by the *PV* of the *best* project for that state. This gives a figure which is substantially greater than the expected value calculated earlier, without perfect information, 1,302. The **expected value of perfect information** is therefore the difference between these two, 30.5. This sets a *maximum* to the value of information, for it is unlikely in the real world that any information about the future is going to be perfect.

Chapter summary

- The theory of probability forms the basis of statistical inference, the drawing of inferences on the basis of a random sample of data. It is the probability basis of random sampling that is the reason for this.

- A convenient definition of the probability of an event is the number of times the event occurs divided by the number of trials (occasions when the event could occur).

- For more complex events, their probabilities can be calculated by combining probabilities, using the addition and multiplication rules.

- The probability of events *A* or *B* occurring is calculated according to the addition rule.

- The probability of *A* and *B* occurring is given by the multiplication rule.

- If *A* and *B* are not independent, then $\Pr(A \text{ and } B) = \Pr(A) \times \Pr(B|A)$, where $\Pr(B|A)$ is the probability of *B* occurring given that *A* has occurred (the conditional probability).

- Tree diagrams are a useful technique for enumerating all the possible paths in series of probability trials, but for large numbers of trials the huge number of possibilities makes the technique impractical.

- For experiments with a large number of trials (e.g. obtaining twenty heads in fifty tosses of a coin) the formulae for combinations and permutations can be used.

- The combinatorial formula *nCr* gives the number of ways of combining *r* similar objects among *n* objects, e.g. the number of orderings of three girls (and hence implicitly two boys also) in five children.

- The permutation formula *nPr* gives the number of orderings of *r* distinct objects among *n*, e.g. three named girls among five children.

Computation and Reasoning

■ The Bayes' theorem provides a formula for calculating a conditional probability, e.g. the probability of someone being a smoker, given they have been diagnosed with cancer. It forms the basis of Bayesian statistics, allowing us to calculate the probability of a hypothesis being true, based on the sample evidence and prior beliefs. Classical statistics disputes this approach.

■ Probabilities can also be used as the basis for decision making in conditions of uncertainty, using as decision criteria expected value maximisation, maximin, maximax or minimax regret.

Key terms and concepts			
probability of an event	frequentist approach	subjective approach
probability experiment	outcome or event	sample space
mutually exclusive	exhaustive	complement
compound event	addition rule	multiplication rule
independent events	tree diagram	combinations
permutations	Bayes' theorem	conditional probability
maximin	minimax	minimax regret
expected value of perfect information		

Exercises

Exercise 1 Given a standard pack of cards, calculate the following probabilities:

(a) drawing an Ace

(b) drawing a court card (i.e. Jack, Queen or King)

(c) drawing a red card

(d) drawing three Aces without replacement

(e) drawing three Aces with replacement

Exercise 2 The following data give duration of unemployment by age, in July 1986.

Age	Duration of unemployment (weeks)				Total (000s)	Economically active (000s)
	≤8	8–26	26–52	>52		
	(Percentage figures)					
16–19	27.2	29.8	24.0	19.0	273.4	1,270
20–24	24.2	20.7	18.3	36.8	442.5	2,000
25–34	14.8	18.8	17.2	49.2	531.4	3,600
35–49	12.2	16.6	15.1	56.2	521.2	4,900
50–59	8.9	14.4	15.6	61.2	388.1	2,560
≥60	18.5	29.7	30.7	21.4	74.8	1,110

The 'economically active' column gives the total of employed plus unemployed in each age category.

(a) In what sense may these figures be regarded as probabilities? What does the figure 27.2 (top left cell) mean following this interpretation?

(b) Assuming the validity of the probability interpretation, which of the following statements are true?

Computation and Reasoning

(i) The probability of an economically active adult aged 25–34, drawn at random, being unemployed is 531.4/3,600.

(ii) If someone who has been unemployed for over one year is drawn at random, the probability that they are aged 16–19 is 19%.

(iii) For those aged 35–49 who became unemployed before July 1985, the probability of their still being unemployed is 56.2%.

(iv) If someone aged 50–59 is drawn at random from the economically active population, the probability of their being unemployed for eight weeks or less is 8.9%.

(v) The probability of someone aged 35–49 drawn at random from the economically active population being unemployed for between 8 and 26 weeks is $0.166 \times 521.2/4,900$.

(c) A person is drawn at random from the population and found to have been unemployed for over one year. What is the probability that they are aged between 16 and 19?

Exercise 3 'Odds' in horserace betting are defined as follows: 3/1 (three to one against) means a horse is expected to win once for every three times it loses; 3/2 means two wins out of five races; 4/5 (five to four *on*) means five wins for every four defeats, etc.

(a) Translate the above odds into 'probabilities' of victory.

(b) In a three-horse race, the odds quoted are 2/1, 6/4, and 1/1. What makes the odds different from probabilities? Why are they different?

(c) Discuss how much the bookmaker would expect to win in the long run at such odds, assuming each horse is backed equally.

Exercise 4 (a) Translate the following odds to 'probabilities': 13/8, 2/1 *on*, 100/30.

(b) In the 2.45 race at Plumpton on 18/10/94 the odds for the five runners were:

Philips Woody	1/1
Gallant Effort	5/2
Satin Noir	11/2
Victory Anthem	9/1
Common Rambler	16/1

Calculate the 'probabilities' and their sum.

(c) Should the bookmaker base his odds on the true probabilities of each horse winning, or on the amount bet on each horse?

Exercise 5 How might you estimate the probability of Peru defaulting on its debt repayments next year?

Exercise 6 How might you estimate the probability of a corporation reneging on its bond payments?

Exercise 7 Judy is 33, unmarried and assertive. She is a graduate in Political Science, and involved in union activities and anti-discrimination movements. Which of the following statements do you think is more probable?

Computation and Reasoning

119

(a) Judy is a bank clerk.

(b) Judy is a bank clerk, active in the feminist movement.

Exercise 8 In March 1994 a news item revealed that a London 'gender' clinic (which reportedly enables you to choose the sex of your child) had just set up in business. Of its first six births, two were of the 'wrong' sex. Assess this from a probability point of view.

Exercise 9 A newspaper advertisement reads 'The sex of your child predicted, or your money back!' Discuss this advertisement from the point of view of (a) the advertiser and (b) the client.

Exercise 10 'Roll six sixes to win a Mercedes!' is the announcement at a fair. You have to roll six dice. If you get six sixes you win the car, valued at £20,000. The entry ticket costs £1. What is your expected gain or loss on this game? The organisers of the fair have to take out insurance against the car being won. This costs £250 for the day. Does this seem a fair premium? If not, why not?

Exercise 11 At another stall, you have to toss a coin numerous times. If a head does not appear in 20 tosses you win £1 billion. The entry fee for the game is £100.

(a) What are your expected winnings?

(b) Would you play?

Exercise 12 A four-engine plane can fly as long as at least two of its engines work. A two-engine plane flies as long as at least one engine works. The probability of an individual engine failure is 1 in 1,000.

(a) Would you feel safer in a four- or two-engine plane, and why? Calculate the probabilities of an accident for each type.

(b) How much safer is one type than the other?

(c) What crucial assumption are you making in your calculation? Do you think it is valid?

Exercise 13 Which of the following events are independent?

(a) Two flips of a fair coin

(b) Two flips of a biased coin

(c) Rainfall on two successive days

(d) Rainfall on St Swithin's day and rain one month later.

Exercise 14 Which of the following events are independent?

(a) A student getting the first two questions correct in a multiple-choice exam

(b) A driver having an accident in successive years

(c) IBM and Compaq earning positive profits next year

(d) Arsenal Football Club winning on successive weekends.

How is the answer to (b) reflected in car insurance premiums?

Computation and Reasoning

120

Exercise 15 Manchester United beat Liverpool 4–2 at soccer, but you do not know the order in which the goals were scored. Draw a tree diagram to display all the possibilities and use it to find (a) the probability that the goals were scored in the order L, MU, MU, MU, L, MU, and (b) the probability that the score was 2–2 at some stage.

Exercise 16 An important numerical calculation on a spacecraft is carried out independently by three computers. If all arrive at the same answer it is deemed correct. If one disagrees it is overruled. If there is no agreement then a fourth computer does the calculation and, if its answer agrees with any of the others, it is deemed correct. The probability of an individual computer getting the answer right is 99%. Use a tree diagram to find:

(a) the probability that the first three computers get the right answer

(b) the probability of getting the right answer

(c) the probability of getting no answer

(d) the probability of getting the wrong answer.

Exercise 17 The French national lottery works as follows. Six numbers from the range 0 to 49 are chosen at random. If you have correctly guessed all six you win the first prize. What are your chances of winning if you are only allowed to choose six numbers? A single entry like this costs one franc. For 210 francs you can choose ten numbers and you win if the six selected numbers are among them. Is this better value than the single entry?

Exercise 18 The UK national lottery works as follows. You choose six (different) numbers in the range 1 to 49. If all six come up in the draw (in any order) you win the first prize, expected to be around £2m. (which could be shared if someone else chooses the six winning numbers).

(a) What is your chance of winning with a single ticket?

(b) You win a second prize if you get five out of six right, *and* your final chosen number matches the 'bonus' number in the draw (also in the range 1 to 49). What is the probability of winning a second prize?

(c) Calculate the probabilities of winning a third, fourth or fifth prize, where a third prize is won by matching five out of the six numbers, a fourth prize by matching four out of six and a fifth prize by matching three out of six.

(d) What is the probability of winning a prize?

(e) The prizes are as follows:

Prize	Value	
First	£2 million	(expected, possibly shared)
Second	£100,000	(expected, for each winner)
Third	£1,500	(expected, for each winner)
Fourth	£65	(expected, for each winner)
Fifth	£10	(guaranteed, for each winner)

Comment upon the distribution of the fund between first, second, etc. prizes.

(f) Why is the fifth prize guaranteed whereas the others are not?

Computation and Reasoning

(g) In the first week of the lottery, 49 million tickets were sold. There were 1,150,000 winners, of which 7 won (a share of) the jackpot, 39 won a second prize, 2,139 won a third prize and 76,731 a fourth prize. Are you surprised by these results or are they as you would expect?

Exercise 19 A coin is either fair or has two heads. You initially assign probabilities of 0.5 to each possibility. The coin is then tossed twice, with two heads appearing. Use Bayes' theorem to work out the posterior probabilities of each possible outcome.

Exercise 20 A test for AIDS is 99% successful, i.e. if you are HIV+ it will detect it in 99% of all tests, and if you are not, it will again be right 99% of the time. Assume that about 1% of the population are HIV+. You take part in a random testing procedure, which gives a positive result. What is the probability that you are HIV+? What implications does your result have for AIDS testing?

Exercise 21 (a) Your initial belief is that a defendant in a court case is guilty with probability 0.5. A witness comes forward claiming he saw the defendant commit the crime. You know the witness is not totally reliable and tells the truth with probability p. Use Bayes' theorem to calculate the posterior probability that the defendant is guilty, based on the witness's evidence.

(b) A second witness, equally unreliable, comes forward and claims she saw the defendant commit the crime. Assuming the witnesses are not colluding, what is your posterior probability of guilt?

(c) If $p < 0.5$, compare the answers to (a) and (b). How do you account for this curious result?

Exercise 22 A man is mugged and claims that the mugger had red hair. In police investigations of such cases, the victim was able to correctly identify the assailant's hair colour 80% of the time. Assuming that 10% of the population have red hair, what is the probability that the assailant in this case did in fact have red hair? Guess the answer first, then find the right answer using Bayes' theorem. What are the implications of your results for juries' interpretation of evidence in court, particularly in relation to racial minorities?

Exercise 23 A firm has a choice of three projects, with profits as indicated below, dependent upon the state of demand.

Project	Demand		
	Low	Middle	High
A	100	140	180
B	130	145	170
C	110	130	200
Probability	0.25	0.45	0.3

(a) Which project should be chosen on the expected value criterion?

(b) Which project should be chosen on the maximin and maximax criteria?

(c) Which project should be chosen on the minimax regret criterion?

(d) What is the expected value of perfect information to the firm?

Computation and Reasoning

Exercise 24 A firm can build a small, medium or large factory, with anticipated profits from each dependent upon the state of demand, as in the table below.

Factory	Demand		
	Low	Middle	High
Small	300	320	330
Medium	270	400	420
Large	50	250	600
Probability	0.3	0.5	0.2

(a) Which project should be chosen on the expected value criterion?

(b) Which project should be chosen on the maximin and maximax criteria?

(c) Which project should be chosen on the minimax regret criterion?

(d) What is the expected value of perfect information to the firm?

Exercise 25 There are 25 people at a party. What is the probability that there are at least two with a birthday in common? (Hint: the *complement* is (much) easier to calculate.)

Exercise 26 This problem is tricky, but amusing. Three gunmen, A, B and C, are shooting at each other. The probabilities that each will hit what they aim at are respectively 1, 0.75, 0.5. They take it in turns to shoot (in alphabetical order) and continue until only one is left alive. Calculate the probabilities of each winning the contest. (Assume they draw lots for the right to shoot first.)

Hint 1: Start with one-on-one gunfights, e.g. the probability of A beating B, or of B beating C.

Hint 2: You'll need the formula for the sum of an infinite series, given in Chapter 1.

Computation and Reasoning

123

13 UNCERTAINTY

In which we see what an agent should do when not all is crystal clear.

13.1 ACTING UNDER UNCERTAINTY

UNCERTAINTY

The logical agents described in Parts III and IV make the epistemological commitment that propositions are true, false, or unknown. When an agent knows enough facts about its environment, the logical approach enables it to derive plans that are guaranteed to work. This is a good thing. Unfortunately, *agents almost never have access to the whole truth about their environment.* Agents must, therefore, act under **uncertainty**. For example, an agent in the wumpus world of Chapter 7 has sensors that report only local information; most of the world is not immediately observable. A wumpus agent often will find itself unable to discover which of two squares contains a pit. If those squares are *en route* to the gold, then the agent might have to take a chance and enter one of the two squares.

The real world is far more complex than the wumpus world. For a logical agent, it might be impossible to construct a complete and correct description of how its actions will work. Suppose, for example, that the agent wants to drive someone to the airport to catch a flight and is considering a plan, A_{90}, that involves leaving home 90 minutes before the flight departs and driving at a reasonable speed. Even though the airport is only about 15 miles away, the agent will not be conclude with certainty that "Plan A_{90} will get us to the airport in time." Instead, it reaches the weaker conclusion "Plan A_{90} will get us to the airport in time, as long as my car doesn't break down or run out of gas, and I don't get into an accident, and there are no accidents on the bridge, and the plane doesn't leave early, and ... ." None of these conditions can be deduced, so the plan's success cannot be inferred. This is an example of the **qualification problem** mentioned in Chapter 10.

If a logical agent cannot conclude that any particular course of action achieves its goal, then it will be unable to act. Conditional planning can overcome uncertainty to some extent, but only if the agent's sensing actions can obtain the required information and only if there are not too many different contingencies. Another possible solution would be to endow the agent with a simple but incorrect theory of the world that *does* enable it to derive a plan;

462

presumably, such plans will work *most* of the time, but problems arise when events contradict the agent's theory. Moreover, handling the tradeoff between the accuracy and usefulness of the agent's theory seems itself to require reasoning about uncertainty. In sum, no purely logical agent will be able to conclude that plan A_{90} is the right thing to do.

Nonetheless, let us suppose that A_{90} *is* in fact the right thing to do. What do we mean by saying this? As we discussed in Chapter 2, we mean that out of all the plans that could be executed, A_{90} is expected to maximize the agent's performance measure, given the information it has about the environment. The performance measure includes getting to the airport in time for the flight, avoiding a long, unproductive wait at the airport, and avoiding speeding tickets along the way. The information the agent has cannot guarantee any of these outcomes for A_{90}, but it can provide some degree of belief that they will be achieved. Other plans, such as A_{120}, might increase the agent's belief that it will get to the airport on time, but also increase the likelihood of a long wait. *The right thing to do—the **rational decision**—therefore depends on both the relative importance of various goals and the likelihood that, and degree to which, they will be achieved.* The remainder of this section hones these ideas, in preparation for the development of the general theories of uncertain reasoning and rational decisions that we present in this and subsequent chapters.

Handling uncertain knowledge

In this section, we look more closely at the nature of uncertain knowledge. We will use a simple diagnosis example to illustrate the concepts involved. Diagnosis—whether for medicine, automobile repair, or whatever—is a task that almost always involves uncertainty. Let us try to write rules for dental diagnosis using first-order logic, so that we can see how the logical approach breaks down. Consider the following rule:

$$\forall p \; Symptom(p, Toothache) \; \Rightarrow \; Disease(p, Cavity) \,.$$

The problem is that this rule is wrong. Not all patients with toothaches have cavities; some of them have gum disease, an abscess, or one of several other problems:

$$\forall p \; Symptom(p, Toothache) \; \Rightarrow$$
$$Disease(p, Cavity) \lor Disease(p, GumDisease) \lor Disease(p, Abscess) \ldots$$

Unfortunately, in order to make the rule true, we have to add an almost unlimited list of possible causes. We could try turning the rule into a causal rule:

$$\forall p \; Disease(p, Cavity) \; \Rightarrow \; Symptom(p, Toothache) \,.$$

But this rule is not right either; not all cavities cause pain. The only way to fix the rule is to make it logically exhaustive: to augment the left-hand side with all the qualifications required for a cavity to cause a toothache. Even then, for the purposes of diagnosis, one must also take into account the possibility that the patient might have a toothache and a cavity that are unconnected.

Trying to use first-order logic to cope with a domain like medical diagnosis thus fails for three main reasons:

◇ **Laziness:** It is too much work to list the complete set of antecedents or consequents needed to ensure an exceptionless rule and too hard to use such rules.

Computation and Reasoning

125

THEORETICAL
IGNORANCE
◇ **Theoretical ignorance**: Medical science has no complete theory for the domain.

PRACTICAL
IGNORANCE
◇ **Practical ignorance**: Even if we know all the rules, we might be uncertain about a particular patient because not all the necessary tests have been or can be run.

The connection between toothaches and cavities is just not a logical consequence in either direction. This is typical of the medical domain, as well as most other judgmental domains: law, business, design, automobile repair, gardening, dating, and so on. The agent's knowledge

DEGREE OF BELIEF

PROBABILITY
THEORY
can at best provide only a **degree of belief** in the relevant sentences. Our main tool for dealing with degrees of belief will be **probability theory**, which assigns to each sentence a numerical degree of belief between 0 and 1. (Some alternative methods for uncertain reasoning are covered in Section 14.7.)

Probability provides a way of **summarizing** *the uncertainty that comes from our laziness and ignorance.* We might not know for sure what afflicts a particular patient, but we believe that there is, say, an 80% chance—that is, a probability of 0.8—that the patient has a cavity if he or she has a toothache. That is, we expect that out of all the situations that are indistinguishable from the current situation as far as the agent's knowledge goes, the patient will have a cavity in 80% of them. This belief could be derived from statistical data—80% of the toothache patients seen so far have had cavities—or from some general rules, or from a combination of evidence sources. The 80% summarizes those cases in which all the factors needed for a cavity to cause a toothache are present and other cases in which the patient has both toothache and cavity but the two are unconnected. The missing 20% summarizes all the other possible causes of toothache that we are too lazy or ignorant to confirm or deny.

Assigning probability of 0 to a given sentence corresponds to an unequivocal belief that the sentence is false, while assigning a probability of 1 corresponds to an unequivocal belief that the sentence is true. Probabilities between 0 and 1 correspond to intermediate degrees of belief in the truth of the sentence. The sentence itself is *in fact* either true or false. It is important to note that a degree of belief is different from a degree of truth. A probability of 0.8 does not mean "80% true" but rather an 80% degree of belief—that is, a fairly strong expectation. Thus, probability theory makes the same ontological commitment as logic—namely, that facts either do or do not hold in the world. Degree of truth, as opposed to degree of belief, is the subject of **fuzzy logic**, which is covered in Section 14.7.

In logic, a sentence such as "The patient has a cavity" is true or false depending on the interpretation and the world; it is true just when the fact it refers to is the case. In probability theory, a sentence such as "The probability that the patient has a cavity is 0.8" is about the agent's beliefs, not directly about the world. These beliefs depend on the percepts that

EVIDENCE
the agent has received to date. These percepts constitute the **evidence** on which probability assertions are based. For example, suppose that the agent has drawn a card from a shuffled pack. Before looking at the card, the agent might assign a probability of 1/52 to its being the ace of spades. After looking at the card, an appropriate probability for the same proposition would be 0 or 1. Thus, an assignment of probability to a proposition is analogous to saying whether a given logical sentence (or its negation) is entailed by the knowledge base, rather than whether or not it is true. Just as entailment status can change when more sentences are

Computation and Reasoning

added to the knowledge base, probabilities can change when more evidence is acquired.[1]

All probability statements must therefore indicate the evidence with respect to which the probability is being assessed. As the agent receives new percepts, its probability assessments are updated to reflect the new evidence. Before the evidence is obtained, we talk about **prior** or **unconditional** probability; after the evidence is obtained, we talk about **posterior** or **conditional** probability. In most cases, an agent will have some evidence from its percepts and will be interested in computing the posterior probabilities of the outcomes it cares about.

Uncertainty and rational decisions

The presence of uncertainty radically changes the way an agent makes decisions. A logical agent typically has a goal and executes any plan that is guaranteed to achieve it. An action can be selected or rejected on the basis of whether it achieves the goal, regardless of what other actions might achieve. When uncertainty enters the picture, this is no longer the case. Consider again the A_{90} plan for getting to the airport. Suppose it has a 95% chance of succeeding. Does this mean it is a rational choice? Not necessarily: There might be other plans, such as A_{120}, with higher probabilities of success. If it is vital not to miss the flight, then it is worth risking the longer wait at the airport. What about A_{1440}, a plan that involves leaving home 24 hours in advance? In most circumstances, this is not a good choice, because, although it almost guarantees getting there on time, it involves an intolerable wait.

PREFERENCES

OUTCOMES

UTILITY THEORY

To make such choices, an agent must first have **preferences** between the different possible **outcomes** of the various plans. A particular outcome is a completely specified state, including such factors as whether the agent arrives on time and the length of the wait at the airport. We will be using **utility theory** to represent and reason with preferences. (The term **utility** is used here in the sense of "the quality of being useful," not in the sense of the electric company or water works.) Utility theory says that every state has a degree of usefulness, or utility, to an agent and that the agent will prefer states with higher utility.

The utility of a state is relative to the agent whose preferences the utility function is supposed to represent. For example, the payoff functions for games in Chapter 6 are utility functions. The utility of a state in which White has won a game of chess is obviously high for the agent playing White, but low for the agent playing Black. Or again, some players (including the authors) might be happy with a draw against the world champion, whereas other players (including the former world champion) might not. There is no accounting for taste or preferences: you might think that an agent who prefers jalapeño bubble-gum ice cream to chocolate chocolate chip is odd or even misguided, but you could not say the agent is irrational. A utility function can even account for altruistic behavior, simply by including the welfare of others as one of the factors contributing to the agent's own utility.

DECISION THEORY

Preferences, as expressed by utilities, are combined with probabilities in the general theory of rational decisions called **decision theory**:

Decision theory = probability theory + utility theory .

---

[1] This is quite different from a sentence's becoming true or false as the world changes. Handling a changing world via probabilities requires the same kinds of mechanisms—situations, intervals, and events—that we used in Chapter 10 for logical representations. These mechanisms are discussed in Chapter 15.

Computation and Reasoning

The fundamental idea of decision theory is that *an agent is rational if and only if it chooses the action that yields the highest expected utility, averaged over all the possible outcomes of the action.* This is called the principle of **Maximum Expected Utility** (MEU). We saw this principle in action in Chapter 6 when we touched briefly on optimal decisions in backgammon. We will see that it is in fact a completely general principle.

Design for a decision-theoretic agent

Figure 13.1 sketches the structure of an agent that uses decision theory to select actions. The agent is identical, at an abstract level, to the logical agent described in Chapter 7. The primary difference is that the decision-theoretic agent's knowledge of the current state is uncertain; the agent's **belief state** is a representation of the probabilities of all possible actual states of the world. As time passes, the agent accumulates more evidence and its belief state changes. Given the belief state, the agent can make probabilistic predictions of action outcomes and hence select the action with highest expected utility. This chapter and the next concentrate on the task of representing and computing with probabilistic information in general. Chapter 15 deals with methods for the specific tasks of representing and updating the belief state and predicting the environment. Chapter 16 covers utility theory in more depth, and Chapter 17 develops algorithms for making complex decisions.

BELIEF STATE

---

function DT-AGENT(*percept*) **returns** an *action*
    static: *belief_state*, probabilistic beliefs about the current state of the world
         action, the agent's action

    update *belief_state* based on *action* and *percept*
    calculate outcome probabilities for actions,
        given action descriptions and current *belief_state*
    select *action* with highest expected utility
        given probabilities of outcomes and utility information
    return *action*

Figure 13.1   A decision-theoretic agent that selects rational actions. The steps will be fleshed out in the next five chapters.

13.2   BASIC PROBABILITY NOTATION

Now that we have set up the general framework for a rational agent, we will need a formal language for representing and reasoning with uncertain knowledge. Any notation for describing degrees of belief must be able to deal with two main issues: the nature of the sentences to which degrees of belief are assigned and the dependence of the degree of belief on the agent's experience. The version of probability theory we present uses an extension of propositional logic for its sentences. The dependence on experience is reflected in the syntactic distinction between prior probability statements, which apply before any evidence is obtained, and conditional probability statements, which include the evidence explicitly.

Propositions

Degrees of belief are always applied to **propositions**—assertions that such-and-such is the case. So far we have seen two formal languages—propositional logic and first-order logic— for stating propositions. Probability theory typically uses a language that is slightly more expressive than propositional logic. This section describes that language. (Section 14.6 discusses ways to ascribe degrees of belief to assertions in first-order logic.)

RANDOM VARIABLE
    The basic element of the language is the **random variable**, which can be thought of as referring to a "part" of the world whose "status" is initially unknown. For example, *Cavity* might refer to whether my lower left wisdom tooth has a cavity. Random variables play a role similar to that of CSP variables in constraint satisfaction problems and that of proposition symbols in propositional logic. We will always capitalize the names of random variables. (However, we still use lowercase, single-letter names to represent an unknown random variable, for example: $P(a) = 1 - P(\neg a)$.)

DOMAIN
    Each random variable has a **domain** of values that it can take on. For example, the domain of *Cavity* might be $\langle true, false \rangle$.[2] (We will use lowercase for the names of values.) The simplest kind of proposition asserts that a random variable has a particular value drawn from its domain. For example, *Cavity = true* might represent the proposition that I do in fact have a cavity in my lower left wisdom tooth.

As with CSP variables, random variables are typically divided into three kinds, depending on the type of the domain:

BOOLEAN RANDOM VARIABLES
◇ **Boolean random variables**, such as *Cavity*, have the domain $\langle true, false \rangle$. We will often abbreviate a proposition such as *Cavity = true* simply by the lowercase name *cavity*. Similarly, *Cavity = false* would be abbreviated by $\neg cavity$.

DISCRETE RANDOM VARIABLES
◇ **Discrete random variables**, which include Boolean random variables as a special case, take on values from a *countable* domain. For example, the domain of *Weather* might be $\langle sunny, rainy, cloudy, snow \rangle$. The values in the domain must be mutually exclusive and exhaustive. Where no confusion arises, we will use, for example, *snow* an an abbreviation for *Weather = snow*.

CONTINUOUS RANDOM VARIABLES
◇ **Continuous random variables** take on values from the real numbers. The domain can be either the entire real line or some subset such as the interval [0,1]. For example, the proposition $X = 4.02$ asserts that the random variable X has the exact value 4.02. Propositions concerning continuous random variables can also be inequalities, such as $X \le 4.02$.

With some exceptions, we will be concentrating on the discrete case.

Elementary, propositions such as *Cavity = true* and *Toothache = false*, can be combined to form complex propositions using all the standard logical connectives. For example,

---

[2] One might expect the domain to be written as a set: $\{ true, false \}$. We write it as a tuple because it will be convenient later to impose an ordering on the values.

Computation and Reasoning

$Cavity = true \land Toothache = false$ is a proposition to which one may ascribe a degree of (dis)belief. As explained in the previous paragraph, this proposition may also be written as $cavity \land \neg toothache$.

Atomic events

ATOMIC EVENT

The notion of an **atomic event** is useful in understanding the foundations of probability theory. An atomic event is a *complete* specification of the state of the world about which the agent is uncertain. It can be thought of as an assignment of particular values to all the variables of which the world is composed. For example, if my world consists of only the Boolean variables $Cavity$ and $Toothache$, then there are just four distinct atomic events; the proposition $Cavity = false \land Toothache = true$ is one such event.[3]

Atomic events have some important properties:

- They are *mutually exclusive*—at most one can actually be the case. For example, $cavity \land toothache$ and $cavity \land \neg toothache$ cannot both be the case.

- The set of all possible atomic events is *exhaustive*—at least one must be the case. That is, the disjunction of all atomic events is logically equivalent to $true$.

- Any particular atomic event entails the truth or falsehood of every proposition, whether simple or complex. This can be seen by using the standard semantics for logical connectives (Chapter 7). For example, the atomic event $cavity \land \neg toothache$ entails the truth of $cavity$ and the falsehood of $cavity \Rightarrow toothache$.

- Any proposition is logically equivalent to the disjunction of all atomic events that entail the truth of the proposition. For example, the proposition $cavity$ is equivalent to disjunction of the atomic events $cavity \land toothache$ and $cavity \land \neg toothache$.

Exercise 13.4 asks you to prove some of these properties.

Prior probability

UNCONDITIONAL

PRIOR PROBABILITY

The **unconditional** or **prior probability** associated with a proposition a is the degree of belief accorded to it *in the absence of any other information*; it is written as $P(a)$. For example, if the prior probability that I have a cavity is 0.1, then we would write

$$P(Cavity = true) = 0.1 \quad \text{or} \quad P(cavity) = 0.1 .$$

It is important to remember that $P(a)$ can be used only when there is no other information. As soon as some new information is known, we must reason with the *conditional* probability of a given that new information. Conditional probabilities are covered in the next section.

Sometimes, we will want to talk about the probabilities of all the possible values of a random variable. In that case, we will use an expression such as $\mathbf{P}(Weather)$, which denotes a *vector* of values for the probabilities of each individual state of the weather. Thus, instead

---

[3] Many standard formulations of probability theory take atomic events, also known as **sample points**, as primitive and define a random variable as a function taking an atomic event as input and returning a value from the appropriate domain. Such an approach is perhaps more general, but also less intuitive.

of writing the four equations

$$P(Weather = sunny) = 0.7$$
$$P(Weather = rain) = 0.2$$
$$P(Weather = cloudy) = 0.08$$
$$P(Weather = snow) = 0.02 \ .$$

we may simply write

$$\mathbf{P}(Weather) = \langle 0.7, 0.2, 0.08, 0.02 \rangle \ .$$

PROBABILITY
DISTRIBUTION

This statement defines a prior **probability distribution** for the random variable *Weather*.

We will also use expressions such as $\mathbf{P}(Weather, Cavity)$ to denote the probabilities of all combinations of the values of a set of random variables.[4] In that case, $\mathbf{P}(Weather, Cavity)$ can be represented by a 4×2 table of probabilities. This is called the **joint probability dis-**

JOINT PROBABILITY
DISTRIBUTION

tribution of *Weather* and *Cavity*.

Sometimes it will be useful to think about the complete set of random variables used to describe the world. A joint probability distribution that covers this complete set is called the

FULL JOINT
PROBABILITY
DISTRIBUTION

full joint probability distribution. For example, if the world consists of just the variables *Cavity*, *Toothache*, and *Weather*, then the full joint distribution is given by

$$\mathbf{P}(Cavity, Toothache, Weather).$$

This joint distribution can be represented as a $2 \times 2 \times 4$ table with 16 entries. A full joint distribution specifies the probability of every atomic event and is therefore a complete specification of one's uncertainty about the world in question. We will see in Section 13.4 that any probabilistic query can be answered from the full joint distribution.

For continuous variables, it is not possible to write out the entire distribution as a table, because there are infinitely many values. Instead, one usually defines the probability that a random variable takes on some value x as a parameterized function of x. For example, let the random variable X denote tomorrow's maximum temperature in Berkeley. Then the sentence

$$P(X = x) = U[18, 26](x)$$

expresses the belief that X is distributed uniformly between 18 and 26 degrees Celsius. (Several useful continuous distributions are defined in Appendix A.) Probability distributions for

PROBABILITY
DENSITY FUNCTIONS

continuous variables are called **probability density functions**. Density functions differ in meaning from discrete distributions. For example, using the temperature distribution given earlier, we find that $P(X = 20.5) = U[18, 26](20.5) = 0.125/C$. This does *not* mean that there's a 12.5% chance that the maximum temperature will be *exactly* 20.5 degrees tomorrow; the probability that this will happen is of course zero. The technical meaning is that the probability that the temperature is in a small region around 20.5 degrees is equal, in the limit, to 0.125 divided by the width of the region in degrees Celsius:

$$\lim_{dx \to 0} P(20.5 \leq X \leq 20.5 + dx)/dx = 0.125/C \ .$$

---

[4] The general notational rule is that the distribution covers all values of the variables that are capitalized. Thus, the expression $\mathbf{P}(Weather, cavity)$ is a four-element vector of probabilities for the conjunction of each weather type with $Cavity = true$.

Computation and Reasoning

Some authors use different symbols for discrete distributions and density functions; we use P in both cases, since confusion seldom arises and the equations are usually identical. Note that probabilities are unitless numbers, whereas density functions are measured with a unit, in this case reciprocal degrees.

Conditional probability

Once the agent has obtained some evidence concerning the previously unknown random variables making up the domain, prior probabilities are no longer applicable. Instead, we use **conditional** or **posterior** probabilities. The notation used is $P(a|b)$, where a and b are any propositions.[5] This is read as "the probability of a, given that *all we know* is b." For example,

CONDITIONAL
PROBABILITY
POSTERIOR
PROBABILITY

$$P(cavity|toothache) = 0.8$$

indicates that if a patient is observed to have a toothache and no other information is yet available, then the probability of the patient's having a cavity will be 0.8. A prior probability, such as $P(cavity)$, can be thought of as a special case of the conditional probability $P(cavity|)$, where the probability is conditioned on no evidence.

Conditional probabilities can be defined in terms of unconditional probabilities. The defining equation is

$$P(a|b) = \frac{P(a \wedge b)}{P(b)} \tag{13.1}$$

which holds whenever $P(b) > 0$. This equation can also be written as

$$P(a \wedge b) = P(a|b)P(b)$$

PRODUCT RULE

which is called the **product rule**. The product rule is perhaps easier to remember: it comes from the fact that, for a and b to be true, we need b to be true, and we also need a to be true given b. We can also have it the other way around:

$$P(a \wedge b) = P(b|a)P(a) .$$

In some cases, it is easier to reason in terms of prior probabilities of conjunctions, but for the most part, we will use conditional probabilities as our vehicle for probabilistic inference.

We can also use the **P** notation for conditional distributions. $\mathbf{P}(X|Y)$ gives the values of $P(X = x_i|Y = y_j)$ for each possible i, j. As an example of how this makes our notation more concise, consider applying the product rule to each case where the propositions a and b assert particular values of X and Y respectively. We obtain the following equations:

$$P(X = x_1 \wedge Y = y_1) = P(X = x_1|Y = y_1)P(Y = y_1) .$$
$$P(X = x_1 \wedge Y = y_2) = P(X = x_1|Y = y_2)P(Y = y_2) .$$
$$\vdots$$

We can combine all these into the single equation

$$\mathbf{P}(X, Y) = \mathbf{P}(X|Y)\mathbf{P}(Y) .$$

Remember that this denotes a set of equations relating the corresponding individual entries in the tables, *not* a matrix multiplication of the tables.

---

[5] The "|" operator has the lowest possible precedence, so $P(a \wedge b|c \vee d)$ means $P((a \wedge b)|(c \vee d))$.

Computation and Reasoning

It is tempting, but wrong, to view conditional probabilities as if they were logical implications with uncertainty added. For example, the sentence $P(a|b) = 0.8$ *cannot* be interpreted to mean "whenever b holds, conclude that $P(a)$ is 0.8." Such an interpretation would be wrong on two counts: first, $P(a)$ always denotes the prior probability of a, not the posterior probability given some evidence; second, the statement $P(a|b) = 0.8$ is immediately relevant just when b is the *only* available evidence. When additional information c is available, the degree of belief in a is $P(a|b \wedge c)$, which may could little relation to $P(a|b)$. For example, c might tell us directly whether a is true or false. If we examine a patient who complains of toothache, and discover a cavity, then we have additional evidence *cavity*, and we conclude (trivially) that $P(cavity|toothache \wedge cavity) = 1.0$.

13.3   THE AXIOMS OF PROBABILITY

So far, we have defined a syntax for propositions and for prior and conditional probability statements about those propositions. Now we must provide some sort of semantics for probability statements. We begin with the basic axioms that serve to define the probability scale and its endpoints:

1. All probabilities are between 0 and 1. For any proposition a,

$$0 \leq P(a) \leq 1 \,.$$

2. Necessarily true (i.e., valid) propositions have probability 1, and necessarily false (i.e., unsatisfiable) propositions have probability 0.

$$P(true) = 1 \qquad P(false) = 0 \,.$$

Next, we need an axiom that connects the probabilities of logically related propositions. The simplest way to do this is to define the probability of a disjunction as follows:

3. The probability of a disjunction is given by

$$P(a \vee b) = P(a) + P(b) - P(a \wedge b) \,.$$

This rule is easily remembered by noting that the cases where a holds, together with the cases where b holds, certainly cover all the cases where $a \vee b$ holds; but summing the two sets of cases counts their intersection twice, so we need to subtract $P(a \wedge b)$.

KOLMOGOROV'S
AXIOMS

These three axioms are often called **Kolmogorov's axioms** in honor of the Russian mathematician Andrei Kolmogorov, who showed how to build up the rest of probability theory from this simple foundation. Notice that the axioms deal only with prior probabilities rather than conditional probabilities; this is because we have already defined the latter in terms of the former via Equation (13.1).

Computation and Reasoning

WHERE DO PROBABILITIES COME FROM?

There has been endless debate over the source and status of probability numbers. The **frequentist** position is that the numbers can come only from *experiments*: if we test 100 people and find that 10 of them have a cavity, then we can say that the probability of a cavity is approximately 0.1. In this view, the assertion "the probability of a cavity is 0.1" means that 0.1 is the fraction that would be observed in the limit of infinitely many samples. From any finite sample, we can estimate the true fraction and also calculate how accurate our estimate is likely to be.

The **objectivist** view is that probabilities are real aspects of the universe—propensities of objects to behave in certain ways—rather than being just descriptions of an observer's degree of belief. For example, that a fair coin comes up heads with probability 0.5 is a propensity of the coin itself. In this view, frequentist measurements are attempts to observe these propensities. Most physicists agree that quantum phenomena are objectively probabilistic, but uncertainty at the macroscopic scale—e.g., in coin tossing—usually arises from ignorance of initial conditions and does not seem consistent with the propensity view.

The **subjectivist** view describes probabilities as a way of characterizing an agent's beliefs, rather than as having any external physical significance. This allows the doctor or analyst to make the numbers up—to say, "In my opinion, I expect the probability of a cavity to be about 0.1." Several more reliable techniques, such as the betting systems described earlier, have also been developed for eliciting probability assessments from humans.

In the end, even a strict frequentist position involves subjective analysis, so the difference probably has little practical importance. The **reference class** problem illustrates the intrusion of subjectivity. Suppose that a frequentist doctor wants to know the chances that a patient has a particular disease. The doctor wants to consider other patients who are similar in important ways—age, symptoms, perhaps sex—and see what proportion of them had the disease. But if the doctor considered everything that is known about the patient—weight to the nearest gram, hair color, mother's maiden name, etc.—the result would be that there are no other patients who are exactly the same and thus no reference class from which to collect experimental data. This has been a vexing problem in the philosophy of science.

Laplace's **principle of indifference** (1816) states that propositions that are syntactically "symmetric" with respect to the evidence should be accorded equal probability. Various refinements have been proposed, culminating in the attempt by Carnap and others to develop a rigorous **inductive logic**, capable of computing the correct probability for any proposition from any collection of observations. Currently, it is believed that no unique inductive logic exists; rather, any such logic rests on a subjective prior probability distribution whose effect is diminished as more observations are collected.

Computation and Reasoning

Using the axioms of probability

We can derive a variety of useful facts from the basic axioms. For example, the familiar rule for negation follows by substituting $\neg a$ for b in axiom 3, giving us:

$$
\begin{aligned}
P(a \vee \neg a) &= P(a) + P(\neg a) - P(a \wedge \neg a) && \text{(by axiom 3 with } b = \neg a) \\
P(true) &= P(a) + P(\neg a) - P(false) && \text{(by logical equivalence)} \\
1 &= P(a) + P(\neg a) && \text{(by axiom 2)} \\
P(\neg a) &= 1 - P(a) && \text{(by algebra)}.
\end{aligned}
$$

The third line of this derivation is itself a useful fact and can be extended from the Boolean case to the general discrete case. Let the discrete variable D have the domain $\langle d_1, \ldots, d_n \rangle$. Then it is easy to show (Exercise 13.2) that

$$
\sum_{i=1}^{n} P(D = d_i) = 1 .
$$

That is, any probability distribution on a single variable must sum to 1.[6] It is also true that any *joint* probability distribution on any *set* of variables must sum to 1: this can be seen simply by creating a single megavariable whose domain is the cross product of the domains of the the original variables.

Recall that any proposition a is equivalent to the disjunction of all the atomic events in which a holds; call this set of events $\mathbf{e}(a)$. Recall also that atomic events are mutually exclusive, so the probability of any conjunction of atomic events is zero, by axiom 2. Hence, from axiom 3, we can derive the following simple relationship: *The probability of a proposition is equal to the sum of the probabilities of the atomic events in which it holds;* that is,

$$
P(a) = \sum_{e_i \in \mathbf{e}(a)} P(e_i) . \tag{13.2}
$$

This equation provides a simple method for computing the probability of any proposition, given a full joint distribution that specifies the probabilities of all atomic events. (See Section 13.4.) In subsequent sections we will derive additional rules for manipulating probabilities. First, however, we will examine the foundation for the axioms themselves.

Why the axioms of probability are reasonable

The axioms of probability can be seen as restricting the set of probabilistic beliefs that an agent can hold. This is somewhat analogous to the logical case, where a logical agent cannot simultaneously believe A, B, and $\neg(A \wedge B)$, for example. There is, however, an additional complication. In the logical case, the semantic definition of conjunction means that at least one of the three beliefs just mentioned *must be false in the world*, so it is unreasonable for an agent to believe all three. With probabilities, on the other hand, statements refer not to the world directly, but to the agent's own state of knowledge. Why, then, can an agent not hold the following set of beliefs, which clearly violates axiom 3?

$$
\begin{aligned}
P(a) &= 0.4 & P(a \wedge b) &= 0.0 \\
P(b) &= 0.3 & P(a \vee b) &= 0.8
\end{aligned} \tag{13.3}
$$

---

[6] For continuous variables, the summation is replaced by an integral: $\int_{-\infty}^{\infty} P(X = x)\, dx = 1$.

Computation and Reasoning

135

This kind of question has been the subject of decades of intense debate between those who advocate the use of probabilities as the only legitimate form for degrees of belief and those who advocate alternative approaches. Here, we give one argument for the axioms of probability, first stated in 1931 by Bruno de Finetti.

The key to de Finetti's argument is the connection between degree of belief and actions. The idea is that if an agent has some degree of belief in a proposition a, then the agent should be able to state odds at which it is indifferent to a bet for or against a. Think of it as a game between two agents: Agent 1 states "my degree of belief in event a is 0.4." Agent 2 is then free to choose whether to bet for or against a, at stakes that are consistent with the stated degree of belief. That is, Agent 2 could choose to bet that a will occur, betting \$4 against Agent 1's \$6. Or Agent 2 could bet \$6 against \$4 that A will not occur.[7] If an agent's degrees of belief do not accurately reflect the world, then you would expect that it would tend to lose money over the long run to an opposing agent whose beliefs more accurately reflect the state of the world.

But de Finetti proved something much stronger: *If Agent 1 expresses a set of degrees of belief that violate the axioms of probability theory then there is a combination of bets Agent 2 that* **guarantees** *that Agent 1 will lose money* **every** *time.* So if you accept the idea that an agent should be willing to "put its money where its probabilities are," then you should accept that it is irrational to have beliefs that violate the axioms of probability.

One might think that this betting game is rather contrived. For example, what if one refuses to bet? Does that end the argument? The answer is that the betting game is an abstract model for the decision-making situation in which every agent is *unavoidably* involved at every moment. Every action (including inaction) is a kind of bet, and every outcome can be seen as a payoff of the bet. Refusing to bet is like refusing to allow time to pass.

We will not provide the proof of de Finetti's theorem, but we will show an example. Suppose that Agent 1 has the set of degrees of belief from Equation (13.3). Figure 13.2 shows that if Agent 2 chooses to bet \$4 on a, \$3 on b, and \$2 on $\neg(a \lor b)$, then Agent 1 always loses money, regardless of the outcomes for a and b.

Agent 1		Agent 2		Outcome for Agent 1			
Proposition	Belief	Bet	Stakes	$a \land b$	$a \land \neg b$	$\neg a \land b$	$\neg a \land \neg b$
a	0.4	a	4 to 6	−6	−6	4	4
b	0.3	b	3 to 7	−7	3	−7	3
$a \lor b$	0.8	$\neg(a \lor b)$	2 to 8	2	2	2	−8
				−11	−1	−1	−1

Figure 13.2   Because Agent 1 has inconsistent beliefs, Agent 2 is able to devise a set of bets that guarantees a loss for Agent 1, no matter what the outcome of a and b.

---

[7]   One might argue that the agent's preferences for different bank balances are such that the possibility of losing \$1 is not counterbalanced by an equal possibility of winning \$1. One possible response is to make the bet amounts small enough to avoid this problem. Savage's analysis (1954) circumvents the issue altogether.

Other strong philosophical arguments have been put forward for the use of probabilities, most notably those of Cox (1946) and Carnap (1950). The world being the way it is, however, practical demonstrations sometimes speak louder than proofs. The success of reasoning systems based on probability theory has been much more effective in making converts. We now look at how the axioms can be deployed to make inferences.

13.4 INFERENCE USING FULL JOINT DISTRIBUTIONS

PROBABILISTIC
INFERENCE

In this section we will describe a simple method for **probabilistic inference**—that is, the computation from observed evidence of posterior probabilities for query propositions. We will use the full joint distribution as the "knowledge base" from which answers to all questions may be derived. Along the way we will also introduce several useful techniques for manipulating equations involving probabilities.

We begin with a very simple example: a domain consisting of just the three Boolean variables *Toothache*, *Cavity*, and *Catch* (the dentist's nasty steel probe catches in my tooth). The full joint distribution is a $2 \times 2 \times 2$ table as shown in Figure 13.3.

	toothache		¬toothache	
	catch	¬catch	catch	¬catch
cavity	0.108	0.012	0.072	0.008
¬cavity	0.016	0.064	0.144	0.576

Figure 13.3   A full joint distribution for the *Toothache, Cavity, Catch* world.

Notice that the probabilities in the joint distribution sum to 1, as required by the axioms of probability. Notice also that Equation (13.2) gives us a direct way to calculate the probability of any proposition, simple or complex: We simply identify those atomic events in which the proposition is true and add up their probabilities. For example, there are six atomic events in which *cavity* $\lor$ *toothache* holds:

$$P(cavity \lor toothache) = 0.108 + 0.012 + 0.072 + 0.008 + 0.016 + 0.064 = 0.28 .$$

One particularly common task is to extract the distribution over some subset of variables or a single variable. For example, adding the entries in the first row gives the unconditional or

MARGINAL
PROBABILITY

marginal probability[8] of *cavity*:

$$P(cavity) = 0.108 + 0.012 + 0.072 + 0.008 = 0.2 .$$

MARGINALIZATION

This process is called **marginalization**, or **summing out**—because the variables other than *Cavity* are summed out. We can write the following general marginalization rule for any sets of variables **Y** and **Z**:

$$\mathbf{P}(\mathbf{Y}) = \sum_{\mathbf{z}} \mathbf{P}(\mathbf{Y}, \mathbf{z}) .\tag{13.4}$$

---

[8] So called because of a common practice among actuaries of writing the sums of observed frequencies in the margins of insurance tables.

Computation and Reasoning

That is, a distribution over $\mathbf{Y}$ can be obtained by summing out all the other variables from any joint distribution containing $\mathbf{Y}$. A variant of this rule involves conditional probabilities instead of joint probabilities, using the product rule:

$$\mathbf{P}(\mathbf{Y}) = \sum_{\mathbf{z}} \mathbf{P}(\mathbf{Y}|\mathbf{z})P(\mathbf{z}) \ . \tag{13.5}$$

This rule is called **conditioning**. Marginalization and conditioning will turn out to be useful rules for all kinds of derivations involving probability expressions.

In most cases, we will be interested in computing *conditional* probabilities of some variables, given evidence about others. Conditional probabilities can be found by first using Equation (13.1) to obtain an expression in terms of unconditional probabilities and then evaluating the expression from the full joint distribution. For example, we can compute the probability of a cavity, given evidence of a toothache, as follows:

$$P(cavity|toothache) = \frac{P(cavity \wedge toothache)}{P(toothache)}$$

$$= \frac{0.108 + 0.012}{0.108 + 0.012 + 0.016 + 0.064} = 0.6 \ .$$

Just to check, we can also compute the probability that there is no cavity, given a toothache:

$$P(\neg cavity|toothache) = \frac{P(\neg cavity \wedge toothache)}{P(toothache)}$$

$$= \frac{0.016 + 0.064}{0.108 + 0.012 + 0.016 + 0.064} = 0.4 \ .$$

Notice that in these two calculations the term $1/P(toothache)$ remains constant, no matter which value of *Cavity* we calculate. In fact, it can be viewed as a **normalization** constant for the distribution $\mathbf{P}(Cavity|toothache)$, ensuring that it adds up to 1. Throughout the chapters dealing with probability, we will use α to denote such constants. With this notation, we can write the two preceding equations in one:

$$\mathbf{P}(Cavity|toothache) = \alpha\, \mathbf{P}(Cavity, toothache)$$

$$= \alpha\, [\mathbf{P}(Cavity, toothache, catch) + \mathbf{P}(Cavity, toothache, \neg catch)]$$

$$= \alpha\, [\langle 0.108, 0.016 \rangle + \langle 0.012, 0.064 \rangle] = \alpha\, \langle 0.12, 0.08 \rangle = \langle 0.6, 0.4 \rangle \ .$$

Normalization will turn out to be a useful shortcut in many probability calculations.

From the example, we can extract a general inference procedure. We will stick to the case in which the query involves a single variable. We will need some notation: let X be the query variable (*Cavity* in the example), let $\mathbf{E}$ be the set of evidence variables (just *Toothache* in the example), let $\mathbf{e}$ be the observed values for them, and let $\mathbf{Y}$ be the remaining unobserved variables (just *Catch* in the example). The query is $\mathbf{P}(X|\mathbf{e})$ and can be evaluated as

$$\mathbf{P}(X|\mathbf{e}) = \alpha\, \mathbf{P}(X, \mathbf{e}) = \alpha \sum_{\mathbf{y}} \mathbf{P}(X, \mathbf{e}, \mathbf{y}) \ , \tag{13.6}$$

where the summation is over all possible $\mathbf{y}$s (i.e., all possible combinations of values of the unobserved variables $\mathbf{Y}$). Notice that together the variables X, $\mathbf{E}$, and $\mathbf{Y}$ constitute the complete set of variables for the domain, so $\mathbf{P}(X, \mathbf{e}, \mathbf{y})$ is simply a subset of probabilities from the full joint distribution. The algorithm is shown in Figure 13.4. It loops over the values

---

function ENUMERATE-JOINT-ASK(X, **e**, **P**) **returns** a distribution over X
   inputs: X, the query variable
         e, observed values for variables **E**
         P, a joint distribution on variables $\{X\} \cup$ **E** $\cup$ **Y**   / * **Y** = *hidden variables* * /

   Q(X) $\leftarrow$ a distribution over X, initially empty
   for each value x_i of X **do**
       Q(x_i) $\leftarrow$ ENUMERATE-JOINT(x_i, **e**, **Y**, [ ], **P**)
   return NORMALIZE(**Q**(X))

---

function ENUMERATE-JOINT(x, **e**, *vars*, *values*, **P**) **returns** a real number
   if EMPTY?(*vars*) **then return P**(x, **e**, *values*)
   $Y \leftarrow$ FIRST(*vars*)
   return $\sum_y$ ENUMERATE-JOINT(x, **e**, REST(*vars*), [$y|values$], **P**)

Figure 13.4   An algorithm for probabilistic inference by enumeration of the entries in a full joint distribution.

of X and the values of Y to enumerate all possible atomic events with **e** fixed, adds up their probabilities from the joint table, and normalizes the results.

Given the full joint distribution to work with, ENUMERATE-JOINT-ASK is a complete algorithm for answering probabilistic queries for discrete variables. It does not scale well, however: For a domain described by n Boolean variables, it requires an input table of size $O(2^n)$ and takes $O(2^n)$ time to process the table. In a realistic problem, there might be hundreds or thousands of random variables to consider, not just three. It quickly becomes completely impractical to define the vast numbers of probabilities required—the experience needed in order to estimate each of the table entries separately simply cannot exist.

For these reasons, the full joint distribution in tabular form is not a practical tool for building reasoning systems (although the historical notes at the end of the chapter includes one real-world application of this method). Instead, it should be viewed as the theoretical foundation on which more effective approaches may be built. The remainder of this chapter introduces some of the basic ideas required in preparation for the development of realistic systems in Chapter 14.

13.5   INDEPENDENCE

Let us expand the full joint distribution in Figure 13.3 by adding a fourth variable, *Weather*. The full joint distribution then becomes **P**(*Toothache, Catch, Cavity, Weather*), which has 32 entries (because *Weather* has four values). It contains four "editions" of the table shown in Figure 13.3, one for each kind of weather. It seems natural to ask what relationship these editions have to each other and to the original three-variable table. For example, how are $P(toothache, catch, cavity, Weather = cloudy)$ and $P(toothache, catch, cavity)$ related?

One way to answer this question is to use the product rule:

$$P(toothache, catch, cavity, Weather = cloudy)$$
$$= P(Weather = cloudy|toothache, catch, cavity)P(toothache, catch, cavity) .$$

Now, unless one is in the deity business, one should not imagine that one's dental problems influence the weather. Therefore, the following assertion seems reasonable:

$$P(Weather = cloudy|toothache, catch, cavity) = P(Weather = cloudy) . \quad (13.7)$$

From this, we can deduce

$$P(toothache, catch, cavity, Weather = cloudy)$$
$$= P(Weather = cloudy)P(toothache, catch, cavity) .$$

A similar equation exists for *every entry* in $\mathbf{P}(Toothache, Catch, Cavity, Weather)$. In fact, we can write the general equation

$$\mathbf{P}(Toothache, Catch, Cavity, Weather) = \mathbf{P}(Toothache, Catch, Cavity)\mathbf{P}(Weather) .$$

Thus, the 32-element table for four variables can be constructed from one 8-element table and one four-element table. This decomposition is illustrated schematically in Figure 13.5(a).

INDEPENDENCE   The property we used in writing Equation (13.7) is called **independence** (also **marginal independence** and **absolute independence**). In particular, the weather is independent of one's dental problems. Independence between propositions a and b can be written as

$$P(a|b) = P(a) \quad \text{or} \quad P(b|a) = P(b) \quad \text{or} \quad P(a \land b) = P(a)P(b) . \quad (13.8)$$

All these forms are equivalent (Exercise 13.7). Independence between variables X and Y can be written as follows (again, these are all equivalent):

$$\mathbf{P}(X|Y) = \mathbf{P}(X) \quad \text{or} \quad \mathbf{P}(Y|X) = \mathbf{P}(Y) \quad \text{or} \quad \mathbf{P}(X, Y) = \mathbf{P}(X)\mathbf{P}(Y) .$$

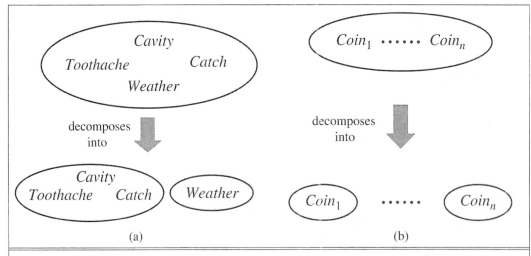

Figure 13.5 Two examples of factoring a large joint distribution into smaller distributions, using absolute independence. (a) Weather and dental problems are independent. (b) Coin flips are independent.

Computation and Reasoning

Independence assertions are usually based on knowledge of the domain. As we have seen, they can dramatically reduce the amount of information necessary to specify the full joint distribution. If the complete set of variables can be divided into independent subsets, then the full joint can be *factored* into separate joint distributions on those subsets. For example, the joint distribution on the outcome of n independent coin flips, $\mathbf{P}(C_1, \ldots, C_n)$, can be represented as the product of n single-variable distributions $\mathbf{P}(C_i)$. In a more practical vein, the independence of dentistry and meteorology is a good thing, because otherwise the practice of dentistry might require intimate knowledge of meteorology and *vice versa*.

When they are available, then, independence assertions can help in reducing the size of the domain representation and the complexity of the inference problem. Unfortunately, clean separation of entire sets of variables by independence is quite rare. Whenever a connection, however indirect, exists between two variables, independence will fail to hold. Moreover, even independent subsets can be quite large—for example, dentistry might involve dozens of diseases and hundreds of symptoms, all of which are interrelated. To handle such problems, we will need more subtle methods than the straightforward concept of independence.

13.6   BAYES' RULE AND ITS USE

On page 470, we defined the **product rule** and pointed out that it can be written in two forms because of the commutativity of conjunction:

$$P(a \wedge b) = P(a|b)P(b)$$
$$P(a \wedge b) = P(b|a)P(a) .$$

Equating the two right-hand sides and dividing by $P(a)$, we get

$$P(b|a) = \frac{P(a|b)P(b)}{P(a)} . \qquad (13.9)$$

BAYES' RULE   This equation is known as **Bayes' rule** (also Bayes' law or Bayes' theorem).[9] This simple equation underlies all modern AI systems for probabilistic inference. The more general case of multivalued variables can be written in the **P** notation as

$$\mathbf{P}(Y|X) = \frac{\mathbf{P}(X|Y)\mathbf{P}(Y)}{\mathbf{P}(X)} .$$

where again this is to be taken as representing a set of equations, each dealing with specific values of the variables. We will also have occasion to use a more general version conditionalized on some background evidence **e**:

$$\mathbf{P}(Y|X, \mathbf{e}) = \frac{\mathbf{P}(X|Y, \mathbf{e})\mathbf{P}(Y|\mathbf{e})}{\mathbf{P}(X|\mathbf{e})} . \qquad (13.10)$$

---

[9]   According to rule 1 on page 1 of Strunk and White's *The Elements of Style*, it should be Bayes's rather than Bayes'. The latter is, however, more commonly used.

Computation and Reasoning

Applying Bayes' rule: The simple case

On the surface, Bayes' rule does not seem very useful. It requires three terms—a conditional probability and two unconditional probabilities—just to compute one conditional probability.

Bayes' rule is useful in practice because there are many cases where we do have good probability estimates for these three numbers and need to compute the fourth. In a task such as medical diagnosis, we often have conditional probabilities on causal relationships and want to derive a diagnosis. A doctor knows that the disease meningitis causes the patient to have a stiff neck, say, 50% of the time. The doctor also knows some unconditional facts: the prior probability that a patient has meningitis is 1/50,000, and the prior probability that any patient has a stiff neck is 1/20. Letting s be the proposition that the patient has a stiff neck and m be the proposition that the patient has meningitis, we have

$$P(s|m) = 0.5$$
$$P(m) = 1/50000$$
$$P(s) = 1/20$$
$$P(m|s) = \frac{P(s|m)P(m)}{P(s)} = \frac{0.5 \times 1/50000}{1/20} = 0.0002 \ .$$

That is, we expect only 1 in 5000 patients with a stiff neck to have meningitis. Notice that, even though a stiff neck is quite strongly indicated by meningitis (with probability 0.5), the probability of meningitis in the patient remains small. This is because the prior probability on stiff necks is much higher than that on meningitis.

Section 13.4 illustrated a process by which one can avoid assessing the probability of the evidence (here, $P(s)$) by instead computing a posterior probability for each value of the query variable (here, m and $\neg m$) and then normalizing the results. The same process can be applied when using Bayes' rule. We have

$$\mathbf{P}(M|s) = \alpha \langle P(s|m)P(m), P(s|\neg m)P(\neg m) \rangle \ .$$

Thus, in order to use this approach we need to estimate $P(s|\neg m)$ instead of $P(s)$. There is no free lunch—sometimes this is easier, sometimes it is harder. The general form of Bayes' rule with normalization is

$$\mathbf{P}(Y|X) = \alpha \, \mathbf{P}(X|Y)\mathbf{P}(Y) \ , \tag{13.11}$$

where α is the normalization constant needed to make the entries in $\mathbf{P}(Y|X)$ sum to 1.

 One obvious question to ask about Bayes' rule is why one might have available the conditional probability in one direction, but not the other. In the meningitis domain, perhaps the doctor knows that a stiff neck implies meningitis in 1 out of 5000 cases; that is, the doctor has quantitative information in the **diagnostic** direction from symptoms to causes. Such a doctor has no need to use Bayes' rule. Unfortunately, *diagnostic knowledge is often more fragile than causal knowledge*. If there is a sudden epidemic of meningitis, the unconditional probability of meningitis, $P(m)$, will go up. The doctor who derived the diagnostic probability $P(m|s)$ directly from statistical observation of patients before the epidemic will have no idea how to update the value, but the doctor who computes $P(m|s)$ from the other three values will see that $P(m|s)$ should go up proportionately with $P(m)$. Most importantly, the causal information $P(s|m)$ is *unaffected* by the epidemic, because it simply reflects the way meningitis works. The use of this kind of direct causal or model-based knowledge provides the crucial robustness needed to make probabilistic systems feasible in the real world.

Using Bayes' rule: Combining evidence

We have seen that Bayes' rule can be useful for answering probabilistic queries conditioned on one piece of evidence—for example, the stiff neck. In particular, we have argued that probabilistic information is often available in the form $P(effect|cause)$. What happens when we have two or more pieces of evidence? For example, what can a dentist conclude if her nasty steel probe catches in the aching tooth of a patient? If we know the full joint distribution (Figure 13.3), one can read off the answer:

$$\mathbf{P}(Cavity|toothache \wedge catch) = \alpha \langle 0.108, 0.016 \rangle \approx \langle 0.871, 0.129 \rangle .$$

We know, however, that such an approach will not scale up to larger numbers of variables.

We can try using use Bayes' rule to reformulate the problem:

$$\mathbf{P}(Cavity|toothache \wedge catch) = \alpha \mathbf{P}(toothache \wedge catch|Cavity)\mathbf{P}(Cavity) . \quad (13.12)$$

For this reformulation to work, we need to know the conditional probabilities of the conjunction *toothache* $\wedge$ *catch* for each value of *Cavity*. That might be feasible for just two evidence variables, but again it will not scale up. If there are n possible evidence variables (X rays, diet, oral hygiene, etc.), then there are 2^n possible combinations of observed values for which we would need to know conditional probabilities. We might as well go back to using the full joint distribution. This is what first led researchers away from probability theory toward approximate methods for evidence combination that, while giving incorrect answers, require fewer numbers to give any answer at all.

Rather than taking this route, we need to find some additional assertions about the domain that will enable us to simplify the expressions. The notion of **independence** in Section 13.5 provides a clue, but needs refining. It would be nice if *Toothache* and *Catch* were independent, but they are not: if the probe catches in the tooth, it probably has a cavity and that probably causes a toothache. These variables *are* independent, however, *given the presence or the absence of a cavity*. Each is directly caused by the cavity, but neither has a direct effect on the other: toothache depends on the state of the nerves in the tooth, whereas the probe's accuracy depends on the dentist's skill, to which the toothache is irrelevant.[10] Mathematically, this property is written as

$$\mathbf{P}(toothache \wedge catch|Cavity) = \mathbf{P}(toothache|Cavity)\mathbf{P}(catch|Cavity) . \quad (13.13)$$

 This equation expresses the **conditional independence** of *toothache* and *catch* given *Cavity*. We can plug it into Equation (13.12) to obtain the probability of a cavity:

$$\mathbf{P}(Cavity|toothache \wedge catch) = \alpha \, \mathbf{P}(toothache|Cavity)\mathbf{P}(catch|Cavity)\mathbf{P}(Cavity).$$

Now the information requirements are the same as for inference using each piece of evidence separately: the prior probability $\mathbf{P}(Cavity)$ for the query variable and the conditional probability of each effect, given its cause.

---

[10] We assume that the patient and dentist are distinct individuals.

The general definition of conditional independence of two variables X and Y, given a third variable Z is

$$\mathbf{P}(X, Y|Z) = \mathbf{P}(X|Z)\mathbf{P}(Y|Z) .$$

In the dentist domain, for example, it seems reasonable to assert conditional independence of the variables *Toothache* and *Catch*, given *Cavity*:

$$\mathbf{P}(\textit{Toothache}, \textit{Catch}|\textit{Cavity}) = \mathbf{P}(\textit{Toothache}|\textit{Cavity})\mathbf{P}(\textit{Catch}|\textit{Cavity}) . \quad (13.14)$$

Notice that this assertion is somewhat stronger than Equation (13.13), which asserts independence only for specific values of *Toothache* and *Catch*. As with absolute independence in Equation (13.8), the equivalent forms

$$\mathbf{P}(X|Y, Z) = \mathbf{P}(X|Z) \quad \text{and} \quad \mathbf{P}(Y|X, Z) = \mathbf{P}(Y|Z)$$

can also be used.

Section 13.5 showed that absolute independence assertions allow a decomposition of the full joint distribution into much smaller pieces. It turns out that the same is true for conditional independence assertions. For example, given the assertion in Equation (13.14), we can derive a decomposition as follows:

$$\mathbf{P}(\textit{Toothache}, \textit{Catch}, \textit{Cavity})$$
$$= \mathbf{P}(\textit{Toothache}, \textit{Catch}|\textit{Cavity})\mathbf{P}(\textit{Cavity}) \quad \text{(product rule)}$$
$$= \mathbf{P}(\textit{Toothache}|\textit{Cavity})\mathbf{P}(\textit{Catch}|\textit{Cavity})\mathbf{P}(\textit{Cavity}) \quad \text{[using (13.14)]}.$$

In this way, the original large table is decomposed into three smaller tables. The original table has seven independent numbers ($2^3 - 1$, because the numbers must sum to 1). The smaller tables contain five independent numbers ($2 \times (2^1 - 1)$ for each conditional probability distribution and $2^1 - 1$ for the prior on *Cavity*). This might not seem to be a major triumph, but the point is that, for n symptoms that are all conditionally independent given *Cavity*, the size of the representation grows as $O(n)$ instead of $O(2^n)$. Thus, *conditional independence assertions can allow probabilistic systems to scale up; moreover, they are much more commonly available than absolute independence assertions.* Conceptually, *Cavity* **separates** *Toothache* and *Catch* because it is a direct cause of both of them. The decomposition of large probabilistic domains into weakly connected subsets via conditional independence is one of the most important developments in the recent history of AI.

SEPARATION

The dentistry example illustrates a commonly occurring pattern in which a single cause directly influences a number of effects, all of which are conditionally independent, given the cause. The full joint distribution can be written as

$$\mathbf{P}(\textit{Cause}, \textit{Effect}_1, \ldots, \textit{Effect}_n) = \mathbf{P}(\textit{Cause}) \prod_i \mathbf{P}(\textit{Effect}_i|\textit{Cause}) .$$

NAIVE BAYES

Such a probability distribution is called a **naive Bayes** model—"naive" because it is often used (as a simplifying assumption) in cases where the "effect" variables are *not* conditionally independent given the cause variable. (The naive Bayes model is sometimes called a **Bayesian classifier**, a somewhat careless usage that has prompted true Bayesians to call it the **idiot Bayes** model.) In practice, naive Bayes systems can work surprisingly well, even when the independence assumption is not true. Chapter 20 describes methods for learning naive Bayes distributions from observations.

IDIOT BAYES

Computation and Reasoning

13.7   THE WUMPUS WORLD REVISITED

We can combine many of the ideas in this chapter to solve probabilistic reasoning problems in the wumpus world. (See Chapter 7 for a complete description of the wumpus world.) Uncertainty arises in the wumpus world because the agent's sensors give only partial, local information about the world. For example, Figure 13.6 shows a situation in which each of the three reachable squares—[1,3], [2,2], and [3,1]—might contain a pit. Pure logical inference can conclude nothing about which square is most likely to be safe, so a logical agent might be forced to choose randomly. We will see that a probabilistic agent can do much better than the logical agent.

Our aim will be to calculate the probability that each of the three squares contains a pit. (For the purposes of this example, we will ignore the wumpus and the gold.) The relevant properties of the wumpus world are that (1) a pit causes breezes in all neighboring squares, and (2) each square other than [1,1] contains a pit with probability 0.2. The first step is to identify the set of random variables we need:

- As in the propositional logic case, we want one Boolean variable P_{ij} for each square, which is true iff square $[i, j]$ actually contains a pit.
- We also have Boolean variables B_{ij} that are true iff square $[i, j]$ is breezy; we include these variables only for the observed squares—in this case, [1,1], [1,2], and [2,1].

The next step is to specify the full joint distribution, $\mathbf{P}(P_{1,1}, \ldots, P_{4,4}, B_{1,1}, B_{1,2}, B_{2,1})$. Applying the product rule, we have

$$\mathbf{P}(P_{1,1}, \ldots, P_{4,4}, B_{1,1}, B_{1,2}, B_{2,1}) =$$
$$\mathbf{P}(B_{1,1}, B_{1,2}, B_{2,1} \mid P_{1,1}, \ldots, P_{4,4})\mathbf{P}(P_{1,1}, \ldots, P_{4,4}) .$$

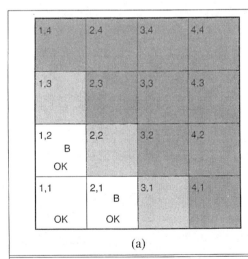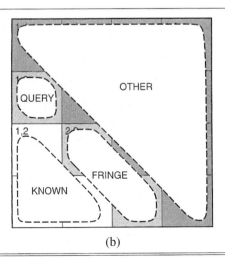

(a)   (b)

Figure 13.6   (a) After finding a breeze in both [1,2] and [2,1], the agent is stuck—there is no safe place to explore. (b) Division of the squares into *Known*, *Fringe*, and *Other*, for a query about [1,3].

Computation and Reasoning

This decomposition makes it very easy to see what the joint probability values should be. The first term is the conditional probability of a breeze configuration, given a pit configuration; this is 1 if the breezes are adjacent to the pits and 0 otherwise. The second term is the prior probability of a pit configuration. Each square contains a pit with probability 0.2, independently of the other squares; hence,

$$\mathbf{P}(P_{1,1},\ldots,P_{4,4}) = \prod_{i,j=1,1}^{4,4} \mathbf{P}(P_{i,j}) \,. \tag{13.15}$$

For a configuration with n pits, this is just $0.2^n \times 0.8^{16-n}$.

In the situation in Figure 13.6(a), the evidence consists of the observed breeze (or its absence) in each square that is visited, combined with the fact that each such square contains no pit. We'll abbreviate these facts as $b = \neg b_{1,1} \wedge b_{1,2} \wedge b_{2,1}$ and $known = \neg p_{1,1} \wedge \neg p_{1,2} \wedge \neg p_{2,1}$. We are interested in answering queries such as $\mathbf{P}(P_{1,3}|known, b)$: how likely is it that [1,3] contains a pit, given the observations so far?

To answer this query, we can follow the standard approach suggested by Equation (13.6) and implemented in the ENUMERATE-JOINT-ASK, namely, summing over entries from the full joint distribution. Let *Unknown* be a composite variable consisting of the $P_{i,j}$ variables for squares other than the *Known* squares and the query square [1,3]. Then, by Equation (13.6), we have

$$\mathbf{P}(P_{1,3}|known, b) = \alpha \sum_{unknown} \mathbf{P}(P_{1,3}, unknown, known, b) \,.$$

The full joint probabilities have already been specified, so we are done—that is, unless we care about computation. There are 12 unknown squares; hence the summation contains $2^{12} = 4096$ terms. In general, the summation grows exponentially with the number of squares.

Intuition suggests that we are missing something here. Surely, one might ask, aren't the other squares irrelevant? The contents of [4,4] don't affect whether [1,3] has a pit! Indeed, this intuition is correct. Let *Fringe* be the variables (other than the query variable) that are adjacent to visited squares, in this case just [2,2] and [3,1]. Also, let *Other* be the variables for the other unknown squares; in this case, there are 10 other squares, as shown in Figure 13.6(b). The key insight is that the observed breezes are *conditionally independent* of the other variables, given the known, fringe, and query variables. The rest is, as they say, a small matter of algebra.

To use the insight, we manipulate the query formula into a form in which the breezes are conditioned on all the other variables, and then we simplify using conditional independence:

$\mathbf{P}(P_{1,3}|known, b)$

$= \alpha \displaystyle\sum_{unknown} \mathbf{P}(b|P_{1,3}, known, unknown)\mathbf{P}(P_{1,3}, known, unknown)$

$\qquad\qquad$ (by the product rule)

$= \alpha \displaystyle\sum_{fringe}\sum_{other} \mathbf{P}(b|known, P_{1,3}, fringe, other)\mathbf{P}(P_{1,3}, known, fringe, other)$

$= \alpha \displaystyle\sum_{fringe}\sum_{other} \mathbf{P}(b|known, P_{1,3}, fringe)\mathbf{P}(P_{1,3}, known, fringe, other) \,,$

Computation and Reasoning

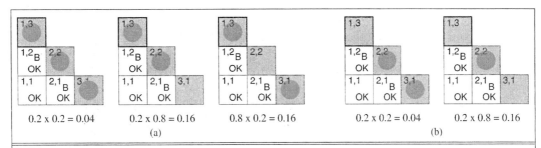

Figure 13.7   Consistent models for the fringe variables $P_{2,2}$ and $P_{3,1}$, showing $P(fringe)$ for each model: (a) three models with $P_{1,3} = true$ showing two or three pits, and (b) two models with $P_{1,3} = false$ showing one or two pits.

where the final step uses conditional independence. Now, the first term in this expression does not depend on the other variables, so we can move the summation inwards:

$$\mathbf{P}(P_{1,3}|known, b)$$
$$= \alpha \sum_{fringe} \mathbf{P}(b|known, P_{1,3}, fringe) \sum_{other} \mathbf{P}(P_{1,3}, known, fringe, other) \ .$$

By independence, as in Equation (13.15), the prior term can be factored, and then the terms can be reordered:

$$\mathbf{P}(P_{1,3}|known, b)$$
$$= \alpha \sum_{fringe} \mathbf{P}(b|known, P_{1,3}, fringe) \sum_{other} \mathbf{P}(P_{1,3})P(known)P(fringe)P(other)$$
$$= \alpha \, P(known)\mathbf{P}(P_{1,3}) \sum_{fringe} \mathbf{P}(b|known, P_{1,3}, fringe)P(fringe) \sum_{other} P(other)$$
$$= \alpha' \, \mathbf{P}(P_{1,3}) \sum_{fringe} \mathbf{P}(b|known, P_{1,3}, fringe)P(fringe) \ ,$$

where the last step folds $P(known)$ into the normalizing constant and uses the fact that $\sum_{other} P(other)$ equals 1.

Now, there are just four terms in the summation over the fringe variables $P_{2,2}$ and $P_{3,1}$. The use of independence and conditional independence has completely eliminated the other squares from consideration. Notice that the expression $\mathbf{P}(b|known, P_{1,3}, fringe)$ is 1 when the fringe is consistent with the breeze observations and 0 otherwise. Thus, for each value of $P_{1,3}$, we sum over the *logical models* for the fringe variables that are consistent with the known facts. (Compare with the enumeration over models in Figure 7.5.) The models and their associated prior probabilities—$P(fringe)$—are shown in Figure 13.7. We have

$$\mathbf{P}(P_{1,3}|known, b) = \alpha' \, \langle 0.2(0.04 + 0.16 + 0.16), \ 0.8(0.04 + 0.16) \rangle \approx \langle 0.31, 0.69 \rangle \ .$$

That is, [1,3] (and [3,1] by symmetry) contains a pit with roughly 31% probability. A similar calculation, which the reader might wish to perform, shows that [2,2] contains a pit with roughly 86% probability. The wumpus agent should definitely avoid [2,2]!

What this section has shown is that even seemingly complicated problems can be formulated precisely in probability theory and solved using simple algorithms. To get *efficient* solutions, independence and conditional independence relationships can be used to simplify the summations required. These relationships often correspond to our natural understanding of how the problem should be decomposed. In the next chapter, we will develop formal representations for such relationships as well as algorithms that operate on those representations to perform probabilistic inference efficiently.

13.8   SUMMARY

This chapter has argued that probability is the right way to reason about uncertainty.

- Uncertainty arises because of both laziness and ignorance. It is inescapable in complex, dynamic, or inaccessible worlds.

- Uncertainty means that many of the simplifications that are possible with deductive inference are no longer valid.

- Probabilities express the agent's inability to reach a definite decision regarding the truth of a sentence. Probabilities summarize the agent's beliefs.

- Basic probability statements include **prior probabilities** and **conditional probabilities** over simple and complex propositions.

- The **full joint probability distribution** specifies the probability of each complete assignment of values to random variables. It is usually too large to create or use in its explicit form.

- The axioms of probability constrain the possible assignments of probabilities to propositions. An agent that violates the axioms will behave irrationally in some circumstances.

- When the full joint distribution is available, it can be used to answer queries simply by adding up entries for the atomic events corresponding to the query propositions.

- **Absolute independence** between subsets of random variables might allow the full joint distribution to be factored into smaller joint distributions. This could greatly reduce complexity, but seldom occurs in practice.

- **Bayes' rule** allows unknown probabilities to be computed from known conditional probabilities, usually in the causal direction. Applying Bayes' rule with many pieces of evidence will in general run into the same scaling problems as does the full joint distribution.

- **Conditional independence** brought about by direct causal relationships in the domain might allow the full joint distribution to be factored into smaller, conditional distributions. The **naive Bayes** model assumes the conditional independence of all effect variables, given a single cause variable, and grows linearly with the number of effects.

- A wumpus-world agent can calculate probabilities for unobserved aspects of the world and use them to make better decisions than a purely logical agent makes.

Computation and Reasoning

BIBLIOGRAPHICAL AND HISTORICAL NOTES

Although games of chance date back at least to around 300 B.C., the mathematical analysis of odds and probability appears to be much more recent. Some work done by Mahaviracarya in India is dated to roughly the ninth century A.D. In Europe, the first attempts date only to the Italian Renaissance, beginning around 1500 A.D. The first significant systematic analyses were produced by Girolamo Cardano around 1565, but they remained unpublished until 1663. By that time, the discovery by Blaise Pascal (in correspondence with Pierre Fermat in 1654) of a systematic way of calculating probabilities had for the first time established probability as a mathematical discipline. The first published textbook on probability was *De Ratiociniis in Ludo Aleae* (Huygens, 1657). Pascal also introduced conditional probability, which is covered in Huygens's textbook. The Rev. Thomas Bayes (1702–1761) introduced the rule for reasoning about conditional probabilities that was named after him. It was published posthumously (Bayes, 1763). Kolmogorov (1950, first published in German in 1933) presented probability theory in a rigorously axiomatic framework for the first time. Rényi (1970) later gave an axiomatic presentation that took conditional probability, rather than absolute probability, as primitive.

Pascal used probability in ways that required both the objective interpretation, as a property of the world based on symmetry or relative frequency, and the subjective interpretation, based on degree of belief—the former in his analyses of probabilities in games of chance, the latter in the famous "Pascal's wager" argument about the possible existence of God. However, Pascal did not clearly realize the distinction between these two interpretations. The distinction was first drawn clearly by James Bernoulli (1654–1705).

Leibniz introduced the "classical" notion of probability as a proportion of enumerated, equally probable cases, which was also used by Bernoulli, although it was brought to prominence by Laplace (1749–1827). This notion is ambiguous between the frequency interpretation and the subjective interpretation. The cases can be thought to be equally probable either because of a natural, physical symmetry between them, or simply because we do not have any knowledge that would lead us to consider one more probable than another. The use of this latter, subjective consideration to justify assigning equal probabilities is known as the *principle of indifference* (Keynes, 1921).

The debate between objectivists and subjectivists became sharper in the 20th century. Kolmogorov (1963), R. A. Fisher (1922), and Richard von Mises (1928) were advocates of the relative frequency interpretation. Karl Popper's (1959, first published in German in 1934) "propensity" interpretation traces relative frequencies to an underlying physical symmetry. Frank Ramsey (1931), Bruno de Finetti (1937), R. T. Cox (1946), Leonard Savage (1954), and Richard Jeffrey (1983) interpreted probabilities as the degrees of belief of specific individuals. Their analyses of degree of belief were closely tied to utilities and to behavior—specifically, to the willingness to place bets. Rudolf Carnap, following Leibniz and Laplace, offered a different kind of subjective interpretation of probability—not as any actual individual's degree of belief, but as the degree of belief that an idealized individual *should* have in a particular proposition a, given a particular body of evidence e. Carnap attempted to go further

Computation and Reasoning

CONFIRMATION than Leibniz or Laplace by making this notion of degree of **confirmation** mathematically precise, as a logical relation between a and **e**. The study of this relation was intended to INDUCTIVE LOGIC constitute a mathematical discipline called **inductive logic**, analogous to ordinary deductive logic (Carnap, 1948, 1950). Carnap was not able to extend his inductive logic much beyond the propositional case, and Putnam (1963) showed that some fundamental difficulties would prevent a strict extension to languages capable of expressing arithmetic.

The question of reference classes is closely tied to the attempt to find an inductive logic. The approach of choosing the "most specific" reference class of sufficient size was formally proposed by Reichenbach (1949). Various attempts have been made, notably by Henry Kyburg (1977, 1983), to formulate more sophisticated policies in order to avoid some obvious fallacies that arise with Reichenbach's rule, but such approaches remain somewhat *ad hoc*. More recent work by Bacchus, Grove, Halpern, and Koller (1992) extends Carnap's methods to first-order theories, thereby avoiding many of the difficulties associated with the straightfoward reference-class method..

Bayesian probabilistic reasoning has been used in AI since the 1960s, especially in medical diagnosis. It was used not only to make a diagnosis from available evidence, but also to select further questions and tests using the theory of information value (Section 16.6) when available evidence was inconclusive (Gorry, 1968; Gorry *et al.*, 1973). One system outperformed human experts in the diagnosis of acute abdominal illnesses (de Dombal *et al.*, 1974). These early Bayesian systems suffered from a number of problems, however. Because they lacked any theoretical model of the conditions they were diagnosing, they were vulnerable to unrepresentative data occurring in situations for which only a small sample was available (de Dombal *et al.*, 1981). Even more fundamentally, because they lacked a concise formalism (such as the one to be described in Chapter 14) for representing and using conditional independence information, they depended on the acquisition, storage, and processing of enormous tables of probabilistic data. Because of these difficulties, probabilistic methods for coping with uncertainty fell out of favor in AI from the 1970s to the mid-1980s. Developments since the late 1980s are described in the next chapter.

The naive Bayes representation for joint distributions has been studied extensively in the pattern recognition literature since the 1950s (Duda and Hart, 1973). It has also been used, often unwittingly, in text retrieval, beginning with the work of Maron (1961). The probabilistic foundations of this technique, described further in Exercise 13.18, were elucidated by Robertson and Sparck Jones (1976). Domingos and Pazzani (1997) provide an explanation for the surprising success of naive Bayesian reasoning even in domains where the independence assumptions are clearly violated.

There are many good introductory textbooks on probability theory, including those by Chung (1979) and Ross (1988). Morris DeGroot (1989) offers a combined introduction to probability and statistics from a Bayesian standpoint, as well as a more advanced text (1970). Richard Hamming's (1991) textbook gives a mathematically sophisticated introduction to probability theory from the standpoint of a propensity interpretation based on physical symmetry. Hacking (1975) and Hald (1990) cover the early history of the concept of probability. Bernstein (1996) gives an entertaining popular account of the story of risk.

Computation and Reasoning

150

EXERCISES

13.1   Show from first principles that $P(a|b \land a) = 1$.

13.2   Using the axioms of probability, prove that any probability distribution on a discrete random variable must sum to 1.

13.3   Would it be rational for an agent to hold the three beliefs $P(A) = 0.4$, $P(B) = 0.3$, and $P(A \lor B) = 0.5$? If so, what range of probabilities would be rational for the agent to hold for $A \land B$? Make up a table like the one in Figure 13.2, and show how it supports your argument about rationality. Then draw another version of the table where $P(A \lor B) = 0.7$. Explain why it is rational to have this probability, even though the table shows one case that is a loss and three that just break even. (*Hint:* what is Agent 1 committed to about the probability of each of the four cases, especially the case that is a loss?)

13.4   This question deals with the properties of atomic events, as discussed on page 468.

    a. Prove that the disjunction of all possible atomic events is logically equivalent to *true*. [*Hint:* Use a proof by induction on the number of random variables.]

    b. Prove that any proposition is logically equivalent to the disjunction of the atomic events that entail its truth.

13.5   Consider the domain of dealing 5-card poker hands from a standard deck of 52 cards, under the assumption that the dealer is fair.

    a. How many atomic events are there in the joint probability distribution (i.e., how many 5-card hands are there)?

    b. What is the probability of each atomic event?

    c. What is the probability of being dealt a royal straight flush? Four of a kind?

13.6   Given the full joint distribution shown in Figure 13.3, calculate the following:

    a. $P(toothache)$

    b. $\mathbf{P}(Cavity)$

    c. $\mathbf{P}(Toothache|cavity)$

    d. $\mathbf{P}(Cavity|toothache \lor catch)$.

13.7   Show that the three forms of independence in Equation (13.8) are equivalent.

13.8   After your yearly checkup, the doctor has bad news and good news. The bad news is that you tested positive for a serious disease and that the test is 99% accurate (i.e., the probability of testing positive when you do have the disease is 0.99, as is the probability of testing negative when you don't have the disease). The good news is that this is a rare disease, striking only 1 in 10,000 people of your age. Why is it good news that the disease is rare? What are the chances that you actually have the disease?

Computation and Reasoning

151

13.9   It is quite often useful to consider the effect of some specific propositions in the context of some general background evidence that remains fixed, rather than in the complete absence of information. The following questions ask you to prove more general versions of the product rule and Bayes' rule, with respect to some background evidence **e**:

a. Prove the conditionalized version of the general product rule:

$$\mathbf{P}(X, Y|\mathbf{e}) = \mathbf{P}(X|Y, \mathbf{e})\mathbf{P}(Y|\mathbf{e}) \ .$$

b. Prove the conditionalized version of Bayes' rule in Equation (13.10).

13.10   Show that the statement

$$\mathbf{P}(A, B|C) = \mathbf{P}(A|C)\mathbf{P}(B|C)$$

is equivalent to either of the statements

$$\mathbf{P}(A|B, C) - \mathbf{P}(A|C) \quad \text{and} \quad \mathbf{P}(B|A, C) = \mathbf{P}(B|C) \ .$$

13.11   Suppose you are given a bag containing n unbiased coins. You are told that $n - 1$ of these coins are normal, with heads on one side and tails on the other, whereas one coin is a fake, with heads on both sides.

a. Suppose you reach into the bag, pick out a coin uniformly at random, flip it, and get a head. What is the (conditional) probability that the coin you chose is the fake coin?

b. Suppose you continue flipping the coin for a total of k times after picking it and see k heads. Now what is the conditional probability that you picked the fake coin?

c. Suppose you wanted to decide whether the chosen coin was fake by flipping it k times. The decision procedure returns FAKE if all k flips come up heads, otherwise it returns NORMAL. What is the (unconditional) probability that this procedure makes an error?

13.12   In this exercise, you will complete the normalization calculation for the meningitis example. First, make up a suitable value for $P(S|\neg M)$, and use it to calculate unnormalized values for $P(M|S)$ and $P(\neg M|S)$ (i.e., ignoring the $P(S)$ term in the Bayes' rule expression). Now normalize these values so that they add to 1.

13.13   This exercise investigates the way in which conditional independence relationships affect the amount of information needed for probabilistic calculations.

a. Suppose we wish to calculate $P(h|e_1, e_2)$ and we have no conditional independence information. Which of the following sets of numbers are sufficient for the calculation?

   (i) $\mathbf{P}(E_1, E_2), \mathbf{P}(H), \mathbf{P}(E_1|H), \mathbf{P}(E_2|H)$
   (ii) $\mathbf{P}(E_1, E_2), \mathbf{P}(H), \mathbf{P}(E_1, E_2|H)$
   (iii) $\mathbf{P}(H), \mathbf{P}(E_1|H), \mathbf{P}(E_2|H)$

b. Suppose we know that $\mathbf{P}(E_1|H, E_2) = \mathbf{P}(E_1|H)$ for all values of H, E_1, E_2. Now which of the three sets are sufficient?

13.14   Let X, Y, Z be Boolean random variables. Label the eight entries in the joint distribution $\mathbf{P}(X, Y, Z)$ as a through h. Express the statement that X and Y are conditionally

Computation and Reasoning

independent given Z as a set of equations relating a through h. How many *nonredundant* equations are there?

13.15   (Adapted from Pearl (1988).) Suppose you are a witness to a nighttime hit-and-run accident involving a taxi in Athens. All taxis in Athens are blue or green. You swear, under oath, that the taxi was blue. Extensive testing shows that, under the dim lighting conditions, discrimination between blue and green is 75% reliable. Is it possible to calculate the most likely color for the taxi? (*Hint:* distinguish carefully between the proposition that the taxi *is* blue and the proposition that it *appears* blue.)

What about now, given that 9 out of 10 Athenian taxis are green?

13.16   (Adapted from Pearl (1988).) Three prisoners, A, B, and C, are locked in their cells. It is common knowledge that one of them will be executed the next day and the others pardoned. Only the governor knows which one will be executed. Prisoner A asks the guard a favor: "Please ask the governor who will be executed, and then take a message to one of my friends B or C to let him know that he will be pardoned in the morning." The guard agrees, and comes back later and tells A that he gave the pardon message to B.

What are A's chances of being executed, given this information? (Answer this *mathematically*, not by energetic waving of hands.)

13.17   Write out a general algorithm for answering queries of the form $\mathbf{P}(Cause|\mathbf{e})$, using a naive Bayes distribution. You should assume that the evidence $\mathbf{e}$ may assign values to *any subset* of the effect variables.

13.18   Text categorization is the task of assigning a given document to one of a fixed set of categories, on the basis of the text it contains. Naive Bayes models are often used for this task. In these models, the query variable is the document category, and the "effect" variables are the presence or absence of each word in the language; the assumption is that words occur independently in documents, with frequencies determined by the document category.

   a. Explain precisely how such a model can be constructed, given as "training data" a set of documents that have been assigned to categories.

   b. Explain precisely how to categorize a new document.

   c. Is the independence assumption reasonable? Discuss.

13.19   In our analysis of the wumpus world, we used the fact that each square contains a pit with probability 0.2, independently of the contents of the other squares. Suppose instead that exactly $N/5$ pits are scattered uniformly at random among the N squares other than [1,1]. Are the variables $P_{i,j}$ and $P_{k,l}$ still independent? What is the joint distribution $\mathbf{P}(P_{1,1}, \ldots, P_{4,4})$ now? Redo the calculation for the probabilities of pits in [1,3] and [2,2].

Computation and Reasoning

153

Computation and Reasoning

154

Topic 2

Algorithms

The following chapters are from
Introduction to the Design &
Analysis of Algorithms
by Anany Levitin

Computation and Reasoning

156

1

Introduction

Two ideas lie gleaming on the jeweler's velvet. The first is the calculus, the second, the algorithm. The calculus and the rich body of mathematical analysis to which it gave rise made modern science possible; but it has been the algorithm that has made possible the modern world.

—David Berlinski, *The Advent of the Algorithm*, 2000

Why do you need to study algorithms? If you are going to be a computer professional, there are both practical and theoretical reasons to study algorithms. From a practical standpoint, you have to know a standard set of important algorithms from different areas of computing; in addition, you should be able to design new algorithms and analyze their efficiency. From the theoretical standpoint, the study of algorithms, sometimes called *algorithmics*, has come to be recognized as the cornerstone of computer science. David Harel, in his delightful book pointedly titled *Algorithmics: the Spirit of Computing,* put it as follows:

> Algorithmics is more than a branch of computer science. It is the core of computer science, and, in all fairness, can be said to be relevant to most of science, business, and technology. [Har92], p. 6.

But even if you are not a student in a computer-related program, there are compelling reasons to study algorithms. To put it bluntly, computer programs would not exist without algorithms. And with computer applications becoming indispensable in almost all aspects of our professional and personal lives, studying algorithms becomes a necessity for more and more people.

Another reason for studying algorithms is their usefulness in developing analytical skills. After all, algorithms can be seen as special kinds of solutions to problems—not answers but rather precisely defined procedures for getting answers. Consequently, specific algorithm design techniques can be interpreted as problem-solving strategies that can be useful regardless of

1

Computation and Reasoning

whether a computer is involved. Of course, the precision inherently imposed by algorithmic thinking limits the kinds of problems that can be solved with an algorithm. You will not find, for example, an algorithm for living a happy life or becoming rich and famous. On the other hand, this required precision has an important educational advantage. Donald Knuth, one of the most prominent computer scientists in the history of algorithmics, put it as follows:

> A person well-trained in computer science knows how to deal with algorithms: how to construct them, manipulate them, understand them, analyze them. This knowledge is preparation for much more than writing good computer programs; it is a general-purpose mental tool that will be a definite aid to the understanding of other subjects, whether they be chemistry, linguistics, or music, etc. The reason for this may be understood in the following way: It has often been said that a person does not really understand something until after teaching it to someone else. Actually, a person does not *really* understand something until after teaching it to a *computer*, i.e., expressing it as an algorithm . . . An attempt to formalize things as algorithms leads to a much deeper understanding than if we simply try to comprehend things in the traditional way. [Knu96], p. 9.

We take up the notion of algorithm in Section 1.1. As examples, we use three algorithms for the same problem: computing the greatest common divisor. There are several reasons for this choice. First, it deals with a problem familiar to everybody from their middle-school days. Second, it makes the important point that the same problem can often be solved by several algorithms. Quite typically, these algorithms differ in their idea, level of sophistication, and efficiency. Third, one of these algorithms deserves to be introduced first, both because of its age—it appeared in Euclid's famous treatise more than two thousand years ago—and its enduring power and importance. Finally, the middle-school procedure for computing the greatest common divisor allows us to highlight a critical requirement every algorithm must satisfy.

Section 1.2 deals with algorithmic problem solving. There we discuss several important issues related to the design and analysis of algorithms. The different aspects of algorithmic problem solving range from analysis of the problem and the means of expressing an algorithm to establishing its correctness and analyzing its efficiency. The section does not contain a magic recipe for designing an algorithm for an arbitrary problem. It is a well-established fact that such a recipe does not exist. Still, the material of Section 1.2 should be useful for organizing your work on designing and analyzing algorithms.

Section 1.3 is devoted to a few problem types that have proven to be particularly important to the study of algorithms and their application. In fact, there are textbooks organized around such problem types. We hold the view—shared by many others—that an organization based on algorithm design techniques is superior. In any case, it is very important to be aware of the principal problem types. Not only are they the most commonly encountered problem types in real-life applications, we use them throughout the book to demonstrate particular algorithm design techniques.

Section 1.4 contains a review of fundamental data structures. It is meant to serve as a reference rather than a deliberate discussion of this topic. If you need a more detailed exposition, there is a wealth of good books on the subject, most of them tailored to a particular programming language.

1.1 Notion of Algorithm

What is an algorithm? Although there is no universally agreed-on wording to describe this notion, there is general agreement about what the concept means:

> An *algorithm* is a sequence of unambiguous instructions for solving a problem, i.e., for obtaining a required output for any legitimate input in a finite amount of time.

This definition can be illustrated by a simple diagram (Figure 1.1).

The reference to "instructions" in the definition implies that there is something or someone capable of understanding and following the instructions given. We call this a "computer," keeping in mind that before the electronic computer

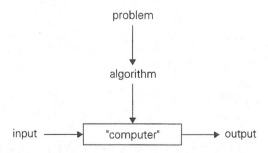

FIGURE 1.1 Notion of algorithm

Computation and Reasoning

was invented, the word "computer" meant a human being involved in performing numeric calculations. Nowadays, of course, "computers" are those ubiquitous electronic devices that have become indispensable in almost everything we do. Note, however, that although the majority of algorithms are indeed intended for eventual computer implementation, the notion of algorithm does not depend on such an assumption.

As examples illustrating the notion of algorithm, we consider in this section three methods for solving the same problem: computing the greatest common divisor of two integers. These examples will help us to illustrate several important points:

- The nonambiguity requirement for each step of an algorithm cannot be compromised.
- The range of inputs for which an algorithm works has to be specified carefully.
- The same algorithm can be represented in several different ways.
- Several algorithms for solving the same problem may exist.
- Algorithms for the same problem can be based on very different ideas and can solve the problem with dramatically different speeds.

Recall that the greatest common divisor of two nonnegative, not-both-zero integers m and n, denoted $\gcd(m, n)$, is defined as the largest integer that divides both m and n evenly, i.e., with a remainder of zero. Euclid of Alexandria (third century B.C.) outlined an algorithm for solving this problem in one of the volumes of his *Elements*, most famous for its systematic exposition of geometry. In modern terms, *Euclid's algorithm* is based on applying repeatedly the equality

$$\gcd(m, n) = \gcd(n, m \bmod n)$$

(where $m \bmod n$ is the remainder of the division of m by n) until $m \bmod n$ is equal to 0; since $\gcd(m, 0) = m$ (why?), the last value of m is also the greatest common divisor of the initial m and n.

For example, $\gcd(60, 24)$ can be computed as follows:

$$\gcd(60, 24) = \gcd(24, 12) = \gcd(12, 0) = 12.$$

(If you are not impressed by this algorithm, try finding the greatest common divisor of larger numbers such as those in Problem 4 of Exercises 1.1.)

Here is a more structured description of this algorithm:

Euclid's algorithm for computing $\gcd(m, n)$

Step 1 If $n = 0$, return the value of m as the answer and stop; otherwise, proceed to Step 2.

Step 2 Divide m by n and assign the value of the remainder to r.

Step 3 Assign the value of n to m and the value of r to n. Go to Step 1.

Alternatively, we can express the same algorithm in a pseudocode:

ALGORITHM *Euclid(m, n)*

    //Computes gcd(m, n) by Euclid's algorithm
    //Input: Two nonnegative, not-both-zero integers m and n
    //Output: Greatest common divisor of m and n
    while $n \neq 0$ **do**
        $r \leftarrow m \bmod n$
        $m \leftarrow n$
        $n \leftarrow r$
    return m

How do we know that Euclid's algorithm eventually comes to a stop? This follows from the observation that the second number of the pair gets smaller with each iteration and it cannot become negative. Indeed, the new value of n on the next iteration is $m \bmod n$, which is always smaller than n. Hence, the value of the second number in the pair eventually becomes 0, and the algorithm stops.

Just as with many other problems, there are several algorithms for solving the greatest common divisor problem. Let us look at the other two methods for this problem. The first is simply based on the definition of the greatest common divisor of m and n as the largest integer that divides both numbers evenly. Obviously, such a common divisor cannot be greater than the smaller of these numbers, which we will denote by $t = \min\{m, n\}$. So we can start by checking whether t divides both m and n: if it does, t is the answer; if it does not, we simply decrease t by 1 and try again. (How do we know that the process will eventually stop?) For example, for numbers 60 and 24, the algorithm will try first 24, then 23, and so on until it reaches 12, where it stops.

Consecutive integer checking algorithm for computing gcd(m, n)

    Step 1 Assign the value of $\min\{m, n\}$ to t.
    Step 2 Divide m by t. If the remainder of this division is 0, go to Step 3; otherwise, go to Step 4.
    Step 3 Divide n by t. If the remainder of this division is 0, return the value of t as the answer and stop; otherwise, proceed to Step 4.
    Step 4 Decrease the value of t by 1. Go to Step 2.

Note that unlike Euclid's algorithm, this algorithm, in the form presented, does not work correctly when one of its input numbers is zero. This example illustrates why it is so important to specify the range of an algorithm's inputs explicitly and carefully.

The third procedure for finding the greatest common divisor should be familiar to you from middle school.

Computation and Reasoning

Middle-school procedure for computing $gcd(m, n)$

> **Step 1** Find the prime factors of m.
>
> **Step 2** Find the prime factors of n.
>
> **Step 3** Identify all the common factors in the two prime expansions found in Step 1 and Step 2. (If p is a common factor occurring p_m and p_n times in m and n, respectively, it should be repeated $\min\{p_m, p_n\}$ times.)
>
> **Step 4** Compute the product of the all the common factors and return it as the greatest common divisor of the numbers given.

Thus, for the numbers 60 and 24, we get

$$60 = 2 \cdot 2 \cdot 3 \cdot 5$$
$$24 = 2 \cdot 2 \cdot 2 \cdot 3$$
$$gcd(60, 24) = 2 \cdot 2 \cdot 3 = 12.$$

Nostalgia for the days when we learned this method should not prevent us from noting that the last procedure is much more complex and slower than Euclid's algorithm. (We will discuss methods for finding and comparing running times of algorithms in the next chapter.) In addition to inferior efficiency, the middle-school procedure does not qualify, in the form presented, as a legitimate algorithm. Why? Because the prime factorization steps are not defined unambiguously: they require a list of prime numbers, and we strongly suspect that your middle-school teacher did not explain how to obtain such a list. You undoubtedly agree that this is not a matter of unnecessary nitpicking. Unless this issue is resolved, we cannot, say, write a program implementing this procedure. (Incidentally, Step 3 is also not defined clearly enough. Its ambiguity is much easier to rectify than that of the factorization steps, however. How would you find common elements in two sorted lists?)

So let us introduce a simple algorithm for generating consecutive primes not exceeding any given integer n. It was probably invented in ancient Greece and is known as the *sieve of Eratosthenes* (ca. 200 B.C.). The algorithm starts by initializing a list of prime candidates with consecutive integers from 2 to n. Then, on the first iteration of the algorithm, it eliminates from the list all multiples of 2, i.e., 4, 6, and so on. Then it moves to the next item on the list, which is 3, and eliminates its multiples. (In this straightforward version, there is an overhead because some numbers, such as 6, are eliminated more than once.) No pass for number 4 is needed: since 4 itself and all its multiples are also multiples of 2, they were already eliminated on a previous pass. (By similar reasoning, we need not consider multiples of any eliminated number.) The next remaining number on the list, which is used on the third pass, is 5. The algorithm continues in this fashion until no more numbers can be eliminated from the list. The remaining integers of the list are the primes needed.

Computation and Reasoning

As an example, consider the application of the algorithm for finding the list of primes not exceeding $n = 25$:

2	3	4	5	6	7	8	9	10	11	12	13	14	15	16	17	18	19	20	21	22	23	24	25
2	**3**		5		7		9		11		13		15		17		19		21		23		25
2	3		5		7				11		13				17		19				23		25
2	3		**5**		7				11		13				17		19				23		

For this example, no more passes are needed because they would eliminate numbers already eliminated on previous iterations of the algorithm. The remaining numbers on the list are the consecutive primes less than or equal to 25.

In general, what is the largest number p whose multiples can still remain on the list? Before we answer this question, let us first note that if p is a number whose multiples are being eliminated on the current pass, then the first multiple we should consider is $p \cdot p$ because all its smaller multiples $2p, \ldots, (p-1)p$ have been eliminated on earlier passes through the list. This observation helps to avoid eliminating the same number more than once. Obviously, $p \cdot p$ should not be larger than n and therefore p cannot exceed $\sqrt{n}$ rounded down (denoted $\lfloor \sqrt{n} \rfloor$ using the so-called floor function). We assume in the following pseudocode that there is a function available for computing $\lfloor \sqrt{n} \rfloor$; alternatively, we could check the inequality $p \cdot p \leq n$ as the loop continuation condition there.

ALGORITHM *Sieve(n)*
    //Implements the sieve of Eratosthenes
    //Input: A positive integer $n \geq 2$
    //Output: Array L of all prime numbers less than or equal to n
    for $p \leftarrow 2$ **to** n **do** $A[p] \leftarrow p$
    for $p \leftarrow 2$ **to** $\lfloor \sqrt{n} \rfloor$ **do**   //see note before pseudocode
        if $A[p] \neq 0$ //p hasn't been eliminated on previous passes
            $j \leftarrow p * p$
            while $j \leq n$ **do**
                $A[j] \leftarrow 0$ //mark an element as eliminated
                $j \leftarrow j + p$
    //copy the remaining elements of A to array L of the primes
    $i \leftarrow 0$
    for $p \leftarrow 2$ **to** n **do**
        if $A[p] \neq 0$
            $L[i] \leftarrow A[p]$
            $i \leftarrow i + 1$
    return L

Computation and Reasoning

So now we can incorporate the sieve of Eratosthenes into the middle-school procedure to get a legitimate algorithm for computing the greatest common divisor of two positive integers. Note that special care needs to be exercised if one or both input numbers are equal to 1: because mathematicians do not consider 1 to be a prime number, strictly speaking, the method does not work for such inputs.

Before we leave this section, one more comment is in order. The examples considered in this section notwithstanding, the majority of algorithms in use today—even those that are implemented as computer programs—do not deal with mathematical problems. Look around for algorithms helping us through our daily routines, both professional and personal. May this ubiquity of algorithms in today's world strengthen your resolve to learn more about these fascinating engines of the information age.

Exercises 1.1

1. Do some research on al-Khorezmi (also al-Khawarizmi), the man from whose name the word "algorithm" is derived. In particular, you should learn what the origins of the words "algorithm" and "algebra" have in common.

2. Given that the official purpose of the U.S. patent system is the promotion of the "useful arts," do you think algorithms are patentable in this country? Should they be?

3. **a.** Write down driving directions for going from your school to your home with the precision required by an algorithm.

   b. Write down a recipe for cooking your favorite dish with the precision required by an algorithm.

4. **a.** Find gcd(31415, 14142) by applying Euclid's algorithm.

   b. Estimate how many times faster it will be to find gcd(31415, 14142) by Euclid's algorithm compared with the algorithm based on checking consecutive integers from $\min\{m, n\}$ down to $\gcd(m, n)$.

5. Prove the equality $\gcd(m, n) = \gcd(n, m \bmod n)$ for every pair of positive integers m and n.

6. What does Euclid's algorithm do for a pair of numbers in which the first number is smaller than the second one? What is the largest number of times this can happen during the algorithm's execution on such an input?

7. **a.** What is the smallest number of divisions made by Euclid's algorithm among all inputs $1 \le m, n \le 10$?

   b. What is the largest number of divisions made by Euclid's algorithm among all inputs $1 \le m, n \le 10$?

8. a. Euclid's algorithm, as presented in Euclid's treatise, uses subtractions rather than integer divisions. Write a pseudocode for this version of Euclid's algorithm.

  b. *Euclid's game* (see [Bog96]) starts with two unequal positive numbers on the board. Two players move in turn. On each move, a player has to write on the board a positive number equal to the difference of two numbers already on the board; this number must be new, i.e., different from all the numbers already on the board. The player who cannot move loses the game. Should you choose to move first or second in this game?

9. Design an algorithm for computing $\lfloor \sqrt{n} \rfloor$.

10. The *extended Euclid's algorithm* determines not only the greatest common divisor d of two positive integers m and n but also integers (not necessarily positive) x and y, such that $mx + ny = d$.

  a. Look up a description of the extended Euclid's algorithm (see, e.g., [KnuI], p. 13) and implement it in the language of your choice.

  b. Modify your program for finding integer solutions to the Diophantine equation $ax + by = c$ with any set of integer coefficients a, b, and c. (Of course, for some coefficients, the equation will have no solutions.)

1.2 Fundamentals of Algorithmic Problem Solving

Let us start by reiterating an important point made in the introduction to this chapter:

> We can consider algorithms to be procedural solutions to problems.

These solutions are not answers but rather specific instructions for getting answers. It is this emphasis on precisely defined constructive procedures that makes computer science distinct from other disciplines. In particular, this distinguishes it from theoretical mathematics whose practitioners are typically satisfied with just proving the existence of a solution to a problem and, possibly, investigating the solution's properties.

We now list and briefly discuss a sequence of steps one typically goes through in designing and analyzing an algorithm (Figure 1.2).

Understanding the Problem

From a practical perspective, the first thing you need to do before designing an algorithm is to understand completely the problem given. Read the problem's description carefully and ask questions if you have any doubts about the problem, do a few small examples by hand, think about special cases, and ask questions again if needed.

Computation and Reasoning

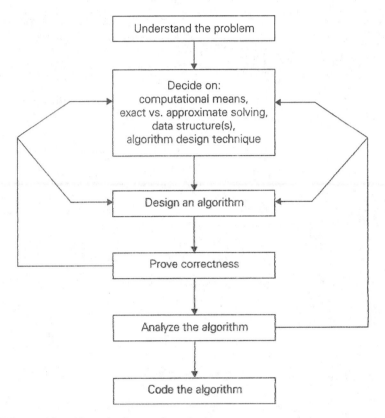

FIGURE 1.2 Algorithm design and analysis process

There are a few types of problems that arise in computing applications quite often. We review them in the next section. If the problem in question is one of them, you might be able to use a known algorithm for solving it. Of course, it helps to understand how such an algorithm works and know its strengths and weaknesses, especially if you have to choose among several available algorithms. But often, you will not find a readily available algorithm and will have to design your own. The sequence of steps outlined in this section should help you in this exciting but not always easy task.

An input to an algorithm specifies an **instance** of the problem the algorithm solves. It is very important to specify exactly the range of instances the algorithm needs to handle. (As an example, recall the variations in the range of instances for the three greatest common divisor algorithms discussed in the previous section.) If you fail to do this, your algorithm may work correctly for a majority of inputs but crash on some "boundary" value. Remember that a correct algorithm is not one that works most of the time but one that works correctly for *all* legitimate inputs.

Do not skimp on this first step of the algorithmic problem-solving process; if you do, you will run the risk of unnecessary rework.

Ascertaining the Capabilities of a Computational Device

Once you completely understand a problem, you need to ascertain the capabilities of the computational device the algorithm is intended for. The vast majority of algorithms in use today are still destined to be programmed for a computer closely resembling the von Neumann machine—a computer architecture outlined by the prominent Hungarian-American mathematician John von Neumann (1903–1957), in collaboration with A. Burks and H. Goldstein, in 1946. The essence of this architecture is captured by the so-called *random-access machine* (*RAM*). Its central assumption is that instructions are executed one after another, one operation at a time. Accordingly, algorithms designed to be executed on such machines are called *sequential algorithms*.

The central assumption of the RAM model does not hold for some newer computers that can execute operations concurrently, i.e., in parallel. Algorithms that take advantage of this capability are called *parallel algorithms*. Still, studying the classic techniques for design and analysis of algorithms under the RAM model remains the cornerstone of algorithmics for the foreseeable future.

Should you worry about the speed and amount of memory of a computer at your disposal? If you are designing an algorithm as a scientific exercise, the answer is a qualified no: as you will see in Section 2.1, most computer scientists prefer to study algorithms in terms independent of specification parameters for a particular computer. If you are designing an algorithm as a practical tool, the answer may depend on a problem you need to solve. Even "slow" computers of today are almost unimaginably fast. Consequently, in many situations, you need not worry about a computer being too slow for the task. There are important problems, however, that are very complex by their nature, have to process huge volumes of data, or deal with applications where time is critical. In such situations, it is imperative to be aware of the speed and memory available on a particular computer system.

Choosing between Exact and Approximate Problem Solving

The next principal decision is to choose between solving the problem exactly or solving it approximately. In the former case, an algorithm is called an *exact algorithm*; in the latter case, an algorithm is called an *approximation algorithm*. Why would one opt for an approximation algorithm? First, there are important problems that simply cannot be solved exactly, such as extracting square roots, solving nonlinear equations, and evaluating definite integrals. Second, available algorithms for solving a problem exactly can be unacceptably slow because of the problem's intrinsic complexity. The most well known of them is the *traveling salesman problem* of finding the shortest tour through n cities; you will see other examples of such difficult problems in Chapters 3, 10, and 11. Third, an approximation algorithm can be a part of a more sophisticated algorithm that solves a problem exactly.

Deciding on Appropriate Data Structures

Some algorithms do not demand any ingenuity in representing their inputs. But others are, in fact, predicated on ingenious data structures. In addition, some of the algorithm design techniques we shall discuss in Chapters 6 and 7 depend intimately on structuring or restructuring data specifying a problem's instance. Many years ago, an influential textbook proclaimed the fundamental importance of both algorithms and data structures for computer programming by its very title: *Algorithms + Data Structures = Programs* [Wir76]. In the new world of object-oriented programming, data structures remain crucially important for both design and analysis of algorithms. We review basic data structures in Section 1.4.

Algorithm Design Techniques

Now, with all the components of the algorithmic problem solving in place, how do you design an algorithm to solve a given problem? This is the main question this book seeks to answer by teaching you several general design techniques.

What is an algorithm design technique?

> An *algorithm design technique* (or "strategy" or "paradigm") is a general approach to solving problems algorithmically that is applicable to a variety of problems from different areas of computing.

Check this book's table of contents and you will see that a majority of its chapters are devoted to individual design techniques. They distill a few key ideas that have proven to be useful in designing algorithms. Learning these techniques is of utmost importance for the following reasons.

First, they provide guidance for designing algorithms for new problems, i.e., problems for which there is no known satisfactory algorithm. Therefore—to use the language of a famous proverb—learning such techniques is akin to learning to fish as opposed to being given a fish caught by somebody else. It is not true, of course, that each of these general techniques will be necessarily applicable to every problem you may encounter. But taken together, they do constitute a powerful collection of tools that you will find quite handy in your studies and work.

Second, algorithms are the cornerstone of computer science. Every science is interested in classifying its principal subject, and computer science is no exception. Algorithm design techniques make it possible to classify algorithms according to an underlying design idea; therefore, they can serve as a natural way to both categorize and study algorithms.

Computation and Reasoning

Methods of Specifying an Algorithm

Once you have designed an algorithm, you need to specify it in some fashion. In Section 1.1, to give you an example, we described Euclid's algorithm in words (in a free and also a step-by-step form) and in pseudocode. These are the two options that are most widely used nowadays for specifying algorithms.

Using a natural language has an obvious appeal; however, the inherent ambiguity of any natural language makes a succinct and clear description of algorithms surprisingly difficult. Nevertheless, being able to do this is an important skill that you should strive to develop in the process of learning algorithms.

A *pseudocode* is a mixture of a natural language and programming language-like constructs. A pseudocode is usually more precise than a natural language, and its usage often yields more succinct algorithm descriptions. Surprisingly, computer scientists have never agreed on a single form of pseudocode, leaving textbook authors to design their own "dialects." Fortunately, these dialects are so close to each other that anyone familiar with a modern programming language should be able to understand them all.

This book's dialect was selected to cause minimal difficulty for a reader. For the sake of simplicity, we omit declarations of variables and use indentation to show the scope of such statements as **for**, **if**, and **while**. As you saw in the previous section, we use an arrow ← for the assignment operation and two slashes // for comments.

In the earlier days of computing, the dominant vehicle for specifying algorithms was a *flowchart*, a method of expressing an algorithm by a collection of connected geometric shapes containing descriptions of the algorithm's steps. This representation technique has proved to be inconvenient for all but very simple algorithms; nowadays, it can be found only in old algorithm books.

The state of the art of computing has not yet reached a point where an algorithm's description—whether in a natural language or a pseudocode—can be fed into an electronic computer directly. Instead, it needs to be converted into a computer program written in a particular computer language. We can look at such a program as yet another way of specifying the algorithm, although it is preferable to consider it as the algorithm's implementation.

Proving an Algorithm's Correctness

Once an algorithm has been specified, you have to prove its *correctness*. That is, you have to prove that the algorithm yields a required result for every legitimate input in a finite amount of time. For example, correctness of Euclid's algorithm for computing the greatest common divisor stems from correctness of the equality $\gcd(m, n) = \gcd(n, m \bmod n)$ (which, in turn, needs a proof; see Problem 5 in Exercises 1.1), the simple observation that the second number gets smaller on every iteration of the algorithm, and the fact that the algorithm stops when the second number becomes 0.

Computation and Reasoning

169

For some algorithms, a proof of correctness is quite easy; for others, it can be quite complex. A common technique for proving correctness is to use mathematical induction because an algorithm's iterations provide a natural sequence of steps needed for such proofs. It might be worth mentioning that although tracing the algorithm's performance for a few specific inputs can be a very worthwhile activity, it cannot prove the algorithm's correctness conclusively. But in order to show that an algorithm is incorrect, you need just one instance of its input for which the algorithm fails. If the algorithm is found to be incorrect, you need to either redesign it under the same decisions regarding the data structures, the design technique, and so on, or, in a more dramatic reversal, to reconsider one or more of those decisions (see Figure 1.2).

The notion of correctness for approximation algorithms is less straightforward than it is for exact algorithms. For an approximation algorithm, we usually would like to be able to show that the error produced by the algorithm does not exceed a predefined limit. You can find examples of such investigations in Chapter 11.

Analyzing an Algorithm

We usually want our algorithms to possess several qualities. After correctness, by far the most important is efficiency. In fact, there are two kinds of algorithm efficiency: time efficiency and space efficiency. *Time efficiency* indicates how fast the algorithm runs; *space efficiency* indicates how much extra memory the algorithm needs. A general framework and specific techniques for analyzing an algorithm's efficiency appear in Chapter 2.

Another desirable characteristic of an algorithm is *simplicity*. Unlike efficiency, which can be precisely defined and investigated with mathematical rigor, simplicity, like beauty, is to a considerable degree in the eye of the beholder. For example, most people would agree that Euclid's algorithm is simpler than the middle-school procedure for computing $gcd(m, n)$, but it is not clear whether Euclid's algorithm is simpler than the consecutive integer checking algorithm. Still, simplicity is an important algorithm characteristic to strive for. Why? Because simpler algorithms are easier to understand and easier to program; consequently, the resulting programs usually contain fewer bugs. There is also the undeniable aesthetic appeal of simplicity. Sometimes simpler algorithms are also more efficient than more complicated alternatives. Unfortunately, it is not always true, in which case a judicious compromise needs to be made.

Yet another desirable characteristic of an algorithm is *generality*. There are, in fact, two issues here: generality of the problem the algorithm solves and the range of inputs it accepts. On the first issue, note that it is sometimes easier to design an algorithm for a problem posed in more general terms. Consider, for example, the problem of determining whether two integers are relatively prime, i.e., whether their only common divisor is equal to 1. It is easier to design an algorithm for a more general problem of computing the greatest common divisor of two integers and, to solve the former problem, check whether the gcd is 1 or not. There are situations, however, where designing a more general algorithm is unnecessary or difficult or even impossible. For example, it is unnecessary to sort a list of n numbers to find its median, which is its $\lceil n/2 \rceil$th smallest element. To give another example, the standard formula for roots of a quadratic equation cannot be generalized to handle polynomials of arbitrary degrees.

As to the range of inputs, your main concern should be designing an algorithm that can handle a range of inputs that is natural for the problem at hand. For example, excluding integers equal to 1 as possible inputs for a greatest common divisor algorithm would be quite unnatural. On the other hand, although the standard formula for the roots of a quadratic equation holds for complex coefficients, we would normally not implement it on this level of generality unless this capability is explicitly required.

If you are not satisfied with the algorithm's efficiency, simplicity, or generality, you must return to the drawing board and redesign the algorithm. In fact, even if your evaluation is positive, it is still worth searching for other algorithmic solutions. Recall the three different algorithms in the previous section for computing the greatest common divisor; generally, you should not expect to get the best algorithm on the first try. At the very least, you should try to fine-tune the algorithm you already have. For example, we made several improvements in our implementation of the sieve of Eratosthenes compared with its initial outline in Section 1.1. (Can you identify them?) You will do well if you keep in mind the following observation of Antoine de Saint-Exupéry, the French writer, pilot, and aircraft designer: "A designer knows he has arrived at perfection not when there is no longer anything to add, but when there is no longer anything to take away."[1]

Coding an Algorithm

Most algorithms are destined to be ultimately implemented as computer programs. Programming an algorithm presents both a peril and an opportunity. The peril lies in the possibility of making the transition from an algorithm to a program either incorrectly or very inefficiently. Some influential computer scientists strongly believe that unless the correctness of a computer program is proven with full mathematical rigor, the program cannot be considered correct. They have developed special techniques for doing such proofs (see [Gri81]), but the power of these techniques of formal verification is limited so far to very small programs. As a practical matter, the validity of programs is still established by testing. Testing of computer programs is an art rather than a science, but that does not mean that there is nothing in it to learn. Do look up books devoted to testing and debugging; even more important, test and debug your program thoroughly whenever you implement an algorithm.

---

[1] I found this call for design simplicity in an essay collection by Jon Bentley [Ben00]; the essays deal with a variety of issues in algorithm design and implementation and are justifiably titled *Programming Pearls*. I wholeheartedly recommend writings of both Jon Bentley and Antoine de Saint-Exupéry.

Computation and Reasoning

Also note that throughout the book, we assume that inputs to algorithms fall within their specified ranges and hence require no verification. When implementing algorithms as programs to be used in actual applications, you should provide such verifications.

Of course, implementing an algorithm correctly is necessary but not sufficient: you would not like to diminish your algorithm's power by an inefficient implementation. Modern compilers do provide a certain safety net in this regard, especially when they are used in their code optimization mode. Still, you need to be aware of such standard tricks as computing a loop's invariant (an expression that does not change its value) outside the loop, collecting common subexpressions, replacing expensive operations by cheap ones, and so on. (See [KP99] and [Ben00] for a good discussion of code tuning and other issues related to algorithm programming.) Typically, such improvements can speed up a program only by a constant factor, whereas a better algorithm can make a difference in running time by orders of magnitude. But once an algorithm is selected, a 10–50% speedup may be worth an effort.

A working program provides an additional opportunity in allowing an empirical analysis of the underlying algorithm. The analysis is based on timing the program on several inputs and then analyzing the results obtained. We discuss the advantages and disadvantages of this approach to analyzing algorithms in Section 2.6.

In conclusion, let us emphasize again the main lesson of the process depicted in Figure 1.2:

As a rule, a good algorithm is a result of repeated effort and rework.

Even if you have been fortunate enough to get an algorithmic idea that seems perfect, you should still try to see whether it can be improved.

Actually, this is good news since it makes the ultimate result so much more enjoyable. (Yes, I did think of naming this book *The Joy of Algorithms*.) On the other hand, how does one know when to stop? In the real world, more often than not a project's schedule and the patience of your boss—whichever happens to be in shorter supply—will stop you. And so it should be: perfection is expensive and in fact not always called for. Designing an algorithm is an engineering-like activity that calls for compromises among competing goals under constraints of available resources, with the designer's time being one of the resources.

In the academic world, the question leads to an interesting but usually difficult investigation of an algorithm's *optimality*. Actually, this question is not about the efficiency of an algorithm but about the complexity of the problem it solves: what is the minimum amount of effort *any* algorithm will need to exert to solve the problem in question? For some problems, the answer to this question is known. For example, any algorithm that sorts an array by comparing values of its elements needs about $n \log_2 n$ comparisons for some arrays of size n (see Section 10.2). But for many seemingly easy problems, such as matrix multiplication, computer scientists do not yet have a final answer.

Computation and Reasoning

Another important issue of algorithmic problem solving is the question of whether or not every problem can be solved by an algorithm. We are not talking here about problems that do not have a solution, such as finding real roots of a quadratic equation with a negative discriminant. For such cases, an output indicating that the problem does not have a solution is all we can and should expect from an algorithm. Nor are we talking about ambiguously stated problems. Even some unambiguous problems that must have a simple yes or no answer are "undecidable," i.e., unsolvable by any algorithm. An example of such a problem appears in Section 10.3. Fortunately, a vast majority of problems in practical computing *can* be solved by an algorithm.

Before leaving this section, let us be sure that you do not have the misconception—possibly caused by the somewhat mechanical nature of the diagram of Figure 1.2—that designing an algorithm is a dull activity. There is nothing further from the truth: inventing (or discovering?) algorithms is a very creative and rewarding process. This book is designed to convince you that this is the case.

Exercises 1.2

1. *(Old World puzzle)* A peasant finds himself on a riverbank with a wolf, a goat, and a head of cabbage. He needs to transport all three to the other side of the river in his boat. However, the boat has room for only the peasant himself and one other item (either the wolf, the goat, or the cabbage). In his absence, the wolf would eat the goat, and the goat would eat the cabbage. Solve this problem for the peasant or prove it has no solution. (Note: The peasant is a vegetarian but does not like cabbage and hence can eat neither the goat nor the cabbage to help him solve the problem. And it goes without saying that the wolf is a protected species.)

2. *(New World puzzle)* There are four people who want to cross a bridge; they all begin on the same side. You have 17 minutes to get them all across to the other side. It is night, and they have one flashlight. A maximum of two people can cross the bridge at one time. Any party that crosses, either one or two people, must have the flashlight with them. The flashlight must be walked back and forth; it cannot be thrown, for example. Each person walks at a different speed: person 1—1 minute to cross the bridge, person 2—2 minutes, person 3—5 minutes, person 4—10 minutes. A pair must walk together at the rate of the slower person's pace. For example, if person 1 and person 4 walk across first, 10 minutes have elapsed when they get to the other side of the bridge. If person 4 returns the flashlight, a total of 20 minutes have passed and you have failed the mission. (Note: According to a rumor on the Internet, interviewers at a well-known software company located near Seattle have given this problem to interviewees.)

Computation and Reasoning

173

3. Which of the following formulas can be considered an algorithm for computing the area of a triangle whose side lengths are given positive numbers a, b, and c?

   a. $S = \sqrt{p(p-a)(p-b)(p-c)}$, where $p = (a+b+c)/2$

   b. $S = \frac{1}{2}bc \sin A$, where A is the angle between sides b and c

   c. $S = \frac{1}{2}ah_a$, where h_a is the height to base a

4. Write a pseudocode for an algorithm for finding real roots of equation $ax^2 + bx + c = 0$ for arbitrary real coefficients a, b, and c. (You may assume the availability of the square root function $sqrt(x)$.)

5. Describe the standard algorithm for finding the binary representation of a positive decimal integer

   a. in English.

   b. in a pseudocode.

6. Describe the algorithm used by your favorite ATM machine in dispensing cash. (You may give your description in either English or a pseudocode, whichever you find more convenient.)

7. a. Can the problem of computing the number π be solved exactly?

   b. How many instances does this problem have?

   c. Look up an algorithm for this problem on the World Wide Web.

8. Give an example of a problem other than computing the greatest common divisor for which you know more than one algorithm. Which of them is simpler? Which is more efficient?

9. Consider the following algorithm for finding the distance between the two closest elements in an array of numbers.

   ALGORITHM *MinDistance*($A[0..n-1]$)
   //Input: Array $A[0..n-1]$ of numbers
   //Output: Smallest distance between two of its elements
   $dmin \leftarrow \infty$
   for $i \leftarrow 0$ **to** $n-1$ **do**
       for $j \leftarrow 0$ **to** $n-1$ **do**
           if $i \neq j$ **and** $|A[i] - A[j]| < dmin$
               $dmin \leftarrow |A[i] - A[j]|$
   return $dmin$

   Make as many improvements as you can in this algorithmic solution to the problem. (If you need to, you may change the algorithm altogether; if not, improve the implementation given.)

Computation and Reasoning

10. One of the most influential books on problem solving, titled *How to Solve It*, [Pol57] was written by the Hungarian-American mathematician George Polya (1887–1985). Polya summarized his ideas in a four-point summary. Find this summary on the Web or better yet in his book, and compare it with the plan outlined in Section 1.2. What do they have in common? How are they different?

1.3 Important Problem Types

In the limitless sea of problems one encounters in computing, there are a few areas that have attracted particular attention from researchers. By and large, interest has been driven either by the problem's practical importance or by some specific characteristics making the problem an interesting research subject; fortunately, these two motivating forces reinforce each other in most cases.

In this section, we take up the most important problem types:

- Sorting
- Searching
- String processing
- Graph problems
- Combinatorial problems
- Geometric problems
- Numerical problems

We use these problems in subsequent chapters of the book to illustrate different algorithm design techniques and methods of algorithm analysis.

Sorting

The *sorting problem* asks us to rearrange the items of a given list in ascending order. Of course, for this problem to be meaningful, the nature of the list's items must allow such an ordering. (Mathematicians would say that there must exist a relation of total ordering.) As a practical matter, we usually need to sort lists of numbers, characters from an alphabet, character strings, and, most important, records similar to those maintained by schools about their students, libraries about their holdings, and companies about their employees. In the case of records, we need to choose a piece of information to guide sorting. For example, we can choose to sort student records in alphabetical order of names or by student number or by student grade point average. Such a specially chosen piece of information is called a *key*. Computer scientists often talk about sorting a list of keys even when the list's items are not records but, say, just integers.

Why would we want a sorted list? Well, sorting makes many questions about the list easier to answer. The most important of them is searching: it is why

Computation and Reasoning

dictionaries, telephone books, class lists, and so on are sorted. You will see other examples of the usefulness of list presorting in Section 6.1. In a similar vein, sorting is used as an auxiliary step in several important algorithms in other areas, e.g., geometric algorithms.

By now, computer scientists have developed dozens of different sorting algorithms. In fact, inventing a new sorting algorithm has been likened to designing the proverbial mousetrap. And we are happy to report that the hunt for a better sorting mousetrap continues. This perseverance is admirable in view of the following facts. On the one hand, there are a few good sorting algorithms that sort an arbitrary array of size n using about $n \log_2 n$ comparisons. On the other hand, no algorithm that sorts by key comparisons (as opposed to, say, comparing small pieces of keys) can do substantially better than that.

There is a reason for this embarrassment of algorithmic riches in the land of sorting. Although some algorithms are indeed better than others, there is no algorithm that would be the best solution in all situations. Some of the algorithms are simple but relatively slow while others are faster but more complex; some work better on randomly ordered inputs while others do better on almost sorted lists; some are suitable only for lists residing in the fast memory while others can be adapted for sorting large files stored on a disk, and so on.

Two properties of sorting algorithms deserve special mention. A sorting algorithm is called *stable* if it preserves the relative order of any two equal elements in its input. In other words, if an input list contains two equal elements in positions i and j where $i < j$, then in the sorted list they have to be in positions i' and j', respectively, such that $i' < j'$. This property can be desirable if, for example, we have a list of students sorted alphabetically and we want to sort it according to student GPA: a stable algorithm will yield a list in which students with the same GPA will still be sorted alphabetically. Generally speaking, algorithms that can exchange keys located far apart are not stable but they usually work faster; you will see how this general comment applies to important sorting algorithms later in the book.

The second notable feature of a sorting algorithm is the amount of extra memory the algorithm requires. An algorithm is said to be *in place* if it does not require extra memory, except, possibly, for a few memory units. There are important sorting algorithms that are in place and those that are not.

Searching

The *searching problem* deals with finding a given value, called a *search key*, in a given set (or a multiset, which permits several elements to have the same value). There are plenty of searching algorithms to choose from. They range from the straightforward sequential search to a spectacularly efficient but limited binary search and algorithms based on representing the underlying set in a different form more conducive to searching. The latter algorithms are of particular importance for real-life applications because they are indispensable for storing and retrieving information from large databases.

For searching, too, there is no single algorithm that fits all situations best. Some algorithms work faster than others but require more memory; some are very fast but applicable only to sorted arrays, and so on. Unlike with sorting algorithms, there is no stability problem, but different issues arise. Specifically, in applications where the underlying data may change frequently relative to the number of searches, searching has to be considered in conjunction with two other operations: addition to and deletion from the data set of an item. In such situations, data structures and algorithms should be chosen to strike a balance among the requirements of each operation. Also, organizing very large data sets for efficient searching (and addition and deletion) poses special challenges with very important implications for practical applications.

String Processing

In recent years, the rapid proliferation of applications dealing with nonnumerical data has intensified interest of researchers and computing practitioners in string-handling algorithms. A *string* is a sequence of characters from an alphabet. Strings of particular interest are text strings, which comprise letters, numbers, and special characters; bit strings, which comprise zeros and ones; and gene sequences, which can be modeled by strings of characters from the four-character alphabet {A, C, G, T}. It should be pointed out, however, that string-processing algorithms have been important for computer science for a long time in conjunction with computer languages and compiling issues.

One particular problem—that of searching for a given word in a text—has attracted special attention from researchers. They call it *string matching*. Several algorithms that exploit the special nature of this type of searching have been invented. We will introduce one very simple algorithm in Chapter 3 and discuss two algorithms based on the remarkable idea of R. Boyer and J. Moore in Chapter 7.

Graph Problems

One of the oldest and most interesting areas in algorithmics is graph algorithms. Informally, a *graph* can be thought of as a collection of points called vertices, some of which are connected by line segments called edges. (A more formal definition is given in the next section.) Graphs are an interesting subject to study for both theoretical and practical reasons. Graphs can be used for modeling a wide variety of real-life applications, including transportation and communication networks, project scheduling, and games. One interesting recent application is an estimation of the Web's diameter, which is the maximum number of links one needs to follow to reach one Web page from another by the most direct route between them.[2]

Basic graph algorithms include graph traversal algorithms (How can one visit all the points in a network?), shortest-path algorithms (What is the best

---

2. This number, according to an estimate by a group of researchers at the University of Notre Dame [AJB99], is just 19.

route between two cities?), and topological sorting for graphs with directed edges (Is a set of courses with their prerequisites consistent or self-contradictory?). Fortunately, these algorithms can be considered illustrations of general design techniques; accordingly, you will find them in corresponding chapters of the book.

Some graph problems are computationally very hard; that is, only very small instances of such problems can be solved in a realistic amount of time even with the fastest computers imaginable. The most widely known graph problems of this type are probably the traveling salesman problem and the graph-coloring problem. The traveling salesman problem, as you recall, is the problem of finding the shortest tour through n cities that visits every city exactly once. The *graph-coloring problem* asks us to assign the smallest number of colors to vertices of a graph so that no two adjacent vertices are the same color. This problem arises in several applications, such as event scheduling: if the events are represented by vertices that are connected by an edge if and only if the corresponding events cannot be scheduled in the same time, a solution to the graph-coloring problem yields an optimal schedule.

Combinatorial Problems

From a more abstract perspective, the traveling salesman problem and the graph-coloring problem are examples of *combinatorial problems*. These are problems that ask (explicitly or implicitly) to find a combinatorial object—such as a permutation, a combination, or a subset—that satisfies certain constraints and has some desired property (e.g., maximizes a value or minimizes a cost).

Generally speaking, combinatorial problems are the most difficult problems in computing from both the theoretical and the practical standpoints. Their difficulty stems from the following facts. First, the number of combinatorial objects typically grows extremely fast with a problem's size, reaching unimaginable magnitudes even for moderate-sized instances. Second, there are no known algorithms for solving most such problems exactly in an acceptable amount of time. Moreover, most computer scientists believe that such algorithms do not exist. This conjecture has been neither proved nor disapproved, and it remains the most important unresolved issue in theoretical computer science. We will discuss this topic in more detail in Section 10.3.

Some combinatorial problems can be solved by efficient algorithms, but they should be considered fortunate exceptions to the rule. The shortest-path problem mentioned earlier is among such exceptions.

Geometric Problems

Geometric algorithms deal with geometric objects such as points, lines, and polygons. Ancient Greeks were very much interested in developing procedures (they did not call them algorithms, of course) for solving a variety of geometric problems, including problems of constructing simple geometric shapes—triangles, circles, and so on—with an unmarked ruler and a compass. Then, for about 2000 years, intense interest in geometric algorithms disappeared, to be resurrected in the age of computers—no more rulers and compasses, just bits, bytes, and good old human ingenuity. Of course, today people are interested in geometric algorithms with quite different applications in mind, such as applications to computer graphics, robotics, and tomography.

We will discuss algorithms for only two classic problems of computational geometry: the closest-pair problem and the convex hull problem. The *closest-pair problem* is self-explanatory: given n points in the plane, find the closest pair among them. The *convex hull problem* asks to find the smallest convex polygon that would include all the points of a given set. If you are interested in other geometric algorithms, you will find a wealth of material in specialized monographs (e.g., [PSh85]) or corresponding chapters of textbooks organized around problem types (e.g., [Sed88]).

Numerical Problems

Numerical problems, another large special area of applications, are problems that involve mathematical objects of continuous nature: solving equations and systems of equations, computing definite integrals, evaluating functions, and so on. The majority of such mathematical problems can be solved only approximately. Another principal difficulty stems from the fact that such problems typically require manipulating real numbers, which can be represented in a computer only approximately. Moreover, a large number of arithmetic operations performed on approximately represented numbers can lead to an accumulation of the round-off error to a point where it can drastically distort an output produced by a seemingly sound algorithm.

Many sophisticated algorithms have been developed over the years in this area, and they continue to play a critical role in many scientific and engineering applications. But in the last 25 years or so, the computing industry has shifted its focus to business applications. These new applications require primarily algorithms for information storage, retrieval, transportation through networks, and presentation to users. As a result of this revolutionary change, numerical analysis has lost its formerly dominating position in both industry and computer science programs. Still, it is important for any computer-literate person to have at least a rudimentary idea about numerical algorithms. We will discuss several classical numerical algorithms in Sections 6.2, 10.4, and 11.4.

Exercises 1.3

1. Consider the algorithm for the sorting problem that sorts an array by counting, for each of its elements, the number of smaller elements and then uses this information to put the element in its appropriate position in the sorted array:

Computation and Reasoning

ALGORITHM *ComparisonCountingSort*($A[0..n-1]$)

//Sorts an array by comparison counting
//Input: Array $A[0..n-1]$ of orderable values
//Output: Array $S[0..n-1]$ of A's elements sorted in nondecreasing order
for $i \leftarrow 0$ **to** $n-1$ **do**
    $Count[i] \leftarrow 0$
for $i \leftarrow 0$ **to** $n-2$ **do**
    for $j \leftarrow i+1$ **to** $n-1$ **do**
        if $A[i] < A[j]$
            $Count[j] \leftarrow Count[j]+1$
        else $Count[i] \leftarrow Count[i]+1$
for $i \leftarrow 0$ **to** $n-1$ **do**
    $S[Count[i]] \leftarrow A[i]$
return S

    a. Apply this algorithm to sorting the list 60, 35, 81, 98, 14, 47.

    b. Is this algorithm stable?

    c. Is it in place?

2. Name the algorithms for the searching problem that you already know. Give a good succinct description of each algorithm in English. (If you know no such algorithms, use this opportunity to design one.)

3. Design a simple algorithm for the string-matching problem.

4. *Königsberg bridge puzzle* The Königsberg bridge puzzle is universally accepted as the problem that gave birth to graph theory. It was solved by the great Swiss-born mathematician Leonhard Euler (1707–1783). The problem asked whether one could, in a single stroll, cross all seven bridges of the city of Königsberg exactly once and return to a starting point. Following is a sketch of the river with its two islands and seven bridges:

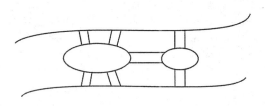

    a. State the problem as a graph problem.

    b. Does this problem have a solution? If you believe it does, draw such a stroll; if you believe it does not, explain why and indicate the smallest number of new bridges that would make such a stroll possible.

Computation and Reasoning

180

5. *Icosian Game* A century after Euler's discovery (see Problem 4), another famous puzzle—this one invented by the renown Irish mathematician Sir William Hamilton (1805–1865)—was presented to the world under the name of the Icosian Game. The game was played on a circular wooden board on which the following graph was carved:

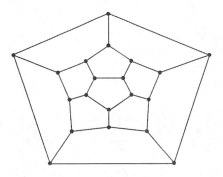

Find a *Hamiltonian circuit*—a path that visits all the graph's vertices exactly once before returning to the starting vertex—for this graph.

6. Consider the following problem: Design an algorithm to determine the best route for a subway passenger to take from one designated station to another in a well-developed subway system similar to those in such cities as Washington, D.C., and London, UK.

   a. The problem's statement is somewhat vague, which is typical of real-life problems. In particular, what reasonable criterion can be used for defining the "best" route?

   b. How would you model this problem by a graph?

7. a. Rephrase the traveling salesman problem in combinatorial object terms.

   b. Rephrase the graph-coloring problem in combinatorial object terms.

8. Consider the following map:

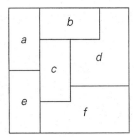

Computation and Reasoning

181

    a. Explain how we can use the graph-coloring problem to color the map so that no two neighboring regions are colored the same.

    b. Use your answer to part (a) to color the map with the smallest number of colors.

  9. Design an algorithm for the following problem: Given a set of n points in the x–y coordinate plane, determine whether all of them lie on the same circumference.

  10. Write a program that reads as its inputs the (x, y) coordinates of endpoints of two line segments P_1Q_1 and P_2Q_2 and determines whether the segments have a common point.

1.4 Fundamental Data Structures

Since the vast majority of algorithms of interest operate on data, particular ways of organizing data play a critical role in the design and analysis of algorithms. A *data structure* can be defined as a particular scheme of organizing related data items. The nature of the data items is dictated by a problem at hand; they can range from elementary data types (e.g., integers or characters) to data structures (e.g., a one-dimensional array of one-dimensional arrays is often used for implementing matrices). There are a few data structures that have proved to be particularly important for computer algorithms. Since you are undoubtedly familiar with most if not all of them, a quick review is provided here.

Linear Data Structures

The two most important elementary data structures are the array and the linked list. A (one-dimensional) *array* is a sequence of n items of the same data type that are stored contiguously in computer memory and made accessible by specifying a value of the array's *index* (Figure 1.3).

In the majority of cases, the index is an integer either between 0 and $n - 1$ (as shown in Figure 1.3) or between 1 and n. Some computer languages allow an array index to range between any two integer bounds *low* and *high*, and some even permit nonnumerical indices to specify, for example, data items corresponding to the 12 months of the year by the month names.

Item [0]	Item [1]	. . .	Item [n–1]

FIGURE 1.3 Array of n elements

Computation and Reasoning

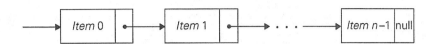

FIGURE 1.4 Singly linked list of n elements

Each and every element of an array can be accessed in the same constant amount of time regardless of where in the array the element in question is located. This feature positively distinguishes arrays from linked lists (see below). It is also assumed that every element of an array occupies the same amount of computer storage.

Arrays are used for implementing a variety of other data structures. Prominent among them is the *string*, a sequence of characters from an alphabet terminated by a special character indicating the string's end. Strings composed of zeros and ones are called *binary strings* or *bit strings*. Strings are indispensable for processing textual data, defining computer languages and compiling programs written in them, and studying abstract computational models. Operations we usually perform on strings differ from those we typically perform on other arrays (say, arrays of numbers). They include computing the string length, comparing two strings to determine which one precedes the other according to the so-called lexicographic order, i.e., in a dictionary, and concatenating two strings (forming one string from two given strings by appending the second to the end of the first).

A *linked list* is a sequence of zero or more elements called *nodes* each containing two kinds of information: some data and one or more links called *pointers* to other nodes of the linked list. (A special pointer called "null" is used to indicate the absence of a node's successor.) In a *singly linked list*, each node except the last one contains a single pointer to the next element (Figure 1.4).

To access a particular node of a linked list, we start with the list's first node and traverse the pointer chain until the particular node is reached. Thus, the time needed to access an element of a singly linked list, unlike that of an array, depends on where in the list the element is located. On the positive side, linked lists do not require any preliminary reservation of the computer memory, and insertions and deletions can be made quite efficiently in a linked list by reconnecting a few appropriate pointers.

We can exploit flexibility of the linked list structure in a variety of ways. For example, it is often convenient to start a linked list with a special node called the *header*. This node often contains information about the linked list such as its current length; it may also contain, in addition to a pointer to the first element, a pointer to the linked list's last element.

Another extension is the structure called the *doubly linked list*, in which every node, except the first and the last, contains pointers to both its successor and its predecessor (Figure 1.5).

The array and linked list are two principal choices in representing another more abstract data structure called a linear list or simply a list. A *list* is a finite

Computation and Reasoning

183

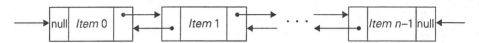

FIGURE 1.5 Doubly linked list of n elements

sequence of data items, i.e., a collection of data items arranged in a certain linear order. The basic operations performed on this data structure are searching for, inserting, and deleting an element.

Two special types of lists, stacks and queues, are particularly important. A *stack* is a list in which insertions and deletions can be done only at the end. This end is called the *top* because a stack is usually visualized not horizontally but vertically (akin to a stack of plates whose "operations" it mimics very closely). As a result, when elements are added to (pushed onto) a stack and deleted from (popped off) it, the structure operates in the "last-in–first-out" (LIFO) fashion, exactly as the stack of plates does if we can remove only the top plate or add another plate to top of the stack. Stacks have a multitude of applications; in particular, they are indispensable for implementing recursive algorithms.

A *queue*, on the other hand, is a list from which elements are deleted from one end of the structure, called the *front* (this operation is called *dequeue*), and new elements are added to the other end, called the *rear* (this operation is called *enqueue*). Consequently, a queue operates in the "first-in–first-out" (FIFO) fashion (akin, say, to a queue of customers served by a single teller in a bank). Queues also have many important applications, including several algorithms for graph problems.

Many important applications require a selection of an item of the highest priority among a dynamically changing set of candidates. A data structure that seeks to satisfy the needs of such applications is called a priority queue. A *priority queue* is a collection of data items from a totally ordered universe (most often, integer or real numbers). The principal operations on a priority queue are finding its largest element, deleting its largest element, and adding a new element. Of course, a priority queue must be implemented so that the last two operations yield a new queue. Straightforward implementations of this data structure can be based on either an array or a sorted array, but neither of these options yields the most efficient solution possible. A better implementation of a priority queue is based on an ingenious data structure called the *heap*. We will discuss heaps (and an important sorting algorithm based on them) in Section 6.4.

Graphs

As mentioned in the previous section, a graph is informally thought of as a collection of points in a plane called "vertices" or "nodes," some of them connected by line segments called "edges" or "arcs." Formally, a *graph* $G = \langle V, E \rangle$ is defined by a pair of two sets: a finite set V of items called *vertices* and a set E of pairs

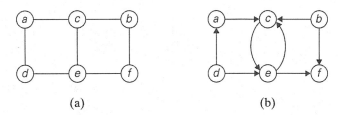

FIGURE 1.6 (a) Undirected graph. (b) Digraph.

of these items called *edges*. If these pairs of vertices are unordered, i.e., a pair of vertices (u, v) is the same as the pair (v, u), we say that the graph G is *undirected*; otherwise, we say that the edge (u, v) is directed from vertex u to vertex v and the graph G itself is called *directed*. Directed graphs are also called *digraphs*.

It is normally convenient to label vertices of a graph or a digraph with letters, integer numbers, or, if an application calls for it, character strings (Figure 1.6). The graph in Figure 1.6a has six vertices and seven edges:

$$V = \{a, b, c, d, e, f\}, \quad E = \{(a, c), \ (a, d), \ (b, c), \ (b, f), \ (c, e), \ (d, e), \ (e, f)\}.$$

The digraph in Figure 1.6b has six vertices and eight directed edges:

$$V = \{a, b, c, d, e, f\}, \quad E = \{(a, c), \ (b, c), \ (b, f), \ (c, e), \ (d, a), \ (d, e), \ (e, c), \ (e, f)\}.$$

Our definition of a graph does not forbid *loops*, or edges connecting vertices to themselves. Unless explicitly stated otherwise, we will consider graphs without loops. Since our definition disallows multiple edges between the same vertices of an undirected graph, we have the following inequality for the number of edges $|E|$ possible in an undirected graph with $|V|$ vertices and no loops:

$$0 \leq |E| \leq |V|(|V| - 1)/2.$$

(We get the largest number of edges in a graph if there is an edge connecting each of its $|V|$ vertices with all $|V| - 1$ other vertices. We have to divide product $|V|(|V| - 1)$ by 2, however, because it includes every edge twice.)

A graph with every pair of its vertices connected by an edge is called *complete*. A standard notation for the complete graph with $|V|$ vertices is $K_{|V|}$. A graph with relatively few possible edges missing is called *dense*; a graph with few edges relative to the number of its vertices is called *sparse*. Whether we are dealing with a dense or sparse graph may influence how we choose to represent the graph and, consequently, the running time of an algorithm being designed or used.

Graph representations Graphs for computer algorithms can be represented in two principal ways: the adjacency matrix and adjacency linked lists. The *adjacency matrix* of a graph with n vertices is an n-by-n boolean matrix with one row and one column for each of the graph's vertices, in which the element in the ith row

Computation and Reasoning

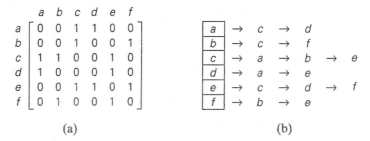

(a)   (b)

FIGURE 1.7 (a) Adjacency matrix and (b) adjacency linked lists of the graph of
Figure 1.6a

and the jth column is equal to 1 if there is an edge from the ith vertex to the jth
vertex and equal to 0 if there is no such edge. For example, the adjacency matrix
for the graph of Figure 1.6a is given in Figure 1.7a. Note that the adjacency matrix
of an undirected graph is always symmetric (why?), i.e., $A[i, j] = A[j, i]$ for every
$0 \le i, j \le n - 1$.

The *adjacency linked lists* of a graph or a digraph is a collection of linked
lists, one for each vertex, that contain all the vertices adjacent to the list's vertex
(i.e., all the vertices connected to it by an edge). Usually, such lists start with a
header identifying a vertex for which the list is compiled. For example, Figure 1.7b
represents the graph of Figure 1.6a via its adjacency linked lists. To put it another
way, adjacency linked lists indicate columns of the adjacency matrix that, for a
given vertex, contain 1's.

If a graph is sparse, the adjacency linked list representation may use less space
than the corresponding adjacency matrix despite the extra storage consumed by
pointers of the linked lists; the situation is exactly opposite for dense graphs. In
general, which of the two representations is more convenient depends on the
nature of the problem, on the algorithm used for solving it, and, possibly, on the
type of input graph (sparse or dense).

Weighted graphs A *weighted graph* (or weighted digraph) is a graph (or digraph)
with numbers assigned to its edges. These numbers are called *weights* or *costs*. An
interest in such graphs is motivated by numerous real-life applications, such as
finding the shortest path between two points in a transportation or communication
network or the traveling salesman problem mentioned earlier.

Both principal representations of a graph can be easily adopted to accommo-
date weighted graphs. If a weighted graph is represented by its adjacency matrix,
then its element $A[i, j]$ will simply contain the weight of the edge from the ith
to the jth vertex if there is such an edge and a special symbol, e.g., ∞, if there is
no such edge. This approach is illustrated in Figure 1.8b. (For some applications,
it is more convenient to put 0's on the main diagonal of the adjacency matrix.)
Adjacency linked lists for a weighted graph will have to include in their nodes not

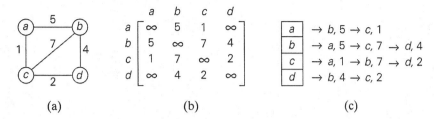

FIGURE 1.8 (a) Weighted graph. (b) Its adjacency matrix. (c) Its adjacency linked lists.

only the name of an adjacent vertex but also the weight of the corresponding edge (Figure 1.8c).

Paths and cycles Among many interesting properties of graphs, two are important for a great number of applications: *connectivity* and *acyclicity*. Both are based on the notion of a path. A *path* from vertex u to vertex v of a graph G can be defined as a sequence of adjacent (connected by an edge) vertices that starts with u and ends with v. If all edges of a path are distinct, the path is said to be *simple*. The *length* of a path is the total number of vertices in a vertex sequence defining the path minus one, which is the same as the number of edges in the path. For example, a, c, b, f is a simple path of length 3 from a to f in the graph of Figure 1.6a, whereas a, c, e, c, b, f is a path (not simple) of length 5 from a to f.

In the case of a directed graph, we are usually interested in directed paths. A *directed path* is a sequence of vertices in which every consecutive pair of the vertices is connected by an edge directed from the vertex listed first to the vertex listed next. For example, a, c, e, f is a directed path from a to f in the graph of Figure 1.6b.

A graph is said to be *connected* if for every pair of its vertices u and v there is a path from u to v. Informally, this property means that if we make a model of a connected graph by connecting some balls representing the graph's vertices with pieces of strings representing its edges, we will be able to hold the entire thing in one hand. If a graph is not connected, such a model will consist of several connected pieces that are called connected components of the graph. Formally, a *connected component* is the maximal (not expandable via an inclusion of an extra vertex adjacent to one of its vertices) subgraph[3] of a given graph. For example, the graphs of Figures 1.6a and 1.8a are connected, while the graph of Figure 1.9 is not because there is no path, for example, from a to f. The graph of Figure 1.9 has two connected components with vertices $\{a, b, c, d, e\}$ and $\{f, g, h, i\}$, respectively.

Graphs with several connected components do happen in real-life applications. A graph representing the Interstate highway system of the United States would be an example (why?).

---

3. A *subgraph* of a given graph $G = \langle V, E \rangle$ is a graph $G' = \langle V', E' \rangle$ such that $V' \subseteq V$ and $E' \subseteq E$.

Computation and Reasoning

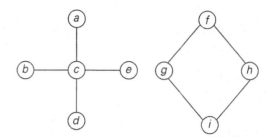

FIGURE 1.9 Graph that is not connected

It is important to know for many applications whether or not a graph under consideration has cycles. A *cycle* is a simple path of a positive length that starts and ends at the same vertex. For example, f, h, i, g, f is a cycle in the graph of Figure 1.9. A graph with no cycles is said to be *acyclic*. We discuss acyclic graphs in the next subsection.

Trees

A *tree* (more accurately, a *free tree*) is a connected acyclic graph (Figure 1.10a). A graph that has no cycles but is not necessarily connected is called a *forest*: each of its connected components is a tree (Figure 1.10b).

Trees have several important properties other graphs do not have. In particular, the number of edges in a tree is always one less than the number of its vertices:

$$|E| = |V| - 1.$$

As the graph of Figure 1.9 demonstrates, this property is necessary but not sufficient for a graph to be a tree. However, for connected graphs it is sufficient and hence provides a convenient way of checking whether a connected graph has a cycle.

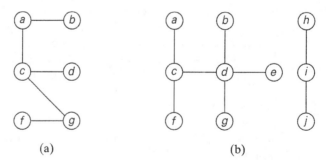

(a)   (b)

FIGURE 1.10 (a) Tree. (b) Forest.

Computation and Reasoning

188

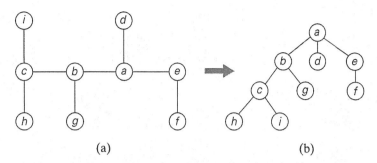

(a)   (b)

FIGURE 1.11 (a) Free tree. (b) Its transformation into a rooted tree.

Rooted trees Another very important property of trees is the fact that for every two vertices in a tree there always exists exactly one simple path from one of these vertices to the other. This property makes it possible to select an arbitrary vertex in a free tree and consider it as the *root* of the so-called *rooted tree.* A rooted tree is usually depicted by placing its root on the top (level 0 of the tree), the vertices adjacent to the root below it (level 1), the vertices two edges apart from the root below that (level 2), etc. Figure 1.11 presents such a transformation from a free tree to a rooted tree.

Rooted trees play a very important role in computer science, a much more important one than free trees do; in fact, for the sake of brevity, they are often referred to as simply "trees." Immediate applications of trees are for describing hierarchies, from file directories to organizational charts of enterprises. There are many less obvious applications, such as implementing dictionaries (see below), efficient storage of very large data sets (Section 7.4), and data encoding (Section 9.4). As we shall see in Chapter 2, trees also are helpful in analysis of recursive algorithms. To finish this far-from-complete list of tree applications, we should mention the so-called *state-space trees* that underline two important algorithm design techniques: backtracking and branch-and-bound (Sections 11.1 and 11.2).

For any vertex v in a tree T, all the vertices on the simple path from the root to that vertex are called *ancestors* of v. The vertex itself is usually considered its own ancestor; the set of ancestors that excludes the vertex itself is referred to as *proper ancestors*. If (u, v) is the last edge of the simple path from the root to vertex v (and $u \neq v$), u is said to be the *parent* of v and v is called a *child* of u; vertices that have the same parent are said to be *siblings*. A vertex with no children is called a *leaf*; a vertex with at least one child is called *parental*. All the vertices for which a vertex v is an ancestor are said to be *descendants* of v. A vertex v with all its descendants is called the *subtree* of T rooted at that vertex. Thus, for the tree of Figure 1.11b, the root of the tree is a; vertices d, g, f, h, and i are leaves while vertices a, b, e, and c are parental; the parent of b is a; the children of b are c and g; the siblings of b are d and e; the vertices of the subtree rooted at b are $\{b, c, g, h, i\}$.

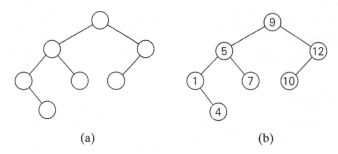

(a)   (b)

FIGURE 1.12 (a) Binary tree. (b) Binary search tree.

The **depth** of a vertex v is the length of the simple path from the root to v. The **height** of a tree is the length of the longest simple path from the root to a leaf. For example, the depth of vertex c of the tree of Figure 1.11b is 2, and the height of the tree is 3. Thus, if we count tree levels top down starting with 0 for the root's level, the depth of a vertex is simply its level in the tree, and the tree's height is the maximum level of its vertices. (You should be alert to the fact that some authors define the height of a tree as the number of levels in it; this makes the height of a tree larger by 1 than the height defined as the length of the longest simple path from the root to a leaf.)

Ordered trees An **ordered tree** is a rooted tree in which all the children of each vertex are ordered. It is convenient to assume that in a tree's diagram, all the children are ordered left to right. A **binary tree** can be defined as an ordered tree in which every vertex has no more than two children and each child is designated as either a **left child** or a **right child** of its parent. The subtree with its root at the left (right) child of a vertex is called the **left (right) subtree** of that vertex. An example of a binary tree is given in Figure 1.12a.

In Figure 1.12b, some numbers are assigned to vertices of the binary tree of Figure 1.12a. Note that a number assigned to each parental vertex is larger than all the numbers in its left subtree and smaller than all the numbers in its right subtree. Such trees are called **binary search trees**. Binary trees and binary search trees have a wide variety of applications in computer science; you will encounter some of them throughout the book. In particular, binary search trees can be generalized to more general kinds of search trees called **multiway search trees**, which are indispensable for efficient storage of very large files on disks.

As you will see later in the book, the efficiency of most important algorithms for binary search trees and their extensions depends on the tree's height. Therefore, the following inequalities for the height h of a binary tree with n nodes are especially important for analysis of such algorithms:

$$\lfloor \log_2 n \rfloor \le h \le n - 1.$$

Computation and Reasoning

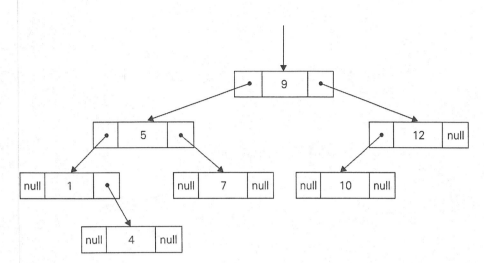

FIGURE 1.13 Standard implementation of the binary search tree of Figure 1.12b.

A binary tree is usually implemented for computing purposes by a collection of nodes corresponding to vertices of the tree. Each node contains some information associated with the vertex (its name or some value assigned to it) and two pointers to the left child and right child of the node, respectively. Figure 1.13 illustrates such an implementation for the binary search tree of Figure 1.12b.

A computer representation of an arbitrary ordered tree can be done by simply providing a parental vertex with the number of pointers equal to the number of its children. This representation may prove to be inconvenient if the number of children varies widely among the nodes. We can avoid this inconvenience by using nodes with just two pointers, as we did for binary trees. Here, however, the left pointer will point to the first child of the vertex while the right pointer will point to its next sibling. Accordingly, this representation is called the *first child–next sibling representation*. Thus, all the siblings of a vertex are linked (via the nodes' right pointers) in a singly linked list, with the first element of the list pointed to by the left pointer of their parent. Figure 1.14a illustrates this representation for the tree of Figure 1.11b. It is not difficult to see that this representation effectively transforms an ordered tree into a binary tree said to be associated with the ordered tree. We get this representation by "rotating" the pointers about 45 degrees clockwise (see Figure 1.14b).

Sets and Dictionaries

The notation of a set plays a central role in mathematics. A *set* can be described as an unordered collection (possibly empty) of distinct items called elements of the set. A specific set is defined either by an explicit listing of its elements (e.g.,

Computation and Reasoning

191

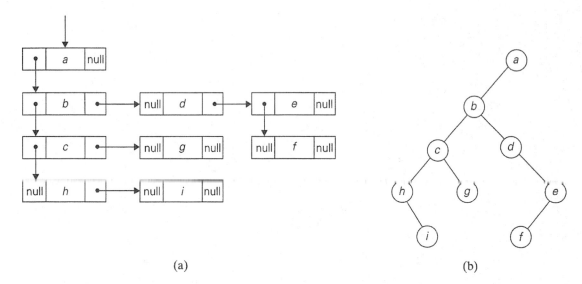

(a)   (b)

FIGURE 1.14 (a) First child–next sibling representation of the graph of Figure
1.11b. (b) Its binary tree representation.

$S = \{2, 3, 5, 7\}$) or by specifying a property that all the set's elements and only they
must satisfy (e.g., $S = \{n: n$ is a prime number and $n < 10\}$). The most important set
operations are checking membership of a given item in a given set (whether a given
item is among the elements of the set), finding the union of two sets (which set
comprises all the elements that belong to either of the two sets or to both of them),
and finding the intersection of two sets (which set comprises all the elements that
belong to both sets).

Sets can be implemented in computer applications in two ways. The first
considers only sets that are subsets of some large set U called the ***universal set***.
If set U has n elements, then any subset S of U can be represented by a bit
string of size n, called a ***bit vector***, in which the ith element is 1 if and only if
the ith element of U is included in set S. Thus, to continue with our example,
if $U = \{1, 2, 3, 4, 5, 6, 7, 8, 9\}$, then $S = \{2, 3, 5, 7\}$ will be represented by the bit
string 011010100. This way of representing sets makes it possible to implement
the standard set operations very fast but at the expense of using a large amount
of storage.[4]

The second and much more frequently used way to represent a set for computing purposes is to use the list structure to indicate the set's elements. Of course,
this option is feasible only for finite sets; fortunately, unlike mathematics, this is

---

4.   It is the first example of a space-for-time tradeoff in this book. We will have much more to say about
     them in Chapter 7.

the kind of sets most computer applications need. Note, however, the two principal points of distinction between sets and lists. First, a set cannot contain identical elements; a list can. This requirement for uniqueness is sometimes circumvented by the introduction of a *multiset* or a *bag*, an unordered collection of items that are not necessarily distinct. Second, a set is an unordered collection of items; therefore, changing the order of its elements does not change the set. A list, defined as an ordered collection of items, is exactly the opposite. This is an important theoretical distinction, but fortunately it is not important for many applications. It is also worth mentioning that if a set is represented by a list, depending on the application at hand, it might be worth maintaining the list in a sorted order.

In computing, the operations we need to perform for a set or a multiset most often are searching for a given item, adding a new item, and deleting an item from the collection. A data structure that implements these three operations is called the *dictionary*. Note the relationship between this data structure and the problem of searching mentioned in Section 1.3; obviously, we are dealing here with searching in a dynamic context. Consequently, an efficient implementation of a dictionary has to strike a compromise between the efficiency of searching and the efficiencies of the other two operations. There are quite a few ways a dictionary can be implemented. They range from an unsophisticated use of arrays (sorted or not) to much more sophisticated techniques such as hashing and balanced search trees, which we will discuss later in the book.

A number of applications in computing require a dynamic partition of some *n*-element set into a collection of disjoints subsets. After being initialized as a collection of *n* one-element subsets, the collection is subjected to a sequence of intermixed union and search operations. This problem is called the *set union problem*. We will discuss efficient algorithmic solutions to this problem in Section 9.2 in conjunction with one of its most important applications.

You may have noticed that in our review of basic data structures we almost always mentioned specific operations that are typically performed for the structure in question. This intimate relationship between data and operations has been recognized by computer scientists for a long time. It has led them in particular to the idea of an *abstract data type* (ADT): a set of abstract objects representing data items with a collection of operations that can be performed on them. As illustrations of this notion, reread, say, our definitions of priority queue and dictionary. Although abstract data types could be implemented in older procedural languages such as Pascal (see, e.g., [AHU83]), it is much more convenient to do so in object-oriented languages, such as C++ and Java, that support abstract data types by means of *classes*.

Exercises 1.4

1. Describe how one can implement each of the following operations on an array so that the time it takes does not depend on the array's size *n*.

Computation and Reasoning

a. Delete the ith element of an array ($1 \leq i \leq n$).

b. Delete the ith element of a sorted array (the remaining array has to stay sorted, of course).

2. If you have to solve the searching problem for a list of n numbers, how can you take advantage of the fact that the list is known to be sorted? Give separate answers for

a. lists represented as arrays.

b. lists represented as linked lists.

3. **a.** Show the stack after each operation of the following sequence that starts with the empty stack:

$$push(a),\ push(b),\ pop,\ push(c),\ push(d),\ pop$$

b. Show the queue after each operation of the following sequence that starts with the empty queue:

$$enqueue(a),\ enqueue(b),\ dequeue,\ enqueue(c),\ enqueue(d),\ dequeue$$

4. **a.** Let A be the adjacency matrix of an undirected graph. Explain what property of the matrix indicates that

   i. the graph is complete.

   ii. the graph has a loop, i.e., an edge connecting a vertex to itself.

   iii. the graph has an isolated vertex, i.e., a vertex with no edges incident with it.

b. Answer the same questions for the adjacency linked list representation.

5. Give a detailed description of an algorithm for transforming a free tree into a tree rooted at a given vertex of the free tree.

6. Prove the inequalities that bracket the height of a binary tree with n vertices:

$$\lfloor \log_2 n \rfloor \leq h \leq n - 1.$$

7. Indicate how the ADT priority queue can be implemented as

a. an (unsorted) array.

b. a sorted array.

c. a binary search tree.

8. How would you implement a dictionary of a reasonably small size n if you knew that all its elements are distinct (e.g., names of 50 states of the United States)? Specify an implementation of each dictionary operation.

9. For each of the following applications, indicate the most appropriate data structure.

a. Answering telephone calls in the order of their known priorities

b. Sending backlog orders to customers in the order they have been received

c. Implementing a calculator for computing simple arithmetical expressions

Computation and Reasoning

194

10. Design an algorithm for checking whether two given words are anagrams, i.e., whether one word can be obtained by permuting the letters of the other. (For example, the words *tea* and *eat* are anagrams.)

SUMMARY

■ An *algorithm* is a sequence of nonambiguous instructions for solving a problem in a finite amount of time. An input to an algorithm specifies an *instance* of the problem the algorithm solves.

■ Algorithms can be specified in a natural language or a pseudocode; they can also be implemented as computer programs.

■ Among several ways to classify algorithms, the two principal alternatives are:
— to group algorithms according to types of problems they solve;
— to group algorithms according to underlying design techniques they are based upon.

■ The important problem types are sorting, searching, string processing, graph problems, combinatorial problems, geometric problems, and numerical problems.

■ Algorithm *design techniques* (or "strategies" or "paradigms") are general approaches to solving problems algorithmically, applicable to a variety of problems from different areas of computing.

■ Although designing an algorithm is undoubtedly a creative activity, one can identify a sequence of interrelated actions involved in such a process. They are summarized in Figure 1.2.

■ A good algorithm is usually a result of repeated efforts and rework.

■ The same problem can often be solved by several algorithms. For example, three algorithms were given for computing the greatest common divisor of two integers: *Euclid's algorithm*, the consecutive integer checking algorithm, and the middle-school algorithm (enhanced by the *sieve of Eratosthenes* for generating a list of primes).

■ Algorithms operate on data. This makes the issue of data structuring critical for efficient algorithmic problem solving. The most important elementary data structures are the *array* and the *linked list*. They are used for representing more abstract data structures such as the *list*, the *stack*, the *queue*, the *graph* (via its *adjacency matrix* or *adjacency linked lists*), the *binary tree,* and the *set*.

■ An abstract collection of objects with several operations that can be performed on them is called an *abstract data type* (ADT). The *list*, the *stack*, the *queue*, the *priority queue,* and the *dictionary* are important examples of abstract data types. Modern object-oriented languages support implementation of ADTs by means of classes.

Computation and Reasoning

195

2

Fundamentals of the Analysis of Algorithm Efficiency

I often say that when you can measure what you are speaking about and express it in numbers you know something about it; but when you cannot express it in numbers your knowledge is a meagre and unsatisfactory kind: it may be the beginning of knowledge but you have scarcely, in your thoughts, advanced to the stage of science, whatever the matter may be.

—Lord Kelvin (1824–1907)

Not everything that can be counted counts, and not everything that counts can be counted.

—Albert Einstein (1879–1955)

This chapter is devoted to analysis of algorithms. The *American Heritage Dictionary* defines "analysis" as "the separation of an intellectual or substantial whole into its constituent parts for individual study." Accordingly, each of the principal dimensions of an algorithm pointed out in Section 1.2 is both a legitimate and desirable subject of study. But the term "analysis of algorithms" is usually used in a narrower technical sense to mean an investigation of an algorithm's efficiency with respect to two resources: running time and memory space. This emphasis on efficiency is easy to explain. First, unlike such dimensions as simplicity and generality, efficiency can be studied in precise quantitative terms. Second, one can argue—although this is hardly always the case, given the speed and memory of today's computers—that the efficiency considerations are of primary importance from the practical point of view. In this chapter, we too limit the discussion to an algorithm's efficiency.

We start with a general framework for analyzing algorithm efficiency in Section 2.1. This section is arguably the most important in the chapter;

Computation and Reasoning

197

the fundamental nature of the topic makes it also one of the most important sections in the entire book.

In Section 2.2, we introduce three notations: O ("big oh"), Ω ("big omega"), and Θ ("big theta"). Borrowed from mathematics, these notations have become *the* language for discussing an algorithm's efficiency.

In Section 2.3, we show how the general framework outlined in Section 2.1 can be systematically applied to analyzing the efficiency of nonrecursive algorithms. The main tool of such an analysis is setting up a sum representing the algorithm's running time and then simplifying the sum by using standard sum manipulation techniques.

In Section 2.4, we show how the general framework outlined in Section 2.1 can be systematically applied to analyzing the efficiency of recursive algorithms. Here, the main tool is not a sum but a special kind of equation called a recurrence relation. We explain how such recurrence relations can be set up and then introduce a method for solving them.

Although we illustrate the analysis framework and the methods of its applications by a variety of examples in the first four sections of this chapter, Section 2.5 is devoted to yet another example—that of the Fibonacci numbers. Introduced 800 years ago, this remarkable sequence appears in a variety of applications both within and outside computer science. A discussion of the Fibonacci sequence serves as a natural vehicle for introducing an important class of recurrence relations not solvable by the method of Section 2.4. We also discuss several algorithms for computing the Fibonacci numbers, mostly for the sake of a few general observations about the efficiency of algorithms and methods of analyzing them.

The methods of Sections 2.3 and 2.4 provide a powerful technique for analyzing the efficiency of many algorithms with mathematical clarity and precision, but these methods are far from being foolproof. The last two sections of the chapter deal with two approaches—empirical analysis and algorithm visualization—that complement the pure mathematical techniques of Sections 2.3 and 2.4. Much newer and, hence, less developed than their mathematical counterparts, these approaches promise to play an important role among the tools available for analysis of algorithm efficiency.

2.1 Analysis Framework

In this section, we outline a general framework for analyzing the efficiency of algorithms. To begin with, there are two kinds of efficiency: time efficiency and space efficiency. *Time efficiency* indicates how fast an algorithm in question runs; *space efficiency* deals with the extra space the algorithm requires. In the early days of electronic computing, both resources—time and space—were at a premium. Half a century of relentless technological innovations have improved the computer's speed and memory size by many orders of magnitude. Now the amount of extra space required by an algorithm is typically not of as much concern, with the caveat that there is still, of course, a difference between the fast main memory, the slower secondary memory, and the cache. The time issue has not diminished quite to the same extent, however. In addition, the research experience has shown that for most problems we can achieve much more spectacular progress in speed than in space. Therefore, following a well-established tradition of algorithm textbooks, we primarily concentrate on time efficiency, but the analytical framework introduced here is applicable to analyzing space efficiency as well.

Measuring an Input's Size

Let us start with the obvious observation that almost all algorithms run longer on larger inputs. For example, it takes longer to sort larger arrays, multiply larger matrices, and so on. Therefore, it is logical to investigate an algorithm's efficiency as a function of some parameter n indicating the algorithm's input size.[1] In most cases, selecting such a parameter is quite straightforward. For example, it will be the size of the list for problems of sorting, searching, finding the list's smallest element, and most other problems dealing with lists. For the problem of evaluating a polynomial $p(x) = a_n x^n + \cdots + a_0$ of degree n, it will be the polynomial's degree or the number of its coefficients, which is larger by one than its degree. We shall see from the discussion that such a minor difference will be inconsequential for the efficiency analysis.

There are situations, of course, where the choice of a parameter indicating an input size does matter. One such example is computing the product of two n-by-n matrices. There are two natural measures of size for this problem. The first and more frequently used is the matrix order n. But the other natural contender is the total number of elements N in the matrices being multiplied. (The latter is also more general since it is applicable to matrices that are not necessarily square.) Since there is a simple formula relating these two measures, we can easily switch from one to the other, but the answer about an algorithm's efficiency will be qualitatively different depending on which of the two measures we use (see Problem 2 in Exercises 2.1).

The choice of an appropriate size metric can be influenced by operations of the algorithm in question. For example, how should we measure an input's size for a spell-checking algorithm? If the algorithm examines individual characters of its input, then we should measure the size by the number of characters; if it works by processing words, we should count their number in the input.

---

[1] Some algorithms require more than one parameter to indicate the size of their inputs (e.g., the number of vertices and the number of edges for algorithms on graphs represented by adjacency linked lists).

Computation and Reasoning

We should make a special note about measuring size of inputs for algorithms involving properties of numbers (e.g., checking whether a given integer n is prime). For such algorithms, computer scientists prefer measuring size by the number b of bits in the n's binary representation:

$$b = \lfloor \log_2 n \rfloor + 1. \tag{2.1}$$

This metric usually gives a better idea about efficiency of algorithms in question.

Units for Measuring Running Time

The next issue concerns units for measuring an algorithm's running time. Of course, we can simply use some standard unit of time measurement—a second, a millisecond, and so on—to measure the running time of a program implementing the algorithm. There are obvious drawbacks to such an approach, however: dependence on the speed of a particular computer, dependence on the quality of a program implementing the algorithm and of the compiler used in generating the machine code, and the difficulty of clocking the actual running time of the program. Since we are after a measure of an *algorithm*'s efficiency, we would like to have a metric that does not depend on these extraneous factors.

One possible approach is to count the number of times each of the algorithm's operations is executed. This approach is both excessively difficult and, as we shall see, usually unnecessary. The thing to do is to identify the most important operation of the algorithm, called the **basic operation**, the operation contributing the most to the total running time, and compute the number of times the basic operation is executed.

As a rule, it is not difficult to identify the basic operation of an algorithm: it is usually the most time-consuming operation in the algorithm's innermost loop. For example, most sorting algorithms work by comparing elements (keys) of a list being sorted with each other; for such algorithms, the basic operation is a key comparison. As another example, algorithms for matrix multiplication and polynomial evaluation require two arithmetic operations: multiplication and addition. On most computers, multiplication of two numbers takes longer than addition, making the former an unquestionable choice for the basic operation.[2]

Thus, the established framework for the analysis of an algorithm's time efficiency suggests measuring it by counting the number of times the algorithm's basic operation is executed on inputs of size n. We will find out how to compute such a count for nonrecursive and recursive algorithms in Sections 2.3 and 2.4, respectively.

Here is an important application. Let c_{op} be the time of execution of an algorithm's basic operation on a particular computer and let $C(n)$ be the number of

---

2. On some computers based on the so-called RISC architecture, it is not necessarily the case (see, for example, the timing data provided by Kernighan and Pike [KP99], pp. 185–186).

times this operation needs to be executed for this algorithm. Then we can estimate the running time $T(n)$ of a program implementing this algorithm on that computer by the formula

$$T(n) \approx c_{op}C(n).$$

Of course, this formula should be used with caution. The count $C(n)$ does not contain any information about operations that are not basic, and, in fact, the count itself is often computed only approximately. Further, the constant c_{op} is also an approximation whose reliability is not easy to assess. Still, unless n is extremely large or very small, the formula can give a reasonable estimate of the algorithm's running time. It also makes it possible to answer such questions as "How much faster would this algorithm run on a machine that is ten times faster that the one we have?" The answer is, obviously, ten times. Or, assuming that $C(n) = \frac{1}{2}n(n-1)$, how much longer will the algorithm run if we double its input size? The answer is about four times longer. Indeed, for all but very small values of n,

$$C(n) = \frac{1}{2}n(n-1) = \frac{1}{2}n^2 - \frac{1}{2}n \approx \frac{1}{2}n^2$$

and therefore

$$\frac{T(2n)}{T(n)} \approx \frac{c_{op}C(2n)}{c_{op}C(n)} \approx \frac{\frac{1}{2}(2n)^2}{\frac{1}{2}n^2} = 4.$$

Note that we were able to answer the last question without actually knowing the value of c_{op}: the value was neatly cancelled out in the ratio. Also note that $\frac{1}{2}$, the multiplicative constant in the formula for the count $C(n)$, was also cancelled out. It is for these reasons that the efficiency analysis framework ignores multiplicative constants and concentrates on the count's *order of growth* to within a constant multiple for large-size inputs.

Orders of Growth

Why this emphasis on the count's order of growth for large input sizes? A difference in running times on small inputs is not what really distinguishes efficient algorithms from inefficient ones. When we have to compute, for example, the greatest common divisor of two small numbers, it is not immediately clear how much more efficient Euclid's algorithm is compared to the other two algorithms discussed in Section 1.1 or even why we should care which of them is faster and by how much. It is only when we have to find the greatest common divisor of two large numbers that the difference in algorithm efficiencies becomes both clear and important. For large values of n, it is the function's order of growth that counts: just look at Table 2.1, which contains values of a few functions particularly important for analysis of algorithms.

Computation and Reasoning

TABLE 2.1 Values (some approximate) of several functions important for analysis of algorithms

n	$\log_2 n$	n	$n \log_2 n$	n^2	n^3	2^n	$n!$
10	3.3	10^1	$3.3 \cdot 10^1$	10^2	10^3	10^3	$3.6 \cdot 10^6$
10^2	6.6	10^2	$6.6 \cdot 10^2$	10^4	10^6	$1.3 \cdot 10^{30}$	$9.3 \cdot 10^{157}$
10^3	10	10^3	$1.0 \cdot 10^4$	10^6	10^9		
10^4	13	10^4	$1.3 \cdot 10^5$	10^8	10^{12}		
10^5	17	10^5	$1.7 \cdot 10^6$	10^{10}	10^{15}		
10^6	20	10^6	$2.0 \cdot 10^7$	10^{12}	10^{18}		

The magnitude of the numbers in Table 2.1 has a profound significance for the analysis of algorithms. The function growing the slowest among these is the logarithmic function. It grows so slowly, in fact, that we should expect a program implementing an algorithm with a logarithmic basic-operation count to run practically instantaneously on inputs of all realistic sizes. Also note that although specific values of such a count depend, of course, on the logarithm's base, the formula

$$\log_a n = \log_a b \, \log_b n$$

makes it possible to switch from one base to another, leaving the count logarithmic but with a new multiplicative constant. This is why we omit a logarithm's base and write simply $\log n$ in situations where we are interested just in a function's order of growth to within a multiplicative constant.

On the other end of the spectrum are the exponential function 2^n and the factorial function $n!$ Both these functions grow so fast that their values become astronomically large even for rather small values of n. (This is the reason why we did not include their values for $n > 10^2$ in Table 2.1.) For example, it would take about $4 \cdot 10^{10}$ years for a computer making one trillion (10^{12}) operations per second to execute 2^{100} operations. Though this is incomparably faster than it would have taken to execute 100! operations, it is still longer than 4.5 billion ($4.5 \cdot 10^9$) years—the estimated age of the planet Earth. Though there is a tremendous difference between the orders of growth of the functions 2^n and $n!$, both are often referred to as "exponential-growth functions" (or simply "exponential") despite the fact that, strictly speaking, only the former should be referred to as such. The bottom line, which is important to remember, is this:

> Algorithms that require an exponential number of operations are practical for solving only problems of very small sizes.

Another way to appreciate the qualitative difference among the orders of growth of the functions in Table 2.1 is to consider how they react to, say, a twofold increase in the value of their argument n. The function $\log_2 n$ increases in value by just 1 (because $\log_2 2n = \log_2 2 + \log_2 n = 1 + \log_2 n$); the linear function increases twofold; the "n-log-n" function $n \log_2 n$ increases slightly more than twofold; the quadratic function n^2 and cubic function n^3 increase fourfold and eightfold, respectively (because $(2n)^2 = 4n^2$ and $(2n)^3 = 8n^3$); the value of 2^n is squared (because $2^{2n} = (2^n)^2$); and $n!$ increases much more than that (yes, even mathematics refuses to cooperate to give a neat answer for $n!$).

Worst-Case, Best-Case, and Average-Case Efficiencies

In the beginning of this section, we established that it is reasonable to measure an algorithm's efficiency as a function of a parameter indicating the size of the algorithm's input. But there are many algorithms for which running time depends not only on an input size but also on the specifics of a particular input. Consider, as an example, sequential search. This is a straightforward algorithm that searches for a given item (some search key K) in a list of n elements by checking successive elements of the list until either a match with the search key is found or the list is exhausted. Here is the algorithm's pseudocode, in which, for simplicity, a list is implemented as an array. (It also assumes that the second condition $A[i] \neq K$ will not be checked if the first one, which checks that the array's index does not exceed its upper bound, fails.)

ALGORITHM *SequentialSearch*($A[0..n-1], K$)

    //Searches for a given value in a given array by sequential search
    //Input: An array $A[0..n-1]$ and a search key K
    //Output: Returns the index of the first element of A that matches K
    //   or -1 if there are no matching elements
    $i \leftarrow 0$
    while $i < n$ **and** $A[i] \neq K$ **do**
        $i \leftarrow i + 1$
    if $i < n$ **return** i
    else return -1

Clearly, the running time of this algorithm can be quite different for the same list size n. In the worst case, when there are no matching elements or the first matching element happens to be the last one on the list, the algorithm makes the largest number of key comparisons among all possible inputs of size n: $C_{worst}(n) = n$.

The *worst-case efficiency* of an algorithm is its efficiency for the worst-case input of size n, which is an input (or inputs) of size n for which the algorithm runs the longest among all possible inputs of that size. The way to determine

Computation and Reasoning

the worst-case efficiency of an algorithm is, in principle, quite straightforward: we analyze the algorithm to see what kind of inputs yield the largest value of the basic operation's count $C(n)$ among all possible inputs of size n and then compute this worst-case value $C_{worst}(n)$. (For sequential search, the answer was obvious. The methods for handling less trivial situations are explained in subsequent sections of this chapter.) Clearly, the worst-case analysis provides very important information about an algorithm's efficiency by bounding its running time from above. In other words, it guarantees that for any instance of size n, the running time will not exceed $C_{worst}(n)$, its running time on the worst-case inputs.

The *best-case efficiency* of an algorithm is its efficiency for the best-case input of size n, which is an input (or inputs) of size n for which the algorithm runs the fastest among all possible inputs of that size. Accordingly, we can analyze the best-case efficiency as follows. First, we determine the kind of inputs for which the count $C(n)$ will be the smallest among all possible inputs of size n. (Note that the best case does not mean the smallest input; it means the input of size n for which the algorithm runs the fastest.) Then we should ascertain the value of $C(n)$ on these most convenient inputs. For example, for sequential search, best-case inputs will be lists of size n with their first elements equal to a search key; accordingly, $C_{best}(n) = 1$.

The analysis of the best-case efficiency is not nearly as important as that of the worst-case efficiency. But it is not completely useless, either. Though we should not expect to get best-case inputs, we might be able to take advantage of the fact that for some algorithms a good best-case performance extends to some useful types of inputs close to being the best-case ones. For example, there is a sorting algorithm (insertion sort) for which the best-case inputs are already sorted arrays on which the algorithm works very fast. Moreover, this good best-case efficiency deteriorates only slightly for almost sorted arrays. Thus, such an algorithm might well be the method of choice for applications dealing with almost sorted arrays. And, of course, if the best-case efficiency of an algorithm is unsatisfactory, we can immediately discard it without further analysis.

It should be clear from our discussion, however, that neither the worst-case analysis nor its best-case counterpart yields the necessary information about an algorithm's behavior on a "typical" or "random" input. This is the information that the *average-case efficiency* seeks to provide. To analyze the algorithm's average-case efficiency, we must make some assumptions about possible inputs of size n.

Let us consider again sequential search. The standard assumptions are that (a) the probability of a successful search is equal to p ($0 \le p \le 1$) and (b) the probability of the first match occurring in the ith position of the list is the same for every i. Under these assumptions—the validity of which is usually difficult to verify, their reasonableness notwithstanding—we can find the average number of key comparisons $C_{avg}(n)$ as follows. In the case of a successful search, the probability of the first match occurring in the ith position of the list is p/n for every i, and the number of comparisons made by the algorithm in such a situation is obviously i. In the case of an unsuccessful search, the number of comparisons is n with the probability of such a search being $(1 - p)$. Therefore,

$$C_{avg}(n) = [1 \cdot \frac{p}{n} + 2 \cdot \frac{p}{n} + \cdots + i \cdot \frac{p}{n} + \cdots + n \cdot \frac{p}{n}] + n \cdot (1 - p)$$

$$= \frac{p}{n}[1 + 2 + \cdots + i + \cdots + n] + n(1 - p)$$

$$= \frac{p}{n}\frac{n(n + 1)}{2} + n(1 - p) = \frac{p(n + 1)}{2} + n(1 - p).$$

This general formula yields some quite reasonable answers. For example, if $p = 1$ (i.e., the search must be successful), the average number of key comparisons made by sequential search is $(n + 1)/2$; i.e., the algorithm will inspect, on average, about half of the list's elements. If $p = 0$ (i.e., the search must be unsuccessful), the average number of key comparisons will be n because the algorithm will inspect all n elements on all such inputs.

As we can see from this very elementary example, investigation of the average-case efficiency is considerably more difficult than investigation of the worst-case and best-case efficiencies. The direct approach for doing it involves dividing all instances of size n into several classes so that for each instance of the class the number of times the algorithm's basic operation is executed is the same. (What were these classes for sequential search?) Then a probability distribution of inputs needs to be obtained or assumed so that the expected value of the basic operation's count can then be derived. The technical implementation of this plan is rarely easy, however, and probabilistic assumptions underlying it in each particular case are usually difficult to verify. Given our quest for simplicity, we mostly quote known results about average-case efficiency of algorithms under discussion. If you are interested in derivations of such results, consult such books as [BvG00], [SF96], [KnuI], [KnuII], and [KnuIII].

Does one really need the average-case efficiency information? The answer is unequivocally yes: there are many important algorithms for which the average-case efficiency is much better than the overly pessimistic worst-case efficiency would lead us to believe. So, without the average-case analysis, computer scientists could have missed many important algorithms. Finally, it should be clear from the preceding discussion that the average-case efficiency cannot be obtained by taking the average of the worst-case and the best-case efficiencies. Even though this average does occasionally coincide with the average-case cost, it is not a legitimate way of performing the average-case analysis.

Yet another type of efficiency is called *amortized efficiency*. It applies not to a single run of an algorithm but rather to a sequence of operations performed on the same data structure. It turns out that in some situations a single operation can be expensive, but the total time for an entire sequence of n such operations is always significantly better than the worst-case efficiency of that single operation multiplied by n. So we can "amortize" the high cost of such a worst-case occurrence over the entire sequence in a manner similar to the way a business would

Computation and Reasoning

205

amortize the cost of an expensive item over the years of the item's productive life. This sophisticated approach was discovered by the American computer scientist Robert Tarjan, who used it, among other applications, in developing an interesting variation of the classic binary search tree (see [Tar87] for a quite readable nontechnical discussion and [Tar85] for a technical account). We will see an example of the usefulness of amortized efficiency in Section 9.2, when we consider algorithms for finding unions of disjoint sets.

Recapitulation of the Analysis Framework

Before we leave this section, let us summarize the main points of the framework outlined above.

- Both time and space efficiencies are measured as functions of the algorithm's input size.
- Time efficiency is measured by counting the number of times the algorithm's basic operation is executed. Space efficiency is measured by counting the number of extra memory units consumed by the algorithm.
- The efficiencies of some algorithms may differ significantly for inputs of the same size. For such algorithms, we need to distinguish between the worst-case, average-case, and best-case efficiencies.
- The framework's primary interest lies in the order of growth of the algorithm's running time (extra memory units consumed) as its input size goes to infinity.

In the next section, we look at formal means to investigate orders of growth. In Sections 2.3 and 2.4 we discuss particular methods for investigating nonrecursive and recursive algorithms, respectively. It is there that you will see how the analysis framework outlined here can be applied to investigating efficiency of specific algorithms. You will encounter many more examples throughout the rest of the book.

Exercises 2.1

1. For each of the following algorithms, indicate (i) a natural size metric for its inputs; (ii) its basic operation; (iii) whether the basic operation count can be different for inputs of the same size.
   a. Computing the sum of n numbers
   b. Computing $n!$
   c. Finding the largest element in a list of n numbers
   d. Euclid's algorithm
   e. Sieve of Eratosthenes
   f. Pen-and-pencil algorithm for multiplying two n-digit decimal integers

2. **a.** Consider the definition-based algorithm for adding two n-by-n matrices. What is its basic operation? How many times is it performed as a function of the matrix order n? As a function of the total number of elements in the input matrices?

   b. Answer the same questions for the definition-based algorithm for matrix multiplication.

3. Consider a variation of sequential search that scans a list to return the number of occurrences of a given search key in the list. Will its efficiency differ from the efficiency of classic sequential search?

4. **a.** There are 22 gloves in a drawer: 5 pairs of red gloves, 4 pairs of yellow, and 2 pairs of green. You select the gloves in the dark and can check them only after a selection has been made. What is the smallest number of gloves you need to select to have at least one matching pair in the best case? in the worst case? (after [Mos01], #18).

   b. Imagine that after washing 5 distinct pairs of socks you discover that two socks are missing. Of course, you would like to have the largest number of complete pairs remaining. Thus, you are left with 4 complete pairs in the best-case scenario and with 3 complete pairs in the worst case. Assuming that the disappearance of each of the 10 socks is the same, find the probability of the best case scenario; the probability of the worst-case scenario; the number of pairs you should expect in the average case (after [Mos01], #48).

5. **a.** Prove formula (2.1) for the number of bits in the binary representation of a positive decimal integer.

   b. What would be the analogous formula for the number of decimal digits?

   c. Explain why, within the accepted analysis framework, it does not matter whether we use binary or decimal digits in measuring n's size.

6. Suggest how any sorting algorithm can be augmented in a way to make the best-case count of its key comparisons equal to just $n - 1$ (n is a list's size, of course). Do you think it would be a worthwhile addition to any sorting algorithm?

7. Gaussian elimination, the classic algorithm for solving systems of n linear equations in n unknowns, requires about $\frac{1}{3}n^3$ multiplications, which is the algorithm's basic operation.

   a. How much longer should we expect Gaussian elimination to work on a system of 1000 equations versus a system of 500 equations?

   b. You are considering buying a computer that is 1000 times faster than the one you currently have. By what factor will the faster computer increase the sizes of systems solvable in the same amount of time as on the old computer?

Computation and Reasoning

207

8. For each of the following functions, indicate how much the function's value will change if its argument is increased fourfold.

    a. $\log_2 n$ **b.** $\sqrt{n}$ **c.** n **d.** n^2 **e.** n^3 **f.** 2^n

9. Indicate whether the first function of each of the following pairs has a smaller, same, or larger order of growth (to within a constant multiple) than the second function.

    a. $n(n+1)$ and $2000n^2$ **b.** $100n^2$ and $0.01n^3$

    c. $\log_2 n$ and $\ln n$ **d.** $\log_2^2 n$ and $\log_2 n^2$

    e. 2^{n-1} and 2^n **f.** $(n-1)!$ and $n!$

10. According to a well-known legend, the game of chess was invented many centuries ago in northwestern India by a sage named Shashi. When he took his invention to his king, the king liked the game so much that he offered the inventor any reward he wanted. Sashi asked for some grain to be obtained as follows: just a single grain of wheat was to be placed on the first square of the chess board, two on the second, four on the third, eight on the fourth, and so on, until all 64 squares had been filled. What would the ultimate result of this algorithm have been?

2.2 Asymptotic Notations and Basic Efficiency Classes

As pointed out in the previous section, the efficiency analysis framework concentrates on the order of growth of an algorithm's basic operation count as the principal indicator of the algorithm's efficiency. To compare and rank such orders of growth, computer scientists use three notations: O (big oh), Ω (big omega), and Θ (big theta). First, we introduce these notations informally and then, after several examples, formal definitions are given. In the following discussion, $t(n)$ and $g(n)$ can be any nonnegative functions defined on the set of natural numbers. In the context we are interested in, $t(n)$ will be an algorithm's running time (usually indicated by its basic operation count $C(n)$), and $g(n)$ will be some simple function to compare the count with.

Informal Introduction

Informally, $O(g(n))$ is the set of all functions with a smaller or same order of growth as $g(n)$ (to within a constant multiple, as n goes to infinity). Thus, to give a few examples, the following assertions are all true:

$$n \in O(n^2), \qquad 100n + 5 \in O(n^2), \qquad \frac{1}{2}n(n-1) \in O(n^2).$$

Indeed, the first two functions are linear and hence have a smaller order of growth than $g(n) = n^2$, while the last one is quadratic and hence has the same order of growth as n^2. On the other hand,

$$n^3 \notin O(n^2), \qquad 0.00001n^3 \notin O(n^2), \qquad n^4 + n + 1 \notin O(n^2).$$

Indeed, the functions n^3 and $0.00001n^3$ are both cubic and hence have a higher order of growth than n^2; and so has the fourth-degree polynomial $n^4 + n + 1$.

The second notation, $\Omega(g(n))$, stands for the set of all functions with a larger or same order of growth as $g(n)$ (to within a constant multiple, as n goes to infinity). For example,

$$n^3 \in \Omega(n^2), \qquad \frac{1}{2}n(n - 1) \in \Omega(n^2), \qquad \text{but } 100n + 5 \notin \Omega(n^2).$$

Finally, $\Theta(g(n))$ is the set of all functions that have the same order of growth as $g(n)$ (to within a constant multiple, as n goes to infinity). Thus, every quadratic function $an^2 + bn + c$ with $a > 0$ is in $\Theta(n^2)$ but so are, among infinitely many others, $n^2 + \sin n$ and $n^2 + \log n$. (Can you explain why?)

We hope that the preceding informal discussion has made you comfortable with the idea behind the three asymptotic notations. So now come the formal definitions.

O-notation

DEFINITION 1   A function $t(n)$ is said to be in $O(g(n))$, denoted $t(n) \in O(g(n))$, if $t(n)$ is bounded above by some constant multiple of $g(n)$ for all large n, i.e., if there exist some positive constant c and some nonnegative integer n_0 such that

$$t(n) \leq cg(n) \text{ for all } n \geq n_0.$$

The definition is illustrated in Figure 2.1 where, for the sake of visual clarity, n is extended to be a real number.

As an example, let us formally prove one of the assertions made in the introduction: $100n + 5 \in O(n^2)$. Indeed,

$$100n + 5 \leq 100n + n \text{ (for all } n \geq 5) = 101n \leq 101n^2.$$

Thus, as values of the constants c and n_0 required by the definition, we can take 101 and 5, respectively.

Note that the definition gives us a lot of freedom in choosing specific values for constants c and n_0. For example, we could also reason that

$$100n + 5 \leq 100n + 5n \text{ (for all } n \geq 1) = 105n$$

to complete the proof with $c = 105$ and $n_0 = 1$.

Computation and Reasoning

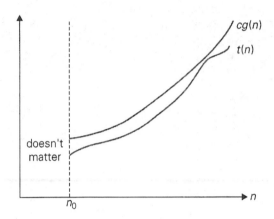

FIGURE 2.1 Big-oh notation: $t(n) \in O(g(n))$

Ω-notation

DEFINITION 2   A function $t(n)$ is said to be in $\Omega(g(n))$, denoted $t(n) \in \Omega(g(n))$, if $t(n)$ is bounded below by some positive constant multiple of $g(n)$ for all large n, i.e., if there exist some positive constant c and some nonnegative integer n_0 such that

$$t(n) \geq cg(n) \text{ for all } n \geq n_0.$$

The definition is illustrated in Figure 2.2.

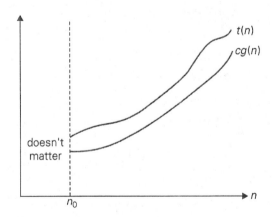

FIGURE 2.2 Big-omega notation: $t(n) \in \Omega(g(n))$

Computation and Reasoning

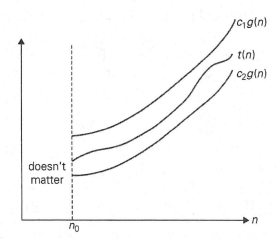

FIGURE 2.3 Big-theta notation: $t(n) \in \Theta(g(n))$

Here is an example of the formal proof that $n^3 \in \Omega(n^2)$:

$$n^3 \geq n^2 \text{ for all } n \geq 0,$$

i.e., we can select $c = 1$ and $n_0 = 0$.

Θ-notation

DEFINITION 3 A function $t(n)$ is said to be in $\Theta(g(n))$, denoted $t(n) \in \Theta(g(n))$, if $t(n)$ is bounded both above and below by some positive constant multiples of $g(n)$ for all large n, i.e., if there exist some positive constant c_1 and c_2 and some nonnegative integer n_0 such that

$$c_2 g(n) \leq t(n) \leq c_1 g(n) \text{ for all } n \geq n_0.$$

The definition is illustrated in Figure 2.3.

For example, let us prove that $\frac{1}{2}n(n-1) \in \Theta(n^2)$. First, we prove the right inequality (the upper bound):

$$\frac{1}{2}n(n-1) = \frac{1}{2}n^2 - \frac{1}{2}n \leq \frac{1}{2}n^2 \text{ for all } n \geq 0.$$

Second, we prove the left inequality (the lower bound):

$$\frac{1}{2}n(n-1) = \frac{1}{2}n^2 - \frac{1}{2}n \geq \frac{1}{2}n^2 - \frac{1}{2}\frac{1}{2}n \text{ (for all } n \geq 2) = \frac{1}{4}n^2.$$

Hence, we can select $c_2 = \frac{1}{4}$, $c_1 = \frac{1}{2}$ and $n_0 = 2$.

Computation and Reasoning

Useful Property Involving the Asymptotic Notations

Using the formal definitions of the asymptotic notations, we can prove their general properties (see Problem 1 in Exercises 2.1 for a few simple examples). The following property, in particular, is useful in analyzing algorithms that comprise two consecutively executed parts.

THEOREM   If $t_1(n) \in O(g_1(n))$ and $t_2(n) \in O(g_2(n))$, then

$$t_1(n) + t_2(n) \in O(\max\{g_1(n), g_2(n)\}).$$

(The analogous assertions are true for the Ω and Θ notations as well.)

PROOF   (As we shall see, the proof will extend to orders of growth the following simple fact about four arbitrary real numbers a_1, b_1, a_2, and b_2: if $a_1 \le b_1$ and $a_2 \le b_2$, then $a_1 + a_2 \le 2 \max\{b_1, b_2\}$.) Since $t_1(n) \in O(g_1(n))$, there exist some constant c_1 and some nonnegative integer n_1 such that

$$t_1(n) \le c_1 g_1(n) \text{ for all } n \ge n_1.$$

Since $t_2(n) \in O(g_2(n))$,

$$t_2(n) \le c_2 g_2(n) \text{ for all } n \ge n_2.$$

Let us denote $c_3 = \max\{c_1, c_2\}$ and consider $n \ge \max\{n_1, n_2\}$ so that we can use both inequalities. Adding the two inequalities above yields the following:

$$\begin{aligned} t_1(n) + t_2(n) &\le c_1 g_1(n) + c_2 g_2(n) \\ &\le c_3 g_1(n) + c_3 g_2(n) = c_3[g_1(n) + g_2(n)] \\ &\le c_3 2 \max\{g_1(n), g_2(n)\}. \end{aligned}$$

Hence, $t_1(n) + t_2(n) \in O(\max\{g_1(n), g_2(n)\})$, with the constants c and n_0 required by the O definition being $2c_3 = 2\max\{c_1, c_2\}$ and $\max\{n_1, n_2\}$, respectively.   ∎

So what does this property imply for an algorithm that comprises two consecutively executed parts? It implies that the algorithm's overall efficiency will be determined by the part with a larger order of growth, i.e., its least efficient part:

$$\left. \begin{array}{|l|} \hline t_1(n) \in O(g_1(n)) \\ \hline t_2(n) \in O(g_2(n)) \\ \hline \end{array} \right\} \quad t_1(n) + t_2(n) \in O(\max\{g_1(n), g_2(n)\})$$

For example, we can check whether an array has identical elements by means of the following two-part algorithm: first, sort the array by applying some known sorting algorithm; second, scan the sorted array to check its consecutive elements for equality. If, for example, a sorting algorithm used in the first part makes no more than $\frac{1}{2}n(n-1)$ comparisons (and hence is in $O(n^2)$) while the second part makes no more than $n-1$ comparisons (and hence is in $O(n)$), the efficiency of the entire algorithm will be in $O(\max\{n^2, n\}) = O(n^2)$.

Computation and Reasoning

Using Limits for Comparing Orders of Growth

Though the formal definitions of O, Ω, and Θ are indispensable for proving their abstract properties, they are rarely used for comparing orders of growth of two specific functions. A much more convenient method for doing so is based on computing the limit of the ratio of two functions in question. Three principal cases may arise:[3]

$$\lim_{n\to\infty} \frac{t(n)}{g(n)} = \begin{cases} 0 & \text{implies that } t(n) \text{ has a smaller order of growth than } g(n) \\ c & \text{implies that } t(n) \text{ has the same order of growth as } g(n) \\ \infty & \text{implies that } t(n) \text{ has a larger order of growth than } g(n). \end{cases}$$

Note that the first two cases mean that $t(n) \in O(g(n))$, the last two mean that $t(n) \in \Omega(g(n))$, and the second case means that $t(n) \in \Theta(g(n))$.

The limit-based approach is often more convenient than the one based on the definitions because it can take advantage of the powerful calculus techniques developed for computing limits, such as L'Hôpital's rule

$$\lim_{n\to\infty} \frac{t(n)}{g(n)} = \lim_{n\to\infty} \frac{t'(n)}{g'(n)}$$

and Stirling's formula

$$n! \approx \sqrt{2\pi n} \left(\frac{n}{e}\right)^n \quad \text{for large values of } n.$$

Here are three examples of using the limit-based approach to comparing orders of growth of two functions.

EXAMPLE 1   Compare orders of growth of $\frac{1}{2}n(n-1)$ and n^2. (This is one of the examples we did above to illustrate the definitions.)

$$\lim_{n\to\infty} \frac{\frac{1}{2}n(n-1)}{n^2} = \frac{1}{2} \lim_{n\to\infty} \frac{n^2-n}{n^2} = \frac{1}{2} \lim_{n\to\infty} (1 - \frac{1}{n}) = \frac{1}{2}.$$

Since the limit is equal to a positive constant, the functions have the same order of growth or, symbolically, $\frac{1}{2}n(n-1) \in \Theta(n^2)$.   ∎

EXAMPLE 2   Compare orders of growth of $\log_2 n$ and $\sqrt{n}$. (Unlike Example 1, the answer here is not immediately obvious.)

$$\lim_{n\to\infty} \frac{\log_2 n}{\sqrt{n}} = \lim_{n\to\infty} \frac{(\log_2 n)'}{(\sqrt{n})'} = \lim_{n\to\infty} \frac{(\log_2 e)\frac{1}{n}}{\frac{1}{2\sqrt{n}}} = 2\log_2 e \lim_{n\to\infty} \frac{\sqrt{n}}{n} = 0.$$

---

3.   The fourth case, in which such a limit does not exist, rarely happens in the actual practice of analyzing algorithms. Still, this possibility makes the limit-based approach to comparing orders of growth less general than the one based on the definitions of O, Ω, and Θ.

Computation and Reasoning

213

Since the limit is equal to zero, $\log_2 n$ has a smaller order of growth than $\sqrt{n}$. (Since $\lim\limits_{n\to\infty} \frac{\log_2 n}{\sqrt{n}} = 0$, we can use the so-called *little-oh notation*: $\log_2 n \in o(\sqrt{n})$. Unlike the big-oh, the little-oh notation is rarely used in analysis of algorithms.)   ■

EXAMPLE 3   Compare orders of growth of $n!$ and 2^n. (We discussed this issue informally in the previous section.) Taking advantage of Stirling's formula, we get

$$\lim_{n\to\infty} \frac{n!}{2^n} = \lim_{n\to\infty} \frac{\sqrt{2\pi n}\left(\frac{n}{e}\right)^n}{2^n} = \lim_{n\to\infty} \sqrt{2\pi n}\,\frac{n^n}{2^n e^n} = \lim_{n\to\infty} \sqrt{2\pi n}\,\left(\frac{n}{2e}\right)^n = \infty.$$

Thus, though 2^n grows very fast, $n!$ grows still faster. We can write symbolically that $n! \in \Omega(2^n)$; note, however, that while big-omega notation does not preclude the possibility that $n!$ and 2^n have the same order of growth, the limit computed here certainly does.   ■

Basic Efficiency Classes

Even though the efficiency analysis framework puts together all the functions whose orders of growth differ by a constant multiple, there are still infinitely many such classes. (For example, the exponential functions a^n have different orders of growth for different values of base a.) Therefore, it may come as a surprise that the time efficiencies of a large number of algorithms fall into only a few classes. These classes are listed in Table 2.2 in increasing order of their orders of growth, along with their names and a few comments.

You could raise a concern that classifying algorithms according to their asymptotic efficiency classes has little practical value because the values of multiplicative constants are usually left unspecified. This leaves open a possibility of an algorithm in a worse efficiency class running faster than an algorithm in a better efficiency class for inputs of realistic sizes. For example, if the running time of one algorithm is n^3 while the running time of the other is $10^6 n^2$, the cubic algorithm will outperform the quadratic algorithm unless n exceeds 10^6. A few such anomalies are indeed known. For example, there exist algorithms for matrix multiplication with a better asymptotic efficiency than the cubic efficiency of the definition-based algorithm (see Section 4.5). Because of their much larger multiplicative constants, however, the value of these more sophisticated algorithms is mostly theoretical.

Fortunately, multiplicative constants usually do not differ that drastically. As a rule, you should expect an algorithm from a better asymptotic efficiency class to outperform an algorithm from a worse class even for moderately sized inputs. This observation is especially true for an algorithm with a better than exponential running time versus an exponential (or worse) algorithm.

Computation and Reasoning

TABLE 2.2 Basic Asymptotic Efficiency Classes

Class	Name	Comments
1	*constant*	Short of best-case efficiencies, very few reasonable examples can be given since an algorithm's running time typically goes to infinity when its input size grows infinitely large.
$\log n$	*logarithmic*	Typically, a result of cutting a problem's size by a constant factor on each iteration of the algorithm (see Section 5.5). Note that a logarithmic algorithm cannot take into account all its input (or even a fixed fraction of it): any algorithm that does so will have at least linear running time.
n	*linear*	Algorithms that scan a list of size n (e.g., sequential search) belong to this class.
$n \log n$	*n-log-n*	Many divide-and-conquer algorithms (see Chapter 4), including mergesort and quicksort in the average case, fall into this category.
n^2	*quadratic*	Typically, characterizes efficiency of algorithms with two embedded loops (see the next section). Elementary sorting algorithms and certain operations on n-by-n matrices are standard examples.
n^3	*cubic*	Typically, characterizes efficiency of algorithms with three embedded loops (see the next section). Several nontrivial algorithms from linear algebra fall into this class.
2^n	*exponential*	Typical for algorithms that generate all subsets of an n-element set. Often, the term "exponential" is used in a broader sense to include this and faster orders of growth as well.
$n!$	*factorial*	Typical for algorithms that generate all permutations of an n-element set.

Exercises 2.2

1. Use the most appropriate notation among O, Θ, and Ω to indicate the time efficiency class of sequential search (see Section 2.1)

   a. in the worst case.

   b. in the best case.

   c. in the average case.

Computation and Reasoning

215

2. Use the informal definitions of O, Θ, and Ω to determine whether the following assertions are true or false.

    a. $n(n+1)/2 \in O(n^3)$ **b.** $n(n+1)/2 \in O(n^2)$

    c. $n(n+1)/2 \in \Theta(n^3)$ **d.** $n(n+1)/2 \in \Omega(n)$

3. For each of the following functions, indicate the class $\Theta(g(n))$ the function belongs to. (Use the simplest $g(n)$ possible in your answers.) Prove your assertions.

    a. $(n^2+1)^{10}$ **b.** $\sqrt{10n^2+7n+3}$

    c. $2n\lg(n+2)^2 + (n+2)^2\lg\frac{n}{2}$ **d.** $2^{n+1} + 3^{n-1}$

    e. $\lfloor \log_2 n \rfloor$

4. **a.** Table 2.1 contains values of several functions that often arise in analysis of algorithms. These values certainly suggest that the functions

$$\log n, \; n, \; n\log n, \; n^2, \; n^3, \; 2^n, \; n!$$

    are listed in increasing order of their order of growth. Do these values prove this fact with mathematical certainty?

    b. Prove that the list is indeed ordered in increasing order of the function order of growth.

5. Order the following functions according to their order of growth (from the lowest to the highest).

$$(n-2)!, \; 5\lg(n+100)^{10}, \; 2^{2n}, \; 0.001n^4 + 3n^3 + 1, \; \ln^2 n, \; \sqrt[3]{n}, \; 3^n.$$

6. **a.** Prove that every polynomial $p(n) = a_k n^k + a_{k-1} n^{k-1} + \cdots + a_0$ with $a_k > 0$ belongs to $\Theta(n^k)$.

    b. Prove that exponential functions a^n have different orders of growth for different values of base $a > 0$.

7. Prove (by using the definitions of the notations involved) or disprove (by giving a specific counterexample) the following assertions.

    a. If $t(n) \in O(g(n))$, then $g(n) \in \Omega(t(n))$.

    b. $\Theta(\alpha g(n)) = \Theta(g(n))$ where $\alpha > 0$.

    c. $\Theta(g(n)) = O(g(n)) \cap \Omega(g(n))$.

    d. For any two nonnegative functions $t(n)$ and $g(n)$ defined on the set of nonnegative integers, either $t(n) \in O(g(n))$, or $t(n) \in \Omega(g(n))$, or both.

8. Prove the section's theorem for

    a. Ω-notation.

    b. Θ-notation.

Computation and Reasoning

9. We mentioned in this section that we can check whether all elements of an array are distinct by a two-staged algorithm based on the array's presorting.

    a. If the presorting is done by an algorithm with the time efficiency known to be in $\Theta(n \log n)$, what will be the time efficiency class of the entire algorithm?

    b. If the sorting algorithm used for presorting needs an extra array of size n, what will be the space efficiency class of the entire algorithm?

10. You are facing a wall that stretches infinitely in both directions. There is a door in the wall, but you know neither how far away nor in which direction. You can see the door only when you are right next to it. Design an algorithm that enables you to reach the door by walking at most $O(n)$ steps where n is the (unknown to you) number of steps between your initial position and the door ([Par95], #652).

2.3 Mathematical Analysis of Nonrecursive Algorithms

In this section, we systematically apply the general framework outlined in Section 2.1 to analyzing the efficiency of nonrecursive algorithms. Let us start with a very simple example that demonstrates all the principal steps typically taken in analyzing such algorithms.

EXAMPLE 1 Consider the problem of finding the value of the largest element in a list of n numbers. For simplicity, we assume that the list is implemented as an array. The following is a pseudocode of a standard algorithm for solving the problem.

ALGORITHM *MaxElement*($A[0..n-1]$)

```
//Determines the value of the largest element in a given array
//Input: An array A[0..n − 1] of real numbers
//Output: The value of the largest element in A
maxval ← A[0]
for i ← 1 to n − 1 do
    if A[i] > maxval
        maxval ← A[i]
return maxval
```

The obvious measure of an input's size here is the number of elements in the array, i.e., n. The operations that are going to be executed most often are in the algorithm's **for** loop. There are two operations in the loop's body: the comparison $A[i] > maxval$ and the assignment $maxval \leftarrow A[i]$. Which of these two operations should we consider basic? Since the comparison is executed on each repetition of the loop and the assignment is not, we should consider the comparison to be the algorithm's basic operation. (Note that the number of comparisons will be the same for all arrays of size n; therefore, in terms of this metric, there is no need to distinguish among the worst, average, and best cases here.)

Let us denote $C(n)$ the number of times this comparison is executed and try to find a formula expressing it as a function of size n. The algorithm makes one comparison on each execution of the loop, which is repeated for each value of the loop's variable i within the bounds between 1 and $n - 1$ (inclusively). Therefore, we get the following sum for $C(n)$:

$$C(n) = \sum_{i=1}^{n-1} 1.$$

This is an easy sum to compute because it is nothing else but 1 repeated $n - 1$ times. Thus,

$$C(n) = \sum_{i=1}^{n-1} 1 = n - 1 \in \Theta(n). \qquad \blacksquare$$

Here is a general plan to follow in analyzing nonrecursive algorithms.

General Plan for Analyzing Efficiency of Nonrecursive Algorithms

1. Decide on a parameter (or parameters) indicating an input's size.
2. Identify the algorithm's basic operation. (As a rule, it is located in its innermost loop.)
3. Check whether the number of times the basic operation is executed depends only on the size of an input. If it also depends on some additional property, the worst-case, average-case, and, if necessary, best-case efficiencies have to be investigated separately.
4. Set up a sum expressing the number of times the algorithm's basic operation is executed.[4]
5. Using standard formulas and rules of sum manipulation, either find a closed-form formula for the count or, at the very least, establish its order of growth.

---

[4] Sometimes, an analysis of a nonrecursive algorithm requires setting not a sum but a recurrence relation for the number of times its basic operation is executed. Setting and solving recurrence relations is much more typical for analyzing recursive algorithms (see Section 2.4).

Before proceeding with further examples, you may want to review Appendix A, which contains a list of summation formulas and rules that are often useful in analysis of algorithms. In particular, we use especially frequently two basic rules of sum manipulation

$$\sum_{i=l}^{u} ca_i = c \sum_{i=l}^{u} a_i \tag{R1}$$

$$\sum_{i=l}^{u} (a_i \pm b_i) = \sum_{i=l}^{u} a_i \pm \sum_{i=l}^{u} b_i \tag{R2}$$

and two summation formulas

$$\sum_{i=l}^{u} 1 = u - l + 1 \text{ where } l \le u \text{ are some lower and upper integer limits} \tag{S1}$$

$$\sum_{i=0}^{n} i = \sum_{i=1}^{n} i = 1 + 2 + \cdots + n = \frac{n(n+1)}{2} \approx \frac{1}{2}n^2 \in \Theta(n^2). \tag{S2}$$

(Note that the formula $\sum_{i=1}^{n-1} 1 = n - 1$, which we used in Example 1, is a special case of formula (S1) for $l = 1$ and $u = n - 1$.)

EXAMPLE 2 Consider the *element uniqueness problem*: check whether all the elements in a given array are distinct. This problem can be solved by the following straightforward algorithm.

ALGORITHM *UniqueElements*($A[0..n-1]$)
    //Checks whether all the elements in a given array are distinct
    //Input: An array $A[0..n-1]$
    //Output: Returns "true" if all the elements in A are distinct
    //   and "false" otherwise.
    for $i \leftarrow 0$ **to** $n - 2$ **do**
        for $j \leftarrow i + 1$ **to** $n - 1$ **do**
            if $A[i] = A[j]$ **return false**
    return true

The natural input's size measure here is again the number of elements in the array, i.e., n. Since the innermost loop contains a single operation (the comparison of two elements), we should consider it as the algorithm's basic operation. Note, however, that the number of element comparisons will depend not only on n but

Computation and Reasoning

219

also on whether there are equal elements in the array and, if there are, which array positions they occupy. We will limit our investigation to the worst case only.

By definition, the worst case input is an array for which the number of element comparisons $C_{worst}(n)$ is the largest among all arrays of size n. An inspection of the innermost loop reveals that there are two kinds of worst-case inputs (inputs for which the algorithm does not exit the loop prematurely): arrays with no equal elements and arrays in which the last two elements are the only pair of equal elements. For such inputs, one comparison is made for each repetition of the innermost loop, i.e., for each value of the loop's variable j between its limits $i + 1$ and $n - 1$; and this is repeated for each value of the outer loop, i.e., for each value of the loop's variable i between its limits 0 and $n - 2$. Accordingly, we get

$$C_{worst}(n) = \sum_{i=0}^{n-2} \sum_{j=i+1}^{n-1} 1 = \sum_{i=0}^{n-2}[(n-1) - (i+1) + 1] = \sum_{i=0}^{n-2}(n - 1 - i)$$

$$= \sum_{i=0}^{n-2}(n-1) - \sum_{i=0}^{n-2} i = (n-1)\sum_{i=0}^{n-2} 1 - \frac{(n-2)(n-1)}{2}$$

$$= (n-1)^2 - \frac{(n-2)(n-1)}{2} = \frac{(n-1)n}{2} \approx \frac{1}{2}n^2 \in \Theta(n^2).$$

We also could have computed the sum $\sum_{i=0}^{n-2}(n - 1 - i)$ faster as follows:

$$\sum_{i=0}^{n-2}(n - 1 - i) = (n-1) + (n-2) + \cdots + 1 \overset{(S2)}{=} \frac{(n-1)n}{2}.$$

Note that this result was perfectly predictable: in the worst case, the algorithm needs to compare all $n(n-1)/2$ distinct pairs of its n elements. ■

EXAMPLE 3   Given two n-by-n matrices A and B, find the time efficiency of the definition-based algorithm for computing their product $C = AB$. By definition, C is an n-by-n matrix whose elements are computed as the scalar (dot) products of the rows of matrix A and the columns of matrix B:

where $C[i, j] = A[i, 0]B[0, j] + \cdots A[i, k]B[k, j] + \cdots + A[i, n - 1]B[n - 1, j]$ for every pair of indices $0 \le i, j \le n - 1$.

ALGORITHM   *MatrixMultiplication*$(A[0..n-1, 0..n-1], B[0..n-1, 0..n-1])$

   //Multiplies two square matrices of order n by the definition-based
   //algorithm
   //Input: Two n-by-n matrices A and B
   //Output: Matrix $C = AB$
   for $i \leftarrow 0$ **to** $n-1$ **do**
      for $j \leftarrow 0$ **to** $n-1$ **do**
         $C[i,j] \leftarrow 0.0$
         for $k \leftarrow 0$ **to** $n-1$ **do**
            $C[i,j] \leftarrow C[i,j] + A[i,k] * B[k,j]$
   return C

We measure an input's size by matrix order n. In the algorithm's innermost loop are two arithmetical operations—multiplication and addition—that, in principle, can compete for designation as the algorithm's basic operation. We consider multiplication as the algorithm's basic operation (see Section 2.1). Note that for this algorithm, we do not have to choose between these two operations because on each repetition of the innermost loop, each of the two is executed exactly once. So by counting one we automatically count the other. Let us set up a sum for the total number of multiplications $M(n)$ executed by the algorithm. (Since this count depends only on the size of the input matrices, we do not have to investigate the worst-case, average-case, and best-case efficiencies separately.)

Obviously, there is just one multiplication executed on each repetition of the algorithm's innermost loop, which is governed by the variable k ranging from the lower bound 0 to the upper bound $n-1$. Therefore, the number of multiplications made for every pair of specific values of variables i and j is

$$\sum_{k=0}^{n-1} 1,$$

and the total number of multiplications $M(n)$ is expressed by the following triple sum:

$$M(n) = \sum_{i=0}^{n-1}\sum_{j=0}^{n-1}\sum_{k=0}^{n-1} 1.$$

Now we can compute this sum by using formula $(S1)$ and rule $(R1)$ (see above). Starting with the innermost sum $\sum_{k=0}^{n-1} 1$, which is equal to n (why?), we get

$$M(n) = \sum_{i=0}^{n-1}\sum_{j=0}^{n-1}\sum_{k=0}^{n-1} 1 = \sum_{i=0}^{n-1}\sum_{j=0}^{n-1} n = \sum_{i=0}^{n-1} n^2 = n^3.$$

Computation and Reasoning

(This example is simple enough so that we could get this result without all the summation machinations. How? The algorithm computes n^2 elements of the product matrix. Each of the product's elements is computed as the scalar (dot) product of an n-element row of the first matrix and an n-element column of the second matrix, which takes n multiplications. So the total number of multiplications is $n \cdot n^2 = n^3$. It is this kind of reasoning we expected you to employ when answering this question in Problem 2 of Exercises 2.1.)

If we now want to estimate the running time of the algorithm on a particular machine, we can do it by the product

$$T(n) \approx c_m M(n) = c_m n^3,$$

where c_m is the time of one multiplication on the machine in question. We would get a more accurate estimate if we took into account the time spent on the additions, too:

$$T(n) \approx c_m M(n) + c_a A(n) = c_m n^3 + c_a n^3 = (c_m + c_a)n^3,$$

where c_a is the time of one addition. Note that the estimates differ only by their multiplicative constants, not by their order of growth. ∎

You should not have the erroneous impression that the plan outlined above always succeeds in analyzing a nonrecursive algorithm. An irregular change in a loop's variable, a sum too complicated to analyze, and the difficulties intrinsic to the average case analysis are just some of the obstacles that can prove to be insurmountable. These caveats notwithstanding, the plan does work for many simple nonrecursive algorithms, as you will see throughout the subsequent chapters of the book.

As a last example, let us consider an algorithm in which the loop's variable changes in a different manner from that of the previous examples.

EXAMPLE 4   The following algorithm finds the number of binary digits in the binary representation of a positive decimal integer.

ALGORITHM   *Binary*(*n*)

    //Input: A positive decimal integer n
    //Output: The number of binary digits in n's binary representation
    count ← 1
    while $n > 1$ **do**
        count ← *count* + 1
        n ← $\lfloor n/2 \rfloor$
    return *count*

First, notice that the most frequently executed operation here is not inside the **while** loop but rather the comparison $n > 1$ that determines whether the loop's body will be executed. Since the number of times the comparison will be executed is larger than the number of repetitions of the loop's body by exactly 1, the choice is not that important.

A more significant feature of this example is the fact that the loop's variable takes on only a few values between its lower and upper limits; therefore we have to use an alternative way of computing the number of times the loop is executed. Since the value of n is about halved on each repetition of the loop, the answer should be about $\log_2 n$. The exact formula for the number of times the comparison $n > 1$ will be executed is actually $\lfloor \log_2 n \rfloor + 1$—the number of bits in the binary representation of n according to formula (2.1). We could also get this answer by applying the analysis technique based on recurrence relations; we discuss this technique in the next section because it is more pertinent to the analysis of recursive algorithms. ∎

Exercises 2.3

1. Compute the following sums.
   a. $1 + 3 + 5 + 7 + \cdots + 999$
   b. $2 + 4 + 8 + 16 + \cdots + 1024$
   c. $\sum_{i=3}^{n+1} 1$ d. $\sum_{i=3}^{n+1} i$ e. $\sum_{i=0}^{n-1} i(i+1)$
   f. $\sum_{j=1}^{n} 3^{j+1}$ g. $\sum_{i=1}^{n} \sum_{j=1}^{n} ij$

2. Find the order of growth of the following sums.
   a. $\sum_{i=0}^{n-1}(i^2+1)^2$ b. $\sum_{i=2}^{n-1} \lg i^2$
   c. $\sum_{i=1}^{n}(i+1)2^{i-1}$ d. $\sum_{i=0}^{n-1} \sum_{j=0}^{i-1}(i+j)$
   Use the $\Theta(g(n))$ notation with the simplest function $g(n)$ possible.

3. The sample variance of n measurements $x_1, \ldots, x_n$ can be computed as

$$\frac{\sum_{i=1}^{n}(x_i - \bar{x})^2}{n - 1} \quad \text{where } \bar{x} = \frac{\sum_{i=1}^{n} x_i}{n}$$

or

$$\frac{\sum_{i=1}^{n} x_i^2 - (\sum_{i=1}^{n} x_i)^2/n}{n - 1}.$$

Find and compare the number of divisions, multiplications, and additions/subtractions (additions and subtractions are usually bunched together) that are required for computing the variance according to each of these formulas.

Computation and Reasoning

4. Consider the following algorithm.

ALGORITHM   *Mystery*(*n*)

//Input: A nonnegative integer *n*
$S \leftarrow 0$
for $i \leftarrow 1$ **to** *n* **do**
     $S \leftarrow S + i * i$
return *S*

a. What does this algorithm compute?
b. What is its basic operation?
c. How many times is the basic operation executed?
d. What is the efficiency class of this algorithm?
e. Suggest an improvement or a better algorithm altogether and indicate its efficiency class. If you cannot do it, try to prove that in fact it cannot be done.

5. Consider the following algorithm.

ALGORITHM   *Secret*(*A*[0..*n* − 1])

//Input: An array *A*[0..*n* − 1] of *n* real numbers
minval ← *A*[0]; *maxval* ← *A*[0]
for $i \leftarrow 1$ **to** *n* − 1 **do**
     if *A*[*i*] < *minval*
          minval ← *A*[*i*]
     if *A*[*i*] > *maxval*
          maxval ← *A*[*i*]
return *maxval* − *minval*

Answer questions a–e of Problem 4 about this algorithm.

6. Consider the following algorithm.

ALGORITHM   *Enigma*(*A*[0..*n* − 1, 0..*n* − 1])

//Input: A matrix *A*[0..*n* − 1, 0..*n* − 1] of real numbers
for $i \leftarrow 0$ **to** *n* − 2 **do**
     for $j \leftarrow i + 1$ **to** *n* − 1 **do**
          if *A*[*i*, *j*] ≠ *A*[*j*, *i*]
               return false
return true

Answer questions a–e of Problem 4 about this algorithm.

Computation and Reasoning

7. Improve the implementation of the matrix multiplication algorithm (see Example 3) by reducing the number of additions made by the algorithm. What effect will this change have on the algorithm's efficiency?

8. What is the efficiency class of the algorithm of Example 4 as a function of the number of bits in n's binary representation?

9. Prove the formula

$$\sum_{i=1}^{n} i = 1 + 2 + \cdots + n = \frac{n(n+1)}{2}$$

either by mathematical induction or by following the insight of a 10-year old schoolboy named Karl Friedrich Gauss (1777–1855), who grew up to become one of the greatest mathematicians of all times.

10. Consider the following version of an important algorithm that we will study later in the book.

ALGORITHM $GE(A[0..n-1, 0..n])$

//Input: An n-by-$n+1$ matrix $A[0..n-1, 0..n]$ of real numbers
for $i \leftarrow 0$ **to** $n-2$ **do**
    for $j \leftarrow i+1$ **to** $n-1$ **do**
        for $k \leftarrow i$ **to** n **do**
            $A[j,k] \leftarrow A[j,k] - A[i,k] * A[j,i] / A[i,i]$

a. Find the time efficiency class of this algorithm.

b. What glaring inefficiency does this pseudocode contain and how can it be eliminated to speed the algorithm up?

2.4 Mathematical Analysis of Recursive Algorithms

In this section, we will see how to apply the general framework for analysis of algorithms to analyzing recursive algorithms. We start with an example often used to introduce novices to the idea of a recursive algorithm.

EXAMPLE 1 Computing the factorial function $F(n) = n!$ for an arbitrary non-negative integer n. Since

$$n! = 1 \cdot \ldots \cdot (n-1) \cdot n = (n-1)! \cdot n \text{ for } n \geq 1$$

and $0! = 1$ by definition, we can compute $F(n) = F(n-1) \cdot n$ with the following recursive algorithm.

Computation and Reasoning

225

ALGORITHM $F(n)$

> //Computes $n!$ recursively
> //Input: A nonnegative integer n
> //Output: The value of $n!$
> **if** $n = 0$ **return** 1
> **else return** $F(n - 1) * n$

For simplicity, we consider n itself as an indicator of this algorithm's input size (rather than the number of bits in its binary expansion). The basic operation of the algorithm is multiplication, whose number of executions we denote $M(n)$.[5] Since the function $F(n)$ is computed according to the formula

$$F(n) = F(n - 1) \cdot n \quad \text{for } n > 0,$$

the number of multiplications $M(n)$ needed to compute it must satisfy the equality

$$M(n) = \underset{\substack{\text{to compute} \\ F(n-1)}}{M(n - 1)} + \underset{\substack{\text{to multiply} \\ F(n-1) \text{ by } n}}{1} \quad \text{for } n > 0.$$

Indeed, $M(n - 1)$ multiplications are spent to compute $F(n - 1)$, and one more multiplication is needed to multiply the result by n.

The last equation defines the sequence $M(n)$ that we need to find. Note that the equation defines $M(n)$ not explicitly, i.e., as a function of n, but implicitly as a function of its value at another point, namely $n - 1$. Such equations are called *recurrence relations* or, for brevity, *recurrences*. Recurrence relations play an important role not only in analysis of algorithms but also in some areas of applied mathematics. They are usually studied in detail in courses on discrete mathematics or discrete structures; a very brief tutorial on them is provided in Appendix B. Our goal now is to solve the recurrence relation $M(n) = M(n - 1) + 1$, i.e., to find an explicit formula for the sequence $M(n)$ in terms of n only.

Note, however, that there is not one but infinitely many sequences that satisfy this recurrence. (Can you give examples of, say, two of them?) To determine a solution uniquely, we need an *initial condition* that tells us the value with which the sequence starts. We can obtain this value by inspecting the condition that makes the algorithm stop its recursive calls:

if $n = 0$ **return** 1.

This tells us two things. First, since the calls stop when $n = 0$, the smallest value of n for which this algorithm is executed and hence $M(n)$ defined is 0. Second,

---

5.   Alternatively, we could count the number of times the comparison $n = 0$ is executed, which is the same as counting the total number of calls made by the algorithm (see Problem 2 in Exercises 2.4).

Computation and Reasoning

by inspecting the code's exiting line, we can see that when $n = 0$, the algorithm performs no multiplications. Thus, the initial condition we are after is

$$M(0) = 0.$$

the calls stop when $n = 0$ ⟶ ⟶ no multiplications when $n = 0$

Thus, we succeed in setting up the recurrence relation and initial condition for the algorithm's number of multiplications $M(n)$:

$$M(n) = M(n - 1) + 1 \text{ for } n > 0, \qquad\qquad \textbf{(2.2)}$$
$$M(0) = 0.$$

Before we embark on a discussion of how to solve this recurrence, let us pause to reiterate an important point. We are dealing here with two recursively defined functions. The first is the factorial function $F(n)$ itself; it is defined by the recurrence

$$F(n) = F(n - 1) \cdot n \text{ for every } n > 0,$$
$$F(0) = 1.$$

The second is the number of multiplications $M(n)$ needed to compute $F(n)$ by the recursive algorithm whose pseudocode was given at the beginning of the section. As we just showed, $M(n)$ is defined by recurrence (2.2). And it is recurrence (2.2) that we need to solve now.

Though it is not difficult to "guess" the solution (what sequence starts with 0 when $n = 0$ and increases by 1 at each step?), it will be more useful to arrive at it in a systematic fashion. Among several techniques available for solving recurrence relations, we use what can be called the ***method of backward substitutions***. The method's idea (and the reason for the name) is immediately clear from the way it applies to solving our particular recurrence:

$M(n) = M(n - 1) + 1$ substitute $M(n - 1) = M(n - 2) + 1$

$\quad = [M(n - 2) + 1] + 1 = M(n - 2) + 2$ substitute $M(n - 2) = M(n - 3) + 1$

$\quad = [M(n - 3) + 1] + 2 = M(n - 3) + 3.$

After inspecting the first three lines, we see an emerging pattern, which makes it possible to predict not only the next line (what would it be?) but also a general formula for the pattern: $M(n) = M(n - i) + i$. Strictly speaking, the correctness of this formula should be proved by mathematical induction, but it is easier to get the solution as follows and then verify its correctness.

What remains to be done is to take advantage of the initial condition given. Since it is specified for $n = 0$, we have to substitute $i = n$ in the pattern's formula to get the ultimate result of our backward substitutions:

$$M(n) = M(n - 1) + 1 = \cdots = M(n - i) + i = \cdots = M(n - n) + n = n.$$

Computation and Reasoning

You should not be disappointed after exerting so much effort to get this "obvious" answer. The benefits of the method illustrated in this simple example will become clear very soon, when we have to solve more difficult recurrences. Also note that the simple iterative algorithm that accumulates the product of n consecutive integers requires the same number of multiplications, and it does so without the overhead of time and space used for maintaining the recursion's stack.

The issue of time efficiency is actually not that important for the problem of computing $n!$, however. As we saw in Section 2.1, the function's values get so large so fast that we can realistically compute its values only for very small n's. Again, we use this example just as a simple and convenient vehicle to introduce the standard approach to analyzing recursive algorithms. ■

Generalizing our experience with investigating the recursive algorithm for computing $n!$, we can now outline a general plan for investigating recursive algorithms.

A General Plan for Analyzing Efficiency of Recursive Algorithms

1. Decide on a parameter (or parameters) indicating an input's size.
2. Identify the algorithm's basic operation.
3. Check whether the number of times the basic operation is executed can vary on different inputs of the same size; if it can, the worst-case, average-case, and best-case efficiencies must be investigated separately.
4. Set up a recurrence relation, with an appropriate initial condition, for the number of times the basic operation is executed.
5. Solve the recurrence or at least ascertain the order of growth of its solution.

EXAMPLE 2   As our next example, we consider another educational workhorse of recursive algorithms: the *Tower of Hanoi* puzzle. In this puzzle, we (or mythical priests, if you do not like to move disks) have n disks of different sizes and three pegs. Initially, all the disks are on the first peg in order of size, the largest on the bottom and the smallest on top. The goal is to move all the disks to the third peg, using the second one as an auxiliary, if necessary. We can move only one disk at a time, and it is forbidden to place a larger disk on top of a smaller one.

The problem has an elegant recursive solution that is illustrated in Figure 2.4. To move $n > 1$ disks from peg 1 to peg 3 (with peg 2 as auxiliary), we first move recursively $n - 1$ disks from peg 1 to peg 2 (with peg 3 as auxiliary), then move the largest disk directly from peg 1 to peg 3, and, finally, move recursively $n - 1$ disks from peg 2 to peg 3 (using peg 1 as auxiliary). Of course, if $n = 1$, we can simply move the single disk directly from the source peg to the destination peg.

Let us apply the general plan to the Tower of Hanoi problem. The number of disks n is the obvious choice for the input size indicator, and so is moving one disk

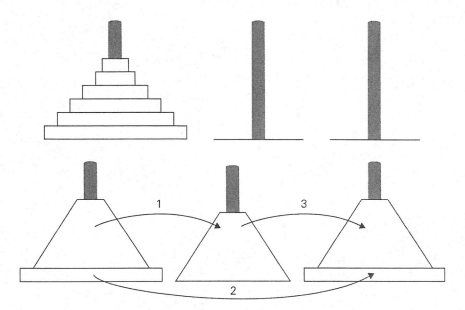

FIGURE 2.4 Recursive solution to the Tower of Hanoi puzzle

as the algorithm's basic operation. Clearly, the number of moves $M(n)$ depends on n only, and we get the following recurrence equation for it:

$$M(n) = M(n-1) + 1 + M(n-1) \text{ for } n > 1.$$

With the obvious initial condition $M(1) = 1$, we have the following recurrence relation for the number of moves $M(n)$:

$$M(n) = 2M(n-1) + 1 \text{ for } n > 1, \qquad (2.3)$$
$$M(1) = 1.$$

We solve this recurrence by the same method of backward substitutions:

$M(n) = 2M(n-1) + 1$ sub. $M(n-1) = 2M(n-2) + 1$

$= 2[2M(n-2) + 1] + 1 = 2^2 M(n-2) + 2 + 1$ sub. $M(n-2) = 2M(n-3) + 1$

$= 2^2 [2M(n-3) + 1] + 2 + 1 = 2^3 M(n-3) + 2^2 + 2 + 1$

The pattern of the first three sums on the left suggests that the next one will be $2^4 M(n-4) + 2^3 + 2^2 + 2 + 1$ and, generally, after i substitutions, we get

$$M(n) = 2^i M(n-i) + 2^{i-1} + 2^{i-2} + \cdots + 2 + 1 = 2^i M(n-i) + 2^i - 1.$$

Computation and Reasoning

229

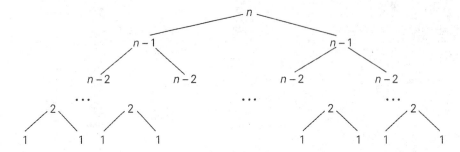

FIGURE 2.5 Tree of recursive calls made by the recursive algorithm for the Tower of Hanoi puzzle

Since the initial condition is specified for $n = 1$, which is achieved for $i = n - 1$, we get the following formula for the solution to recurrence (2.3):

$$M(n) = 2^{n-1}M(n - (n - 1)) + 2^{n-1} - 1$$
$$= 2^{n-1}M(1) + 2^{n-1} - 1 = 2^{n-1} + 2^{n-1} - 1 = 2^n - 1.$$

Thus, we have an exponential algorithm, which will run for an unimaginably long time even for moderate values of n (see Problem 5 in Exercises 2.4). This is not due to the fact that this particular algorithm is poor; in fact, it is not difficult to prove that this is the most efficient algorithm possible for this problem. It is the problem's intrinsic difficulty that makes it so computationally difficult. Still, this example makes an important general point:

> You should be careful with recursive algorithms because their succinctness may mask their inefficiency.

When a recursive algorithm makes more than a single call to itself, it is useful for analysis purposes to construct a tree of its recursive calls. In this tree, nodes correspond to recursive calls, and we can label them with the value of the parameter (or, more generally, parameters) of the calls. For the Tower of Hanoi example, the tree is given in Figure 2.5. By counting the number of nodes in the tree, we can get the total number of calls made by the Tower of Hanoi algorithm:

$$C(n) = \sum_{l=0}^{n-1} 2^l \text{ (where } l \text{ is the level in the tree above)} = 2^n - 1.$$

The number agrees, as it should, with the move count obtained earlier. ∎

EXAMPLE 3   As our next example, we investigate a recursive version of the algorithm discussed at the end of Section 2.3.

ALGORITHM *BinRec(n)*

//Input: A positive decimal integer n
//Output: The number of binary digits in n's binary representation
if $n = 1$ **return** 1
else return $BinRec(\lfloor n/2 \rfloor) + 1$

Let us set up a recurrence and an initial condition for the number of additions $A(n)$ made by the algorithm. The number of additions made in computing $BinRec(\lfloor n/2 \rfloor)$ is $A(\lfloor n/2 \rfloor)$, plus one more addition is made by the algorithm to increase the returned value by 1. This leads to the recurrence

$$A(n) = A(\lfloor n/2 \rfloor) + 1 \text{ for } n > 1. \qquad (2.4)$$

Since the recursive calls end when n is equal to 1 and there are no additions made then, the initial condition is

$$A(1) = 0.$$

The presence of $\lfloor n/2 \rfloor$ in the function's argument makes the method of backward substitutions stumble on values of n that are not powers of 2. Therefore, the standard approach to solving such a recurrence is to solve it only for $n = 2^k$ and then take advantage of the theorem called the *smoothness rule* (see Appendix B) which claims that under very broad assumptions the order of growth observed for $n = 2^k$ gives a correct answer about the order of growth for all values of n. (Alternatively, after getting a solution for powers of 2, we can sometimes finetune this solution to get a formula valid for an arbitrary n.) So let us apply this recipe to our recurrence, which for $n = 2^k$ takes the form

$$A(2^k) = A(2^{k-1}) + 1 \text{ for } k > 0,$$
$$A(2^0) = 0.$$

Now backward substitutions encounter no problems:

$$A(2^k) = A(2^{k-1}) + 1 \qquad \text{substitute } A(2^{k-1}) = A(2^{k-2}) + 1$$
$$= [A(2^{k-2}) + 1] + 1 = A(2^{k-2}) + 2 \quad \text{substitute } A(2^{k-2}) = A(2^{k-3}) + 1$$
$$= [A(2^{k-3}) + 1] + 2 = A(2^{k-3}) + 3 \qquad \cdots$$
$$\cdots$$
$$= A(2^{k-i}) + i$$
$$\cdots$$
$$= A(2^{k-k}) + k.$$

Thus, we end up with

$$A(2^k) = A(1) + k = k$$

or, after returning to the original variable $n = 2^k$ and, hence, $k = \log_2 n$,

$$A(n) = \log_2 n \in \Theta(\log n).$$

Computation and Reasoning

In fact, we can prove (Problem 6 in Exercises 2.4) that the exact solution for an arbitrary value of n is given by just a slightly more refined formula $A(n) = \lfloor \log_2 n \rfloor$.

∎

This section provides an introduction to analysis of recursive algorithms. These techniques will be used throughout the book and expanded further as necessary. In the next section in particular we discuss the Fibonacci numbers; their analysis involves more difficult recurrence relations to be solved by a method different from backward substitutions.

Exercises 2.4

1. Solve the following recurrence relations.

    a. $x(n) = x(n-1) + 5$ for $n > 1$, $x(1) = 0$

    b. $x(n) = 3x(n-1)$ for $n > 1$, $x(1) = 4$

    c. $x(n) = x(n-1) + n$ for $n > 0$, $x(0) = 0$

    d. $x(n) = x(n/2) + n$ for $n > 1$, $x(1) = 1$ (solve for $n = 2^k$)

    e. $x(n) = x(n/3) + 1$ for $n > 1$, $x(1) = 1$ (solve for $n = 3^k$)

2. Set up and solve a recurrence relation for the number of calls made by $F(n)$, the recursive algorithm for computing $n!$.

3. Consider the following recursive algorithm for computing the sum of the first n cubes: $S(n) = 1^3 + 2^3 + \cdots + n^3$.

    ALGORITHM $S(n)$

    //Input: A positive integer n
    //Output: The sum of the first n cubes
    if $n = 1$ **return** 1
    else return $S(n-1) + n * n * n$

    a. Set up and solve a recurrence relation for the number of times the algorithm's basic operation is executed.

    b. How does this algorithm compare with the straightforward nonrecursive algorithm for computing this function?

4. Consider the following recursive algorithm.

    ALGORITHM $Q(n)$

    //Input: A positive integer n
    if $n = 1$ **return** 1
    else return $Q(n-1) + 2 * n - 1$

Computation and Reasoning

232

    a. Set up a recurrence relation for this function's values and solve it to determine what this algorithm computes.

    b. Set up a recurrence relation for the number of multiplications made by this algorithm and solve it.

    c. Set up a recurrence relation for the number of additions/subtractions made by this algorithm and solve it.

5. a. In the original version of the Tower of Hanoi puzzle, as it was published by Edouard Lucas, a French mathematician, in the 1890s, the world will end after 64 disks have been moved from a mystical Tower of Brahma. Estimate the number of years it will take if priests could move one disk per minute. (Assume that priests do not eat, sleep, or die.)

    b. How many moves are made by the ith largest disk ($1 \leq i \leq n$) in this algorithm?

    c. Design a nonrecursive algorithm for the Tower of Hanoi puzzle.

6. a. Prove that the exact number of additions made by the recursive algorithm $BinRec(n)$ for an arbitrary positive decimal integer n is $\lfloor \log_2 n \rfloor$.

    b. Set up a recurrence relation and solve it for the number of additions made by the nonrecursive version of this algorithm (see Section 2.3, Example 4).

7. a. Design a recursive algorithm for computing 2^n for any nonnegative integer n which is based on the formula: $2^n = 2^{n-1} + 2^{n-1}$.

    b. Set up a recurrence relation for the number of additions made by the algorithm and solve it.

    c. Draw a tree of recursive calls for this algorithm and count the number of calls made by the algorithm.

    d. Is it a good algorithm for solving this problem?

8. Consider the following recursive algorithm.

ALGORITHM $Min1(A[0..n-1])$

    //Input: An array $A[0..n-1]$ of real numbers
    if $n = 1$ **return** $A[0]$
    else $temp \leftarrow Min1(A[0..n-2])$
        if $temp \leq A[n-1]$ **return** $temp$
        else return $A[n-1]$

    a. What does this algorithm compute?

    b. Set up a recurrence relation for the algorithm's basic operation count and solve it.

Computation and Reasoning

9. Consider another algorithm for solving the problem of Exercise 8, which recursively divides an array into two halves: call $Min2(A[0..n-1])$ where

    ALGORITHM $Min2(A[l..r])$

    > **if** $l = r$ **return** $A[l]$
    > **else** $temp1 \leftarrow Min2(A[l..\lfloor(l+r)/2\rfloor])$
    > $temp2 \leftarrow Min2(A[\lfloor(l+r)/2\rfloor+1..r])$
    >   **if** $temp1 \leq temp2$ **return** $temp1$
    >   **else return** $temp2$

    a. Set up a recurrence relation for the algorithm's basic operation and solve it.

    b. Which of the algorithms *Min1* or *Min2* is faster? Can you suggest an algorithm for the problem they solve that would be more efficient than both of them?

10. The determinant of an n-by-n matrix

$$
A = \begin{bmatrix} a_{11} & & a_{1n} \\ a_{21} & & a_{2n} \\ \vdots & & \\ a_{n1} & & a_{nn} \end{bmatrix},
$$

denoted det A, can be defined as a_{11} for $n = 1$ and, for $n > 1$, by the recursive formula

$$
\det A = \sum_{j=1}^{n} s_j a_{1j} \det A_j,
$$

where s_j is +1 if j is odd and -1 if j is even, a_{1j} is the element in row 1 and column j, and A_j is the $(n-1)$-by-$(n-1)$ matrix obtained from matrix A by deleting its row 1 and column j.

    a. Set up a recurrence relation for the number of multiplications made by the algorithm implementing this recursive definition.

    b. Without solving the recurrence, what can you say about the solution's order of growth as compared to $n!$?

2.5   Example: Fibonacci Numbers

In this section, we consider the *Fibonacci numbers*, a famous sequence

$$0,\ 1,\ 1,\ 2,\ 3,\ 5,\ 8,\ 13,\ 21,\ 34,\ \ldots \tag{2.5}$$

that can be defined by the simple recurrence

$$F(n) = F(n-1) + F(n-2) \text{ for } n > 1 \tag{2.6}$$

Computation and Reasoning

and two initial conditions

$$F(0) = 0, \; F(1) = 1. \tag{2.7}$$

The Fibonacci numbers were introduced by Leonardo Fibonacci in 1202 as a solution to a problem about the size of a rabbit population. Many more examples of Fibonacci-like numbers have since been discovered in the natural world, and they have even been used in predicting prices of stocks and commodities. There are some interesting applications of the Fibonacci numbers in computer science as well. For example, worst-case inputs for Euclid's algorithm happen to be consecutive elements of the Fibonacci sequence. Our discussion goals are quite limited here, however. First, we find an explicit formula for the nth Fibonacci number $F(n)$, and then we briefly discuss algorithms for computing it.

Explicit Formula for the *n*th Fibonacci Number

If we try to apply the method of backward substitutions to solve recurrence (2.6), we will fail to get an easily discernible pattern. Instead, let us take advantage of a theorem that describes solutions to a *homogeneous second-order linear recurrence with constant coefficients*

$$ax(n) + bx(n-1) + cx(n-2) = 0, \tag{2.8}$$

where a, b, and c are some fixed real numbers ($a \neq 0$) called the coefficients of the recurrence and $x(n)$ is an unknown sequence to be found. According to this theorem—see Theorem 1 in Appendix B—recurrence (2.8) has an infinite number of solutions that can be obtained by one of the three formulas. Which of the three formulas applies for a particular case depends on the number of real roots of the quadratic equation with the same coefficients as recurrence (2.8):

$$ar^2 + br + c = 0. \tag{2.9}$$

Quite logically, equation (2.9) is called the *characteristic equation* for recurrence (2.8).

Let us apply this theorem to the case of the Fibonacci numbers. To do so, recurrence (2.6) needs to be rewritten as

$$F(n) - F(n-1) - F(n-2) = 0. \tag{2.10}$$

Its characteristic equation is

$$r^2 - r - 1 = 0,$$

with the roots

$$r_{1,2} = \frac{1 \pm \sqrt{1 - 4(-1)}}{2} = \frac{1 \pm \sqrt{5}}{2}.$$

Computation and Reasoning

235

Since this characteristic equation has two distinct real roots, we have to use the formula indicated in Case 1 of Theorem 1:

$$F(n) = \alpha \left(\frac{1 + \sqrt{5}}{2} \right)^n + \beta \left(\frac{1 - \sqrt{5}}{2} \right)^n.$$

So far, we have ignored initial conditions (2.7). Now we take advantage of them to find specific values of parameters α and β. We do this by substituting 0 and 1—the values of n for which the initial conditions are given—into the last formula and equating the results to 0 and 1 (the values of $F(0)$ and $F(1)$ according to (2.7)), respectively:

$$F(0) = \alpha \left(\frac{1+\sqrt{5}}{2} \right)^0 + \beta \left(\frac{1-\sqrt{5}}{2} \right)^0 = 0$$

$$F(1) = \alpha \left(\frac{1+\sqrt{5}}{2} \right)^1 + \beta \left(\frac{1-\sqrt{5}}{2} \right)^1 = 1.$$

After some standard algebraic simplifications, we get the following system of two linear equations in two unknowns α and β:

$$\begin{aligned} \alpha \quad + \quad & \beta \quad = \quad 0 \\ \left(\frac{1+\sqrt{5}}{2} \right)\alpha \quad + \quad & \left(\frac{1-\sqrt{5}}{2} \right)\beta \quad = \quad 1. \end{aligned}$$

Solving the system (e.g., by substituting $\beta = -\alpha$ into the second equation and solving the equation obtained for α), we get the values $\alpha = 1/\sqrt{5}$ and $\beta = -1/\sqrt{5}$ for the unknowns. Thus,

$$F(n) = \frac{1}{\sqrt{5}} \left(\frac{1 + \sqrt{5}}{2} \right)^n - \frac{1}{\sqrt{5}} \left(\frac{1 - \sqrt{5}}{2} \right)^n = \frac{1}{\sqrt{5}}(\phi^n - \hat{\phi}^n), \qquad \textbf{(2.11)}$$

where $\phi = (1 + \sqrt{5})/2 \approx 1.61803$ and $\hat{\phi} = -1/\phi \approx -0.61803$.[6] It is hard to believe that formula (2.11), which includes arbitrary integer powers of irrational numbers, yields nothing else but all the elements of Fibonacci sequence (2.5), but it does!

One of the benefits of formula (2.11) is that it immediately implies that $F(n)$ grows exponentially (remember Fibonacci's rabbits?), i.e., $F(n) \in \Theta(\phi^n)$. It follows from the observation that $\hat{\phi}$ is between -1 and 0, and, hence, $\hat{\phi}^n$ gets infinitely small as n goes to infinity. In fact, one can prove that the impact of the second term $\frac{1}{\sqrt{5}}\hat{\phi}^n$ on the value of $F(n)$ can be obtained by rounding off the value of the first term to the nearest integer. In other words, for every nonnegative integer n,

$$F(n) = \frac{1}{\sqrt{5}}\phi^n \text{ rounded to the nearest integer.} \qquad \textbf{(2.12)}$$

---

6. Constant ϕ is known as the **golden ratio**. Since antiquity, it has been considered the most pleasing ratio of a rectangle's two sides to the human eye and might have been consciously used by ancient architects and sculptors.

Computation and Reasoning

Algorithms for Computing Fibonacci Numbers

Though the Fibonacci numbers have many fascinating properties, we limit our discussion to a few remarks about algorithms for computing them. Actually, the sequence grows so fast that it is the size of the numbers rather than a time-efficient method for computing them that should be of primary concern here. Also, for the sake of simplicity, we consider such operations as additions and multiplications at unit cost in the algorithms that follow. Since the Fibonacci numbers grow infinitely large (and grow rapidly), a more detailed analysis than the one offered here is warranted. These caveats notwithstanding, the algorithms we outline and their analysis are useful examples for a student of design and analysis of algorithms.

To begin with, we can use recurrence (2.6) and initial condition (2.7) for the obvious recursive algorithm for computing $F(n)$.

ALGORITHM $F(n)$

//Computes the nth Fibonacci number recursively by using its definition
//Input: A nonnegative integer n
//Output: The nth Fibonacci number
if $n \leq 1$ **return** n
else return $F(n-1) + F(n-2)$

Before embarking on its formal analysis, can you tell whether this is an efficient algorithm? Well, we need to do a formal analysis anyway. The algorithm's basic operation is clearly addition, so let $A(n)$ be the number of additions performed by the algorithm in computing $F(n)$. Then the numbers of additions needed for computing $F(n-1)$ and $F(n-2)$ are $A(n-1)$ and $A(n-2)$, respectively, and the algorithm needs one more addition to compute their sum. Thus, we get the following recurrence for $A(n)$:

$$A(n) = A(n-1) + A(n-2) + 1 \text{ for } n > 1, \qquad \textbf{(2.13)}$$
$$A(0) = 0, \ A(1) = 0.$$

The recurrence $A(n) - A(n-1) - A(n-2) = 1$ is quite similar to recurrence (2.10) but its right-hand side is not equal to zero. Such recurrences are called **_inhomogeneous recurrences_**. There are general techniques for solving inhomogeneous recurrences (see Appendix B or any textbook on discrete mathematics), but for this particular recurrence, a special trick leads to a faster solution. We can reduce our inhomogeneous recurrence to a homogeneous one by rewriting it as

$$[A(n) + 1] - [A(n-1) + 1] - [A(n-2) + 1] = 0$$

and substituting $B(n) = A(n) + 1$:

$$B(n) - B(n-1) - B(n-2) = 0$$
$$B(0) = 1, \quad B(1) = 1.$$

Computation and Reasoning

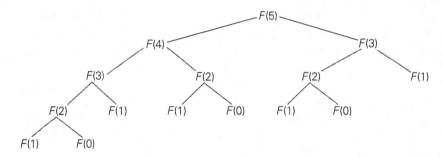

FIGURE 2.6 Tree of recursive calls for computing the Fibonacci number for $n = 5$

This homogeneous recurrence can be solved exactly in the same manner as recurrence (2.10) was solved to find an explicit formula for $F(n)$. But it can actually be avoided by noting that $B(n)$ is, in fact, the same recurrence as $F(n)$ except that it starts with two ones and thus runs one step ahead of $F(n)$. So $B(n) = F(n + 1)$, and

$$A(n) = B(n) - 1 = F(n + 1) - 1 = \frac{1}{\sqrt{5}} (\phi^{n+1} - \hat{\phi}^{n+1}) - 1.$$

Hence, $A(n) \in \Theta(\phi^n)$ and, if we measure the size of n by the number of bits $b = \lfloor \log_2 n \rfloor + 1$ in its binary representation, the efficiency class will be even worse, namely doubly exponential.

The poor efficiency class of the algorithm could be anticipated by the nature of recurrence (2.13). Indeed, it contains two recursive calls with the sizes of smaller instances only slightly smaller than size n. (Have you encountered such a situation before?) We can also see the reason behind the algorithm's inefficiency by looking at a recursive tree of calls tracing the algorithm's execution. An example of such a tree for $n = 5$ is given in Figure 2.6. Note that the same values of the function are being evaluated again and again, which is clearly extremely inefficient.

We can obtain a much faster algorithm by simply computing the successive elements of the Fibonacci sequence iteratively, as is done in the following algorithm.

ALGORITHM   *Fib*(n)

    //Computes the nth Fibonacci number iteratively by using its definition
    //Input: A nonnegative integer n
    //Output: The nth Fibonacci number
    $F[0] \leftarrow 0$; $F[1] \leftarrow 1$
    for $i \leftarrow 2$ **to** n **do**
        $F[i] \leftarrow F[i - 1] + F[i - 2]$
    return $F[n]$

This algorithm clearly makes $n - 1$ additions. Hence, it is linear as a function of n and "only" exponential as a function of the number of bits b in n's binary representation. Note that using an extra array for storing all the preceding elements of the Fibonacci sequence can be avoided: storing just two values is necessary to accomplish the task (see Problem 6 in Exercises 2.5).

The third alternative for computing the nth Fibonacci number lies in using formula (2.12). The efficiency of the algorithm will obviously be determined by the efficiency of an exponentiation algorithm used for computing ϕ^n. If it is done by simply multiplying ϕ by itself $n - 1$ times, the algorithm will be in $\Theta(n) = \Theta(2^b)$. There are faster algorithms for the exponentiation problem. For example, we will discuss $\Theta(\log n) = \Theta(b)$ algorithms for this problem in Chapters 5 and 6. Note also that special care should be exercised in implementing this approach to computing the nth Fibonacci number. Since all its intermediate results are irrational numbers, we would have to make sure that their approximations in the computer are accurate enough so that the final round-off yields a correct result.

Finally, there exists a $\Theta(\log n)$ algorithm for computing the nth Fibonacci number that manipulates only integers. It is based on the equality

$$\begin{bmatrix} F(n-1) & F(n) \\ F(n) & F(n+1) \end{bmatrix} = \begin{bmatrix} 0 & 1 \\ 1 & 1 \end{bmatrix}^n \quad \text{for } n \geq 1$$

and an efficient way of computing matrix powers.

Exercises 2.5

1. Find a Web site dedicated to applications of the Fibonacci numbers and study it.

2. Check by direct substitutions that the function $\frac{1}{\sqrt{5}}(\phi^n - \hat{\phi}^n)$ indeed satisfies recurrence (2.6) for every $n > 1$ and initial conditions (2.7) for $n = 0$ and 1.

3. The maximum values of the Java primitive types int and long are $2^{31} - 1$ and $2^{63} - 1$, respectively. Find the smallest n for which the nth Fibonacci number is not going to fit in a memory allocated for
   a. the type int.   **b.** the type long.

4. Find the number of different ways to climb an n-stage ladder when each step is either one or two stages. (For example, a 3-stage ladder can be climbed three ways: 1-1-1, 1-2, and 2-1.) [Tuc80]

5. Consider the recursive definition-based algorithm for computing the nth Fibonacci number $F(n)$. Let $C(n)$ and $Z(n)$ be the number of times $F(1)$ and $F(0)$, respectively, are computed. Prove that
   a. $C(n) = F(n)$ **b.** $Z(n) = F(n-1)$.

6. Improve algorithm *Fib* so that it requires only $\Theta(1)$ space.

Computation and Reasoning

7. Prove the equality

$$\begin{bmatrix} F(n-1) & F(n) \\ F(n) & F(n+1) \end{bmatrix} = \begin{bmatrix} 0 & 1 \\ 1 & 1 \end{bmatrix}^{n} \quad \text{for } n \geq 1.$$

8. How many modulo divisions are made by Euclid's algorithm on two consecutive Fibonacci numbers $F(n)$ and $F(n-1)$ as the algorithm's input?

9. a. Prove *Cassini's identity*:

$$F(n+1)F(n-1) - [F(n)]^2 = (-1)^n \text{ for every } n \geq 1.$$

b. Consider the following paradox, which is based on Cassini's identity. Take an 8-by-8 chessboard (more generally, any $F(n)$-by-$F(n)$ board divided into $[F(n)]^2$ squares). Cut it into two trapezoids and two triangles as shown in the left portion of the figure below. Then reassemble it as shown in the right portion of the figure. The area of the left rectangle is $8 \times 8 = 64$ squares, while the area of the right rectangle is $13 \times 5 = 65$ squares. Explain the paradox.

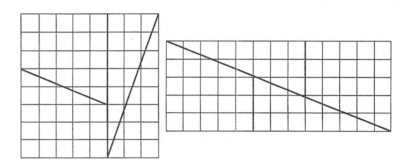

10. In a language of your choice, implement three algorithms for computing the last five digits of the nth Fibonacci number that are based on (a) the recursive definition-based algorithm $F(n)$; (b) the iterative definition-based algorithm $Fib(n)$; (c) the space-efficient version of $Fib(n)$. Do an experiment to find the largest value of n for which your programs run under 1 minute on your computer.

2.6 Empirical Analysis of Algorithms

In Sections 2.3 and 2.4, we saw how algorithms, both nonrecursive and recursive, can be analyzed mathematically. Though these techniques can be applied successfully to many simple algorithms, the power of mathematics, even when enhanced

Computation and Reasoning

240

with more advanced techniques (see [SF96], [PB84], [GKP94], and [GK82]), is far from limitless. In fact, even some seemingly simple algorithms have proved to be very difficult to analyze with mathematical precision and certainty. As we pointed out in Section 2.2, this is especially true for average-case analysis.

The principal alternative to the mathematical analysis of an algorithm's efficiency is its empirical analysis. This approach implies the steps spelled out in the following plan.

A General Plan for Empirical Analysis of Algorithm Efficiency

1. Understand the experiment's purpose.
2. Decide on the efficiency metric M to be measured and the measurement unit (an operation's count vs. a time unit).
3. Decide on characteristics of the input sample (its range, size, and so on).
4. Prepare a program implementing the algorithm (or algorithms) for the experimentation.
5. Generate a sample of inputs.
6. Run the algorithm (or algorithms) on the sample's inputs and record the data observed.
7. Analyze the data obtained.

Let us discuss these steps one at a time. There are several different goals one can pursue in analyzing algorithms empirically. They include checking the accuracy of a theoretical assertion about the algorithm's efficiency, comparing the efficiency of several algorithms for solving the same problem or different implementations of the same algorithm, developing a hypothesis about the algorithm's efficiency class, and ascertaining the efficiency of the program implementing the algorithm on a particular machine. Obviously, an experiment's design should depend on the question the experimenter seeks to answer.

In particular, the experiment's goal should influence, if not dictate, how the algorithm's efficiency is to be measured. The first alternative is to insert a counter (or counters) in a program implementing the algorithm to count the number of times the algorithm's basic operation is executed. This is usually a straightforward operation; you should only be mindful of the possibility that the basic operation is located in several places in the program and all its executions need to be accounted for. As straightforward as this task usually is, you should always test the modified program to ensure that it works correctly, in terms of both the problem it solves and the counts it yields.

The second alternative is to time the program implementing the algorithm in question. The easiest way to do this is to use a system's command, such as the `time` command in UNIX. Alternatively, we can measure the running time of a code fragment by asking for the system's time right before the fragment's start (t_{start}) and just after its completion (t_{finish}) and then computing the difference between the two ($t_{finish} - t_{start}$).[7] In C and C++, you can use the function clock for this purpose; in Java, the method currentTimeMillis() in the System class is available.

It is important to keep several facts in mind, however. First, a system's time is typically not very accurate, and you might get somewhat different results on repeated runs of the same program on the same inputs. An obvious remedy is to make several such measurements and then take their average (or the median) as the sample's observation point. Second, given the high speed of modern computers, the running time may fail to register at all and be reported as zero. The standard trick to overcome this obstacle is to run the program in an extra loop many times, measure the total running time, and then divide it by the number of the loop's repetitions. Third, on a computer running under a time-sharing system (such as UNIX), the reported time may include the time spent by the CPU on other programs, which obviously defeats the purpose of the experiment. Therefore you should take care to ask the system for the time devoted specifically to execution of your program. (In UNIX, this time is called the "user time," and it is automatically provided by the time command.)

Thus, measuring the physical running time has several disadvantages, both principal (dependence on a particular machine being the most important of them) and technical, not shared by counting a basic operation's executions. On the other hand, the physical running time provides very specific information about an algorithm's performance in a particular computing environment, which can be of more importance to the experimenter than, say, the algorithm's asymptotic efficiency class. In addition, measuring time spent on different segments of a program can pinpoint a bottleneck in the program's performance that can be missed by an abstract deliberation about the algorithm's basic operation. Getting such data—called *profiling*—is an important resource in the empirical analysis of an algorithm's running time; the data in question can usually be obtained from the system's tools available in most computing environments.

Whether you decide to measure the efficiency by basic operation counting or by time clocking, you will need to decide on a sample of inputs for the experiment. Often, the goal is to use a sample representing a "typical" input; so the challenge is to understand what a "typical" input is. For some classes of algorithms—e.g., algorithms for the traveling salesman problem discussed later in the book—researchers have developed a set of instances they use for benchmarking. But much more often than not, an input sample has to be developed by the

---

7.   If the system time is given in units called "ticks," the difference should be divided by a constant indicating the number of ticks per time unit.

Computation and Reasoning

experimenter. Typically, you will have to make decisions about the sample size (it is sensible to start with a relatively small sample and increase it later if necessary), the range of input sizes in your sample (typically neither trivially small, nor excessively huge), and a procedure for generating inputs in the range chosen. On the last issue, the sizes can either adhere to some pattern (e.g., 1000, 2000, 3000, ..., 10,000 or 500, 1000, 2000, 4000, ..., 128000) or be generated randomly (e.g., uniformly distributed between the smallest and largest values).

The principal advantage of size changing according to a pattern is that its impact is easier to analyze. For example, if a sample's sizes are generated by doubling, we can compute the ratios $M(2n)/M(n)$ of the observed metric M (the count or the time) and see whether the ratios exhibit a behavior typical of algorithms in one of the basic efficiency classes (see Section 2.2). The major disadvantage of nonrandom sizes is the possibility that the algorithm under investigation exhibits atypical behavior on the sample chosen. For example, if all the sizes in a sample are even and an algorithm under investigation runs much more slowly on odd-size inputs, the empirical results will be quite misleading.

Another important issue concerning sizes in an experiment's sample is whether several instances of the same size should be included. If you expect the observed metric to vary considerably on instances of the same size, it is probably wise to include several instances for every size in the sample. (There are well-developed methods in statistics to help the experimenter make such decisions. You will find no shortage of books on this subject.) Of course, if several instances of the same size are included in the sample, the averages or medians of the observed values for each size should be computed and investigated instead of or in addition to individual sample points.

Much more often than not, an empirical analysis of an algorithm's efficiency requires generating random numbers. Even if we decide to use a pattern for input sizes, we typically want instances themselves generated randomly. Generating random numbers on a digital computer is known to present a difficult problem because, in principle, the problem can be solved only approximately. This is the reason computer scientists prefer to call such numbers *pseudorandom*. As a practical matter, the easiest and most natural way of getting such numbers is to take advantage of a random number generator available in computer language libraries. Typically, its output will be a value of a (pseudo)random variable uniformly distributed in the interval between 0 and 1. If a different (pseudo)random variable is desired, an appropriate transformation needs to be made. For example, if x is a continuous random variable uniformly distributed on the interval $0 \le x < 1$, the variable $y = l + \lfloor x(r - l) \rfloor$ will be uniformly distributed among the integer values between integers l and $r - 1$ where l and r are two integers $(l < r)$.

Alternatively, you can implement one of several known algorithms for generating (pseudo)random numbers. The most widely used and thoroughly studied of such algorithms is the so-called *linear congruential method*.

Computation and Reasoning

ALGORITHM *Random(n, m, seed, a, b)*

//Generates a sequence of n pseudorandom numbers according to the linear
//congruential method
//Input: A positive integer n and positive integer parameters $m, seed, a, b$
//Output: A sequence $r_1, \ldots, r_n$ of n pseudorandom integers uniformly
//   distributed among integer values between 0 and $m - 1$
//Note: Pseudorandom numbers between 0 and 1 can be obtained
//   by treating the integers generated as digits after the decimal point
$r_0 \leftarrow seed$
for $i \leftarrow 1$ **to** n **do**
    $r_i \leftarrow (a * r_{i-1} + b) \bmod m$

The simplicity of the algorithm's code is misleading because the devil lies in the details of choosing the algorithm's parameters. Here is a partial list of recommendations based on the results of a sophisticated mathematical analysis (see [KnuII], pp. 184–185, for details): *seed* may be chosen arbitrarily and is often set to the current date and time; m should be large and may be conveniently taken as 2^w where w is the computer's word size; a should be selected as an integer between $0.01m$ and $0.99m$ with no particular pattern in its digits but such that $a \bmod 8 = 5$; the value of b can be chosen as 1.

The empirical data obtained as the result of an experiment need to be recorded and then presented for an analysis. Data can be represented in a table or graphically in a ***scatterplot***, that is by points in a Cartesian coordinate system. It is a good idea to use both these options whenever it is feasible because both methods have their unique strengths and weaknesses.

The principal advantage of tabulated data lies in the opportunity to manipulate it easily. For example, we can compute the ratios $M(n)/g(n)$ where $g(n)$ is a candidate to represent the efficiency class of the algorithm in question. If the algorithm is indeed in $\Theta(g(n))$, most likely these ratios will converge to some positive constant as n gets large. (Note that careless novices sometimes assume that this constant must be 1, which is, of course, incorrect according to the definition of $\Theta(g(n))$.) Or we can compute the ratios $M(2n)/M(n)$ and see how the running time reacts to doubling of its input size. As we discussed in Section 2.2, such ratios should change only slightly for logarithmic algorithms and most likely converge to 2, 4, and 8 for linear, quadratic, and cubic algorithms, respectively—to name the most obvious and convenient cases.

On the other hand, the form of a scatterplot may also help in ascertaining the algorithm's probable efficiency class. For a logarithmic algorithm, the scatterplot will have a concave shape (Figure 2.7a); this fact distinguishes it from all the other basic efficiency classes. For a linear algorithm, the points will tend to aggregate around a straight line or, more generally, to be contained between two straight lines (Figure 2.7b). Scatterplots of functions in $\Theta(n \lg n)$ and $\Theta(n^2)$ will

Computation and Reasoning

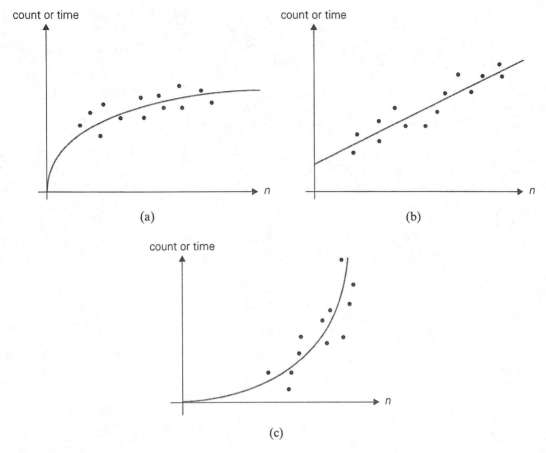

count or time

count or time

count or time

(a)

(b)

(c)

FIGURE 2.7 Typical scatterplots: (a) logarithmic; (b) linear; (c) one of the convex functions

have a convex shape (Figure 2.7c), making them difficult to differentiate. A scatterplot of a cubic algorithm will also have a convex shape but it will show a much more rapid increase in the metric's values. An exponential algorithm will most probably require a logarithmic scale for the vertical axis, in which the values of $\log_a M(n)$ rather than those of $M(n)$ are plotted. (The logarithm's base that is used most often is 2 or 10.) In such a coordinate system, a scatterplot of a truly exponential algorithm should resemble a linear function because $M(n) \approx ca^n$ implies $\log_b M(n) \approx \log_b c + n \log_b a$.

One of the possible applications of the empirical analysis is to attempt predicting the algorithm's performance on a sample size not included in the experiment's sample. For example, if we observe that the ratios $M(n)/g(n)$ are close to some constant c for instances in the sample, we can approximate $M(n)$ by the product

Computation and Reasoning

245

$cg(n)$ for other values of n. Though this approach is sensible, it should be used with caution, especially for values of n that are outside of the range of the sample's values. (Mathematicians call such predictions *extrapolation* as opposed to *interpolation*, which deals with values within the sample's range.) In particular, no claims about accuracy of estimates obtained in this fashion can usually be made. Of course, we can also try unleashing the standard techniques of statistical data analysis and prediction. Note, however, that the majority of such techniques are based on specific probabilistic assumptions that may or may not be valid for the experimental data in question.

It seems appropriate to end this section by pointing out the basic differences between mathematical and empirical analyses of algorithms. The principal strength of the mathematical analysis is its independence of specific inputs; its principal weakness is its limited applicability, especially for investigating the average-case efficiency. The principal strength of the empirical analysis lies in its applicability to any algorithm, but its results can depend on the particular sample of instances and the computer used in the experiment.

----------- Exercises 2.6 -----------

1. Consider a well-known sorting algorithm (we shall study it more closely later in the book) with a counter inserted to count the number of key comparisons.

   ALGORITHM   *SortAnalysis*$(A[0..n-1])$
       //Input: An array $A[0..n-1]$ of n orderable elements
       //Output: The total number of key comparisons made
       $count \leftarrow 0$
       for $i \leftarrow 1$ **to** $n-1$ **do**
           $v \leftarrow A[i]$
           $j \leftarrow i-1$
           while $j \geq 0$ **and** $A[j] > v$ **do**
               $count \leftarrow count + 1$
               $A[j+1] \leftarrow A[j]$
               $j \leftarrow j-1$
           $A[j+1] \leftarrow v$
       return *count*

   Is the comparison counter inserted in the right place? If you believe it is, prove it; if you believe it is not, make an appropriate correction.

2. **a.** Run the program of Problem 1, with a properly inserted counter (or counters) for the number of key comparisons, on 20 random arrays of sizes 1000, 1500, 2000, 2500, . . . , 9000, 9500.

Computation and Reasoning

   b. Analyze the data obtained to form a hypothesis about the algorithm's average-case efficiency.

   c. Estimate the number of key comparisons we should expect for a randomly generated array of size 10,000 sorted by the same algorithm.

3. Repeat Problem 2 by measuring the program's running time in milliseconds.

4. Hypothesize a likely efficiency class of an algorithm based on the following empirical observations of its basic operation's count:

size	1000	2000	3000	4000	5000	6000	7000	8000	9000	10000
count	11,966	24,303	39,992	53,010	67,272	78,692	91,274	113,063	129,799	140,538

5. What scale transformation will make a logarithmic scatterplot look like a linear one?

6. How can we distinguish a scatterplot for an algorithm in $\Theta(\lg \lg n)$ from a scatterplot for an algorithm in $\Theta(\lg n)$?

7. **a.** Find empirically the largest number of divisions made by Euclid's algorithm for computing $\gcd(m, n)$ for $1 \le n \le m \le 100$.

   b. For each positive integer k, find empirically the smallest pair of integers $1 \le n \le m \le 100$ for which Euclid's algorithm needs to make k divisions in order to find $\gcd(m, n)$.

8. The average-case efficiency of Euclid's algorithm on inputs of size n can be measured by the average number of divisions $D_{avg}(n)$ made by the algorithm in computing $\gcd(n, 1), \gcd(n, 2), \ldots, \gcd(n, n)$. For example,

$$D_{avg}(5) = \frac{1}{5}(1 + 2 + 3 + 2 + 1) = 1.8.$$

   Produce a scatterplot of $D_{avg}(n)$ and indicate the algorithm's likely average-case efficiency class.

9. Run an experiment to ascertain the efficiency class of the sieve of Eratosthenes (see Section 1.1).

10. Run a timing experiment for the three algorithms for computing $\gcd(m, n)$ presented in Section 1.1.

2.7 Algorithm Visualization

In addition to the mathematical and empirical analyses of algorithms, there is yet a third way to study algorithms. It is called *algorithm visualization* and can be defined as the use of images to convey some useful information about algorithms.

Computation and Reasoning

That information can be a visual illustration of an algorithm's operation, of its performance on different kinds of inputs, or of its execution speed versus that of other algorithms for the same problem. To accomplish this goal, an algorithm visualization uses graphic elements (points, line segments, two- or three-dimensional bars, and so on) to represent some "interesting events" in the algorithm's operation.

There are two principal variations of algorithm visualization:

- static algorithm visualization
- dynamic algorithm visualization, also called *algorithm animation*.

Static algorithm visualization shows an algorithm's progress through a series of still images. Algorithm animation, on the other hand, shows a continuous movie-like presentation of an algorithm's operations. Animation is an arguably more sophisticated option, and it is, of course, much more difficult to implement.

Early efforts in the area of algorithm visualization go back to the 1970s. The watershed event happened in 1981 with the appearance of the algorithm visualization classic, a 30-minute color sound film titled *Sorting Out Sorting*. The film was produced at the University of Toronto by Ronald Baecker with the assistance of D. Sherman [Bae81, Bae98]. It contained visualizations of nine well-known sorting algorithms (more than half of them will be discussed later in the book) and provided quite a convincing demonstration of their relative speeds.

The success of *Sorting Out Sorting* made sorting algorithms a perennial favorite for algorithm animation. Indeed, the sorting problem lends itself quite naturally to visual presentation via vertical or horizontal bars or sticks of different heights or lengths, which are rearranged according to their sizes (Figure 2.8). This presentation is convenient, however, only for illustrating actions of a typical sorting algorithm on small inputs. For larger files, *Sorting Out Sorting* used the ingenious idea of presenting data by a scatterplot of points on a coordinate plane, with the first coordinate representing an item's position in the file and the second one representing the item's value; with such a representation, the process of sorting looks like a transformation of a "random" scatterplot of points into the points along a frame's diagonal (Figure 2.9). In addition, most sorting algorithms work by comparing and exchanging two given items at a time—an event that can be animated relatively easily.

Since the appearance of *Sorting Out Sorting*, a great number of algorithm animations have been created. They range in scope from one particular algorithm to a group of algorithms for the same problem (e.g., sorting) or the same application area (e.g., geometric algorithms) and general-purpose animation systems. The most widely known of the general-purpose systems include BALSA [BS84], TANGO [Sta90], and ZEUS [Bro91]; a comparative review of their features along with those of nine other packages can be found in [PBS93]. A good general-purpose animation system should allow a user to not only watch and interact with existing animations of a wide variety of algorithms; they should also provide facilities for creating new animations. Experience has shown that creating such systems is a difficult but not impossible task.

Computation and Reasoning

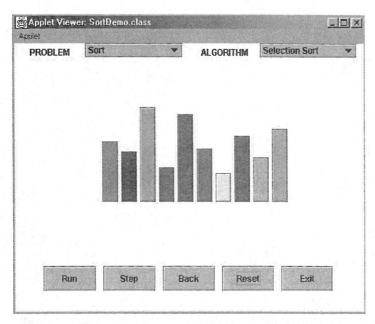

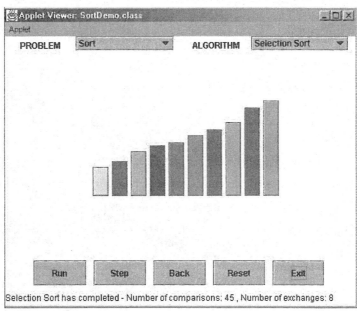

FIGURE 2.8 Initial and final screens of a typical visualization of a sorting algorithm using the bar representation

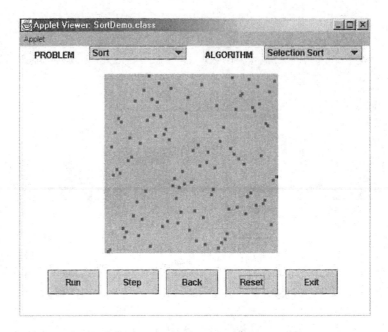

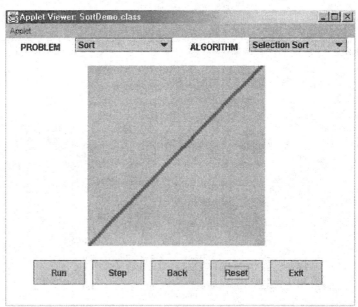

FIGURE 2.9 Initial and final screens of a typical visualization of a sorting algorithm using the scatterplot representation

Computation and Reasoning

The appearance of Java and the World Wide Web has given a new impetus to algorithm animation. You are advised to start an exploration with an up-to-date site containing a collection of links to sites devoted to algorithm animation. Since the Web world is notorious for its instability, no specific Web addresses appear here; a search for the phrase "algorithm animation" or "algorithm visualization" with a good search engine should do the trick. While you peruse and evaluate different algorithm animations, you may want to keep in mind the "ten commandments of algorithm animations." This list of desirable features of an animation's user interface was suggested by Peter Gloor [Glo98], who was a principal developer of Animated Algorithms, another well-known algorithm visualization system:

1. Be consistent.
2. Be interactive.
3. Be clear and concise.
4. Be forgiving to the user.
5. Adapt to the knowledge level of the user.
6. Emphasize the visual component.
7. Keep the user interested.
8. Incorporate both symbolic and iconic representations.
9. Include algorithm's analysis (run statistics) and comparisons with other algorithms for the same problem.
10. Include execution history.

There are two principal applications of algorithm visualization: research and education. The application to education seeks to help students learning algorithms. Potential benefits for researchers are based on expectations that algorithm visualization may help uncover some unknown features of algorithms. For example, one researcher used a visualization of the recursive Tower of Hanoi algorithm in which odd- and even-numbered disks were two different colors. He noticed that two disks of the same color never came in direct contact during the algorithm's execution. This observation helped him in developing a better nonrecursive version of the classic algorithm. Though some successes in both education and research applications have been reported, they are not as impressive as one might expect. Experience has shown that creating sophisticated software systems is not going to be enough. A deeper understanding of human perception of images will be required before the true potential of algorithm animation is fulfilled.

SUMMARY

■ There are two kinds of algorithm efficiency: time efficiency and space efficiency. *Time efficiency* indicates how fast the algorithm runs; *space efficiency* deals with the extra space it requires.

■ An algorithm's time efficiency is principally measured as a function of its input size by counting the number of times its basic operation is executed. A *basic operation* is the operation that contributes most toward running time. Typically, it is the most time-consuming operation in the algorithm's innermost loop.

■ For some algorithms, the running time may differ considerably for inputs of the same size, leading to *worst-case* efficiency, *average-case* efficiency, and *best-case* efficiency.

■ The established framework for analyzing an algorithm's time efficiency is primarily grounded in the order of growth of the algorithm's running time as its input size goes to infinity.

■ The notations O, Ω, and Θ are used to indicate and compare the asymptotic orders of growth of functions expressing algorithm efficiencies.

■ The efficiencies of a large number of algorithms fall into the following few classes: *constant, logarithmic, linear, "n-log-n," quadratic, cubic,* and *exponential*.

■ The main tool for analyzing the time efficiency of a nonrecursive algorithm is to set up a sum expressing the number of executions of its basic operation and ascertain the sum's order of growth.

■ The main tool for analyzing the time efficiency of a recursive algorithm is to set up a recurrence relation expressing the number of executions of its basic operation and ascertain the solution's order of growth.

■ Succinctness of a recursive algorithm may mask its inefficiency.

■ The *Fibonacci numbers* are an important sequence of integers in which every element is equal to the sum of its two immediate predecessors. There are several algorithms for computing the Fibonacci numbers with drastically different efficiencies.

■ Empirical analysis of an algorithm is performed by running a program implementing the algorithm on a sample of inputs and analyzing the data observed (the basic operation's count or physical running time). This often involves generating pseudorandom numbers. The applicability to any algorithm is the principal strength of this approach; the dependence of results on the particular computer and instance sample is its main weakness.

■ *Algorithm visualization* is the use of images to convey useful information about algorithms. The two principal variations of algorithm visualization are static algorithm visualization and dynamic algorithm visualization (also called *algorithm animation*).

Computation and Reasoning

3

Brute Force

Science is as far removed from brute force as this sword from a crowbar.
—Edward Lytton (1803–1873), *Leila*, Book II, Chapter I

Doing a thing well is often a waste of time.
—Robert Byrne, master pool and billiards player and writer

After discussing the framework and methods for algorithm analysis in the preceding chapter of the book, we are ready to embark on a discussion of algorithm design techniques. Each of the next seven chapters is devoted to a particular design strategy. The subject of this chapter is brute force—the simplest of the design strategies. It can be described as follows:

> **Brute force** is a straightforward approach to solving a problem, usually directly based on the problem's statement and definitions of the concepts involved.

The "force" implied by the strategy's definition is that of a computer and not that of one's intellect. "Just do it!" would be another way to describe the prescription of the brute-force approach. And often, the brute-force strategy is indeed the one that is easiest to apply.

As an example, consider the exponentiation problem: compute a^n for a given number a and a nonnegative integer n. Though this problem might seem trivial, it provides a useful vehicle for illustrating several algorithm design techniques, including the brute-force approach. (Also note that computing a^n mod m for some large integers is a principal component of a leading encryption algorithm.) By the definition of exponentiation,

$$a^n = \underbrace{a * \cdots * a}_{n \text{ times}}.$$

This suggests simply computing a^n by multiplying 1 by a n times.

Computation and Reasoning

We have already encountered at least two brute-force algorithms in the book: the consecutive integer checking algorithm for computing $gcd(m, n)$ (Section 1.1) and the definition-based algorithm for matrix multiplication (Section 2.3). Many other examples are given later in this chapter. (Can you identify a few algorithms you already know as being based on the brute-force approach?)

Though rarely a source of clever or efficient algorithms, the brute-force approach should not be overlooked as an important algorithm design strategy. First, unlike some of the other strategies, brute force is applicable to a very wide variety of problems. (In fact, it seems to be the only general approach for which it is more difficult to point out problems it *cannot* tackle.) In particular, brute force is used for many elementary but important algorithmic tasks such as computing the sum of n numbers, finding the largest element in a list, and so on. Second, for some important problems (e.g., sorting, searching, matrix multiplication, string matching), the brute-force approach yields reasonable algorithms of at least some practical value with no limitation on instance size. Third, the expense of designing a more efficient algorithm may be unjustifiable if only a few instances of a problem need to be solved and a brute-force algorithm can solve those instances with acceptable speed. Fourth, even if too inefficient in general, a brute-force algorithm can still be useful for solving small-size instances of a problem. Finally, a brute-force algorithm can serve an important theoretical or educational purpose, e.g., as a yardstick with which to judge more efficient alternatives for solving a problem.

3.1 Selection Sort and Bubble Sort

In this section, we consider the application of the brute-force approach to the problem of sorting: given a list of n orderable items (e.g., numbers, characters from some alphabet, character strings), rearrange them in nondecreasing order. As we mentioned in Section 1.3, dozens of algorithms have been developed for solving this very important problem. You might have learned several of them in the past. If you have, try to forget them for the time being and look at the problem afresh.

Now, after your mind is unburdened of previous knowledge of sorting algorithms, ask yourself a question: "What would be the most straightforward method for solving the sorting problem?" Reasonable people may disagree on the answer to this question. The two algorithms discussed here—selection sort and bubble sort—seem to be the two prime candidates. The first of these two algorithms seems to be much better than the second, both because it is a better algorithm overall and because it implements the brute-force approach more clearly.

Selection Sort

We start selection sort by scanning the entire given list to find its smallest element and exchange it with the first element, putting the smallest element in its final position in the sorted list. Then we scan the list, starting with the second element, to find the smallest among the last $n - 1$ elements and exchange it with the second element, putting the second smallest element in its final position. Generally, on the ith pass through the list, which we number from 0 to $n - 2$, the algorithm searches for the smallest item among the last $n - i$ elements and swaps it with A_i:

$$A_0 \leq A_1 \leq \cdots \leq A_{i-1} \mid A_i, \ldots, A_{min}, \ldots, A_{n-1}$$

in their final positions $\qquad$ the last $n-i$ elements

After $n - 1$ passes, the list is sorted.

Here is a pseudocode of this algorithm, which, for simplicity, assumes that the list is implemented as an array.

ALGORITHM *SelectionSort(A[0..n − 1])*

//The algorithm sorts a given array by selection sort
//Input: An array $A[0..n − 1]$ of orderable elements
//Output: Array $A[0..n − 1]$ sorted in ascending order
for $i \leftarrow 0$ **to** $n - 2$ **do**
$\quad min \leftarrow i$
$\quad$**for** $j \leftarrow i + 1$ **to** $n - 1$ **do**
$\quad\quad$**if** $A[j] < A[min] \quad min \leftarrow j$
$\quad$swap $A[i]$ and $A[min]$

As an example, the action of the algorithm on the list 89, 45, 68, 90, 29, 34, 17 is illustrated in Figure 3.1.

The analysis of selection sort is straightforward. The input's size is given by the number of elements n; the algorithm's basic operation is the key comparison $A[j] < A[min]$. The number of times it is executed depends only on the array's size and is given by the following sum:

$$C(n) = \sum_{i=0}^{n-2} \sum_{j=i+1}^{n-1} 1 = \sum_{i=0}^{n-2}[(n - 1) - (i + 1) + 1] = \sum_{i=0}^{n-2}(n - 1 - i).$$

We have already encountered the last sum in analyzing the algorithm of Example 2 in Section 2.3 (so you should be able to compute it now on your own). Whether you compute this sum by distributing the summation symbol or by immediately getting the sum of decreasing integers, the answer, of course, must be the same:

$$C(n) = \sum_{i=0}^{n-2} \sum_{j=i+1}^{n-1} 1 = \sum_{i=0}^{n-2}(n - 1 - i) = \frac{(n - 1)n}{2}.$$

Computation and Reasoning

255

```
| 89   45   68   90   29   34   17
  17 | 45   68   90   29   34   89
  17   29 | 68   90   45   34   89
  17   29   34 | 90   45   68   89
  17   29   34   45 | 90   68   89
  17   29   34   45   68 | 90   89
  17   29   34   45   68   89 | 90
```

FIGURE 3.1 Selection sort's operation on the list 89, 45, 68, 90, 29, 34, 17. Each line corresponds to one iteration of the algorithm, i.e., a pass through the list's tail to the right of the vertical bar; an element in bold indicates the smallest element found. Elements to the left of the vertical bar are in their final positions and are not considered in this and subsequent iterations.

Thus, selection sort is a $\Theta(n^2)$ algorithm on all inputs. Note, however, that the number of key swaps is only $\Theta(n)$ or, more precisely, $n - 1$ (one for each repetition of the i loop). This property distinguishes selection sort positively from many other sorting algorithms.

Bubble Sort

Another brute-force application to the sorting problem is to compare adjacent elements of the list and exchange them if they are out of order. By doing it repeatedly, we end up "bubbling up" the largest element to the last position on the list. The next pass bubbles up the second largest element, and so on until, after $n - 1$ passes, the list is sorted. Pass i $(0 \le i \le n - 2)$ of bubble sort can be represented by the following diagram:

$$A_0, \ldots, A_j \overset{?}{\leftrightarrow} A_{j+1}, \ldots, \ A_{n-i-1} \mid \underset{\text{in their final positions}}{A_{n-i} \le \cdots \le A_{n-1}}$$

Here is a pseudocode of this algorithm.

ALGORITHM *BubbleSort(A[0..n − 1])*

    //The algorithm sorts array $A[0..n - 1]$ by bubble sort
    //Input: An array $A[0..n - 1]$ of orderable elements
    //Output: Array $A[0..n - 1]$ sorted in ascending order
    for $i \leftarrow 0$ **to** $n - 2$ **do**
        for $j \leftarrow 0$ **to** $n - 2 - i$ **do**
            if $A[j + 1] < A[j]$ swap $A[j]$ and $A[j + 1]$

The action of the algorithm on the list 89, 45, 68, 90, 29, 34, 17 is illustrated as an example in Figure 3.2.

Computation and Reasoning

256

89 $\overset{?}{\leftrightarrow}$ 45		68	90	29	34	17
45	89 $\overset{?}{\leftrightarrow}$ 68		90	29	34	17
45	68	89 $\overset{?}{\leftrightarrow}$ 90 $\overset{?}{\leftrightarrow}$	29		34	17
45	68	89	29	90 $\overset{?}{\leftrightarrow}$ 34		17
45	68	89	29	34	90 $\overset{?}{\leftrightarrow}$ 17	
45	68	89	29	34	17	|90
45 $\overset{?}{\leftrightarrow}$ 68 $\overset{?}{\leftrightarrow}$ 89 $\overset{?}{\leftrightarrow}$ 29				34	17	|90
45	68	29	89 $\overset{?}{\leftrightarrow}$ 34		17	|90
45	68	29	34	89 $\overset{?}{\leftrightarrow}$ 17		|90
45	68	29	34	17	|89	90

etc.

FIGURE 3.2 The first two passes of bubble sort on the list 89, 45, 68, 90, 29, 34, 17. A new line is shown after a swap of two elements is done. The elements to the right of the vertical bar are in their final positions and are not considered in subsequent iterations of the algorithm.

The number of key comparisons for the bubble sort version given above is the same for all arrays of size n; it is obtained by a sum that is almost identical to the sum for selection sort:

$$C(n) = \sum_{i=0}^{n-2} \sum_{j=0}^{n-2-i} 1 = \sum_{i=0}^{n-2} [(n-2-i) - 0 + 1]$$

$$= \sum_{i=0}^{n-2} (n-1-i) = \frac{(n-1)n}{2} \in \Theta(n^2).$$

The number of key swaps, however, depends on the input. For the worst case of decreasing arrays, it is the same as the number of key comparisons:

$$S_{worst}(n) = C(n) = \frac{(n-1)n}{2} \in \Theta(n^2).$$

As is often the case with an application of the brute-force strategy, the first version of an algorithm obtained can often be improved with a modest amount of effort. Specifically, we can improve the crude version of bubble sort given by exploiting the following observation: if a pass through the list makes no exchanges, the list has been sorted and we can stop the algorithm (Problem 9a in Exercises 3.1). Though the new version runs faster on some inputs, it is still in $\Theta(n^2)$ in the worst and average cases. In fact, even among elementary sorting methods, bubble sort is an inferior choice, and, if it were not for its catchy name, you would

Computation and Reasoning

probably have never heard of it. However, the general lesson you just learned is important and worth repeating:

> A first application of the brute-force approach often results in an algorithm that can be improved with a modest amount of effort.

Exercises 3.1

1. **a.** Give an example of an algorithm that should not be considered an application of the brute-force approach.

   b. Give an example of a problem that cannot be solved by a brute-force algorithm.

2. **a.** What is the efficiency of the brute-force algorithm for computing a^n as a function of n? As a function of the number of bits in the binary representation of n?

   b. If you are to compute $a^n \bmod m$ where $a > 1$ and n is a large positive integer, how would you circumvent the problem of a very large magnitude of a^n?

3. For each of the algorithms in Problems 4, 5, and 6 of Exercises 2.3, tell whether or not the algorithm is based on the brute-force approach.

4. **a.** Design a brute-force algorithm for computing the value of a polynomial

   $$p(x) = a_n x^n + a_{n-1} x^{n-1} + \cdots + a_1 x + a_0$$

   at a given point x_0 and determine its worst-case efficiency class.

   b. If the algorithm you designed is in $\Theta(n^2)$, design a linear algorithm for this problem.

   c. Is it possible to design an algorithm with a better than linear efficiency for this problem?

5. Sort the list E, X, A, M, P, L, E in alphabetical order by selection sort.

6. Is selection sort stable? (The definition of a stable sorting algorithm was given in Section 1.3.)

7. Is it possible to implement selection sort for linked lists with the same $\Theta(n^2)$ efficiency as the array version?

8. Sort the list E, X, A, M, P, L, E in alphabetical order by bubble sort.

9. **a.** Prove that if bubble sort makes no exchanges on its pass through a list, the list is sorted and the algorithm can be stopped.

   b. Write a pseudocode of the method that incorporates this improvement.

   c. Prove that the worst-case efficiency of the improved version is quadratic.

10. Is bubble sort stable?

3.2 Sequential Search and Brute-Force String Matching

We saw in the previous section two applications of the brute-force approach to the sorting problem. Here we discuss two applications of this strategy to the problem of searching. The first deals with the canonical problem of searching for an item of a given value in a given list. The second is different in that it deals with the string-matching problem.

Sequential Search

We have already encountered a brute-force algorithm for the general searching problem: it is called sequential search (see Section 2.1). To repeat, the algorithm simply compares successive elements of a given list with a given search key until either a match is encountered (successful search) or the list is exhausted without finding a match (unsuccessful search). A simple extra trick is often employed in implementing sequential search: if we append the search key to the end of the list, the search for the key will have to be successful, and therefore we can eliminate a check for the list's end on each iteration of the algorithm. Here is a pseudocode for this enhanced version, with its input implemented as an array.

ALGORITHM *SequentialSearch2*($A[0..n]$, K)

    //The algorithm implements sequential search with a search key as a sentinel
    //Input: An array A of n elements and a search key K
    //Output: The position of the first element in $A[0..n-1]$ whose value is
    //   equal to K or -1 if no such element is found
    $A[n] \leftarrow K$
    $i \leftarrow 0$
    while $A[i] \neq K$ **do**
        $i \leftarrow i + 1$
    if $i < n$ **return** i
    else return -1

Another straightforward improvement can be incorporated in sequential search if a given list is known to be sorted: searching in such a list can be stopped as soon as an element greater than or equal to the search key is encountered.

Sequential search provides an excellent illustration of the brute-force approach, with its characteristic strength (simplicity) and weakness (inferior efficiency). The efficiency results obtained in Section 2.1 for the standard version of sequential search change for the enhanced version only very slightly, so that the algorithm remains linear in both worst and average cases. We will discuss

Computation and Reasoning

later in the book several searching algorithms with a better time efficiency in the average case.

Brute-Force String Matching

Recall the string-matching problem introduced in Section 1.3: given a string of n characters called the **text** and a string of m characters ($m \leq n$) called the **pattern**, find a substring of the text that matches the pattern. To put it more precisely, we want to find i—the index of the leftmost character of the first matching substring in the text—such that $t_i = p_0, \ldots, t_{i+j} = p_j, \ldots, t_{i+m-1} = p_{m-1}$:

$$
\begin{array}{ccccccccc}
t_0 & \cdots & t_i & \cdots & t_{i+j} & \cdots & t_{i+m-1} & \cdots & t_{n-1} \quad \text{text } T \\
& & \updownarrow & & \updownarrow & & \updownarrow & & \\
& & p_0 & \cdots & p_j & \cdots & p_{m-1} & \text{pattern } P &
\end{array}
$$

If matches other than the first one need to be found, a string-matching algorithm can simply continue working until the entire text is exhausted.

A brute-force algorithm for the string-matching problem is quite obvious: align the pattern against the first m characters of the text and start matching the corresponding pairs of characters from left to right until either all m pairs of the characters match (then the algorithm can stop) or a mismatching pair is encountered. In the latter case, the pattern is shifted one position to the right and character comparisons are resumed, starting again with the first character of the pattern and its counterpart in the text. Note that the last position in the text that can still be a beginning of a matching substring is $n - m$ (provided the text's positions are indexed from 0 to $n - 1$). Beyond that position, there are not enough characters to match the entire pattern; hence, the algorithm need not make any comparisons there.

ALGORITHM   *BruteForceStringMatch*$(T[0..n-1], P[0..m-1])$
　　//The algorithm implements brute-force string matching.
　　//Input: An array $T[0..n-1]$ of n characters representing a text;
　　//　　an array $P[0..m-1]$ of m characters representing a pattern.
　　//Output: The position of the first character in the text that starts the first
　　//　　matching substring if the search is successful and -1 otherwise.
　　for $i \leftarrow 0$ **to** $n - m$ **do**
　　　　$j \leftarrow 0$
　　　　while $j < m$ **and** $P[j] = T[i + j]$ **do**
　　　　　　$j \leftarrow j + 1$
　　　　if $j = m$ **return** i
　　return -1

An operation of the algorithm is illustrated in Figure 3.3.

```
N  O  B  O  D  Y  _  N  O  T  I  C  E  D  _  H  I  M
N  O  T
   N  O  T
      N  O  T
         N  O  T
            N  O  T
               N  O  T
                  N  O  T
```

FIGURE 3.3 An example of brute-force string matching. (The pattern's characters that are compared with their text counterparts are in bold type.)

Note that for this example, the algorithm shifts the pattern almost always after a single character comparison. However, the worst case is much worse: the algorithm may have to make all m comparisons before shifting the pattern, and this can happen for each of the $n - m + 1$ tries. (Problem 6 asks you to give a specific example of such a situation.) Thus, in the worst case, the algorithm is in $\Theta(nm)$. For a typical word search in a natural language text, however, we should expect that most shifts would happen after very few comparisons (check the example again). Therefore the average-case efficiency should be considerably better than the worst-case efficiency. Indeed it is: for searching in random texts, it has been shown to be linear, i.e., $\Theta(n + m) = \Theta(n)$. There are several more sophisticated and more efficient algorithms for string searching. The most widely known of them—by R. Boyer and J. Moore—will be outlined in Section 7.2 along with its simplification suggested by R. Horspool.

Exercises 3.2

1. Find the number of comparisons made by the sentinel version of sequential search
   a. in the worst case.
   b. in the average case if the probability of a successful search is p $(0 \le p \le 1)$.

2. As shown in Section 2.1, the average number of key comparisons made by sequential search (without a sentinel, under standard assumptions about its inputs) is given by the formula

$$C_{avg}(n) = \frac{p(n+1)}{2} + n(1-p),$$

where p is the probability of a successful search. Determine, for a fixed n, the values of p $(0 \le p \le 1)$ for which this formula yields the largest value of $C_{avg}(n)$ and the smallest value of $C_{avg}(n)$.

Computation and Reasoning

3. Design and run an experiment to compare running times of the two versions of sequential search outlined in Sections 2.1 and 3.2.

4. Determine the number of character comparisons that will be made by the brute-force algorithm in searching for the pattern GANDHI in the text

    THERE_IS_MORE_TO_LIFE_THAN_INCREASING_ITS_SPEED

    (Assume that the length of the text—it is 47 characters long—is known before the search starts.)

5. How many comparisons (both successful and unsuccessful) will be made by the brute-force string-matching algorithm in searching for each of the following patterns in the binary text of 1000 zeros?
        a. 00001   **b.** 10000   **c.** 01010

6. Give an example of a text of length n and a pattern of length m that constitutes the worst-case input for the brute-force searching algorithm. Exactly how many character comparisons will be made for such input?

7. Write a pseudocode of the brute-force string matching that returns, for a given pattern, the total number of matching substrings in a given text.

8. If you are to search for a pattern containing an infrequent character such as Q or Z in an English text, how could you modify the brute-force algorithm to take advantage of this information?

9. A popular diversion in the United States, word find, asks the player to find each of a given set of words in a square table filled with single letters. A word can read horizontally, vertically, or diagonally in any direction. Design a brute-force algorithm for this game and implement it as a computer program.

10. Write a program for playing Battleship (a classic strategy game) on the computer which is based on a version of brute-force pattern matching. The rules of the game are as follows. There are two opponents in the game (in this case, a human player and the computer). The game is played on two identical boards (10-by-10 tables of squares) on which each opponent places his or her ships, not seen by the opponent. Each player has five ships, each of which occupies a certain number of squares on the board: a destroyer (2 squares), a submarine (3 squares), a cruiser (3 squares), a battleship (4 squares), and an aircraft carrier (5 squares). Each ship is placed either horizontally or vertically, with no two ships touching each other. The game is played by the opponents taking turns "shooting" at each other's ships. A result of every shot is displayed as either a hit or a miss. In case of a hit, the player gets to go again and keeps playing until this player misses. The goal is to sink all the opponent's ships before the opponent succeeds in doing it first. (To sink a ship, all squares occupied by the ship must be hit.)

3.3 Closest-Pair and Convex-Hull Problems by Brute Force

In this section, we consider a straightforward approach to two well-known problems dealing with a finite set of points on the plane. These problems, aside from their theoretical interest, arise in two important applied areas: computational geometry and operations research.

Closest-Pair Problem

The closest-pair problem calls for finding the two closest points in a set of n points. For simplicity, we consider the two-dimensional case of the problem, though the problem can be posed for points in higher-dimensional spaces as well. We assume that the points in question are specified in a standard fashion by their (x, y) Cartesian coordinates and that the distance between two points $P_i = (x_i, y_i)$ and $P_j = (x_j, y_j)$ is the standard Euclidean distance

$$d(P_i, P_j) = \sqrt{(x_i - x_j)^2 + (y_i - y_j)^2}.$$

The brute-force approach to solving this problem leads to the following obvious algorithm: compute the distance between each pair of distinct points and find a pair with the smallest distance. Of course, we do not want to compute the distance between the same pair of points twice. To avoid doing so, we consider only the pairs of points (P_i, P_j) for which $i < j$.

ALGORITHM *BruteForceClosestPoints(P)*

    //Input: A list P of n ($n \geq 2$) points $P_1 = (x_1, y_1), \ldots, P_n = (x_n, y_n)$
    //Output: Indices *index*1 and *index*2 of the closest pair of points
    $dmin \leftarrow \infty$
    for $i \leftarrow 1$ **to** $n - 1$ **do**
        for $j \leftarrow i + 1$ **to** n **do**
            $d \leftarrow sqrt((x_i - x_j)^2 + (y_i - y_j)^2)$ //*sqrt* is the square root function
            if $d < dmin$
                $dmin \leftarrow d$; $index1 \leftarrow i$; $index2 \leftarrow j$
    return $index1, index2$

The basic operation of the algorithm is computing the Euclidean distance between two points. In the age of electronic calculators with the square-root button, one might be led to believe that computing the square root is as simple an operation as, say, addition or multiplication. It is not, however. For starters, even for most integers, square roots are irrational numbers that therefore can be found only approximately. Moreover, computing such approximations is not a trivial matter. But, in fact, computing square roots can be avoided! (Can you think

Computation and Reasoning

how?) The trick is to realize that we can simply ignore the square root function and compare the values $(x_i - x_j)^2 + (y_i - y_j)^2$ themselves. We can do this because the smaller a number of which we take the square root, the smaller its square root, or, as mathematicians say, the square root function is strictly increasing.

So, if we replace $d \leftarrow sqrt((x_i - x_j)^2 + (y_i - y_j)^2)$ by $dsqr \leftarrow (x_i - x_j)^2 + (y_i - y_j)^2$, the basic operation of the algorithm will be squaring a number. The number of times it will be executed can be computed as follows:

$$C(n) = \sum_{i=1}^{n-1} \sum_{j=i+1}^{n} 2 = 2 \sum_{i=1}^{n-1} (n-i)$$

$$= 2[(n-1) + (n-2) + \cdots + 1] = (n-1)n \in \Theta(n^2).$$

In Chapter 4, we will discuss an $n \log n$ algorithm for this problem.

Convex-Hull Problem

On to the other problem—computing the convex hull. We start with a definition of a convex set.

DEFINITION   A set of points (finite or infinite) on the plane is called *convex* if for any two points P and Q in the set, the entire line segment with the end points at P and Q belongs to the set.

All the sets depicted in Figure 3.4a are convex, and so are a straight line, a triangle, a rectangle, and, more generally, any convex polygon,[1] a circle, the entire plane. On the other hand, the sets depicted in Figure 3.4b, any finite set of two or more distinct points, the boundary of any convex polygon, and a circumference are examples of sets that are not convex.

Now we are ready for the notion of the convex hull. Intuitively, the convex hull of a set of n points in the plane is the smallest convex polygon that contains all of them (either inside or on its boundary). If this formulation does not quite fire up your enthusiasm, consider the problem as one of barricading n sleeping tigers by a fence of the shortest length. This interpretation is due to D. Harel [Har92]; it is somewhat lively, however, because the fence's posts have to be erected right at the spots where some of the tigers sleep! There is another, much tamer interpretation of this notion. Imagine that the points in question are represented by nails driven into a large sheet of plywood representing the plane. Take a rubber band and stretch it to include all the nails, then let it snap into place. The convex hull is the area bounded by the snapped rubber band (Figure 3.5).

---

1.   By a triangle, rectangle, and, more generally, a convex polygon, we mean here a region, i.e., the set of points both inside and on the boundary of the shape in question.

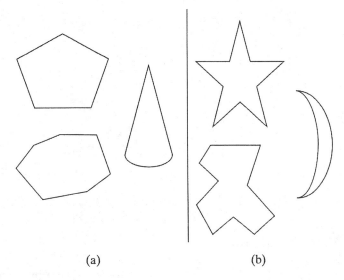

(a)   (b)

FIGURE 3.4 (a) Convex sets. (b) Sets that are not convex.

A formal definition of the convex hull that is applicable to arbitrary sets, including sets of points that happen to lie on the same line, follows.

DEFINITION The *convex hull* of a set S of points is the smallest convex set containing S. (The "smallest" requirement means that the convex hull of S must be a subset of any convex set containing S.)

If S is convex, its convex hull is obviously S itself. If S is a set of two points, its convex hull is the line segment connecting these points. If S is a set of three points not on the same line, its convex hull is the triangle with the vertices at the

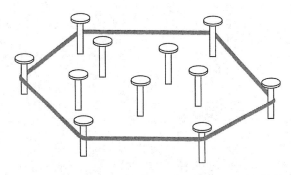

FIGURE 3.5 A rubber band interpretation of the convex hull

Computation and Reasoning

265

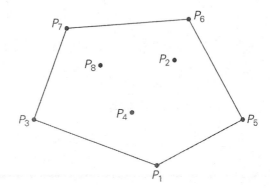

FIGURE 3.6 The convex hull for this set of eight points is the convex polygon with its vertices at P_1, P_5, P_6, P_7, and P_3.

three points given; if three points do lie on the same line, the convex hull is the line segment with its end points at the two points that are farthest apart. For an example of the convex hull for a larger set, see Figure 3.6.

A study of the examples makes the following theorem an expected result.

THEOREM   The convex hull of any set S of $n > 2$ points (not all on the same line) is a convex polygon with the vertices at some of the points of S. (If all the points do lie on the same line, the polygon degenerates to a line segment but still with the end points at two points of S.)

The *convex-hull problem* is the problem of constructing the convex hull for a given set S of n points. To solve it, we need to find the points that will serve as the vertices of the polygon in question. Mathematicians call vertices of such a polygon "extreme points." By definition, an *extreme point* of a convex set is a point of this set that is not a middle point of any line segment with end points in the set. For example, the extreme points of a triangle are its three vertices, the extreme points of a circle are all the points of its circumference, the extreme points of the convex hull of the set of eight points in Figure 3.6 are P_1, P_5, P_6, P_7, and P_3.

Extreme points have several special properties other points of a convex set do not have. One of them is exploited by a very important algorithm called the *simplex method*. This algorithm solves *linear programming* problems, problems of finding a minimum or a maximum of a linear function of n variables subject to linear constraints (see Problem 9 in Exercises 3.3 for an example and Section 6.6 for a general discussion). Here, however, we are interested in extreme points because their identification solves the convex-hull problem. Actually, to solve this problem completely, we need to know a bit more than just which of n points of a given set are extreme points of the set's convex hull: we need to know which

Computation and Reasoning

pairs of points need to be connected to form the boundary of the convex hull. Note that this issue can also be addressed by listing the extreme points in a clockwise or a counterclockwise order.

So how can we solve the convex-hull problem in a brute-force manner? If you do not see an immediate plan for a frontal attack, do not be dismayed: the convex-hull problem is one with no obvious algorithmic solution. Nevertheless, there is a simple but inefficient algorithm that is based on the following observation about line segments making up a boundary of the convex hull: a line segment connecting two points P_i and P_j of a set of n points is a part of its convex hull's boundary if and only if all the other points of the set lie on the same side of the straight line through these two points.[2] (Verify this property for the set of Figure 3.6.) Repeating this test for every pair of points yields a list of line segments that make up the convex hull's boundary.

A few elementary facts from analytical geometry are needed to implement this algorithm. First, the straight line through two points (x_1, y_1), (x_2, y_2) in the coordinate plane can be defined by the equation

$$ax + by = c,$$

where $a = y_2 - y_1, b = x_1 - x_2, c = x_1y_2 - y_1x_2$.

Second, such a line divides the plane into two half-planes: for all the points in one of them $ax + by > c$, while for all the points in the other $ax + by < c$. (For the points on the line itself, of course, $ax + by = c$.) Thus, to check whether certain points lie on the same side of the line, we can simply check whether the expression $ax + by - c$ has the same sign at each of these points. We leave the implementation details as an exercise.

What is the time efficiency of this algorithm? It is in $O(n^3)$: for each of $n(n-1)/2$ pairs of distinct points, we may need to find the sign of $ax + by - c$ for each of the other $n-2$ points. There are much more efficient algorithms for this important problem, and we will discuss one of them later in the book.

Exercises 3.3

1. Can you design a faster algorithm than the one based on the brute-force strategy to solve the closest-pair problem for n points $x_1, \ldots, x_n$ on the real line?

2. **a.** There are several alternative ways to define a distance between two points $P_1 = (x_1, y_1)$ and $P_2 = (x_2, y_2)$. In particular, the so-called *Manhattan distance* is defined as

$$d_M(P_1, P_2) = |x_1 - x_2| + |y_1 - y_2|.$$

---

2. For the sake of simplicity, we assume here that no three points of a given set lie on the same line. A modification needed for the general case is left for the exercises.

Prove that d_M satisfies the following axioms that every distance function must satisfy:

    i. $d_M(P_1, P_2) \geq 0$ for any two points P_1 and P_2, and $d_M(P_1, P_2) = 0$ if and only if $P_1 = P_2$;

    ii. $d_M(P_1, P_2) = d_M(P_2, P_1)$;

    iii. $d_M(P_1, P_2) \leq d_M(P_1, P_3) + d_M(P_3, P_2)$ for any P_1, P_2, and P_3.

b. Sketch all the points in the x, y coordinate plane whose Manhattan distance to the origin $(0,0)$ is equal to 1. Do the same for the Euclidean distance.

c. True or false: A solution to the closest-pair problem does not depend on which of the two metrics—d_E (Euclidean) or d_M (Manhattan)—is used.

3. The closest-pair problem can be posed in k-dimensional space in which the Euclidean distance between two points $P' = (x'_1, \ldots, x'_k)$ and $P'' = (x''_1, \ldots, x''_k)$ is defined as

$$d(P', P'') = \sqrt{\sum_{s=1}^{k} (x'_s - x''_s)^2}.$$

What will be the efficiency class of the brute-force algorithm for the k-dimensional closest-pair problem?

4. Find the convex hulls of the following sets and identify their extreme points (if they have any).

    a. a line segment

    b. a square

    c. the boundary of a square

    d. a straight line

5. What is the largest and what is the smallest number of extreme points the convex hull of a set of n distinct points can have?

6. Design a linear-time algorithm to determine one extreme point of the convex hull of a set of n points in the plane.

7. What modification needs to be made in the brute-force algorithm for the convex-hull problem to handle more than two points on the same straight line?

8. Write a program implementing the brute-force algorithm for the convex-hull problem.

9. Consider the following small instance of the linear programming problem:

$$\begin{aligned} \text{maximize} \quad & 3x + 5y \\ \text{subject to} \quad & x + y \leq 4 \\ & x + 3y \leq 6 \\ & x \geq 0, y \geq 0 \end{aligned}$$

a. Sketch, in the Cartesian plane, the problem's *feasible region*, or set of points satisfying all the problem's constraints.

b. Identify the region's extreme points.

c. Solve the optimization problem given by using the following theorem: Linear programming problem with a nonempty bounded feasible region always has a solution, which can be found at one of the extreme points of its feasible region.

3.4 Exhaustive Search

Many important problems require finding an element with a special property in a domain that grows exponentially (or faster) with an instance size. Typically, such problems arise in situations that involve—explicitly or implicitly—combinatorial objects such as permutations, combinations, and subsets of a given set. Many such problems are optimization problems: they ask to find an element that maximizes or minimizes some desired characteristic such as a path's length or an assignment's cost.

Exhaustive search is simply a brute-force approach to combinatorial problems. It suggests generating each and every element of the problem's domain, selecting those of them that satisfy the problem's constraints, and then finding a desired element (e.g., the one that optimizes some objective function). Note that though the idea of exhaustive search is quite straightforward, its implementation typically requires an algorithm for generating certain combinatorial objects. We delay a discussion of such algorithms until Chapter 5 and assume here that they exist. We illustrate exhaustive search by applying it to three important problems: the traveling salesman problem, the knapsack problem, and the assignment problem.

Traveling Salesman Problem

The *traveling salesman problem* has been intriguing researchers for the last 100 years by its seemingly simple formulation, important applications, and interesting connections to other combinatorial problems. In layman's terms, the problem asks to find the shortest tour through a given set of n cities that visits each city exactly once before returning to the city where it started. The problem can be conveniently modeled by a weighted graph, with the graph's vertices representing the cities and the edge weights specifying the distances. Then the problem can be stated as the problem of finding the shortest *Hamiltonian circuit* of the graph. (A Hamiltonian circuit is defined as a cycle that passes through all the vertices of the graph exactly once. It is named after the Irish mathematician Sir William Rowan Hamilton (1805–1865), who became interested in such cycles as an application of his algebraic discoveries.)

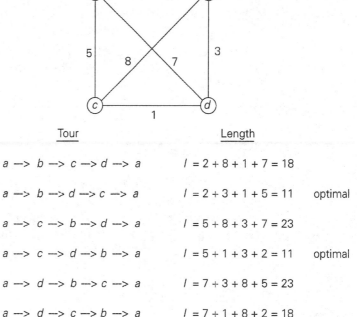

Tour	Length	
$a \longrightarrow b \longrightarrow c \longrightarrow d \longrightarrow a$	$l = 2 + 8 + 1 + 7 = 18$	
$a \longrightarrow b \longrightarrow d \longrightarrow c \longrightarrow a$	$l = 2 + 3 + 1 + 5 = 11$	optimal
$a \longrightarrow c \longrightarrow b \longrightarrow d \longrightarrow a$	$l = 5 + 8 + 3 + 7 = 23$	
$a \longrightarrow c \longrightarrow d \longrightarrow b \longrightarrow a$	$l = 5 + 1 + 3 + 2 = 11$	optimal
$a \longrightarrow d \longrightarrow b \longrightarrow c \longrightarrow a$	$l = 7 + 3 + 8 + 5 = 23$	
$a \longrightarrow d \longrightarrow c \longrightarrow b \longrightarrow a$	$l = 7 + 1 + 8 + 2 = 18$	

FIGURE 3.7 A solution to a small instance of the traveling salesman problem by exhaustive search

It is easy to see that a Hamiltonian circuit can be also defined as a sequence of $n + 1$ adjacent vertices $v_{i_0}, v_{i_1}, \ldots, v_{i_{n-1}}, v_{i_0}$, where the first vertex of the sequence is the same as the last one while all the other $n - 1$ vertices are distinct. Further, we can assume, with no loss of generality, that all circuits start and end at one particular vertex (they are cycles after all, are they not?). Thus, we can get all the tours by generating all the permutations of $n - 1$ intermediate cities, compute the tour lengths, and find the shortest among them. Figure 3.7 presents a small instance of the problem and its solution by this method.

An inspection of Figure 3.7 reveals three pairs of tours that differ only by the tour's direction. Hence, we can cut the number of vertex permutations by half. We can, for example, choose any two intermediate vertices, say, B and C, and then consider only permutations in which B precedes C. (This trick implicitly defines a tour's direction.)

This improvement cannot brighten the efficiency picture much, however. The total number of permutations needed will still be $(n - 1)!/2$, which makes the exhaustive-search approach impractical for all but very small values of n. On the other hand, if you always see your glass as half-full, you can claim that cutting the work by half is nothing to sneeze at, even if you solve a small instance of the problem, especially by hand. Also note that had we not limited our investigation to the circuits starting at the same vertex, the number of permutations would have been even larger by a factor of n.

Knapsack Problem

Here is another well-known problem in computer science. Given n items of known weights $w_1, \ldots, w_n$ and values $v_1, \ldots, v_n$ and a knapsack of capacity W, find the most valuable subset of the items that fit into the knapsack. If you do not like an idea of putting yourself in the shoes of a thief who wants to steal the most valuable loot that fits into his knapsack, think about a transport plane that has to deliver the most valuable set of items to a remote location without exceeding its capacity. Figure 3.8a presents a small instance of the knapsack problem.

The exhaustive search approach to this problem leads to considering all the subsets of the set of n items given, computing the total weight of each subset in order to identify feasible subsets (i.e., the ones with the total weight not exceeding the knapsack's capacity), and finding a subset of the largest value among them. As an example, the solution to the instance of Figure 3.8a is given in Figure 3.8b. Since the number of subsets of an n-element set is 2^n, the exhaustive search leads to a $\Omega(2^n)$ algorithm no matter how efficiently individual subsets are generated.

Thus, for both the traveling salesman and knapsack problems, exhaustive search leads to algorithms that are extremely inefficient on every input. In fact, these two problems are the best-known examples of so-called **NP-hard problems**. No polynomial-time algorithm is known for any *NP*-hard problem. Moreover, most computer scientists believe that such algorithms do not exist, although this very important conjecture has never been proven. More sophisticated approaches—backtracking and branch-and-bound (see Sections 11.1 and 11.2)—enable us to solve some but not all instances of these (and similar) problems in less than exponential time. Alternatively, we can use one of many approximation algorithms, such as those described in Section 11.3.

Assignment Problem

In our third example of a problem that can be solved by exhaustive search, there are n people who need to be assigned to execute n jobs, one person per job. (That is, each person is assigned to exactly one job and each job is assigned to exactly one person.) The cost that would accrue if the ith person is assigned to the jth job is a known quantity $C[i, j]$ for each pair $i, j = 1, \ldots, n$. The problem is to find an assignment with the smallest total cost.

Computation and Reasoning

271

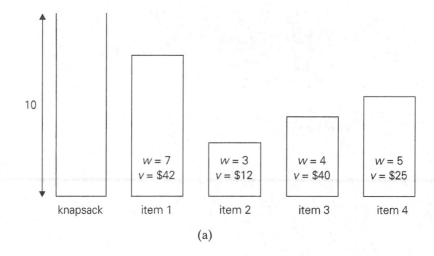

(a)

Subset	Total weight	Total value
Ø	0	$ 0
{1}	7	$42
{2}	3	$12
{3}	4	$40
{4}	5	$25
{1, 2}	10	$36
{1, 3}	11	not feasible
{1, 4}	12	not feasible
{2, 3}	7	$52
{2, 4}	8	$37
{3, 4}	**9**	**$65**
{1, 2, 3}	14	not feasible
{1, 2, 4}	15	not feasible
{1, 3, 4}	16	not feasible
{2, 3, 4}	12	not feasible
{1, 2, 3, 4}	19	not feasible

(b)

FIGURE 3.8 (a) Instance of the knapsack problem. (b) Its solution by exhaustive search. (The information about the optimal selection is in bold.)

Computation and Reasoning

A small instance of this problem follows, with the table's entries representing the assignment costs $C[i, j]$:

	Job 1	Job 2	Job 3	Job 4
Person 1	9	2	7	8
Person 2	6	4	3	7
Person 3	5	8	1	8
Person 4	7	6	9	4

It is easy to see that an instance of the assignment problem is completely specified by its cost matrix C. In terms of this matrix, the problem calls for a selection of one element in each row of the matrix so that all selected elements are in different columns and the total sum of the selected elements is the smallest possible. Note that no obvious strategy for finding a solution works here. For example, we cannot select the smallest element in each row because the smallest elements may happen to be in the same column. In fact, the smallest element in the entire matrix need not be a component of an optimal solution. Thus, opting for the exhaustive search may appear as an unavoidable evil.

We can describe feasible solutions to the assignment problem as n-tuples $\langle j_1, \ldots, j_n \rangle$ in which the ith component, $i = 1, \ldots, n$, indicates the column of the element selected in the ith row (i.e., the job number assigned to the ith person). For example, for the cost matrix above, $\langle 2, 3, 4, 1 \rangle$ indicates a feasible assignment of Person 1 to Job 2, Person 2 to Job 3, Person 3 to Job 4, and Person 4 to Job 1. The requirements of the assignment problem imply that there is a one-to-one correspondence between feasible assignments and permutations of the first n integers. Therefore the exhaustive approach to the assignment problem would require generating all the permutations of integers $1, 2, \ldots, n$, computing the total cost of each assignment by summing up the corresponding elements of the cost matrix, and finally selecting the one with the smallest sum. A few first iterations of applying this algorithm to the instance given above are shown in Figure 3.9; you are asked to complete it in the section's exercises.

$$C = \begin{bmatrix} 9 & 2 & 7 & 8 \\ 6 & 4 & 3 & 7 \\ 5 & 8 & 1 & 8 \\ 7 & 6 & 9 & 4 \end{bmatrix}$$

<1, 2, 3, 4>	cost = 9 + 4 + 1 + 4 = 18
<1, 2, 4, 3>	cost = 9 + 4 + 8 + 9 = 30
<1, 3, 2, 4>	cost = 9 + 3 + 8 + 4 = 24
<1, 3, 4, 2>	cost = 9 + 3 + 8 + 6 = 26 etc.
<1, 4, 2, 3>	cost = 9 + 7 + 8 + 9 = 33
<1, 4, 3, 2>	cost = 9 + 7 + 1 + 6 = 23

FIGURE 3.9 First few iterations of solving a small instance of the assignment problem by exhaustive search

Computation and Reasoning

273

Since the number of permutations to be considered for the general case of the assignment problem is $n!$, exhaustive search is impractical for all but very small instances of the problem. Fortunately, there is a much more efficient algorithm for this problem called the ***Hungarian method*** after the Hungarian mathematicians König and Egerváry whose work underlies the method (see, e.g., [KB95]).

This is good news: the fact that a problem's domain grows exponentially (or faster) does not necessarily imply that there can be no efficient algorithm for solving it. In fact, we will see several other examples of such problems later in the book. However, such examples are more of an exception from the rule. More often than not, there are no known polynomial-time algorithms for problems whose domains grow exponentially (provided, we want to solve them exactly). And, as mentioned, such algorithms quite possibly do not exist.

Exercises 3.4

1. **a.** Assuming that each tour can be generated in constant time, what will be the efficiency class of the exhaustive-search algorithm outlined in the text for the traveling salesman problem?

   b. If this algorithm is programmed on a computer that makes 1 billion additions per second, estimate the maximum number of cities for which the problem can be solved in

   i. one hour.

   ii. 24-hours.

   iii. one year.

   iv. one century.

2. Outline an exhaustive-search algorithm for the Hamiltonian circuit problem.

3. Outline an algorithm to determine whether a connected graph represented by its adjacency matrix has a Eulerian circuit. What is the efficiency class of your algorithm?

4. Complete the application of exhaustive search to the instance of the assignment problem started in the text.

5. Give an example of the assignment problem whose optimal solution does not include the smallest element of its cost matrix.

6. Write a report on the Hungarian method.

7. Consider the ***partition problem***: given n positive integers, partition them into two disjoint subsets with the same sum of their elements. (Of course, the problem does not always have a solution.) Design an exhaustive search algorithm for this problem. Try to minimize the number of subsets the algorithm needs to generate.

Computation and Reasoning

8. Consider the *clique problem*: given a graph G and a positive integer k, determine whether the graph contains a *clique* of size k, i.e., a complete subgraph of k vertices. Design an exhaustive-search algorithm for this problem.

9. Explain how exhaustive search can be applied to the sorting problem and determine the efficiency class of such an algorithm.

10. A magic square of order n is an arrangement of the numbers from 1 to n^2 in an n-by-n matrix, with each number occurring exactly once, so that each row, each column, and each main diagonal has the same sum.
    a. Prove that if a magic square of order n exists, the sum in question must be equal to $n(n^2 + 1)/2$.
    b. Design an exhaustive search algorithm for generating all magic squares of order n.
    c. Go to the Internet or your library and find a better algorithm for generating magic squares.
    d. Implement the two algorithms—the exhaustive search and the one you've found—and run an experiment to determine the largest value of n for which each of the algorithms is able to find a magic square of order n in less than one minute of your computer's time.

SUMMARY

■ *Brute force* is a straightforward approach to solving a problem, usually directly based on the problem's statement and definitions of the concepts involved.

■ The principal strengths of the brute-force approach are wide applicability and simplicity; its principal weakness is subpar efficiency of most brute-force algorithms.

■ A first application of the brute-force approach often results in an algorithm that can be improved with a modest amount of effort.

■ The following noted algorithms can be considered as examples of the brute-force approach:
   — definition-based algorithm for matrix multiplication
   — *selection sort*
   — *sequential search*
   — straightforward string matching algorithm.

■ *Exhaustive search* is a brute-force approach to combinatorial problems. It suggests generating each and every combinatorial object of the problem,

Computation and Reasoning

selecting those of them that satisfy the problem's constraints and then finding a desired object.

■ The *traveling salesman problem,* the *knapsack problem,* and the *assignment problem* are typical examples of problems that can be solved, at least theoretically, by exhaustive-search algorithms.

■ Exhaustive search is impractical for all but very small instances of problems it can be applied to.

4

Divide-and-Conquer

Whatever man prays for, he prays for a miracle. Every prayer reduces itself
to this—Great God, grant that twice two be not four.
—Ivan Turgenev (1818–1883), Russian novelist and short-story writer

Divide-and-conquer is probably the best-known general algorithm design
technique. Though its fame may have something to do with its catchy
name, it is well deserved: quite a few very efficient algorithms are specific implementations of this general strategy. Divide-and-conquer algorithms work
according to the following general plan:

1. A problem's instance is divided into several smaller instances of the same
   problem, ideally of about the same size.
2. The smaller instances are solved (typically recursively, though sometimes
   a different algorithm is employed when instances become small enough).
3. If necessary, the solutions obtained for the smaller instances are combined
   to get a solution to the original problem.

The divide-and-conquer technique is diagrammed in Figure 4.1, which depicts
the case of dividing a problem into two smaller subproblems, by far the most
widely occurring case (at least for divide-and-conquer algorithms designed to
be executed on a single-processor computer).

As an example, let us consider the problem of computing the sum of n
numbers $a_0, \ldots, a_{n-1}$. If $n > 1$, we can divide the problem into two instances
of the same problem: to compute the sum of the first $\lfloor n/2 \rfloor$ numbers and to
compute the sum of the remaining $\lceil n/2 \rceil$ numbers. (Of course, if $n = 1$, we
simply return a_0 as the answer.) Once each of these two sums is computed (by
applying the same method, i.e., recursively), we can add their values to get the
sum in question:

$$a_0 + \cdots + a_{n-1} = (a_0 + \cdots + a_{\lfloor n/2 \rfloor - 1}) + (a_{\lfloor n/2 \rfloor} + \cdots + a_{n-1}).$$

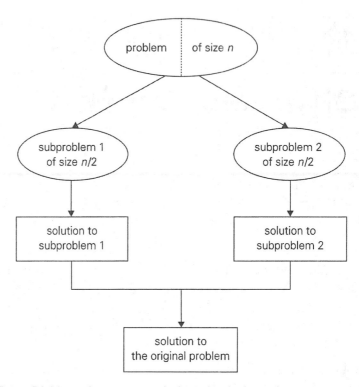

FIGURE 4.1 Divide-and-conquer technique (typical case)

Is this an efficient way to compute the sum of n numbers? A moment of reflection (why could it be more efficient than the brute-force summation?), a small example of summing, say, four numbers by this algorithm, a formal analysis (which follows), and common sense (we do not compute sums this way, do we?) all lead to a negative answer to this question.

Thus, not every divide-and-conquer algorithm is necessarily more efficient than even a brute-force solution. But often our prayers to the Goddess of Algorithmics—see the chapter's epigraph—*are* answered, and the time spent on executing the divide-and-conquer plan turns out to be smaller than solving a problem by a different method. In fact, the divide-and-conquer approach yields some of the most important and efficient algorithms in computer science. We discuss a few classic examples of such algorithms in this chapter. Though we consider only sequential algorithms here, it is worth keeping in mind that the divide-and-conquer technique is ideally suited for parallel computations, in which each subproblem can be solved simultaneously by its own processor.

The sum example illustrates the most typical case of divide-and-conquer: a problem's instance of size n is divided into two instances of size $n/2$. More generally, an instance of size n can be divided into several instances of size n/b, with a of them needing to be solved. (Here, a and b are constants; $a \geq 1$ and $b > 1$.). Assuming that size n is a power of b, to simplify our analysis, we get the following recurrence for the running time $T(n)$:

$$T(n) = aT(n/b) + f(n), \qquad (4.1)$$

where $f(n)$ is a function that accounts for the time spent on dividing the problem into smaller ones and on combining their solutions. (For the summation example, $a = b = 2$ and $f(n) = 1$.) Recurrence (4.1) is called the **general divide-and-conquer recurrence**. Obviously, the order of growth of its solution $T(n)$ depends on the values of the constants a and b and the order of growth of the function $f(n)$. The efficiency analysis of many divide-and-conquer algorithms is greatly simplified by the following theorem (see Appendix B).

MASTER THEOREM   If $f(n) \in \Theta(n^d)$ where $d \geq 0$ in recurrence equation (4.1), then

$$T(n) \in \begin{cases} \Theta(n^d) & \text{if } a < b^d \\ \Theta(n^d \log n) & \text{if } a = b^d \\ \Theta(n^{\log_b a}) & \text{if } a > b^d \end{cases}$$

(Analogous results hold for the O and Ω notations, too.)

For example, the recurrence equation for the number of additions $A(n)$ made by the divide-and-conquer summation algorithm (see above) on inputs of size $n = 2^k$ is

$$A(n) = 2A(n/2) + 1.$$

Thus, for this example, $a = 2$, $b = 2$, and $d = 0$; hence, since $a > b^d$,

$$A(n) \in \Theta(n^{\log_b a}) = \Theta(n^{\log_2 2}) = \Theta(n).$$

Note that we were able to find the solution's efficiency class without going through the drudgery of solving the recurrence. But, of course, this approach can only establish a solution's order of growth to within an unknown multiplicative constant while solving a recurrence equation with a specific initial condition yields an exact answer (at least for n's that are powers of b).

Computation and Reasoning

4.1 Mergesort

Mergesort is a perfect example of a successful application of the divide-and-conquer technique. It sorts a given array $A[0..n-1]$ by dividing it into two halves $A[0..\lfloor n/2 \rfloor - 1]$ and $A[\lfloor n/2 \rfloor..n-1]$, sorting each of them recursively, and then merging the two smaller sorted arrays into a single sorted one.

ALGORITHM *Mergesort*($A[0..n-1]$)

    //Sorts array $A[0..n-1]$ by recursive mergesort
    //Input: An array $A[0..n-1]$ of orderable elements
    //Output: Array $A[0..n-1]$ sorted in nondecreasing order
    if $n > 1$
        copy $A[0..\lfloor n/2 \rfloor - 1]$ to $B[0..\lfloor n/2 \rfloor - 1]$
        copy $A[\lfloor n/2 \rfloor..n-1]$ to $C[0..\lceil n/2 \rceil - 1]$
        Mergesort($B[0..\lfloor n/2 \rfloor - 1]$)
        Mergesort($C[0..\lceil n/2 \rceil - 1]$)
        Merge(B, C, A)

The ***merging*** of two sorted arrays can be done as follows. Two pointers (array indices) are initialized to point to the first elements of the arrays being merged. Then the elements pointed to are compared and the smaller of them is added to a new array being constructed; after that, the index of that smaller element is incremented to point to its immediate successor in the array it was copied from. This operation is continued until one of the two given arrays is exhausted, and then the remaining elements of the other array are copied to the end of the new array.

ALGORITHM *Merge*($B[0..p-1], C[0..q-1], A[0..p+q-1]$)

    //Merges two sorted arrays into one sorted array
    //Input: Arrays $B[0..p-1]$ and $C[0..q-1]$ both sorted
    //Output: Sorted array $A[0..p+q-1]$ of the elements of B and C
    $i \leftarrow 0;\ j \leftarrow 0;\ k \leftarrow 0$
    while $i < p$ **and** $j < q$ **do**
        if $B[i] \le C[j]$
            $A[k] \leftarrow B[i];\ i \leftarrow i+1$
        else $A[k] \leftarrow C[j];\ j \leftarrow j+1$
        $k \leftarrow k+1$
    if $i = p$
        copy $C[j..q-1]$ to $A[k..p+q-1]$
    else copy $B[i..p-1]$ to $A[k..p+q-1]$

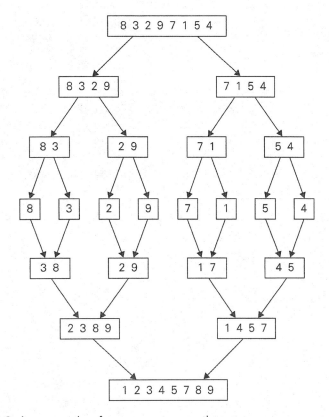

FIGURE 4.2 An example of mergesort operation

The operation of the algorithm on the list 8, 3, 2, 9, 7, 1, 5, 4 is illustrated in Figure 4.2.

How efficient is mergesort? Assuming for simplicity that n is a power of 2, the recurrence relation for the number of key comparisons $C(n)$ is

$$C(n) = 2C(n/2) + C_{merge}(n) \text{ for } n > 1, \ C(1) = 0.$$

Let us analyze $C_{merge}(n)$, the number of key comparisons performed during the merging stage. At each step, exactly one comparison is made, after which the total number of elements in the two arrays still needed to be processed is reduced by one. In the worst case, neither of the two arrays becomes empty before the other one contains just one element (e.g., smaller elements may come from the alternating arrays). Therefore, for the worst case, $C_{merge}(n) = n - 1$, and we have the recurrence

$$C_{worst}(n) = 2C_{worst}(n/2) + n - 1 \text{ for } n > 1, \ C_{worst}(1) = 0.$$

Computation and Reasoning

Hence, according to the Master Theorem, $C_{worst}(n) \in \Theta(n \log n)$ (why?). In fact, it is easy to find the exact solution to the worst-case recurrence for $n = 2^k$:

$$C_{worst}(n) = n \log_2 n - n + 1.$$

The number of key comparisons made by mergesort in the worst case comes very close to the theoretical minimum[1] that any general comparison-based sorting algorithm can have. The principal shortcoming of mergesort is the linear amount of extra storage the algorithm requires. Though merging can be done in place, the resulting algorithm is quite complicated and, since it has a significantly larger multiplicative constant, the in-place mergesort is of theoretical interest only.

Exercises 4.1

1. **a.** Write a pseudocode for a divide-and-conquer algorithm for finding a position of the largest element in an array of n numbers.

   b. What will be your algorithm's output for arrays with several elements of the largest value?

   c. Set up and solve a recurrence relation for the number of key comparisons made by your algorithm.

   d. How does this algorithm compare with the brute-force algorithm for this problem?

2. **a.** Write a pseudocode for a divide-and-conquer algorithm for finding values of both the largest and smallest elements in an array of n numbers.

   b. Set up and solve a recurrence relation for the number of key comparisons made by your algorithm.

   c. How does this algorithm compare with the brute-force algorithm for this problem?

3. **a.** Write a pseudocode for a divide-and-conquer algorithm for the exponentiation problem of computing a^n where $a > 0$ and n is a positive integer.

   b. Set up and solve (for $n = 2^k$) a recurrence relation for the number of multiplications made by this algorithm.

   c. How does this algorithm compare with the brute-force algorithm for this problem?

4. While discussing the framework for design and analysis of algorithms in Chapter 2, we mentioned that logarithm bases are irrelevant in most contexts arising in analysis of algorithms. Is it true for both assertions of the Master Theorem that include logarithms?

---

1. As we shall see in Section 10.2, this theoretical minimum is $\lceil \log_2 n! \rceil \approx \lceil n \log_2 n - 1.44n \rceil$.

5. Find the order of growth for solutions of the following recurrences.
   a. $T(n) = 4T(n/2) + n$, $T(1) = 1$
   b. $T(n) = 4T(n/2) + n^2$, $T(1) = 1$
   c. $T(n) = 4T(n/2) + n^3$, $T(1) = 1$

6. Apply mergesort to sort the list E, X, A, M, P, L, E in alphabetical order.

7. Is mergesort a stable sorting algorithm?

8. a. Solve the recurrence relation for the number of key comparisons made by mergesort in the worst case. (You may assume that $n = 2^k$.)
   b. Set up a recurrence relation for the number of key comparisons made by mergesort on best-case inputs and solve it for $n = 2^k$.
   c. Set up a recurrence relation for the number of key moves made by the version of mergesort given in Section 4.1. Does taking the number of key moves into account change the algorithm's efficiency class?

9. We can implement mergesort without a recursion by starting with merging adjacent elements of a given array, then merging sorted pairs, and so on. Implement this bottom-up version of mergesort in the language of your choice.

10. *Triomino Puzzle* A triomino is an L-shaped tile formed by three adjacent squares of a chess board. The problem is to cover any 2^n-by-2^n chessboard with one missing square (anywhere on the board) with triominos. Triominos should cover all the squares except the missing one with no overlaps.

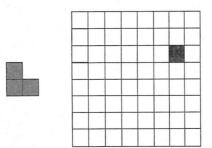

Design a divide-and-conquer algorithm for this problem.

4.2 Quicksort

Quicksort is another important sorting algorithm that is based on the divide-and-conquer approach. Unlike mergesort, which divides its input's elements according to their position in the array, quicksort divides them according to their value. Specifically, it rearranges elements of a given array $A[0..n-1]$ to achieve its

Computation and Reasoning

partition, a situation where all the elements before some position s are smaller than or equal to $A[s]$ and all the elements after position s are greater than or equal to $A[s]$:

$$\underbrace{A[0]\ldots A[s-1]}_{\text{all are } \leq A[s]}\ A[s]\ \underbrace{A[s+1]\ldots A[n-1]}_{\text{all are } \geq A[s]}$$

Obviously, after a partition has been achieved, $A[s]$ will be in its final position in the sorted array, and we can continue sorting the two subarrays of the elements preceding and following $A[s]$ independently (e.g., by the same method).

ALGORITHM *Quicksort(A[l..r])*

   //Sorts a subarray by quicksort
   //Input: A subarray $A[l..r]$ of $A[0..n-1]$, defined by its left and right indices
   // l and r
   //Output: The subarray $A[l..r]$ sorted in nondecreasing order
   if $l < r$
       $s \leftarrow$ *Partition(A[l..r])* //s is a split position
       Quicksort(A[l..s − 1])
       Quicksort(A[s + 1..r])

A partition of $A[0..n-1]$ and, more generally, of its subarray $A[l..r]$ ($0 \leq l < r \leq n-1$) can be achieved by the following algorithm. First, we select an element with respect to whose value we are going to divide the subarray. Because of its guiding role, we call this element the ***pivot***. There are several different strategies for selecting a pivot; we will return to this issue when we analyze the algorithm's efficiency. For now, we use the simplest strategy of selecting the subarray's first element: $p = A[l]$.

There are also several alternative procedures for rearranging elements to achieve a partition. Here we use an efficient method based on two scans of the subarray: one is left-to-right and the other right-to-left, each comparing the subarray's elements with the pivot. The left-to-right scan starts with the second element. Since we want elements smaller than the pivot to be in the first part of the subarray, this scan skips over elements that are smaller than the pivot and stops on encountering the first element greater than or equal to the pivot. The right-to-left scan starts with the last element of the subarray. Since we want elements larger than the pivot to be in the second part of the subarray, this scan skips over elements that are larger than the pivot and stops on encountering the first element smaller than or equal to the pivot.

Three situations may arise, depending on whether or not the scanning indices have crossed. If scanning indices i and j have not crossed, i.e., $i < j$, we simply exchange $A[i]$ and $A[j]$ and resume the scans by incrementing i and decrementing j, respectively:

		$\rightarrow i$			$j\leftarrow$	
p	all are $\leq p$	$\geq p$	. . .	$\leq p$	all are $\geq p$	

If the scanning indices have crossed over, i.e., $i > j$, we have partitioned the array after exchanging the pivot with $A[j]$:

		$j\leftarrow$	$\rightarrow i$	
p	all are $\leq p$	$\leq p$	$\geq p$	all are $\geq p$

Finally, if the scanning indices stop while pointing to the same element, i.e., $i = j$, the value they are pointing to must be equal to p (why?). Thus, we have partitioned the array:

		$\rightarrow i = j \leftarrow$	
p	all are $\leq p$	$= p$	all are $\geq p$

We can combine the last case with the case of crossed-over indices ($i > j$) by exchanging the pivot with $A[j]$ whenever $i \geq j$.

Here is a pseudocode implementing this partitioning procedure.

ALGORITHM *Partition*($A[l..r]$)

//Partitions a subarray by using its first element as a pivot
//Input: A subarray $A[l..r]$ of $A[0..n-1]$, defined by its left and right
//   indices l and r ($l < r$)
//Output: A partition of $A[l..r]$, with the split position returned as
//   this function's value
$p \leftarrow A[l]$
$i \leftarrow l; \quad j \leftarrow r + 1$
repeat
    repeat $i \leftarrow i + 1$ **until** $A[i] \geq p$
    repeat $j \leftarrow j - 1$ **until** $A[j] \leq p$
    swap($A[i], A[j]$)
until $i \geq j$
swap($A[i], A[j]$)   //undo last swap when $i \geq j$
swap($A[l], A[j]$)
return j

Computation and Reasoning

285

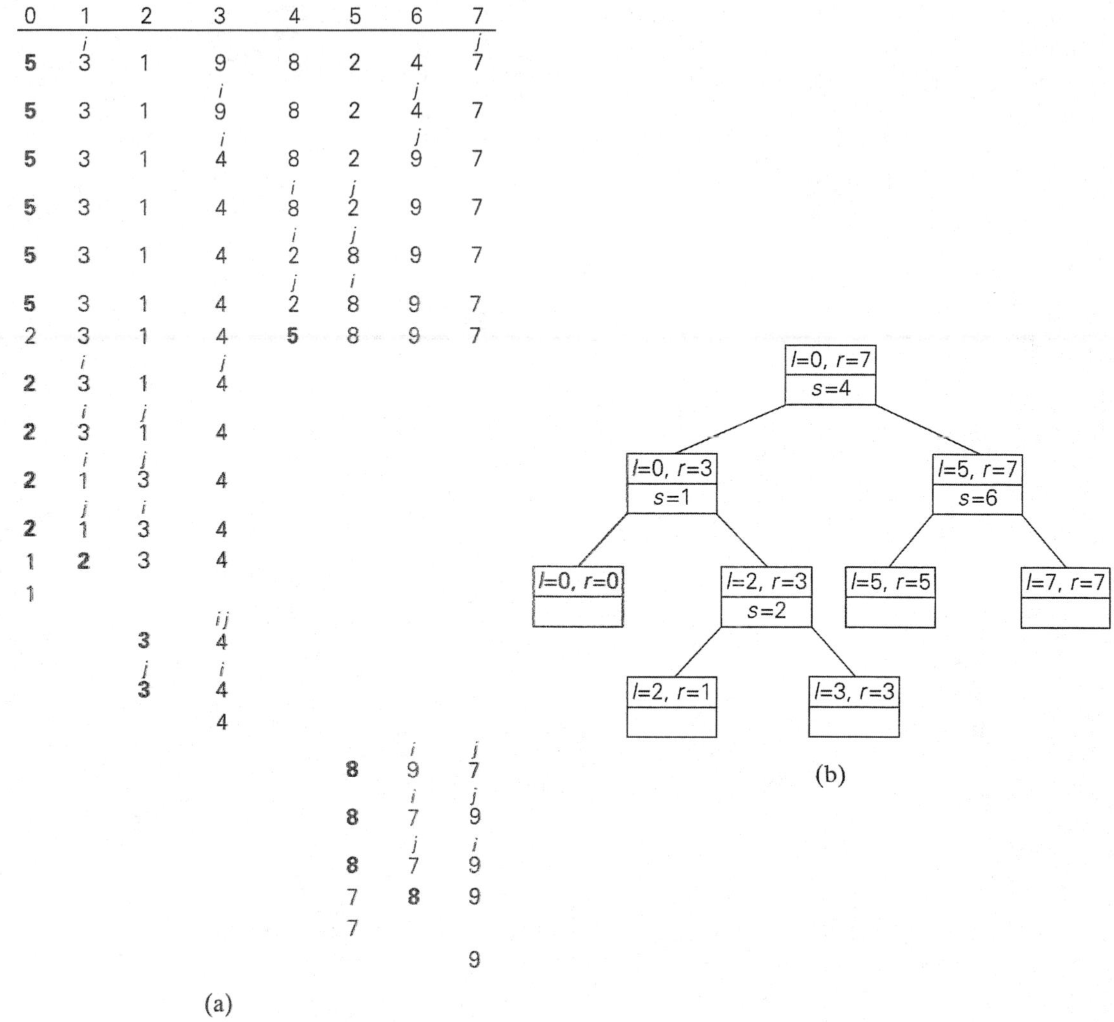

0	1	2	3	4	5	6	7
	i						*j*
5	3	1	9	8	2	4	7
			i			*j*	
5	3	1	9	8	2	4	7
			i			*j*	
5	3	1	4	8	2	9	7
				i	*j*		
5	3	1	4	8	2	9	7
				i	*j*		
5	3	1	4	2	8	9	7
				j	*i*		
5	3	1	4	2	8	9	7
2	3	1	4	**5**	8	9	7

	i		*j*	
2	3	1	4	
	i	*j*		
2	3	1	4	
	i	*j*		
2	1	3	4	
	j	*i*		
2	1	3	4	
1	**2**	3	4	
1				

	ij	
3	4	
	j	*i*
3	4	
	4	

	i	*j*
8	9	7
	i	*j*
8	7	9
	j	*i*
8	7	9
7	**8**	9
7		
		9

(a)

(b)

FIGURE 4.3 An example of Quicksort operation. (a) The array's transformations with pivots shown in bold. (b) The tree of recursive calls to *Quicksort* with input values *l* and *r* of subarray bounds and split position *s* of a partition obtained.

Note that, in this form, index *i* can go out of bounds of the subarray. Rather than checking for this possibility every time index *i* is incremented, we can append to array $A[0..n-1]$ a "sentinel" that would prevent index *i* from advancing beyond position *n*. Note that the more sophisticated method of pivot selection mentioned at the end of the section makes such a sentinel unnecessary.

An example of sorting an array by quicksort is given in Figure 4.3.

We start our discussion of quicksort's efficiency by noting that the number of key comparisons made before a partition is achieved is $n + 1$ if the scanning indices cross over, n if they coincide (why?). If all the splits happen in the middle of corresponding subarrays, we will have the best case. The number of key comparisons in the best case, $C_{best}(n)$ will satisfy the recurrence

$$C_{best}(n) = 2C_{best}(n/2) + n \text{ for } n > 1, \quad C_{best}(1) = 0.$$

According to the Master Theorem, $C_{best}(n) \in \Theta(n \log_2 n)$; solving it exactly for $n = 2^k$ yields $C_{best}(n) = n \log_2 n$.

In the worst case, all the splits will be skewed to the extreme: one of the two subarrays will be empty while the size of the other will be just one less than the size of a subarray being partitioned. This unfortunate situation will happen, in particular, for increasing arrays, i.e., for inputs for which the problem is already solved! Indeed, if $A[0..n-1]$ is a strictly increasing array and we use $A[0]$ as the pivot, the left-to-right scan will stop on $A[1]$ while the right-to-left scan will go all the way to reach $A[0]$, indicating the split at position 0:

$$j \leftarrow \quad i \rightarrow$$

$A[0]$	$A[1]$	$\cdots$	$A[n-1]$

So, after making $n + 1$ comparisons to get to this partition and exchanging the pivot $A[0]$ with itself, the algorithm will find itself with the strictly increasing array $A[1..n-1]$ to sort. This sorting of strictly increasing arrays of diminishing sizes will continue until the last one $A[n-2..n-1]$ has been processed. The total number of key comparisons made will be equal to

$$C_{worst}(n) = (n + 1) + n + \cdots + 3 = \frac{(n+1)(n+2)}{2} - 3 \in \Theta(n^2).$$

Thus, the question about the utility of quicksort comes to its average-case behavior. Let $C_{avg}(n)$ be the average number of key comparisons made by quicksort on a randomly ordered array of size n. Assuming that the partition split can happen in each position s $(0 \le s \le n - 1)$ with the same probability $1/n$, we get the following recurrence relation

$$C_{avg}(n) = \frac{1}{n} \sum_{s=0}^{n-1} [(n + 1) + C_{avg}(s) + C_{avg}(n - 1 - s)] \text{ for } n > 1,$$

$$C_{avg}(0) = 0, \quad C_{avg}(1) = 0.$$

Though solving this recurrence is easier than one might expect, it is still much trickier than the worst- and best-case analyses and we will leave it for the exercises. Its solution turns out to be

$$C_{avg}(n) \approx 2n \ln n \approx 1.38n \log_2 n.$$

Computation and Reasoning

Thus, on the average, quicksort makes only 38% more comparisons than in the best case. Moreover, its innermost loop is so efficient that it runs faster than mergesort (and heapsort, another $n \log n$ algorithm that we will discuss in Chapter 6) on randomly ordered arrays, justifying the name given to the algorithm by its inventor, the prominent British computer scientist C.A.R. Hoare.[2]

Given the importance of quicksort, there have been persistent efforts over the years to refine the basic algorithm. Among several improvements discovered by researchers are: better pivot selection methods (such as the ***median-of-three partitioning*** that uses as a pivot the median of the leftmost, rightmost, and the middle element of the array); switching to a simpler sort on smaller subfiles; and recursion elimination (so called nonrecursive quicksort). According to R. Sedgewick [Sed98], the world's leading expert on quicksort, these improvements in combination can cut the running time of the algorithm by 20%–25%.

We should also point out that the idea of partitioning can be useful in applications other than sorting. In particular, it underlines a fast algorithm for the important ***selection problem*** discussed in Section 5.6.

Exercises 4.2

1. Apply quicksort to sort the list

$$E, \ X, \ A, \ M, \ P, \ L, \ E$$

   in alphabetical order. Draw the tree of the recursive calls made.

2. For the partitioning procedure outlined in Section 4.2:
   a. Prove that if the scanning indices stop while pointing to the same element, i.e., $i = j$, the value they are pointing to must be equal to p.
   b. Prove that when the scanning indices stop, j cannot point to an element more than one position to the left of the one pointed to by i.
   c. Why is it worth stopping the scans after encountering an element equal to the pivot?

3. Is quicksort a stable sorting algorithm?

4. Give an example of an array of n elements for which the sentinel mentioned in the text is actually needed. What should be its value? Also explain why a single sentinel suffices for any input.

---

2. The young Hoare invented his algorithm while trying to sort words of a Russian dictionary for a machine translation project from Russian to English. Says Hoare, "My first thought on how to do this was bubblesort and, by an amazing stroke of luck, my second thought was Quicksort." It is hard to disagree with his overall assessment: "I have been very lucky. What a wonderful way to start a career in Computing, by discovering a new sorting algorithm!" [Hoa96]

5. For the version of quicksort given in the text:
   a. Are arrays made up of all equal elements the worst-case input, the best-case input, or neither?
   b. Are strictly decreasing arrays the worst-case input, the best-case input, or neither?

6. a. With the median-of-three pivot selection, will increasing arrays be the worst-case input, the best-case input, or neither?
   b. Answer the same question for decreasing arrays.

7. Solve the average-case recurrence for quicksort.

8. Design an algorithm to rearrange elements of a given array of n real numbers so that all its negative elements precede all its positive elements. Your algorithm should be both time- and space-efficient.

9. Implement quicksort in the language of your choice. Run your program on a sample of inputs to verify the theoretical assertions about the algorithm's efficiency.

10. *Nuts-and-Bolts Problem* You are given a collection of n bolts of different widths and n corresponding nuts. You are allowed to try a nut and bolt together, from which you can determine whether the nut is larger than the bolt, smaller than the bolt, or matches the bolt exactly. However, there is no way to compare two nuts together or two bolts together. The problem is to match each bolt to its nut. Design an algorithm for this problem with average-case efficiency in $\Theta(n \log n)$. [Raw91]

4.3 Binary Search

Binary search is a remarkably efficient algorithm for searching in a sorted array. It works by comparing a search key K with the array's middle element $A[m]$. If they match, the algorithm stops; otherwise, the same operation is repeated recursively for the first half of the array if $K < A[m]$ and for the second half if $K > A[m]$:

$$K$$
$$\updownarrow$$
$$\underbrace{A[0] \ldots A[m-1]}_{\substack{\text{search here if} \\ K < A[m]}} \quad A[m] \quad \underbrace{A[m+1] \ldots A[n-1]}_{\substack{\text{search here if} \\ K > A[m]}}.$$

As an example, let us apply binary search to searching for $K = 70$ in the array

3	14	27	31	39	42	55	70	74	81	85	93	98

Computation and Reasoning

289

The iterations of the algorithm are given in the following table:

index	0	1	2	3	4	5	6	7	8	9	10	11	12
value	3	14	27	31	39	42	55	70	74	81	85	93	98
iteration 1	l						m						r
iteration 2								l		m			r
iteration 3									l,m	r			

Though binary search is clearly based on a recursive idea, it can be easily implemented as a nonrecursive algorithm, too. Here is a pseudocode for this nonrecursive version:

ALGORITHM *BinarySearch*$(A[0..n - 1], K)$
    //Implements nonrecursive binary search
    //Input: An array $A[0..n - 1]$ sorted in ascending order and
    //   a search key K
    //Output: An index of the array's element that is equal to K
    //   or −1 if there is no such element
    $l \leftarrow 0; r \leftarrow n - 1$
    while $l \le r$ **do**
        $m \leftarrow \lfloor (l + r)/2 \rfloor$
        if $K = A[m]$ **return** m
        else if $K < A[m]$ $r \leftarrow m - 1$
        else $l \leftarrow m + 1$
    return −1

The standard way to analyze the efficiency of binary search is to count the number of times the search key is compared with an element of the array. Moreover, for the sake of simplicity, we will count the so-called three-way comparisons. This assumes that after one comparison of K with $A[m]$, the algorithm can determine whether K is smaller, equal to, or larger than $A[m]$.

How many such comparisons does the algorithm make on an array of n elements? The answer obviously depends not only on n but also on the specifics of a particular instance of the problem. Let us find the number of key comparisons in the worst case $C_w(n)$. The worst case inputs include all arrays that do not contain a given search key (and, in fact, some cases of successful searches as well). Since after one comparison the algorithm faces the same situation but for an array half the size, we get the following recurrence relation for $C_w(n)$:

$$C_w(n) = C_w(\lfloor n/2 \rfloor) + 1 \text{ for } n > 1, \ C_w(1) = 1. \tag{4.2}$$

(Stop and convince yourself that $n/2$ must be, indeed, rounded down and that the initial condition must be written as specified.)

As we discussed in Section 2.4, the standard way of solving recurrences such as recurrence (4.2) is to assume that $n = 2^k$ and solve the resulting recurrence by backward substitutions or another method. We leave this as a straightforward exercise to obtain the solution

$$C_w(2^k) = k + 1 = \log_2 n + 1. \tag{4.3}$$

Actually, one can prove that the solution given by formula (4.3) for $n = 2^k$ can be tweaked to get a solution valid for an arbitrary positive integer n:

$$C_w(n) = \lfloor \log_2 n \rfloor + 1 = \lceil \log_2(n + 1) \rceil. \tag{4.4}$$

Let us verify by substitution that function $C_w(n) = \lfloor \log_2 n \rfloor + 1$ indeed satisfies equation (4.2) for any positive even number n. (You are asked to do this for odd n's in Exercises 4.3). If n is positive and even, $n = 2i$ where $i > 0$. The left-hand side of equation (4.2) for $n = 2i$ is

$$C_w(n) = \lfloor \log_2 n \rfloor + 1 = \lfloor \log_2 2i \rfloor + 1 = \lfloor \log_2 2 + \log_2 i \rfloor + 1$$
$$= (1 + \lfloor \log_2 i \rfloor) + 1 = \lfloor \log_2 i \rfloor + 2.$$

The right-hand side of equation (4.2) for $n = 2i$ is

$$C_w(\lfloor n/2 \rfloor) + 1 = C_w(\lfloor 2i/2 \rfloor) + 1 = C_w(i) + 1$$
$$= (\lfloor \log_2 i \rfloor + 1) + 1 = \lfloor \log_2 i \rfloor + 2.$$

Since both expressions are the same, we proved the assertion.

Formula (4.4) deserves attention. First, it implies that the worst-case efficiency of binary search is in $\Theta(\log n)$. (Incidentally, we could get this fact by applying the Master Theorem, but this approach would not give us the value of the multiplicative constant.) Second, it is the answer we should have fully expected: since the algorithm simply reduces the size of the remaining array by about half on each iteration, the number of such iterations needed to reduce the initial size n to the final size 1 has to be about $\log_2 n$. Third, to reiterate the point made in Section 2.1, the logarithmic function grows so slowly that its values remain small even for very large values of n. In particular, according to formula (4.4), it will take no more than $\lfloor \log_2 10^3 \rfloor + 1 = 10$ three-way comparisons to find an element of a given value (or establish that there is no such element) in any sorted array of 1000 elements, and it will take no more than $\lfloor \log_2 10^6 \rfloor + 1 = 20$ comparisons to do it for any sorted array of size one million!

What can we say about the average-case efficiency of binary search? A sophisticated analysis shows that the average number of key comparisons made by binary search is only slightly smaller than that in the worst case:

$$C_{avg}(n) \approx \log_2 n.$$

(More accurate formulas for the average number of comparisons in a successful and an unsuccessful search are $C_{avg}^{yes}(n) \approx \log_2 n - 1$ and $C_{avg}^{no}(n) \approx \log_2(n + 1)$, respectively.)

Though binary search is an optimal searching algorithm if we restrict our operations only to comparisons between keys (see Section 10.2), there are searching algorithms (see interpolation search in Section 5.6 and hashing in Section 7.3) with a better average-case efficiency, and one of them (hashing) does not even require the array to be sorted! These algorithms do require some special calculations in addition to key comparisons, however. Finally, the idea behind binary search has several applications beyond searching (see, e.g., [Ben00]). In addition, it can be applied to solving nonlinear equations in one unknown; we will discuss this continuous analogue of binary search, called the method of bisection, in Section 11.4.

Before we leave this section, one other remark about binary search needs to be made. Binary search is sometimes presented as the quintessential example of a divide-and-conquer algorithm. This interpretation is flawed because, in fact, binary search is a very atypical case of divide-and-conquer. Indeed, according to the definition given at the beginning of this chapter, the divide-and-conquer technique divides a problem into *several* subproblems, each of which needs to be solved. That is not the case for binary search where, instead, only one of the two subproblems needs to be solved. Therefore, if binary search is to be considered as a divide-and-conquer algorithm, it should be looked on as a degenerative case of this technique. As a matter of fact, binary search fits much better into the class of decrease-by-half algorithms, which we discuss in Section 5.5. Why then is this discussion of binary search in this chapter? Partly because of tradition and partly because a bad example can sometimes make a point that a good example cannot.

——————— **Exercises 4.3** ———————

1. a. What is the largest number of key comparisons made by binary search in searching for a key in the following array?

3	14	27	31	39	42	55	70	74	81	85	93	98

   b. List all the keys of this array that will require the largest number of key comparisons when searched for by binary search.

   c. Find the average number of key comparisons made by binary search in a successful search in this array. (Assume that each key is searched for with the same probability.)

   d. Find the average number of key comparisons made by binary search in an unsuccessful search in this array. (Assume that searches for keys in each of the 14 intervals formed by the array's elements are equally likely.)

2. Solve the recurrence $C_w(n) = C_w(\lfloor n/2 \rfloor) + 1$ for $n > 1$, $C_w(1) = 1$ for $n = 2^k$ by backward substitutions.

3. **a.** Prove the equality

$$\lfloor \log_2 n \rfloor + 1 = \lceil \log_2(n + 1) \rceil \text{ for } n \geq 1.$$

   b. Prove that the function $C_w(n) = \lfloor \log_2 n \rfloor + 1$ solves recurrence relation (4.2) for every positive odd integer n.

4. Estimate how many times faster an average successful search will be in a sorted array of 100,000 elements if it is done by binary search versus sequential search.

5. Sequential search can be used with about the same efficiency whether a list is implemented as an array or as a linked list. Is it also true for binary search? (Of course, we assume that a list is sorted for binary search.)

6. How can we use binary search for range searching, i.e., for finding all the elements in a sorted array whose values fall between two given values L and U (inclusively), $L \leq U$? What is the worst-case efficiency of this algorithm?

7. Write a pseudocode for a recursive version of binary search.

8. Design a version of binary search that uses only two-way comparisons such as $\leq$ and $=$. Implement your algorithm in the language of your choice and carefully debug it (such programs are notorious for being prone to bugs).

9. Analyze the time efficiency of the two-way comparison version designed in Problem 8.

10. A version of the popular problem-solving task involves presenting people with an array of 42 pictures—seven rows of six pictures each—and asking them to identify the target picture by asking questions that can be answered yes or no. Further, people are then required to identify the picture with as few questions as possible. Suggest the most efficient algorithm for this problem and indicate the largest number of questions that may be necessary.

Computation and Reasoning

293

4.4 Binary Tree Traversals and Related Properties

In this section, we see how the divide-and-conquer technique can be applied to binary trees. A **binary tree** T is defined as a finite set of nodes that is either empty or consists of a root and two disjoint binary trees T_L and T_R called, respectively, the left and right subtree of the root. We usually think of a binary tree as a special case of an ordered tree (Figure 4.4). (This standard interpretation was an alternative definition of a binary tree in Section 1.4.)

Since the definition itself divides a binary tree into two smaller structures of the same type, the left subtree and the right subtree, many problems about binary trees can be solved by applying the divide-conquer technique. As an example, we consider a recursive algorithm for computing the height of a binary tree. Recall that the height of a tree is defined as the length of the longest path from the root to a leaf. Hence, it can be computed as the maximum of the heights of the root's left and right subtrees plus 1. (We add 1 to account for the extra level of the root.) Also note that it is convenient to define the height of the empty tree as -1. Thus, we have the following recursive algorithm.

ALGORITHM *Height(T)*

//Computes recursively the height of a binary tree
//Input: A binary tree T
//Output: The height of T
if $T = \varnothing$ **return** -1
else return $\max\{Height(T_L), Height(T_R)\} + 1$

We measure the problem's instance size by the number of nodes $n(T)$ in a given binary tree T. Obviously, the number of comparisons made to compute the maximum of two numbers and the number of additions $A(n(T))$ made by the

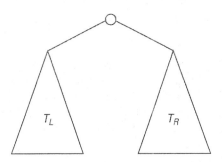

FIGURE 4.4 A standard representation of a binary tree

Computation and Reasoning

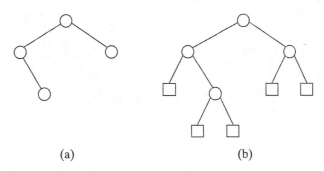

(a)   (b)

FIGURE 4.5 (a) Binary tree. (b) Its extension. Internal nodes are shown as circles; external nodes are shown as squares.

algorithm are the same. We have the following recurrence relation for $A(n(T))$

$$A(n(T)) = A(n(T_L)) + A(n(T_R)) + 1 \text{ for } n(T) > 0,$$
$$A(0) = 0.$$

Before we solve this recurrence (can you tell what its solution is?), let us note that addition is not the most frequently executed operation of this algorithm. What is? Checking—and this is very typical for binary tree algorithms—that the tree is not empty. For example, for the empty tree, the comparison $T = \oslash$ is executed once but there are no additions, and for a single-node tree, the comparison and addition numbers are three and one, respectively.

It helps in analysis of tree algorithms to draw the tree's extension by replacing the empty subtrees by special nodes. The extra nodes (shown by little squares in Figure 4.5) are called *external*; the original nodes (shown by little circles) are called *internal*. By definition, the extension of the empty binary tree is a single external node.

It is easy to see that the height algorithm makes exactly one addition for every internal node of the extended tree, and it makes one comparison to check whether the tree is empty for every internal and external node. Thus, to ascertain the algorithm's efficiency we need to know how many external nodes an extended binary tree with n internal nodes can have. Checking Figure 4.5 and a few similar examples, it is easy to hypothesize (and, in fact, not difficult to prove) that the number of external nodes x is always one more than the number of internal nodes n:

$$x = n + 1. \tag{4.5}$$

Let us prove this equality by induction in the number of internal nodes $n \geq 0$. The induction's basis is true because for $n = 0$ we have the empty tree with 1 external node by definition. For the general case, let us assume that

$$x = k + 1$$

Computation and Reasoning

295

for any extended binary tree with $0 \leq k < n$ internal nodes. Let T be an extended binary tree with n internal nodes and x external nodes, let n_L and x_L be the numbers of internal and external nodes in the left subtree of T, respectively, and let n_R and x_R be the numbers of internal and external nodes in the right subtree of T, respectively. Since $n > 0$, T has a root, which is its internal node, and hence $n = n_L + n_R + 1$. Using the equality assumed to be correct for the left and right subtrees, we obtain the following:

$$x = x_L + x_R = (n_L + 1) + (n_R + 1) = (n_L + n_R + 1) + 1 = n + 1,$$

which completes the proof.

Returning to algorithm *Height*, the number of comparisons to check whether the tree is empty is

$$C(n) = n + x = 2n + 1,$$

while the number of additions is

$$A(n) = n.$$

The most important divide-and-conquer algorithms for binary trees are the three classic traversals: preorder, inorder, and postorder. All three traversals visit nodes of a binary tree recursively, i.e., by visiting the tree's root and its left and right subtrees. They differ just by the timing of the root's visit:

In the *preorder traversal*, the root is visited before the left and right subtrees are visited (in that order).

In the *inorder traversal*, the root is visited after visiting its left subtree but before visiting the right subtree.

In the *postorder traversal*, the root is visited after visiting the left and right subtrees (in that order).

A pseudocode for these traversals is quite straightforward. (These traversals are also a standard feature of data structures textbooks.) As to their efficiency analysis, it is identical to the one just discussed because a recursive call is made for each node of an extended binary tree.

Finally, we should note that, obviously, not all questions about binary trees require traversals of both left and right subtrees. For example, the find and insert operations for a binary search tree require processing only one of the two subtrees. Hence, they should be considered not as applications of divide-and-conquer but rather as examples of the variable-size decrease technique to be discussed in Section 5.6.

―――――――――― **Exercises 4.4** ――――――――――

1. Design a divide-and-conquer algorithm for computing the number of levels in a binary tree. (In particular, the algorithm should return 0 and 1 for the

empty and single-node trees, respectively.) What is the efficiency class of your algorithm?

2. Traverse the following binary tree:

   a. in preorder;   **b.** in inorder;   **c.** in postorder.

   Show the contents of the traversal's stack as the algorithm progresses.

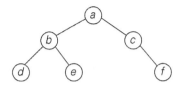

3. Write a pseudocode for one of the classic traversal algorithms (preorder, inorder, and postorder) for binary trees. Assuming that your algorithm is recursive, find the number of recursive calls made.

4. What is the largest number of nodes that can be on the inorder traversal stack at the same time? Describe trees for which this maximum is actually achieved.

5. In which order—preorder, inorder, postorder, or none of these—does the height computation algorithm of this section find the heights of all the subtrees of an input tree?

6. Which of the three classic traversal algorithms yields a sorted list if applied to a binary search tree? Prove this property.

7. In a rooted ordered tree, each internal node has a positive number of ordered children, each serving as a root of an ordered subtree. Design an algorithm for computing the height of a rooted ordered tree. (Assume that the smallest rooted ordered tree is a single node and that its height is 0.)

8. The following algorithm seeks to compute the number of leaves in a binary tree.

   ALGORITHM *LeafCounter(T)*

      //Computes recursively the number of leaves in a binary tree
      //Input: A binary tree T
      //Output: The number of leaves in T
      if $T = \oslash$ **return** 0
      else return *LeafCounter*(T_L)+ *LeafCounter*(T_R)

   Is this algorithm correct? If it is, prove it; if it is not, make an appropriate correction.

9. The *internal path length I* of an extended binary tree is defined as the sum of the lengths of the paths—taken over all internal nodes—from the root to

each internal node. Similarly, the ***external path length*** E of an extended binary tree is defined as the sum of the lengths of the paths—taken over all external nodes—from the root to each external node. Prove that $E = I + 2n$ where n is the number of internal nodes in the tree.

10. Write a program for computing the internal path length of a binary search tree. Use it to investigate empirically the average number of key comparisons for searching in a randomly generated binary search tree.

4.5 Multiplication of Large Integers and Strassen's Matrix Multiplication

In this section, we examine two surprising algorithms for seemingly straightforward tasks: multiplying two numbers and multiplying two square matrices. Both seek to decrease the total number of multiplications performed at the expense of a slight increase in the number of additions. Both do it by exploiting the divide-and-conquer idea.

Multiplication of Large Integers

Some applications, notably modern cryptology, require manipulation of integers that are over 100 decimal digits long. Obviously, such integers are too long to fit in a single word of a modern computer, and hence they require special treatment. This practical need supports investigations of algorithms for efficient manipulation of large integers. In this section, we outline an interesting algorithm for multiplying such numbers. Obviously, if we use the classic pen-and-pencil algorithm for multiplying two n-digit integers, each of the n digits of the first number is multiplied by each of the n digits of the second number for the total of n^2 digit multiplications. (If one of the numbers has fewer digits than the other, we can pad a shorter number with leading zeros to equal their lengths.) Though it might appear that it would be impossible to design an algorithm with fewer than n^2 digit multiplications, it proves not to be the case. The miracle of divide-and-conquer comes to the rescue to accomplish this feat.

To demonstrate the basic idea of the algorithm, let us start with a case of two-digit integers, say, 23 and 14. These numbers can be represented as follows:

$$23 = 2 \cdot 10^1 + 3 \cdot 10^0 \text{ and } 14 = 1 \cdot 10^1 + 4 \cdot 10^0.$$

Now let us multiply them:

$$23 = (2 \cdot 10^1 + 3 \cdot 10^0) * (1 \cdot 10^1 + 4 \cdot 10^0)$$
$$= (2 * 1)10^2 + (3 * 1 + 2 * 4)10^1 + (3 * 4)10^0.$$

The last formula yields the correct answer of 322, of course, but it uses the same four digit multiplications as the pen-and-pencil algorithm. Fortunately, we can compute the middle term with just one digit multiplication by taking advantage of the products $(2 * 1)$ and $(3 * 4)$ that need to be computed anyway:

$$3 * 1 + 2 * 4 = (2 + 3) * (1 + 4) - (2 * 1) - (3 * 4).$$

Of course, there is nothing special about the numbers we just multiplied. For any pair of two-digit numbers $a = a_1 a_0$ and $b = b_1 b_0$, their product c can be computed by the formula

$$c = a * b = c_2 10^2 + c_1 10^1 + c_0,$$

where

$c_2 = a_1 * b_1$ is the product of their first digits,

$c_0 = a_0 * b_0$ is the product of their second digits,

$c_1 = (a_1 + a_0) * (b_1 + b_0) - (c_2 + c_0)$ is the product of the sum of the a's digits and the sum of the b's digits minus the sum of c_2 and c_0.

Now we apply this trick to multiplying two n-digit integers a and b where n is a positive even number. Let us divide both numbers in the middle—after all, we promised to take advantage of the divide-and-conquer technique. We denote the first half of the a's digits by a_1 and the second half by a_0; for b, the notations are b_1 and b_0, respectively. In these notations, $a = a_1 a_0$ implies that $a = a_1 10^{n/2} + a_0$ and $b = b_1 b_0$ implies that $b = b_1 10^{n/2} + b_0$. Therefore, taking advantage of the same trick we used for two-digit numbers, we get

$$\begin{aligned} c = a * b &= (a_1 10^{n/2} + a_0) * (b_1 10^{n/2} + b_0) \\ &= (a_1 * b_1) 10^n + (a_1 * b_0 + a_0 * b_1) 10^{n/2} + (a_0 * b_0) \\ &= c_2 10^n + c_1 10^{n/2} + c_0, \end{aligned}$$

where

$c_2 = a_1 * b_1$ is the product of their first halves,

$c_0 = a_0 * b_0$ is the product of their second halves,

$c_1 = (a_1 + a_0) * (b_1 + b_0) - (c_2 + c_0)$ is the product of the sum of the a's halves and the sum of the b's halves minus the sum of c_2 and c_0.

If $n/2$ is even, we can apply the same method for computing the products c_2, c_0, and c_1. Thus, if n is a power of 2, we have a recursive algorithm for computing the product of two n-digit integers. In its pure form, the recursion is stopped when n becomes one. It can also be stopped when we deem n small enough to multiply the numbers of that size directly.

Computation and Reasoning

299

How many digit multiplications does this algorithm make? Since multiplication of n-digit numbers requires three multiplications of $n/2$-digit numbers, the recurrence for the number of multiplications $M(n)$ will be

$$M(n) = 3M(n/2) \text{ for } n > 1, \ M(1) = 1.$$

Solving it by backward substitutions for $n = 2^k$ yields

$$M(2^k) = 3M(2^{k-1}) = 3[3M(2^{k-2})] = 3^2 M(2^{k-2})$$
$$= \cdots = 3^i M(2^{k-i}) = \cdots = 3^k M(2^{k-k}) = 3^k.$$

Since $k = \log_2 n$,

$$M(n) = 3^{\log_2 n} = n^{\log_2 3} \approx n^{1.585}.$$

(On the last step, we take advantage of the following property of logarithms: $a^{\log_b c} = c^{\log_b a}$.)

You should keep in mind that for moderately large integers this algorithm will probably run longer than the classic one. Brassard and Bratley ([BB96], pp. 70–71) report that in their experiments the divide-and-conquer algorithm started to outperform the pen-and-pencil method on integers over 600 digits long. If you program in an object-oriented language such as Java, C++, or Smalltalk, you should also be aware that these languages have special classes for dealing with large integers.

Strassen's Matrix Multiplication

Now that we have seen that the divide-and-conquer approach can reduce the number of one-digit multiplications in multiplying two integers, we should not be surprised that a similar feat can be accomplished for multiplying matrices. Such an algorithm was published by V. Strassen in 1969 [Str69]. The principal insight of the algorithm lies in the discovery that we can find the product C of two 2-by-2 matrices A and B with just seven multiplications as opposed to eight required by the brute-force algorithm (see Example 3, Section 2.3). This is accomplished by using the following formulas:

$$\begin{bmatrix} c_{00} & c_{01} \\ c_{10} & c_{11} \end{bmatrix} = \begin{bmatrix} a_{00} & a_{01} \\ b_{10} & b_{11} \end{bmatrix} * \begin{bmatrix} b_{00} & b_{01} \\ b_{10} & b_{11} \end{bmatrix}$$
$$= \begin{bmatrix} m_1 + m_4 - m_5 + m_7 & m_3 + m_5 \\ m_2 + m_4 & m_1 + m_3 - m_2 + m_6 \end{bmatrix},$$

where

$$m_1 = (a_{00} + a_{11}) * (b_{00} + b_{11})$$
$$m_2 = (a_{10} + a_{11}) * b_{00}$$
$$m_3 = a_{00} * (b_{01} - b_{11})$$
$$m_4 = a_{11} * (b_{10} - b_{00})$$
$$m_5 = (a_{00} + a_{01}) * b_{11}$$
$$m_6 = (a_{10} - a_{00}) * (b_{00} + b_{01})$$
$$m_7 = (a_{01} - a_{11}) * (b_{10} + b_{11}).$$

Thus, to multiply two 2-by-2 matrices, Strassen's algorithm makes seven multiplications and 18 additions/subtractions, whereas the brute-force algorithm requires eight multiplications and four additions. These numbers should not lead us to multiplying 2-by-2 matrices by Strassen's algorithm. Its importance stems from its *asymptotic* superiority as matrix order n goes to infinity.

Let A and B be two n-by-n matrices where n is a power of two. (If n is not a power of two, matrices can be padded with rows and columns of zeros.) We can divide A, B, and their product C into four $n/2$-by-$n/2$ submatrices each as follows:

$$\begin{bmatrix} C_{00} & C_{01} \\ C_{10} & C_{11} \end{bmatrix} = \begin{bmatrix} A_{00} & A_{01} \\ A_{10} & A_{11} \end{bmatrix} * \begin{bmatrix} B_{00} & B_{01} \\ B_{10} & B_{11} \end{bmatrix}$$

It is not difficult to verify that one can treat these submatrices as numbers to get the correct product. For example, C_{00} can be computed either as $A_{00} * B_{00} + A_{01} * B_{10}$ or as $M_1 + M_4 - M_5 + M_7$ where M_1, M_4, M_5, and M_7 are found by Strassen's formulas, with the numbers replaced by the corresponding submatrices. If the seven products of $n/2$-by-$n/2$ matrices are computed recursively by the same method, we have Strassen's algorithm for matrix multiplication.

Let us evaluate the asymptotic efficiency of this algorithm. If $M(n)$ is the number of multiplications made by Strassen's algorithm in multiplying two n-by-n matrices (where n is a power of 2), we get the following recurrence relation for it:

$$M(n) = 7M(n/2) \text{ for } n > 1, \ M(1) = 1.$$

Since $n = 2^k$,

$$M(2^k) = 7M(2^{k-1}) = 7[7M(2^{k-2})] = 7^2 M(2^{k-2}) = \cdots$$
$$= 7^i M(2^{k-i}) \cdots = 7^k M(2^{k-k}) = 7^k.$$

Since $k = \log_2 n$,

$$M(n) = 7^{\log_2 n} = n^{\log_2 7} \approx n^{2.807},$$

which is smaller than n^3 required by the brute-force algorithm.

Since this saving in the number of multiplications was achieved at the expense of making extra additions, we must check the number of additions $A(n)$ made by

Computation and Reasoning

Strassen's algorithm. To multiply two matrices of order $n > 1$, the algorithm needs to multiply seven matrices of order $n/2$ and make 18 additions of matrices of size $n/2$; when $n = 1$, no additions are made since two numbers are simply multiplied. These observations yield the following recurrence relation:

$$A(n) = 7A(n/2) + 18(n/2)^2 \text{ for } n > 1, \ A(1) = 0.$$

Though one can obtain a closed-form solution to this recurrence (see Problem 8), here we simply establish the solution's order of growth. According to the Master Theorem stated in the beginning of the chapter, $A(n) \in \Theta(n^{\log_2 7})$. In other words, the number of additions has the same order of growth as the number of multiplications. This puts Strassen's algorithm in $\Theta(n^{\log_2 7})$, which is a better efficiency class than $\Theta(n^3)$ of the brute-force method.

Since the time of Strassen's discovery, several other algorithms for multiplying two n-by-n matrices of real numbers in a time in $O(n^\alpha)$ with progressively smaller constants α have been invented. The fastest algorithm so far is that of Coopersmith and Winograd [CW87] with its efficiency in $O(n^{2.376})$. The decreasing values of the exponents have been obtained at the expense of increasing complexity of these algorithms. Because of large multiplicative constants, none of them is of practical value. However, they are interesting from a theoretical point of view. On one hand, they get closer and closer to the best theoretical lower bound known for matrix multiplication, which is n^2 multiplications, though the gap between this bound and the best available algorithm remains unresolved. On the other hand, matrix multiplication is known to be computationally equivalent to some other important problems such as solving systems of linear equations.

───────── **Exercises 4.5** ─────────

1. What are the smallest and largest numbers of digits the product of two decimal n-digit numbers can have?

2. Compute $2101 * 1130$ by applying the divide-and-conquer algorithm outlined in the text.

3. **a.** Prove the equality $a^{\log_b c} = c^{\log_b a}$, which was used twice in Section 4.5.

   b. Why is $n^{\log_2 3}$ better than $3^{\log_2 n}$ as a closed-form formula for $M(n)$?

4. **a.** Why did we not include multiplications by 10^n in the multiplication count $M(n)$ of the large-integer multiplication algorithm?

   b. In addition to assuming that n is a power of 2, we made, for the sake of simplicity, another more subtle assumption in setting up a recurrence relation for $M(n)$, which is not always true (it does not change the final answer, however). What is this assumption?

Computation and Reasoning

5. How many one-digit additions are made by the pen-and-pencil algorithm in multiplying two n-digit numbers? (You may disregard potential carries.)

6. Verify the formulas underlying Strassen's algorithm for multiplying 2-by-2 matrices.

7. Apply Strassen's algorithm to compute

$$\begin{bmatrix} 1 & 0 & 2 & 1 \\ 4 & 1 & 1 & 0 \\ 0 & 1 & 3 & 0 \\ 5 & 0 & 2 & 1 \end{bmatrix} * \begin{bmatrix} 0 & 1 & 0 & 1 \\ 2 & 1 & 0 & 4 \\ 2 & 0 & 1 & 1 \\ 1 & 3 & 5 & 0 \end{bmatrix}$$

exiting the recursion when $n = 2$, i.e., computing the products of 2-by-2 matrices by the brute-force algorithm.

8. Solve the recurrence for the number of additions required by Strassen's algorithm. (Assume that n is a power of 2.)

9. V. Pan [Pan78] has discovered a divide-and-conquer matrix multiplication algorithm that is based on multiplying two 70-by-70 matrices using 143,640 multiplications. Find the asymptotic efficiency of Pan's algorithm (you may ignore additions) and compare it with that of Strassen's algorithm.

10. Practical implementations of Strassen's algorithm usually switch to the brute-force method after matrix sizes become smaller than some "crossover point." Run an experiment to determine such crossover point on your computer system.

4.6 Closest-Pair and Convex-Hull Problems by Divide-and-Conquer

In Section 3.3, we discussed the brute-force approach to solving two classic problems of computational geometry: the closest-pair problem and the convex-hull problem. We saw that the two-dimensional versions of these problems can be solved by brute-force algorithms in $\Theta(n^2)$ and $O(n^3)$, respectively. In this section, we discuss more sophisticated and asymptotically more efficient algorithms for these problems, which are based on the divide-and-conquer technique.

Closest-Pair Problem

Let $P_1 = (x_1, y_1), \ldots, P_n = (x_n, y_n)$ be a set S of n points in the plane, where n, for simplicity, is a power of two. With no loss of generality, we can assume that the points are ordered in ascending order of their x coordinates. (If they were not, we can sort them in $O(n \log n)$ time, e.g., by mergesort.) We can divide the points given into two subsets S_1 and S_2 of $n/2$ points each by drawing a vertical line $x = c$

Computation and Reasoning

303

so that $n/2$ points lie to the left of or on the line itself and $n/2$ points lie to the right of or on the line. (One way of finding an appropriate value for constant c for doing this is to use the median μ of the x coordinates.)

Following the divide-and-conquer approach, we can find recursively the closest pairs for the left subset S_1 and the right subset S_2. Let d_1 and d_2 be the smallest distances between pairs of points in S_1 and S_2, respectively, and let $d = \min\{d_1, d_2\}$. Unfortunately, d is not necessarily the smallest distance between all pairs of points in S_1 and S_2 because a closer pair of points can lie on the opposite sides of the separating line. So, as a step of combining the solutions to the smaller subproblems, we need to examine such points. Obviously, we can limit our attention to the points in the symmetric vertical strip of width $2d$ since the distance between any other pair of points is greater than d (Figure 4.6a). Let C_1 and C_2 be the subsets of points in the left and right parts of the strip, respectively.

Now, for every point $P(x, y)$ in C_1, we need to inspect points in C_2 that may be closer to P than d. Obviously, such points must have their y coordinates in the interval $[y - d, y + d]$. The critical insight here is an observation that there can be no more than six such points because any pair of points in C_2 is at least d apart from each other. (Recall that $d \leq d_2$ where d_2 is the smallest distance between pairs of points to the right of the dividing line.) The worst case is illustrated in Figure 4.6b.

Another important observation is that we can maintain lists of points in C_1 and C_2 sorted in ascending order of their y coordinates. (You can think of these lists as projections of the points on the dividing line.) Moreover, this ordering can be maintained not by resorting points on each iteration but rather by merging two previously sorted lists (see algorithm *Merge* in Section 4.1). We can process the C_1 points sequentially while a pointer into the C_2 list may oscillate within an interval of width $2d$ to fetch up to six candidates for computing their distances to a current point P of the C_1 list. The time $M(n)$ for this "merging" of solutions to the smaller subproblems is in $O(n)$.

Now we have the following recurrence for $T(n)$, the running time of this algorithm on n presorted points:

$$T(n) = 2T(n/2) + M(n).$$

Applying the O version of the Master Theorem (with $a = 2$, $b = 2$, and $d = 1$), we get $T(n) \in O(n \log n)$. The possible necessity to presort input points does not change the overall efficiency class if sorting is done by a $O(n \log n)$ algorithm. In fact, this is the best efficiency class we can achieve because it has been proved that any algorithm for this problem must be in $\Omega(n \log n)$ (see [PSh85], p. 188).

Convex-Hull Problem

There are, in fact, several divide-and-conquer algorithms for the convex-hull problem of finding the smallest convex polygon that contains n given points in the plane. We look at the simplest though not the most efficient among them. This

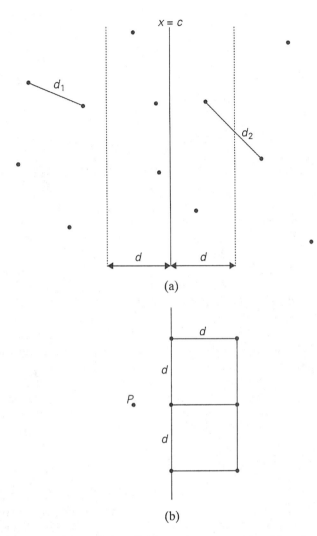

FIGURE 4.6 (a) Idea of the divide-and-conquer algorithm for the closest-pair
problem. (b) The six points that may need to be examined for
point P.

algorithm is sometimes called *quickhull* because its operations resemble those of
quicksort.

Let $P_1 = (x_1, y_1), \ldots, P_n = (x_n, y_n)$ be a set S of n points in the plane. We
assume that the points are sorted in increasing order of their x coordinates, with
ties resolved by increasing order of the y coordinates of the points involved. It
is not difficult to prove the geometrically obvious fact that the leftmost point P_1
and the rightmost point P_n must belong to the set's convex hull (Figure 4.7). Let

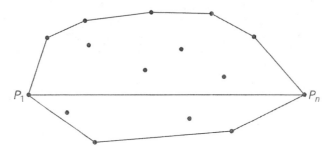

FIGURE 4.7 Upper and lower hulls of a set of points

$\overrightarrow{P_1P_n}$ be the straight line through points P_1 to P_n directed from P_1 to P_n. This line separates the points into two sets: S_1 is the set of points to the left of or on this line and S_2 is the set of points to the right of or on this line. (We say that point p_3 is to the left of the line $\overrightarrow{p_1p_2}$ directed from point p_1 to point p_2 if $p_1p_2p_3$ forms a counterclockwise cycle. Later, we cite an analytical way to check this condition, based on checking the sign of a determinant formed by the coordinates of the three points.)

The convex hull of S_1 consists of the line segment with the end points at P_1 and P_n and an upper boundary made up of a polygonal chain, i.e., a sequence of line segments connecting some points of S_1. The upper boundary is called the *upper hull*. Similarly, the polygonal chain, which serves as the lower boundary of the convex hull of set S_2, is called the *lower hull*. The fact that the convex hull of the entire set S is composed of the upper and lower hulls, which can be constructed independently and in a similar fashion, is a very useful observation that is exploited by several algorithms for this problem.

For concreteness, let us discuss how the algorithm called quickhull proceeds to construct the upper hull; the lower hull can be constructed in the same manner. First, the algorithm identifies vertex P_{max} in S_1, which is the farthest from the line $\overrightarrow{P_1P_n}$ (Figure 4.8) If there is a tie, the point that maximizes the angle $\angle P_{max}P_1P_n$ can be selected. (Note that point P_{max} maximizes the area of the triangle with two vertices at P_1 and P_n and the third at some other point of S_1.) Then the algorithm identifies all the points of set S_1 that are to the left of the line $\overrightarrow{P_1P_{max}}$; these are the points that, along with P_1 and P_{max}, will make up the set $S_{1,1}$. The points of S_1 to the left of the line $\overrightarrow{P_{max}P_n}$ will make up, along with P_{max} and P_n, the set $S_{1,2}$. It is not difficult to prove that there are no points to the left of both these lines. The points inside $\triangle P_1P_{max}P_n$ can be eliminated from further consideration. Therefore, the algorithm can continue constructing the upper hulls of $S_{1,1}$ and $S_{1,2}$ recursively and then simply concatenate them to get the upper hull of the entire S_1.

Now we have to figure out how the algorithm's geometric operations can be implemented. Fortunately, we can take advantage of the following very useful fact from analytical geometry: if $p_1 = (x_1, y_1)$, $p_2 = (x_1, y_1)$, and $p_3 = (x_3, y_3)$ are three

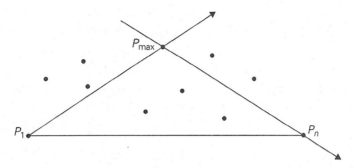

FIGURE 4.8 The idea of quickhull

arbitrary points in the plane, then the area of the triangle $\triangle p_1 p_2 p_3$ is equal to one half of the magnitude of the determinant

$$\begin{vmatrix} x_1 & y_1 & 1 \\ x_2 & y_2 & 1 \\ x_3 & y_3 & 1 \end{vmatrix} = x_1 y_2 + x_3 y_1 + x_2 y_3 - x_3 y_2 - x_2 y_1 - x_1 y_3,$$

while the sign of this expression is positive if and only if the point $p_3 = (x_3, y_3)$ is to the left of the line $\overrightarrow{p_1 p_2}$. Using this formula, we can check in constant time whether a point lies to the left of a line determined by two other points as well as find the distance from the point to the line.

Quickhull has the same efficiency as quicksort: it is in $\Theta(n \log n)$ in the average case but in $\Theta(n^2)$ in the worst case. Though the latter is an improvement over the efficiency of the brute-force algorithm of Section 3.3, there are, as we mentioned above, more sophisticated divide-and-conquer algorithms for this problem with the worst-case efficiency in $\Theta(n \log n)$ (see, e.g., [PSh85]).

Exercises 4.6

1. **a.** For the one-dimensional version of the closest-pair problem, i.e., for the problem of finding two closest numbers among a given set of n real numbers, design an algorithm that is directly based on the divide-and-conquer technique and determine its efficiency class.

   b. Is it a good algorithm for this problem?

2. Consider the version of the divide-and-conquer two-dimensional closest-pair algorithm in which we simply sort each of the two sets C_1 and C_2 in ascending order of their y coordinates on each recursive call. Assuming that sorting is done by mergesort, set up an approximate recurrence relation for the running time in the worst case and solve it for $n = 2^k$.

Computation and Reasoning

3. Implement the divide-and-conquer closest-pair algorithm, outlined in this section, in the language of your choice.

4. Find a visualization of an algorithm for the closest-pair problem on the Web. What algorithm does this visualization represent?

5. The ***Voronoi polygon*** for a point P of a set S of points in the plane is defined to be the perimeter of the set of all points in the plane closer to P than to any other point in S. The union of all the Voronoi polygons of the points in S is called the ***Voronoi diagram*** of S.

   a. What is the Voronoi diagram for a set of three points?

   b. Find a visualization of an algorithm for generating the Voronoi diagram on the Web and study a few examples of such diagrams. Based on your observations, can you tell how the solution to the previous question is generalized to the general case?

6. Explain how one can find point $P_{\max}$ in the quickhull algorithm analytically.

7. Describe in geometric terms inputs for which the set S_1 of the quickhull algorithm would be empty. What would be the set's upper hull in this situation?

8. What is the best-case efficiency of quickhull?

9. Give a specific example of inputs that make the quickhull algorithm run in quadratic time.

10. Implement the quickhull algorithm in the language of your choice.

SUMMARY

- *Divide-and-conquer* is a general algorithm design technique that solves a problem's instance by dividing it into several smaller instances (ideally, of equal size), solving each of them recursively, and then combining their solutions to get a solution to the original instance of the problem. Many efficient algorithms are based on this technique, although it can be both inapplicable and inferior to simpler algorithmic solutions.

- Time efficiency $T(n)$ of many divide-and-conquer algorithms satisfies the equation $T(n) = aT(n/b) + f(n)$. The *Master Theorem* establishes the order of growth of this equation's solutions.

- *Mergesort* is a divide-and-conquer sorting algorithm. It works by dividing an input array into two halves, sorting them recursively, and then *merging* the two sorted halves to get the original array sorted. The algorithm's time efficiency is in $\Theta(n \log n)$ in all cases, with the number of key comparisons being very close to the theoretical minimum. Its principal drawback is a significant extra storage requirement.

Computation and Reasoning

308

- *Quicksort* is a divide-and-conquer sorting algorithm that works by partitioning its input's elements according to their value relative to some preselected element. Quicksort is noted for its superior efficiency among $n \log n$ algorithms for sorting randomly ordered arrays but also for the quadratic worst-case efficiency.

- *Binary search* is a $O(\log n)$ algorithm for searching in sorted arrays. It is an atypical example of an application of the divide-and-conquer technique because it needs to solve just one problem of half the size on each of its iterations.

- The classic traversals of a binary tree—*preorder*, *inorder*, and *postorder*—and similar algorithms that require recursive processing of both left and right subtrees can be considered examples of the divide-and-conquer technique. Their analysis is helped by replacing all the empty subtrees of a given tree with special *external nodes*.

- There is a divide-and-conquer algorithm for multiplying two n-digit integers that requires about $n^{1.585}$ one-digit multiplications.

- *Strassen's algorithm* needs only seven multiplications to multiply two 2-by-2 matrices but requires more additions than the definition-based algorithm. By exploiting the divide-and-conquer technique, this algorithm can multiply two n-by-n matrices with about $n^{2.807}$ multiplications.

- The divide-and-conquer technique can be successfully applied to two important problems of computational geometry: the closest-pair problem and the convex-hull problem.

Computation and Reasoning

309

Computation and Reasoning

310

Topic 3

Prolog

The following chapters are from
Prolog: Programming for Artificial Intelligence
Third Edition
by Ivan Bratko

chapter 1

Introduction to Prolog

This chapter reviews basic mechanisms of Prolog through an example program. Although the treatment is largely informal many important concepts are introduced such as: Prolog clauses, facts, rules and procedures. Prolog's built-in backtracking mechanism and the distinction between declarative and procedural meanings of a program are discussed.

1.1 Defining relations by facts

Prolog is a programming language for symbolic, non-numeric computation. It is specially well suited for solving problems that involve objects and relations between objects. Figure 1.1 shows an example: a family relation. The fact that Tom is a parent of Bob can be written in Prolog as:

```
parent( tom, bob).
```

Here we choose parent as the name of a relation; tom and bob are its arguments. For reasons that will become clear later we write names like tom with an initial lower-case letter. The whole family tree of Figure 1.1 is defined by the following Prolog program:

```
parent( pam, bob).
parent( tom, bob).
```

3

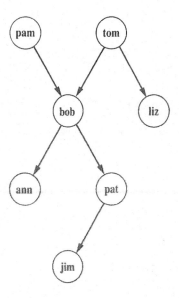

Figure 1.1   A family tree.

```
parent( tom, liz).
parent( bob, ann).
parent( bob, pat).
parent( pat, jim).
```

This program consists of six *clauses*. Each of these clauses declares one fact about the parent relation. For example, parent(tom, bob) is a particular *instance* of the **parent** relation. Such an instance is also called a *relationship*. In general, a relation is defined as the set of all its instances.

When this program has been communicated to the Prolog system, Prolog can be posed some questions about the **parent** relation. For example: Is Bob a parent of Pat? This question can be communicated to the Prolog system by typing into the terminal:

```
?-  parent( bob, pat).
```

Having found this as an asserted fact in the program, Prolog will answer:

```
yes
```

A further query can be:

```
?-  parent( liz, pat).
```

Prolog answers:

```
no
```

Computation and Reasoning

314

because the program does not mention anything about Liz being a parent of Pat. It also answers 'no' to the question:

   ?- parent(tom, ben).

because the program has not even heard of the name Ben.

   More interesting questions can also be asked. For example: Who is Liz's parent?

   ?- parent(X, liz).

Prolog's answer will not be just 'yes' or 'no' this time. Prolog will tell us what is the value of X such that the above statement is true. So the answer is:

   X = tom

The question Who are Bob's children? can be communicated to Prolog as:

   ?- parent(bob, X).

This time there is more than just one possible answer. Prolog first answers with one solution:

   X = ann

We may now request another solution (by typing a semicolon), and Prolog will find:

   X = pat

If we request more solutions again, Prolog will answer 'no' because all the solutions have been exhausted.

   Our program can be asked an even broader question: Who is a parent of whom? Another formulation of this question is:

   Find X and Y such that X is a parent of Y.

This is expressed in Prolog by:

   ?- parent(X, Y).

Prolog now finds all the parent-child pairs one after another. The solutions will be displayed one at a time as long as we tell Prolog we want more solutions, until all the solutions have been found. The answers are output as:

   X = pam
   Y = bob;

   X = tom
   Y = bob;

   X = tom
   Y = liz;

   ...

We can stop the stream of solutions by typing a return instead of a semicolon.

Computation and Reasoning

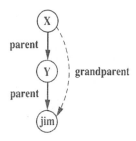

Figure 1.2   The **grandparent** relation expressed as a composition of two **parent** relations.

Our example program can be asked still more complicated questions like: Who is a grandparent of Jim? As our program does not directly know the **grandparent** relation this query has to be broken down into two steps, as illustrated by Figure 1.2.

(1)   Who is a parent of Jim? Assume that this is some Y.

(2)   Who is a parent of Y? Assume that this is some X.

Such a composed query is written in Prolog as a sequence of two simple ones:

   ?- parent(Y, jim), parent(X, Y).

The answer will be:

   X = bob
   Y = pat

Our composed query can be read: Find such X and Y that satisfy the following two requirements:

   parent(Y, jim)   and   parent(X, Y)

If we change the order of the two requirements the logical meaning remains the same:

   parent(X, Y)   and   parent(Y, jim)

We can indeed do this in our Prolog program, and the query:

   ?- parent(X, Y), parent(Y, jim).

will produce the same result.
   In a similar way we can ask: Who are Tom's grandchildren?

   ?- parent(tom, X), parent(X, Y).

Prolog's answers are:

   X = bob
   Y = ann;

Computation and Reasoning

316

X = bob
Y = pat

Yet another question could be: Do Ann and Pat have a common parent? This can be expressed again in two steps:

(1)   Who is a parent, X, of Ann?

(2)   Is (this same) X a parent of Pat?

The corresponding question to Prolog is then:

  ?- parent(X, ann), parent(X, pat).

The answer is:

X = bob

Our example program has helped to illustrate some important points:

- It is easy in Prolog to define a relation, such as the **parent** relation, by stating the n-tuples of objects that satisfy the relation.

- The user can easily query the Prolog system about relations defined in the program.

- A Prolog program consists of *clauses*. Each clause terminates with a full stop.

- The arguments of relations can (among other things) be: concrete objects, or constants (such as **tom** and **ann**), or general objects such as X and Y. Objects of the first kind in our program are called *atoms*. Objects of the second kind are called *variables*.

- Questions to the system consist of one or more *goals*. A sequence of goals, such as:

    parent(X, ann), parent(X, pat)

  means the conjunction of the goals:

    X is a parent of Ann, and
    X is a parent of Pat.

  The word 'goals' is used because Prolog accepts questions as goals that are to be satisfied.

- An answer to a question can be either positive or negative, depending on whether the corresponding goal can be satisfied or not. In the case of a positive answer we say that the corresponding goal was *satisfiable* and that the goal *succeeded*. Otherwise the goal was *unsatisfiable* and it *failed*.

- If several answers satisfy the question then Prolog will find as many of them as desired by the user.

Computation and Reasoning

Exercises

1.1   Assuming the **parent** relation as defined in this section (see Figure 1.1), what will be Prolog's answers to the following questions?

(a)   ?- parent(jim, X).

(b)   ?- parent(X, jim).

(c)   ?- parent(pam, X), parent(X, pat).

(d)   ?- parent(pam, X), parent(X, Y), parent(Y, jim).

1.2   Formulate in Prolog the following questions about the **parent** relation:

(a)   Who is Pat's parent?

(b)   Does Liz have a child?

(c)   Who is Pat's grandparent?

1.2   Defining relations by rules

Our example program can be easily extended in many interesting ways. Let us first add the information on the sex of the people that occur in the **parent** relation. This can be done by simply adding the following facts to our program:

```
female( pam).
male( tom).
male( bob).
female( liz).
female( pat).
female( ann).
male( jim).
```

The relations introduced here are **male** and **female**. These relations are unary (or one-place) relations. A binary relation like **parent** defines a relation between *pairs* of objects; on the other hand, unary relations can be used to declare simple yes/no properties of objects. The first unary clause above can be read: Pam is a female. We could convey the same information declared in the two unary relations with one binary relation, sex, instead. An alternative piece of program would then be:

```
sex( pam, feminine).
sex( tom, masculine).
sex( bob, masculine).
...
```

As our next extension to the program let us introduce the **offspring** relation as the inverse of the **parent** relation. We could define offspring in a similar way as the

parent relation; that is, by simply providing a list of simple facts about the **offspring** relation, each fact mentioning one pair of people such that one is an offspring of the other. For example:

offspring(liz, tom).

However, the offspring relation can be defined much more elegantly by making use of the fact that it is the inverse of **parent**, and that **parent** has already been defined. This alternative way can be based on the following logical statement:

For all X and Y,
   Y is an offspring of X if
     X is a parent of Y.

This formulation is already close to the formalism of Prolog. The corresponding Prolog clause which has the same meaning is:

offspring(Y, X) :- parent(X, Y).

This clause can also be read as:

For all X and Y,
   if X is a parent of Y then
   Y is an offspring of X.

Prolog clauses such as:

offspring(Y, X) :- parent(X, Y).

are called *rules*. There is an important difference between facts and rules. A fact like:

parent(tom, liz).

is something that is always, unconditionally, true. On the other hand, rules specify things that are true if some condition is satisfied. Therefore we say that rules have:

- a condition part (the right-hand side of the rule) and
- a conclusion part (the left-hand side of the rule).

The conclusion part is also called the *head* of a clause and the condition part the *body* of a clause. For example:

offspring(Y, X) :- parent(X, Y).

      head   body

If the condition **parent(X, Y)** is true then a logical consequence of this is **offspring(Y, X)**.

How rules are actually used by Prolog is illustrated by the following example. Let us ask our program whether Liz is an offspring of Tom:

?- offspring(liz, tom).

Computation and Reasoning

319

There is no fact about offsprings in the program, therefore the only way to consider this question is to apply the rule about offsprings. The rule is general in the sense that it is applicable to any objects X and Y; therefore it can also be applied to such particular objects as liz and tom. To apply the rule to liz and tom, Y has to be substituted with liz, and X with tom. We say that the variables X and Y become instantiated to:

X = tom   and   Y = liz

After the instantiation we have obtained a special case of our general rule. The special case is:

offspring(liz, tom) :- parent(tom, liz).

The condition part has become:

parent(tom, liz)

Now Prolog tries to find out whether the condition part is true. So the initial goal:

offspring(liz, tom)

has been replaced with the subgoal:

parent(tom, liz)

This (new) goal happens to be trivial as it can be found as a fact in our program. This means that the conclusion part of the rule is also true, and Prolog will answer the question with yes.

Let us now add more family relations to our example program. The specification of the mother relation can be based on the following logical statement:

For all X and Y,
   X is the mother of Y if
   X is a parent of Y and
   X is a female.

This is translated into Prolog as the following rule:

mother(X, Y) :- parent(X, Y), female(X).

A comma between two conditions indicates the conjunction of the conditions, meaning that *both* conditions have to be true.

Relations such as parent, offspring and mother can be illustrated by diagrams such as those in Figure 1.3. These diagrams conform to the following conventions. Nodes in the graphs correspond to objects – that is, arguments of relations. Arcs between nodes correspond to binary (or two-place) relations. The arcs are oriented so as to point from the first argument of the relation to the second argument. Unary relations are indicated in the diagrams by simply marking the corresponding objects

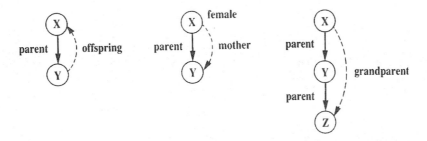

Figure 1.3 Definition graphs for the relations **offspring**, **mother** and **grandparent** in terms of other relations.

with the name of the relation. The relations that are being defined are represented by dashed arcs. So each diagram should be understood as follows: if the relations shown by solid arcs hold, then the relation shown by a dashed arc also holds. The **grandparent** relation can be, according to Figure 1.3, immediately written in Prolog as:

grandparent(X, Z) :- parent(X, Y), parent(Y, Z).

At this point it will be useful to make a comment on the layout of our programs. Prolog gives us almost full freedom in choosing the layout of the program. So we can insert spaces and new lines as it best suits our taste. In general we want to make our programs look nice and tidy, and, above all, easy to read. To this end we will often choose to write the head of a clause and each goal of the body on a separate line. When doing this, we will indent goals in order to make the difference between the head and the goals more visible. For example, the **grandparent** rule would be, according to this convention, written as follows:

grandparent(X, Z) :-
    parent(X, Y),
    parent(Y, Z).

Figure 1.4 illustrates the **sister** relation:

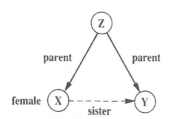

Figure 1.4 Defining the **sister** relation.

Computation and Reasoning

For any X and Y,
    X is a sister of Y if
    (1) both X and Y have the same parent, and
    (2) X is a female.

The graph in Figure 1.4 can be translated into Prolog as:

```
sister( X, Y)  :-
    parent( Z, X),
    parent( Z, Y),
    female( X).
```

Notice the way in which the requirement 'both X and Y have the same parent' has been expressed. The following logical formulation was used: some Z must be a parent of X, and this *same* Z must be a parent of Y. An alternative, but less elegant way would be to say: Z1 is a parent of X, and Z2 is a parent of Y, and Z1 is equal to Z2.
    We can now ask:

```
?- sister( ann, pat).
```

The answer will be 'yes', as expected (see Figure 1.1). Therefore we might conclude that the sister relation, as defined, works correctly. There is, however, a rather subtle flaw in our program, which is revealed if we ask the question Who is Pat's sister?:

```
?- sister( X, pat).
```

Prolog will find two answers, one of which may come as a surprise:

```
X = ann;
```

```
X = pat
```

So, Pat is a sister to herself?! This is probably not what we had in mind when defining the sister relation. However, according to our rule about sisters Prolog's answer is perfectly logical. Our rule about sisters does not mention that X and Y must not be the same if X is to be a sister of Y. As this is not required Prolog (rightfully) assumes that X and Y can be the same, and will as a consequence find that any female who has a parent is a sister of herself.
    To correct our rule about sisters we have to add that X and Y must be different. We will see in later chapters how this can be done in several ways, but for the moment we will assume that a relation different is already known to Prolog, and that:

```
different( X, Y)
```

is satisfied if and only if X and Y are not equal. An improved rule for the sister relation can then be:

```
sister( X, Y)  :-
    parent( Z, X),
    parent( Z, Y),
    female( X),
    different( X, Y).
```

Some important points of this section are:

- Prolog programs can be extended by simply adding new clauses.
- Prolog clauses are of three types: *facts*, *rules* and *questions*.
- *Facts* declare things that are always, unconditionally true.
- *Rules* declare things that are true depending on a given condition.
- By means of *questions* the user can ask the program what things are true.
- Prolog clauses consist of the *head* and the *body*. The body is a list of *goals* separated by commas. Commas are understood as conjunctions.
- Facts are clauses that have a head and the empty body. Questions only have the body. Rules have the head and the (non-empty) body.
- In the course of computation, a variable can be substituted by another object. We say that a variable becomes *instantiated*.
- Variables are assumed to be universally quantified and are read as 'for all'. Alternative readings are, however, possible for variables that appear only in the body. For example:

  hasachild(X) :- parent(X, Y).

  can be read in two ways:

  (a) *For all* X and Y,
      if X is a parent of Y then
      X has a child.

  (b) *For all* X,
      X has a child if
      there is *some* Y such that X is a parent of Y.

Exercises

1.3   Translate the following statements into Prolog rules:

(a) Everybody who has a child is happy (introduce a one-argument relation **happy**).

(b) For all X, if X has a child who has a sister then X has two children (introduce new relation **hastwochildren**).

1.4   Define the relation **grandchild** using the **parent** relation. Hint: It will be similar to the **grandparent** relation (see Figure 1.3).

1.5   Define the relation **aunt(X, Y)** in terms of the relations **parent** and **sister**. As an aid you can first draw a diagram in the style of Figure 1.3 for the **aunt** relation.

Computation and Reasoning

1.3 Recursive rules

Let us add one more relation to our family program, the **predecessor** relation. This relation will be defined in terms of the **parent** relation. The whole definition can be expressed with two rules. The first rule will define the direct (immediate) predecessors and the second rule the indirect predecessors. We say that some X is an indirect predecessor of some Z if there is a parentship chain of people between X and Z, as illustrated in Figure 1.5. In our example of Figure 1.1, Tom is a direct predecessor of Liz and an indirect predecessor of Pat.

The first rule is simple and can be formulated as:

For all X and Z,
    X is a predecessor of Z if
    X is a parent of Z.

This is straightforwardly translated into Prolog as:

```
predecessor( X, Z) :-
    parent( X, Z).
```

The second rule, on the other hand, is more complicated because the chain of parents may present some problems. One attempt to define indirect predecessors could be as shown in Figure 1.6. According to this, the predecessor relation would be defined by a set of clauses as follows:

```
predecessor( X, Z) :-
    parent( X, Z).

predecessor( X, Z) :-
    parent( X, Y),
    parent( Y, Z).
```

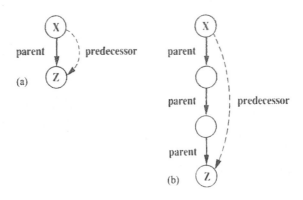

Figure 1.5 Examples of the **predecessor** relation: (a) X is a direct predecessor of Z; (b) X is an indirect predecessor of Z.

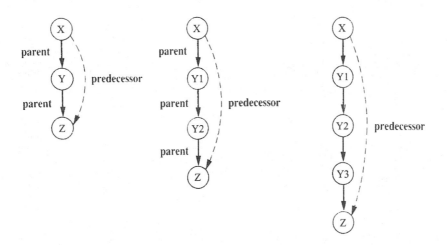

Figure 1.6 Predecessor-successor pairs at various distances.

```
predecessor( X, Z) :-
   parent( X, Y1),
   parent( Y1, Y2),
   parent( Y2, Z).

predecessor( X, Z) :-
   parent( X, Y1),
   parent( Y1, Y2),
   parent( Y2, Y3),
   parent( Y3, Z).
```

...

This program is lengthy and, more importantly, it only works to some extent. It would only discover predecessors to a certain depth in a family tree because the length of the chain of people between the predecessor and the successor would be limited according to the length of our predecessor clauses.

There is, however, an elegant and correct formulation of the **predecessor** relation: it will be correct in the sense that it will work for predecessors at any depth. The key idea is to define the **predecessor** relation in terms of itself. Figure 1.7 illustrates the idea:

For all X and Z,
    X is a predecessor of Z if
    there is a Y such that
    (1) X is a parent of Y and
    (2) Y is a predecessor of Z.

A Prolog clause with the above meaning is:

```
predecessor( X, Z) :-
   parent( X, Y),
   predecessor( Y, Z).
```

Computation and Reasoning

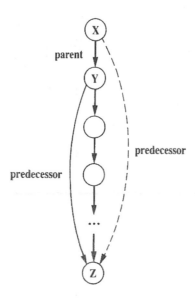

Figure 1.7   Recursive formulation of the **predecessor** relation.

We have thus constructed a complete program for the **predecessor** relation, which consists of two rules: one for direct predecessors and one for indirect predecessors. Both rules are rewritten together here:

predecessor(X, Z) :-
  parent(X, Z).

predecessor(X, Z) :-
  parent(X, Y),
  predecessor(Y, Z).

The key to this formulation was the use of **predecessor** itself in its definition. Such a definition may look surprising in view of the question: When defining something, can we use this same thing that has not yet been completely defined? Such definitions are, in general, called *recursive* definitions. Logically, they are perfectly correct and understandable, which is also intuitively obvious if we look at Figure 1.7. But will the Prolog system be able to use recursive rules? It turns out that Prolog can indeed very easily use recursive definitions. Recursive programming is, in fact, one of the fundamental principles of programming in Prolog. It is not possible to solve tasks of any significant complexity in Prolog without the use of recursion.

Going back to our program, we can ask Prolog: Who are Pam's successors? That is: Who is a person that has Pam as his or her predecessor?

  ?- predecessor(pam, X).

X = bob;

X = ann;

Computation and Reasoning

326

X = pat;

X = jim

Prolog's answers are, of course, correct and they logically follow from our definition of the **predecessor** and the **parent** relation. There is, however, a rather important question: *How* did Prolog actually use the program to find these answers?

An informal explanation of how Prolog does this is given in the next section. But first let us put together all the pieces of our family program, which was extended gradually by adding new facts and rules. The final form of the program is shown in Figure 1.8. Looking at Figure 1.8, two further points are in order here: the

```
parent( pam, bob).        % Pam is a parent of Bob
parent( tom, bob).
parent( tom, liz).
parent( bob, ann).
parent( bob, pat).
parent( pat, jim).

female( pam).             % Pam is female
male( tom).               % Tom is male
male( bob).
female( liz).
female( ann).
female( pat).
male( jim).

offspring( Y, X) :-       % Y is an offspring of X if
    parent( X, Y).        % X is a parent of Y

mother( X, Y) :-          % X is the mother of Y if
    parent( X, Y),        % X is a parent of Y and
    female( X).           % X is female

grandparent( X, Z) :-     % X is a grandparent of Z if
    parent( X, Y),        % X is a parent of Y and
    parent( Y, Z).        % Y is a parent of Z

sister( X, Y) :-          % X is a sister of Y if
    parent( Z, X),
    parent( Z, Y),        % X and Y have the same parent and
    female( X),           % X is female and
    different( X, Y).      % X and Y are different

predecessor( X, Z) :-     % Rule pr1: X is a predecessor of Z
    parent( X, Z).

predecessor( X, Z) :-     % Rule pr2: X is a predecessor of Z
    parent( X, Y),
    predecessor( Y, Z).
```

Figure 1.8 The family program.

Computation and Reasoning

327

first will introduce the term 'procedure', the second will be about comments in programs.

The program in Figure 1.8 defines several relations – **parent**, **male**, **female**, **predecessor**, etc. The **predecessor** relation, for example, is defined by two clauses. We say that these two clauses are *about* the **predecessor** relation. Sometimes it is convenient to consider the whole set of clauses about the same relation. Such a set of clauses is called a *procedure*.

In Figure 1.8, the two rules about the **predecessor** relation have been distinguished by the names 'pr1' and 'pr2', added as *comments* to the program. These names will be used later as references to these rules. Comments are, in general, ignored by the Prolog system. They only serve as a further clarification to the person who reads the program. Comments are distinguished in Prolog from the rest of the program by being enclosed in special brackets '/∗' and '∗/'. Thus comments in Prolog look like this:

```
/∗ This is a comment ∗/
```

Another method, more practical for short comments, uses the percent character '%'. Everything between '%' and the end of the line is interpreted as a comment:

```
% This is also a comment
```

Exercise

1.6   Consider the following alternative definition of the **predecessor** relation:

```
predecessor( X, Z) :-
    parent( X, Z).

predecessor( X, Z) :-
    parent( Y, Z),
    predecessor( X, Y).
```

Does this also seem to be a correct definition of predecessors? Can you modify the diagram of Figure 1.7 so that it would correspond to this new definition?

1.4   How Prolog answers questions

This section gives an informal explanation of *how* Prolog answers questions. A question to Prolog is always a sequence of one or more goals. To answer a question, Prolog tries to satisfy all the goals. What does it mean to *satisfy* a goal? To satisfy a goal means to demonstrate that the goal is true, assuming that the relations in the program are true. In other words, to satisfy a goal means to demonstrate that the goal *logically follows* from the facts and rules in the program. If the question contains variables, Prolog also has to find what are the particular objects (in place of variables) for which the goals are satisfied. The particular instantiation of variables to these objects is displayed to the user. If Prolog cannot demonstrate for some instantiation of variables that the goals logically follow from the program, then Prolog's answer to the question will be 'no'.

An appropriate view of the interpretation of a Prolog program in mathematical terms is then as follows: Prolog accepts facts and rules as a set of axioms, and the user's question as a *conjectured theorem*; then it tries to prove this theorem – that is, to demonstrate that it can be logically derived from the axioms.

We will illustrate this view by a classical example. Let the axioms be:

All men are fallible.
Socrates is a man.

A theorem that logically follows from these two axioms is:

Socrates is fallible.

The first axiom above can be rewritten as:

For all X, if X is a man then X is fallible.

Accordingly, the example can be translated into Prolog as follows:

    fallible(X) :- man(X).   % All men are fallible
    man(socrates).   % Socrates is a man
    ?- fallible(socrates).   % Socrates is fallible?
    yes

A more complicated example from the family program of Figure 1.8 is:

    ?- predecessor(tom, pat).

We know that **parent(bob, pat)** is a fact. Using this fact and rule *pr1* we can conclude **predecessor(bob, pat)**. This is a *derived* fact: it cannot be found explicitly in our program, but it can be derived from facts and rules in the program. An inference step, such as this, can be written in a more compact form as:

    parent(bob, pat) ==> predecessor(bob, pat)

This can be read: from **parent(bob, pat)** it follows that **predecessor(bob, pat)**, by rule *pr1*. Further, we know that **parent(tom, bob)** is a fact. Using this fact and the derived fact **predecessor(bob, pat)** we can conclude **predecessor(tom, pat)**, by rule *pr2*. We have thus shown that our goal statement **predecessor(tom, pat)** is true. This whole inference process of two steps can be written as:

    parent(bob, pat) ==> predecessor(bob, pat)
    parent(tom, bob) *and* predecessor(bob, pat) ==> predecessor(tom, pat)

Computation and Reasoning

329

We have thus shown *what* can be a sequence of steps that satisfy a goal – that is, make it clear that the goal is true. Let us call this a proof sequence. We have not, however, shown *how* the Prolog system actually finds such a proof sequence.

Prolog finds the proof sequence in the inverse order to that which we have just used. Instead of starting with simple facts given in the program, Prolog starts with the goals and, using rules, substitutes the current goals with new goals, until new goals happen to be simple facts. Given the question:

    ?- predecessor(tom, pat).

Prolog will try to satisfy this goal. In order to do so it will try to find a clause in the program from which the above goal could immediately follow. Obviously, the only clauses relevant to this end are *pr1* and *pr2*. These are the rules about the **predecessor** relation. We say that the heads of these rules *match* the goal.

The two clauses, *pr1* and *pr2*, represent two alternative ways for Prolog to proceed. Prolog first tries that clause which appears first in the program:

    predecessor(X, Z) :- parent(X, Z).

Since the goal is **predecessor(tom, pat)**, the variables in the rule must be instantiated as follows:

    X = tom, Z = pat

The original goal **predecessor(tom, pat)** is then replaced by a new goal:

    parent(tom, pat)

This step of using a rule to transform a goal into another goal, as above, is graphically illustrated in Figure 1.9. There is no clause in the program whose head matches the goal **parent(tom, pat)**, therefore this goal fails. Now Prolog *backtracks* to the original goal in order to try an alternative way to derive the top goal **predecessor(tom, pat)**. The rule *pr2* is thus tried:

    predecessor(X, Z) :-
        parent(X, Y),
        predecessor(Y, Z).

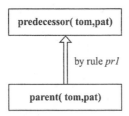

Figure 1.9   The first step of the execution. The top goal is true if the bottom goal is true.

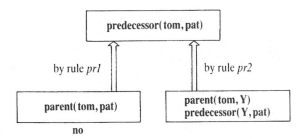

Figure 1.10 Execution trace continued from Figure 1.9.

As before, the variables X and Z become instantiated as:

X = **tom**, Z = **pat**

But Y is not instantiated yet. The top goal **predecessor(tom, pat)** is replaced by two goals:

parent(tom, Y),
predecessor(Y, pat)

This executional step is shown in Figure 1.10, which is an extension to the situation we had in Figure 1.9.

Being now faced with *two* goals, Prolog tries to satisfy them in the order in which they are written. The first one is easy as it matches one of the facts in the program. The matching forces Y to become instantiated to **bob**. Thus the first goal has been satisfied, and the remaining goal has become:

predecessor(bob, pat)

To satisfy this goal the rule *pr1* is used again. Note that this (second) application of the same rule has nothing to do with its previous application. Therefore, Prolog uses a new set of variables in the rule each time the rule is applied. To indicate this we shall rename the variables in rule *pr1* for this application as follows:

predecessor(X′, Z′) :-
parent(X′, Z′).

The head has to match our current goal **predecessor(bob, pat)**. Therefore:

X′ = **bob**, Z′ = **pat**

The current goal is replaced by:

parent(bob, pat)

This goal is immediately satisfied because it appears in the program as a fact. This completes the execution trace, which is graphically shown in Figure 1.11.

Computation and Reasoning

331

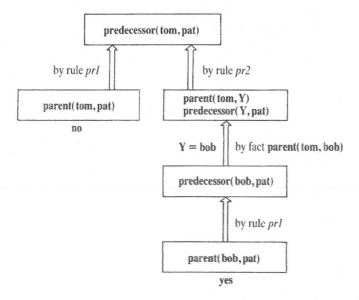

Figure 1.11 The complete execution trace to satisfy the goal predecessor(tom, pat). The right-hand branch proves the goal is satisfiable.

The graphical illustration of the execution trace in Figure 1.11 has the form of a tree. The nodes of the tree correspond to goals, or to lists of goals that are to be satisfied. The arcs between the nodes correspond to the application of (alternative) program clauses that transform the goals at one node into the goals at another node. The top goal is satisfied when a path is found from the root node (top goal) to a leaf node labelled 'yes'. A leaf is labelled 'yes' if it is a simple fact. The execution of Prolog programs is the searching for such paths. During the search Prolog may enter an unsuccessful branch. When Prolog discovers that a branch fails it automatically *backtracks* to the previous node and tries to apply an alternative clause at that node.

Exercise

1.7   Try to understand how Prolog derives answers to the following questions, using the program of Figure 1.8. Try to draw the corresponding derivation diagrams in the style of Figures 1.9 to 1.11. Will any backtracking occur at particular questions?

(a) ?- parent(pam, bob).

(b) ?- mother(pam, bob).

(c) ?- grandparent(pam, ann).

(d) ?- grandparent(bob, jim).

1.5 Declarative and procedural meaning of programs

In our examples so far it has always been possible to understand the results of the program without exactly knowing *how* the system actually found the results. It therefore makes sense to distinguish between two levels of meaning of Prolog programs; namely,

- the *declarative meaning* and

- the *procedural meaning.*

The declarative meaning is concerned only with the *relations* defined by the program. The declarative meaning thus determines *what* will be the output of the program. On the other hand, the procedural meaning also determines *how* this output is obtained; that is, how the relations are actually evaluated by the Prolog system.

The ability of Prolog to work out many procedural details on its own is considered to be one of its specific advantages. It encourages the programmer to consider the declarative meaning of programs relatively independently of their procedural meaning. Since the results of the program are, in principle, determined by its declarative meaning, this should be (in principle) sufficient for writing programs. This is of practical importance because the declarative aspects of programs are usually easier to understand than the procedural details. To take full advantage of this, the programmer should concentrate mainly on the declarative meaning and, whenever possible, avoid being distracted by the executional details. These should be left to the greatest possible extent to the Prolog system itself.

This declarative approach indeed often makes programming in Prolog easier than in typical procedurally oriented programming languages such as C or Pascal. Unfortunately, however, the declarative approach is not always sufficient. It will later become clear that, especially in large programs, the procedural aspects cannot be completely ignored by the programmer for practical reasons of executional efficiency. Nevertheless, the declarative style of thinking about Prolog programs should be encouraged and the procedural aspects ignored to the extent that is permitted by practical constraints.

Summary

- Prolog programming consists of defining relations and querying about relations.

- A program consists of *clauses*. These are of three types: *facts*, *rules* and *questions*.

- A relation can be specified by *facts*, simply stating the n-tuples of objects that satisfy the relation, or by stating *rules* about the relation.

Computation and Reasoning

333

- A *procedure* is a set of clauses about the same relation.

- Querying about relations, by means of *questions*, resembles querying a database. Prolog's answer to a question consists of a set of objects that satisfy the question.

- In Prolog, to establish whether an object satisfies a query is often a complicated process that involves logical inference, exploring among alternatives and possibly *backtracking*. All this is done automatically by the Prolog system and is, in principle, hidden from the user.

- Two types of meaning of Prolog programs are distinguished: declarative and procedural. The declarative view is advantageous from the programming point of view. Nevertheless, the procedural details often have to be considered by the programmer as well.

- The following concepts have been introduced in this chapter:

  clause, fact, rule, question
  the head of a clause, the body of a clause
  recursive rule, recursive definition
  procedure
  atom, variable
  instantiation of a variable
  goal
  goal is satisfiable, goal succeeds
  goal is unsatisfiable, goal fails
  backtracking
  declarative meaning, procedural meaning

References

Various implementations of Prolog use different syntactic conventions. However, most of them follow the tradition of the so-called Edinburgh syntax (also called DEC-10 syntax, established by the historically influential implementation of Prolog for the DEC-10 computer; Pereira *et al.* 1978; Bowen 1981). The Edinburgh syntax also forms the basis of the ISO international standard for Prolog ISO/IEC 13211-1 (Deransart *et al.* 1996). Major Prolog implementations now largely comply with the standard. In this book we use a subset of the standard syntax, with some small and insignificant differences. In rare cases of such differences, there is a note to this effect at an appropriate place.

Bowen, D.L. (1981) *DECsystem-10 Prolog User's Manual*. University of Edinburgh: Department of Artificial Intelligence.
Deransart, P., Ed-Bdali, A. and Ceroni, L. (1996) *Prolog: The Standard*. Berlin: Springer-Verlag.
Pereira, L.M., Pereira, F. and Warren, D.H.D. (1978) *User's Guide to DECsystem-10 Prolog*. University of Edinburgh: Department of Artificial Intelligence.

chapter 2

Syntax and Meaning of Prolog Programs

This chapter gives a systematic treatment of the syntax and semantics of basic concepts of Prolog, and introduces structured data objects. The topics included are:

- simple data objects (atoms, numbers, variables)
- structured objects
- matching as the fundamental operation on objects
- declarative (or non-procedural) meaning of a program
- procedural meaning of a program
- relation between the declarative and procedural meanings of a program
- altering the procedural meaning by reordering clauses and goals.

Most of these topics have already been reviewed in Chapter 1. Here the treatment will become more formal and detailed.

25

Computation and Reasoning

2.1 Data objects

Figure 2.1 shows a classification of data objects in Prolog. The Prolog system recognizes the type of an object in the program by its syntactic form. This is possible because the syntax of Prolog specifies different forms for each type of data object. We have already seen a method for distinguishing between atoms and variables in Chapter 1: variables start with upper-case letters whereas atoms start with lower-case letters. No additional information (such as data-type declaration) has to be communicated to Prolog in order to recognize the type of an object.

2.1.1 Atoms and numbers

In Chapter 1 we have seen some simple examples of atoms and variables. In general, however, they can take more complicated forms – that is, strings of the following characters:

- upper-case letters A, B, ..., Z
- lower-case letters a, b, ..., z
- digits 0, 1, 2, ..., 9
- special characters such as $+ - * / < > = : . \& \_ \sim$

Atoms can be constructed in three ways:

(1) Strings of letters, digits and the underscore character, '_', starting with a lower-case letter:

    anna
    nil
    x25
    x_25
    x_25AB
    x_
    x___y
    alpha_beta_procedure
    miss_Jones
    sarah_jones

(2) Strings of special characters:

    <--->
    ======>
    ...
    .:.
    ::=

When using atoms of this form, some care is necessary because some strings of special characters already have a predefined meaning; an example is ':-'.

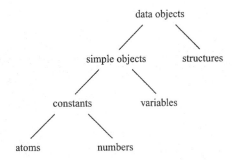

Figure 2.1 Data objects in Prolog.

(3)   Strings of characters enclosed in single quotes. This is useful if we want, for example, to have an atom that starts with a capital letter. By enclosing it in quotes we make it distinguishable from variables:

    'Tom'
    'South_America'
    'Sarah Jones'

Numbers used in Prolog include integer numbers and real numbers. The syntax of integers is simple, as illustrated by the following examples:

    1   1313   0   −97

Not all integer numbers can be represented in a computer, therefore the range of integers is limited to an interval between some smallest and some largest number permitted by a particular Prolog implementation.

We will assume the simple syntax of real numbers, as shown by the following examples:

    3.14   −0.0035   100.2

Real numbers are not very heavily used in typical Prolog programming. The reason for this is that Prolog is primarily a language for symbolic, non-numeric computation. In symbolic computation, integers are often used, for example, to count the number of items in a list; but there is typically less need for real numbers.

Apart from this lack of necessity to use real numbers in typical Prolog applications, there is another reason for avoiding real numbers. In general, we want to keep the meaning of programs as neat as possible. The introduction of real numbers somewhat impairs this neatness because of numerical errors that arise due to rounding when doing arithmetic. For example, the evaluation of the expression

    $10000 + 0.0001 - 10000$

may result in 0 instead of the correct result 0.0001.

Computation and Reasoning

2.1.2   Variables

Variables are strings of letters, digits and underscore characters. They start with an upper-case letter or an underscore character:

X
Result
Object2
Participant_list
ShoppingList
_x23
_23

When a variable appears in a clause once only, we do not have to invent a name for it. We can use the so-called 'anonymous' variable, which is written as a single underscore character. For example, let us consider the following rule:

hasachild(X) :- parent(X, Y).

This rule says: for all X, X has a child if X is a parent of some Y. We are defining the property **hasachild** which, as it is meant here, does not depend on the name of the child. Thus, this is a proper place in which to use an anonymous variable. The clause above can thus be rewritten:

hasachild(X) :- parent(X, _).

Each time a single underscore character occurs in a clause it represents a new anonymous variable. For example, we can say that there is somebody who has a child if there are two objects such that one is a parent of the other:

somebody_has_child :- parent(_, _).

This is equivalent to:

somebody_has_child :- parent(X, Y).

But this is, of course, quite different from:

somebody_has_child :- parent(X, X).

If the anonymous variable appears in a question clause then its value is not output when Prolog answers the question. If we are interested in people who have children, but not in the names of the children, then we can simply ask:

?- parent(X, _).

The *lexical scope* of variable names is one clause. This means that, for example, if the name X15 occurs in two clauses, then it signifies two different variables. But each occurrence of X15 within the same clause means the same variable. The situation is different for constants: the same atom always means the same object in any clause – that is, throughout the whole program.

Computation and Reasoning

2.1.3 Structures

Structured objects (or simply *structures*) are objects that have several components. The components themselves can, in turn, be structures. For example, the date can be viewed as a structure with three components: day, month, year. Although composed of several components, structures are treated in the program as single objects. In order to combine the components into a single object we have to choose a *functor*. A suitable functor for our example is **date**. Then the date 1 May 2001 can be written as:

date(1, may, 2001)

(see Figure 2.2).

All the components in this example are constants (two integers and one atom). Components can also be variables or other structures. Any day in May can be represented by the structure:

date(Day, may, 2001)

Note that **Day** is a variable and can be instantiated to any object at some later point in the execution.

This method for data structuring is simple and powerful. It is one of the reasons why Prolog is so naturally applied to problems that involve symbolic manipulation.

Syntactically, all data objects in Prolog are *terms*. For example,

may

and

date(1, may, 2001)

are terms.

All structured objects can be pictured as trees (see Figure 2.2 for an example). The root of the tree is the functor, and the offsprings of the root are the components. If a component is also a structure then it is a subtree of the tree that corresponds to the whole structured object.

Our next example will show how structures can be used to represent some simple geometric objects (see Figure 2.3). A point in two-dimensional space is defined by its

Figure 2.2 Date is an example of a structured object: (a) as it is represented as a tree; (b) as it is written in Prolog.

Computation and Reasoning

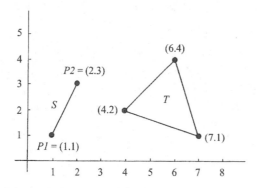

Figure 2.3 Some simple geometric objects.

two coordinates; a line segment is defined by two points; and a triangle can be defined by three points. Let us choose the following functors:

> **point**   for points,
> **seg**   for line segments, and
> **triangle** for triangles.

Then the objects in Figure 2.3 can be represented as follows:

> P1 = **point**(1,1)
> P2 = **point**(2,3)
> S = **seg**(P1, P2) = **seg**(point(1,1), point(2,3))
> T = **triangle**(point(4,2), point(6,4), point(7,1))

The corresponding tree representation of these objects is shown in Figure 2.4. In general, the functor at the root of the tree is called the *principal functor* of the term.

If in the same program we also had points in three-dimensional space then we could use another functor, **point3**, say, for their representation:

> **point3**(X, Y, Z)

We can, however, use the same name, **point**, for points in both two and three dimensions, and write for example:

> **point**(X1, Y1)   and   **point**(X, Y, Z)

If the same name appears in the program in two different roles, as is the case for point above, the Prolog system will recognize the difference by the number of arguments, and will interpret this name as two functors: one of them with two arguments and the other one with three arguments. This is so because each functor is defined by two things:

(1)   the name, whose syntax is that of atoms;

(2)   the *arity* – that is, the number of arguments.

Computation and Reasoning

340

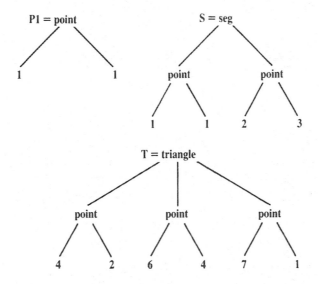

Figure 2.4 Tree representation of the objects in Figure 2.3.

As already explained, all structured objects in Prolog are trees, represented in the program by terms. We will study two more examples to illustrate how naturally complicated data objects can be represented by Prolog terms. Figure 2.5 shows the tree structure that corresponds to the arithmetic expression:

$$(a + b) * (c - 5)$$

According to the syntax of terms introduced so far this can be written, using the symbols '∗', '+' and '−' as functors, as follows:

∗(+(a, b), −(c, 5))

This is, of course, a legal Prolog term; but this is not the form that we would normally like to have. We would normally prefer the usual, infix notation as used in mathematics. In fact, Prolog also allows us to use the infix notation so that the symbols '∗', '+' and '−' are written as infix operators. Details of how the programmer can define his or her own operators will be discussed in Chapter 3.

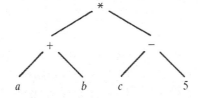

Figure 2.5 A tree structure that corresponds to the arithmetic expression $(a + b) * (c - 5)$.

Computation and Reasoning

341

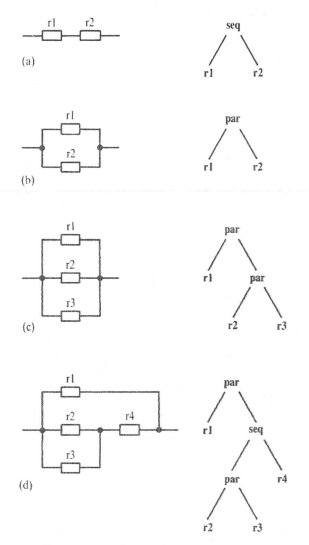

Figure 2.6   Some simple electric circuits and their tree representations: (a) sequential composition of resistors r1 and r2; (b) parallel composition of two resistors; (c) parallel composition of three resistors; (d) parallel composition of r1 and another circuit.

As the last example we consider some simple electric circuits shown in Figure 2.6. The right-hand side of the figure shows the tree representation of these circuits. The atoms **r1**, **r2**, **r3** and **r4** are the names of the resistors. The functors **par** and **seq** denote the parallel and the sequential compositions of resistors respectively. The corresponding Prolog terms are:

```
seq( r1, r2)
par( r1, r2)
par( r1, par( r2, r3) )
par( r1, seq( par( r2, r3), r4) )
```

Exercises

2.1 Which of the following are syntactically correct Prolog objects? What kinds of object are they (atom, number, variable, structure)?

(a) Diana

(b) diana

(c) 'Diana'

(d) _diana

(e) 'Diana goes south'

(f) goes(diana, south)

(g) 45

(h) 5(X, Y)

(i) +(north, west)

(j) three(Black(Cats))

2.2 Suggest a representation for rectangles, squares and circles as structured Prolog objects. Use an approach similar to that in Figure 2.4. For example, a rectangle can be represented by four points (or maybe three points only). Write some example terms that represent some concrete objects of these types using the suggested representation.

2.2 Matching

In the previous section we have seen how terms can be used to represent complex data objects. The most important operation on terms is *matching*. Matching alone can produce some interesting computation.

Given two terms, we say that they *match* if:

(1) they are identical, or

(2) the variables in both terms can be instantiated to objects in such a way that after the substitution of variables by these objects the terms become identical.

For example, the terms date(D, M, 2001) and date(D1, may, Y1) match. One instantiation that makes both terms identical is:

- D is instantiated to D1
- M is instantiated to **may**
- Y1 is instantiated to 2001

This instantiation is more compactly written in the familiar form in which Prolog outputs results:

D = D1
M = may
Y1 = 2001

On the other hand, the terms date(D, M, 2001) and date(D1, M1, 1444) do not match, nor do the terms date(X, Y, Z) and point(X, Y, Z).

Matching is a process that takes as input two terms and checks whether they match. If the terms do not match we say that this process *fails*. If they do match then the process *succeeds* and it also instantiates the variables in both terms to such values that the terms become identical.

Let us consider again the matching of the two dates. The request for this operation can be communicated to the Prolog system by the following question, using the operator '=':

?- date(D, M, 2001) = date(D1, may, Y1).

We have already mentioned the instantiation D = D1, M = may, Y1 = 2001, which achieves the match. There are, however, other instantiations that also make both terms identical. Two of them are as follows:

D = 1
D1 = 1
M = may
Y1 = 2001

D = third
D1 = third
M = may
Y1 = 2001

These two instantiations are said to be *less general* than the first one because they constrain the values of the variables D and D1 more strongly than necessary. For making both terms in our example identical, it is only important that D and D1 have the same value, although this value can be anything. Matching in Prolog always results in the *most general* instantiation. This is the instantiation that commits the variables to the least possible extent, thus leaving the greatest possible freedom for further instantiations if further matching is required. As an example consider the following question:

?- date(D, M, 2001) = date(D1, may, Y1),
   date(D, M, 2001) = date(15, M, Y).

To satisfy the first goal, Prolog instantiates the variables as follows:

D = D1
M = may
Y1 = 2001

After having satisfied the second goal, the instantiation becomes more specific as follows:

D = 15
D1 = 15
M = may
Y1 = 2001
Y = 2001

This example also shows that variables, during the execution of consecutive goals, typically become instantiated to increasingly more specific values.

The general rules to decide whether two terms, S and T, match are as follows:

(1)   If S and T are constants then S and T match only if they are the same object.

(2)   If S is a variable and T is anything, then they match, and S is instantiated to T. Conversely, if T is a variable then T is instantiated to S.

(3)   If S and T are structures then they match only if

    (a)   S and T have the same principal functor, and

    (b)   all their corresponding components match.

    The resulting instantiation is determined by the matching of the components.

The last of these rules can be visualized by considering the tree representation of terms, as in the example of Figure 2.7. The matching process starts at the root (the principal functors). As both functors match, the process proceeds to the arguments where matching of the pairs of corresponding arguments occurs. So the whole matching process can be thought of as consisting of the following sequence of (simpler) matching operations:

triangle = triangle,
point(1,1) = X,
A = point(4,Y),
point(2,3) = point(2,Z).

The whole matching process succeeds because all the matchings in the sequence succeed. The resulting instantiation is:

X = point(1,1)
A = point(4,Y)
Z = 3

Computation and Reasoning

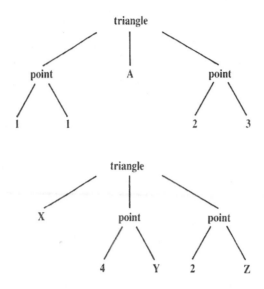

Figure 2.7 Matching **triangle(point(1,1), A, point(2,3))** = **triangle(X, point(4,Y), point(2,Z))**.

The following example will illustrate how matching alone can be used for interesting computation. Let us return to the simple geometric objects of Figure 2.4, and define a piece of program for recognizing horizontal and vertical line segments. 'Vertical' is a property of segments, so it can be formalized in Prolog as a unary relation. Figure 2.8 helps to formulate this relation. A segment is vertical if the *x*-coordinates of its end-points are equal, otherwise there is no other restriction on the segment. The property 'horizontal' is similarly formulated, with only *x* and *y* interchanged. The following program, consisting of two facts, does the job:

vertical(seg(point(X,Y), point(X,Y1))).

horizontal(seg(point(X,Y), point(X1,Y))).

The following conversation is possible with this program:

?- vertical(seg(point(1,1), point(1,2))).

yes

?- vertical(seg(point(1,1), point(2,Y))).

no

?- horizontal(seg(point(1,1), point(2,Y))).

Y = 1

The first question was answered 'yes' because the goal in the question matched one of the facts in the program. For the second question no match was possible. In the third question, Y was forced to become 1 by matching the fact about horizontal segments.

Computation and Reasoning

346

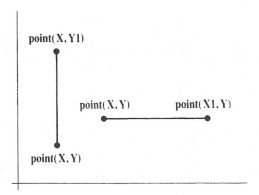

Figure 2.8   Illustration of vertical and horizontal line segments.

A more general question to the program is: Are there any vertical segments that start at the point (2,3)?

?- vertical(seg(point(2,3), P)).

P = point(2,Y)

This answer means: Yes, any segment that ends at any point (2,Y), which means anywhere on the vertical line $x = 2$. It should be noted that Prolog's actual answer would probably not look as neat as above, but (depending on the Prolog implementation used) something like this:

P = point(2,_136)

This is, however, only a cosmetic difference. Here _136 is a variable that has not been instantiated. _136 is a legal variable name that the system has constructed during the execution. The system has to generate new names in order to rename the user's variables in the program. This is necessary for two reasons: first, because the same name in different clauses signifies different variables, and second, in successive applications of the same clause, its 'copy' with a new set of variables is used each time.

Another interesting question to our program is: Is there a segment that is both vertical and horizontal?

?- vertical(S), horizontal(S).

S = seg(point(X,Y), point(X,Y))

This answer by Prolog says: Yes, any segment that is degenerated to a point has the property of being vertical and horizontal at the same time. The answer was, again, derived simply by matching. As before, some internally generated names may appear in the answer, instead of the variable names X and Y.

Computation and Reasoning

347

Exercises

2.3   Will the following matching operations succeed or fail? If they succeed, what are the resulting instantiations of variables?

(a)   **point(A, B) = point(1, 2)**

(b)   **point(A, B) = point(X, Y, Z)**

(c)   **plus(2, 2) = 4**

(d)   **+(2, D) = +(E, 2)**

(e)   **triangle(point(−1,0), P2, P3) = triangle(P1, point(1,0), point(0,Y))**

The resulting instantiation defines a family of triangles. How would you describe this family?

2.4   Using the representation for line segments as described in this section, write a term that represents any vertical line segment at $x = 5$.

2.5   Assume that a rectangle is represented by the term **rectangle(P1, P2, P3, P4)** where the P's are the vertices of the rectangle positively ordered. Define the relation:

regular(R)

which is true if R is a rectangle whose sides are vertical and horizontal.

2.3 Declarative meaning of Prolog programs

We have already seen in Chapter 1 that Prolog programs can be understood in two ways: declaratively and procedurally. In this and the next section we will consider a more formal definition of the declarative and procedural meanings of programs in basic Prolog. But first let us look at the difference between these two meanings again.
    Consider a clause:

P :- Q, R.

where P, Q and R have the syntax of terms. Some alternative declarative readings of this clause are:

P is true if Q and R are true.
From Q and R follows P.

Two alternative procedural readings of this clause are:

To solve problem P, *first* solve the subproblem Q and *then* the subproblem R.
To satisfy P, *first* satisfy Q and *then* R.

Computation and Reasoning

Thus the difference between the declarative readings and the procedural ones is that the latter do not only define the logical relations between the head of the clause and the goals in the body, but also the *order* in which the goals are processed.

Let us now formalize the declarative meaning.

The declarative meaning of programs determines whether a given goal is true, and if so, for what values of variables it is true. To precisely define the declarative meaning we need to introduce the concept of *instance* of a clause. An instance of a clause C is the clause C with each of its variables substituted by some term. A *variant* of a clause C is such an instance of the clause C where each variable is substituted by another variable. For example, consider the clause:

hasachild(X) :- parent(X, Y).

Two variants of this clause are:

hasachild(A) :- parent(A, B).
hasachild(X1) :- parent(X1, X2).

Instances of this clause are:

hasachild(peter) :- parent(peter, Z).
hasachild(barry) :- parent(barry, small(caroline)).

Given a program and a goal G, the declarative meaning says:

A goal G is true (that is, satisfiable, or logically follows from the program) if and only if:

(1)   there is a clause C in the program such that

(2)   there is a clause instance I of C such that

    (a)   the head of I is identical to G, and

    (b)   all the goals in the body of I are true.

This definition extends to Prolog questions as follows. In general, a question to the Prolog system is a *list* of goals separated by commas. A list of goals is true if *all* the goals in the list are true for the *same* instantiation of variables. The values of the variables result from the most general instantiation.

A comma between goals thus denotes the *conjunction* of goals: they *all* have to be true. But Prolog also accepts the *disjunction* of goals: *any one* of the goals in a disjunction has to be true. Disjunction is indicated by a semicolon. For example,

P :- Q; R.

is read: P is true if Q is true *or* R is true. The meaning of this clause is thus the same as the meaning of the following two clauses together:

P :- Q.
P :- R.

Computation and Reasoning

The comma binds stronger than the semicolon. So the clause:

P :- Q, R; S, T, U.

is understood as:

P :- (Q, R); (S, T, U).

and means the same as the clauses:

P :- Q, R.
P :- S, T, U.

Exercises

2.6   Consider the following program:

f(1, one).
f(s(1), two).
f(s(s(1)), three).
f(s(s(s(X))), N) :-
    f(X, N).

How will Prolog answer the following questions? Whenever several answers are possible, give at least two.

(a) ?- f(s(1), A).

(b) ?- f(s(s(1)), two).

(c) ?- f(s(s(s(s(s(s(1)))))), C).

(d) ?- f(D, three).

2.7   The following program says that two people are relatives if

(a) one is a predecessor of the other, or

(b) they have a common predecessor, or

(c) they have a common successor:

relatives(X, Y) :-
    predecessor(X, Y).

relatives(X, Y) :-
    predecessor(Y, X).

relatives(X, Y) :-   % X and Y have a common predecessor
    predecessor(Z, X),
    predecessor(Z, Y).

relatives(X, Y) :-   % X and Y have a common successor
    predecessor(X, Z),
    predecessor(Y, Z).

Can you shorten this program by using the semicolon notation?

2.8   Rewrite the following program without using the semicolon notation.

translate(Number, Word) :-
 Number = 1, Word = one;
 Number = 2, Word = two;
 Number = 3, Word = three.

2.4   Procedural meaning

The procedural meaning specifies *how* Prolog answers questions. To answer a question means to try to satisfy a list of goals. They can be satisfied if the variables that occur in the goals can be instantiated in such a way that the goals logically follow from the program. Thus the procedural meaning of Prolog is a procedure for executing a list of goals with respect to a given program. To 'execute goals' means: try to satisfy them.

Let us call this procedure **execute**. As shown in Figure 2.9, the inputs to and the outputs from this procedure are:

input: a program and a goal list
output: a success/failure indicator and an instantiation of variables

The meaning of the two output results is as follows:

(1)   The success/failure indicator is 'yes' if the goals are satisfiable and 'no' otherwise. We say that 'yes' signals a *successful* termination and 'no' a *failure*.

(2)   An instantiation of variables is only produced in the case of a successful termination; in the case of failure there is no instantiation.

In Chapter 1, we have in effect already discussed informally what procedure **execute** does, under the heading 'How Prolog answers questions'. What follows in the rest of this section is just a more formal and systematic description of this

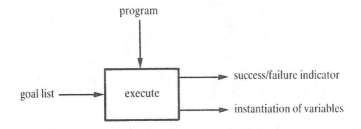

Figure 2.9 Input/output view of the procedure that executes a list of goals.

Computation and Reasoning

process, and can be skipped without seriously affecting the understanding of the rest of the book.

Particular operations in the goal execution process are illustrated by the example in Figure 2.10. It may be helpful to study Figure 2.10 before reading the following general description.

To execute a list of goals:

G1, G2, ..., Gm

the procedure execute does the following:

- If the goal list is empty then terminate with *success*.

- If the goal list is not empty then continue with (the following) operation called 'SCANNING'.

- *SCANNING*: Scan through the clauses in the program from top to bottom until the first clause, C, is found such that the head of C matches the first goal G1. If there is no such clause then terminate with *failure*.

  If there is such a clause C of the form

      H :- B1, ..., Bn.

  then rename the variables in C to obtain a variant C' of C, such that C' and the list G1, ..., Gm have no common variables. Let C' be

      H' :- B1', ..., Bn'.

  Match G1 and H'; let the resulting instantiation of variables be S.

  In the goal list G1, G2, ..., Gm, replace G1 with the list B1', ..., Bn', obtaining a new goal list

      B1', ..., Bn', G2, ..., Gm

  (Note that if C is a fact then $n = 0$ and the new goal list is shorter than the original one; such shrinking of the goal list may eventually lead to the empty list and thereby a successful termination.)

  Substitute the variables in this new goal list with new values as specified in the instantiation S, obtaining another goal list

      B1'', ..., Bn'', G2', ..., Gm'

- Execute (recursively with this same procedure) this new goal list. If the execution of this new goal list terminates with success then terminate the execution of the original goal list also with success. If the execution of the new goal list is not successful then abandon this new goal list and go back to SCANNING through the program. Continue the scanning with the clause that immediately follows the clause C (C is the clause that was last used) and try to find a successful termination using some other clause.

Computation and Reasoning

352

PROGRAM

big(bear).	% Clause 1
big(elephant).	% Clause 2
small(cat).	% Clause 3
brown(bear).	% Clause 4
black(cat).	% Clause 5
gray(elephant).	% Clause 6
dark(Z) :- black(Z).	% Clause 7: Anything black is dark
dark(Z) :- brown(Z).	% Clause 8: Anything brown is dark

QUESTION

?- dark(X), big(X).   % Who is dark and big?

EXECUTION TRACE

(1) Initial goal list: **dark(X), big(X)**.

(2) Scan the program from top to bottom looking for a clause whose head matches the first goal **dark(X)**. Clause 7 found:

    dark(Z) :- black(Z).

Replace the first goal by the instantiated body of clause 7, giving a new goal list:

    black(X), big(X)

(3) Scan the program to find a match with **black(X)**. Clause 5 found: **black(cat)**. This clause has no body, so the goal list, properly instantiated, shrinks to:

    big(cat)

(4) Scan the program for the goal **big(cat)**. No clause found. Therefore backtrack to step (3) and undo the instantiation X = cat. Now the goal list is again:

    black(X), big(X)

Continue scanning the program below clause 5. No clause found. Therefore backtrack to step (2) and continue scanning below clause 7. Clause 8 is found:

    dark(Z) :- brown(Z).

Replace the first goal in the goal list by **brown(X)**, giving:

    brown(X), big(X)

(5) Scan the program to match **brown(X)**, finding **brown(bear)**. This clause has no body, so the goal list shrinks to:

    big(bear)

(6) Scan the program and find clause **big(bear)**. It has no body so the goal list shrinks to empty. This indicates successful termination, and the corresponding variable instantiation is:

    X = bear

Figure 2.10 An example to illustrate the procedural meaning of Prolog: a sample trace of the procedure **execute**.

Computation and Reasoning

This procedure is more compactly written in a Pascal-like notation in Figure 2.11.

Several additional remarks are in order here regarding the procedure **execute** as presented. First, it was not explicitly described how the final resulting instantiation of variables is produced. It is the instantiation S which led to a successful termination, and was possibly further refined by additional instantiations that were done in the nested recursive calls to **execute**.

Whenever a recursive call to **execute** fails, the execution returns to SCANNING, continuing at the program clause C that had been last used before. As the application of the clause C did not lead to a successful termination Prolog has to try an alternative clause to proceed. What effectively happens is that Prolog abandons this whole part of the unsuccessful execution and backtracks to the point (clause C) where this failed branch of the execution was started. When the procedure backtracks to a certain point, all the variable instantiations that were done after that point are undone. This ensures that Prolog systematically examines all the possible alternative paths of execution until one is found that eventually succeeds, or until all of them have been shown to fail.

We have already seen that even after a successful termination the user can force the system to backtrack to search for more solutions. In our description of **execute** this detail was left out.

Of course, in actual implementations of Prolog, several other refinements have to be added to **execute**. One of them is to reduce the amount of scanning through the program clauses to improve efficiency. So a practical Prolog implementation will not scan through all the clauses of the program, but will only consider the clauses about the relation in the current goal.

Exercise

2.9   Consider the program in Figure 2.10 and simulate, in the style of Figure 2.10, Prolog's execution of the question:

?- **big**(X), **dark**(X).

Compare your execution trace with that of Figure 2.10 when the question was essentially the same, but with the goals in the order:

?- **dark**(X), **big**(X).

In which of the two cases does Prolog have to do more work before the answer is found?

Computation and Reasoning

procedure *execute* (*Program, GoalList, Success*);

Input arguments:
   Program: list of clauses
   GoalList: list of goals
Output argument:
   Success: truth value; *Success* will become true if *GoalList* is true with respect to *Program*
Local variables:
   Goal: goal
   OtherGoals: list of goals
   Satisfied: truth value
   MatchOK: truth value
   Instant: instantiation of variables
   $H, H', B1, B1', \ldots, Bn, Bn'$: goals
Auxiliary functions:
   empty(L): returns true if L is the empty list
   head(L): returns the first element of list L
   tail(L): returns the rest of L
   append(L1,L2): appends list *L2* at the end of list *L1*
   match(T1,T2,MatchOK,Instant): tries to match terms *T1* and *T2*; if
      succeeds then *MatchOK* is true and *Instant* is the corresponding instantiation of variables
   substitute(Instant,Goals): substitutes variables in *Goals* according to instantiation *Instant*

begin
   if *empty(GoalList)* **then** *Success* := *true*
   else
      begin
         Goal := *head(GoalList)*;
         OtherGoals := *tail(GoalList)*;
         Satisfied := *false*;
         while not *Satisfied* **and** *"more clauses in program"* **do**
            begin
               Let next clause in Program be
                  $H :\text{-} B1, \ldots, Bn.$
               Construct a variant of this clause
                  $H' :\text{-} B1', \ldots, Bn'.$
               match(Goal,H',MatchOK,Instant);
               if *MatchOK* **then**
                  begin
                     NewGoals := *append([B1',\ldots,Bn']*, *OtherGoals)*;
                     NewGoals := *substitute(Instant,NewGoals)*;
                     execute(Program,NewGoals,Satisfied)
                  end
            end;
         Success := *Satisfied*
      end
end;

Figure 2.11 Executing Prolog goals.

Computation and Reasoning

2.5 Example: monkey and banana

The monkey and banana problem is used as a simple example of problem solving. Our Prolog program for this problem will show how the mechanisms of matching and backtracking can be used in such exercises. We will develop the program in the non-procedural way, and then study its procedural behaviour in detail. The program will be compact and illustrative.

We will use the following variation of the problem. There is a monkey at the door into a room. In the middle of the room a banana is hanging from the ceiling. The monkey is hungry and wants to get the banana, but he cannot stretch high enough from the floor. At the window of the room there is a box the monkey may use. The monkey can perform the following actions: walk on the floor, climb the box, push the box around (if it is already at the box) and grasp the banana if standing on the box directly under the banana. Can the monkey get the banana?

One important task in programming is that of finding a representation of the problem in terms of the programming language used. In our case we can think of the 'monkey world' as always being in some *state* that can change in time. The current state is determined by the positions of the objects. For example, the initial state of the world is determined by:

(1)   Monkey is at door.

(2)   Monkey is on floor.

(3)   Box is at window.

(4)   Monkey does not have banana.

It is convenient to combine all of these four pieces of information into one structured object. Let us choose the word 'state' as the functor to hold the four components together. Figure 2.12 shows the initial state represented as a structured object.

Our problem can be viewed as a one-person game. Let us now formalize the rules of the game. First, the goal of the game is a situation in which the monkey has the banana; that is, any state in which the last component is 'has':

state(_, _, _, has)

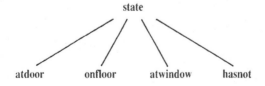

Figure 2.12   The initial state of the monkey world represented as a structured object. The four components are: horizontal position of monkey, vertical position of monkey, position of box, monkey has or has not banana.

Second, what are the allowed moves that change the world from one state to another? There are four types of moves:

(1) grasp banana,

(2) climb box,

(3) push box,

(4) walk around.

Not all moves are possible in every possible state of the world. For example, the move 'grasp' is only possible if the monkey is standing on the box directly under the banana (which is in the middle of the room) and does not have the banana yet. Such rules can be formalized in Prolog as a three-place relation named **move**:

move(State1, Move, State2)

The three arguments of the relation specify a move thus:

State1 ⟶ State2
        Move

State1 is the state before the move, **Move** is the move executed and **State2** is the state after the move.

The move 'grasp', with its necessary precondition on the state before the move, can be defined by the clause:

```
move( state( middle, onbox, middle, hasnot),    % Before move
      grasp,                                      % Move
      state( middle, onbox, middle, has) ).       % After move
```

This fact says that after the move the monkey has the banana, and he has remained on the box in the middle of the room.

In a similar way we can express the fact that the monkey on the floor can walk from any horizontal position Pos1 to any position Pos2. The monkey can do this regardless of the position of the box and whether it has the banana or not. All this can be defined by the following Prolog fact:

```
move( state( Pos1, onfloor, Box, Has),
      walk( Pos1, Pos2),                           % Walk from Pos1 to Pos2
      state( Pos2, onfloor, Box, Has) ).
```

Note that this clause says many things, including, for example:

• the move executed was 'walk from some position Pos1 to some position Pos2';

• the monkey is on the floor before and after the move;

Computation and Reasoning

357

- the box is at some point **Box** which remained the same after the move;
- the 'has banana' status **Has** remains the same after the move.

The clause actually specifies a whole set of possible moves because it is applicable to any situation that matches the specified state before the move. Such a specification is therefore sometimes also called a move *schema*. Using Prolog variables, such schemas can be easily programmed in Prolog.

The other two types of moves, 'push' and 'climb', can be similarly specified.

The main kind of question that our program will have to answer is: Can the monkey in some initial state **State** get the banana? This can be formulated as a predicate

    canget(State)

where the argument **State** is a state of the monkey world. The program for **canget** can be based on two observations:

(1)   For any state in which the monkey already has the banana, the predicate **canget** must certainly be true; no move is needed in this case. This corresponds to the Prolog fact:

        canget(state(_, _, _, has)).

(2)   In other cases one or more moves are necessary. The monkey can get the banana in any state **State1** if there is some move **Move** from **State1** to some state **State2**, such that the monkey can then get the banana in state **State2** (in zero or more moves). This principle is illustrated in Figure 2.13. A Prolog clause that corresponds to this rule is:

        canget(State1) :-
          move(State1, Move, State2),
          canget(State2).

This completes our program, which is shown in Figure 2.14.

The formulation of **canget** is recursive and is similar to that of the **predecessor** relation of Chapter 1 (compare Figures 2.13 and 1.7). This principle is used in Prolog again and again.

We have developed our monkey and banana program in the non-procedural way. Let us now study its *procedural* behaviour by considering the following question

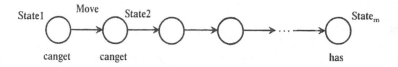

Figure 2.13 Recursive formulation of **canget**.

Computation and Reasoning

358

```
% move( State1, Move, State2): making Move in State1 results in State2;
%    a state is represented by a term:
%      state( MonkeyHorizontal, MonkeyVertical, BoxPosition, HasBanana)

move( state( middle, onbox, middle, hasnot),      % Before move
        grasp,                                     % Grasp banana
        state( middle, onbox, middle, has) ).      % After move

move( state( P, onfloor, P, H),
        climb,                                     % Climb box
        state( P, onbox, P, H) ).

move( state( P1, onfloor, P1, H),
        push( P1, P2),                             % Push box from P1 to P2
        state( P2, onfloor, P2, H) ).

move( state( P1, onfloor, B, H),
        walk( P1, P2),                             % Walk from P1 to P2
        state( P2, onfloor, B, H) ).

% canget( State): monkey can get banana in State

canget( state( _, _, _, has) ).                    % can 1: Monkey already has it

canget( State1) :-                                 % can 2: Do some work to get it
        move( State1, Move, State2),               % Do something
        canget( State2).                           % Get it now
```

Figure 2.14   A program for the monkey and banana problem.

to the program:

> ?- canget(state(atdoor, onfloor, atwindow, hasnot)).

Prolog's answer is 'yes'. The process carried out by Prolog to reach this answer proceeds, according to the procedural semantics of Prolog, through a sequence of goal lists. It involves some search for the right moves among the possible alternative moves. At some point this search will take a wrong move leading to a dead branch. At this stage, backtracking will help it to recover. Figure 2.15 illustrates this search process.

To answer the question Prolog had to backtrack once only. A right sequence of moves was found almost straight away. The reason for this efficiency of the program was the order in which the clauses about the move relation occurred in the program. The order in our case (luckily) turned out to be quite suitable. However, less lucky orderings are possible. According to the rules of the game, the monkey could just as easily try to walk here or there without ever touching the box, or aimlessly push the box around. A more thorough investigation will reveal, as shown in the following section, that the ordering of clauses is, in the case of our program, in fact critical.

Computation and Reasoning

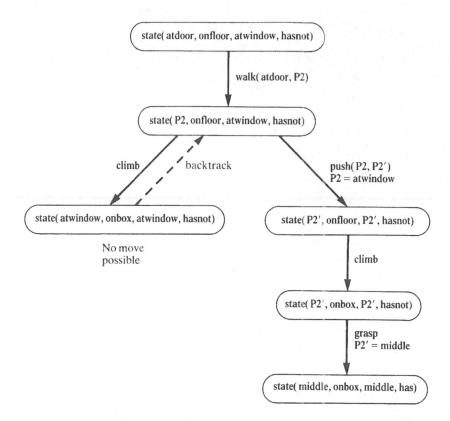

Figure 2.15   The monkey's search for the banana. The search starts at the top node and proceeds downwards, as indicated. Alternative moves are tried in the left-to-right order. Backtracking occurred once only.

2.6   Order of clauses and goals

2.6.1   Danger of indefinite looping

Consider the following clause:

    p :- p.

This says that 'p is true if p is true'. This is declaratively perfectly correct, but procedurally is quite useless. In fact, such a clause can cause problems to Prolog. Consider the question:

    ?- p.

Using the clause above, the goal p is replaced by the same goal p; this will be in turn replaced by p, etc. In such a case Prolog will enter an infinite loop not noticing that no progress is being made.

This example is a simple way of getting Prolog to loop indefinitely. However, similar looping could have occurred in some of our previous example programs if we changed the order of clauses, or the order of goals in the clauses. It will be instructive to consider some examples.

In the monkey and banana program, the clauses about the **move** relation were ordered thus: grasp, climb, push, walk (perhaps 'unclimb' should be added for completeness). These clauses say that grasping is possible, climbing is possible, etc. According to the procedural semantics of Prolog, the order of clauses indicates that the monkey prefers grasping to climbing, climbing to pushing, etc. This order of preferences in fact helps the monkey to solve the problem. But what could happen if the order was different? Let us assume that the 'walk' clause appears first. The execution of our original goal of the previous section

   ?- canget(state(atdoor, onfloor, atwindow, hasnot)).

would this time produce the following trace. The first four goal lists (with variables appropriately renamed) are the same as before:

   (1)   canget(state(atdoor, onfloor, atwindow, hasnot))

The second clause of canget ('can2') is applied, producing:

   (2)   move(state(atdoor, onfloor, atwindow, hasnot), M′, S2′),
         canget(S2′)

By the move walk(atdoor, P2′) we get:

   (3)   canget(state(P2′, onfloor, atwindow, hasnot))

Using the clause 'can2' again the goal list becomes:

   (4)   move(state(P2′, onfloor, atwindow, hasnot), M″, S2″),
         canget(S2″)

Now the difference occurs. The first clause whose head matches the first goal above is now 'walk' (and not 'climb' as before). The instantiation is

   S2″ = state(P2″, onfloor, atwindow, hasnot)

Therefore the goal list becomes:

   (5)   canget(state(P2″, onfloor, atwindow, hasnot))

Applying the clause 'can2' we obtain:

   (6)   move(state(P2″, onfloor, atwindow, hasnot), M‴, S2‴),
         canget(S2‴)

Again, 'walk' is now tried first, producing:

(7)   canget(state(P2''', onfloor, atwindow, hasnot))

Let us now compare the goals (3), (5) and (7). They are the same apart from one variable; this variable is, in turn, P', P'' and P'''. As we know, the success of a goal does not depend on particular names of variables in the goal. This means that from goal list (3) the execution trace shows no progress. We can see, in fact, that the same two clauses, 'can2' and 'walk', are used repetitively. The monkey walks around without ever trying to use the box. As there is no progress made this will (theoretically) go on for ever: Prolog will not realize that there is no point in continuing along this line.

This example shows Prolog trying to solve a problem in such a way that a solution is never reached, although a solution exists. Such situations are not unusual in Prolog programming. Infinite loops are, also, not unusual in other programming languages. What *is* unusual in comparison with other languages is that a Prolog program may be declaratively correct, but at the same time be procedurally incorrect in that it is not able to produce an answer to a question. In such cases Prolog may not be able to satisfy a goal because it tries to reach an answer by choosing a wrong path.

A natural question to ask at this point is: Can we not make some more substantial change to our program so as to drastically prevent any danger of looping? Or shall we always have to rely just on a suitable ordering of clauses and goals? As it turns out programs, especially large ones, would be too fragile if they just had to rely on some suitable ordering. There are several other methods that preclude infinite loops, and these are much more general and robust than the ordering method itself. These techniques will be used regularly later in the book, especially in those chapters that deal with path finding, problem solving and search.

2.6.2   Program variations through reordering of clauses and goals

Already in the example programs of Chapter 1 there was a latent danger of producing a cycling behaviour. Our program to specify the predecessor relation in Chapter 1 was:

```
predecessor( Parent, Child) :-
    parent( Parent, Child).

predecessor( Predecessor, Successor) :-
    parent( Predecessor, Child),
    predecessor( Child, Successor).
```

Let us analyze some variations of this program. All the variations will clearly have the same declarative meaning, but not the same procedural meaning. According to the declarative semantics of Prolog we can, without affecting the declarative meaning, change:

(1)   the order of clauses in the program, and

(2)   the order of goals in the bodies of clauses.

The **predecessor** procedure consists of two clauses, and one of them has two goals in the body. There are, therefore, four variations of this program, all with the same declarative meaning. The four variations are obtained by:

(1)   swapping both clauses, and

(2)   swapping the goals for each order of clauses.

The corresponding four procedures, called **pred1**, **pred2**, **pred3** and **pred4**, are shown in Figure 2.16.

....

% Four versions of the predecessor program

% The original version

pred1(X, Z) :-
  parent(X, Z).

pred1(X, Z) :-
  parent(X, Y),
  pred1(Y, Z).

% Variation a: swap clauses of the original version

pred2(X, Z) :-
  parent(X, Y),
  pred2(Y, Z).

pred2(X, Z) :-
  parent(X, Z).

% Variation b: swap goals in second clause of the original version

pred3(X, Z) :-
  parent(X, Z).

pred3(X, Z) :-
  pred3(X, Y),
  parent(Y, Z).

% Variation c: swap goals and clauses of the original version

pred4(X, Z) :-
  pred4(X, Y),
  parent(Y, Z).

pred4(X, Z) :-
  parent(X, Z).

....

Figure 2.16   Four versions of the **predecessor** program.

Computation and Reasoning

363

There are important differences in the behaviour of these four declaratively equivalent procedures. To demonstrate these, consider the parent relation as shown in Figure 1.1 of Chapter 1. Now, what happens if we ask whether Tom is a predecessor of Pat using the four variations of the predecessor relation:

```
?- pred1( tom, pat).

yes

?- pred2( tom, pat).

yes

?- pred3( tom, pat).

yes

?- pred4( tom, pat).
```

In the last case Prolog cannot find the answer. This is manifested on the terminal by a Prolog message such as 'More core needed' or 'Stack overflow'.

Figure 1.11 in Chapter 1 showed the trace of pred1 (in Chapter 1 called predecessor) produced for the above question. Figure 2.17 shows the corresponding traces for pred2, pred3 and pred4. Figure 2.17(c) clearly shows that pred4 is hopeless, and Figure 2.17(a) indicates that pred2 is rather inefficient compared to pred1: pred2 does much more searching and backtracking in the family tree.

This comparison should remind us of a general practical heuristic in problem solving: it is usually best to try the simplest idea first. In our case, all the versions of the predecessor relation are based on two ideas:

(1) the simpler idea is to check whether the two arguments of the predecessor relation satisfy the parent relation;

(2) the more complicated idea is to find somebody 'between' both people (somebody who is related to them by the parent and predecessor relations).

Of the four variations of the predecessor relation, pred1 does simplest things first. On the contrary, pred4 always tries complicated things first. pred2 and pred3 are in between the two extremes. Even without a detailed study of the execution traces, pred1 should be preferred merely on the grounds of the rule 'try simple things first'. This rule will be in general a useful guide in programming.

Our four variations of the predecessor procedure can be further compared by considering the question: What types of questions can particular variations answer, and what types can they not answer? It turns out that pred1 and pred2 are both able to reach an answer for any type of question about predecessors; pred4 can never reach an answer; and pred3 sometimes can and sometimes cannot. One example in which pred3 fails is:

```
?- pred3( liz, jim).
```

This question again brings the system into an infinite sequence of recursive calls. Thus **pred3** also cannot be considered procedurally correct.

2.6.3 Combining declarative and procedural views

The foregoing section has shown that the order of goals and clauses does matter. Furthermore, there are programs that are declaratively correct, but do not work in practice. Such discrepancies between the declarative and procedural meaning may

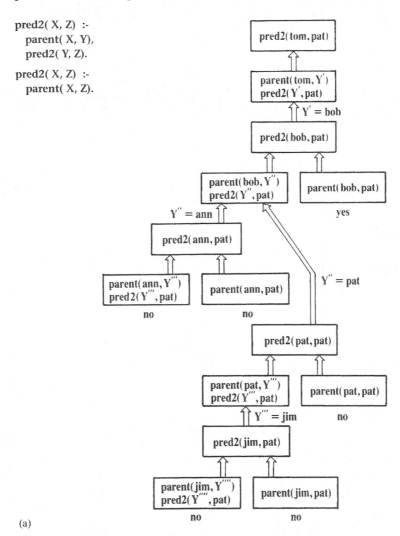

(a)

Figure 2.17 The behaviour of three formulations of the **predecessor** relation on the question: Is Tom a predecessor of Pat?

Computation and Reasoning

365

pred3(X, Z) :-
    parent(X, Z).

pred3(X, Z) :-
    pred3(X, Y),
    parent(Y, Z).

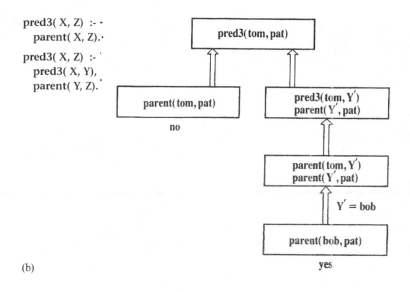

(b)

pred4(X, Z) :-
    pred4(X, Y),
    parent(Y, Z).

pred4(X, Z) :-
    parent(X, Z).

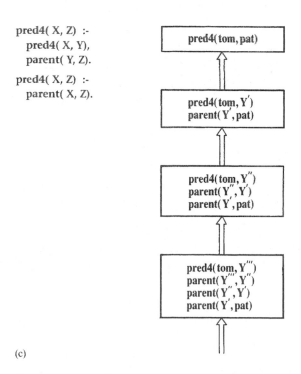

(c)

Figure 2.17 *contd*

Computation and Reasoning

366

appear annoying. One may argue: Why not simply forget about the declarative meaning? This argument can be brought to an extreme with a clause such as:

```
predecessor( X, Z) :- predecessor( X, Z).
```

which is declaratively correct, but is completely useless as a working program.

The reason why we should not forget about the declarative meaning is that progress in programming technology is achieved by moving away from procedural details toward declarative aspects, which are normally easier to formulate and understand. The system itself, not the programmer, should carry the burden of filling in the procedural details. Prolog does help toward this end, although, as we have seen in this section, it only helps partially: sometimes it does work out the procedural details itself properly, and sometimes it does not. The philosophy adopted by many is that it is better to have at least *some* declarative meaning rather than *none* ('none' is the case in most other programming languages). The practical aspect of this view is that it is often rather easy to get a working program once we have a program that is declaratively correct. Consequently, a useful practical approach that often works is to concentrate on the declarative aspects of the problem, then test the resulting program, and if it fails procedurally try to rearrange the clauses and goals into a suitable order.

2.7   The relation between Prolog and logic

Prolog is related to mathematical logic, so its syntax and meaning can be specified most concisely with references to logic. Prolog is indeed often defined that way. However, such an introduction to Prolog assumes that the reader is familiar with certain concepts of mathematical logic. These concepts are, on the other hand, certainly not necessary for understanding and using Prolog as a programming tool, which is the aim of this book. For the reader who is especially interested in the relation between Prolog and logic, the following are some basic links to mathematical logic, together with some appropriate references.

Prolog's syntax is that of the *first-order predicate logic* formulas written in the so-called *clause form* (a conjunctive normal form in which quantifiers are not explicitly written), and further restricted to Horn clauses only (clauses that have at most one positive literal). Clocksin and Mellish (1987) give a Prolog program that transforms a first-order predicate calculus formula into the clause form. The procedural meaning of Prolog is based on the *resolution principle* for mechanical theorem proving introduced by Robinson in his classic paper (1965). Prolog uses a special strategy for resolution theorem proving called SLD. An introduction to the first-order predicate calculus and resolution-based theorem proving can be found in several general books on artificial intelligence (Genesereth and Nilsson 1987; Ginsberg 1993; Poole *et al.* 1998; Russell and Norvig 1995; see also Flach 1994). Mathematical questions regarding the properties of Prolog's procedural meaning with respect to logic are analyzed by Lloyd (1991).

Matching in Prolog corresponds to what is called *unification* in logic. However, we avoid the word unification because matching, for efficiency reasons in most Prolog systems, is implemented in a way that does not exactly correspond to unification (see Exercise 2.10). But from the practical point of view this approximation to unification is quite adequate. Proper unification requires the so-called *occurs check*: does a given variable occur in a given term? The occurs check would make matching inefficient.

Exercise

2.10   What happens if we ask Prolog:

    ?-   X = f(X).

Should this request for matching succeed or fail? According to the definition of unification in logic this should fail, but what happens according to our definition of matching in Section 2.2? Try to explain why many Prolog implementations answer the question above with:

    X = f(f(f(f(f(f(f(f(f(f(f(f(f(...

Summary

So far we have covered a kind of basic Prolog, also called 'pure Prolog'. It is 'pure' because it corresponds closely to formal logic. Extensions whose aim is to tailor the language toward some practical needs will be covered later in the book (Chapters 3, 5, 6, 7). Important points of this chapter are:

- Simple objects in Prolog are *atoms*, *variables* and *numbers*. Structured objects, or *structures*, are used to represent objects that have several components.

- Structures are constructed by means of *functors*. Each functor is defined by its name and arity.

- The type of object is recognized entirely by its syntactic form.

- The *lexical* scope of variables is one clause. Thus the same variable name in two clauses means two different variables.

- Structures can be naturally pictured as trees. Prolog can be viewed as a language for processing trees.

- The *matching* operation takes two terms and tries to make them identical by instantiating the variables in both terms.

- Matching, if it succeeds, results in the *most general* instantiation of variables.

- The *declarative semantics* of Prolog defines whether a goal is true with respect to a given program, and if it is true, for what instantiation of variables it is true.

- A comma between goals means the conjunction of goals. A semicolon between goals means the disjunction of goals.

- The *procedural semantics* of Prolog is a procedure for satisfying a list of goals in the context of a given program. The procedure outputs the truth or falsity of the goal list and the corresponding instantiations of variables. The procedure automatically backtracks to examine alternatives.

- The declarative meaning of programs in 'pure Prolog' does not depend on the order of clauses and the order of goals in clauses.

- The procedural meaning does depend on the order of goals and clauses. Thus the order can affect the efficiency of the program; an unsuitable order may even lead to infinite recursive calls.

- Given a declaratively correct program, changing the order of clauses and goals can improve the program's efficiency while retaining its declarative correctness. Reordering is one method of preventing indefinite looping.

- There are other more general techniques, apart from reordering, to prevent indefinite looping and thereby make programs procedurally robust.

- Concepts discussed in this chapter are:

  data objects: atom, number, variable, structure
  term
  functor, arity of a functor
  principal functor of a term
  matching of terms
  most general instantiation
  declarative semantics
  instance of a clause, variant of a clause
  procedural semantics
  executing goals

References

Clocksin, W.F. and Mellish, C.S. (1987) *Programming in Prolog*, second edition. Berlin: Springer-Verlag.

Flach, P. (1994) *Simply Logical: Intelligent Reasoning by Example*. Chichester, UK: Wiley.

Genesereth, M.R. and Nilsson, N.J. (1987) *Logical Foundation of Artificial Intelligence*. Palo Alto, CA: Morgan Kaufmann.

Ginsberg, M. (1993) *Essentials of Artificial Intelligence*. San Francisco, CA: Morgan Kaufmann.

Lloyd, J.W. (1991) *Foundations of Logic Programming*, second edition. Berlin: Springer-Verlag.

Computation and Reasoning

Robinson, A.J. (1965) A machine-oriented logic based on the resolution principle. *JACM* **12**: 23–41.

Poole, D., Mackworth, A. and Gaebel, R. (1998) *Computational Intelligence: A Logical Approach.* Oxford University Press.

Russell, S. and Norvig, P. (1995) *Artificial Intelligence: A Modern Approach.* Englewood Cliffs, NJ: Prentice Hall.

Computation and Reasoning

Lists, Operators, Arithmetic

In this chapter we will study a special notation for lists, one of the simplest and most useful structures, and some programs for typical operations on lists. We will also look at simple arithmetic and the operator notation, which often improves the readability of programs. Basic Prolog of Chapter 2, extended with these three additions, becomes a convenient framework for writing interesting programs.

3.1   Representation of lists

The *list* is a simple data structure widely used in non-numeric programming. A list is a sequence of any number of items, such as **ann, tennis, tom, skiing**. Such a list can be written in Prolog as:

[ann, tennis, tom, skiing]

This is, however, only the external appearance of lists. As we have already seen in Chapter 2, all structured objects in Prolog are trees. Lists are no exception to this.

How can a list be represented as a standard Prolog object? We have to consider two cases: the list is either empty or non-empty. In the first case, the list is simply written as a Prolog atom, []. In the second case, the list can be viewed as consisting of two things:

(1)   the first item, called the *head* of the list;

(2)   the remaining part of the list, called the *tail*.

61

For our example list,

[ann, tennis, tom, skiing]

the head is ann and the tail is the list:

[tennis, tom, skiing]

In general, the head can be anything (any Prolog object, for example, a tree or a variable); the tail has to be a list. The head and the tail are then combined into a structure by a special functor,

.(Head, Tail)

Since Tail is in turn a list, it is either empty or it has its own head and tail. Therefore, to represent lists of any length no additional principle is needed. Our example list is then represented as the term:

.(ann, .(tennis, .(tom, .(skiing, [ ]))))

Figure 3.1 shows the corresponding tree structure. Note that the empty list appears in our term. This is because the one but last tail is a single item list:

[skiing]

This list has the empty list as its tail:

[skiing] = .(skiing, [ ])

This example shows how the general principle for structuring data objects in Prolog also applies to lists of any length. As our example also shows, the straight-forward notation with dots and possibly deep nesting of subterms in the tail part can produce rather confusing expressions. This is the reason why Prolog provides the neater notation for lists, so that they can be written as sequences of items enclosed in square brackets. A programmer can use both notations, but the square bracket notation is, of course, normally preferred. We will be aware, however, that this is

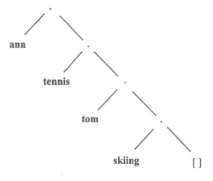

Figure 3.1   Tree representation of the list [ann, tennis, tom, skiing].

only a cosmetic improvement and that our lists will be internally represented as binary trees. When such terms are output they will be automatically converted into their neater form. Thus the following conversation with Prolog is possible:

```
?- List1 = [a,b,c],
   List2 = .( a, .( b, .( c, [] ) ) ).

List1 = [a,b,c]
List2 = [a,b,c]

?- Hobbies1 = .( tennis, .( music, [] ) ),
   Hobbies2 = [ skiing, food],
   L = [ ann, Hobbies1, tom, Hobbies2].

Hobbies1 = [ tennis, music]
Hobbies2 = [ skiing, food]
L = [ ann, [tennis,music], tom, [skiing,food] ]
```

This example also reminds us that the elements of a list can be objects of any kind; in particular they can also be lists.

It is often practical to treat the whole tail as a single object. For example, let:

```
L = [a,b,c]
```

Then we could write:

```
Tail = [b,c]   and   L = .( a, Tail)
```

To express this in the square bracket notation for lists, Prolog provides another notational extension, the vertical bar, which separates the head and the tail:

```
L = [ a | Tail]
```

The vertical bar notation is in fact more general: we can list any number of elements followed by ' | ' and the list of remaining items. Thus alternative ways of writing the above list are:

```
[a,b,c] = [a | [b,c] ] = [a,b | [c] ] = [a,b,c | [] ]
```

To summarize:

- A list is a data structure that is either empty or consists of two parts: a *head* and a *tail*. The tail itself has to be a list.
- Lists are handled in Prolog as a special case of binary trees. For improved readability Prolog provides a special notation for lists, thus accepting lists written as:

    ```
    [ Item1, Item2, ...]
    ```

  or

    ```
    [ Head | Tail]
    ```

  or

    ```
    [ Item1, Item2, ... | Others]
    ```

Computation and Reasoning

3.2 Some operations on lists

Lists can be used to represent sets, although there is a difference: the order of elements in a set does not matter while the order of items in a list does; also, the same object can occur repeatedly in a list. Still, the most common operations on lists are similar to those on sets. Among them are:

- checking whether some object is an element of a list, which corresponds to checking for the set membership;

- concatenation of two lists, obtaining a third list, which may correspond to the union of sets;

- adding a new object to a list, or deleting some object from it.

In the remainder of this section we give programs for these and some other operations on lists.

3.2.1 Membership

Let us implement the membership relation as:

member(X, L)

where X is an object and L is a list. The goal member(X, L) is true if X occurs in L. For example,

member(b, [a,b,c])

is true,

member(b, [a,[b,c]])

is not true, but

member([b,c], [a,[b,c]])

is true. The program for the membership relation can be based on the following observation:

X is a member of L if either:
(1) X is the head of L, or
(2) X is a member of the tail of L.

This can be written in two clauses; the first is a simple fact and the second is a rule:

member(X, [X | Tail]).

member(X, [Head | Tail]) :-
    member(X, Tail).

3.2.2 Concatenation

For concatenating lists we will define the relation:

conc(L1, L2, L3)

Here L1 and L2 are two lists, and L3 is their concatenation. For example,

conc([a,b], [c,d], [a,b,c,d])

is true, but

conc([a,b], [c,d], [a,b,a,c,d])

is false. In the definition of **conc** we will have again two cases, depending on the first argument, L1:

(1)   If the first argument is the empty list then the second and the third arguments must be the same list (call it L); this is expressed by the following Prolog fact:

conc([ ], L, L).

(2)   If the first argument of **conc** is a non-empty list then it has a head and a tail and must look like this:

[X | L1]

Figure 3.2 illustrates the concatenation of [X | L1] and some list L2. The result of the concatenation is the list [X | L3] where L3 is the concatenation of L1 and L2. In Prolog this is written as:

conc([X | L1], L2, [X | L3]) :-
    conc(L1, L2, L3).

This program can now be used for concatenating given lists, for example:

?- conc([a,b,c], [1,2,3], L).

L = [a,b,c,1,2,3]

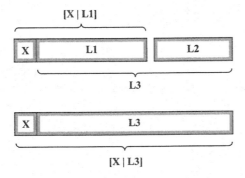

Figure 3.2   Concatenation of lists.

Computation and Reasoning

375

?- conc([a,[b,c],d], [a,[ ],b], L).

L = [a, [b,c], d, a, [ ], b]

Although the conc program looks rather simple it can be used flexibly in many other ways. For example, we can use conc in the inverse direction for *decomposing* a given list into two lists, as follows:

?- conc(L1, L2, [a,b,c]).

L1 = [ ]
L2 = [a,b,c];

L1 = [a]
L2 = [b,c];

L1 = [a,b]
L2 = [c];

L1 = [a,b,c]
L2 = [ ];

no

It is possible to decompose the list [a,b,c] in four ways, all of which were found by our program through backtracking.

We can also use our program to look for a certain pattern in a list. For example, we can find the months that precede and the months that follow a given month, as in the following goal:

?- conc(Before, [may | After],
        [jan,feb,mar,apr,may,jun,jul,aug,sep,oct,nov,dec]).

Before = [jan,feb,mar,apr]
After = [jun,jul,aug,sep,oct,nov,dec].

Further we can find the immediate predecessor and the immediate successor of May by asking:

?- conc(_, [Month1,may,Month2 | _],
        [jan,feb,mar,apr,may,jun,jul,aug,sep,oct,nov,dec]).

Month1 = apr
Month2 = jun

Further still, we can, for example, delete from some list, L1, everything that follows three successive occurrences of z in L1 together with the three z's. For example:

?- L1 = [a,b,z,z,c,z,z,z,d,e],
   conc(L2, [z,z,z | _], L1).

L1 = [a,b,z,z,c,z,z,z,d,e]
L2 = [a,b,z,z,c]

We have already programmed the membership relation. Using conc, however, the membership relation could be elegantly programmed by the clause:

```
member1( X, L) :-
    conc( L1, [X | L2], L).
```

This clause says: X is a member of list L if L can be decomposed into two lists so that the second one has X as its head. Of course, member1 defines the same relation as member. We have just used a different name to distinguish between the two implementations. Note that the above clause can be written using anonymous variables as:

```
member1( X, L) :-
    conc( _, [X | _], L).
```

It is interesting to compare both implementations of the membership relation, member and member1. member has a rather straightforward procedural meaning, which is as follows:

To check whether some X is a member of some list L:
(1) first check whether the head of L is equal to X, and then
(2) check whether X is a member of the tail of L.

On the other hand, the declarative reading of member1 is straightforward, but its procedural meaning is not so obvious. An interesting exercise is to find how member1 actually computes something. An example execution trace will give some idea: let us consider the question:

```
?- member1( b, [a,b,c] ).
```

Figure 3.3 shows the execution trace. From the trace we can infer that member1 behaves similarly to member. It scans the list, element by element, until the item in question is found or the list is exhausted.

Exercises

3.1 (a) Write a goal, using conc, to delete the last three elements from a list L producing another list L1. Hint: L is the concatenation of L1 and a three-element list.

(b) Write a goal to delete the first three elements and the last three elements from a list L producing list L2.

3.2 Define the relation

last(Item, List)

so that Item is the last element of a list List. Write two versions: (a) using the conc relation, (b) without conc.

Computation and Reasoning

377

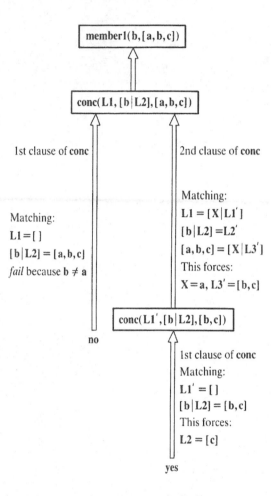

Figure 3.3 Procedure **member1** finds an item in a given list by sequentially searching the list.

3.2.3   Adding an item

To add an item to a list, it is easiest to put the new item in front of the list so that it becomes the new head. If X is the new item and the list to which X is added is L then the resulting list is simply:

   [X | L]

So we actually need no procedure for adding a new element in front of the list. Nevertheless, if we want to define such a procedure explicitly, it can be written as the fact:

   add(X, L, [X | L]).

Computation and Reasoning

3.2.4 Deleting an item

Deleting an item, X, from a list, L, can be programmed as a relation

del(X, L, L1)

where L1 is equal to the list L with the item X removed. The **del** relation can be defined similarly to the membership relation. We have, again, two cases:

(1)   If X is the head of the list then the result after the deletion is the tail of the list.

(2)   If X is in the tail then it is deleted from there.

del(X, [X | Tail], Tail).

del(X, [Y | Tail], [Y | Tail1]) :-
    del(X, Tail, Tail1).

Like **member**, **del** is also non-deterministic. If there are several occurrences of X in the list then **del** will be able to delete any one of them by backtracking. Of course, each alternative execution will only delete one occurrence of X, leaving the others untouched. For example:

?- del(a, [a,b,a,a], L).

L = [b,a,a];

L = [a,b,a];

L = [a,b,a];

no

del will fail if the list does not contain the item to be deleted.

del can also be used in the inverse direction, to add an item to a list by inserting the new item anywhere in the list. For example, if we want to insert a at any place in the list [1,2,3] then we can do this by asking the question: What is L such that after deleting a from L we obtain [1,2,3]?

?- del(a, L, [1,2,3]).

L = [a,1,2,3];

L = [1,a,2,3];

L = [1,2,a,3];

L = [1,2,3,a];

no

In general, the operation of inserting X at any place in some list **List** giving **BiggerList** can be defined by the clause:

insert(X, List, BiggerList) :-
    del(X, BiggerList, List).

In **member1** we elegantly implemented the membership relation by using **conc**. We can also use **del** to test for membership. The idea is simple: some X is a member of **List** if X can be deleted from **List**:

```
member2( X, List) :-
    del( X, List, _).
```

3.2.5 Sublist

Let us now consider the sublist relation. This relation has two arguments, a list L and a list S such that S occurs within L as its sublist. So,

> sublist([c,d,e], [a,b,c,d,e,f])

is true, but

> sublist([c,e], [a,b,c,d,e,f])

is not. The Prolog program for **sublist** can be based on the same idea as **member1**, only this time the relation is more general (see Figure 3.4). Accordingly, the relation can be formulated as:

S is a sublist of L if:
(1) L can be decomposed into two lists, L1 and L2, and
(2) L2 can be decomposed into two lists, S and some L3.

As we have seen before, the **conc** relation can be used for decomposing lists. So the above formulation can be expressed in Prolog as:

```
sublist( S, L) :-
    conc( L1, L2, L),
    conc( S, L3, L2).
```

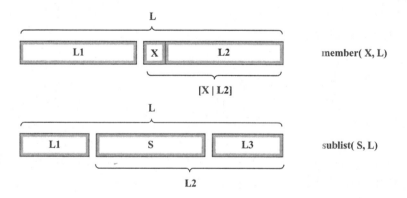

Figure 3.4 The **member** and **sublist** relations.

Computation and Reasoning

380

Of course, the **sublist** procedure can be used flexibly in several ways. Although it was designed to check if some list occurs as a sublist within another list it can also be used, for example, to find all sublists of a given list:

```
?- sublist( S, [a,b,c] ).
S = [ ];
S = [a];
S = [a,b];
S = [a,b,c];
S = [ ];
S = [b];
...
```

3.2.6   Permutations

Sometimes it is useful to generate permutations of a given list. To this end, we will define the **permutation** relation with two arguments. The arguments are two lists such that one is a permutation of the other. The intention is to generate permutations of a list through backtracking using the **permutation** procedure, as in the following example:

```
?- permutation( [a,b,c], P).
P = [a,b,c];
P = [a,c,b];
P = [b,a,c];
...
```

The program for **permutation** can be, again, based on the consideration of two cases, depending on the first list:

(1)   If the first list is empty then the second list must also be empty.

(2)   If the first list is not empty then it has the form [X | L], and a permutation of such a list can be constructed as shown in Figure 3.5: first permute L obtaining L1 and then insert X at any position into L1.

Two Prolog clauses that correspond to these two cases are:

```
permutation( [], [] ).

permutation( [X | L], P) :-
   permutation( L, L1),
   insert( X, L1, P).
```

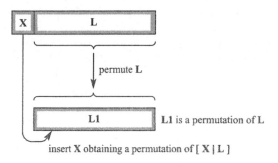

Figure 3.5 One way of constructing a permutation of the list [X | L].

One alternative to this program would be to delete an element, X, from the first list, permute the rest of it obtaining a list P, and then add X in front of P. The corresponding program is:

permutation2([ ], [ ]).

permutation2(L, [X | P]) :-
   del(X, L, L1),
   permutation2(L1, P).

It is instructive to do some experiments with our permutation programs. Its normal use would be something like this:

?- **permutation**([red,blue,green], P).

This would result in all six permutations, as intended:

P = [red, blue, green];

P = [red, green, blue];

P = [blue, red, green];

P = [blue, green, red];

P = [green, red, blue];

P = [green, blue, red];

no

Another attempt to use **permutation** is:

?- **permutation**(L, [a,b,c]).

Our first version, **permutation**, will now instantiate L successfully to all six permutations. If the user then requests more solutions, the program would never answer 'no' because it would get into an infinite loop trying to find another permutation when there is none. Our second version, **permutation2**, will in this case find only the first (identical) permutation and then immediately get into an infinite loop. Thus, some care is necessary when using these permutation programs.

Computation and Reasoning

382

Exercises

3.3   Define two predicates

evenlength(List)   and   **oddlength(List)**

so that they are true if their argument is a list of even or odd length respectively. For example, the list [a,b,c,d] is 'evenlength' and [a,b,c] is 'oddlength'.

3.4   Define the relation

reverse(List, ReversedList)

that reverses lists. For example, **reverse([a,b,c,d], [d,c,b,a])**.

3.5   Define the predicate **palindrome(List)**. A list is a palindrome if it reads the same in the forward and in the backward direction. For example, [m,a,d,a,m].

3.6   Define the relation

shift(List1, List2)

so that **List2** is **List1** 'shifted rotationally' by one element to the left. For example,

    ?- shift([1,2,3,4,5], L1),
       shift(L1, L2).

produces:

    L1 = [2,3,4,5,1]
    L2 = [3,4,5,1,2]

3.7   Define the relation

translate(List1, List2)

to translate a list of numbers between 0 and 9 to a list of the corresponding words. For example:

translate([3,5,1,3], [three,five,one,three])

Use the following as an auxiliary relation:

means(0, zero).   means(1, one).   means(2, two).   ...

3.8   Define the relation

subset(Set, Subset)

where **Set** and **Subset** are two lists representing two sets. We would like to be able to use this relation not only to check for the subset relation, but also to generate all possible subsets of a given set. For example:

Computation and Reasoning

383

```
?- subset( [a,b,c], S).
S = [a,b,c];
S = [a,b];
S = [a,c];
S = [a];
S = [b,c];
S = [b];
...
```

3.9   Define the relation

    dividelist(List, List1, List2)

so that the elements of List are partitioned between List1 and List2, and List1 and List2 are of approximately the same length. For example, dividelist([a,b,c,d,e], [a,c,e], [b,d]).

3.10   Rewrite the monkey and banana program of Chapter 2 as the relation

    canget(State, Actions)

to answer not just 'yes' or 'no', but to produce a sequence of monkey's actions represented as a list of moves. For example:

    Actions = [walk(door,window), push(window,middle), climb, grasp]

3.11   Define the relation

    flatten(List, FlatList)

where List can be a list of lists, and FlatList is List 'flattened' so that the elements of List's sublists (or sub-sublists) are reorganized as one plain list. For example:

    ?- flatten([a,b,[c,d],[ ],[[[e]]],f], L).
    L = [a,b,c,d,e,f]

3.3 Operator notation

In mathematics we are used to writing expressions like

$$2*a + b*c$$

where $+$ and $*$ are operators, and 2, a, b, are arguments. In particular, $+$ and $*$ are said to be *infix* operators because they appear *between* the two arguments. Such expressions can be represented as trees, as in Figure 3.6, and can be written as Prolog terms with $+$ and $*$ as functors:

$$+(*(2,a), *(b,c))$$

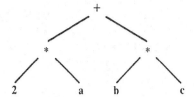

Figure 3.6   Tree representation of the expression 2∗a + b∗c.

Since we would normally prefer to have such expressions written in the usual, infix style with operators, Prolog caters for this notational convenience. Prolog will therefore accept our expression written simply as:

  2∗a + b∗c

This will be, however, only the external representation of this object, which will be automatically converted into the usual form of Prolog terms. Such a term will be output for the user, again, in its external, infix form.

Thus operators in Prolog are merely a notational extension. If we write **a + b**, Prolog will handle it exactly as if it had been written +(a,b). In order that Prolog properly understands expressions such as a + b∗c, Prolog has to know that ∗ binds stronger than +. We say that + has higher precedence than ∗. So the precedence of operators decides what is the correct interpretation of expressions. For example, the expression **a + b∗c** can be, in principle, understood either as

  +(a, ∗(b,c))

or as

  ∗(+(a,b), c)

The general rule is that the operator with the highest precedence is the principal functor of the term. If expressions containing + and ∗ are to be understood according to our normal conventions, then + has to have a higher precedence than ∗. Then the expression **a + b∗c** means the same as **a + (b∗c)**. If another interpretation is intended, then it has to be explicitly indicated by parentheses – for example, **(a + b)∗c**.

A programmer can define his or her own operators. So, for example, we can define the atoms **has** and **supports** as infix operators and then write in the program facts like:

  peter has information.
  floor supports table.

These facts are exactly equivalent to:

  has(peter, information).
  supports(floor, table).

Computation and Reasoning

385

A programmer can define new operators by inserting into the program special kinds of clauses, sometimes called *directives*, which act as operator definitions. An operator definition must appear in the program before any expression containing that operator. For our example, the operator **has** can be properly defined by the directive:

:- op(600, xfx, has).

This tells Prolog that we want to use 'has' as an operator, whose precedence is 600 and its type is 'xfx', which is a kind of infix operator. The form of the specifier 'xfx' suggests that the operator, denoted by 'f', is between the two arguments denoted by 'x'.

Notice that operator definitions do not specify any operation or action. In principle, *no operation on data is associated with an operator* (except in very special cases). Operators are normally used, as functors, only to combine objects into structures and not to invoke actions on data, although the word 'operator' appears to suggest an action.

Operator names are atoms. An operator's precedence must be in some range which depends on the implementation. We will assume that the range is between 1 and 1200.

There are three groups of operator types which are indicated by type specifiers such as xfx. The three groups are:

(1)   infix operators of three types:

   xfx   xfy   yfx

(2)   prefix operators of two types:

   fx   fy

(3)   postfix operators of two types:

   xf   yf

The specifiers are chosen so as to reflect the structure of the expression where 'f' represents the operator and 'x' and 'y' represent arguments. An 'f' appearing between the arguments indicates that the operator is infix. The prefix and postfix specifiers have only one argument, which follows or precedes the operator respectively.

There is a difference between 'x' and 'y'. To explain this we need to introduce the notion of the *precedence of argument*. If an argument is enclosed in parentheses or it is an unstructured object then its precedence is 0; if an argument is a structure then its precedence is equal to the precedence of its principal functor. 'x' represents an argument whose precedence must be strictly lower than that of the operator. 'y' represents an argument whose precedence is lower or equal to that of the operator.

These rules help to disambiguate expressions with several operators of the same precedence. For example, the expression

a – b – c

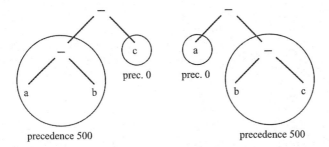

Figure 3.7 · Two interpretations of the expression **a − b − c** assuming that '−' has precedence 500. If '−' is of type **yfx**, then interpretation 2 is invalid because the precedence of **b − c** is not less than the precedence of '−'.

is normally understood as (a − b) − c, and not as a − (b − c). To achieve the normal interpretation the operator '−' has to be defined as yfx. Figure 3.7 shows why the second interpretation is then ruled out.

As another example consider the prefix operator **not**. If **not** is defined as **fy** then the expression

   not not p

is legal; but if **not** is defined as **fx** then this expression is illegal because the argument to the first **not** is **not p**, which has the same precedence as **not** itself. In this case the expression has to be written with parentheses:

   not(not p)

For convenience, some operators are predefined in the Prolog system so that they can be readily used, and no definition is needed for them. What these operators are and what their precedences are depends on the implementation of Prolog. We will assume that this set of 'standard' operators is as if defined by the clauses in Figure 3.8. The operators in this figure are a subset of those defined in the Prolog standard, plus the operator **not**. As Figure 3.8 also shows, several operators can be declared by one clause if they all have the same precedence and if they are all of the same type. In this case the operators' names are written as a list.

The use of operators can greatly improve the readability of programs. As an example let us assume that we are writing a program for manipulating Boolean expressions. In such a program we may want to state, for example, one of de Morgan's equivalence theorems, which can in mathematics be written as:

   ∼(A & B)   <⟹>   ∼A ∨ ∼B

One way to state this in Prolog is by the clause:

   equivalence(not(and(A, B)), or(not(A), not(B))).

Computation and Reasoning

```
:- op( 1200, xfx, [ :-, -->] ).
:- op( 1200, fx [ :-, ?-] ).
:- op( 1100, xfy, ';' ).
:- op( 1050, xfy, -> ).
:- op( 1000, xfy, ',' ).
:- op( 900, fy, [ not, '\+'] ).
:- op( 700, xfx, [ =, \=, ==, \==, =.. ] ).
:- op( 700, xfx, [ is, =:=, =\=, < , =< , > , >=, @<, @=<, @>, @>=] ).
:- op( 500, yfx, [ + , - ] ).
:- op( 400, yfx, [ *, /, //, mod] ).
:- op( 200, xfx, **).
:- op( 200, xfy, ^).
:- op( 200, fy, - ).
```

Figure 3.8 A set of predefined operators.

However, it is in general a good programming practice to try to retain as much resemblance as possible between the original problem notation and the notation used in the program. In our example, this can be achieved almost completely by using operators. A suitable set of operators for our purpose can be defined as:

```
:- op( 800, xfx, <===>).
:- op( 700, xfy, v).
:- op( 600, xfy, &).
:- op( 500, fy, ~).
```

Now the de Morgan's theorem can be written as the fact:

$\sim$(A & B) <===> $\sim$A v $\sim$B.

According to our specification of operators above, this term is understood as shown in Figure 3.9.

To summarize:

- The readability of programs can be often improved by using the operator notation. Operators can be infix, prefix or postfix.

- In principle, no operation on data is associated with an operator except in special cases. Operator definitions do not define any action, they only introduce new notation. Operators, as functors, only hold together components of structures.

- A programmer can define his or her own operators. Each operator is defined by its name, precedence and type.

- The precedence is an integer within some range, usually between 1 and 1200. The operator with the highest precedence in the expression is the principal functor of the expression. Operators with lowest precedence bind strongest.

Computation and Reasoning

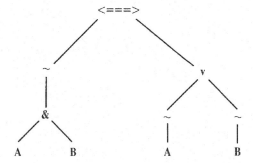

Figure 3.9 Interpretation of the term ~(A & B) <===> ~A v ~B.

- The type of an operator depends on two things: (1) the position of the operator with respect to the arguments, and (2) the precedence of the arguments compared to the precedence of the operator itself. In a specifier like xfy, x indicates an argument whose precedence is strictly lower than that of the operator; y indicates an argument whose precedence is less than or equal to that of the operator.

Exercises

3.12   Assuming the operator definitions

        :- op(300, xfx, plays).
        :- op(200, xfy, and).

then the following two terms are syntactically legal objects:

        Term1 = jimmy plays football and squash
        Term2 = susan plays tennis and basketball and volleyball

How are these terms understood by Prolog? What are their principal functors and what is their structure?

3.13   Suggest an appropriate definition of operators ('was', 'of', 'the') to be able to write clauses like

        diana was the secretary of the department.

and then ask Prolog:

        ?- Who was the secretary of the department.

        Who = diana

        ?- diana was What.

        What = the secretary of the department

Computation and Reasoning

389

3.14   Consider the program:

        t(0+1, 1+0).

        t(X+0+1, X+1+0).

        t(X+1+1, Z) :-
           t(X+1, X1),
           t(X1+1, Z).

How will this program answer the following questions if '+' is an infix operator of type yfx (as usual):

(a)   ?- **t(0+1, A).**

(b)   ?- **t(0+1+1, B).**

(c)   ?- **t(1+0+1+1+1, C).**

(d)   ?- **t(D, 1+1+1+0).**

3.15   In the previous section, relations involving lists were written as:

    member(Element, List),
    conc(List1, List2, List3),
    del(Element, List, NewList), ...

Suppose that we would prefer to write these relations as:

    Element in List,
    concatenating List1 and List2 gives List3,
    deleting Element from List gives NewList, ...

Define 'in', 'concatenating', 'and', etc. as operators to make this possible. Also, redefine the corresponding procedures.

3.4   Arithmetic

Some of the predefined operators can be used for basic arithmetic operations. These are:

+	addition
−	subtraction
*	multiplication
/	division
**	power
//	integer division
mod	modulo, the remainder of integer division

Notice that this is an exceptional case in which an operator may in fact invoke an operation. But even in such cases an additional indication to perform arithmetic will be necessary. The following question is a naive attempt to request arithmetic computation:

?- X = 1 + 2.

Prolog will 'quietly' answer

X = 1 + 2

and not X = 3 as we might possibly expect. The reason is simple: the expression 1 + 2 merely denotes a Prolog term where + is the functor and 1 and 2 are its arguments. There is nothing in the above goal to force Prolog to actually activate the addition operation. A special predefined operator, is, is provided to circumvent this problem. The is operator will force evaluation. So the right way to invoke arithmetic is:

?- X is 1 + 2.

Now the answer will be:

X = 3

The addition here was carried out by a special procedure that is associated with the operator is. We call such procedures *built-in procedures*.

Different implementations of Prolog may use somewhat different notations for arithmetics. For example, the '/' operator may denote integer division or real division. In this book, '/' denotes real division, the operator // denotes integer division, and **mod** denotes the remainder. Accordingly, the question:

?- X is 5/2,
    Y is 5//2,
    Z is 5 mod 2.

is answered by:

X = 2.5
Y = 2
Z = 1

The left argument of the is operator is a simple object. The right argument is an arithmetic expression composed of arithmetic operators, numbers and variables. Since the is operator will force the evaluation, all the variables in the expression must already be instantiated to numbers at the time of execution of this goal. The precedence of the predefined arithmetic operators (see Figure 3.8) is such that the associativity of arguments with operators is the same as normally in mathematics. Parentheses can be used to indicate different associations. Note that +, −, *, / and **div** are defined as yfx, which means that evaluation is carried out from left to right. For example,

X is 5 − 2 − 1

Computation and Reasoning

391

is interpreted as:

X is $(5 - 2) - 1$

Prolog implementations usually also provide standard functions such as sin(X), cos(X), atan(X), log(X), exp(X), etc. These functions can appear to the right of operator is.

Arithmetic is also involved when *comparing* numerical values. We can, for example, test whether the product of 277 and 37 is greater than 10000 by the goal:

?- 277 * 37 > 10000.

yes

Note that, similarly to is, the '>' operator also forces the evaluation.

Suppose that we have in the program a relation born that relates the names of people with their birth years. Then we can retrieve the names of people born between 1980 and 1990 inclusive with the following question:

?- born(Name, Year),
    Year >= 1980,
    Year =< 1990.

The comparison operators are as follows:

X > Y	X is greater than Y
X < Y	X is less than Y
X >= Y	X is greater than or equal to Y
X =< Y	X is less than or equal to Y
X =:= Y	the values of X and Y are equal
X =\= Y	the values of X and Y are not equal

Notice the difference between the matching operator '=' and '=:='; for example, in the goals X = Y and X =:= Y. The first goal will cause the matching of the objects X and Y, and will, if X and Y match, possibly instantiate some variables in X and Y. There will be no evaluation. On the other hand, X =:= Y causes the arithmetic evaluation and cannot cause any instantiation of variables. These differences are illustrated by the following examples:

?- 1 + 2 =:= 2 + 1.

yes

?- 1 + 2 = 2 + 1.

no

?- 1 + A = B + 2.

A = 2
B = 1

Let us further illustrate the use of arithmetic operations by two simple examples. The first is computing the greatest common divisor; the second, counting the items in a list.

Given two positive integers, X and Y, their greatest common divisor, D, can be found according to three cases:

(1)   If X and Y are equal then D is equal to X.

(2)   If X < Y then D is equal to the greatest common divisor of X and the difference Y − X.

(3)   If Y < X then do the same as in case (2) with X and Y interchanged.

It can be easily shown by an example that these three rules actually work. Choosing, for example, X = 20 and Y = 25, the above rules would give D = 5 after a sequence of subtractions.

These rules can be formulated into a Prolog program by defining a three-argument relation, say:

    gcd(X, Y, D)

The three rules are then expressed as three clauses, as follows:

    gcd(X, X, X).

    gcd(X, Y, D) :-
        X < Y,
        Y1 is Y − X,
        gcd(X, Y1, D).

    gcd(X, Y, D) :-
        Y < X,
        gcd(Y, X, D).

Of course, the last goal in the third clause could be equivalently replaced by the two goals:

    X1 is X − Y,
    gcd(X1, Y, D)

Our next example involves counting, which usually requires some arithmetic. An example of such a task is to establish the length of a list; that is, we have to count the items in the list. Let us define the procedure:

    length(List, N)

which will count the elements in a list List and instantiate N to their number. As was the case with our previous relations involving lists, it is useful to consider two cases:

(1)   If the list is empty then its length is 0.

(2)   If the list is not empty then List = [Head | Tail]; then its length is equal to 1 plus the length of the tail Tail.

Computation and Reasoning

These two cases correspond to the following program:

```
length( [ ], 0).

length( [_ | Tail], N) :-
  length( Tail, N1),
  N is 1 + N1.
```

An application of length can be:

```
?- length( [a,b,[c,d],e], N).

N = 4
```

Note that in the second clause of length, the two goals of the body cannot be swapped. The reason for this is that N1 has to be instantiated before the goal:

```
N is 1 + N1
```

can be processed. With the built-in procedure is, a relation has been introduced that is sensitive to the order of processing and therefore the procedural considerations have become vital.

It is interesting to see what happens if we try to program the length relation without the use of is. Such an attempt can be:

```
length1( [ ], 0).

length1( [_ | Tail], N) :-
  length1( Tail, N1),
  N = 1 + N1.
```

Now the goal

```
?- length1( [a,b,[c,d],e], N).
```

will produce the answer:

```
N = 1+(1+(1+(1+0))).
```

The addition was never explicitly forced and was therefore not carried out at all. But in length1 we can, unlike in length, swap the goals in the second clause:

```
length1( [_ | Tail], N) :-
  N = 1 + N1,
  length1( Tail, N1).
```

This version of length1 will produce the same result as the original version. It can also be written shorter, as follows,

```
length1( [_ | Tail], 1 + N) :-
  length1( Tail, N).
```

still producing the same result. We can, however, use length1 to find the number of elements in a list as follows:

?- **length1**([a,b,c], N), **Length is N.**

N = 1+(1+(1+0))
Length = 3

Finally we note that the predicate **length** is often provided as a built-in predicate. To summarize:

- Built-in procedures can be used for doing arithmetic.
- Arithmetic operations have to be explicitly requested by the built-in procedure **is**. There are built-in procedures associated with the predefined operators +, −, *, /, **div** and **mod**.
- At the time that evaluation is carried out, all arguments must be already instantiated to numbers.
- The values of arithmetic expressions can be compared by operators such as <, =<, etc. These operators force the evaluation of their arguments.

Exercises

3.16   Define the relation

   max(X, Y, Max)

so that **Max** is the greater of two numbers X and Y.

3.17   Define the predicate

   maxlist(List, Max)

so that **Max** is the greatest number in the list of numbers **List**.

3.18   Define the predicate

   sumlist(List, Sum)

so that **Sum** is the sum of a given list of numbers **List**.

3.19   Define the predicate

   ordered(List)

which is true if **List** is an ordered list of numbers. For example,

   ordered([1,5,6,6,9,12]).

3.20   Define the predicate

   subsum(Set, Sum, SubSet)

so that **Set** is a list of numbers, **SubSet** is a subset of these numbers, and the sum of the numbers in **SubSet** is **Sum**. For example:

```
?- subsum( [1,2,5,3,2], 5, Sub).
Sub = [1,2,2];
Sub = [2,3];
Sub = [5];
...
```

3.21 Define the procedure

between(N1, N2, X)

which, for two given integers N1 and N2, generates through backtracking all the integers X that satisfy the constraint N1 $\leq$ X $\leq$ N2.

3.22 Define the operators 'if', 'then', 'else' and ':=' so that the following becomes a legal term:

if X > Y then Z := X else Z := Y

Choose the precedences so that 'if' will be the principal functor. Then define the relation 'if' as a small interpreter for a kind of 'if-then-else' statement of the form

if Val1 > Val2 then Var := Val3 else Var := Val4

where Val1, Val2, Val3 and Val4 are numbers (or variables instantiated to numbers) and Var is a variable. The meaning of the 'if' relation should be: if the value of Val1 is greater than the value of Val2 then Var is instantiated to Val3, otherwise to Val4. Here is an example of the use of this interpreter:

```
?- X = 2, Y = 3,
   Val2 is 2*X,
   Val4 is 4*X,
   if Y > Val2 then Z := Y else Z := Val4,
   if Z > 5 then W := 1 else W := 0.

X  = 2
Y  = 3
Z  = 8
W = 1
Val2 = 4
Val4 = 8
```

Summary

- The list is a frequently used structure. It is either empty or consists of a *head* and a *tail* which is a list as well. Prolog provides a special notation for lists.

- Common operations on lists, programmed in this chapter, are: list membership, concatenation, adding an item, deleting an item, sublist.

- The *operator notation* allows the programmer to tailor the syntax of programs toward particular needs. Using operators the readability of programs can be greatly improved.

- New operators are defined by the directive **op**, stating the name of an operator, its type and precedence.

- In principle, there is no operation associated with an operator; operators are merely a syntactic device providing an alternative syntax for terms.

- Arithmetic is done by built-in procedures. Evaluation of an arithmetic expression is forced by the procedure is and by the comparison predicates <, =<, etc.

- Concepts introduced in this chapter are:

    list, head of list, tail of list
    list notation
    operators, operator notation
    infix, prefix and suffix operators
    precedence of an operator
    arithmetic built-in procedures

Computation and Reasoning

397

Using Structures: Example Programs

Data structures, with matching, backtracking and arithmetic, are a powerful programming tool. In this chapter we will develop the skill of using this tool through programming examples: retrieving structured information from a database, simulating a non-deterministic automaton, travel planning, and eight queens on the chessboard. We will also see how the principle of data abstraction can be carried out in Prolog. The programming examples in this chapter can be read selectively.

4.1 Retrieving structured information from a database

This exercise develops techniques of representing and manipulating structured data objects. It also illustrates Prolog as a natural database query language.

A database can be naturally represented in Prolog as a set of facts. For example, a database about families can be represented so that each family is described by one clause. Figure 4.1 shows how the information about each family can be structured. Each family has three components: husband, wife and children. As the number of children varies from family to family the children are represented by a list that is capable of accommodating any number of items. Each person is, in turn, represented by a structure of four components: name, surname, date of birth, job. The job information is 'unemployed', or it specifies the working organization and salary. The family of Figure 4.1 can be stored in the database by the clause:

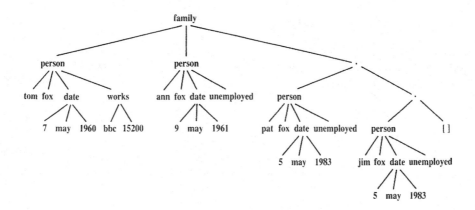

Figure 4.1 Structuring information about the family.

```
family(
    person( tom, fox, date(7,may,1960), works(bbc,15200) ),
    person( ann, fox, date(9,may,1961), unemployed),
    [ person( pat, fox, date(5,may,1983), unemployed),
      person( jim, fox, date(5,may,1983), unemployed) ] ).
```

Our database would then be comprised of a sequence of facts like this describing all families that are of interest to our program.

Prolog is, in fact, a very suitable language for retrieving the desired information from such a database. One nice thing about Prolog is that we can refer to objects without actually specifying all the components of these objects. We can merely indicate the *structure* of objects that we are interested in, and leave the particular components in the structures unspecified or only partially specified. Figure 4.2 shows some examples. So we can refer to all Armstrong families by:

```
family( person( _, armstrong, _, _), _, _)
```

The underscore characters denote different anonymous variables; we do not care about their values. Further, we can refer to all families with three children by the term:

```
family( _, _, [_, _, _] )
```

To find all married women that have at least three children we can pose the question:

```
?- family( _, person( Name, Surname, _, _), [_, _, _ | _]).
```

The point of these examples is that we can specify objects of interest not by their content, but by their structure. We only indicate their structure and leave their arguments as unspecified slots.

Computation and Reasoning

399

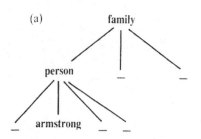

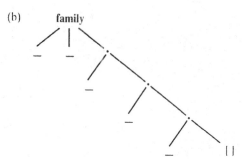

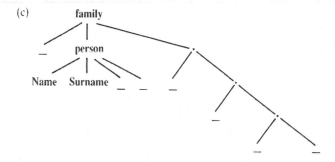

Figure 4.2 Specifying objects by their structural properties: (a) any Armstrong family; (b) any family with exactly three children; (c) any family with at least three children. Structure (c) makes provision for retrieving the wife's name through the instantiation of the variables **Name** and **Surname**.

We can provide a set of procedures that can serve as a utility to make the interaction with the database more comfortable. Such utility procedures could be part of the user interface. Some useful utility procedures for our database are:

```
husband( X) :-                          % X is a husband
   family( X, _, _).

wife( X) :-                             % X is a wife
   family( _, X, _).

child( X) :-                            % X is a child
   family( _, _, Children),
   member( X, Children).                % X in list Children

exists( Person) :-                      % Any person in the database
   husband( Person)
   ;
   wife( Person)
   ;
   child( Person).
```

dateofbirth(person(_, _, Date, _), Date).

salary(person(_, _, _, works(_, S)), S).   % Salary of working person

salary(person(_, _, _, unemployed), 0).   % Salary of unemployed

We can use these utilities, for example, in the following queries to the database:

- Find the names of all the people in the database:

    ?- exists(person(Name, Surname, _, _)).

- Find all children born in 2000:

    ?- child(X),
       dateofbirth(X, date(_, _, 2000)).

- Find all employed wives:

    ?- wife(person(Name, Surname, _, works(_, _))).

- Find the names of unemployed people who were born before 1973:

    ?- exists(person(Name, Surname, date(_, _, Year), unemployed)),
       Year < 1973.

- Find people born before 1960 whose salary is less than 8000:

    ?- exists(Person),
       dateofbirth(Person, date(_, _, Year)),
       Year < 1960,
       salary(Person, Salary),
       Salary < 8000.

- Find the names of families with at least three children:

    ?- family(person(_, Name, _, _), _, [_, _, _ | _]).

To calculate the total income of a family it is useful to define the sum of salaries of a list of people as a two-argument relation:

total(List_of_people, Sum_of_their_salaries)

This relation can be programmed as:

total([], 0).   % Empty list of people

total([Person | List], Sum) :-
    salary(Person, S),   % S: salary of first person
    total(List, Rest),   % Rest: sum of salaries of others
    Sum is S + Rest.

The total income of families can then be found by the question:

    ?- family(Husband, Wife, Children),
       total([Husband, Wife | Children], Income).

Computation and Reasoning

401

Let the **length** relation count the number of elements of a list, as defined in Section 3.4. Then we can specify all families that have an income per family member of less than 2000 by:

```
?- family( Husband, Wife, Children),
   total( [Husband, Wife | Children], Income),
   length( [Husband, Wife | Children], N),      % N: size of family
   Income/N < 2000.
```

Exercises

4.1   Write queries to find the following from the family database:

(a) names of families without children;

(b) all employed children;

(c) names of families with employed wives and unemployed husbands;

(d) all the children whose parents differ in age by at least 15 years.

4.2   Define the relation

    twins(Child1, Child2)

to find twins in the family database.

4.2 Doing data abstraction

Data abstraction can be viewed as a process of organizing various pieces of information into natural units (possibly hierarchically), thus structuring the information into some conceptually meaningful form. Each such unit of information should be easily accessible in the program. Ideally, all the details of implementing such a structure should be invisible to the user of the structure – the programmer can then just concentrate on objects and relations between them. The point of the process is to make the use of information possible without the programmer having to think about the details of how the information is actually represented.

Let us discuss one way of carrying out this principle in Prolog. Consider our family example of the previous section again. Each family is a collection of pieces of information. These pieces are all clustered into natural units such as a person or a family, so they can be treated as single objects. Assume again that the family information is structured as in Figure 4.1. In the previous section, each family was represented by a Prolog clause. Here, a family will be represented as a structured object, for example:

    FoxFamily = family(person(tom, fox, _, _), _, _)

Let us now define some relations through which the user can access particular components of a family without knowing the details of Figure 4.1. Such relations can be called *selectors* as they select particular components. The name of such a selector relation will be the name of the component to be selected. The relation will have two arguments: first, the object that contains the component, and second, the component itself:

selector_relation(Object, Component_selected)

Here are some selectors for the family structure:

husband(family(Husband, _, _), Husband).

wife(family(_, Wife, _), Wife).

children(family(_, _, ChildList), ChildList).

We can also define selectors for particular children:

firstchild(Family, First) :-
  children(Family, [First | _]).

secondchild(Family, Second) :-
  children(Family, [_, Second | _]).

  . . .

We can generalize this to selecting the Nth child:

nthchild(N, Family, Child) :-
  children(Family, ChildList),
  nth_member(N, ChildList, Child).   % Nth element of a list

Another interesting object is a person. Some related selectors according to Figure 4.1 are:

firstname(person(Name, _, _, _), Name).

surname(person(_, Surname, _, _), Surname).

born(person(_, _, Date, _), Date).

How can we benefit from selector relations? Having defined them, we can now forget about the particular way that structured information is represented. To create and manipulate this information, we just have to know the names of the selector relations and use these in the rest of the program. In the case of complicated representations, this is easier than always referring to the representation explicitly. In our family example in particular, the user does not have to know that the children are represented as a list. For example, assume that we want to say that Tom Fox and Jim Fox belong to the same family and that Jim is the second child of Tom. Using the selector relations above, we can define two persons, call them **Person1** and **Person2**, and the family. The following list of goals does this:

firstname(Person1, tom), surname(Person1, fox),   % Person1 is Tom Fox
firstname(Person2, jim), surname(Person2, fox),   % Person2 is Jim Fox
husband(Family, Person1),
secondchild(Family, Person2)

As a result, the variables Person1, Person2 and Family are instantiated as:

Person1 = person(tom, fox, _, _)

Person2 = person(jim, fox, _, _)

Family = family(person(tom, fox, _, _), _, [_, person(jim, fox) | _])

The use of selector relations also makes programs easier to modify. Imagine that we would like to improve the efficiency of a program by changing the representation of data. All we have to do is to change the definitions of the selector relations, and the rest of the program will work unchanged with the new representation.

Exercise

4.3   Complete the definition of **nthchild** by defining the relation

nth_member(N, List, X)

which is true if X is the Nth member of List.

4.3 Simulating a non-deterministic automaton

This exercise shows how an abstract mathematical construct can be translated into Prolog. In addition, our resulting program will turn out to be much more flexible than initially intended.

A *non-deterministic finite automaton* is an abstract machine that reads as input a string of symbols and decides whether to *accept* or to *reject* the input string. An automaton has a number of *states* and it is always in one of the states. It can change its state by moving from the current state to another state. The internal structure of the automaton can be represented by a transition graph such as that in Figure 4.3. In this example, s_1, s_2, s_3 and s_4 are the *states* of the automaton. Starting from the initial state (s_1 in our example), the automaton moves from state to state while reading the input string. Transitions depend on the current input symbol, as indicated by the arc labels in the transition graph.

A transition occurs each time an input symbol is read. Note that transitions can be non-deterministic. In Figure 4.3, if the automaton is in state s_1 and the current input symbol is *a* then it can transit into s_1 or s_2. Some arcs are labelled *null* denoting the 'null symbol'. These arcs correspond to 'silent moves' of the automaton. Such a

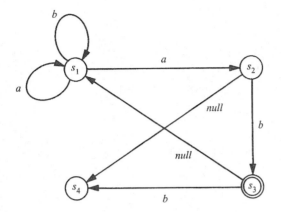

Figure 4.3   An example of a non-deterministic finite automaton.

move is said to be *silent* because it occurs without any reading of input, and the observer, viewing the automaton as a black box, will not be able to notice that any transition has occurred.

The state s_3 is double circled, which indicates that it is a *final state*. The automaton is said to *accept* the input string if there is a transition path in the graph such that

(1)   it starts with the initial state,

(2)   it ends with a final state, and

(3)   the arc labels along the path correspond to the complete input string.

It is entirely up to the automaton to decide which of the possible moves to execute at any time. In particular, the automaton may choose to make or not to make a silent move, if it is available in the current state. But abstract non-deterministic machines of this kind have a magic property: if there is a choice then they always choose a 'right' move; that is, a move that leads to the acceptance of the input string, if such a move exists. The automaton in Figure 4.3 will, for example, accept the strings *ab* and *aabaab*, but it will reject the strings *abb* and *abba*. It is easy to see that this automaton accepts any string that terminates with *ab*, and rejects all others.

In Prolog, an automaton can be specified by three relations:

(1)   a unary relation **final** which defines the final states of the automaton;

(2)   a three-argument relation **trans** which defines the state transitions so that

>   **trans(S1, X, S2)**

>   means that a transition from a state S1 to S2 is possible when the current input symbol X is read;

(3)   a binary relation

> silent(S1, S2)

> meaning that a silent move is possible from S1 to S2.

For the automaton in Figure 4.3 these three relations are:

> final(s3).

> trans(s1, a, s1).
> trans(s1, a, s2).
> trans(s1, b, s1).
> trans(s2, b, s3).
> trans(s3, b, s4).

> silent(s2, s4).
> silent(s3, s1).

We will represent input strings as Prolog lists. So the string *aab* will be represented by [a,a,b]. Given the description of the automaton, the simulator will process a given input string and decide whether the string is accepted or rejected. By definition, the non-deterministic automaton accepts a given string if (starting from an initial state), after having read the whole input string, the automaton can (possibly) be in its final state. The simulator is programmed as a binary relation, **accepts**, which defines the acceptance of a string from a given state. So

> accepts(State, String)

is true if the automaton, starting from the state **State** as initial state, accepts the string **String**. The **accepts** relation can be defined by three clauses. They correspond to the following three cases:

(1)   The empty string, [], is accepted from a state **State** if **State** is a final state.

(2)   A non-empty string is accepted from **State** if reading the first symbol in the string can bring the automaton into some state **State1**, and the rest of the string is accepted from **State1**. Figure 4.4(a) illustrates.

(3)   A string is accepted from **State** if the automaton can make a silent move from **State** to **State1** and then accept the (whole) input string from **State1**. Figure 4.4(b) illustrates.

These rules can be translated into Prolog as:

> accepts(State, [ ]) :-   % Accept empty string
>   final(State).
>
> accepts(State, [X | Rest]) :-   % Accept by reading first symbol
>   trans(State, X, State1),
>   accepts(State1, Rest).
>
> accepts(State, String) :-   % Accept by making silent move
>   silent(State, State1),
>   accepts(State1, String).

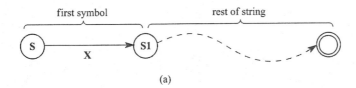

(a)

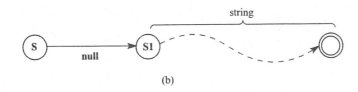

(b)

Figure 4.4 Accepting a string: (a) by reading its first symbol X; (b) by making a silent move.

The program can be asked, for example, about the acceptance of the string *aaab* by:

?- accepts(s1, [a,a,a,b]).

yes

As we have already seen, Prolog programs are often able to solve more general problems than problems for which they were originally developed. In our case, we can also ask the simulator which state our automaton can be in initially so that it will accept the string *ab*:

?- accepts(S, [a,b]).

S = s1;

S = s3

Amusingly, we can also ask: What are all the strings of length 3 that are accepted from state s_1?

?- accepts(s1, [X1,X2,X3]).

X1 = a
X2 = a
X3 = b;

X1 = b
X2 = a
X3 = b;

no

If we prefer the acceptable input strings to be typed out as lists then we can formulate the question as:

Computation and Reasoning

407

?- String = [_, _, _], accepts(s1, String).

String = [a,a,b];

String = [b,a,b];

no

We can make further experiments asking even more general questions, such as: From what states will the automaton accept input strings of length 7?

Further experimentation could involve modifications in the structure of the automaton by changing the relations **final**, **trans** and **silent**. The automaton in Figure 4.3 does not contain any cyclic 'silent path' (a path that consists only of silent moves). If in Figure 4.3 a new transition

silent(s1, s3)

is added then a 'silent cycle' is created. But our simulator may now get into trouble. For example, the question

?- accepts(s1, [a]).

would induce the simulator to cycle in state s_1 indefinitely, all the time hoping to find some way to the final state.

Exercises

4.4   Why could cycling not occur in the simulation of the original automaton in Figure 4.3, when there was no 'silent cycle' in the transition graph?

4.5   Cycling in the execution of **accepts** can be prevented, for example, by counting the number of moves made so far. The simulator would then be requested to search only for paths of some limited length. Modify the **accepts** relation this way. Hint: Add a third argument: the maximum number of moves allowed:

accepts(State, String, MaxMoves)

4.4 Travel agent

In this section we will construct a program that gives advice on planning air travel. The program will be a rather simple advisor, yet it will be able to answer some useful questions, such as:

- What days of the week is there a direct evening flight from Ljubljana to London?
- How can I get from Ljubljana to Edinburgh on Thursday?

- I have to visit Milan, Ljubljana and Zurich, starting from London on Tuesday and returning to London on Friday. In what sequence should I visit these cities so that I have no more than one flight each day of the tour?

The program will be centred around a database holding the flight information. This will be represented as a three-argument relation:

   timetable(Place1, Place2, ListOfFlights)

where **ListOfFlights** is a list of structured items of the form:

   DepartureTime / ArrivalTime / FlightNumber / ListOfDays

Here the operator '/' only holds together the components of the structure, and of course does not mean arithmetic division. **ListOfDays** is either a list of weekdays or the atom **alldays**. One clause of the **timetable** relation can be, for example:

   timetable(london, edinburgh,
          [9:40 / 10:50 / ba4733 / alldays,
          19:40 / 20:50 / ba4833 / [mo,tu,we,th,fr,su]]).

The times are represented as structured objects with two components, hours and minutes, combined by the operator ':'.

The main problem is to find exact routes between two given cities on a given day of the week. This will be programmed as a four-argument relation:

   route(Place1, Place2, Day, Route)

Here **Route** is a sequence of flights that satisfies the following criteria:

(1)   the start point of the route is **Place1**;

(2)   the end point is **Place2**;

(3)   all the flights are on the same day of the week, **Day**;

(4)   all the flights in **Route** are in the **timetable** relation;

(5)   there is enough time for transfer between flights.

The route is represented as a list of structured objects of the form:

   From / To / FlightNumber / Departure_time

We will also use the following auxiliary predicates:

(1)   **flight(Place1, Place2, Day, FlightNum, DepTime, ArrTime)**

   This says that there is a flight, **FlightNum**, between **Place1** and **Place2** on the day of the week **Day** with the specified departure and arrival times.

(2)   **deptime(Route, Time)**

   Departure time of **Route** is **Time**.

Computation and Reasoning

409

(3)   transfer(Time1, Time2)

> There is at least 40 minutes between Time1 and Time2, which should be sufficient for transfer between two flights.

The problem of finding a route is reminiscent of the simulation of the non-deterministic automaton of the previous section. The similarities of both problems are as follows:

- The states of the automaton correspond to the cities.

- A transition between two states corresponds to a flight between two cities.

- The **transition** relation of the automaton corresponds to the **timetable** relation.

- The automaton simulator finds a path in the transition graph between the initial state and a final state; the travel planner finds a route between the start city and the end city of the tour.

Not surprisingly, therefore, the route relation can be defined similarly to the **accepts** relation, with the exception that here we have no 'silent moves'. We have two cases:

(1)   Direct flight connection: if there is a direct flight between places Place1 and Place2 then the route consists of this flight only:

        route(Place1, Place2, Day, [Place1 / Place2 / Fnum / Dep]) :-
        flight(Place1, Place2, Day, Fnum, Dep, Arr).

(2)   Indirect flight connection: the route between places P1 and P2 consists of the first flight, from P1 to some intermediate place P3, followed by a route between P3 to P2. In addition, there must be enough time between the arrival of the first flight and the departure of the second flight for transfer.

        route(P1, P2, Day, [P1 / P3 / Fnum1 / Dep1 | RestRoute]) :-
        route(P3, P2, Day, RestRoute),
        flight(P1, P3, Day, Fnum1, Dep1, Arr1),
        deptime(RestRoute, Dep2),
        transfer(Arr1, Dep2).

The auxiliary relations **flight**, **transfer** and **deptime** are easily programmed and are included in the complete travel planning program in Figure 4.5. Also included is an example timetable database.

Our route planner is extremely simple and may examine paths that obviously lead nowhere. Yet it will suffice if the flight database is not large. A really large database would require more intelligent planning to cope with the large number of potential candidate paths.

Some example questions to the program are as follows:

% A FLIGHT ROUTE PLANNER

:- op(50, xfy, :).

% route(Place1, Place2, Day, Route):
%   Route is a sequence of flights on Day, starting at Place1, ending at Place2

```
route( P1, P2, Day, [ P1 / P2 / Fnum / Deptime ] )  :-        % Direct flight
    flight( P1, P2, Day, Fnum, Deptime, _).

route( P1, P2, Day, [ (P1/P3/Fnum1/Dep1) | RestRoute] )  :-   % Indirect connection
    route( P3, P2, Day, RestRoute),
    flight( P1, P3, Day, Fnum1, Dep1, Arr1),
    deptime( RestRoute, Dep2),                                % Departure time of Route
    transfer( Arr1, Dep2).                                    % Enough time for transfer

flight( Place1, Place2, Day, Fnum, Deptime, Arrtime)  :-
    timetable( Place1, Place2, Flightlist),
    member( Deptime / Arrtime / Fnum / Daylist , Flightlist),
    flyday( Day, Daylist).

flyday( Day, Daylist)  :-
    member( Day, Daylist).

flyday( Day, alldays)  :-
    member( Day, [mo,tu,we,th,fr,sa,su] ).

deptime( [ P1 / P2 / Fnum / Dep | _], Dep).

transfer( Hours1:Mins1, Hours2:Mins2)  :-
    60 * (Hours2 − Hours1) + Mins2 − Mins1 >= 40.

member( X, [X | L] ).

member( X, [Y | L] )  :-
    member( X, L).
```

% A FLIGHT DATABASE

```
timetable( edinburgh, london,
        [  9:40 / 10:50 / ba4733 / alldays,
          13:40 / 14:50 / ba4773 / alldays,
          19:40 / 20:50 / ba4833 / [mo,tu,we,th,fr,su] ] ).

timetable( london, edinburgh,
        [  9:40 / 10:50 / ba4732 / alldays,
          11:40 / 12:50 / ba4752 / alldays,
          18:40 / 19:50 / ba4822 / [mo,tu,we,th,fr] ] ).

timetable( london, ljubljana,
        [ 13:20 / 16:20 / jp212 / [mo,tu,we,fr,su],
          16:30 / 19:30 / ba473 / [mo,we,th,sa] ] ).

timetable( london, zurich,
        [  9:10 / 11:45 / ba614 / alldays,
          14:45 / 17:20 / sr805 / alldays ] ).
```

Figure 4.5 A flight route planner and an imaginary flight timetable.

Computation and Reasoning

411

Figure 4.5 *contd*

```
timetable( london, milan,
            [  8:30 / 11:20 / ba510 / alldays,
              11:00 / 13:50 / az459 / alldays ] ).
timetable( ljubljana, zurich,
            [ 11:30 / 12:40 / jp322 / [tu,th] ] ).
timetable( ljubljana, london,
            [ 11:10 / 12:20 / jp211 / [mo,tu,we,fr,su],
              20:30 / 21:30 / ba472 / [mo,we,th,sa] ] ).
timetable( milan, london,
            [  9:10 / 10:00 / az458 / alldays,
              12:20 / 13:10 / ba511 / alldays ] ).
timetable( milan, zurich,
            [  9:25 / 10:15 / sr621 / alldays,
              12:45 / 13:35 / sr623 / alldays ] ).
timetable( zurich, ljubljana,
            [ 13:30 / 14:40 / jp323 / [tu,th] ] ).
timetable( zurich, london,
            [  9:00 /  9:40 / ba613 / [mo,tu,we,th,fr,sa],
              16:10 / 16:55 / sr806 / [mo,tu,we,th,fr,su] ] ).
timetable( zurich, milan,
            [  7:55 /  8:45 / sr620 / alldays ] ).
```

- What days of the week is there a direct evening flight from Ljubljana to London?

  ```
  ?- flight( ljubljana, london, Day, _, DeptHour: _, _), DeptHour >= 18.

  Day = mo;
  Day = we;
  ...
  ```

- How can I get from Ljubljana to Edinburgh on Thursday?

  ```
  ?- route( ljubljana, edinburgh, th, R).

  R = [ ljubljana / zurich / jp322 / 11:30, zurich / london / sr806 / 16:10,
        london / edinburgh / ba4822 / 18:40]
  ```

- How can I visit Milan, Ljubljana and Zurich, starting from London on Tuesday and returning to London on Friday, with no more than one flight each day of the tour? This question is somewhat trickier. It can be formulated by using the permutation relation, programmed in Chapter 3. We are asking for a permutation of the cities Milan, Ljubljana and Zurich such that the corresponding flights are possible on successive days:

```
?- permutation( [milan, ljubljana, zurich], [City1, City2, City3] ),
   flight( london, City1, tu, FN1, _, _),
   flight( City1, City2, we, FN2, _, _),
   flight( City2, City3, th, FN3, _, _),
   flight( City3, london, fr, FN4, _, _).

City1 = milan
City2 = zurich
City3 = ljubljana
FN1 = ba510
FN2 = sr621
FN3 = jp323
FN4 = jp211
```

Finally let us note that this program is susceptible to indefinite loops, which happens for example if we ask it to find a route not in the timetable:

```
?- route ( moscow, edinburgh, mo, R).
```

It is better therefore to keep questions safe by limiting the length of the route. We can use the usual trick with conc:

```
?- conc( R, _, [_,_,_,_]), route( moscow, edinburgh, mo, R).

no
```

The conc goal limits the list R to length 4 and also forces the search to consider shortest routes first.

4.5 The eight queens problem

The problem here is to place eight queens on the empty chessboard in such a way that no queen attacks any other queen. The solution will be programmed as a unary predicate

```
solution( Pos)
```

which is true if and only if Pos represents a position with eight queens that do not attack each other. It will be interesting to compare various ideas for programming this problem. Therefore we will present three programs based on somewhat different representations of the problem.

4.5.1 Program 1

First we have to choose a representation of the board position. One natural choice is to represent the position by a list of eight items, each of them corresponding to one queen. Each item in the list will specify a square of the board on which the

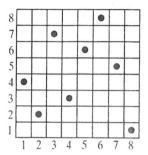

Figure 4.6   A solution to the eight queens problem. This position can be specified by the list [1/4, 2/2, 3/7, 4/3, 5/6, 6/8, 7/5, 8/1].

corresponding queen is sitting. Further, each square can be specified by a pair of coordinates (X and Y) on the board, where each coordinate is an integer between 1 and 8. In the program we can write such a pair as:

X/Y

where, of course, the '/' operator is not meant to indicate division, but simply combines both coordinates together into a square. Figure 4.6 shows one solution of the eight queens problem and its list representation.

Having chosen this representation, the problem is to find such a list of the form:

[X1/Y1, X2/Y2, X3/Y3, ..., X8/Y8]

which satisfies the no-attack requirement. Our procedure **solution** will have to search for a proper instantiation of the variables X1, Y1, X2, Y2, ..., X8, Y8. As we know that all the queens will have to be in different columns to prevent vertical attacks, we can immediately constrain the choice and so make the search task easier. We can thus fix the X-coordinates so that the solution list will fit the following, more specific template:

[1/Y1, 2/Y2, 3/Y3, ..., 8/Y8]

We are interested in the solution on a board of size 8 by 8. However, in programming, the key to the solution is often in considering a more general problem. Paradoxically, it is often the case that the solution for the more general problem is easier to formulate than that for the more specific, original problem. The original problem is then simply solved as a special case of the more general problem.

The creative part of the problem is to find the correct generalization of the original problem. In our case, a good idea is to generalize the number of queens (the number of columns in the list) from 8 to any number, including zero. The **solution** relation can then be formulated by considering two cases:

Case 1   The list of queens is empty: the empty list is certainly a solution because there is no attack.

Computation and Reasoning

414

Case 2   The list of queens is non-empty: then it looks like this:

[X/Y | Others]

In case 2, the first queen is at some square X/Y and the other queens are at squares specified by the list **Others**. If this is to be a solution then the following conditions must hold:

(1)   There must be no attack between the queens in the list **Others**; that is, **Others** itself must also be a solution.

(2)   X and Y must be integers between 1 and 8.

(3)   A queen at square X/Y must not attack any of the queens in the list **Others**.

To program the first condition we can simply use the **solution** relation itself. The second condition can be specified as follows: Y will have to be a member of the list of integers between 1 and 8 – that is, [1,2,3,4,5,6,7,8]. On the other hand, we do not have to worry about X since the solution list will have to match the template in which the X-coordinates are already specified. So X will be guaranteed to have a proper value between 1 and 8. We can implement the third condition as another relation, **noattack**. All this can then be written in Prolog as follows:

```
solution( [X/Y | Others] )  :-
  solution( Others),
  member( Y, [1,2,3,4,5,6,7,8] ),
  noattack( X/Y, Others).
```

It now remains to define the **noattack** relation:

```
noattack( Q, Qlist)
```

Again, this can be broken down into two cases:

(1)   If the list **Qlist** is empty then the relation is certainly true because there is no queen to be attacked.

(2)   If **Qlist** is not empty then it has the form [Q1 | Qlist1] and two conditions must be satisfied:

(a)   the queen at Q must not attack the queen at Q1, and

(b)   the queen at Q must not attack any of the queens in **Qlist1**.

To specify that a queen at some square does not attack another square is easy: the two squares must not be in the same row, the same column or the same diagonal. Our solution template guarantees that all the queens are in different columns, so it only remains to specify explicitly that:

•   the Y-coordinates of the queens are different, and

•   they are not in the same diagonal, either upward or downward; that is, the distance between the squares in the X-direction must not be equal to that in the Y-direction.

Computation and Reasoning

....

% solution(BoardPosition) if BoardPosition is a list of non-attacking queens

solution([]).

solution([X/Y | Others]) :-   % First queen at X/Y, other queens at Others
   solution(Others),
   member(Y, [1,2,3,4,5,6,7,8]),
   noattack(X/Y, Others).   % First queen does not attack others

noattack(_, []).   % Nothing to attack

noattack(X/Y, [X1/Y1 | Others]) :-
   Y =\= Y1,   % Different Y-coordinates
   Y1 – Y =\= X1 – X,   % Different diagonals
   Y1 – Y =\= X – X1,
   noattack(X/Y, Others).

member(Item, [Item | Rest]).

member(Item, [First | Rest]) :-
   member(Item, Rest).

% A solution template

template([1/Y1,2/Y2,3/Y3,4/Y4,5/Y5,6/Y6,7/Y7,8/Y8]).

....

Figure 4.7   Program 1 for the eight queens problem.

Figure 4.7 shows the complete program. To alleviate its use a template list has been added. This list can be retrieved in a question for generating solutions. So we can now ask:

   ?- template(S), solution(S).

and the program will generate solutions as follows:

   S = [1/4, 2/2, 3/7, 4/3, 5/6, 6/8, 7/5, 8/1];
   S = [1/5, 2/2, 3/4, 4/7, 5/3, 6/8, 7/6, 8/1];
   S = [1/3, 2/5, 3/2, 4/8, 5/6, 6/4, 7/7, 8/1];
   ...

Exercise

4.6   When searching for a solution, the program of Figure 4.7 explores alternative values for the Y-coordinates of the queens. At which place in the program is the order of alternatives defined? How can we easily modify the program to change the order? Experiment with different orders with the view of studying the time efficiency of the program.

4.5.2   Program 2

In the board representation of program 1, each solution had the form

[1/Y1, 2/Y2, 3/Y3, ..., 8/Y8]

because the queens were simply placed in consecutive columns. No information is lost if the X-coordinates were omitted. So a more economical representation of the board position can be used, retaining only the Y-coordinates of the queens:

[Y1, Y2, Y3, ..., Y8]

To prevent the horizontal attacks, no two queens can be in the same row. This imposes a constraint on the Y-coordinates. The queens have to occupy all the rows 1, 2, ..., 8. The choice that remains is the *order* of these eight numbers. Each solution is therefore represented by a permutation of the list

[1,2,3,4,5,6,7,8]

Such a permutation, S, is a solution if all the queens are safe. So we can write:

```
solution( S) :-
    permutation( [1,2,3,4,5,6,7,8], S),
    safe( S).
```

We have already programmed the **permutation** relation in Chapter 3, but the **safe** relation remains to be specified. We can split its definition into two cases:

(1)   S is the empty list: this is certainly safe as there is nothing to be attacked.

(2)   S is a non-empty list of the form [Queen | Others]. This is safe if the list Others is safe, and Queen does not attack any queen in the list Others.

In Prolog, this is:

```
safe( [] ).

safe( [Queen | Others] ) :-
    safe( Others),
    noattack( Queen, Others).
```

The **noattack** relation here is slightly trickier. The difficulty is that the queens' positions are only defined by their Y-coordinates, and the X-coordinates are not explicitly present. This problem can be circumvented by a small generalization of the **noattack** relation, as illustrated in Figure 4.8. The goal

noattack(Queen,Others)

is meant to ensure that Queen does not attack Others when the X-distance between Queen and Others is equal to 1. What is needed is the generalization of the X-distance between Queen and Others. So we add this distance as the third argument of the **noattack** relation:

noattack(Queen, Others, Xdist)

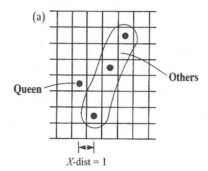 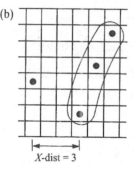

Figure 4.8   (a) X-distance between **Queen** and **Others** is 1. (b) X-distance between **Queen** and **Others** is 3.

Accordingly, the **noattack** goal in the **safe** relation has to be modified to

noattack(Queen, Others, 1)

The **noattack** relation can now be formulated according to two cases, depending on the list **Others**: if **Others** is empty then there is no target and certainly no attack; if **Others** is non-empty then **Queen** must not attack the first queen in **Others** (which is **Xdist** columns from **Queen**) and also the tail of **Others** at **Xdist** + 1. This leads to the program shown in Figure 4.9.

4.5.3   Program 3

Our third program for the eight queens problem will be based on the following reasoning. Each queen has to be placed on some square; that is, into some column, some row, some upward diagonal and some downward diagonal. To make sure that all the queens are safe, each queen must be placed in a different column, a different row, a different upward and a different downward diagonal. It is thus natural to consider a richer representation with four coordinates:

x columns
y rows
u upward diagonals
v downward diagonals

The coordinates are not independent: given x and y, u and v are determined (Figure 4.10 illustrates). For example, as:

$u = x - y$
$v = x + y$

....

% solution(Queens) if Queens is a list of Y-coordinates of eight non-attacking queens

```
solution( Queens) :-
    permutation( [1,2,3,4,5,6,7,8], Queens),
    safe( Queens).

permutation( [], [] ).

permutation( [Head | Tail], PermList) :-
    permutation( Tail, PermTail),
    del( Head, PermList, PermTail).        % Insert Head in permuted Tail
```

% del(Item, List, NewList): deleting Item from List gives NewList

```
del( Item, [Item | List], List).

del( Item, [First | List], [First | List1] ) :-
    del( Item, List, List1).
```

% safe(Queens) if Queens is a list of Y-coordinates of non-attacking queens

```
safe( [] ).

safe( [Queen | Others] ) :-
    safe( Others),
    noattack( Queen, Others, 1).

noattack( _, [], _).

noattack( Y, [Y1 | Ylist], Xdist) :-
    Y1 – Y =\= Xdist,
    Y – Y1 =\= Xdist,
    Dist1 is Xdist + 1,
    noattack( Y, Ylist, Dist1).
```

....

Figure 4.9   Program 2 for the eight queens problem.

The domains for all four dimensions are:

$$Dx = [1,2,3,4,5,6,7,8]$$

$$Dy = [1,2,3,4,5,6,7,8]$$

$$Du = [-7,-6,-5,-4,-3,-2,-1,0,1,2,3,4,5,6,7]$$

$$Dv = [2,3,4,5,6,7,8,9,10,11,12,13,14,15,16]$$

The eight queens problem can now be stated as follows: select eight 4-tuples (X,Y,U,V) from the domains (X from Dx, Y from Dy, etc.), never using the same element twice from any of the domains. Of course, once X and Y are chosen, U and V are determined. The solution can then be, roughly speaking, as follows: given all four domains, select the position of the first queen, delete the corresponding items from the four domains, and then use the rest of the domains for placing the rest of the queens. A program based on this idea is shown in Figure 4.11. The board

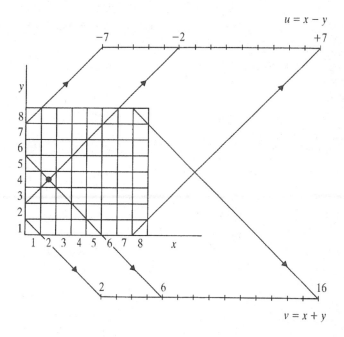

Figure 4.10 The relation between columns, rows, upward and downward diagonals. The indicated square has coordinates: $x = 2$, $y = 4$, $u = 2 - 4 = -2$, $v = 2 + 4 = 6$.

```
% solution( Ylist) if Ylist is a list of Y-coordinates of eight non-attacking queens

solution( Ylist) :-
    sol( Ylist,                                       % Y-coordinates of queens
        [1,2,3,4,5,6,7,8],                            % Domain for X-coordinates
        [1,2,3,4,5,6,7,8],                            % Domain for Y-coordinates
        [-7,-6,-5,-4,-3,-2,-1,0,1,2,3,4,5,6,7],       % Upward diagonals
        [2,3,4,5,6,7,8,9,10,11,12,13,14,15,16] ).     % Downward diagonals

sol( [], [], Dy, Du, Dv).

sol( [Y | Ylist], [X | Dx1], Dy, Du, Dv) :-
    del( Y, Dy, Dy1),                                 % Choose a Y-coordinate
    U is X−Y,                                          % Corresponding upward diagonal
    del( U, Du, Du1),                                 % Remove it
    V is X+Y,                                          % Corresponding downward diagonal
    del( V, Dv, Dv1),                                 % Remove it
    sol( Ylist, Dx1, Dy1, Du1, Dv1).                  % Use remaining values

del( Item, [Item | List], List).

del( Item, [First | List], [First | List1] ) :-
    del( Item, List, List1).
```

Figure 4.11 Program 3 for the eight queens problem.

Computation and Reasoning

420

position is, again, represented by a list of Y-coordinates. The key relation in this program is

sol(Ylist, Dx, Dy, Du, Dv)

which instantiates the Y-coordinates (in Ylist) of the queens, assuming that they are placed in consecutive columns taken from Dx. All Y-coordinates and the corresponding U and V-coordinates are taken from the lists Dy, Du and Dv. The top procedure, **solution**, can be invoked by the question:

?- solution(S).

This will cause the invocation of **sol** with the complete domains that correspond to the problem space of eight queens.

The **sol** procedure is general in the sense that it can be used for solving the N-queens problem (on a chessboard of size N by N). It is only necessary to properly set up the domains Dx, Dy, etc.

It is practical to mechanize the generation of the domains. For that we need a procedure

gen(N1, N2, List)

which will, for two given integers N1 and N2, produce the list:

List = [N1, N1 + 1, N1 + 2, ..., N2 − 1, N2]

Such a procedure is:

```
gen( N, N, [N] ).

gen( N1, N2, [N1 | List] ) :-
    N1 < N2,
    M is N1 + 1,
    gen( M, N2, List).
```

The top level relation, **solution**, has to be accordingly generalized to

solution(N, S)

where N is the size of the board and S is a solution represented as a list of Y-coordinates of N queens. The generalized **solution** relation is:

```
solution( N, S) :-
    gen( 1, N, Dxy),                    % Dxy – domain for X and Y
    Nu1 is 1 − N, Nu2 is N − 1,
    gen( Nu1, Nu2, Du),
    Nv2 is N + N,
    gen( 2, Nv2, Dv),
    sol( S, Dxy, Dxy, Du, Dv).
```

For example, a solution to the 12-queens problem would be generated by:

?- solution(12, S).

S = [1,3,5,8,10,12,6,11,2,7,9,4]

Computation and Reasoning

4.5.4 Concluding remarks

The three solutions to the eight queens problem show how the same problem can be approached in different ways. We also varied the representation of data. Sometimes the representation was more economical, sometimes it was more explicit and partially redundant. The drawback of the more economical representation is that some information always has to be recomputed when it is required.

At several points, the key step toward the solution was to generalize the problem. Paradoxically, by considering a more general problem, the solution became easier to formulate. This generalization principle is a kind of standard technique that can often be applied.

Of the three programs, the third one illustrates best how to approach general problems of constructing under constraints a structure from a given set of elements.

A natural question is: Which of the three programs is most efficient? In this respect, program 2 is far inferior while the other two programs are similar. The reason is that permutation-based program 2 constructs complete permutations while the other two programs are able to recognize and reject unsafe permutations when they are only partially constructed. Program 3 avoids some of the arithmetic computation that is essentially captured in the redundant board representation this program uses.

Exercise

4.7   Let the squares of the chessboard be represented by pairs of their coordinates of the form X/Y, where both X and Y are between 1 and 8.

(a) Define the relation jump(Square1, Square2) according to the knight jump on the chessboard. Assume that Square1 is always instantiated to a square while Square2 can be uninstantiated. For example:

   ?- jump(1/1, S).

   S = 3/2;

   S = 2/3;

   no

(b) Define the relation knightpath(Path) where Path is a list of squares that represent a legal path of a knight on the empty chessboard.

(c) Using this knightpath relation, write a question to find any knight's path of length 4 moves from square 2/1 to the opposite edge of the board (Y = 8) that goes through square 5/4 after the second move.

Computation and Reasoning

422

Summary

The examples of this chapter illustrate some strong points and characteristic features of Prolog programming:

- A database can be naturally represented as a set of Prolog facts.

- Prolog's mechanisms of querying and matching can be flexibly used for retrieving structured information from a database. In addition, utility procedures can be easily defined to further alleviate the interaction with a particular database.

- *Data abstraction* can be viewed as a programming technique that makes the use of complex data structures easier, and contributes to the clarity of programs. It is easy in Prolog to carry out the essential principles of data abstraction.

- Abstract mathematical constructs, such as automata, can often be readily translated into executable Prolog definitions.

- As in the case of eight queens, the same problem can be approached in different ways by varying the representation of the problem. Often, introducing redundancy into the representation saves computation. This entails trading space for time.

- Often, the key step toward a solution is to generalize the problem. Paradoxically, by considering a more general problem the solution may become easier to formulate.

Computation and Reasoning

423

chapter 5

Controlling Backtracking

We have already seen that a programmer can control the execution of a program through the ordering of clauses and goals. In this chapter we will look at another control facility, called 'cut', for preventing backtracking. The cut also extends the expressive power of Prolog and enables the definition of a kind of negation, called 'negation as failure' and associated with the 'closed world assumption'.

5.1   Preventing backtracking

Prolog will automatically backtrack if this is necessary for satisfying a goal. Automatic backtracking is a useful programming concept because it relieves the programmer of the burden of programming backtracking explicitly. On the other hand, uncontrolled backtracking may cause inefficiency in a program. Therefore we sometimes want to control, or to prevent, backtracking. We can do this in Prolog by using the 'cut' facility.

Let us first study the behaviour of a simple example program whose execution involves some unnecessary backtracking. We will identify those points at which the backtracking is useless and leads to inefficiency.

Consider the double-step function shown in Figure 5.1. The relation between X and Y can be specified by three rules:

Rule 1:   if X < 3 then Y = 0

Rule 2:   if $3 \leq X$ and X < 6 then Y = 2

Rule 3:   if $6 \leq X$ then Y = 4

114

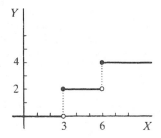

Figure 5.1 A double-step function.

This can be written in Prolog as a binary relation:

f(X, Y)

as follows:

f(X, 0) :- X < 3.	% Rule 1
f(X, 2) :- 3 =< X, X < 6.	% Rule 2
f(X, 4) :- 6 =< X.	% Rule 3

This program, of course, assumes that before f(X, Y) is executed X is already instantiated to a number, as this is required by the comparison operators.

We will make two experiments with this program. Each experiment will reveal some source of inefficiency in the program, and we will remove each source in turn by using the cut mechanism.

5.1.1 Experiment 1

Let us analyze what happens when the following question is posed:

?- f(1, Y),   2 < Y.

When executing the first goal, f(1, Y), Y becomes instantiated to 0. So the second goal becomes

2 < 0

which fails, and so does the whole goal list. This is straightforward, but before admitting that the goal list is not satisfiable, Prolog tries, through backtracking, two useless alternatives. The detailed trace is shown in Figure 5.2.

The three rules about the f relation are mutually exclusive so that one of them at most will succeed. Therefore we, not Prolog, know that as soon as one rule succeeds there is no point in trying to use the others, as they are bound to fail. In the example of Figure 5.2, rule 1 has become known to succeed at the point indicated by 'CUT'. In order to prevent futile backtracking at this point we have to tell Prolog explicitly

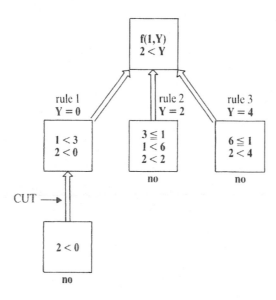

Figure 5.2   At the point marked 'CUT' we already know that the rules 2 and 3 are bound to fail.

not to backtrack. We can do this by using the cut mechanism. The 'cut' is written as ! and is inserted between goals as a kind of pseudo-goal. Our program, rewritten with cuts, is:

f(X, 0) :- X < 3, !.

f(X, 2) :- 3 =< X, X < 6, !.

f(X, 4) :- 6 =< X.

The ! symbol will now prevent backtracking at the points at which it appears in the program. If we now ask:

?- f(1, Y), 2 < Y.

Prolog will produce the same left-hand branch as in Figure 5.2. This branch will fail at the goal 2 < 0. Now Prolog will try to backtrack, but not beyond the point marked ! in the program. The alternative branches that correspond to 'rule 2' and 'rule 3' will not be generated.

The new program, equipped with cuts, is in general more efficient than the original version without cuts. When the execution fails, the new program will in general recognize this sooner than the original program.

To conclude, we have improved the efficiency by adding cuts. If the cuts are now removed in this example, the program will still produce the same result; it will perhaps only spend more time. In our case, by introducing the cut we only changed the procedural meaning of the program; that is, the results of the program were not affected. We will see later that using a cut may affect the results as well.

5.1.2   Experiment 2

Let us now perform a second experiment with the second version of our program. Suppose we ask:

```
?- f( 7, Y).

Y = 4
```

Let us analyze what has happened. All three rules were tried before the answer was obtained. This produced the following sequence of goals:

Try rule 1:   7 < 3 fails, backtrack and try rule 2 (cut was not reached)

Try rule 2:   3 ≦ 7 succeeds, but then 7 < 6 fails, backtrack and try rule 3 (cut was not reached)

Try rule 3:   6 ≦ 7 succeeds

This trace reveals another source of inefficiency. First it is established that X < 3 is not true (7 < 3 fails). The next goal is 3 =< X (3 =< 7 succeeds). But we know that once the first test has failed the second test is bound to succeed as it is the negation of the first. Therefore the second test is redundant and the corresponding goal can be omitted. The same is true about the goal 6 =< X in rule 3. This leads to the following, more economical formulation of the three rules:

if X < 3 then Y = 0,
otherwise if X < 6 then Y = 2,
otherwise Y = 4.

We can now omit the conditions in the program that are guaranteed to be true whenever they are executed. This leads to the third version of the program:

```
f( X, 0) :- X < 3, !.
f( X, 2) :- X < 6, !.
f( X, 4).
```

This program produces the same results as our original version, but is more efficient than both previous versions. But what happens if we *now* remove the cuts? The program becomes:

```
f( X, 0) :- X < 3.
f( X, 2) :- X < 6.
f( X, 4).
```

This may produce multiple solutions, some of which are not correct. For example:

```
?- f( 1, Y).

Y = 0;
```

Y = 2;

Y = 4;

no

It is important to notice that, in contrast to the second version of the program, this time the cuts do not only affect the procedural behaviour, but also change the results of the program.

A more precise meaning of the cut mechanism is as follows:

Let us call the 'parent goal' the goal that matched the head of the clause containing the cut. When the cut is encountered as a goal it succeeds immediately, but it commits the system to all choices made between the time the 'parent goal' was invoked and the time the cut was encountered. All the remaining alternatives between the parent goal and the cut are discarded.

To clarify this definition consider a clause of the form:

H :- B1, B2, ..., Bm, !, ..., Bn.

Let us assume that this clause was invoked by a goal G that matched H. Then G is the parent goal. At the moment that the cut is encountered, the system has already found some solution of the goals B1, ..., Bm. When the cut is executed, this (current) solution of B1, ..., Bm becomes frozen and all possible remaining alternatives are discarded. Also, the goal G now becomes committed to this clause: any attempt to match G with the head of some other clause is precluded.

Let us apply these rules to the following example:

C :- P, Q, R, !, S, T, U.

C :- V.

A :- B, C, D.

?- A.

Here A, B, C, D, P, etc. have the syntax of terms. The cut will affect the execution of the goal C as illustrated by Figure 5.3. Backtracking will be possible within the goal list P, Q, R; however, as soon as the cut is reached, all alternative solutions of the goal list P, Q, R are suppressed. The alternative clause about C,

C :- V.

will also be discarded. However, backtracking will still be possible within the goal list S, T, U. The 'parent goal' of the clause containing the cut is the goal C in the clause:

A :- B, C, D.

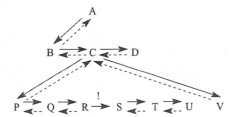

Figure 5.3 The effect of the cut on the execution. Starting with A, the solid arrows indicate the sequence of calls; the dashed arrows indicate backtracking. There is 'one way traffic' between R and S.

Therefore the cut will only affect the execution of the goal C. On the other hand, it will be 'invisible' from goal A. So automatic backtracking within the goal list B, C, D will remain active regardless of the cut within the clause used for satisfying C.

5.2 Examples using cut

5.2.1 Computing maximum

The procedure for finding the larger of two numbers can be programmed as a relation

max(X, Y, Max)

where Max = X if X is greater than or equal to Y, and Max is Y if X is less than Y. This corresponds to the following two clauses:

max(X, Y, X) :- X >= Y.

max(X, Y, Y) :- X < Y.

These two rules are mutually exclusive. If the first one succeeds then the second one will fail. If the first one fails then the second must succeed. Therefore a more economical formulation, with 'otherwise', is possible:

If X ≥ Y then Max = X,
otherwise Max = Y.

This is written in Prolog using a cut as:

max(X, Y, X) :- X >= Y, !.

max(X, Y, Y).

Computation and Reasoning

429

It should be noted that the use of this procedure requires care. It is safe if in the goal max(X,Y,Max) the argument Max is not instantiated. The following example of incorrect use illustrates the problem:

    ?- max(3, 1, 1).

    yes

The following reformulation of **max** overcomes this limitation:

    max(X, Y, Max) :-
        X >= Y, !, Max = X
        ;
        Max = Y.

5.2.2   Single-solution membership

We have been using the relation

    member(X, L)

for establishing whether X is in list L. The program was:

    member(X, [X | L]).

    member(X, [Y | L]) :- member(X, L).

This is non-deterministic: if X occurs several times then any occurrence can be found. Let us now change **member** into a deterministic procedure which will find only the first occurrence. The change is simple: we only have to prevent back-tracking as soon as X is found, which happens when the first clause succeeds. The modified program is:

    member(X, [X | L]) :- !.

    member(X, [Y | L]) :- member(X, L).

This program will generate just one solution. For example:

    ?- member(X, [a,b,c]).

    X = a;

    no

5.2.3   Adding an element to a list without duplication

Often we want to add an item X to a list L so that X is added only if X is not yet in L. If X is already in L then L remains the same because we do not want to have redundant duplicates in L. The **add** relation has three arguments:

    add(X, L, L1)

Computation and Reasoning

430

where X is the item to be added, L is the list to which X is to be added and L1 is the resulting new list. Our rule for adding can be formulated as:

If X is a member of list L then L1 = L,
otherwise L1 is equal to L with X inserted.

It is easiest to insert X in front of L so that X becomes the head of L1. This is then programmed as follows:

```
add( X, L, L)  :-  member( X, L), !.
add( X, L, [X | L] ).
```

The behaviour of this procedure is illustrated by the following example:

```
?- add( a, [b,c], L).
L = [a,b,c]
?- add( X, [b,c], L).
L = [b,c]
X = b
?- add( a, [b,c,X], L).
L = [b,c,a]
X = a
```

Similar to the foregoing example with **max**, add(X, L1, L2) is intended to be called with L2 uninstantiated. Otherwise the result may be unexpected: for example add(a, [a], [a,a]) succeeds.

This example is instructive because we cannot easily program the 'non-duplicate add' without the use of cut or another construct derived from the cut. If we omit the cut in the foregoing program then the **add** relation will also add duplicate items. For example:

```
?- add( a, [a,b,c], L).
L = [a,b,c];
L = [a,a,b,c]
```

So the cut is necessary here to specify the intended relation, and not only to improve efficiency. The next example also illustrates this point.

5.2.4 Classification into categories

Assume we have a database of results of tennis games played by members of a club. The pairings were not arranged in any systematic way, so each player just played some other players. The results are in the program represented as facts like:

```
beat( tom, jim).
beat( ann, tom).
beat( pat, jim).
```

We want to define a relation

```
class( Player, Category)
```

that ranks the players into categories. We have just three categories:

winner: every player who won all his or her games is a winner
fighter: any player that won some games and lost some
sportsman: any player who lost all his or her games

For example, if all the results available are just those above then Ann and Pat are winners, Tom is a fighter and Jim is a sportsman.

It is easy to specify the rule for a fighter:

X is a fighter if
  there is some Y such that X beat Y and
  there is some Z such that Z beat X.

Now a rule for a winner:

X is a winner if
  X beat some Y and
  X was not beaten by anybody.

This formulation contains 'not' which cannot be directly expressed with our present Prolog facilities. So the formulation of **winner** appears trickier. The same problem occurs with **sportsman**. The problem can be circumvented by combining the definition of **winner** with that of **fighter**, and using the 'otherwise' connective. Such a formulation is:

If X beat somebody and X was beaten by somebody
  then X is a fighter,
  otherwise if X beat somebody
    then X is a winner,
    otherwise if X got beaten by somebody
      then X is a sportsman.

This formulation can be readily translated into Prolog. The mutual exclusion of the three alternative categories is indicated by the cuts:

```
class( X, fighter) :-
  beat( X, _),
  beat( _, X), !.

class( X, winner) :-
  beat( X, _), !.
```

Computation and Reasoning

432

```
class( X, sportsman) :-
    beat( _, X).
```

Notice that the cut in the clause for **winner** is not necessary. Care is needed when using such procedures containing cuts. Here is what can happen:

```
?- class( tom, C).

C = fighter;                        % As intended

no

?- class( tom, sportsman).

yes                                 % Not as intended
```

The call of **class** is safe if the second argument is not instantiated. Otherwise we may get an unintended result.

Exercises

5.1   Let a program be:

```
p( 1).
p( 2) :- !.
p( 3).
```

Write all Prolog's answers to the following questions:

(a) ?- p(X).

(b) ?- p(X), p(Y).

(c) ?- p(X), !, p(Y).

5.2   The following relation classifies numbers into three classes: positive, zero and negative:

```
class( Number, positive) :- Number > 0.
class( 0, zero).
class( Number, negative) :- Number < 0.
```

Define this procedure in a more efficient way using cuts.

5.3   Define the procedure

```
split( Numbers, Positives, Negatives)
```

which splits a list of numbers into two lists: positive ones (including zero) and negative ones. For example:

```
split( [3,−1,0,5,−2], [3,0,5], [−1,−2] )
```

Propose two versions: one with a cut and one without.

Computation and Reasoning

5.3 Negation as failure

'Mary likes all animals but snakes'. How can we say this in Prolog? It is easy to express one part of this statement: Mary likes any X if X is an animal. This is in Prolog:

```
likes( mary, X)  :-  animal( X).
```

But we have to exclude snakes. This can be done by using a different formulation:

> If X is a snake then 'Mary likes X' is not true,
> otherwise if X is an animal then Mary likes X.

That something is not true can be said in Prolog by using a special goal, **fail**, which always fails, thus forcing the parent goal to fail. The above formulation is translated into Prolog, using **fail**, as follows:

```
likes( mary, X)  :-
   snake( X), !, fail.

likes( mary, X)  :-
   animal( X).
```

The first rule here will take care of snakes: if X is a snake then the cut will prevent backtracking (thus excluding the second rule) and **fail** will cause the failure. These two clauses can be written more compactly as one clause:

```
likes( mary, X)  :-
   snake( X), !, fail
   ;
   animal( X).
```

We can use the same idea to define the relation

```
different( X, Y)
```

which is true if X and Y are different. We have to be more precise, however, because 'different' can be understood in several ways:

- X and Y are not literally the same;
- X and Y do not match;
- the values of arithmetic expressions X and Y are not equal.

Let us choose here that X and Y are different if they do not match. The key to saying this in Prolog is:

> If X and Y match then **different**(X, Y) fails,
> otherwise **different**(X, Y) succeeds.

We again use the cut and fail combination:

different(X, X) :- !, fail.

different(X, Y).

This can also be written as one clause:

different(X, Y) :-
X = Y, !, fail
;
true.

true is a goal that always succeeds.

These examples indicate that it would be useful to have a unary predicate 'not' such that

not(Goal)

is true if Goal is not true. We will now define the **not** relation as follows:

If Goal succeeds then **not(Goal)** fails,
otherwise **not(Goal)** succeeds.

This definition can be written in Prolog as:

not(P) :-
P, !, fail
;
true.

Henceforth, we will assume that **not** is a built-in Prolog procedure that behaves as defined here. We will also assume that **not** is defined as a prefix operator, so that we can also write the goal

not(snake(X))

as:

not snake(X)

Some Prolog implementations, in fact, support this notation. If not, then we can always define **not** ourselves. Alternatively, **not** Goal is written as \+ Goal. This more mysterious notation is also recommended in the Prolog standard for the following reason. **not** defined as failure, as here, does not exactly correspond to negation in mathematical logic. This difference can cause unexpected behaviour if **not** is used without care. This will be discussed later in the chapter.

Nevertheless, **not** is a useful facility and can often be used advantageously in place of cut. Our two examples can be rewritten with **not** as:

likes(mary, X) :-
animal(X),
not snake(X).

```
solution( [] ).

solution( [X/Y | Others] )  :-
  solution( Others),
  member( Y, [1,2,3,4,5,6,7,8] ),              % Usual member predicate
  not attacks( X/Y, Others).

attacks( X/Y, Others)  :-
  member( X1/Y1, Others),
  ( Y1 = Y;
    Y1 is Y + X1 − X;
    Y1 is Y − X1 + X ).
```

Figure 5.4 Another eight queens program.

```
different( X, Y )  :-
  not( X = Y).
```

This certainly looks better than our original formulations. It is more natural and is easier to read.

Our tennis classification program of the previous section can also be rewritten, using not, in a way that is closer to the initial definition of the three categories:

```
class( X, fighter )  :-
  beat( X, _ ),
  beat( _, X).

class( X, winner )  :-
  beat( X, _ ),
  not beat( _, X).

class( X, sportsman )  :-
  beat( _, X),
  not beat( X, _ ).
```

As another example of the use of **not** let us reconsider program 1 for the eight queens problem of the previous chapter (Figure 4.7). We specified the **no_attack** relation between a queen and other queens. This relation can be formulated also as the negation of the **attack** relation. Figure 5.4 shows a program modified accordingly.

Exercises

5.4   Given two lists, **Candidates** and **RuledOut**, write a sequence of goals (using **member** and **not**) that will through backtracking find all the items in **Candidates** that are not in RuledOut.

5.5   Define the set subtraction relation

    set_difference(Set1, Set2, SetDifference)

where all the three sets are represented as lists. For example:

    set_difference([a,b,c,d], [b,d,e,f], [a,c])

5.6   Define the predicate

    unifiable(List1, Term, List2)

where **List2** is the list of all the members of **List1** that match **Term**, but are not instantiated by this matching. For example:

    ?- unifiable([X, b, t(Y)], t(a), List).

    List = [X, t(Y)]

Note that X and Y have to remain uninstantiated although the matching with **t(a)** does cause their instantiation. Hint: Use **not(Term1 = Term2)**. If **Term1 = Term2** succeeds then **not(Term1 = Term2)** fails and the resulting instantiation is undone!

5.4   Problems with cut and negation

Using the cut facility we get something, but not for nothing. The advantages and disadvantages of using cut were illustrated by examples in the previous sections. Let us summarize, first the advantages:

(1)   With cut we can often improve the efficiency of the program. The idea is to explicitly tell Prolog: do not try other alternatives because they are bound to fail.

(2)   Using cut we can specify mutually exclusive rules; so we can express rules of the form:

    if condition P *then* conclusion Q,
    otherwise conclusion R

In this way, cut enhances the expressive power of the language.

The reservations against the use of cut stem from the fact that we can lose the valuable correspondence between the declarative and procedural meaning of programs. If there is no cut in the program we can change the order of clauses and goals, and this will only affect the efficiency or termination of the program, not the declarative meaning. On the other hand, in programs with cuts, a change in the order of clauses may affect the declarative meaning. This means that we can get different results. The following example illustrates:

```
p :- a, b.
p :- c.
```

The declarative meaning of this program is: p is true if and only if a and b are both true or c is true. This can be written as a logic formula:

$$p \iff (a \,\&\, b) \lor c$$

We can change the order of the two clauses and the declarative meaning remains the same. Let us now insert a cut:

```
p :- a, !, b.
p :- c.
```

The declarative meaning is now:

$$p \iff (a \,\&\, b) \lor (\sim a \,\&\, c)$$

If we swap the clauses,

```
p :- c.
p :- a, !, b.
```

then the meaning becomes:

$$p \iff c \lor (a \,\&\, b)$$

The important point is that when we use the cut facility we have to pay more attention to the procedural aspects. Unfortunately, this additional difficulty increases the probability of a programming error.

In our examples in the previous sections we have seen that sometimes the removal of a cut from the program can change the declarative meaning of the program. But there were also cases in which the cut had no effect on the declarative meaning. The use of cuts of the latter type is less delicate, and therefore cuts of this kind are sometimes called 'green cuts'. From the point of view of readability of programs, green cuts are 'innocent' and their use is quite acceptable. When reading a program, green cuts can simply be ignored.

On the contrary, cuts that do affect the declarative meaning are called 'red cuts'. Red cuts are the ones that make programs hard to understand, and they should be used with special care.

Cut is often used in combination with a special goal, fail. In particular, we defined the negation of a goal (not) as the failure of the goal. The negation, so defined, is just a special, more restricted way of using cut. For reasons of clarity we will prefer to use not instead of the *cut–fail* combination (whenever possible), because the negation is intuitively clearer than the *cut–fail* combination.

It should be noted that not may also cause problems, and so should also be used with care. The problem is that not, as defined here, does not correspond exactly to negation in mathematics. If we ask Prolog:

?- not human(mary).

Prolog will probably answer 'yes'. But this should not be understood as Prolog saying 'Mary is not human'. What Prolog really means to say is: 'There is not enough information in the program to prove that Mary is human'. This arises because when processing a **not** goal, Prolog does not try to prove this goal directly. Instead, it tries to prove the opposite, and if the opposite cannot be proved then Prolog assumes that the **not** goal succeeds.

Such reasoning is based on the so-called *closed world assumption*. According to this assumption *the world is closed* in the sense that everything that exists is stated in the program or can be derived from the program. Accordingly then, if something is not in the program (or cannot be derived from it) then it is not true and consequently its negation is true. This deserves special care because we do not normally assume that 'the world is closed'. When we do not explicitly enter the clause

human(mary).

into our program, we do not mean to imply that Mary is not human.

To further study the special care that **not** requires, consider the following example about restaurants:

good_standard(jeanluis).

expensive(jeanluis).

good_standard(francesco).

reasonable(Restaurant) :-
    not expensive(Restaurant).

If we ask:

?- good_standard(X), reasonable(X).

Prolog will answer:

X = francesco

If we ask apparently the same question

?- reasonable(X), good_standard(X).

then Prolog will answer:

no

The reader is invited to trace the program to understand why we get different answers. The key difference between both questions is that the variable X is, in the first case, already instantiated when reasonable(X) is executed, whereas X is not yet instantiated in the second case. The general hint is: **not Goal** works safely if the variables in **Goal** are instantiated at the time **not Goal** is called. Otherwise we may get unexpected results due to reasons explained in the sequel.

Computation and Reasoning

439

The problem with uninstantiated negated goals arises from unfortunate change of the quantification of variables in negation as failure. In the usual interpretation in Prolog, the question:

?- expensive(X).

means: Does there *exist* X such that expensive(X) is true? If yes, what is X? So X is *existentially* quantified. Accordingly Prolog answers X = jeanluis. But the question:

?- not expensive(X).

is not interpreted as: Does there exist X such that not expensive(X)? The expected answer would be X = francesco. But Prolog answers 'no' because negation as failure changes the quantification to universal. The question not expensive(X) is interpreted as:

not(exists X such that expensive(X))

This is equivalent to:

For *all* X: not expensive(X)

We have discussed problems with cut, which also indirectly occur in not, in detail. The intention has been to warn users about the necessary care, not to definitely discourage the use of cut. Cut is useful and often necessary. And after all, the kind of complications that are incurred by cut in Prolog commonly occur when programming in other languages as well.

Summary

- The cut facility prevents backtracking. It is used both to improve the efficiency of programs and to enhance the expressive power of the language.

- Efficiency is improved by explicitly telling Prolog (with cut) not to explore alternatives that we know are bound to fail.

- Cut makes it possible to formulate mutually exclusive conclusions through rules of the form:

    if Condition *then* Conclusion1 *otherwise* Conclusion2

- Cut makes it possible to introduce *negation as failure*: not Goal is defined through the failure of Goal.

- Two special goals are sometimes useful: true always succeeds, fail always fails.

- There are also some reservations against cut: inserting a cut may destroy the correspondence between the declarative and procedural meaning of a program. Therefore, it is part of good programming style to use cut with care and not to use it without reason.

- not defined through failure does not exactly correspond to negation in mathematical logic. Therefore, the use of **not** also requires special care.

References

The distinction between 'green cuts' and 'red cuts' was proposed by van Emden (1982). Le (1993) proposes a different negation for Prolog which is mathematically advantageous, but computationally more expensive.

Le, T.V. (1993) *Techniques of Prolog Programming*. John Wiley & Sons.
van Emden, M. (1982) Red and green cuts. *Logic Programming Newsletter*: 2.

Topic 4

Theory of Computation

The following chapters are from
Languages and Machines: An Introduction to the
Theory of Computer Science
Third Edition
by Thomas A. Sudkamp

Computation and Reasoning

444

CHAPTER 1

Mathematical Preliminaries

Set theory and discrete mathematics provide the mathematical foundation for formal language theory, computability theory, and the analysis of computational complexity. We begin our study of these topics with a review of the notation and basic operations of set theory. Cardinality measures the size of a set and provides a precise definition of an infinite set. One of the interesting results of the investigations into the properties of sets by German mathematician Georg Cantor is that there are different sizes of infinite sets. While Cantor's work showed that there is a complete hierarchy of sizes of infinite sets, it is sufficient for our purposes to divide infinite sets into two classes: countable and uncountable. A set is countably infinite if it has the same number of elements as the set of natural numbers. Sets with more elements than the natural numbers are uncountable.

In this chapter we will use a construction known as the *diagonalization argument* to show that the set of functions defined on the natural numbers is uncountably infinite. After we have agreed upon what is meant by the terms *effective procedure* and *computable function* (reaching this consensus is a major goal of Part III of this book), we will be able to determine the size of the set of functions that can be algorithmically computed. A comparison of the sizes of these two sets will establish the existence of functions whose values cannot be computed by any algorithmic process.

While a set may consist of an arbitrary collection of objects, we are interested in sets whose elements can be mechanically produced. Recursive definitions are introduced to generate the elements of a set. The relationship between recursively generated sets and mathematical induction is developed, and induction is shown to provide a general proof technique for establishing properties of elements in recursively generated infinite sets.

7

This chapter ends with a review of directed graphs and trees, structures that will be used throughout the book to graphically illustrate the concepts of formal language theory and the theory of computation.

1.1 Set Theory

We assume that the reader is familiar with the notions of elementary set theory. In this section, the concepts and notation of that theory are briefly reviewed. The symbol $\in$ signifies membership; $x \in X$ indicates that x is a member or element of the set X. A slash through a symbol represents *not*, so $x \notin X$ signifies that x is not a member of X. Two sets are equal if they contain the same members. Throughout this book, sets are denoted by capital letters. In particular, X, Y, and Z are used to represent arbitrary sets. Italics are used to denote the elements of a set. For example, symbols and strings of the form a, b, A, B, $aaaa$, and abc represent elements of sets.

Brackets { } are used to indicate a set definition. Sets with a small number of members can be defined explicitly; that is, their members can be listed. The sets

$$X = \{1, 2, 3\}$$
$$Y = \{a, b, c, d, e\}$$

are defined in an explicit manner. Sets having a large finite or infinite number of members must be defined implicitly. A set is defined implicitly by specifying conditions that describe the elements of the set. The set consisting of all perfect squares is defined by

$$\{n \mid n = m^2 \text{ for some natural number } m\}.$$

The vertical bar | in an implicit definition is read "such that." The entire definition is read "the set of n such that n equals m squared for some natural number m."

The previous example mentioned the set of **natural numbers**. This important set, denoted **N**, consists of the numbers 0, 1, 2, 3, ... The **empty set**, denoted $\emptyset$, is the set that has no members and can be defined explicitly by $\emptyset = \{ \}$.

A set is determined completely by its membership; the order in which the elements are presented in the definition is immaterial. The explicit definitions

$$X = \{1, 2, 3\}, \ Y = \{2, 1, 3\}, \ Z = \{1, 3, 2, 2, 2\}$$

describe the same set. The definition of Z contains multiple instances of the number 2. Repetition in the definition of a set does not affect the membership. Set equality requires that the sets have exactly the same members, and this is the case; each of the sets X, Y, and Z has the natural numbers 1, 2, and 3 as its members.

A set Y is a **subset** of X, written $Y \subseteq X$, if every member of Y is also a member of X. The empty set is trivially a subset of every set. Every set X is a subset of itself. If Y is a subset of X and Y ≠ X, then Y is called a **proper subset** of X. The set of all subsets of X is called the **power set** of X and is denoted $\mathcal{P}(X)$.

Example 1.1.1

Let $X = \{1, 2, 3\}$. The subsets of X are

$$\emptyset \qquad \{1\} \qquad \{2\} \qquad \{3\}$$
$$\{1, 2\} \quad \{2, 3\} \quad \{3, 1\} \quad \{1, 2, 3\}. \qquad\qquad \square$$

Set operations are used to construct new sets from existing ones. The **union** of two sets is defined by

$$X \cup Y = \{z \mid z \in X \text{ or } z \in Y\}.$$

The *or* is inclusive. This means that z is a member of $X \cup Y$ if it is a member of X or Y or both. The **intersection** of two sets is the set of elements common to both. This is defined by

$$X \cap Y = \{z \mid z \in X \text{ and } z \in Y\}.$$

Two sets whose intersection is empty are said to be **disjoint**. The union and intersection of n sets, $X_1, X_2, \ldots, X_n$, are defined by

$$\bigcup_{i=1}^{n} X_i = X_1 \cup X_2 \cup \cdots \cup X_n = \{x \mid x \in X_i, \text{ for some } i = 1, 2, \ldots, n\}$$

$$\bigcap_{i=1}^{n} X_i = X_1 \cap X_2 \cap \cdots \cap X_n = \{x \mid x \in X_i, \text{ for all } i = 1, 2, \ldots, n\},$$

respectively.

Subsets $X_1, X_2, \ldots, X_n$ of a set X are said to **partition** X if

i) $X = \bigcup_{i=1}^{n} X_i$

ii) $X_i \cap X_j = \emptyset$, for $1 \le i, j \le n$, and $i \ne j$.

For example, the set of even natural numbers (zero is considered even) and the set of odd natural numbers partition **N**.

The **difference** of sets X and Y, $X - Y$, consists of the elements of X that are not in Y:

$$X - Y = \{z \mid z \in X \text{ and } z \notin Y\}.$$

Let X be a subset of a universal set U. The **complement** of X with respect to U is the set of elements in U but not in X. In other words, the complement of X with respect to U is the set $U - X$. When the universe U is known, the complement of X with respect to U is denoted $\overline{X}$. The following identities, known as *DeMorgan's Laws,* exhibit the relationships

Computation and Reasoning

447

between union, intersection, and complement when X and Y are subsets of a set U and complementation is taken with respect to U:

i) $\overline{(X \cup Y)} = \overline{X} \cap \overline{Y}$

ii) $\overline{(X \cap Y)} = \overline{X} \cup \overline{Y}$.

Example 1.1.2

Let $X = \{0, 1, 2, 3\}$, $Y = \{2, 3, 4, 5\}$, and let $\overline{X}$ and $\overline{Y}$ denote the complement of X and Y with respect to N. Then

$$X \cup Y = \{0, 1, 2, 3, 4, 5\} \qquad \overline{X} = \{n \mid n > 3\}$$

$$X \cap Y = \{2, 3\} \qquad \overline{Y} = \{0, 1\} \cup \{n \mid n > 5\}$$

$$X - Y = \{0, 1\} \qquad \overline{X} \cap \overline{Y} = \{n \mid n > 5\}$$

$$Y - X = \{4, 5\} \qquad \overline{(X \cup Y)} = \{n \mid n > 5\}$$

The final two sets in the right-hand column exhibit the equality required by DeMorgan's Law. □

The definition of subset provides the method for proving that a set X is a subset of Y; we must show that every element of X is also an element of Y. When X is finite, we can explicitly check each element of X for membership in Y. When X contains infinitely many elements, a different approach is needed. The strategy is to show that an arbitrary element of X is in Y.

Example 1.1.3

We will show that $X = \{8n - 1 \mid n > 0\}$ is a subset of $Y = \{2m + 1 \mid m \text{ is odd}\}$. To gain a better understanding of the sets X and Y, it is useful to generate some of the elements of X and Y:

$$X: \ 8 \cdot 1 - 1 = 7, \ 8 \cdot 2 - 1 = 15, \ 8 \cdot 3 - 1 = 23, \ 8 \cdot 4 - 1 = 31, \ldots$$

$$Y: \ 2 \cdot 1 + 1 = 3, \ 2 \cdot 3 + 1 = 7, \ 2 \cdot 5 + 1 = 11, \ 2 \cdot 7 + 1 = 13, \ldots$$

To establish the inclusion, we must show that every element of X is also an element of Y. An arbitrary element x of X has the form $8n - 1$, for some $n > 0$. Let $m = 4n - 1$. Then m is an odd natural number and

$$2m + 1 = 2(4n - 1) + 1$$
$$= 8n - 2 + 1$$
$$= 8n - 1$$
$$= x.$$

Thus x is also in Y and $X \subseteq Y$. □

Computation and Reasoning

448

Set equality can be defined using set inclusion; sets X and Y are equal if $X \subseteq Y$ and $Y \subseteq X$. This simply states that every element of X is also an element of Y and vice versa. When establishing the equality of two sets, the two inclusions are usually proved separately and combined to yield the equality.

Example 1.1.4

We prove that the sets

$$X = \{n \mid n = m^2 \text{ for some natural number } m > 0\}$$

$$Y = \{n^2 + 2n + 1 \mid n \geq 0\}$$

are equal. First, we show that every element of X is also an element of Y. Let $x \in X$; then $x = m^2$ for some natural number $m > 0$. Let m_0 be that number. Then x can be written

$$x = (m_0)^2$$
$$= (m_0 - 1 + 1)^2$$
$$= (m_0 - 1)^2 + 2(m_0 - 1) + 1.$$

Letting $n = m_0 - 1$, we see that $x = n^2 + 2n + 1$ with $n \geq 0$. Consequently, x is a member of the set Y.

We now establish the opposite inclusion. Let $y = (n_0)^2 + 2n_0 + 1$ be an element of Y. Factoring yields $y = (n_0 + 1)^2$. Thus y is the square of a natural number greater than zero and therefore an element of X.

Since $X \subseteq Y$ and $Y \subseteq X$, we conclude that $X = Y$.   □

1.2   Cartesian Product, Relations, and Functions

The **Cartesian product** is a set operation that builds a set consisting of ordered pairs of elements from two existing sets. The Cartesian product of sets X and Y, denoted $X \times Y$, is defined by

$$X \times Y = \{[x, y] \mid x \in X \text{ and } y \in Y\}.$$

A **binary relation** on X and Y is a subset of $X \times Y$. The ordering of the natural numbers can be used to generate a relation LT (less than) on the set $N \times N$. This relation is the subset of $N \times N$ defined by

$$LT = \{[i, j] \mid i < j \text{ and } i, j \in N\}.$$

The notation $[i, j] \in LT$ indicates that i is less than j, for example, $[0, 1]$, $[0, 2] \in LT$ and $[1, 1] \notin LT$.

Computation and Reasoning

449

The Cartesian product can be generalized to construct new sets from any finite number of sets. If x_1, x_2, . . . , x_n are n elements, then $[x_1, x_2, . . . , x_n]$ is called an **ordered n-tuple**. An ordered pair is simply another name for an ordered 2-tuple. Ordered 3-tuples, 4-tuples, and 5-tuples are commonly referred to as triples, quadruples, and quintuples, respectively. The Cartesian product of n sets $X_1, X_2, . . . , X_n$ is defined by

$$X_1 \times X_2 \times \cdots \times X_n = \{[x_1, x_2, . . . , x_n] \mid x_i \in X_i, \text{ for } i = 1, 2, . . . , n\}.$$

An ***n*-ary relation** on $X_1, X_2, . . . , X_n$ is a subset of $X_1 \times X_2 \times \cdots \times X_n$. 1-ary, 2-ary, and 3-ary relations are called *unary*, *binary*, and *ternary*, respectively.

Example 1.2.1

Let $X = \{1, 2, 3\}$ and $Y = \{a, b\}$. Then

a) $X \times Y = \{[1, a], [1, b], [2, a], [2, b], [3, a], [3, b]\}$

b) $Y \times X = \{[a, 1], [a, 2], [a, 3], [b, 1], [b, 2], [b, 3]\}$

c) $Y \times Y = \{[a, a], [a, b], [b, a], [b, b]\}$

d) $X \times Y \times Y = \{[1, a, a], [1, b, a], [2, a, a], [2, b, a], [3, a, a], [3, b, a],$
$[1, a, b], [1, b, b], [2, a, b], [2, b, b], [3, a, b], [3, b, b]\}$ □

Informally, a **function** from a set X to a set Y is a mapping of elements of X to elements of Y in which each element of X is mapped to at most one element of Y. A function f from X to Y is denoted $f : X \rightarrow Y$. The element of Y assigned by the function f to an element $x \in X$ is denoted $f(x)$. The set X is called the **domain** of the function and the elements of X are the arguments or operands of the function f. The **range** of f is the subset of Y consisting of the members of Y that are assigned to elements of X. Thus the range of a function $f : X \rightarrow Y$ is the set $\{y \in Y \mid y = f(x) \text{ for some } x \in X\}$.

The relationship that assigns to each person his or her age is a function from the set of people to the natural numbers. Note that an element in the range may be assigned to more than one element of the domain—there are many people who have the same age. Moreover, not all natural numbers are in the range of the function; it is unlikely that the number 1000 is assigned to anyone.

The domain of a function is a set, but this set is often the Cartesian product of two or more sets. A function

$$f : X_1 \times X_2 \times \cdots \times X_n \rightarrow Y$$

is said to be an ***n*-variable function** or operation. The value of the function with variables x_1, x_2, . . . , x_n is denoted $f(x_1, x_2, . . . , x_n)$. Functions with one, two, or three variables are often referred to as *unary*, *binary*, and *ternary* operations. The function $sq : N \rightarrow N$ that assigns n^2 to each natural number is a unary operation. When the domain of a function consists of the Cartesian product of a set X with itself, the function is simply said to be a binary operation on X. Addition and multiplication are examples of binary operations on N.

A function f relates members of the domain to members of the range of f. A natural definition of function is in terms of this relation. A **total function** f from X to Y is a binary relation on X × Y that satisfies the following two properties:

i) For each $x \in$ X, there is a $y \in$ Y such that $[x, y] \in f$.

ii) If $[x, y_1] \in f$ and $[x, y_2] \in f$, then $y_1 = y_2$.

Condition (i) guarantees that each element of X is assigned a member of Y, hence the term *total*. The second condition ensures that this assignment is unique. The previously defined relation LT is not a total function since it does not satisfy the second condition. A relation on N × N representing *greater than* fails to satisfy either of the conditions. Why?

Example 1.2.2

Let X = {1, 2, 3} and Y = {a, b}. The eight total functions from X to Y are listed below.

x	$f(x)$		x	$f(x)$		x	$f(x)$		x	$f(x)$
1	a		1	a		1	a		1	b
2	a		2	a		2	b		2	a
3	a		3	b		3	a		3	a

x	$f(x)$		x	$f(x)$		x	$f(x)$		x	$f(x)$
1	a		1	b		1	b		1	b
2	b		2	a		2	b		2	b
3	b		3	b		3	a		3	b

□

A **partial function** f from X to Y is a relation on X × Y in which $y_1 = y_2$ whenever $[x, y_1] \in f$ and $[x, y_2] \in f$. A partial function f is defined for an argument x if there is a $y \in$ Y such that $[x, y] \in f$. Otherwise, f is undefined for x. A total function is simply a partial function defined for all elements of the domain.

Although functions have been formally defined in terms of relations, we will use the standard notation $f(x) = y$ to indicate that y is the value assigned to x by the function f, that is, that $[x, y] \in f$. The notation $f(x) \uparrow$ indicates that the partial function f is undefined for the argument x. The notation $f(x) \downarrow$ is used to show that $f(x)$ is defined without explicitly giving its value.

Integer division defines a binary partial function *div* from N × N to N. The quotient obtained from the division of i by j, when defined, is assigned to $div(i, j)$. For example, $div(3, 2) = 1$, $div(4, 2) = 2$, and $div(1, 2) = 0$. Using the previous notation, $div(i, 0) \uparrow$ and $div(i, j) \downarrow$ for all values of j other than zero.

A total function $f : X \rightarrow Y$ is said to be **one-to-one** if each element of X maps to a distinct element in the range. Formally, f is one-to-one if $x_1 \neq x_2$ implies $f(x_1) \neq f(x_2)$. A function $f : X \rightarrow Y$ is said to be **onto** if the range of f is the entire set Y. A total function that is both one-to-one and onto defines a correspondence between the elements of domain and the range.

Example 1.2.3

The functions f, g, and s are defined from N to N − {0}, the set of positive natural numbers.

 i) $f(n) = 2n + 1$

 ii) $g(n) = \begin{cases} 1 & \text{if } n = 0 \\ n & \text{otherwise} \end{cases}$

iii) $s(n) = n + 1$

The function f is one-to-one but not onto; the range of f consists of the odd numbers. The mapping from N to N − {0} defined by g is clearly onto but not one-to-one since $g(0) = g(1) = 1$. The function s is both one-to-one and onto, defining a correspondence that maps each natural number to its successor.   □

Example 1.2.4

In the preceding example we noted that the function $f(n) = 2n + 1$ is one-to-one, but not onto the set N − {0}. It is, however, a mapping from N to the set of odd natural numbers that is both one-to-one and onto. We will use f to demonstrate how to prove that a function has these properties.

One-to-one: To prove that a function is one-to-one, we show that n and m must be the same whenever $f(n) = f(m)$. The assumption $f(n) = f(m)$ yields,

$$2n + 1 = 2m + 1 \qquad \text{or}$$
$$2n = 2m, \qquad \text{and finally,}$$
$$n = m.$$

It follows that $n \neq m$ implies $f(n) \neq f(m)$, and f is one-to-one.

Onto: To establish that f maps N onto the set of odd natural numbers, we must show that every odd natural number is in the range of f. If m is an odd natural number, it can be written $m = 2n + 1$ for some $n \in$ N. Then $f(n) = 2n + 1 = m$ and m is in the range of f.   □

1.3 Equivalence Relations

A binary relation over a set X has been formally defined as a subset of the Cartesian product X × X. Informally, we use a relation to indicate whether a property holds between two elements of a set. An ordered pair is in the relation if its elements satisfy the prescribed condition. For example, the property *is less than* defines a binary relation on the set of natural numbers. The relation defined by this property is the set LT = {[i, j] | i < j}.

Infix notation is often used to express membership in many common binary relations. In this standard usage, $i < j$ indicates that i is less than j and consequently the pair $[i, j]$ is in the relation LT defined above.

We now consider a type of relation, known as an equivalence relation, that can be used to partition the underlying set. Equivalence relations are generally denoted using the infix notation $a \equiv b$ to indicate that a is equivalent to b.

Definition 1.3.1

A binary relation $\equiv$ over a set X is an **equivalence relation** if it satisfies

   i) *Reflexivity:* $a \equiv a$, for all $a \in X$
  ii) *Symmetry:* $a \equiv b$ implies $b \equiv a$, for all $a, b \in X$
 iii) *Transitivity:* $a \equiv b$ and $b \equiv c$ implies $a \equiv c$, for all $a, b, c \in X$.

Definition 1.3.2

Let $\equiv$ be an equivalence relation over X. The **equivalence class** of an element $a \in X$ defined by the relation $\equiv$ is the set $[a]_{\equiv} = \{b \in X \mid a \equiv b\}$.

Example 1.3.1

Let $\equiv_P$ be the parity relation over N defined by $n \equiv_P m$ if, and only if, n and m have the same parity (even or odd). To prove that $\equiv_P$ is an equivalence relation, we must show that it is symmetric, reflexive, and transitive.

   i) *Reflexivity:* For every natural number n, n has the same parity as itself and $n \equiv_P n$.
  ii) *Symmetry:* If $n \equiv_P m$, then n and m have the same parity and $m \equiv_P n$.
 iii) *Transitivity:* If $n \equiv_P m$ and $m \equiv_P k$, then n and m have the same parity and m and k have the same parity. It follows that n and k have the same parity and $n \equiv_P k$.

The two equivalence classes of the parity relation $\equiv_P$ are $[0]_{\equiv_P} = \{0, 2, 4, \ldots\}$ and $[1]_{\equiv_P} = \{1, 3, 5, \ldots\}$.   □

An equivalence class is usually written $[a]_{\equiv}$, where a is an element in the class. In the preceding example, $[0]_{\equiv_P}$ was used to represent the set of even natural numbers. Lemma 1.3.3 shows that if $a \equiv b$, then $[a]_{\equiv} = [b]_{\equiv}$. Thus the element chosen to represent the class is irrelevant.

Lemma 1.3.3

Let $\equiv$ be an equivalence relation over X and let a and b be elements of X. Then either $[a]_{\equiv} = [b]_{\equiv}$ or $[a]_{\equiv} \cap [b]_{\equiv} = \emptyset$.

Proof.   Assume that the intersection of $[a]_{\equiv}$ and $[b]_{\equiv}$ is not empty. Then there is some element c that is in both of the equivalence classes. Using symmetry and transitivity, we show that $[b]_{\equiv} \subseteq [a]_{\equiv}$. Since c is in both $[a]_{\equiv}$ and $[b]_{\equiv}$, we know $a \equiv c$ and $b \equiv c$. By symmetry, $c \equiv b$. Using transitivity, we conclude that $a \equiv b$.

Computation and Reasoning

453

Now let d be any element in $[b]_\equiv$. Then $b \equiv d$. The combination of $a \equiv b$, $b \equiv d$, and transitivity yields $a \equiv d$. That is, $d \in [a]_\equiv$. We have shown that every element in $[b]_\equiv$ is also in $[a]_\equiv$, so $[b]_\equiv \subseteq [a]_\equiv$. By a similar argument, we can establish that $[a]_\equiv \subseteq [b]_\equiv$. The two inclusions combine to produce the desired set equality.   ∎

Theorem 1.3.4

Let $\equiv$ be an equivalence relation over X. The equivalence classes of $\equiv$ partition X.

Proof.   By Lemma 1.3.3, we know that the equivalence classes form a disjoint family of subsets of X. Let a be any element of X. By reflexivity, $a \in [a]_\equiv$. Thus each element of X is in one of the equivalence classes. It follows that the union of the equivalence classes is the entire set X.   ∎

1.4   Countable and Uncountable Sets

Cardinality is a measure that compares the size of sets. Intuitively, the cardinality of a set is the number of elements in the set. This informal definition is sufficient when dealing with finite sets; the cardinality can be obtained by counting the elements of the set. There are obvious difficulties in extending this approach to infinite sets.

Two finite sets can be shown to have the same number of elements by constructing a one-to-one correspondence between the elements of the sets. For example, the mapping

$$a \longrightarrow 1$$
$$b \longrightarrow 2$$
$$c \longrightarrow 3$$

demonstrates that the sets $\{a, b, c\}$ and $\{1, 2, 3\}$ have the same size. This approach, comparing the size of sets using mappings, works equally well for sets with a finite or infinite number of members.

Definition 1.4.1

i)   Two sets X and Y have the same cardinality if there is a total one-to-one function from X onto Y.

ii) The cardinality of a set X is less than or equal to the cardinality of a set Y if there is total one-to-one function from X into Y.

Note that the two definitions differ only by the extent to which the mapping covers the set Y. If the range of the one-to-one mapping is all of Y, then the two sets have the same cardinality.

The cardinality of a set X is denoted $card(X)$. The relationships in (i) and (ii) are denoted $card(X) = card(Y)$ and $card(X) \leq card(Y)$, respectively. The cardinality of X is said to be strictly less than that of Y, written $card(X) < card(Y)$, if $card(X) \leq card(Y)$ and $card(X) \neq card(Y)$. The Schröder-Bernstein Theorem establishes the familiar relationship between $\leq$ and $=$ for cardinality. The proof of the Schröder-Bernstein Theorem is left as an exercise.

Computation and Reasoning

Theorem 1.4.2 (Schröder-Bernstein)

If $card(X) \leq card(Y)$ and $card(Y) \leq card(X)$, then $card(X) = card(Y)$.

The cardinality of a finite set is denoted by the number of elements in the set. Thus $card(\{a, b\}) = 2$. A set that has the same cardinality as the set of natural numbers is said to be **countably infinite** or **denumerable.** Intuitively, a set is denumerable if its members can be put into an order and counted. The mapping f that establishes the correspondence with the natural numbers provides such an ordering; the first element is $f(0)$, the second $f(1)$, the third $f(2)$, and so on. The term **countable** refers to sets that are either finite or denumerable. A set that is not countable is said to be **uncountable.**

The set $N - \{0\}$ is countably infinite; the function $s(n) = n + 1$ defines a one-to-one mapping from N onto $N - \{0\}$. It may seem paradoxical that the set $N - \{0\}$, obtained by removing an element from N, has the same number of elements of N. Clearly, there is no one-to-one mapping of a finite set onto a proper subset of itself. It is this property that differentiates finite and infinite sets.

Definition 1.4.3

A set is **infinite** if it has a proper subset of the same cardinality.

Example 1.4.1

The set of odd natural numbers is countably infinite. The function $f(n) = 2n + 1$ from Example 1.2.4 establishes the one-to-one correspondence between N and the odd numbers.

□

A set is countably infinite if its elements can be put in a one-to-one correspondence with the natural numbers. A diagram of a mapping from N onto a set graphically illustrates the countability of the set. The one-to-one correspondence between the natural numbers and the set of all integers

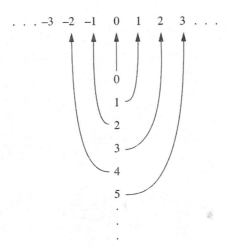

Computation and Reasoning

455

exhibits the countability of the set of integers. This correspondence is defined by the function

$$f(n) = \begin{cases} div(n,\,2) + 1 & \text{if } n \text{ is odd} \\ -\,div(n,\,2) & \text{if } n \text{ is even.} \end{cases}$$

Example 1.4.2

The points of an infinite two-dimensional grid can be used to show that $\mathbf{N} \times \mathbf{N}$, the set of ordered pairs of natural numbers, is denumerable. The grid is constructed by labeling the axes with the natural numbers. The position defined by the ith entry on the horizontal axis and the jth entry on the vertical axis represents the ordered pair $[i,\,j]$.

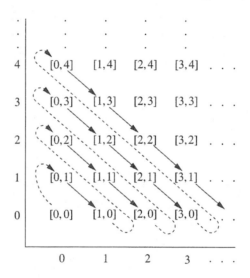

The elements of the grid can be listed sequentially by following the arrows in the diagram. This creates the correspondence

0	1	2	3	4	5	6	7	...
$\updownarrow$	$\updownarrow$	$\updownarrow$	$\updownarrow$	$\updownarrow$	$\updownarrow$	$\updownarrow$	$\updownarrow$	
$[0, 0]$	$[0, 1]$	$[1, 0]$	$[0, 2]$	$[1, 1]$	$[2, 0]$	$[0, 3]$	$[1, 2]$	...

that demonstrates the countability of $\mathbf{N} \times \mathbf{N}$. The one-to-one correspondence outlined above maps the ordered pair $[i,\,j]$ to the natural number $((i + j)(i + j + 1)/2) + i$.   □

The sets of interest in language theory and computability are almost exclusively finite or denumerable. We state, without proof, several closure properties of countable sets.

Theorem 1.4.4

i) The union of two countable sets is countable.

ii) The Cartesian product of two countable sets is countable.

iii) The set of finite subsets of a countable set is countable.

iv) The set of finite-length sequences consisting of elements of a nonempty countable set is countably infinite.

The preceding theorem indicates that the property of countability is retained under many standard set-theoretic operations. Each of these closure results can be established by constructing a one-to-one correspondence between the new set and a subset of the natural numbers.

A set is uncountable if it is impossible to sequentially list its members. The following proof technique, known as *Cantor's diagonalization argument,* is used to show that there is an uncountable number of total functions from N to N. Two total functions $f : N \to N$ and $g : N \to N$ are equal if they have the same value for every element in the domain. That is, $f = g$ if $f(n) = g(n)$ for all $n \in N$. To show that two functions are distinct, it suffices to find a single input value for which the functions differ.

Assume that the set of total functions from the natural numbers to the natural numbers is denumerable. Then there is a sequence $f_0, f_1, f_2, \ldots$ that contains all the functions. The values of the functions are exhibited in the two-dimensional grid with the input values on the horizontal axis and the functions on the vertical axis.

	0	1	2	3	4	
f_0	$f_0(0)$	$f_0(1)$	$f_0(2)$	$f_0(3)$	$f_0(4)$	$\cdots$
f_1	$f_1(0)$	$f_1(1)$	$f_1(2)$	$f_1(3)$	$f_1(4)$	$\cdots$
f_2	$f_2(0)$	$f_2(1)$	$f_2(2)$	$f_2(3)$	$f_2(4)$	$\cdots$
f_3	$f_3(0)$	$f_3(1)$	$f_3(2)$	$f_3(3)$	$f_3(4)$	$\cdots$
f_4	$f_4(0)$	$f_4(1)$	$f_4(2)$	$f_4(3)$	$f_4(4)$	$\cdots$
$\vdots$	$\vdots$	$\vdots$	$\vdots$	$\vdots$	$\vdots$	

Consider the function $f : N \to N$ defined by $f(n) = f_n(n) + 1$. The values of f are obtained by adding 1 to the values on the diagonal of the grid, hence the name diagonalization. By the definition of f, $f(i) \neq f_i(i)$ for every i. Consequently, f is not in the sequence $f_0, f_1, f_2, \ldots$. This is a contradiction since the sequence was assumed to contain all the total functions. The assumption that the number of functions is countably infinite leads to a contradiction. It follows that the set is uncountable.

Diagonalization is a general proof technique for demonstrating that a set is not countable. As seen in the preceding example, establishing uncountability using diagonalization is a proof by contradiction. The first step is to assume that the set is countable and therefore its members can be exhaustively listed. The contradiction is achieved by producing a member of the set that cannot occur anywhere in the list. No conditions are put on the listing of the elements other than that it must contain all the elements of the set. Producing a contradiction by diagonalization shows that there is no possible exhaustive listing of the elements and consequently that the set is uncountable. This technique is exhibited again in the following examples.

Computation and Reasoning

457

Example 1.4.3

A function f from **N** to **N** has a *fixed point* if there is some natural number i such that $f(i) = i$. For example, $f(n) = n^2$ has fixed points 0 and 1, while $f(n) = n^2 + 1$ has no fixed points. We will show that the number of functions that do not have fixed points is uncountable. The argument is similar to the proof that the number of all functions from **N** to **N** is uncountable, except that we now have an additional condition that must be met when constructing an element that is not in the listing.

Assume that the number of the functions without fixed points is countable. Then these functions can be listed $f_0, f_1, f_2, \ldots$. To obtain a contradiction to our assumption that the set is countable, we construct a function that has no fixed points and is not in the list. Consider the function $f(n) = f_n(n) + n + 1$. The addition of $n + 1$ in the definition of f ensures that $f(n) > n$ for all n. Thus f has no fixed points. By an argument similar to that given above, $f(i) \neq f_i(i)$ for all i. Consequently, the listing $f_0, f_1, f_2, \ldots$ is not exhaustive, and we conclude that the number of functions without fixed points is uncountable. $\square$

Example 1.4.4

$\mathcal{P}(\mathbf{N})$, the set of subsets of **N**, is uncountable. Assume that the set of subsets of **N** is countable. Then they can be listed $N_0, N_1, N_2, \ldots$. Define a subset D of **N** as follows: For every natural number j,

$$j \in D \text{ if, and only if, } j \notin N_j.$$

By our construction, $0 \in D$ if $0 \notin N_0$, $1 \in D$ if $1 \notin N_1$, and so on. The set D is clearly a set of natural numbers. By our assumption, $N_0, N_1, N_2, \ldots$ is an exhaustive listing of the subsets of **N**. Hence, $D = N_i$ for some i. Is the number i in the set D? By definition of D,

$$i \in D \text{ if, and only if, } i \notin N_i.$$

But since $D = N_i$, this becomes

$$i \in D \text{ if, and only if, } i \notin D,$$

which is a contradiction. Thus, our assumption that $\mathcal{P}(\mathbf{N})$ is countable must be false and we conclude that $\mathcal{P}(\mathbf{N})$ is uncountable.

To appreciate the "diagonal" technique, consider a two-dimensional grid with the natural numbers on the horizontal axis and the vertical axis labeled by the sets $N_0, N_1, N_2, \ldots$. The position of the grid designated by row N_i and column j contains *yes* if $j \in N_i$. Otherwise, the position defined by N_i and column j contains *no*. The set D is constructed by considering the relationship between the entries along the diagonal of the grid: the number j and the set N_j. By the way that we have defined D, the number j is an element of D if, and only if, the entry in the position labeled by N_j and j is *no*. $\square$

Computation and Reasoning

458

1.5   Diagonalization and Self-Reference

In addition to its use in cardinality proofs, diagonalization provides a method for demonstrating that certain properties or relations are inherently contradictory. These results are used in nonexistence proofs since there can be no object that satisfies such a property. Diagonalization proofs of nonexistence frequently depend upon contradictions that arise from self-reference—an object analyzing its own actions, properties, or characteristics. Russell's paradox, the undecidability of the Halting Problem for Turing Machines, and Gödel's proof of the undecidability of number theory are all based on contradictions associated with self-reference.

The diagonalization proofs in the preceding section used a table with operators listed on the vertical axis and their arguments on the horizontal axis to illustrate the relationship between the operators and arguments. In each example, the operators were of a different type than their arguments. In self-reference, the same family of objects comprises the operators and their arguments. We will use the *barber's paradox*, an amusing simplification of Russell's paradox, to illustrate diagonalization and self-reference.

The barber's paradox is concerned with who shaves whom in a mythical town. We are told that every man who is able to shave himself does so and that the barber of the town (a man himself) shaves all and only the people who cannot shave themselves. We wish to consider the possible truth of such a statement and the existence of such a town. In this case, the set of males in the town make up both the operators and the arguments; they are doing the shaving and being shaved. Let $M = \{p_1, p_2, p_3, \ldots, p_i, \ldots\}$ be the set of all males in the town. A tabular representation of the shaving relationship has the form

	p_1	p_2	p_3	$\cdots$	p_i	$\cdots$
p_1	-	-	-	$\cdots$	-	$\cdots$
p_2	-	-	-	$\cdots$	-	$\cdots$
p_3	-	-	-	$\cdots$	-	$\cdots$
$\vdots$	$\vdots$	$\vdots$	$\vdots$	$\ddots$	-	$\cdots$
p_i	-	-	-	$\cdots$	-	$\cdots$
$\vdots$	$\vdots$	$\vdots$	$\vdots$	$\vdots$	$\vdots$	$\ddots$

where the i, jth position of the table has a 1 if p_i shaves p_j and a 0 otherwise. Every column will have one entry with a 1 and all the other entries will be 0; each person either shaves himself or is shaved by the barber. The barber must be one of the people in the town, so he is p_i for some value i. What is the value of the position i, i in the table? This is classic self-reference; we are asking what occurs when a particular object is simultaneously the operator (the person doing the shaving) and the operand (the person being shaved).

Who shaves the barber? If the barber is able to shave himself, then he cannot do so since he shaves only people who are unable to shave themselves. If he is unable to shave himself,

Computation and Reasoning

then he must shave himself since he shaves everyone who cannot shave themselves. We have shown that the properties describing the shaving habits of the town are contradictory so such a town cannot exist.

Russell's paradox follows the same pattern, but its consequences were much more significant than the nonexistence of a mythical town. One of the fundamental tenets of set theory as proposed by Cantor in the late 1800s was that any property or condition that can be described defines a set—the set of objects that satisfy the condition. There may be no objects, finitely many, or infinitely many that satisfy the property, but regardless of the number or the type of elements, the objects form a set. Russell devised an argument based on self-reference to show that this claim cannot be true.

The relationship examined by Russell's paradox is that of the membership of one set in another. For each set X we ask the question, "Is a set Y an element of X?" This is not an unreasonable question, since one set can certainly be an element of another. The table below gives both some negative and positive examples of this question.

X	Y	$Y \in X$?
$\{a\}$	$\{a\}$	no
$\{\{a\}, b\}$	$\{a\}$	yes
$\{\{a\}, a, \emptyset\}$	$\emptyset$	yes
$\{\{a, b\}, \{a\}\}$	$\{\{a\}\}$	no
$\{\{\{a\}, b\}, b\}$	$\{\{a\}, b\}$	yes

It is important to note that the question is not whether Y is a subset of X, but whether it is an element of X.

The membership relation can be depicted by the table

	X_1	X_2	X_3	...	X_i	...
X_1	-	-	-	...	-	...
X_2	-	-	-	...	-	...
X_3	-	-	-	...	-	...
$\vdots$	$\vdots$	$\vdots$	$\vdots$	$\ddots$	-	...
X_i	-	-	-	...	-	...
$\vdots$	$\vdots$	$\vdots$	$\vdots$	$\vdots$	$\vdots$	$\ddots$

where axes are labeled by the sets. A table entry $[i, j]$ is 1 if X_j is an element of X_i and 0 if X_j is not an element of X_i.

A question of self-reference can be obtained by identifying the operator and the operand in the membership question. That is, we ask if a set X_i is an element of itself. The diagonal entry $[i, i]$ in the preceding table contains the answer to the question, "Is X_i an element of X_i?" Now consider the property that a set is not an element of itself. Does this property define a set? There are clearly examples of sets that satisfy the property; the set $\{a\}$ is not an element of itself. The satisfaction of the property is indicated by the complement of the diagonal. A set X_i is not an element of itself if, and only if, entry $[i, i]$ is 0.

Assume that $S = \{X \mid X \notin X\}$ is a set. Is S in S? If S is an element of itself, then it is not in S by the definition of S. Moreover, if S is not in S, then it must be in S since it is not an element of itself. This is an obvious contradiction. We were led to this contradiction by our assumption that the collection of sets that satisfy the property $X \notin X$ form a set.

We have constructed a describable property that cannot define a set. This shows that Cantor's assertion about the universality of sets is demonstrably false. The ramifications of Russell's paradox were far-reaching. The study of set theory moved from a foundation based on naive definitions to formal systems of axioms and inference rules and helped initiate the formalist philosophy of mathematics. In Chapter 12 we will use self-reference to establish a fundamental result in the theory of computer science, the undecidability of the Halting Problem.

1.6 Recursive Definitions

Many, in fact most, of the sets of interest in formal language and automata theory contain an infinite number of elements. Thus it is necessary that we develop techniques to describe, generate, or recognize the elements that belong to an infinite set. In the preceding section we described the set of natural numbers utilizing ellipsis dots (. . .). This seemed reasonable since everyone reading this text is familiar with the natural numbers and knows what comes after 0, 1, 2, 3. However, this description would be totally inadequate for an alien unfamiliar with our base 10 arithmetic system and numeric representations. Such a being would have no idea that the symbol 4 is the next element in the sequence or that 1492 is a natural number.

In the development of a mathematical theory, such as the theory of languages or automata, the theorems and proofs may utilize only the definitions of the concepts of that theory. This requires precise definitions of both the objects of the domain and the operations. A method of definition must be developed that enables our friend the alien, or a computer that has no intuition, to generate and "understand" the properties of the elements of a set.

A **recursive definition** of a set X specifies a method for constructing the elements of the set. The definition utilizes two components: a basis and a set of operations. The basis consists of a finite set of elements that are explicitly designated as members of X. The operations are used to construct new elements of the set from the previously defined members. The recursively defined set X consists of all elements that can be generated from the basis elements by a finite number of applications of the operations.

The key word in the process of recursively defining a set is *generate*. Clearly, no process can list the complete set of natural numbers. Any particular number, however, can be obtained by beginning with zero and constructing an initial sequence of the natural numbers. This intuitively describes the process of recursively defining the set of natural numbers. This idea is formalized in the following definition.

Computation and Reasoning

Definition 1.6.1

A recursive definition of **N**, the set of natural numbers, is constructed using the successor function s.

i) Basis: $0 \in \mathbf{N}$.

ii) Recursive step: If $n \in \mathbf{N}$, then $s(n) \in \mathbf{N}$.

iii) Closure: $n \in \mathbf{N}$ only if it can be obtained from 0 by a finite number of applications of the operation s.

The basis explicitly states that 0 is a natural number. In (ii), a new natural number is defined in terms of a previously defined number and the successor operation. The closure section guarantees that the set contains only those elements that can be obtained from 0 using the successor operator. Definition 1.6.1 generates an infinite sequence 0, $s(0)$, $s(s(0))$, $s(s(s(0)))$, ... This sequence is usually abbreviated 0, 1, 2, 3, ... However, anything that can be done with the familiar Arabic numerals could also be done with the more cumbersome unabbreviated representation.

The essence of a recursive procedure is to define complicated processes or structures in terms of simpler instances of the same process or structure. In the case of the natural numbers, "simpler" often means smaller. The recursive step of Definition 1.6.1 defines a number in terms of its predecessor.

The natural numbers have now been defined, but what does it mean to understand their properties? We usually associate operations of addition, multiplication, and subtraction with the natural numbers. We may have learned these by brute force, either through memorization or tedious repetition. For the alien or a computer to perform addition, the meaning of "add" must be appropriately defined. One cannot memorize the sum of all possible combinations of natural numbers, but we can use recursion to establish a method by which the sum of any two numbers can be mechanically calculated. The successor function is the only operation on the natural numbers that has been introduced. Thus the definition of addition may use only 0 and s.

Definition 1.6.2

In the following recursive definition of the sum of m and n, the recursion is done on n, the second argument of the sum.

i) Basis: If $n = 0$, then $m + n = m$.

ii) Recursive step: $m + s(n) = s(m + n)$.

iii) Closure: $m + n = k$ only if this equality can be obtained from $m + 0 = m$ using finitely many applications of the recursive step.

The closure step is often omitted from a recursive definition of an operation on a given domain. In this case, it is assumed that the operation is defined for all the elements of the domain. The operation of addition given above is defined for all elements of $\mathbf{N} \times \mathbf{N}$.

The sum of m and the successor of n is defined in terms of the simpler case, the sum of m and n, and the successor operation. The choice of n as the recursive operand was arbitrary; the operation could also have been defined in terms of m, with n fixed.

Computation and Reasoning

Following the construction given in Definition 1.6.2, the sum of any two natural numbers can be computed using 0 and s, the primitives used in the definition of the natural numbers. Example 1.6.1 traces the recursive computation of $3 + 2$.

Example 1.6.1

The numbers 3 and 2 abbreviate $s(s(s(0)))$ and $s(s(0))$, respectively. The sum is computed recursively by

$$s(s(s(0))) + s(s(0))$$
$$= s(s(s(s(0))) + s(0))$$
$$= s(s(s(s(s(0))) + 0))$$
$$= s(s(s(s(s(0))))) \qquad \text{(basis case)}.$$

This final value is the representation of the number 5. □

Figure 1.1 illustrates the process of recursively generating a set X from basis X_0. Each of the concentric circles represents a stage of the construction. X_1 represents the basis elements and the elements that can be obtained from them using a single application of an operation defined in the recursive step. X_i contains the elements that can be constructed with i or fewer operations. The generation process in the recursive portion of the definition produces a countably infinite sequence of nested sets. The set X can be thought of as the infinite union of the X_i's. Let x be an element of X and let X_j be the first set in which x occurs. This means that x can be constructed from the basis elements using exactly j applications of the operators. Although each element of X can be generated by a finite number of applications of the operators, there is no upper bound on the number of applications needed to generate the entire set X. This property, generation using a finite but unbounded number of operations, is a fundamental property of recursive definitions.

The successor operator can be used recursively to define relations on the set $N \times N$. The Cartesian product $N \times N$ is often portrayed by the grid of points representing the ordered pairs. Following the standard conventions, the horizontal axis represents the first component of the ordered pair and the vertical axis the second. The shaded area in Figure 1.2(a) contains the ordered pairs $[i, j]$ in which $i < j$. This set is the relation LT, less than, that was described in Section 1.2.

Example 1.6.2

The relation LT is defined as follows:

i) Basis: $[0, 1] \in$ LT.
ii) Recursive step: If $[m, n] \in$ LT, then $[m, s(n)] \in$ LT and $[s(m), s(n)] \in$ LT.
iii) Closure: $[m, n] \in$ LT only if it can be obtained from $[0, 1]$ by a finite number of applications of the operations in the recursive step.

Computation and Reasoning

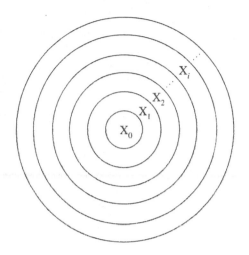

Recursive generation of X:

$X_0 = \{x \mid x$ is a basis element$\}$

$X_{i+1} = X_i \cup \{x \mid x$ can be generated by $i+1$ operations$\}$

$X = \{x \mid x \in X_j$ for some $j \geq 0\}$

FIGURE 1.1   Nested sequence of sets in recursive definition.

Using the infinite union description of recursive generation, the definition of LT generates the sequence LT_i of nested sets where

$$LT_0 = \{[0, 1]\}$$

$$LT_1 = LT_0 \cup \{[0, 2], \ [1, 2]\}$$

$$LT_2 = LT_1 \cup \{[0, 3], \ [1, 3], \ [2, 3]\}$$

$$LT_3 = LT_2 \cup \{[0, 4], \ [1, 4], \ [2, 4], \ [3, 4]\}$$

$$\vdots$$

$$LT_i = LT_{i-1} \cup \{[j, i+1] \mid j = 0, 1, \ldots, i\}$$

$$\vdots$$

$\square$

The construction of LT shows that the generation of an element in a recursively defined set may not be unique. The ordered pair $[1, 3] \in LT_2$ is generated by the two distinct sequences of operations:

Basis:	[0, 1]	[0, 1]
1:	$[0, s(1)] = [0, 2]$	$[s(0), s(1)] = [1, 2]$
2:	$[s(0), s(2)] = [1, 3]$	$[1, s(2)] = [1, 3].$

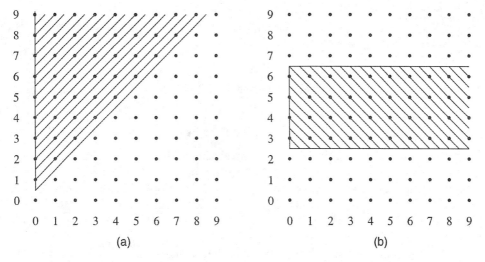

FIGURE 1.2 Relations on **N** × **N**.

Example 1.6.3

The shaded area in Figure 1.2(b) contains all the ordered pairs with second component 3, 4, 5, or 6. A recursive definition of this set, call it X, is given below.

  i) Basis: [0, 3], [0, 4], [0, 5], and [0, 6] are in X.

 ii) Recursive step: If $[m, n] \in$ X, then $[s(m), n] \in$ X.

iii) Closure: $[m, n] \in$ X only if it can be obtained from the basis elements by a finite number of applications of the operation in the recursive step.

The sequence of sets X_i generated by this recursive process is defined by

$$X_i = \{[j, 3], \ [j, 4], \ [j, 5], \ [j, 6] \mid j = 0, 1, \ldots, i\}. \qquad \square$$

1.7 Mathematical Induction

Establishing relationships between the elements of sets and operations on the sets requires the ability to construct proofs that verify the hypothesized properties. It is impossible to prove that a property holds for every member in an infinite set by considering each element individually. The principle of mathematical induction gives sufficient conditions for proving that a property holds for every element in a recursively defined set. Induction uses the family of nested sets generated by the recursive process to extend a property from the basis to the entire set.

Computation and Reasoning

Principle of Mathematical Induction   Let X be a set defined by recursion from the basis X_0 and let $X_0, X_1, X_2, \ldots, X_i, \ldots$ be the sequence of sets generated by the recursive process. Also let **P** be a property defined on the elements of X. If it can be shown that

i) **P** holds for each element in X_0,

ii) whenever **P** holds for every element in the sets $X_0, X_1, \ldots, X_i$, **P** also holds for every element in X_{i+1},

then, by the principle of mathematical induction, **P** holds for every element in X.

The soundness of the principle of mathematical induction can be intuitively exhibited using the sequence of sets constructed in the recursive definition of X. Shading the circle X_i indicates that **P** holds for every element of X_i. The first condition requires that the interior set be shaded. Condition (ii) states that the shading can be extended from any circle to the next concentric circle. Figure 1.3 illustrates how this process eventually shades the entire set X.

The justification for the principle of mathematical induction should be clear from the preceding argument. Another justification can be obtained by assuming that conditions (i) and (ii) are satisfied but **P** is not true for every element in X. If **P** does not hold for all elements of X, then there is at least one set X_i for which **P** does not universally hold. Let X_j be the first such set. Since condition (i) asserts that **P** holds for all elements of X_0, j cannot be zero. Now **P** holds for all elements of X_{j-1} by our choice of j. Condition (ii) then requires that **P** hold for all elements in X_j. This implies that there is no first set in the sequence for which the property **P** fails. Consequently, **P** must be true for all the X_i's, and therefore for X.

An inductive proof consists of three distinct steps. The first step is proving that the property **P** holds for each element of a basis set. This corresponds to establishing condition (i) in the definition of the principle of mathematical induction. The second is the statement of the inductive hypothesis. The inductive hypothesis is the assumption that the property **P** holds for every element in the sets $X_0, X_1, \ldots, X_n$. The inductive step then proves, using the inductive hypothesis, that **P** can be extended to each element in X_{n+1}. Completing the inductive step satisfies the requirements of the principle of mathematical induction. Thus, it can be concluded that **P** is true for all elements of X.

In Example 1.6.2, a recursive definition was given to generate the relation LT, which consists of ordered pairs $[i, j]$ that satisfy $i < j$. Does every ordered pair generated by the definition satisfy this inequality? We will use this question to illustrate the steps of an inductive proof on a recursively defined set.

The first step is to explicitly show that the inequality is satisfied for all elements in the basis. The basis of the recursive definition of LT is the set $\{[0, 1]\}$. The basis step of the inductive proof is satisfied since $0 < 1$.

The inductive hypothesis states the assumption that $x < y$ for all ordered pairs $[x, y] \in$ LT_n. In the inductive step we must prove that $i < j$ for all ordered pairs $[i, j] \in LT_{n+1}$. The recursive step in the definition of LT relates the sets LT_{n+1} and LT_n. Let $[i, j]$ be an ordered

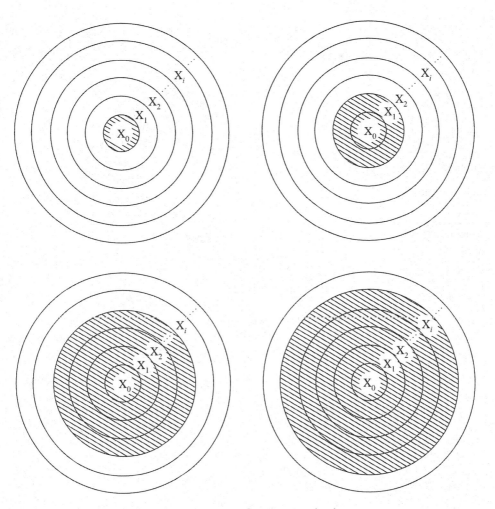

FIGURE 1.3   Principle of mathematical induction.

pair in LT_{n+1}. Then either $[i, j] = [x, s(y)]$ or $[i, j] = [s(x), s(y)]$ for some $[x, y] \in LT_n$. By the inductive hypothesis, $x < y$. If $[i, j] = [x, s(y)]$, then

$$i = x < y < s(y) = j.$$

Similarly, if $[i, j] = [s(x), s(y)]$, then

$$i = s(x) < s(y) = j.$$

In either case, $i < j$ and the inequality is extended to all ordered pairs in LT_{n+1}. This completes the requirements for an inductive proof and consequently the inequality holds for all ordered pairs in LT.

In the proof that every ordered pair $[i,\ j]$ in the relation LT satisfies $i < j$, the inductive step used only the assumption that the property was true for the elements generated by the preceding application of the recursive step. This type of proof is sometimes referred to as *simple induction*. When the inductive step utilizes the full strength of the inductive hypothesis—that the property holds for all the previously generated elements—the proof technique is called *strong induction*. Example 1.7.1 uses strong induction to establish a relationship between the number of operators and the number of parentheses in an arithmetic expression.

Example 1.7.1

A set E of arithmetic expressions is defined recursively from symbols $\{a, b\}$, operators $+$ and $-$, and parentheses as follows:

i) Basis: a and b are in E.

ii) Recursive step: If u and v are in E, then $(u + v)$, $(u - v)$, and $(-v)$ are in E.

iii) Closure: An expression is in E only if it can be obtained from the basis by a finite number of applications of the recursive step.

The recursive definition generates the expressions $(a + b)$, $(a + (b + b))$, $((a + a) - (b - a))$ in one, two, and three applications of the recursive step, respectively. We will use induction to prove that the number of parentheses in an expression u is twice the number of operators. That is, $n_p(u) = 2n_o(u)$, where $n_p(u)$ is the number of parentheses in u and $n_o(u)$ is the number of operators.

Basis: The basis for the induction consists of the expressions a and b. In this case, $n_p(a) = 0 = 2n_o(a)$ and $n_p(b) = 0 = 2n_o(b)$.

Inductive Hypothesis: Assume that $n_p(u) = 2n_o(u)$ for all expressions generated by n or fewer iterations of the recursive step, that is, for all u in E_n.

Inductive Step: Let w be an expression generated by $n + 1$ applications of the recursive step. Then $w = (u + v)$, $w = (u - v)$, or $w = (-v)$ where u and v are strings in E_n. By the inductive hypothesis,

$$n_p(u) = 2n_o(u)$$

$$n_p(v) = 2n_o(v).$$

If $w = (u + v)$ or $w = (u - v)$,

$$n_p(w) = n_p(u) + n_p(v) + 2$$

$$n_o(w) = n_o(u) + n_o(v) + 1.$$

Computation and Reasoning

468

Consequently,

$$2n_o(w) = 2n_o(u) + 2n_o(v) + 2 = n_p(u) + n_p(v) + 2 = n_p(w).$$

If $w = (-v)$, then

$$2n_o(w) = 2(n_o(v) + 1) = 2n_o(v) + 2 = n_p(v) + 2 = n_p(w).$$

Thus the property $n_p(w) = 2n_o(w)$ holds for all $w \in E_{n+1}$ and we conclude, by mathematical induction, that it holds for all expressions in E.   □

Frequently, inductive proofs use the natural numbers as the underlying recursively defined set. A recursive definition of this set with basis $\{0\}$ is given in Definition 1.6.1. The nth application of the recursive step produces the natural number n, and the corresponding inductive step consists of extending the satisfaction of the property under consideration from $0, \ldots, n$ to $n + 1$.

Example 1.7.2

Induction is used to prove that $0 + 1 + \cdots + n = n(n + 1)/2$. Using the summation notation, we can write the preceding expression as

$$\sum_{i=0}^{n} i = n(n + 1)/2.$$

Basis: The basis is $n = 0$. The relationship is explicitly established by computing the values of each of the sides of the desired equality.

$$\sum_{i=0}^{0} i = 0 = 0(0 + 1)/2.$$

Inductive Hypothesis: Assume for all values $k = 1, 2, \ldots, n$ that

$$\sum_{i=0}^{k} i = k(k + 1)/2.$$

Inductive Step: We need to prove that

$$\sum_{i=0}^{n+1} i = (n + 1)(n + 1 + 1)/2 = (n + 1)(n + 2)/2.$$

The inductive hypothesis establishes the result for the sum of the sequence containing n or fewer integers. Combining the inductive hypothesis with the properties of addition, we obtain

$$\sum_{i=0}^{n+1} i = \sum_{i=0}^{n} i + (n+1) \qquad \text{(associativity of +)}$$

$$= n(n+1)/2 + (n+1) \qquad \text{(inductive hypothesis)}$$

$$= (n+1)(n/2+1) \qquad \text{(distributive property)}$$

$$= (n+1)(n+2)/2.$$

Since the conditions of the principle of mathematical induction have been established, we conclude that the result holds for all natural numbers. $\qquad \square$

Each step in the proof must follow from previously established properties of the operators or the inductive hypothesis. The strategy of an inductive proof is to manipulate the formula to contain an instance of the property applied to a simpler case. When this is accomplished, the inductive hypothesis may be invoked. After the application of the inductive hypothesis, the remainder of the proof often consists of algebraic manipulation to produce the desired result.

1.8   Directed Graphs

A mathematical structure consists of a set or sets, distinguished elements from the sets, and functions and relations on the sets. A *distinguished element* is an element of a set that has special properties that differentiate it from the other elements. The natural numbers, as defined in Definition 1.6.1, can be expressed as a structure (N, s, 0). The set N contains the natural numbers, s is a unary function on N, and 0 is a distinguished element of N. Zero is distinguished because of its explicit role in the definition of the natural numbers.

Graphs are frequently used to portray the essential features of a mathematical entity in a diagram, which aids the intuitive understanding of the concept. Formally, a **directed graph** is a mathematical structure consisting of a set N and a binary relation A on N. The elements of N are called the *nodes,* or *vertices,* of the graph and the elements of A are called *arcs* or *edges.* The relation A is referred to as the *adjacency relation.* A node y is said to be *adjacent* to x when $[x, y] \in$ A. An arc from x to y in a directed graph is depicted by an arrow from x to y. Using the arrow metaphor, y is called the head of the arc and x the tail. The *in-degree* of a node x is the number of arcs with x as the head. The *out-degree* of x is the number of arcs with x as the tail. Node a in Figure 1.4 has in-degree two and out-degree one.

A **path** from a node x to a node y in a directed graph G = (N, A) is a sequence of nodes and arcs $x_0, [x_0, x_1], x_1, [x_1, x_2], x_2, \ldots, x_{n-1}, [x_{n-1}, x_n], x_n$ of G with $x = x_0$ and $y = x_n$. The node x is the initial node of the path and y is the terminal node. Each pair

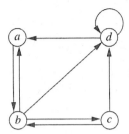

N = {a, b, c, d}		Node	In-degree	Out-degree
A = {[a, b], [b, a], [b, c],		a	2	1
[b, d], [c, b], [c, d],		b	2	3
[d, a], [d, d]}		c	1	2
		d	3	2

FIGURE 1.4   Directed graph.

of nodes x_i, x_{i+1} in the path is connected by the arc $[x_i, x_{i+1}]$. The length of a path is the number of arcs in the path. We will frequently describe a path simply by sequentially listing its arcs.

There is a path of length zero from any node to itself called the **null path**. A path of length one or more that begins and ends with the same node is called a *cycle*. A cycle is *simple* if it does not contain a cyclic subpath. The path $[a, b]$, $[b, c]$, $[c, d]$, $[d, a]$ in Figure 1.4 is a simple cycle of length four. A directed graph containing at least one cycle is said to be *cyclic*. A graph with no cycles is said to be *acyclic*.

The arcs of a directed graph often designate more than the adjacency of the nodes. A labeled directed graph is a structure (N, L, A) where L is the set of labels and A is a relation on N × N × L. An element $[x, y, v] \in$ A is an arc from x to y labeled by v. The label on an arc specifies a relationship between the adjacent nodes. The labels on the graph in Figure 1.5 indicate the distances of the legs of a trip from Chicago to Minneapolis, Seattle, San Francisco, Dallas, St. Louis, and back to Chicago.

An **ordered tree**, or simply a tree, is an acyclic directed graph in which each node is connected by a unique path from a distinguished node called the **root** of the tree. The root has in-degree zero and all other nodes have in-degree one. A tree is a structure (N, A, r) where N is the set of nodes, A is the adjacency relation, and $r \in$ N is the root of the tree. The terminology of trees combines a mixture of references to family trees and to those of the arboreal nature. Although a tree is a directed graph, the arrows on the arcs are usually omitted in the illustrations of trees. Figure 1.6(a) gives a tree T with root x_1.

A node y is called a **child** of a node x, and x the parent of y, if y is adjacent to x. Accompanying the adjacency relation is an order on the children of any node. When a tree is drawn, this ordering is usually indicated by listing the children of a node in a left-to-right manner according to the ordering. The order of the children of x_2 in T is x_4, x_5, and x_6.

Computation and Reasoning

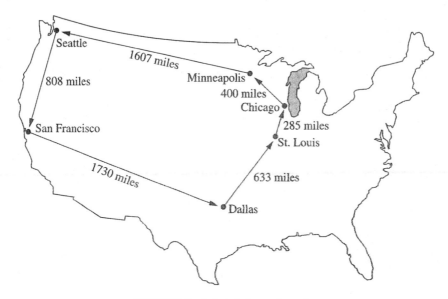

FIGURE 1.5   Labeled directed graph.

A node with out-degree zero is called a **leaf**. All other nodes are referred to as internal nodes. The *depth* of the root is zero; the depth of any other node is the depth of its parent plus one. The height or depth of a tree is the maximum of the depths of the nodes in the tree.

A node y is called a *descendant* of a node x, and x an *ancestor* of y, if there is a path from x to y. With this definition, each node is an ancestor and descendant of itself. The ancestor and descendant relations can be defined recursively using the adjacency relation (Exercises 43 and 44). The *minimal common ancestor* of two nodes x and y is an ancestor of both and a descendant of all other common ancestors. In the tree in Figure 1.6(a), the minimal common ancestor of x_{10} and x_{11} is x_5, of x_{10} and x_6 is x_2, and of x_{10} and x_{14} is x_1.

A subtree of a tree T is a subgraph of T that is a tree in its own right. The set of descendants of a node x and the restriction of the adjacency relation to this set form a subtree with root x. This tree is called the subtree generated by x.

The ordering of siblings in the tree can be extended to a relation LEFTOF on N × N. LEFTOF attempts to capture the property of one node being to the left of another in the diagram of a tree. For two nodes x and y, neither of which is an ancestor of the other, the relation LEFTOF is defined in terms of the subtrees generated by the minimal common ancestor of the nodes. Let z be the minimal common ancestor of x and y and let z_1, z_2, . . . , z_n be the children of z in their correct order. Then x is in the subtree generated by one of the children of z, call it z_i. Similarly, y is in the subtree generated by z_j for some j. Since z is the minimal common ancestor of x and y, $i \neq j$. If $i < j$, then $[x, y] \in$ LEFTOF; $[y, x] \in$ LEFTOF otherwise. With this definition, no node is LEFTOF one of its ancestors. If x_{13} were to the left of x_{12}, then x_{10} must also be to the left of x_5, since they are both the first

Computation and Reasoning

472

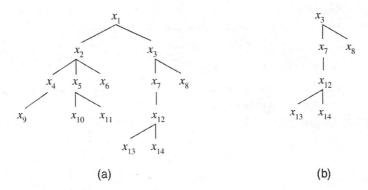

FIGURE 1.6 (a) Tree with root x_1. (b) Subtree generated by x_3.

child of their parent. The appearance of being to the left or right of an ancestor is a feature of the diagram, not a property of the ordering of the nodes.

The relation LEFTOF can be used to order the set of leaves of a tree. The **frontier** of a tree is constructed from the leaves in the order generated by the relation LEFTOF. The frontier of T is the sequence x_9, x_{10}, x_{11}, x_6, x_{13}, x_{14}, x_8.

When a family of graphs is defined recursively, the principle of mathematical induction can be used to prove that properties hold for all graphs in the family. We will use induction to demonstrate a relationship between the number of leaves and the number of arcs in strictly binary trees, trees in which each node is either a leaf or has two children.

Example 1.8.1

A tree in which each node has at most two children is called a **binary tree**. If each node is a leaf or has exactly two children, the tree is called *strictly binary*. The family of strictly binary trees can be defined recursively as follows:

i) Basis: A directed graph $T = (\{r\}, \emptyset, r)$ is a strictly binary tree.

ii) Recursive step: If $T_1 = (N_1, A_1, r_1)$ and $T_2 = (N_2, A_2, r_2)$ are strictly binary trees, where N_1 and N_2 are disjoint and $r \notin N_1 \cup N_2$, then

$$T = (N_1 \cup N_2 \cup \{r\},\ A_1 \cup A_2 \cup \{[r, r_1],\ [r, r_2]\},\ r)$$

is a strictly binary tree.

iii) Closure: T is a strictly binary tree only if it can be obtained from the basis elements by a finite number of applications of the construction given in the recursive step.

A strictly binary tree is either a single node or is constructed from two distinct strictly binary trees by the addition of a root and arcs to the two subtrees. Let $lv(T)$ and $arc(T)$ denote the number of leaves and arcs in a strictly binary tree T. We prove by induction that $2\,lv(T) - 2 = arc(T)$ for all strictly binary trees.

Computation and Reasoning

Basis: The basis consists of strictly binary trees of the form $(\{r\},\ \emptyset,\ r)$. The equality clearly holds in this case since a tree of this form has one leaf and no arcs.

Inductive Hypothesis: Assume that every strictly binary tree T generated by n or fewer applications of the recursive step satisfies $2\,lv(T) - 2 = arc(T)$.

Inductive Step: Let T be a strictly binary tree generated by $n + 1$ applications of the recursive step in the definition of the family of strictly binary trees. T is built from a node r and two previously constructed strictly binary trees T_1 and T_2 with roots r_1 and r_2, respectively.

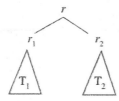

The node r is not a leaf since it has arcs to the roots of T_1 and T_2. Consequently, $lv(T) = lv(T_1) + lv(T_2)$. The arcs of T consist of the arcs of the component trees plus the two arcs from r.

  Since T_1 and T_2 are strictly binary trees generated by n or fewer applications of the recursive step, we may employ the inductive hypothesis to establish the desired equality. By the inductive hypothesis,

$$2\,lv(T_1) - 2 = arc(T_1)$$
$$2\,lv\,(T_2) - 2 = arc(T_2).$$

Now,

$$
\begin{aligned}
arc(T) &= arc(T_1) + arc(T_2) + 2 \\
&= 2\,lv(T_1) - 2 + 2\,lv(T_2) - 2 + 2 \\
&= 2(lv(T_1) + lv(T_2)) - 2 \\
&= 2(lv(T)) - 2,
\end{aligned}
$$

as desired.   □

Exercises

1. Let $X = \{1, 2, 3, 4\}$ and $Y = \{0, 2, 4, 6\}$. Explicitly define the sets described in parts (a) to (e).

   a) $X \cup Y$ d) $Y - X$

   b) $X \cap Y$ e) $\mathcal{P}(X)$

   c) $X - Y$

Computation and Reasoning

2. Let X = {a, b, c} and Y = {1, 2}.

   a) List all the subsets of X.

   b) List the members of X × Y.

   c) List all total functions from Y to X.

3. Let X = {3^n | $n > 0$} and Y = {$3n$ | $n \geq 0$}. Prove that X ⊆ Y.

4. Let X = {$n^3 + 3n^2 + 3n$ | $n \geq 0$} and Y = {$n^3 - 1$ | $n > 0$}. Prove that X = Y.

 *5. Prove DeMorgan's Laws. Use the definition of set equality to establish the identities.

6. Give functions $f : N \to N$ that satisfy the following.

   a) f is total and one-to-one but not onto.

   b) f is total and onto but not one-to-one.

   c) f is total, one-to-one, and onto but not the identity.

   d) f is not total but is onto.

7. Prove that the function $f : N \to N$ defined by $f(n) = n^2 + 1$ is one-to-one but not onto.

8. Let $f : R^+ \to R^+$ be the function defined by $f(x) = 1/x$, where R^+ denotes the set of positive real numbers. Prove that f is one-to-one and onto.

9. Give an example of a binary relation on N × N that is

   a) reflexive and symmetric but not transitive.

   b) reflexive and transitive but not symmetric.

   c) symmetric and transitive but not reflexive.

10. Let ≡ be the binary relation on N defined by $n \equiv m$ if, and only if, $n = m$. Prove that ≡ is an equivalence relation. Describe the equivalence classes of ≡.

11. Let ≡ be the binary relation on N defined by $n \equiv m$ for all $n, m \in N$. Prove that ≡ is an equivalence relation. Describe the equivalence classes of ≡.

12. Show that the binary relation LT, less than, is not an equivalence relation.

13. Let $\equiv_p$ be the binary relation on N defined by $n \equiv_p m$ if n mod $p = m$ mod p. For $p \geq 2$, prove that $\equiv_p$ is an equivalence relation. Describe the equivalence classes of $\equiv_p$.

14. Let $X_1, \ldots, X_n$ be a partition of a set X. Define an equivalence relation ≡ on X whose equivalence classes are precisely the sets $X_1, \ldots, X_n$.

15. A binary relation ≡ is defined on ordered pairs of natural numbers as follows: $[m, n] \equiv [j, k]$ if, and only if, $m + k = n + j$. Prove that ≡ is an equivalence relation in N × N.

16. Prove that the set of even natural numbers is denumerable.

17. Prove that the set of even integers is denumerable.

* **18.** Prove that the set of nonnegative rational numbers is denumerable.

19. Prove that the union of two disjoint countable sets is countable.

20. Prove that there are an uncountable number of total functions from N to {0, 1}.

21. A total function f from N to N is said to be *repeating* if $f(n) = f(n+1)$ for some $n \in$ N. Otherwise, f is said to be *nonrepeating*. Prove that there are an uncountable number of repeating functions. Also prove that there are an uncountable number of nonrepeating functions.

22. A total function f from N to N is *monotone increasing* if $f(n) < f(n+1)$ for all $n \in$ N. Prove that there are an uncountable number of monotone increasing functions.

23. Prove that there are uncountably many total functions from N to N that have a fixed point. See Example 1.4.3 for the definition of a fixed point.

24. A total function f from N to N is *nearly identity* if $f(n) = n - 1$, n, or $n + 1$ for every n. Prove that there are uncountably many nearly identity functions.

* **25.** Prove that the set of real numbers in the interval [0, 1] is uncountable. *Hint:* Use the diagonalization argument on the decimal expansion of real numbers. Be sure that each number is represented by only one infinite decimal expansion.

26. Let F be the set of total functions of the form $f : \{0, 1\} \rightarrow$ N (functions that map from {0, 1} to the natural numbers). Is the set of such functions countable or uncountable? Prove your answer.

27. Prove that the binary relation on sets defined by X $\equiv$ Y if, and only if, $card(\text{X}) = card(\text{Y})$ is an equivalence relation.

* **28.** Prove the Schröder-Bernstein Theorem.

29. Give a recursive definition of the relation *is equal to* on N $\times$ N using the operator s.

30. Give a recursive definition of the relation *greater than* on N $\times$ N using the successor operator s.

31. Give a recursive definition of the set of points $[m, n]$ that lie on the line $n = 3m$ in N $\times$ N. Use s as the operator in the definition.

32. Give a recursive definition of the set of points $[m, n]$ that lie on or under the line $n = 3m$ in N $\times$ N. Use s as the operator in the definition.

33. Give a recursive definition of the operation of multiplication of natural numbers using the operations s and addition.

34. Give a recursive definition of the predecessor operation

$$pred(n) = \begin{cases} 0 & \text{if } n = 0 \\ n - 1 & \text{otherwise} \end{cases}$$

using the operator s.

Computation and Reasoning

476

35. Subtraction on the set of natural numbers is defined by

$$n \div m = \begin{cases} n - m & \text{if } n > m \\ 0 & \text{otherwise.} \end{cases}$$

   This operation is often called *proper subtraction*. Give a recursive definition of proper subtraction using the operations s and $pred$.

36. Let X be a finite set. Give a recursive definition of the set of subsets of X. Use union as the operator in the definition.

* 37. Give a recursive definition of the set of finite subsets of $\mathbf{N}$. Use union and the successor s as the operators in the definition.

38. Prove that $2 + 5 + 8 + \cdots + (3n - 1) = n(3n + 1)/2$ for all $n > 0$.

39. Prove that $1 + 2 + 2^2 + \cdots + 2^n = 2^{n+1} - 1$ for all $n \geq 0$.

40. Prove $1 + 2^n < 3^n$ for all $n > 2$.

41. Prove that 3 is a factor of $n^3 - n + 3$ for all $n \geq 0$.

42. Let $P = \{A, B\}$ be a set consisting of two proposition letters (Boolean variables). The set E of well-formed conjunctive and disjunctive Boolean expressions over P is defined recursively as follows:

   i) Basis: $A, B \in$ E.

   ii) Recursive step: If $u, v \in$ E, then $(u \lor v) \in$ E and $(u \land v) \in$ E.

   iii) Closure: An expression is in E only if it is obtained from the basis by a finite number of iterations of the recursive step.

   a) Explicitly give the Boolean expressions in the sets E_0, E_1, and E_2.

   b) Prove by mathematical induction that for every Boolean expression in E, the number of occurrences of proposition letters is one more than the number of operators. For an expression u, let $n_p(u)$ denote the number of proposition letters in u and $n_o(u)$ denote the number of operators in u.

   c) Prove by mathematical induction that, for every Boolean expression in E, the number of left parentheses is equal to the number of right parentheses.

43. Give a recursive definition of all the nodes in a directed graph that can be reached by paths from a given node x. Use the adjacency relation as the operation in the definition. This definition also defines the set of descendants of a node in a tree.

44. Give a recursive definition of the set of ancestors of a node x in a tree.

45. List the members of the relation LEFTOF for the tree in Figure 1.6(a).

Computation and Reasoning

46. Using the tree below, give the values of each of the items in parts (a) to (e).

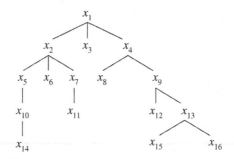

a) the depth of the tree

b) the ancestors of x_{11}

c) the minimal common ancestor of x_{14} and x_{11}, of x_{15} and x_{11}

d) the subtree generated by x_2

e) the frontier of the tree

47. Prove that a strictly binary tree with n leaves contains $2n - 1$ nodes.

48. A **complete binary tree** of depth n is a strictly binary tree in which every node on levels $1, 2, \ldots, n - 1$ is a parent and each node on level n is a leaf. Prove that a complete binary tree of depth n has $2^{n+1} - 1$ nodes.

Bibliographic Notes

The topics presented in this chapter are normally covered in a first course in discrete mathematics. A comprehensive presentation of the discrete mathematical structures important to the foundations of computer science can be found in Bobrow and Arbib [1974].

There are a number of classic books that provide detailed presentations of the topics introduced in this chapter. An introduction to set theory can be found in Halmos [1974], Stoll [1963], and Fraenkel, Bar-Hillel, and Levy [1984]. The latter begins with an excellent description of Russell's paradox and other antinomies arising in set theory. The diagonalization argument was originally presented by Cantor in 1874 and is reproduced in Cantor [1947]. The texts by Wilson [1985], Ore [1963], Bondy and Murty [1977], and Busacker and Saaty [1965] introduce the theory of graphs. Induction, recursion, and their relationship to theoretical computer science are covered in Wand [1980].

Computation and Reasoning

CHAPTER 2

Languages

The concept of language includes a variety of seemingly distinct categories including natural languages, computer languages, and mathematical languages. A general definition of language must encompass all of these various types of languages. In this chapter, a purely set-theoretic definition of language is given: A language is a set of strings over an alphabet. The alphabet is the set of symbols of the language and a string over the alphabet is a finite sequence of symbols from the alphabet.

Although strings are inherently simple structures, their importance in communication and computation cannot be overemphasized. The sentence "The sun did not shine" is a string of English words. The alphabet of the English language is the set of words and punctuation symbols that can occur in sentences. The mathematical equation

$$p = (n \times r \times t)/v$$

is a string consisting of variable names, operators, and parentheses. A digital photograph is stored as a bit string, a sequence of 0's and 1's. In fact, all data stored and manipulated by computers are represented as bit strings. As computer users, we frequently input information to the computer and receive output in the form of text strings. The source code of a computer program is a text string made up of the keywords, identifiers, and special symbols that constitute the alphabet of the programming language. Because of the importance of strings, we begin this chapter by formally defining the notion of string and studying the properties of operations on strings.

Languages of interest are not made up of arbitrary strings; not all strings of English words are sentences and not all strings of source code are legitimate computer programs. Languages consist of strings that satisfy certain requirements and restrictions that define the

41

syntax of the language. In this chapter, we will use recursive definitions and set operations to enforce syntactic restrictions on the strings of a language.

We will also introduce the family of languages defined by regular expressions. A regular expression describes a pattern and the language associated with the regular expression consists of all strings that match the pattern. Although we introduce the regular expressions via a set-theoretic construction, as we progress we will see that these languages occur naturally as the languages generated by regular grammars and accepted by finite-state machines. The chapter concludes by examining the use of regular expressions in searching and pattern matching.

2.1   Strings and Languages

The description of a language begins with the identification of its alphabet, the set of symbols that occur in the language. The elements of the language are finite-length strings of alphabet symbols. Consequently, the study of languages requires an understanding of the operations that generate and manipulate strings. In this section we give precise definitions of a string over an alphabet and of the basic string operations.

The sole requirement for an alphabet is that it consists of a finite number of indivisible objects. The alphabet of a natural language, like English or French, consists of the words and punctuation marks of the language. The symbols in the alphabet of the language are considered to be indivisible objects. The word *language* cannot be divided into *lang* and *uage*. The word *format* has no relation to the words *for* and *mat*; these are all distinct members of the alphabet. A string over this alphabet is a sequence of words and punctuation symbols. The sentence that you have just read is such a string. The alphabet of a computer language consists of the permissible keywords, identifiers, and symbols of the language. A string over this alphabet is a sequence of source code.

Because the elements of the alphabet of a language are indivisible, we will generally denote them by single characters. Letters a, b, c, d, e, with or without subscripts, are used to represent the elements of an alphabet and Σ is used to denote an alphabet. Strings over an alphabet are represented by letters occurring near the end of the alphabet. In particular, p, q, u, v, w, x, y, z are used to denote strings. The notation used for natural languages and computer languages provides an exception to this convention. In these cases, the alphabet consists of the indivisible elements of the particular language.

A string has been defined informally as a sequence of elements from an alphabet. In order to establish the properties of strings, the set of strings over an alphabet is defined recursively. The basis consists of the string containing no elements. This string is called the **null string** and denoted λ. The primitive operator used in the definition consists of adjoining a single element from the alphabet to the right-hand side of an existing string.

Definition 2.1.1

Let Σ be an alphabet. Σ^*, the set of strings over Σ, is defined recursively as follows:

i) Basis: $\lambda \in \Sigma^*$.

ii) Recursive step: If $w \in \Sigma^*$ and $a \in \Sigma$, then $wa \in \Sigma^*$.

iii) Closure: $w \in \Sigma^*$ only if it can be obtained from λ by a finite number of applications of the recursive step.

For any nonempty alphabet Σ, Σ^* contains infinitely many elements. If $\Sigma = \{a\}$, Σ^* contains the strings $\lambda, a, aa, aaa, \ldots$. The length of a string w, intuitively the number of elements in the string or formally the number of applications of the recursive step needed to construct the string from the elements of the alphabet, is denoted $length(w)$. If Σ contains n elements, there are n^k strings of length k in Σ^*.

Example 2.1.1

Let $\Sigma = \{a, b, c\}$. The elements of Σ^* include

Length 0: λ

Length 1: $a\ b\ c$

Length 2: $aa\ ab\ ac\ ba\ bb\ bc\ ca\ cb\ cc$

Length 3: $aaa\ aab\ aac\ aba\ abb\ abc\ aca\ acb\ acc$

$baa\ bab\ bac\ bba\ bbb\ bbc\ bca\ bcb\ bcc$

$caa\ cab\ cac\ cba\ cbb\ cbc\ cca\ ccb\ ccc$ □

By our informal definition, a language consists of strings over an alphabet. For example, the English language consists of those strings of words that we call sentences. Not all strings of words form sentences, only those satisfying certain conditions on the order and type of the constituent words. The collection of rules, requirements, and restrictions that specify the correctly formed sentences defines the syntax of the language. These observations lead to our formal definition of language; a language consists of a subset of the set of all possible strings over the alphabet.

Definition 2.1.2

A **language** over an alphabet Σ is a subset of Σ^*.

Since strings are the elements of a language, we must examine the properties of strings and the operations on them. Concatenation, taking two strings and "gluing them together," is the fundamental operation in the generation of strings. A formal definition of concatenation is given by recursion on the length of the second string in the concatenation. At this point, the primitive operation of adjoining a single member of the alphabet to the right-hand side of a string is the only operation on strings that has been introduced. Thus any new operation must be defined in terms of it.

Definition 2.1.3

Let $u, v \in \Sigma^*$. The **concatenation** of u and v, written uv, is a binary operation on Σ^* defined as follows:

i) Basis: If $length(v) = 0$, then $v = \lambda$ and $uv = u$.

ii) Recursive step: Let v be a string with $length(v) = n > 0$. Then $v = wa$, for some string w with length $n - 1$ and $a \in \Sigma$, and $uv = (uw)a$.

Example 2.1.2

Let $u = ab$, $v = ca$, and $w = bb$. Then

$$uv = abca \qquad\qquad vw = cabb$$
$$(uv)w = abcabb \qquad u(vw) = abcabb. \qquad\qquad \Box$$

The result of the concatenation of u, v, and w is independent of the order in which the operations are performed. Mathematically, this property is known as *associativity*. Theorem 2.1.4 proves that concatenation is an associative binary operation.

Theorem 2.1.4

Let u, v, $w \in \Sigma^*$. Then $(uv)w = u(vw)$.

Proof. The proof is by induction on the length of the string w. The string w was chosen for compatibility with the recursive definition of strings, which builds on the right-hand side of an existing string.

Basis: $length(w) = 0$. Then $w = \lambda$, and $(uv)w = uv$ by the definition of concatenation. On the other hand, $u(vw) = u(v) = uv$.

Inductive Hypothesis: Assume that $(uv)w = u(vw)$ for all strings w of length n or less.

Inductive Step: We need to prove that $(uv)w = u(vw)$ for all strings w of length $n + 1$. Let w be such a string. Then $w = xa$ for some string x of length n and $a \in \Sigma$ and

$$
\begin{aligned}
(uv)w &= (uv)(xa) &&\text{(substitution, } w = xa) \\
&= ((uv)x)a &&\text{(definition of concatenation)} \\
&= (u(vx))a &&\text{(inductive hypothesis)} \\
&= u((vx)a) &&\text{(definition of concatenation)} \\
&= u(v(xa)) &&\text{(definition of concatenation)} \\
&= u(vw) &&\text{(substitution, } xa = w). \qquad\blacksquare
\end{aligned}
$$

Since associativity guarantees the same result regardless of the order of the operations, parentheses are omitted from a sequence of applications of concatenation. Exponents are used to abbreviate the concatenation of a string with itself. Thus uu may be written u^2, uuu may be written u^3, and so on. For completeness, u^0, which represents concatenating u with itself zero times, is defined to be the null string. The operation of concatenation is not commutative. For strings $u = ab$ and $v = ba$, $uv = abba$ and $vu = baab$. Note that $u^2 = abab$ and not $aabb = a^2b^2$.

Substrings can be defined using the operation of concatenation. Intuitively, u is a substring of v if u "occurs inside of" v. Formally, u is a *substring* of v if there are strings

x and y such that $v = xuy$. A *prefix* of v is a substring u in which x is the null string in the decomposition of v. That is, $v = uy$. Similarly, u is a *suffix* of v if $v = xu$.

The reversal of a string is the string written backward. The reversal of $abbc$ is $cbba$. Like concatenation, this unary operation is also defined recursively on the length of the string. Removing an element from the right-hand side of a string constructs a smaller string that can then be used in the recursive step of the definition. Theorem 2.1.6 establishes the relationship between the operations of concatenation and reversal.

Definition 2.1.5

Let u be a string in Σ^*. The **reversal** of u, denoted u^R, is defined as follows:

 i) Basis: If $length(u) = 0$, then $u = \lambda$ and $\lambda^R = \lambda$.

 ii) Recursive step: If $length(u) = n > 0$, then $u = wa$ for some string w with length $n - 1$ and some $a \in \Sigma$, and $u^R = aw^R$.

Theorem 2.1.6

Let $u, \ v \in \Sigma^*$. Then $(uv)^R = v^R u^R$.

Proof.   The proof is by induction on the length of the string v.

Basis: If $length(v) = 0$, then $v = \lambda$ and $(uv)^R = u^R$. Similarly, $v^R u^R = \lambda^R u^R = u^R$.

Inductive Hypothesis: Assume $(uv)^R = v^R u^R$ for all strings v of length n or less.

Inductive Step: We must prove that, for any string v of length $n + 1$, $(uv)^R = v^R u^R$. Let v be a string of length $n + 1$. Then $v = wa$, where w is a string of length n and $a \in \Sigma$. The inductive step is established by

$$(uv)^R = (u(wa))^R$$

$$= ((uw)a)^R \qquad \text{(associativity of concatenation)}$$

$$= a(uw)^R \qquad \text{(definition of reversal)}$$

$$= a(w^R u^R) \qquad \text{(inductive hypothesis)}$$

$$= (aw^R)u^R \qquad \text{(associativity of concatenation)}$$

$$= (wa)^R u^R \qquad \text{(definition of reversal)}$$

$$= v^R u^R. \qquad\qquad\qquad \blacksquare$$

2.2   Finite Specification of Languages

A language has been defined as a set of strings over an alphabet. Languages of interest do not consist of arbitrary sets of strings but rather of strings that satisfy some prescribed syntactic requirements. The specification of a language requires an unambiguous description of the strings of the language. A finite language can be explicitly defined by enumerating its elements. Several infinite languages with simple syntactic requirements are defined recursively in the examples that follow.

Computation and Reasoning

483

Example 2.2.1

The language L of strings over $\{a, b\}$ in which each string begins with an a and has even length is defined by

i) Basis: aa, $ab \in L$.

ii) Recursive step: If $u \in L$, then uaa, uab, uba, $ubb \in L$.

iii) Closure: A string $u \in L$ only if it can be obtained from the basis elements by a finite number of applications of the recursive step.

The strings in L are built by adjoining two elements to the right-hand side of a previously constructed string. The basis ensures that each string in L begins with an a. Adding substrings of length two maintains the even parity.   □

Example 2.2.2

The language L over the alphabet $\{a, b\}$ defined by

i) Basis: $\lambda \in L$;

ii) Recursive step: If $u \in L$, then ua, $uab \in L$;

iii) Closure: A string $u \in L$ only if it can be obtained from the basis element by a finite number of applications of the recursive step;

consists of strings in which each occurrence of b is immediately preceded by an a. For example, λ, a, $abaab$ are in L and bb, bab, abb are not in L.   □

The recursive step in the preceding examples concatenated elements to the end of an existing string. Breaking a string into substrings permits the addition of elements anywhere within the original string. This technique is illustrated in the following example.

Example 2.2.3

Let L be the language over the alphabet $\{a, b\}$ defined by

i) Basis: $\lambda \in L$.

ii) Recursive step: If $u \in$ and u can be written $u = xyz$, then $xaybz \in L$ and $xaybz \in L$.

iii) Closure: A string $u \in L$ only if it can be obtained from the basis element by a finite number of applications of the recursive step.

The language L consists of all strings with the same number of a's and b's. The first construction in the recursive step, $xaybz \in L$, consists of the following three actions:

1. Select a string u that is already in L.

2. Divide u into three substrings x, y, z such that $u = xyz$. Note that any of the substrings may be λ.

3. Insert an a between x and y and a b between y and z.

Taken together, the two rules can be intuitively interpreted as "insert one a and one b anywhere in the string u."   □

Recursive definitions provide a tool for defining the strings of a language. Examples 2.2.1, 2.2.2, and 2.2.3 have shown that requirements on order, positioning, and parity can be obtained using a recursive generation of strings. The process of generating strings using a single recursive definition, however, is unsuitable for enforcing the complex syntactic requirements of natural or computer languages.

Another technique for constructing languages is to use set operations to construct complex sets of strings from simpler ones. An operation defined on strings can be extended to an operation on sets, hence on languages. Descriptions of infinite languages can then be constructed from finite sets using the set operations. The next two definitions introduce operations on sets of strings that will be used for both language definition and pattern specification.

Definition 2.2.1

The concatenation of languages X and Y, denoted XY, is the language

$$XY = \{uv \mid u \in X \text{ and } v \in Y\}.$$

The concatenation of X with itself n times is denoted X^n. X^0 is defined as $\{\lambda\}$.

Example 2.2.4

Let $X = \{a, b, c\}$ and $Y = \{abb, ba\}$. Then

$$XY = \{aabb, babb, cabb, aba, bba, cba\}$$
$$X^0 = \{\lambda\}$$
$$X^1 = X = \{a, b, c\}$$
$$X^2 = XX = \{aa, ab, ac, ba, bb, bc, ca, cb, cc\}$$
$$X^3 = X^2X = \{aaa, aab, aac, aba, abb, abc, aca, acb, acc,$$
$$baa, bab, bac, bba, bbb, bbc, bca, bcb, bcc,$$
$$caa, cab, cac, cba, cbb, cbc, cca, ccb, ccc\}.$$ □

The sets in the previous example should look familiar. For each i, X^i contains the strings of length i in Σ^* given in Example 2.1.1. This observation leads to another set operation, the Kleene star of a set X, denoted X^*. Using the $*$ operator, the strings over a set can be defined with the operations of concatenation and union rather than with the primitive operation of Definition 2.1.1.

Computation and Reasoning

Definition 2.2.2

Let X be a set. Then

$$X^* = \bigcup_{i=0}^{\infty} X^i \quad \text{and} \quad X^+ = \bigcup_{i=1}^{\infty} X^i.$$

The set X^* contains all strings that can be built from the elements of X. If X is an alphabet, X^+ is the set of all nonnull strings over X. An alternative definition of X^+ using concatenation and the Kleene star is $X^+ = XX^*$.

The definition of a formal language requires an unambiguous specification of the strings that belong to the language. Describing languages informally lacks the rigor required for a precise definition. Consider the language over $\{a, b\}$ consisting of all strings that contain the substring bb. Does this mean that a string in the language contains exactly one occurrence of bb, or are multiple substrings bb permitted? This could be answered by specifically describing the strings as containing exactly one or at least one occurrence of bb. However, these types of questions are inherent in the imprecise medium provided by natural languages.

The precision afforded by set operations can be used to give an unambiguous description of the strings of a language. Example 2.2.5 gives a set theoretic definition of the strings that contain the substring bb. In this definition it is clear that the language contains all strings in which bb occurs at least once.

Example 2.2.5

The language $L = \{a, b\}^*\{bb\}\{a, b\}^*$ consists of the strings over $\{a, b\}$ that contain the substring bb. The concatenation of $\{bb\}$, which contains the single string bb, ensures the presence of bb in every string in L. The sets $\{a, b\}^*$ permit any number of a's and b's, in any order, to precede and follow the occurrence of bb. In particular, additional copies of the substring bb may occur before or after the occurrence ensured by the concatenation of $\{bb\}$. □

Example 2.2.6

Concatenation can be used to specify the order of components of strings. Let L be the language that consists of all strings that begin with aa or end with bb. The set $\{aa\}\{a, b\}^*$ describes the strings with prefix aa. Similarly, $\{a, b\}^*\{bb\}$ is the set of strings with suffix bb. Thus $L = \{aa\}\{a, b\}^* \cup \{a, b\}^*\{bb\}$. □

Example 2.2.7

Let $L_1 = \{bb\}$ and $L_2 = \{\lambda, bb, bbbb\}$ be languages over $\{b\}$. The languages L_1^* and L_2^* both contain precisely the strings consisting of an even number of b's. Note that λ, with length zero, is an element of both L_1^* and L_2^*. □

Example 2.2.8

The set $\{aa, bb, ab, ba\}^*$ consists of all even-length strings over $\{a, b\}$. The repeated concatenation constructs strings by adding two elements at a time. The set of strings of odd length can be defined by $\{a, b\}^* - \{aa, bb, ab, ba\}^*$. This set can also be obtained by concatenating a single element to the even-length strings. Thus the odd-length strings are also defined by $\{aa, bb, ab, ba\}^*\{a, b\}$. □

2.3   Regular Sets and Expressions

In the previous section we used set operations to construct new languages from existing ones. The operators were selected to ensure that certain patterns occurred in the strings of the language. In this section we follow the approach of constructing languages from set operations but limit the sets and operations that are allowed in the construction process.

A set of strings is regular if it can be generated from the empty set, the set containing the null string, and sets containing a single element of the alphabet using union, concatenation, and the Kleene star operation. The regular sets, defined recursively in Definition 2.3.1, comprise a family of languages that play an important role in formal languages, pattern recognition, and the theory of finite-state machines.

Definition 2.3.1

Let Σ be an alphabet. The **regular sets** over Σ are defined recursively as follows:

i) Basis: $\emptyset$, $\{\lambda\}$ and $\{a\}$, for every $a \in \Sigma$, are regular sets over Σ.

ii) Recursive step: Let X and Y be regular sets over Σ. The sets

$$X \cup Y$$
$$XY$$
$$X^*$$

   are regular sets over Σ.

iii) Closure: X is a regular set over Σ only if it can be obtained from the basis elements by a finite number of applications of the recursive step.

A language is called **regular** if it is defined by a regular set. The following examples show how regular sets can be used to describe the strings of a language.

Example 2.3.1

The language from Example 2.2.5, the set of strings containing the substring bb, is a regular set over $\{a, b\}$. From the basis of the definition, $\{a\}$ and $\{b\}$ are regular sets. The union of $\{a\}$ and $\{b\}$ and the Kleene star operation produce $\{a, b\}^*$, the set of all strings over

$\{a, b\}$. By concatenation, $\{b\}\{b\} = \{bb\}$ is regular. Applying concatenation twice yields $\{a, b\}^*\{bb\}\{a, b\}^*$.   □

Example 2.3.2

The set of strings that begin and end with an a and contain at least one b is regular over $\{a, b\}$. The strings in this set could be described intuitively as "an a, followed by any string, followed by a b, followed by any string, followed by an a." The concatenation

$$\{a\}\{a, b\}^*\{b\}\{a, b\}^*\{a\}$$

exhibits the regularity of the set.   □

By definition, regular sets are those that can be built from the empty set, the set containing the null string, and the sets containing a single element of the alphabet using the operations of union, concatenation, and Kleene star. Regular expressions are used to abbreviate the descriptions of regular sets. The regular sets $\emptyset$, $\{\lambda\}$, and $\{a\}$ are represented by $\emptyset$, λ, and a, removing the need for the set brackets $\{\ \}$. The set operations of union, Kleene star, and concatenation are designated by $\cup$, *, and juxtaposition, respectively. Parentheses are used to indicate the order of the operations.

Definition 2.3.2

Let Σ be an alphabet. The **regular expressions** over Σ are defined recursively as follows:

  i) Basis: $\emptyset$, λ, and a, for every $a \in \Sigma$, are regular expressions over Σ.

 ii) Recursive step: Let u and v be regular expressions over Σ. The expressions

$$(u \cup v)$$

$$(uv)$$

$$(u^*)$$

are regular expressions over Σ.

iii) Closure: u is a regular expression over Σ only if it can be obtained from the basis elements by a finite number of applications of the recursive step.

Since union and concatenation are associative, parentheses can be omitted from expressions consisting of a sequence of one of these operations. To further reduce the number of parentheses, a precedence is assigned to the operators. The priority designates the Kleene star as the most binding operation, followed by concatenation and union. Employing these conventions, regular expressions for the sets in Examples 2.3.1 and 2.3.2 are $(a \cup b)^*bb(a \cup b)^*$ and $a(a \cup b)^*b(a \cup b)^*a$, respectively. The notation u^+ is used to abbreviate the expression uu^*. Similarly, u^2 denotes the regular expression uu, u^3 denotes u^2u, and so on.

Example 2.3.3

The set $\{bawab \mid w \in \{a, b\}^*\}$ is regular over $\{a, b\}$. The following table demonstrates the recursive generation of a regular set and the corresponding regular expression definition of the language. The column on the right gives the justification for the regularity of each of the components used in the recursive operations.

Set	Expression	Justification
1. $\{a\}$	a	Basis
2. $\{b\}$	b	Basis
3. $\{a\}\{b\} = \{ab\}$	ab	1, 2, concatenation
4. $\{a\} \cup \{b\} = \{a, b\}$	$a \cup b$	1, 2, union
5. $\{b\}\{a\} = \{ba\}$	ba	2, 1, concatenation
6. $\{a, b\}^*$	$(a \cup b)^*$	4, Kleene star
7. $\{ba\}\{a, b\}^*$	$ba(a \cup b)^*$	5, 6, concatenation
8. $\{ba\}\{a, b\}^*\{ab\}$	$ba(a \cup b)^* ab$	7, 3, concatenation

□

The preceding example illustrates how regular sets and regular expressions are generated from the basic regular sets. Every regular set can be obtained by a finite sequence of operations in the manner shown in Example 2.3.3.

A regular expression defines a pattern and a string is in the language of the expression only if it matches the pattern. Concatenation specifies order; a string w is in uv only if it consists of a string from u followed by one from v. The Kleene star permits repetition and $\cup$ selection. The pattern specified by the regular expression in Example 2.3.3 requires ba to begin the string, ab to end it, and any combination of a's and b's to occur between the required prefix and suffix. The following examples further illustrate the ability of regular expressions to describe patterns.

Example 2.3.4

The regular expressions $(a \cup b)^*aa(a \cup b)^*$ and $(a \cup b)^*bb(a \cup b)^*$ represent the regular sets with strings containing aa and bb, respectively. Combining these two expressions with the $\cup$ operator yields the expression $(a \cup b)^*aa(a \cup b)^* \cup (a \cup b)^*bb(a \cup b)^*$ representing the set of strings over $\{a, b\}$ that contain the substring aa or bb. □

Example 2.3.5

A regular expression for the set of strings over $\{a, b\}$ that contain exactly two b's must explicitly ensure the presence of two b's. Any number of a's may occur before, between, and after the b's. Concatenating the required subexpressions produces $a^*ba^*ba^*$. □

Computation and Reasoning

489

Example 2.3.6

The regular expressions

  i) $a^*ba^*b(a \cup b)^*$

 ii) $(a \cup b)^*ba^*ba^*$

iii) $(a \cup b)^*b(a \cup b)^*b(a \cup b)^*$

define the set of strings over $\{a, b\}$ containing two or more b's. As in Example 2.3.5, the presence of at least two b's is ensured by the two instances of the expression b in the concatenation.   ☐

Example 2.3.7

Consider the regular set defined by the expression $a^*(a^*ba^*ba^*)^*$. The expression inside the parentheses is the regular expression from Example 2.3.5 representing the strings with exactly two b's. The Kleene star generates the concatenation of any number of these strings. The result is the null string (no repetitions of the pattern) and all strings with a positive, even number of b's. Strings consisting of only a's are not included in $(a^*ba^*ba^*)^*$. Concatenating a^* to the beginning of the expression produces the set consisting of all strings with an even number of b's. Another regular expression for this set is $a^*(ba^*ba^*)^*$.   ☐

Example 2.3.8

The ability of substrings to share elements complicates the construction of a regular expression for the set of strings that begin with ba, end with ab, and contain the substring aa. The expression $ba(a \cup b)^*aa(a \cup b)^*ab$ explicitly inserts each of the three components. Every string represented by this expression must contain at least four a's. However, the string $baab$ satisfies the specification but only has two a's. A regular expression for this language is

$$ba(a \cup b)^*aa(a \cup b)^*ab$$
$$\cup \ baa(a \cup b)^*ab$$
$$\cup \ ba(a \cup b)^*aab$$
$$\cup \ baab.$$ ☐

    The construction of a regular expression is a positive process; features of the desired strings are explicitly inserted into the expression using concatenation, union, or the Kleene star. There is no negative operation to omit strings that have a particular property. To construct a regular expression for the set of strings that do not have a property, it is necessary to formulate the condition in a positive manner and construct the regular expression using the reformulation of the language. The next two examples illustrate this approach.

Example 2.3.9

To construct a regular expression for the set of strings over $\{a, b\}$ that do not end in aaa, we must ensure that aaa is not a suffix of any string described by the expression. The possible endings for a string with a b in one of the final three positions are b, ba, or baa. The first part of the regular expression

$$(a \cup b)^*(b \cup ba \cup baa) \cup \lambda \cup a \cup aa$$

defines these strings. The final three expressions represent the special case of strings of length zero, one, and two that do not contain a b.   □

Example 2.3.10

The language L defined by $c^*(b \cup ac^*)^*$ consists of all strings over $\{a, b, c\}$ that do not contain the substring bc. The outer c^* and the ac^* inside the parentheses allow any number of a's and c's to occur in any order. A b can be followed by another b or a string from ac^*. The a at the beginning of ac^* blocks a b from directly preceding a c. To help develop your understanding of the representation of sets by expressions, convince yourself that both $acabacc$ and $bbaaacc$ are in the set represented by $c^*(b \cup ac^*)^*$.   □

Examples 2.3.6 and 2.3.7 show that the regular expression definition of a language is not unique. Two expressions that represent the same set are called *equivalent*. The identities in Table 2.1 can be used to algebraically manipulate regular expressions to construct equivalent expressions. These identities are the regular expression formulation of properties of union, concatenation, and the Kleene star operation.

Identity 5 follows from the commutativity of the union of sets. Identities 9 and 10 are the distributive laws of union and concatenation translated to the regular expression notation. The final set of expressions provides a number of equivalent representations of all strings made from elements of u and v. The identities in Table 2.1 can be used to simplify or to establish the equivalence of regular expressions.

Example 2.3.11

A regular expression is constructed to represent the set of strings over $\{a, b\}$ that do not contain the substring aa. A string in this set may contain a prefix of any number of b's. All a's must be followed by at least one b or terminate the string. The regular expression $b^*(ab^+)^* \cup b^*(ab^+)^*a$ generates the desired set by partitioning it into two disjoint subsets;

TABLE 2.1   Regular Expression Identities

1.	$\emptyset u = u\emptyset = \emptyset$
2.	$\lambda u = u\lambda = u$
3.	$\emptyset^* = \lambda$
4.	$\lambda^* = \lambda$
5.	$u \cup v = v \cup u$
6.	$u \cup \emptyset = u$
7.	$u \cup u = u$
8.	$u^* = (u^*)^*$
9.	$u(v \cup w) = uv \cup uw$
10.	$(u \cup v)w = uw \cup vw$
11.	$(uv)^*u = u(vu)^*$
12.	$(u \cup v)^* = (u^* \cup v)^*$
	$= u^*(u \cup v)^* = (u \cup vu^*)^*$
	$= (u^*v^*)^* = u^*(vu^*)^*$
	$= (u^*v)^*u^*$

the first consists of strings that end in b and the second of strings that end in a. This expression can be simplified using the identities from Table 2.1 as follows:

$$b^*(ab^+)^* \cup b^*(ab^+)^*a$$

$$= b^*(ab^+)^*(\lambda \cup a)$$

$$= b^*(abb^*)^*(\lambda \cup a)$$

$$= (b \cup ab)^*(\lambda \cup a). \qquad \qquad \square$$

While regular expressions allow us to describe many complex patterns, it is important to note that there are languages that cannot be defined by any regular expression. In Chapter 6 we will see that there is no regular expression that defines the language $\{a^i b^i \mid i \geq 0\}$.

2.4   Regular Expressions and Text Searching

A common application of regular expressions, perhaps the most common for the majority of computer users, is the specification of patterns for searching documents and files. In this section we will examine the use of regular expressions in two types of text searching applications.

The major difference between the use of regular expressions for language definition and for text searching is the scope of the desired match. A string is in the language defined by a regular expression if the entire string matches the pattern specified by regular expression.

For example, a string matches ab^+ only if it begins with an a and is followed by one or more b's.

In text searching we are looking for the occurrence of a substring in the text that matches the desired pattern. Thus the words

about

abbot

rehabilitate

tabulate

abominable

would all be considered to match the pattern ab^+. In fact, abominable would match it twice!

This brings up a difference between two types of text searching that can be described (somewhat simplistically) as off-line and online searching. By off-line search we mean that a search program is run, the input to the program is a pattern and a file, and the output consists of the lines or the text in the file that match the pattern. Frequently, off-line file searching is done using operating system utilities or programs written in a language designed for searching. GREP and awk are examples of the utilities available for file searching, and Perl is a programming language designed for file searching. We will use GREP, which is an acronym for "Global search for Regular Expression and Print," to illustrate this type of regular expression search.

Online search tools are provided by web browsers, text editors, and word processing systems. The objective is to interactively find the first, the next, or to sequentially find all occurrences of substrings that match the search pattern. The "Find" command in Microsoft Word will be used to demonstrate the differences between online and off-line pattern matching.

Since the desired patterns are generally entered on a keyboard, the regular expression notation used by search utilities should be concise and not contain superscripts. Although there is no uniform syntax for regular expressions in search applications, the notation used in the majority of the applications has many features in common. We will use the extended regular expression notation of GREP to illustrate the description of patterns for text searching.

The alphabet of the file or document frequently consists of the ASCII character set, which is given in Appendix III. This is considerably larger than the two or three element alphabets that we have used in most of our examples of regular expressions. With the alphabet $\{a, b\}$, the regular expression for any string is $(a \cup b)^*$. To write the expression for any string of ASCII characters using this format would require several lines and would be extremely inconvenient to enter on a keyboard. Two notational conventions, bracket expressions and range expressions, were introduced to facilitate the description of patterns over an extended alphabet.

The bracket notation [ ] is used to represent the union of alphabet symbols. For example, [abcd] is equivalent to the expression $(a \cup b \cup c \cup d)$. Adding a caret immediately

TABLE 2.2   Extended Regular Expression Operations

Operation	Symbol	Example	Regular Expression
concatenation		ab	ab
		[a-c][AB]	$aA \cup aB \cup bA \cup bB \cup cA \cup cB$
Kleene star	*	[ab]*	$(a \cup b)^*$
disjunction	|	[ab]*|A	$(a \cup b)^* \cup A$
zero or more	+	[ab]+	$(a \cup b)^+$
zero or one	?	a?	$(a \cup \lambda)$
one character	.	a.a	$a(a \cup b)a \qquad$ if $\Sigma = \{a, b\}$
n-times	{n}	a{4}	$aaaa = a^4$
n or more times	{n,}	a{4,}	$aaaaa^*$
n to m times	{n,m}	a{4,6}	$aaaa \cup aaaaa \cup aaaaaa$

after the left bracket produces the complement of the union, thus [^abcd] designates all characters other than a, b, c, and d.

Range expressions use the ordering of the ASCII character set to describe a sequence of characters. For example, A-Z is the range expression that designates all capital letters. In the ASCII table these are the characters numbered from 65 to 90. Range expressions can be arguments in bracket expressions; [a-zA-Z0-9] represents the set of all letters and digits. In addition, certain frequently occurring subsets of characters are given there own mnemonic identifiers. For example, [:digit:], [:alpha:], and [:alnum:] are shorthand for [0-9], [a-zA-Z], and [a-zA-Z0-9]. The extended regular expression notation also includes symbols \< and \> that require the match to occur at the beginning or the end of a word.

Along with the standard operations of ∪, concatenation, and *, the extended regular expression notation of GREP contains additional operations on expressions. These operations do not extend the type of patterns that can be expressed, rather they are introduced to simplify the representation of patterns. A description of the extended regular expression operations are given in Table 2.2. A set of priorities and parentheses combine to define the scope of the operations.

The input to GREP is a pattern and file to be searched. GREP performs a line-by-line search on the file. If a line contains a substring that matches the pattern, the line is printed and the search continues with the subsequent line. To demonstrate pattern matching using extended regular expressions, we will search a file caesar containing Caesar's comments to his wife in Shakespeare's *Julius Caesar*, Act 2, Scene 2.

```
Cowards die many times before their deaths;
The valiant never taste of death but once.
Of all the wonders that I yet have heard.
It seems to me most strange that men should fear;
```

Computation and Reasoning

```
Seeing that death, a necessary end,
Will come when it will come.
```

We begin by looking for matches of the pattern m[a-z]n. This is matched by a substring of length three consisting of an m and an n separated by any single lowercase letter. The result of the search is

```
C:> grep -E "m[a-z]n" caesar
Cowards die many times before their deaths;
It seems to me most strange that men should fear;
```

The option -E in the GREP call indicates that the extended regular expression notation is used to describe the pattern, and the quotation marks delimit the pattern. The substring man in many and the word men match this pattern and the lines containing these strings are printed.

The search is now changed to find occurrences of m and n separated by any number of lowercase letters and blanks.

```
C:> grep -E "m[a-z ]*n" caesar
Cowards die many times before their deaths;
It seems to me most strange that men should fear;
Will come when it will come.
```

The final line is added to the output because the pattern is matched by the substring me when. The pattern m[a-z]*n is matched six times in the line

```
It seems to me most strange that men should fear;
```

However, GREP does not need to find all matches; finding one is sufficient for a line to be selected for output.

The extended regular expression notation can be used to describe more complicated patterns of interest that may occur in text. Consider the task of finding lines in a text file that contain a person's name. To determine the form of names, we initially consider the potential strings that occur as parts of a name:

  i) First name or initial: [A-Z][a-z]+|[A-Z][.]

  ii) Middle name, initial, or neither: ([A-Z][a-z]+|[A-Z][.])?

  iii) Family name: [A-Z][a-z]+

A string that can occur in the first position is either a name or an initial. In the former case, the string begins with a capital letter followed by a string of lowercase letters. An initial is simply a capital letter followed by a period. The same expressions can be used for middle names and family names. The ? indicates that no middle name or initial is required. These expressions are concatenated with blanks

  ([A-Z][a-z]+|[A-Z][.])[ ](([A-Z][a-z]+|[A-Z][.])[ ])?([A-Z][a-z]+)

to produce a general pattern for matching names.

Computation and Reasoning

495

The preceding expression will match E. B. White, Edgar Allen Poe, and Alan Turing. Since pattern matching is restricted to the form of the strings and not any underlying meaning (that is, pattern matching checks syntax and not semantics), the expression will also match Buckingham Palace and U. S. Mail. Moreover, the pattern will not match Vincent van Gogh, Dr. Watson, or Aristotle. Additional conditions would need to be added to the expression to match these variations of names.

Unlike off-line analysis, search commands in web browsers or word processors interactively find occurrences of strings that match an input pattern. A substring matching a pattern may span several lines. The pattern m*n in the Microsoft Word "Find" command searches for substrings beginning with m and ending with n; any string may separate the m and n. The search finds and highlights the first substring beginning at or after the current location of the cursor that matches the pattern. Repeating the search by clicking "next" highlights successive matches of the pattern. The substrings identified as matches of m*n in the file caesar follow, with the matching substrings highlighted.

> Cowards die *many* times before their deaths;
>
> Cowards die many ti*mes before their deaths;*
> *The valiant ne*ver taste of death but once.
>
> It see*ms to me most stran*ge that men should fear;
>
> It seems to *me most stran*ge that men should fear;
>
> It seems to me *most stran*ge that men should fear;
>
> It seems to me most strange that *men* should fear;
>
> Will co*me when* it will come.

Notice that not all matching substrings are highlighted. The pattern m*n is matched by any substring that begins with an occurrence of m and extends to any subsequent occurrence of n. The search only highlights the first matching substring for every m in the file.

In Chapter 6 we will see that a regular expression can be converted into a finite-state machine. The computation of the resulting machine will find the strings or substrings that match the pattern described by the expression. The restrictions on the operations used in regular expressions—intersection and set difference are not allowed—facilitate the automatic conversion from the description of a pattern to the implementation of a search algorithm.

Exercises

1. Give a recursive definition of the length of a string over Σ. Use the primitive operation from the definition of string.

Computation and Reasoning

2. Using induction on i, prove that $(w^R)^i = (w^i)^R$ for any string w and all $i \geq 0$.

3. Prove, using induction on the length of the string, that $(w^R)^R = w$ for all strings $w \in \Sigma^*$.

4. Let $X = \{aa, bb\}$ and $Y = \{\lambda, b, ab\}$.

   a) List the strings in the set XY.

   b) How many strings of length 6 are there in X^*?

   c) List the strings in the set Y^* of length three or less.

   d) List the strings in the set X^*Y^* of length four or less.

5. Let L be the set of strings over $\{a, b\}$ generated by the recursive definition

      i) Basis: $b \in L$.

      ii) Recursive step: if u is in L then $ub \in L$, $uab \in L$, and $uba \in L$, and $bua \in L$.

      iii) Closure: a string v is in L only if it can be obtained from the basis by a finite number of iterations of the recursive step.

   a) List the elements in the sets L_0, L_1, and L_2.

   b) Is the string $bbaaba$ in L? If so, trace how it is produced. If not, explain why not.

   c) Is the string $bbaaaabb$ in L? If so, trace how it is produced. If not, explain why not.

6. Give a recursive definition of the set of strings over $\{a, b\}$ that contain at least one b and have an even number of a's before the first b. For example, bab, aab, and $aaaababababab$ are in the set, while aa, abb are not.

7. Give a recursive definition of the set $\{a^i b^j \mid 0 \leq i \leq j \leq 2i\}$.

8. Give a recursive definition of the set of strings over $\{a, b\}$ that contain twice as many a's as b's.

9. Prove that every string in the language defined in Example 2.2.1 has even length. The proof is by induction on the recursive generation of the strings.

10. Prove that every string in the language defined in Example 2.2.2 has at least as many a's as b's. Let $n_a(u)$ denote the number of a's in the string u and $n_b(u)$ denote the number of b's in u. The inductive proof should establish the inequality $n_a(u) \geq n_b(u)$.

11. Let L be the language over $\{a, b\}$ generated by the recursive definition

      i) Basis: $\lambda \in L$.

      ii) Recursive step: If $u \in L$ then $aaub \in L$.

      iii) Closure: A string w is in L only if it can be obtained from the basis by a finite number of applications of the recursive step.

   a) Give the sets L_0, L_1, and L_2 generated by the recursive definition.

   b) Give an implicit definition of the set of strings defined by the recursive definition.

   c) Prove by mathematical induction that for every string u in L, the number of a's in u is twice the number b's in u. Let $n_a(u)$ and $n_b(u)$ denote the number of a's and the number of b's in u, respectively.

Computation and Reasoning

* 12. A **palindrome** over an alphabet Σ is a string in Σ* that is spelled the same forward and backward. The set of palindromes over Σ can be defined recursively as follows:

   i) Basis: λ and a, for all $a \in \Sigma$, are palindromes.

   ii) Recursive step: If w is a palindrome and $a \in \Sigma$, then awa is a palindrome.

   iii) Closure: w is a palindrome only if it can be obtained from the basis elements by a finite number of applications of the recursive step.

   The set of palindromes can also be defined by $\{w \mid w = w^R\}$. Prove that these two definitions generate the same set.

13. Let $L_1 = \{aaa\}^*$, $L_2 = \{a, b\}\{a, b\}\{a, b\}\{a, b\}$, and $L_3 = L_2^*$. Describe the strings that are in the languages L_2, L_3, and $L_1 \cap L_3$.

For Exercises 14 through 38, give a regular expression that represents the described set.

14. The set of strings over $\{a, b, c\}$ in which all the a's precede the b's, which in turn precede the c's. It is possible that there are no a's, b's, or c's.

15. The same set as Exercise 14 without the null string.

16. The set of strings over $\{a, b, c\}$ with length three.

17. The set of strings over $\{a, b, c\}$ with length less than three.

18. The set of strings over $\{a, b, c\}$ with length greater than three.

19. The set of strings over $\{a, b\}$ that contain the substring ab and have length greater than two.

20. The set of strings of length two or more over $\{a, b\}$ in which all the a's precede the b's.

21. The set of strings over $\{a, b\}$ that contain the substring aa and the substring bb.

22. The set of strings over $\{a, b\}$ in which the substring aa occurs at least twice. *Hint:* Beware of the substring aaa.

23. The set of strings over $\{a, b, c\}$ that begin with a, contain exactly two b's, and end with cc.

* 24. The set of strings over $\{a, b\}$ that contain the substring ab and the substring ba.

25. The set of strings over $\{a, b, c\}$ in which every b is immediately followed by at least one c.

26. The set of strings over $\{a, b\}$ in which the number of a's is divisible by three.

27. The set of strings over $\{a, b, c\}$ in which the total number of b's and c's is three.

* 28. The set of strings over $\{a, b\}$ in which every a is either immediately preceded or immediately followed by b, for example, $baab$, aba, and b.

29. The set of strings over $\{a, b, c\}$ that do not contain the substring aa.

30. The set of strings over $\{a, b\}$ that do not begin with the substring aaa.

31. The set of strings over $\{a, b\}$ that do not contain the substring aaa.

* 32. The set of strings over $\{a, b\}$ that do not contain the substring aba.

Computation and Reasoning

33. The set of strings over $\{a, b\}$ in which the substring aa occurs exactly once.

34. The set of strings of odd length over $\{a, b\}$ that contain the substring bb.

35. The set of strings of even length over $\{a, b, c\}$ that contain exactly one a.

36. The set of strings of odd length over $\{a, b\}$ that contain exactly two b's.

37. The set of strings over $\{a, b\}$ with an even number of a's or an odd number of b's.

* 38. The set of strings over $\{a, b\}$ with an even number of a's and an even number of b's. This is tricky; a strategy for constructing this expression is presented in Chapter 6.

39. Use the regular expression identities in Table 2.1 to establish the following identities:

    a) $(ba)^+(a^*b^* \cup a^*) = (ba)^*ba^+(b^* \cup \lambda)$

    b) $b^+(a^*b^* \cup \lambda)b = b(b^*a^* \cup \lambda)b^+$

    c) $(a \cup b)^* = (a \cup b)^*b^*$

    d) $(a \cup b)^* = (a^* \cup ba^*)^*$

    e) $(a \cup b)^* = (b^*(a \cup \lambda)b^*)^*$

40. Write the output that would be printed by a search of the file caesar described in Section 2.4 with the following extended regular expressions.

    a) `[Cc]`

    b) `[K-Z]`

    c) `\<[a-z]{6}\>`

    d) `\<[a-z]{6}\>|\<[a-z]{7}\>`

41. Design an extended regular expression to search for addresses. For this exercise, an address will consist of

    i) a number,

    ii) a street name, and

    iii) a street type identifier or abbreviation.

Your pattern should match addresses of the form `1428 Elm Street`, `51095 Tobacco Rd.`, and `1600 Pennsylvania Avenue`. Do not be concerned if your regular expression does not identify all possible addresses.

Bibliographic Notes

Regular expressions were developed by Kleene [1956] for studying the properties of neural networks. McNaughton and Yamada [1960] proved that the regular sets are closed under the operations of intersection and complementation. An axiomatization of the algebra of regular expressions can be found in Salomaa [1966].

CHAPTER 3

Context-Free Grammars

In this chapter we present a rule-based approach for generating the strings of a language. Borrowing the terminology of natural languages, we call a syntactically correct string a **sentence** of the language. A small subset of the English language is used to illustrate the components of the string-generation process. The alphabet of our miniature language is the set {*a, the, John, Jill, hamburger, car, drives, eats, slowly, frequently, big, juicy, brown*}. The elements of the alphabet are called the **terminal symbols** of the language. Capitalization, punctuation, and other important features of written languages are ignored in this example.

The sentence-generation procedure should construct the strings *John eats a hamburger* and *Jill drives frequently*. Strings of the form *Jill* and *car John slowly* should not result from this process. Additional symbols are used during the construction of sentences to enforce the syntactic restrictions of the language. These intermediate symbols, known as **variables** or **nonterminals**, are represented by enclosing them in angle brackets ⟨ ⟩.

Since the generation procedure constructs sentences, the initial variable is named ⟨*sentence*⟩. The generation of a sentence consists of replacing variables by strings of a specific form. Syntactically correct replacements are given by a set of transformation rules. Two possible rules for the variable ⟨*sentence*⟩ are

1. ⟨*sentence*⟩ → ⟨*noun-phrase*⟩⟨*verb-phrase*⟩

2. ⟨*sentence*⟩ → ⟨*noun-phrase*⟩⟨*verb*⟩⟨*direct-object-phrase*⟩

An informal interpretation of rule 1 is that a sentence may be formed by a noun phrase followed by a verb phrase. At this point, of course, neither of the variables ⟨*noun-phrase*⟩ nor ⟨*verb-phrase*⟩ has been defined. The second rule gives an alternative definition of sentence, a noun phrase followed by a verb followed by a direct object phrase. The existence of multiple transformations indicates that syntactically correct sentences may have several different forms.

65

A noun phrase may contain either a proper or a common noun. A common noun is preceded by a determiner, while a proper noun stands alone. This feature of the syntax of the English language is represented by rules 3 and 4.

Rules for the variables that generate noun and verb phrases are given below. Rather than rewriting the left-hand side of alternative rules for the same variable, we list the right-hand sides of the rules sequentially. Numbering the rules is not a feature of the generation process, merely a notational convenience.

3. ⟨noun-phrase⟩ → ⟨proper-noun⟩
4.   → ⟨determiner⟩⟨common-noun⟩
5. ⟨proper-noun⟩ → John
6.   → Jill
7. ⟨common-noun⟩ → car
8.   → hamburger
9. ⟨determiner⟩ → a
10.   → the
11. ⟨verb-phrase⟩ → ⟨verb⟩⟨adverb⟩
12.   → ⟨verb⟩
13. ⟨verb⟩ → drives
14.   → eats
15. ⟨adverb⟩ → slowly
16.   → frequently

With the exception of ⟨direct-object-phrase⟩, rules have been defined for each of the variables that have been introduced.

The application of a rule transforms one string to another. The transformation consists of replacing an occurrence of the variable on the left-hand side of the → with the string on the right-hand side. The generation of a sentence consists of repeated rule applications to transform the variable ⟨sentence⟩ into a string of terminal symbols.

For example, the sentence *Jill drives frequently* is generated by the following transformations:

Derivation	Rule Applied
⟨sentence⟩ ⇒ ⟨noun-phrase⟩⟨verb-phrase⟩	1
⇒ ⟨proper-noun⟩⟨verb-phrase⟩	3
⇒ Jill ⟨verb-phrase⟩	6
⇒ Jill ⟨verb⟩⟨adverb⟩	11
⇒ Jill drives ⟨adverb⟩	13
⇒ Jill drives frequently	16

The symbol ⇒, used to designate a rule application, is read "derives." The column on the right gives the number of the rule that was applied to achieve the transformation. The derivation terminates when all variables have been removed from the derived string. The resulting string, consisting solely of terminal symbols, is a sentence of the language. The set of terminal strings derivable from the variable ⟨*sentence*⟩ is the language generated by the rules of our example.

To complete the set of rules, the transformations for ⟨*direct-object-phrase*⟩ must be given. Before designing rules, we must decide upon the form of the strings that we wish to generate. In our language we will allow the possibility of any number of adjectives, including repetitions, to precede the direct object. This requires a set of rules capable of generating each of the following strings:

John eats a hamburger

John eats a big hamburger

John eats a big juicy hamburger

John eats a big brown juicy hamburger

John eats a big big brown juicy hamburger

As can be seen by the potential repetition of the adjectives, the rules of the grammar must be capable of generating strings of arbitrary length. The use of a recursive definition allows the elements of an infinite set to be generated by a finite specification. Following that example, recursion is introduced into the string-generation process, that is, into the rules.

17. ⟨*adjective-list*⟩ → ⟨*adjective*⟩⟨*adjective-list*⟩
18.   → λ
19. ⟨*adjective*⟩ → *big*
20.   → *juicy*
21.   → *brown*

The definition of ⟨*adjective-list*⟩ follows the standard recursive pattern. Rule 17 defines ⟨*adjective-list*⟩ in terms of itself, while rule 18 provides the basis of the recursive definition. The λ on the right-hand side of rule 18 indicates that the application of this rule replaces ⟨*adjective-list*⟩ with the null string. Repeated applications of rule 17 generate a sequence of adjectives. Rules for ⟨*direct-object-phrase*⟩ are constructed using ⟨*adjective-list*⟩:

22. ⟨*direct-object-phrase*⟩ → ⟨*adjective-list*⟩⟨*proper-noun*⟩
23.   → ⟨*determiner*⟩⟨*adjective-list*⟩⟨*common-noun*⟩

Computation and Reasoning

503

The sentence *John eats a big juicy hamburger* can be derived by the following sequence of rule applications:

Derivation	Rule Applied
⟨sentence⟩ ⟹ ⟨noun-phrase⟩ ⟨verb⟩ ⟨direct-object-phrase⟩	2
⟹ ⟨proper-noun⟩ ⟨verb⟩ ⟨direct-object-phrase⟩	3
⟹ John ⟨verb⟩ ⟨direct-object-phrase⟩	5
⟹ John eats ⟨direct-object-phrase⟩	14
⟹ John eats ⟨determiner⟩ ⟨adjective-list⟩ ⟨common-noun⟩	23
⟹ John eats a ⟨adjective-list⟩ ⟨common-noun⟩	9
⟹ John eats a ⟨adjective⟩ ⟨adjective-list⟩ ⟨common-noun⟩	17
⟹ John eats a big ⟨adjective-list⟩ ⟨common-noun⟩	19
⟹ John eats a big ⟨adjective⟩ ⟨adjective-list⟩ ⟨common-noun⟩	17
⟹ John eats a big juicy ⟨adjective-list⟩ ⟨common-noun⟩	20
⟹ John eats a big juicy ⟨common-noun⟩	18
⟹ John eats a big juicy hamburger	8

The generation of sentences is strictly a function of the rules. The string *the car eats slowly* is a sentence in the language since it has the form ⟨noun-phrase⟩ ⟨verb-phrase⟩ outlined by rule 1. This illustrates the important distinction between syntax and semantics; the generation of sentences is concerned with the form of the derived string without regard to any underlying meaning that may be associated with the terminal symbols.

By rules 3 and 4, a noun phrase consists of a proper noun or a common noun preceded by a determiner. The variable ⟨adjective-list⟩ may be incorporated into the ⟨noun-phrase⟩ rules, permitting adjectives to modify a noun:

3′. ⟨noun-phrase⟩ → ⟨adjective-list⟩ ⟨proper-noun⟩

4′.   → ⟨determiner⟩ ⟨adjective-list⟩ ⟨common-noun⟩

With this modification, the string *big John eats frequently* can be derived from the variable ⟨sentence⟩.

3.1   Context-Free Grammars and Languages

We will now define a formal system, the context-free grammar, that is used to generate the strings of a language. The natural language example was presented to motivate the components and features of string generation using a context-free grammar.

Definition 3.1.1

A **context-free grammar** is a quadruple (V, Σ, P, S) where V is a finite set of variables, Σ (the alphabet) is a finite set of terminal symbols, P is a finite set of rules, and S is a distinguished element of V called the start symbol. The sets V and Σ are assumed to be disjoint.

A **rule** is written $A \rightarrow w$ where $A \in V$ and $w \in (V \cup \Sigma)^*$. A rule of this form is called an A rule, referring to the variable on the left-hand side. Since the null string is in $(V \cup \Sigma)^*$, λ may occur on the right-hand side of a rule. A rule of the form $A \rightarrow \lambda$ is called a **null** or λ-**rule**.

Italics are used to denote the variables and terminals of a context-free grammar. Terminals are represented by lowercase letters occurring at the beginning of the alphabet, that is, a, b, c, ... Following the conventions introduced for strings, the letters p, q, u, v, w, x, y, z, with or without subscripts, represent arbitrary members of $(V \cup \Sigma)^*$. Variables will be denoted by capital letters. As in the natural language example, variables are referred to as the *nonterminal symbols* of the grammar.

Grammars are used to generate properly formed strings over the prescribed alphabet. The fundamental step in the generation process consists of transforming a string by the application of a rule. The application of $A \rightarrow w$ to the variable A in uAv produces the string uwv. This is denoted $uAv \Rightarrow uwv$. The prefix u and suffix v define the *context* in which the variable A occurs. The grammars introduced in this chapter are called context-free because of the general applicability of the rules. An A rule can be applied to the variable A whenever and wherever it occurs; the context places no limitations on the applicability of a rule.

A string w is derivable from v if there is a finite sequence of rule applications that transforms v to w; that is, if a sequence of transformations

$$v \Rightarrow w_1 \Rightarrow w_2 \Rightarrow \cdots \Rightarrow w_n = w$$

can be constructed from the rules of the grammar. The derivability of w from v is denoted $v \overset{*}{\Rightarrow} w$. The set of strings derivable from v, being constructed by a finite but unbounded number of rule applications, can be defined recursively.

Definition 3.1.2

Let $G = (V, \Sigma, P, S)$ be a context-free grammar and $v \in (V \cup \Sigma)^*$. The set of strings **derivable** from v is defined recursively as follows:

i)   Basis: v is derivable from v.

ii) Recursive step: If $u = xAy$ is derivable from v and $A \rightarrow w \in P$, then xwy is derivable from v.

iii) Closure: A string is derivable from v only if it can be generated from v by a finite number of applications of the recursive step.

Note that the definition of a rule uses the $\rightarrow$ notation, while its application uses $\Rightarrow$. The symbol $\overset{*}{\Rightarrow}$ denotes derivability and $\overset{+}{\Rightarrow}$ designates derivability utilizing one or more rule applications. The length of a derivation is the number of rule applications employed. A derivation of w from v of length n is denoted $v \overset{n}{\Rightarrow} w$. When more than one grammar is being considered, the notation $v \overset{*}{\Rightarrow} w$ will be used to explicitly indicate that the derivation utilizes rules of the grammar G.

A language has been defined as a set of strings over an alphabet. A grammar consists of an alphabet and a method of generating strings. These strings may contain both variables and terminals. The start symbol of the grammar, assuming the role of ⟨sentence⟩ in the natural language example, initiates the process of generating acceptable strings. The language of the grammar G is the set of terminal strings derivable from the start symbol. We now state this as a definition.

Definition 3.1.3

Let $G = (V, \Sigma, P, S)$ be a context-free grammar.

i) A string $w \in (V \cup \Sigma)^*$ is a **sentential form** of G if there is a derivation $S \overset{*}{\Rightarrow} w$ in G.

ii) A string $w \in \Sigma^*$ is a **sentence** of G if there is a derivation $S \overset{*}{\Rightarrow} w$ in G.

iii) The **language** of G, denoted L(G), is the set $\{w \in \Sigma^* \mid S \overset{*}{\Rightarrow} w\}$.

A sentential form is a string that is derivable from the start symbol of the grammar. Referring back to the natural language example, the derivation

$$\langle sentence \rangle \Rightarrow \langle noun\text{-}phrase \rangle \langle verb\text{-}phrase \rangle$$
$$\Rightarrow \langle proper\text{-}noun \rangle \langle verb\text{-}phrase \rangle$$
$$\Rightarrow Jill \langle verb\text{-}phrase \rangle$$

shows that *Jill* ⟨verb-phrase⟩ is a sentential form of that grammar. It is not yet a sentence, it still contains variables, but it has the form of a sentence. A sentence is a sentential form that contains only terminal symbols. The language of a grammar consists of the sentences generated by the grammar. A set of strings over an alphabet Σ is said to be a **context-free language** if it is generated by a context-free grammar.

The use of recursion is necessary for a finite set of rules to generate strings of arbitrary length and languages with infinitely many strings. Recursion is introduced into grammars through the rules. A rule of the form $A \rightarrow uAv$ is called **recursive** since it defines the variable A in terms of itself. Rules of the form $A \rightarrow Av$ and $A \rightarrow uA$ are called *left-recursive* and *right-recursive*, respectively, indicating the location of recursion in the rule.

Because of the importance of recursive rules, we examine the form of strings produced by repeated applications of the recursive rules $A \rightarrow aAb$, $A \rightarrow aA$, $A \rightarrow Ab$, and $A \rightarrow AA$:

$A \Rightarrow aAb$	$A \Rightarrow aA$	$A \Rightarrow Ab$	$A \Rightarrow AA$
$\Rightarrow aAb$	$\Rightarrow aA$	$\Rightarrow Ab$	$\Rightarrow AAA$
$\Rightarrow aaAbb$	$\Rightarrow aaA$	$\Rightarrow Abb$	$\Rightarrow AAAA$
$\Rightarrow aaaAbbb$	$\Rightarrow aaaA$	$\Rightarrow Abbb$	$\Rightarrow AAAAA$
$\vdots$	$\vdots$	$\vdots$	$\vdots$

A derivation employing the rule $A \rightarrow aAb$ generates any number of a's followed by the same number of b's. Rules of this form are necessary for producing strings that contain symbols in

$$G = (V, \Sigma, P, S)$$
$$V = \{S, A\}$$
$$\Sigma = \{a, b\}$$
$$P: \quad S \to AA$$
$$A \to AAA \mid bA \mid Ab \mid a$$

$S \Rightarrow AA$	$S \Rightarrow AA$	$S \Rightarrow AA$	$S \Rightarrow AA$
$\Rightarrow aA$	$\Rightarrow AAAA$	$\Rightarrow Aa$	$\Rightarrow aA$
$\Rightarrow aAAA$	$\Rightarrow aAAA$	$\Rightarrow AAAa$	$\Rightarrow aAAA$
$\Rightarrow abAAA$	$\Rightarrow abAAA$	$\Rightarrow AAbAa$	$\Rightarrow aAAa$
$\Rightarrow abaAA$	$\Rightarrow abaAA$	$\Rightarrow AAbaa$	$\Rightarrow abAAa$
$\Rightarrow ababAA$	$\Rightarrow ababAA$	$\Rightarrow AbAbaa$	$\Rightarrow abAbAa$
$\Rightarrow ababaA$	$\Rightarrow ababaA$	$\Rightarrow Ababaa$	$\Rightarrow ababAa$
$\Rightarrow ababaa$	$\Rightarrow ababaa$	$\Rightarrow ababaa$	$\Rightarrow ababaa$
(a)	(b)	(c)	(d)

FIGURE 3.1   Sample derivations of *ababaa* in G.

matched pairs, such as left and right parentheses. The right recursive rule $A \to aA$ generates any number of a's preceding the variable A, and the left recursive $A \to Ab$ generates any number of b's following A. Each application of the rule $A \to AA$, which is both left- and right-recursive, produces an additional A. The repetitive application of a recursive rule can be terminated at any time by the application of a different A rule.

A variable A is called *recursive* if there is a derivation $A \overset{+}{\Rightarrow} uAv$. A derivation of the form $A \Rightarrow w \overset{+}{\Rightarrow} uAv$, where A is not in w, is said to be *indirectly recursive*. Note that, due to indirect recursion, a variable A may be recursive even if there are no recursive A rules.

A grammar G that generates the language consisting of strings with a positive, even number of a's is given in Figure 3.1. The rules are written using the shorthand $A \to u \mid v$ to abbreviate $A \to u$ and $A \to v$. The vertical bar $\mid$ is read "or." Four distinct derivations of the terminal string *ababaa* are shown in Figure 3.1. The definition of derivation permits the transformation of any variable in the string. Each rule application in derivations (a) and (b) in the figure transforms the first variable occurring in a left-to-right reading of the string. Derivations with this property are called *leftmost*. Derivation (c) is *rightmost*, since the rightmost variable has a rule applied to it. These derivations demonstrate that there may be more than one derivation of a string in a context-free grammar.

Figure 3.1 exhibits the flexibility of derivations in a context-free grammar. The essential feature of a derivation is not the order in which the rules are applied, but the manner in which each variable is transformed into a terminal string. The transformation is graphically depicted by a derivation or parse tree. The tree structure indicates the rule applied to each variable but does not designate the order of the rule applications. The leaves of the derivation tree can be ordered to yield the result of a derivation represented by the tree.

Definition 3.1.4

Let $G = (V, \Sigma, P, S)$ be a context-free grammar and let $S \overset{*}{\Rightarrow} w$ be a derivation in G. The **derivation tree**, DT, of $S \overset{*}{\Rightarrow} w$ is an ordered tree that can be built iteratively as follows:

i) Initialize DT with root S.

Computation and Reasoning

ii) If $A \to x_1 x_2 \ldots x_n$ with $x_i \in (V \cup \Sigma)$ is the rule in the derivation applied to the string uAv, then add $x_1, x_2, \ldots, x_n$ as the children of A in the tree.

iii) If $A \to \lambda$ is the rule in the derivation applied to the string uAv, then add λ as the only child of A in the tree.

The ordering of the leaves also follows this iterative process. Initially, the only leaf is S and the ordering is obvious. When the rule $A \to x_1 x_2 \ldots x_n$ is used to generate the children of A, each x_i becomes a leaf and A is replaced in the ordering of the leaves by the sequence $x_1, x_2, \ldots, x_n$. The application of a rule $A \to \lambda$ simply replaces A by the null string. Figure 3.2 traces the construction of the tree corresponding to derivation (a) of Figure 3.1. The ordering of the leaves is given along with each of the trees.

The order of the leaves in a derivation tree is independent of the derivation from which the tree was generated. The ordering provided by the iterative process is identical to the ordering of the leaves given by the relation LEFTOF in Section 1.8. The frontier of the derivation tree is the string generated by the derivation.

Figure 3.3 gives the derivation trees for each of the derivations in Figure 3.1. The trees generated by derivations (a) and (d) are identical, indicating that each variable is transformed into a terminal string in the same manner. The only difference between these derivations is the order of the rule applications.

A derivation tree can be used to produce several derivations that generate the same string. The rule applied to a variable A can be reconstructed from the children of A in the tree. The rightmost derivation

$$
\begin{aligned}
S &\Rightarrow AA \\
&\Rightarrow AAAA \\
&\Rightarrow AAAa \\
&\Rightarrow AAbAa \\
&\Rightarrow AAbaa \\
&\Rightarrow AbAbaa \\
&\Rightarrow Ababaa \\
&\Rightarrow ababaa
\end{aligned}
$$

is obtained from the derivation tree (a) in Figure 3.3. Notice that this derivation is different from the rightmost derivation (c) in Figure 3.1. In the latter derivation, the second variable in the string AA is transformed using the rule $A \to a$, while $A \to AAA$ is used in the preceding derivation. The two trees graphically illustrate the distinct transformations.

As we have seen, the context-free applicability of rules allows a great deal of flexibility in the constructions of derivations. Lemma 3.1.5 shows that a derivation may be broken into subderivations from each variable in the string. Derivability was defined recursively, the length of derivations being finite but unbounded. Consequently, we may use mathematical induction to establish that a property holds for all derivations from a given string.

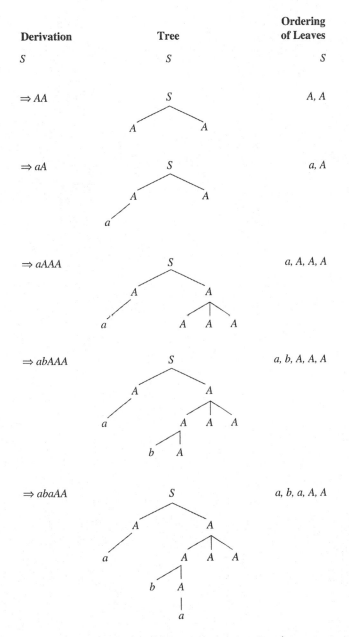

Derivation	Tree	Ordering of Leaves
S	S	S
$\Rightarrow AA$		A, A
$\Rightarrow aA$		a, A
$\Rightarrow aAAA$		a, A, A, A
$\Rightarrow abAAA$		a, b, A, A, A
$\Rightarrow abaAA$		a, b, a, A, A

FIGURE 3.2   Construction of derivation tree. *(continued on next page)*

Computation and Reasoning

509

Derivation	Tree	Ordering of Leaves
$\Rightarrow ababAA$		a, b, a, b, A, A
$\Rightarrow ababaA$		a, b, a, b, a, A
$\Rightarrow ababaa$		a, b, a, b, a, a

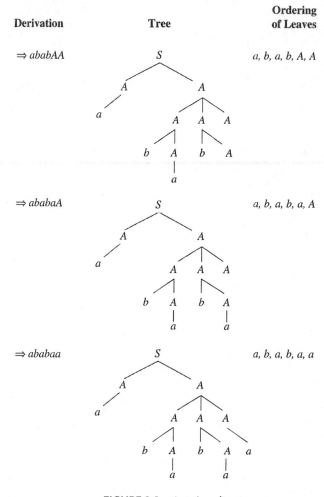

FIGURE 3.2   *(continued)*

Lemma 3.1.5

Let G be a context-free grammar and $v \overset{n}{\Rightarrow} w$ be a derivation in G where v can be written

$$v = w_1 A_1 w_2 A_2 \ldots w_k A_k w_{k+1},$$

with $w_i \in \Sigma^*$. Then there are strings $p_i \in (\Sigma \cup V)^*$ that satisfy

i) $A_i \overset{t_i}{\Rightarrow} p_i$

ii) $w = w_1 p_1 w_2 p_2 \ldots w_k p_k w_{k+1}$

iii) $\displaystyle\sum_{i=1}^{k} t_i = n.$

Computation and Reasoning

510

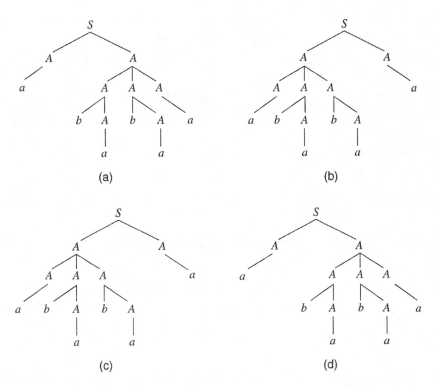

FIGURE 3.3   Trees corresponding to the derivations in Figure 3.1.

Proof.   The proof is by induction on the length of the derivation of w from v.

Basis: The basis consists of derivations of the form $v \overset{0}{\Rightarrow} w$. In this case, $w = v$ and each A_i is equal to the corresponding p_i. The desired derivations have the form $A_i \overset{0}{\Rightarrow} p_i$.

Inductive Hypothesis: Assume that all derivations $v \overset{n}{\Rightarrow} w$ can be decomposed into derivations from the A_i's, the variables of v, which together form a derivation of w from v of length n.

Inductive Step: Let $v \overset{n+1}{\Longrightarrow} w$ be a derivation in G with

$$v = w_1 A_1 w_2 A_2 \ldots w_k A_k w_{k+1},$$

where $w_i \in \Sigma^*$. The derivation can be written $v \Rightarrow u \overset{n}{\Rightarrow} w$. This reduces the original derivation to the application of a single rule and derivation of length n, the latter of which is suitable for the invocation of the inductive hypothesis.

The first rule application in the derivation, $v \Rightarrow u$, transforms one of the variables in v, call it A_j, with a rule of the form

$$A_j \rightarrow u_1 B_1 u_2 B_2 \ldots u_m B_m u_{m+1},$$

Computation and Reasoning

511

where each $u_i \in \Sigma^*$. The string u is obtained from v by replacing A_j by the right-hand side of the A_j rule. Making this substitution, u can be written as

$$w_1 A_1 \ldots A_{j-1} w_j u_1 B_1 u_2 B_2 \ldots u_m B_m u_{m+1} w_{j+1} A_{j+1} \ldots w_k A_k w_{k+1}.$$

Since w is derivable from u using n rule applications, the inductive hypothesis asserts that there are strings $p_1, \ldots, p_{j-1}, q_1, \ldots, q_m$, and $p_{j+1}, \ldots, p_k$ that satisfy

i) $A_i \overset{t_i}{\Rightarrow} p_i$ for $i = 1, \ldots, j-1, j+1, \ldots, k$
   $B_i \overset{s_i}{\Rightarrow} q_i$ for $i = 1, \ldots, m$;

ii) $w = w_1 p_1 w_2 \ldots p_{j-1} w_j u_1 q_1 u_2 \ldots u_m q_m u_{m+1} w_{j+1} p_{j+1} \ldots w_k p_k w_{k+1}$; and

iii) $\sum_{i=1}^{j-1} t_i + \sum_{i=j+1}^{k} t_i + \sum_{i=1}^{m} s_i = n$.

Combining the rule $A_j \to u_1 B_1 u_2 B_2 \ldots u_m B_m u_{m+1}$ with the derivations $B_i \overset{*}{\Rightarrow} q_i$, we obtain a derivation

$$A_j \overset{*}{\Rightarrow} u_1 q_1 u_2 q_2 \ldots u_m q_m u_{m+1} = p_j$$

whose length is the sum of lengths of the derivations from the B_i's plus one. The derivations $A_i \overset{*}{\Rightarrow} p_i$, $i = 1, \ldots, k$, provide the desired decomposition of the derivation of w from v. ∎

Lemma 3.1.5 demonstrates the flexibility and modularity of derivations in context-free grammars. Every complex derivation can be broken down into subderivations of the constituent variables. This modularity will be exploited in the design of complex languages by using variables to define smaller and more manageable subsets of the language. These independently defined sublanguages are then combined by additional rules to produce the syntax of the entire language.

3.2   Examples of Grammars and Languages

Context-free grammars have been introduced to generate languages. Formal languages, like computer languages and natural languages, have requirements that the strings must satisfy in order to be syntactically correct. Grammars for these languages must generate precisely the desired strings and no others. There are two natural approaches that we may take to help develop our understanding of the relationship between grammars and languages. One is to begin with an informal specification of a language and then construct a grammar that generates it. This is the approach followed in the design of programming languages—the syntax is selected and the language designer produces a set of rules that defines the correctly formed strings. Conversely, we may begin with the rules of a grammar and analyze them to determine the form of the strings of the language. This is the approach frequently taken when checking the syntax of the source code of a computer program. The syntax of the programming is specified by a set of grammatical rules, such as the definition of the programming language Java given in Appendix IV. The syntax of constants, identifiers, statements, and entire programs is correct if the source code is derivable from the appropriate variables in the grammar.

Initially, determining the relationship between strings and rules may seem difficult. With experience, you will recognize frequently occurring patterns in strings and the rules that produce them. The goal of this section is to analyze examples to help you develop an intuitive understanding of language definition using context-free grammars.

In each of the examples a grammar is defined by listing its rules. The variables and terminals of the grammar are those occurring in the rules. The variable S is the start symbol of each grammar.

Example 3.2.1

Let G be the grammar given by the rules

$$S \to aSa \mid aBa$$
$$B \to bB \mid b.$$

Then $L(G) = \{a^n b^m a^n \mid n > 0, \ m > 0\}$. The rule $S \to aSa$ recursively builds an equal number of a's on each end of the string. The recursion is terminated by the application of the rule $S \to aBa$, ensuring at least one leading and one trailing a. The recursive B rule then generates any number of b's. To remove the variable B from the string and obtain a sentence of the language, the rule $B \to b$ must be applied, forcing the presence of at least one b. □

Example 3.2.2

The relationship between the number of leading a's and trailing d's in the language $\{a^n b^m c^m d^{2n} \mid n \geq 0, \ m > 0\}$ indicates that a recursive rule is needed to generate them. The same is true of the b's and c's. Derivations in the grammar

$$S \to aSdd \mid A$$
$$A \to bAc \mid bc$$

generate strings in an *outside-to-inside* manner. The S rules produce the a's and d's while the A rules generate the b's and c's. The rule $A \to bc$, whose application terminates the recursion, ensures the presence of the substring bc in every string in the language. □

Example 3.2.3

Recall that a string w is a palindrome if $w = w^R$. A grammar is constructed to generate the set of palindromes over $\{a, b\}$. The rules of the grammar mimic the recursive definition of palindromes given in Exercise 2.12. The basis of the set of palindromes consists of the strings λ, a, and b. The S rules

$$S \to a \mid b \mid \lambda$$

immediately generate these strings. The recursive part of the definition consists of adding the same symbol to each side of an existing palindrome. The rules

$$S \rightarrow aSa \mid bSb$$

capture the recursive generation process.   □

Example 3.2.4

The first recursive rule of

$$S \rightarrow aSb \mid aSbb \mid \lambda$$

generates a trailing b for every a, while the second generates two b's for each a. Thus there is at least one b for every a and at most two. The language of the grammar is $\{a^n b^m \mid 0 \leq n \leq m \leq 2n\}$.   □

Example 3.2.5

Consider the grammar

$$S \rightarrow abScB \mid \lambda$$
$$B \rightarrow bB \mid b.$$

The recursive S rule generates an equal number of ab's and cB's. The B rules generate b^+. In a derivation each occurrence of B may produce a different number of b's. For example, in the derivation

$$S \Rightarrow abScB$$
$$\Rightarrow ababScBcB$$
$$\Rightarrow ababcBcB$$
$$\Rightarrow ababcbcB$$
$$\Rightarrow ababcbcbB$$
$$\Rightarrow ababcbcbb,$$

the first occurrence of B generates a single b and the second occurrence produces bb. The language of the grammar is the set $\{(ab)^n (cb^{m_n})^n \mid n \geq 0, \ m_n > 0\}$. The superscript m_n indicates that the number of b's produced by each occurrence of B may be different since b^{m_i} need not equal b^{m_j} when $i \neq j$.   □

Example 3.2.6

Let G_1 and G_2 be the grammars

$$\begin{array}{ll} G_1\colon\ S \rightarrow AB & \qquad G_2\colon\ S \rightarrow aS \mid aA \\ \qquad A \rightarrow aA \mid a & \qquad\quad A \rightarrow bA \mid \lambda. \\ \qquad B \rightarrow bB \mid \lambda & \end{array}$$

Both of these grammars generate the language a^+b^*. The A rules in G_1 provide the standard method of generating a nonnull string of a's. The use of the λ-rule to terminate the derivation allows the possibility of having no b's. The rules in grammar G_2 build the strings of a^+b^* in a left-to-right manner.   □

Example 3.2.7

The grammars G_1 and G_2 generate the strings over $\{a, b\}$ that contain exactly two b's. That is, the language of the grammars is $a^*ba^*ba^*$.

$$G_1: S \to AbAbA \qquad G_2: S \to aS \mid bA$$
$$A \to aA \mid \lambda \qquad\qquad A \to aA \mid bC$$
$$\qquad\qquad\qquad\qquad C \to aC \mid \lambda$$

G_1 requires only two variables since the three instances of a^* are generated by the same A rules. The second builds the strings in a left-to-right manner, requiring a distinct variable for the generation of each sequence of a's.   □

Example 3.2.8

The grammars from Example 3.2.7 can be modified to generate strings with at least two b's.

$$G_1: S \to AbAbA \qquad G_2: S \to aS \mid bA$$
$$A \to aA \mid bA \mid \lambda \qquad\qquad A \to aA \mid bC$$
$$\qquad\qquad\qquad\qquad C \to aC \mid bC \mid \lambda$$

In G_1, any string can be generated before, between, and after the two b's produced by the S rule. A derivation in G_2 produces the first b using the rule $S \to bA$ and the second b with $A \to bC$. The derivation finishes using applications of the C rules, which can generate any string of a's and b's.   □

Two grammars that generate the same language are said to be *equivalent*. Examples 3.2.6, 3.2.7, and 3.2.8 show that equivalent grammars may produce the strings of a language by significantly different derivations. In later chapters we will see that rules having particular forms may facilitate the mechanical determination of the syntactic correctness of strings.

Example 3.2.9

A grammar is given that generates the language consisting of even-length strings over $\{a, b\}$. The strategy can be generalized to construct strings of length divisible by three, by four, and so forth. The variables S and O serve as counters. An S occurs in a sentential form when an even number of terminals has been generated. An O records the presence of an odd number of terminals.

$$S \rightarrow aO \mid bO \mid \lambda$$

$$O \rightarrow aS \mid bS$$

The application of $S \rightarrow \lambda$ completes the derivation of a terminal string. Until this occurs, a derivation alternates between applications of S and O rules.   □

Example 3.2.10

Let L be the language over $\{a, b\}$ consisting of all strings with an even number of b's. The grammar

$$S \rightarrow aS \mid bB \mid \lambda$$

$$B \rightarrow aB \mid bS \mid bC$$

$$C \rightarrow aC \mid \lambda$$

that generates L combines the techniques presented in the previous examples, Example 3.2.9 for the even number of b's and Example 3.2.7 for the arbitrary number of a's. Deleting all rules containing C yields another grammar that generates L.   □

Example 3.2.11

Exercise 2.38 requested a regular expression for the language over $\{a, b\}$ consisting of strings with an even number of a's and an even number of b's. It was noted at the time that a regular expression for this language was quite complex. The flexibility provided by string generation with rules makes the construction of a context-free grammar for this language straightforward. The variables are chosen to represent the parities of the number of a's and b's in the derived string. The variables of the grammar with their interpretations are

Variable	Interpretation
S	Even number of a's and even number of b's
A	Even number of a's and odd number of b's
B	Odd number of a's and even number of b's
C	Odd number of a's and odd number of b's

The application of a rule adds one terminal symbol to the derived string and updates the variable to reflect the new status. The rules of the grammar are

$$S \rightarrow aB \mid bA \mid \lambda$$

$$A \rightarrow aC \mid bS$$

$$B \rightarrow aS \mid bC$$

$$C \rightarrow aA \mid bB.$$

When the variable S is present, the derived string has an even number of a's and an even number of b's. The application of $S \rightarrow \lambda$ removes the variable from the sentential form, producing a string that satisfies the language specification. □

Example 3.2.12

The rules of a grammar are designed to impose a structure on the strings in the language. This structure may consist of ensuring the presence or absence of certain combinations of elements of the alphabet. We construct a grammar with alphabet $\{a, b, c\}$ whose language consists of all strings that do not contain the substring abc. The variables are used to determine how far the derivation has progressed toward generating the string abc.

$$S \rightarrow bS \mid cS \mid aB \mid \lambda$$
$$B \rightarrow aB \mid cS \mid bC \mid \lambda$$
$$C \rightarrow aB \mid bS \mid \lambda$$

The strings are built in a left-to-right manner. At most one variable is present in a sentential form. If an S is present, no progress has been made toward deriving abc. The variable B occurs when the previous terminal is an a. The variable C is present only when preceded by ab. Thus, the C rules cannot generate the terminal c. □

3.3 Regular Grammars

Regular grammars are an important subclass of context-free grammars that play a prominent role in the lexical analysis and parsing of programming languages. Regular grammars are obtained by placing restrictions on the form of the right-hand side of the rules. In Chapter 6 we will show that regular grammars generate precisely the languages that are defined by regular expressions or accepted by finite-state machines.

Definition 3.3.1

A **regular grammar** is a context-free grammar in which each rule has one of the following forms:

i) $A \rightarrow a$,

ii) $A \rightarrow aB$, or

iii) $A \rightarrow \lambda$,

where $A, B \in V$, and $a \in \Sigma$.

Derivations in regular grammars have a particularly nice form; there is at most one variable present in a sentential form and that variable, if present, is the rightmost symbol in the string. Each rule application adds a terminal to the derived string until a rule of the form $A \rightarrow a$ or $A \rightarrow \lambda$ terminates the derivation. These properties are illustrated using the regular grammar G_1

$$S \rightarrow aS \mid aA$$
$$A \rightarrow bA \mid \lambda$$

from Example 3.2.6 that generates the language a^+b^*. The derivation of $aabb$,

$$S \Rightarrow aS$$
$$\Rightarrow aaA$$
$$\Rightarrow aabA$$
$$\Rightarrow aabbA$$
$$\Rightarrow aabb,$$

shows the left-to-right generation of the prefix of terminal symbols. The derivation ends with the application of the rule $A \rightarrow \lambda$.

A language generated by a regular grammar is called a *regular* language. You may recall that the family of regular languages was introduced in Chapter 2 as the set of languages described by regular expressions. There is no conflict with what might appear to be two different definitions of the same term, since we will show that regular expressions and regular grammars define the same family of languages.

A regular language may be generated by both regular and nonregular grammars. The grammars G_1 and G_2 from Example 3.2.6 both generate the language a^+b^*. The grammar G_1 is not regular because the rule $S \rightarrow AB$ does not have the specified form. A language is regular if it is generated by some regular grammar; the existence of nonregular grammars that also generate the language is irrelevant. The grammars constructed in Examples 3.2.9, 3.2.10, 3.2.11, and 3.2.12 provide additional examples of regular grammars.

Example 3.3.1

We will construct a regular grammar that generates the same language as the context-free grammar

$$G: S \rightarrow abSA \mid \lambda$$
$$A \rightarrow Aa \mid \lambda.$$

The language of G is $\lambda \cup (ab)^+a^*$. The equivalent regular grammar

$$S \rightarrow aB \mid \lambda$$
$$B \rightarrow bS \mid bA$$
$$A \rightarrow aA \mid \lambda$$

Computation and Reasoning

518

generates the strings in a left-to-right manner. The S and B rules generate a prefix from the set $(ab)^*$. If a string has a suffix of a's, the rule $B \rightarrow bA$ is applied. The A rules are used to generate the remainder of the string.   □

3.4 Verifying Grammars

The grammars in the previous sections were built to generate specific languages. An intuitive argument was given to show that the grammar did indeed generate the correct set of strings. No matter how convincing the argument, the possibility of error exists. A proof is required to guarantee that a grammar generates precisely the desired strings.

To prove that the language of a grammar G is identical to a given language L, the inclusions $L \subseteq L(G)$ and $L(G) \subseteq L$ must be established. To demonstrate the techniques involved, we will prove that the language of the grammar

$$G: S \rightarrow AASB \mid AAB$$
$$A \rightarrow a$$
$$B \rightarrow bbb$$

is the set $L = \{a^{2n}b^{3n} \mid n > 0\}$.

A terminal string is in the language of a grammar if it can be derived from the start symbol using the rules of the grammar. The inclusion $\{a^{2n}b^{3n} \mid n > 0\} \subseteq L(G)$ is established by showing that every string in L is derivable in G. Since L contains an infinite number of strings, we cannot construct a derivation for every string in L. Unfortunately, this is precisely what is required. The apparent dilemma is solved by providing a derivation schema. The schema consists of a pattern that can be followed to construct a derivation for any string in L. A string of the form $a^{2n}b^{3n}$, for $n > 0$, can be derived by the following sequence of rule applications:

Derivation	Rule Applied
$S \overset{n-1}{\Longrightarrow} (AA)^{n-1}SB^{n-1}$	$S \rightarrow AASB$
$\Rightarrow (AA)^n B^n$	$S \rightarrow AAB$
$\overset{2n}{\Longrightarrow} (aa)^n B^n$	$A \rightarrow a$
$\overset{n}{\Longrightarrow} (aa)^n (bbb)^n$	$B \rightarrow bbb$
$= a^{2n}b^{3n}$	

where the superscripts on the $\Rightarrow$ specify the number of applications of the rule. The preceding schema provides a "recipe," that, when followed, can produce a derivation for any string in L.

The opposite inclusion, $L(G) \subseteq \{a^{2n}b^{3n} \mid n > 0\}$, requires each terminal string derivable in G to have the form specified by the set L. The derivation of a string in the language consists of a finite number of rule applications, indicating the suitability of a proof by induction. The first difficulty is to determine exactly what we need to prove. We wish to establish a relationship between the a's and b's in all terminal strings derivable in G. A necessary condition for a string w to be a member of L is that three times the number of a's in the string be equal to twice the number of b's. Letting $n_x(u)$ be the number of occurrences of the symbol x in the string u, this relationship can be expressed by $3n_a(u) = 2n_b(u)$.

This numeric relationship between the symbols in a terminal string clearly is not true for every string derivable from S. Consider the derivation

$$S \Rightarrow AASB$$
$$\Rightarrow aASB.$$

The string $aASB$, which is derivable in G, contains one a and no b's.

To account for the intermediate sentential forms that occur in a derivation, relationships between the variables and terminals that hold for all steps in the derivation must be determined. When a terminal string is derived, no variables will remain and the relationships should yield the required structure of the string.

The interactions of the variables and the terminals in the rules of G must be examined to determine their effect on the derivations of terminal strings. The rule $A \rightarrow a$ guarantees that every A will eventually be replaced by a single a. The number of a's present at the termination of a derivation consists of those already in the string and the number of A's in the string. The sum $n_a(u) + n_A(u)$ represents the number of a's that must be generated in deriving a terminal string from u. Similarly, every B will be replaced by the string bbb. The number of b's in a terminal string derivable from u is $n_b(u) + 3n_B(u)$. These observations are used to construct condition (i), establishing the correspondence of variables and terminals that holds for each step in the derivation.

i) $3(n_a(u) + n_A(u)) = 2(n_b(u) + 3n_B(u))$.

The string $aASB$, which we have seen is derivable in G, satisfies this condition since $n_a(aASB) + n_A(aASB) = 2$ and $n_b(aASB) + 3n_B(aASB) = 3$.

Conditions (ii) and (iii) are

ii) $n_A(u) + n_a(u) > 1$, and

iii) the a's and A's in a sentential form precede the S, which precedes the b's and B's.

All strings in $\{a^{2n}b^{3n} \mid n > 0\}$ contain at least two a's and three b's. Conditions (i) and (ii) combine to yield this property. Condition (iii) prescribes the order of the symbols in a derivable string. Not all of the symbols must be present in each string; strings derivable from S by one rule application do not contain any terminal symbols.

After the appropriate relationships have been determined, we must prove that they hold for every string derivable from S. The basis of the induction consists of all strings that can be obtained by derivations of length one (the S rules). The inductive hypothesis asserts that the conditions are satisfied for all strings derivable by n or fewer rule applications. The inductive step consists of showing that the application of an additional rule preserves the relationships.

There are two derivations of length one, $S \Rightarrow AASB$ and $S \Rightarrow AAB$. For each of these strings, $3(n_a(u) + n_A(u)) = 2(n_b(u) + 3n_B(u)) = 6$. By observation, conditions (ii) and (iii) hold for the two strings.

The inductive hypothesis asserts that (i), (ii), and (iii) are satisfied by all strings derivable by n or fewer rule applications. We now use the inductive hypothesis to show that the three properties hold for all strings generated by derivations of $n + 1$ rule applications.

Let w be a string derivable from S by a derivation $S \overset{n+1}{\Longrightarrow} w$ of length $n + 1$. To use the inductive hypothesis, we write the derivation of length $n + 1$ as a derivation of length n followed by a single rule application:

$$S \overset{n}{\Rightarrow} u \Rightarrow w.$$

Written in this form, it is clear that the string u is derivable by n rule applications. The inductive hypothesis asserts that properties (i), (ii), and (iii) hold for u. The inductive step requires that we show that the application of one rule to u preserves these properties.

For any sentential form v, we let $j(v) = 3(n_a(v) + n_A(v))$ and $k(v) = 2(n_b(v) + 3n_B(v))$. By the inductive hypothesis, $j(u) = k(u)$ and $j(u)/3 > 1$. The effects of the application of an additional rule on the constituents of the string u are given in the following table.

Rule	$j(w)$	$k(w)$	$j(w)/3$
$S \to AASB$	$j(u) + 6$	$k(u) + 6$	$j(u)/3 + 2$
$S \to AAB$	$j(u) + 6$	$k(u) + 6$	$j(u)/3 + 2$
$A \to a$	$j(u)$	$k(u)$	$j(u)/3$
$B \to bbb$	$j(u)$	$k(u)$	$j(u)/3$

Since $j(u) = k(u)$, we conclude that $j(w) = k(w)$. Similarly, $j(w)/3 > 1$ follows from the inductive hypothesis that $j(u)/3 > 1$. The ordering of the symbols is preserved by noting that each rule application either replaces S by an appropriately ordered sequence of variables or transforms a variable to the corresponding terminal.

We have shown that the three conditions hold for every string derivable in G. Since there are no variables in a string $w \in L(G)$, condition (i) implies $3n_a(w) = 2n_b(w)$. Condition (ii) guarantees the existence of a's and b's, while (iii) prescribes the order. Thus $L(G) \subseteq \{a^{2n}b^{3n} \mid n > 0\}$. Having established the opposite inclusions, we conclude that the language of G is $\{a^{2n}b^{3n} \mid n > 0\}$.

As illustrated by the preceding argument, proving that a grammar generates a certain language is a complicated process. This, of course, was an extremely simple grammar with only a few rules. The inductive process is straightforward after the correct relationships have been determined. The most challenging part of the inductive proof is determining the relationships between the variables and the terminals that must hold in the intermediate sentential forms. The relationships are sufficient if, when all references to the variables are removed, they yield the desired structure of the terminal strings.

As seen in the preceding argument, establishing that a grammar G generates a language L requires two distinct arguments:

i) that all strings of L are derivable in G, and

ii) that all strings generated by G are in L.

The former is accomplished by providing a derivation schema that can be used to produce a derivation for any sting in L. The latter uses induction to show that each sentential form satisfies conditions that lead to the generation of a string in L. The following examples further illustrate the steps involved in these proofs.

Example 3.4.1

Let G be the grammar

$$S \rightarrow aS \mid bB \mid \lambda$$
$$B \rightarrow aB \mid bS \mid bC$$
$$C \rightarrow aC \mid \lambda$$

given in Example 3.2.10. We will prove that $L(G) = a^*(a^*ba^*ba^*)^*$, the set of all strings over $\{a, b\}$ with an even number of b's. It is not true that every string derivable from S has an even number of b's. The derivation $S \Rightarrow bB$ produces a single b. To derive a terminal string, every B must eventually be transformed into a b. Consequently, we conclude that the desired relationship asserts that $n_b(u) + n_B(u)$ is even. When a terminal string w is derived, $n_B(w) = 0$ and $n_b(w)$ is even.

We will prove that $n_b(u) + n_B(u)$ is even for all strings derivable from S. The proof is by induction on the length of the derivations.

Basis: Derivations of length one. There are three such derivations:

$$S \Rightarrow aS$$
$$S \Rightarrow bB$$
$$S \Rightarrow \lambda.$$

By inspection, $n_b(u) + n_B(u)$ is even for these strings.

Inductive Hypothesis: Assume that $n_b(u) + n_B(u)$ is even for all strings u that can be derived with n rule applications.

Inductive Step: To complete the proof, we need to show that $n_b(w) + n_B(w)$ is even whenever w can be obtained by a derivation of the form $S \overset{n+1}{\Longrightarrow} w$. The key step is to reformulate the derivation to apply the inductive hypothesis. A derivation of w of length $n + 1$ can be written $S \overset{n}{\Rightarrow} u \Rightarrow w$.

By the inductive hypothesis, $n_b(u) + n_B(u)$ is even. We show that the result of the application of any rule to u preserves the parity of $n_b(u) + n_B(u)$. The table

Rule	$n_b(w) + n_B(w)$
$S \to aS$	$n_b(u) + n_B(u)$
$S \to bB$	$n_b(u) + n_B(u) + 2$
$S \to \lambda$	$n_b(u) + n_B(u)$
$B \to aB$	$n_b(u) + n_B(u)$
$B \to bS$	$n_b(u) + n_B(u)$
$B \to bC$	$n_b(u) + n_B(u)$
$C \to aC$	$n_b(u) + n_B(u)$
$C \to \lambda$	$n_b(u) + n_B(u)$

gives the value of $n_b(w) + n_B(w)$ when the corresponding rule is applied to u. Each of the rules leaves the total number of B's and b's fixed except the second, which adds two to the total. Thus the sum of the b's and B's in a string obtained from u by the application of a rule is even. Since a terminal string contains no B's, we have shown that every string in L(G) has an even number of b's.

To complete the proof, the opposite inclusion, $L(G) \subseteq a^*(a^*ba^*ba^*)^*$, must also be established. To accomplish this, we show that every string in $a^*(a^*ba^*ba^*)^*$ is derivable in G. A string in $a^*(a^*ba^*ba^*)^*$ has the form

$$a^{n_1}ba^{n_2}ba^{n_3} \ldots a^{n_{2k}}ba^{n_{2k+1}}, \ k \geq 0.$$

Any string in a^* can be derived using the rules $S \to aS$ and $S \to \lambda$. All other strings in L(G) can be generated by a derivation of the form

Derivation	Rule Applied
$S \overset{n_1}{\Longrightarrow} a^{n_1}S$	$S \to aS$
$\Longrightarrow a^{n_1}bB$	$S \to bB$
$\overset{n_2}{\Longrightarrow} a^{n_1}ba^{n_2}B$	$B \to aB$
$\Longrightarrow a^{n_1}ba^{n_2}bS$	$B \to bS$
$\vdots$	
$\overset{n_{2k}}{\Longrightarrow} a^{n_1}ba^{n_2}ba^{n_3} \ldots a^{n_{2k}}B$	$B \to aB$
$\Longrightarrow a^{n_1}ba^{n_2}ba^{n_3} \ldots a^{n_{2k}}bC$	$B \to bC$
$\overset{n_{2k+1}}{\Longrightarrow} a^{n_1}ba^{n_2}ba^{n_3} \ldots a^{n_{2k}}ba^{n_{2k+1}}C$	$C \to aC$
$\Longrightarrow a^{n_1}ba^{n_2}ba^{n_3} \ldots a^{n_{2k}}ba^{n_{2k+1}}$	$C \to \lambda$

$\square$

Computation and Reasoning

Example 3.4.2

Let G be the grammar

$$S \rightarrow aASB \mid \lambda$$
$$A \rightarrow ad \mid d$$
$$B \rightarrow bb.$$

We show that every string in L(G) has at least as many b's as a's. The number of b's in a terminal string depends upon the b's and B's in the intermediate steps of the derivation. Each B generates two b's, while an A generates at most one a. We will prove, for every sentential form u of G, that $n_a(u) + n_A(u) \leq n_b(u) + 2n_B(u)$. Let $j(u) = n_a(u) + n_A(u)$ and $k(u) = n_b(u) + 2n_B(u)$.

Basis: There are two derivations of length one

Rule	$j(u)$	$k(u)$
$S \Rightarrow aASB$	2	2
$S \Rightarrow \lambda$	0	0

and $j(u) \leq k(u)$ for both of the derivable strings.

Inductive Hypothesis: Assume that $j(u) \leq k(u)$ for all strings u derivable from S in n or fewer rule applications.

Inductive Step: We need to prove that $j(w) \leq k(w)$ whenever $S \overset{n+1}{\Longrightarrow} w$. The derivation of w can be rewritten $S \overset{n}{\Rightarrow} u \Rightarrow w$ and, by the inductive hypothesis, $j(u) \leq k(u)$. We must show that the inequality is preserved by an additional rule application. The effect of each rule application on j and k is indicated in the following table.

Rule	$j(w)$	$k(w)$
$S \rightarrow aASB$	$j(u) + 2$	$k(u) + 2$
$S \rightarrow \lambda$	$j(u)$	$k(u)$
$B \rightarrow bb$	$j(u)$	$k(u)$
$A \rightarrow ad$	$j(u)$	$k(u)$
$A \rightarrow d$	$j(u) - 1$	$k(u)$

The first rule adds 2 to each side of an inequality, maintaining the inequality. The final rule subtracts 1 from the smaller side, reinforcing the inequality. For a string $w \in$ L(G), the inequality yields $n_a(w) \leq n_b(w)$ as desired.   □

Example 3.4.3

In Example 3.2.2 the grammar

$$G: \; S \rightarrow aSdd \mid A$$
$$A \rightarrow bAc \mid bc$$

was constructed to generate the language $L = \{a^n b^m c^m d^{2n} \mid n \geq 0,\ m > 0\}$. We develop relationships among the variables and terminals that are sufficient to prove that $L(G) \subseteq L$. The S and the A rules enforce the numeric relationships between the a's and d's and the b's and c's. In a derivation of G, the start symbol is removed by an application of the rule $S \to A$. The presence of an A guarantees that a b will eventually be generated. These observations lead to the following four conditions for every sentential form u of G:

  i) $2n_a(u) = n_d(u)$.

  ii) $n_b(u) = n_c(u)$.

  iii) $n_S(u) + n_A(u) + n_b(u) > 0$.

  iv) The a's precede the b's, which precede the S or A, which precede the c's, which precede the d's.

The equalities guarantee that the terminals occur in correct numerical relationships. The description of the language also demands that the terminals occur in a specified order. The final condition ensures that the order is maintained at each step in the derivation. □

3.5 Leftmost Derivations and Ambiguity

The language of a grammar is the set of terminal strings that can be derived, in any manner, from the start symbol. A terminal string may be generated by a number of different derivations. For example, Figure 3.1 gave a grammar and four derivations of the string *ababaa* using the rules of the grammar. Any one of the derivations is sufficient to exhibit the syntactic correctness of the string.

The derivations using the natural language example that introduced this chapter were all given as leftmost derivations. This is a natural technique for readers of English since the leftmost variable is the first encountered when reading a string. To reduce the number of derivations that must be considered in determining whether a string is in the language of a grammar, we now prove that every string in the language is derivable in a leftmost manner.

Theorem 3.5.1

Let $G = (V,\ \Sigma,\ P,\ S)$ be a context-free grammar. A string w is in L(G) if, and only if, there is a leftmost derivation of w from S.

Proof.   Clearly, $w \in L(G)$ whenever there is a leftmost derivation of w from S. We must establish the "only if" clause of the equivalence, that is, that every string in the L(G) is derivable in a leftmost manner. Let

$$S \Rightarrow w_1 \Rightarrow w_2 \Rightarrow w_3 \Rightarrow \cdots \Rightarrow w_n = w$$

be a, not necessarily leftmost, derivation of w in G. The independence of rule applications in a context-free grammar is used to build a leftmost derivation of w. Let w_k be the first sentential form in the derivation to which the rule application is not leftmost. If there is no such k, the derivation is already leftmost and there is nothing to show. We will show that

Computation and Reasoning

the rule applications can be reordered so that the first $k+1$ rule applications are leftmost. This procedure can be repeated, $n-k$ times if necessary, to produce a leftmost derivation.

By the choice of w_k, the derivation $S \overset{k}{\Rightarrow} w_k$ is leftmost. Assume that A is the leftmost variable in w_k and B is the variable transformed in the $k+1$st step of the derivation. Then w_k can be written $u_1 A u_2 B u_3$ with $u_1 \in \Sigma^*$. The application of a rule $B \to v$ to w_k has the form

$$w_k = u_1 A u_2 B u_3 \Rightarrow u_1 A u_2 v u_3 = w_{k+1}.$$

Since w is a terminal string, an A rule must eventually be applied to the leftmost variable in w_k. Let the first rule application that transforms the variable A occur at the $j+1$st step in the original derivation. Then the application of the rule $A \to p$ can be written

$$w_j = u_1 A q \Rightarrow u_1 p q = w_{j+1}.$$

The rules applied in steps $k+2$ to j transform the string $u_2 v u_3$ into q. The derivation is completed by the subderivation

$$w_{j+1} \overset{*}{\Rightarrow} w_n = w.$$

The original derivation has been divided into five distinct subderivations. The first k rule applications are already leftmost, so they are left intact. To construct a leftmost derivation, the rule $A \to p$ is applied to the leftmost variable at step $k+1$. The context-free nature of rule applications permits this rearrangement. A derivation of w that is leftmost for the first $k+1$ rule applications is obtained as follows:

$$
\begin{aligned}
S \overset{k}{\Rightarrow} w_k &= u_1 A u_2 B u_3 \\
&\Rightarrow u_1 p u_2 B u_3 && \text{(applying } A \to p\text{)} \\
&\Rightarrow u_1 p u_2 v u_3 && \text{(applying } B \to v\text{)} \\
&\overset{j-k-1}{\Longrightarrow} u_1 p q = w_{j+1} && \text{(using the derivation } u_2 v u_3 \overset{*}{\Rightarrow} q\text{)} \\
&\overset{n-j-1}{\Longrightarrow} w_n. && \text{(using the derivation } w_{j+1} \overset{*}{\Rightarrow} w_n\text{)}
\end{aligned}
$$

Every time this procedure is repeated, the derivation becomes "more" leftmost. If the length of a derivation is n, then at most n iterations are needed to produce a leftmost derivation of w. ∎

Theorem 3.5.1 does not guarantee that all sentential forms of the grammar can be generated by a leftmost derivation. Only leftmost derivations of terminal strings are assured. Consider the grammar

$$
\begin{aligned}
S &\to AB \\
A &\to aA \mid \lambda \\
B &\to bB \mid \lambda
\end{aligned}
$$

that generates a^*b^*. The sentential form A can be obtained by the rightmost derivation $S \Rightarrow AB \Rightarrow A$. It is easy to see that there is no leftmost derivation of A.

A similar result (Exercise 31) establishes the sufficiency of using rightmost derivations for the generation of terminal strings. Leftmost and rightmost derivations of w from v are explicitly denoted $v \stackrel{*}{\underset{L}{\Rightarrow}} w$ and $v \stackrel{*}{\underset{R}{\Rightarrow}} w$.

Restricting our attention to leftmost derivations eliminates many of the possible derivations of a string. Is this reduction sufficient to establish a canonical derivation? That is, is there a unique leftmost derivation of every string in the language of a grammar? Unfortunately, the answer is no. Two distinct leftmost derivations of the string $ababaa$ were given in Figure 3.1.

The possibility of a string having several leftmost derivations introduces the notion of ambiguity. Ambiguity in formal languages is similar to ambiguity encountered frequently in natural languages. The sentence *Jack was given a book by Hemingway* has two distinct structural decompositions. The prepositional phrase *by Hemingway* can modify either the verb *was given* or the noun *book*. Each of these structural decompositions represents a syntactically correct sentence.

The compilation of a computer program utilizes the derivation produced by the parser to generate machine-language code. The compilation of a program that has two derivations uses only one of the possible interpretations to produce the executable code. An unfortunate programmer may then be faced with debugging a program that is completely correct according to the language definition but does not perform as expected. To avoid this possibility—and help maintain the sanity of programmers everywhere—the definitions of computer languages should be constructed so that no ambiguity can occur. The preceding discussion of ambiguity leads to the following definition.

Definition 3.5.2

A context-free grammar G is **ambiguous** if there is a string $w \in L(G)$ that can be derived by two distinct leftmost derivations. A grammar that is not ambiguous is called **unambiguous**.

Example 3.5.1

Let G be the grammar

$$S \rightarrow aS \mid Sa \mid a$$

that generates a^+. G is ambiguous since the string aa has two distinct leftmost derivations:

$$S \Rightarrow aS \qquad S \Rightarrow Sa$$
$$\Rightarrow aa \qquad \Rightarrow aa.$$

The language a^+ is also generated by the unambiguous grammar

$$S \rightarrow aS \mid a.$$

Computation and Reasoning

This grammar, being regular, has the property that all strings are generated in a left-to-right manner. The variable S remains as the rightmost symbol of the string until the recursion is halted by the application of the rule $S \rightarrow a$.   □

The previous example demonstrates that ambiguity is a property of grammars, not of languages. When a grammar is shown to be ambiguous, it is often possible to construct an equivalent unambiguous grammar. This is not always the case. There are some context-free languages that cannot be generated by any unambiguous grammar. Such languages are called **inherently ambiguous**. The syntax of most programming languages, which require unambiguous derivations, is sufficiently restrictive to avoid inherent ambiguity.

Example 3.5.2

Let G be the grammar

$$S \rightarrow bS \mid Sb \mid a$$

with language b^*ab^*. The leftmost derivations

$$
\begin{array}{ll}
S \Rightarrow bS & S \Rightarrow Sb \\
 \Rightarrow bSb & \Rightarrow bSb \\
 \Rightarrow bab & \Rightarrow bab
\end{array}
$$

exhibit the ambiguity of G. The ability to generate the b's in either order must be eliminated to obtain an unambiguous grammar. L(G) is also generated by the unambiguous grammars

$$
\begin{array}{ll}
G_1: S \rightarrow bS \mid aA & G_2: S \rightarrow bS \mid A \\
 A \rightarrow bA \mid \lambda & A \rightarrow Ab \mid a.
\end{array}
$$

In G_1, the sequence of rule applications in a leftmost derivation is completely determined by the string being derived. The only leftmost derivation of the string b^nab^m has the form

$$
\begin{aligned}
S &\overset{n}{\Rightarrow} b^n S \\
&\Rightarrow b^n aA \\
&\overset{m}{\Rightarrow} b^n ab^m A \\
&\Rightarrow b^n ab^m.
\end{aligned}
$$

A derivation in G_2 initially generates the leading b's, followed by the trailing b's, and finally the a.   □

A grammar is unambiguous if, at each step in a leftmost derivation, there is only one rule whose application can lead to a derivation of the desired string. This does not mean that there is only one applicable rule, but rather that the application of any other rule makes it impossible to complete a derivation of the string.

Consider the possibilities encountered in constructing a leftmost derivation of the string *bbabb* using the grammar G_2 from Example 3.5.2. There are two *S* rules that can initiate a derivation. Derivations initiated with the rule $S \rightarrow A$ generate strings beginning with *a*. Consequently, a derivation of *bbabb* must begin with the application of the rule $S \rightarrow bS$. The second *b* is generated by another application of the same rule. At this point, the derivation continues using $S \rightarrow A$. Another application of $S \rightarrow bS$ would generate the prefix *bbb*. The suffix *bb* is generated by two applications of $A \rightarrow Ab$. The derivation is successfully completed with an application of $A \rightarrow a$. Since the terminal string specifies the exact sequence of rule applications, the grammar is unambiguous.

Example 3.5.3

The grammar from Example 3.2.4 that generates the language $L = \{a^n b^m \mid 0 \leq n \leq m \leq 2n\}$ is ambiguous. The string *aabbb* can be generated by the derivations

$$\begin{array}{ll} S \Rightarrow aSb & S \Rightarrow aSbb \\ \Rightarrow aaSbbb & \Rightarrow aaSbbb \\ \Rightarrow aabbb & \Rightarrow aabbb. \end{array}$$

A strategy for unambiguously generating the strings of L is to initially produce *a*'s with a single matching *b*. This is followed by generating *a*'s with two *b*'s. An unambiguous grammar that produces the strings of L in this manner is

$$S \rightarrow aSb \mid A \mid \lambda$$
$$A \rightarrow aAbb \mid abb. \qquad\qquad \square$$

A derivation tree depicts the transformation of the variables in a derivation. There is a natural one-to-one correspondence between leftmost (rightmost) derivations and derivation trees. Definition 3.1.4 outlines the construction of a derivation tree directly from a leftmost derivation. Conversely, a unique leftmost derivation of a string *w* can be extracted from a derivation tree with frontier *w*. Because of this correspondence, ambiguity is often defined in terms of derivation trees. A grammar G is ambiguous if there is a string in L(G) that is the frontier of two distinct derivation trees. Figure 3.3 shows that the two leftmost derivations of the string *ababaa* given in Figure 3.1 generate distinct derivation trees.

3.6   Context-Free Grammars and Programming Language Definition

In the preceding sections we used context-free grammars to generate "toy" languages using an alphabet with only a few elements and a small number of rules. These examples demonstrated the ability of context-free rules to produce strings that satisfy particular syntactic requirements. A programming language has a larger alphabet and more complicated syntax, increasing the number and complexity of the rules needed to define the language.

The first formal specification of a high-level programming language was given for the language ALGOL 60 by John Backus [1959] and Peter Naur [1963]. The system employed by Backus and Naur is now referred to as *Backus-Naur form*, or *BNF*. The programming language Java, whose specification was given in BNF, will be used to illustrate principles of the syntactic definition of a programming language. A complete formal definition of Java is given in Appendix IV.

A BNF description of a language is a context-free grammar; the only difference is the notation used to define the rules. We will give the rules using the context-free notation, with one exception. The subscript *opt* after a variable or a terminal indicates that it is optional. This notation reduces the number of rules that need to be written, but rules with optional components can easily be transformed into equivalent context-free rules. For example, $A \rightarrow B_{opt}$ and $A \rightarrow B_{opt}C$ can be replaced by the rules $A \rightarrow B \mid \lambda$ and $A \rightarrow BC \mid C$, respectively.

The notational conventions used in the Java rules are the same as the natural language example at the beginning of the chapter. The names of the variables indicate the components of the language that they generate and are enclosed in $\langle \ \rangle$. Java keywords are given in bold, and other terminal symbols are represented by character strings delimited by blanks.

The design of a programming language, like the design of a complex program, is greatly simplified utilizing modularity to develop subsets of the grammar independently. The techniques you have used in building small rule sets provide the skills needed to design a grammar for larger languages with more complicated syntaxes. These techniques include using rules to ensure the presence or relative position of elements and using recursion to generate sequences and to nest parentheses.

To illustrate the principles of language design, we will examine rules that define literals, identifiers, and arithmetic expressions in Java. Literals, strings that have a fixed type and value, are frequently used to initialize variables, to set the bounds on repetitive statements, and to store standard messages to be output. The rule for the variable $\langle Literal \rangle$ defines the types of Java literals. The Java literals, along with the variables that generate them, are

Literal	Variable	Examples
Boolean	$< BooleanLiteral >$	**true**, **false**
Character	$< CharacterLiteral >$	'a', '\n' (linefeed escape sequence), 'π',
String	$< StringLiteral >$	"" (empty string),
		"This is a nonempty string"
Integer	$< IntegerLiteral >$	0, 356, 1234L (long), 077 (octal),
		0x1ab2 (hex)
Floating point	$< FloatingPointLiteral >$	2., .2, 2.0, 12.34, 2e3, 6.2e-5
Null	$< NullLiteral >$	**null**

Each floating point literal can have an f, F, d, or D as a suffix to indicate its precision. The definitions for the complete set of Java literals are given in rules 143–167 in Appendix IV.

Computation and Reasoning

We will consider the rules that define the floating point literals, since they have the most interesting syntactic variations. The four ⟨*FloatingPointLiteral*⟩ rules specify the general form of floating point literals.

⟨*FloatingPointLiteral*⟩ → ⟨*Digits*⟩ . ⟨*Digits*⟩$_{opt}$⟨*ExponentPart*⟩$_{opt}$⟨*FloatTypeSuffix*⟩$_{opt}$ |

. ⟨*Digits*⟩ ⟨*ExponentPart*⟩$_{opt}$⟨*FloatTypeSuffix*⟩$_{opt}$ |

⟨*Digits*⟩ ⟨*ExponentPart*⟩⟨*FloatTypeSuffix*⟩$_{opt}$ |

⟨*Digits*⟩ ⟨*ExponentPart*⟩$_{opt}$⟨*FloatTypeSuffix*⟩

The variables ⟨*Digits*⟩, ⟨*ExponentPart*⟩, and ⟨*FloatTypeSuffix*⟩ generate the components that make up the literal. The variable ⟨*Digits*⟩ generates a string of digits using recursion. The nonrecursive rule ensures the presence of at least one digit.

⟨*Digits*⟩ → ⟨*Digit*⟩ | ⟨*Digits*⟩⟨*Digit*⟩

⟨*Digit*⟩ → 0 | ⟨*NonZeroDigit*⟩

⟨*NonZeroDigit*⟩ → 1 | 2 | 3 | 4 | 5 | 6 | 7 | 8 | 9

⟨*ExponentPart*⟩ → ⟨*ExponentIndicator*⟩⟨*SignedInteger*⟩

⟨*ExponentIndicator*⟩ → e | E

⟨*SignedInteger*⟩ → ⟨*Sign*⟩$_{opt}$⟨*Digits*⟩

⟨*Sign*⟩ → + | −

⟨*FloatTypeSuffix*⟩ → f | F | d | D

The subscript *opt* in the rule ⟨*SignedInteger*⟩ → ⟨*Sign*⟩$_{opt}$⟨*Digits*⟩ indicates that a signed integer may begin with + or −, but the sign is not necessary.

The first ⟨*FloatingPointLiteral*⟩ rule generates literals of the form 1., 1.1, 1.1e, 1.e, 1.1ef, 1.f, 1.1f, and 1.ef. The leading string of digits and decimal point are required; all other components are optional. The second rule generates literals that begin with a decimal point, and the last two rules define the floating point literals without decimal points.

Identifiers are used as names of variables, types, methods, and so forth. Identifiers are defined by the rules

⟨*Identifier*⟩ → ⟨*IdentifierChars*⟩

⟨*IdentifierChars*⟩ → ⟨*JavaLetter*⟩ | ⟨*JavaLetter*⟩⟨*JavaLetterOrDigit*⟩

where the Java letters include the letters A to Z and a to z, the underscore _, and the dollar sign $, along with other characters represented in the Unicode encoding.

The definition of statements in Java begins with the variable ⟨*Statement*⟩:

⟨*Statement*⟩ → ⟨*StatementWithoutTrailing Substatement*⟩ | ⟨*LabeledStatement*⟩ |

⟨*IfThenStatement*⟩ | ⟨*IfThenElseStatement*⟩ |

⟨*WhileStatement*⟩ | ⟨*ForStatement*⟩.

Statements without trailing substatements include blocks and the **do** and **switch** statements. The entire set of statements is given in rules 73–75 in Appendix IV. Like the rules for the literals, the statement rules define the high-level structure of a statement. For example, **if-then** and **do** statements are defined by

$$\langle IfThenStatement \rangle \rightarrow \textbf{if } (\langle Expression \rangle) \langle Statement \rangle$$

$$\langle DoStatement \rangle \rightarrow \textbf{do } \langle Statement \rangle \textbf{ while } (\langle Expression \rangle).$$

The occurrence of the variable $\langle Statement \rangle$ on the right-hand side of the preceding rules generates the statements to be executed after the condition in the **if-then** statement and in the loop in the **do** loop.

The evaluation of expressions is the key to numeric computation and checking the conditions in **if-then, do, while,** and **switch** statements. The syntax of expressions is defined by the rules 118–142 in Appendix IV. The syntax is complicated because Java has numeric and Boolean expressions that may utilize postfix, prefix, or infix operators. Rather than describing individual rules, we will look at several subderivations that occur in the derivation of a simple arithmetic assignment.

The first steps transform the variable $\langle Expression \rangle$ to an assignment:

$$\langle Expression \rangle \Rightarrow \langle AssignmentExpression \rangle$$
$$\Rightarrow \langle Assignment \rangle$$
$$\Rightarrow \langle LeftHandSide \rangle \langle AssignmentOperator \rangle \langle AssignmentExpression \rangle$$
$$\Rightarrow \langle ExpressionName \rangle \langle AssignmentOperator \rangle \langle AssignmentExpression \rangle$$
$$\Rightarrow \langle Identifier \rangle \langle AssignmentOperator \rangle \langle AssignmentExpression \rangle$$
$$\Rightarrow \langle Identifier \rangle = \langle AssignmentExpression \rangle.$$

The next step is to derive $\langle AdditiveExpression \rangle$ from $\langle AssignmentExpression \rangle$.

$$\langle AssignmentExpression \rangle \Rightarrow \langle ConditionalExpression \rangle$$
$$\Rightarrow \langle ConditionalOrExpression \rangle$$
$$\Rightarrow \langle ConditionalAndExpression \rangle$$
$$\Rightarrow \langle InclusiveOrExpression \rangle$$
$$\Rightarrow \langle ExclusionOrExpression \rangle$$
$$\Rightarrow \langle AndExpression \rangle$$
$$\Rightarrow \langle EqualityExpression \rangle$$
$$\Rightarrow \langle RelationalExpression \rangle$$
$$\Rightarrow \langle ShiftExpression \rangle$$
$$\Rightarrow \langle AdditiveExpression \rangle.$$

Derivations beginning with ⟨*AdditiveExpression*⟩ produce correctly formed expressions with additive operators, multiplicative operators, and parentheses. For example,

$$⟨AdditiveExpression⟩ \Rightarrow ⟨AdditiveExpression⟩ + ⟨MultiplicativeExpression⟩$$
$$\Rightarrow ⟨MultiplicativeExpression⟩ + ⟨MultiplicativeExpression⟩$$
$$\Rightarrow ⟨UnaryExpression⟩ + ⟨MultiplicativeExpression⟩$$
$$\overset{*}{\Rightarrow} ⟨Identifier⟩ + ⟨MultiplicativeExpression⟩$$
$$\Rightarrow ⟨Identifier⟩ +$$
$$⟨MultiplicativeExpression⟩ * ⟨MultiplicativeExpression⟩$$

begins such a derivation. Derivations from ⟨*UnaryExpression*⟩ can produce literals, variables, or (⟨*Expression*⟩) to obtain nested parentheses.

The rules that define identifiers, literals, and expressions show how the design of a large language is decomposed into creating rules for frequently recurring subsets of the language. The resulting variables ⟨*Identifier*⟩, ⟨*Literal*⟩, and ⟨*Expression*⟩ become the building blocks for higher-level rules.

The start symbol of the grammar is ⟨*CompilationUnit*⟩ and the derivation of a Java program begins with the rule

$$⟨CompulationUnit⟩ \rightarrow ⟨PackageDeclaration⟩_{opt} ⟨ImportDeclarations⟩_{opt}$$
$$⟨TypeDeclarations⟩_{opt}.$$

A string of terminal symbols derivable from this rule is a syntactically correct Java program.

Exercises

1. Let G be the grammar

$$S \rightarrow abSc \mid A$$
$$A \rightarrow cAd \mid cd.$$

a) Give a derivation of *ababccddcc*.
b) Build the derivation tree for the derivation in part (a).
c) Use set notation to define L(G).

2. Let G be the grammar

$$S \rightarrow ASB \mid \lambda$$
$$A \rightarrow aAb \mid \lambda$$
$$B \rightarrow bBa \mid ba.$$

a) Give a leftmost derivation of *aabbba*.
b) Give a rightmost derivation of *abaabbbabbaa*.

c) Build the derivation tree for the derivations in parts (a) and (b).

d) Use set notation to define L(G).

3. Let G be the grammar

$$S \rightarrow SAB \mid \lambda$$
$$A \rightarrow aA \mid a$$
$$B \rightarrow bB \mid \lambda.$$

a) Give a leftmost derivation of *abbaab*.

b) Give two leftmost derivations of *aa*.

c) Build the derivation tree for the derivations in part (b).

d) Give a regular expression for L(G).

4. Let DT be the derivation tree

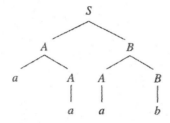

a) Give a leftmost derivation that generates the tree DT.

b) Give a rightmost derivation that generates the tree DT.

c) How many different derivations are there that generate DT?

5. Give the leftmost and rightmost derivations corresponding to each of the derivation trees given in Figure 3.3.

6. For each of the following context-free grammars, use set notation to define the language generated by the grammar.

a) $S \rightarrow aaSB \mid \lambda$
   $B \rightarrow bB \mid b$

b) $S \rightarrow aSbb \mid A$
   $A \rightarrow cA \mid c$

c) $S \rightarrow abSdc \mid A$
   $A \rightarrow cdAba \mid \lambda$

d) $S \rightarrow aSb \mid A$
   $A \rightarrow cAd \mid cBd$
   $B \rightarrow aBb \mid ab$

e) $S \rightarrow aSB \mid aB$
   $B \rightarrow bb \mid b$

7. Construct a grammar over $\{a, b, c\}$ whose language is $\{a^n b^{2n} c^m \mid n, m > 0\}$.

8. Construct a grammar over $\{a, b, c\}$ whose language is $\{a^n b^m c^{2n+m} \mid n, m > 0\}$.

9. Construct a grammar over $\{a, b, c\}$ whose language is $\{a^n b^m c^i \mid 0 \leq n + m \leq i\}$.

10. Construct a grammar over $\{a, b\}$ whose language is $\{a^m b^n \mid 0 \le n \le m \le 3n\}$.

11. Construct a grammar over $\{a, b\}$ whose language is $\{a^m b^i a^n \mid i = m + n\}$.

12. Construct a grammar over $\{a, b\}$ whose language contains precisely the strings with the same number of a's and b's.

* 13. Construct a grammar over $\{a, b\}$ whose language contains precisely the strings of odd length that have the same symbol in the first and middle positions.

14. For each of the following regular grammars, give a regular expression for the language generated by the grammar.

a) $S \to aA$
   $A \to aA \mid bA \mid b$

b) $S \to aA$
   $A \to aA \mid bB$
   $B \to bB \mid \lambda$

c) $S \to aS \mid bA$
   $A \to bB$
   $B \to aB \mid \lambda$

d) $S \to aS \mid bA \mid \lambda$
   $A \to aA \mid bS$

For Exercises 15 through 25, give a regular grammar that generates the described language.

15. The set of strings over $\{a, b, c\}$ in which all the a's precede the b's, which in turn precede the c's. It is possible that there are no a's, b's, or c's.

16. The set of strings over $\{a, b\}$ that contain the substring aa and the substring bb.

17. The set of strings over $\{a, b\}$ in which the substring aa occurs at least twice. (*Hint:* Beware of the substring aaa.)

18. The set of strings over $\{a, b\}$ that contain the substring ab and the substring ba.

19. The set of strings over $\{a, b\}$ in which the number of a's is divisible by three.

20. The set of strings over $\{a, b\}$ in which every a is either immediately preceded or immediately followed by b, for example, $baab$, aba, and b.

21. The set of strings over $\{a, b\}$ that do not contain the substring aba.

22. The set of strings over $\{a, b\}$ in which the substring aa occurs exactly once.

23. The set of strings of odd length over $\{a, b\}$ that contain exactly two b's.

* 24. The set of strings over $\{a, b, c\}$ with an odd number of occurrences of the substring ab.

25. The set of strings over $\{a, b\}$ with an even number of a's or an odd number of b's.

26. The grammar in Figure 3.1 generates $(b^*ab^*ab^*)^+$, the set of all strings with a positive, even number of a's. Prove this.

27. Prove that the grammar given in Example 3.2.2 generates the prescribed language.

28. Let G be the grammar

$$S \to aSb \mid B$$
$$B \to bB \mid b.$$

Prove that $L(G) = \{a^n b^m \mid 0 \le n < m\}$.

Computation and Reasoning

535

29. Let G be the grammar

$$S \to aSaa \mid B$$
$$B \to bbBdd \mid C$$
$$C \to bd.$$

   a) What is L(G)?

   b) Prove that L(G) is the set given in part (a).

* 30. Let G be the grammar

$$S \to aSbS \mid aS \mid \lambda.$$

Prove that every prefix of a string in L(G) has at least as many a's as b's.

31. Let G be a context-free grammar and $w \in$ L(G). Prove that there is a rightmost derivation of w in G.

32. Let G be the grammar

$$S \to aS \mid Sb \mid ab.$$

   a) Give a regular expression for L(G).

   b) Construct two leftmost derivations of the string $aabb$.

   c) Build the derivation trees for the derivations from part (b).

   d) Construct an unambiguous grammar equivalent to G.

33. For each of the following grammars, give a regular expression or set-theoretic definition for the language of the grammar. Show that the grammar is ambiguous and construct an equivalent unambiguous grammar.

   a) $S \to aaS \mid aaaaaS \mid \lambda$

   b) $S \to aSA \mid \lambda$
      $A \to bA \mid \lambda$

   c) $S \to aSb \mid aAb$
      $A \to cAd \mid B$
      $B \to aBb \mid \lambda$

   d) $S \to AaSbB \mid \lambda$
      $A \to aA \mid a$
      $B \to bB \mid \lambda$

  *e) $S \to A \mid B$
      $A \to abA \mid \lambda$
      $B \to aBb \mid \lambda$

34. Let G be the grammar

$$S \rightarrow aA \mid \lambda$$
$$A \rightarrow aA \mid bB$$
$$B \rightarrow bB \mid b.$$

   a) Give a regular expression for L(G).

   b) Prove that G is unambiguous.

35. Let G be the grammar

$$S \rightarrow aS \mid aA \mid a$$
$$A \rightarrow aAb \mid ab.$$

   a) Give a set-theoretic definition of L(G).

   b) Prove that G is unambiguous.

36. Let G be the grammar

$$S \rightarrow aS \mid bA \mid \lambda$$
$$A \rightarrow bA \mid aS \mid \lambda.$$

Give a regular expression for L(G). Is G ambiguous? If so, give an unambiguous grammar that generates L(G). If not, prove it.

37. Construct unambiguous grammars for the languages $L_1 = \{a^n b^n c^m \mid n, m > 0\}$ and $L_2 = \{a^n b^m c^m \mid n, m > 0\}$. Construct a grammar G that generates $L_1 \cup L_2$. Prove that G is ambiguous. This is an example of an inherently ambiguous language. Explain, intuitively, why every grammar generating $L_1 \cup L_2$ must be ambiguous.

38. Use the definition of Java in Appendix IV to construct a derivation of the string $1.3e2$ from the variable $\langle Literal \rangle$.

* 39. Let G_1 and G_2 be the following grammars:

$$
\begin{array}{ll}
G_1 : S \rightarrow aABb & \quad G_2 : S \rightarrow AABB \\
\quad A \rightarrow aA \mid a & \quad\quad A \rightarrow AA \mid a \\
\quad B \rightarrow bB \mid b & \quad\quad B \rightarrow BB \mid b.
\end{array}
$$

   a) For each variable X, show that the right-hand side of every X rule of G_1 is derivable from the corresponding variable X using the rules of G_2. Use this to conclude that $L(G_1) \subseteq L(G_2)$.

   b) Prove that $L(G_1) = L(G_2)$.

* 40. A **right-linear grammar** is a context-free grammar, each of whose rules has one of the following forms:

    i) $A \rightarrow w$, or

    ii) $A \rightarrow wB$,

    where $w \in \Sigma^*$. Prove that a language L is generated by a right-linear grammar if, and only if, L is generated by a regular grammar.

41. Try to construct a regular grammar that generates the language $\{a^n b^n \mid n \geq 0\}$. Explain why none of your attempts succeed.

42. Try to construct a context-free grammar that generates the language $\{a^n b^n c^n \mid n \geq 0\}$. Explain why none of your attempts succeed.

Bibliographic Notes

Context-free grammars were introduced by Chomsky [1956], [1959]. Backus-Naur form was developed by Backus [1959]. This formalism was used to define the programming language ALGOL; see Naur [1963]. The BNF definition of Java is given in Appendix IV. The equivalence of context-free languages and the languages generated by BNF definitions was noted by Ginsburg and Rice [1962].

Properties of ambiguity are examined in Floyd [1962], Cantor [1962], and Chomsky and Schutzenberger [1963]. Inherent ambiguity was first noted in Parikh [1966]. A proof that the language in Exercise 37 is inherently ambiguous can be found in Harrison [1978]. Closure properties for ambiguous and inherently ambiguous languages were established by Ginsburg and Ullian [1966a, 1966b].

CHAPTER 5

Finite Automata

In this chapter we introduce the family of abstract computing devices known as finite-state machines. The computations of a finite-state machine determine whether a string satisfies a set of conditions or matches a prescribed pattern. Finite-state machines share properties common to many mechanical devices; they process input and generate output. A vending machine takes coins as input and returns food or beverages as output. A combination lock expects a sequence of numbers and opens the lock if the input sequence is correct. The input to a finite-state machine is a string and the result of a computation indicates acceptability of the string. The set of strings that are accepted makes up the language of the machine.

The preceding examples of machines exhibit a property that we take for granted in mechanical computation, determinism. When the appropriate amount of money is inserted into a vending machine, we are upset if nothing is forthcoming. Similarly, we expect the combination to open the lock and all other sequences to fail. Initially, we require finite-state machines to be deterministic. This condition will be relaxed to examine the effects of nondeterminism on the capabilities of finite-state computation.

5.1 A Finite-State Machine

A formal definition of a machine is not concerned with the hardware involved in the operation of the machine, but rather with a description of the internal operations as the machine processes the input. A vending machine may be built with levers, a combination lock with tumblers, and an electronic entry system is controlled by a microchip, but all accept

145

input and produce an affirmative or negative response. What sort of description encompasses the features of each of these seemingly different types of mechanical computation?

A simple newspaper vending machine, similar to those found on many street corners, is used to illustrate the components of a finite-state machine. The input to the machine consists of nickels, dimes, and quarters. When 30 cents is inserted, the cover of the machine may be opened and a paper removed. If the total of the coins exceeds 30 cents, the machine graciously accepts the overpayment and does not give change.

The newspaper machine on the street corner has no memory, at least not as we usually conceive of memory in a computing machine. However, the machine "knows" that an additional 5 cents will unlatch the cover when 25 cents has previously been inserted. This knowledge is acquired by the machine's altering its internal state whenever input is received and processed.

A machine state represents the status of an ongoing computation. The internal operation of the vending machine can be described by the interactions of the following seven states. The names of the states, given in italics, indicate the progress made toward opening the cover.

- *Needs 30 cents*: The state of the machine before any coins are inserted
- *Needs 25 cents*: The state after a nickel has been input
- *Needs 20 cents*: The state after two nickels or a dime have been input
- *Needs 15 cents*: The state after three nickels or a dime and a nickel have been input
- *Needs 10 cents*: The state after four nickels, a dime and two nickels, or two dimes have been input
- *Needs 5 cents*: The state after a quarter, five nickels, two dimes and a nickel, or one dime and three nickels have been input
- *Needs 0 cents*: The state that represents having at least 30 cents input

The insertion of a coin causes the machine to alter its state. When 30 cents or more is input, the state *needs 0 cents* is entered and the latch is opened. Such a state is called *accepting* since it indicates the correctness of the input.

The design of the machine must represent each of the components symbolically. Rather than a sequence of coins, the input to the abstract machine is a string of symbols. A labeled directed graph known as a **state diagram** is often used to represent the transformations of the internal state of the machine. The nodes of the state diagram are the states described above. The *needs m cents* node is represented simply by m in the state diagram. The state of the machine at the beginning of a computation is designated $\times\!\bigcirc$. The initial state for the newspaper vending machine is the node *30*.

The arcs are labeled n, d, or q, representing the input of a nickel, dime, or quarter. An arc from node x to node y labeled v indicates that processing input v when the machine is in state x causes the machine to enter state y. Figure 5.1 gives the state diagram for the newspaper vending machine. The arc labeled d from node *15* to *5* represents the change of state of the machine when 15 cents has previously been processed and a dime is input. The

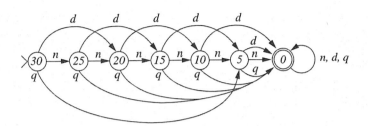

FIGURE 5.1 State diagram of newspaper vending machine.

cycles of length one from node *0* to itself indicate that any input that increases the total past 30 cents leaves the latch unlocked.

Input to the machine consists of strings from $\{n, d, q\}^*$. The sequence of states entered during the processing of an input string can be traced by following the arcs in the state diagram. The machine is in its initial state at the beginning of a computation. The arc labeled by the first input symbol is traversed, specifying the subsequent machine state. The next symbol of the input string is processed by traversing the appropriate arc from the current node, the node reached by traversal of the previous arc. This procedure is repeated until the entire input string has been processed. The string is accepted if the computation terminates in the accepting state. The string *dndn* is accepted by the vending machine, while the string *nndn* is not accepted since the computation terminates in state *5*.

5.2 Deterministic Finite Automata

The analysis of the vending machine required separating the fundamentals of the design from the implementational details. The implementation-independent description is often referred to as an *abstract machine*. We now introduce a class of abstract machines whose computations can be used to determine the acceptability of input strings.

Definition 5.2.1

A **deterministic finite automaton (DFA)** is a quintuple $M = (Q, \Sigma, \delta, q_0, F)$, where Q is a finite set of states, Σ a finite set called the *alphabet*, $q_0 \in Q$ a distinguished state known as the *start state*, F a subset of Q called the *final* or *accepting states*, and δ a total function from $Q \times \Sigma$ to Q known as the *transition function*.

We have referred to a deterministic finite automaton as an abstract machine. To reveal its mechanical nature, the operation of a DFA is described in terms of components that are present in many familiar computing machines. An automaton can be thought of as a machine consisting of five components: a single internal register, a set of values for the register, a tape, a tape reader, and an instruction set.

The states of a DFA represent the internal status of the machine and are often denoted $q_0, q_1, q_2, \ldots, q_n$. The register of the machine, also called the finite control, contains

Computation and Reasoning

one of the states as its value. At the beginning of a computation, the value of the register is q_0, the start state of the DFA.

The input is a finite sequence of elements from the alphabet Σ. The tape stores the input until needed by the computation. The tape is divided into squares, each square capable of holding one element from the alphabet. Since there is no upper bound to the length of an input string, the tape must be of unbounded length. The input to a computation of the automaton is placed on an initial segment of the tape.

The tape head reads a single square of the input tape. The body of the machine consists of the tape head and the register. The position of the tape head is indicated by placing the body of the machine under the tape square being scanned. The current state of the automaton is indicated by the value on the register. The initial configuration of a computation with input *baba* is depicted

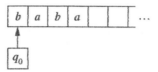

A computation of an automaton consists of the execution of a sequence of instructions. The execution of an instruction alters the state of the machine and moves the tape head one square to the right. The instruction set is obtained from the transition function of the DFA. The machine state and the symbol scanned determine the instruction to be executed. The action of a machine in state q_i scanning an a is to reset the state to $\delta(q_i, a)$. Since δ is a total function, there is exactly one instruction specified for every combination of state and input symbol, hence the *deterministic* in deterministic finite automaton.

The objective of a computation of an automaton is to determine the acceptability of the input string. A computation begins with the tape head scanning the leftmost square of the tape and the register containing the state q_0. The state and symbol are used to select the instruction. The machine then alters its state as prescribed by the instruction, and the tape head moves to the right. The transformation of a machine by the execution of an instruction cycle is exhibited in Figure 5.2. The instruction cycle is repeated until the tape head scans a blank square, at which time the computation terminates. An input string is **accepted** if the computation terminates in an accepting state; otherwise it is rejected. The computation in Figure 5.2 exhibits the acceptance of the string *aba*.

Definition 5.2.2

Let $M = (Q, \Sigma, \delta, q_0, F)$ be a DFA. The **language** of M, denoted L(M), is the set of strings in Σ^* accepted by M.

A DFA can be considered to be a language acceptor; the language of the machine is simply the set of strings accepted by its computations. The language of the machine in Figure 5.2 is the set of all strings over $\{a, b\}$ that end in a.

A DFA is a read-only machine that processes the input in a left-to-right manner; once an input symbol has been read, it has no further effect on the computation. At any point during the computation, the result depends only on the current state and the unprocessed

$$M: \quad Q = \{q_0, q_1\} \qquad \delta(q_0, a) = q_1$$
$$\Sigma = \{a, b\} \qquad \delta(q_0, b) = q_0$$
$$F = \{q_1\} \qquad \delta(q_1, a) = q_1$$
$$\delta(q_1, b) = q_0$$

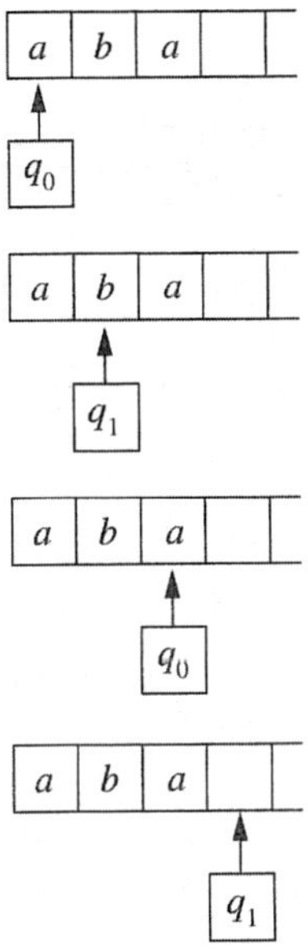

FIGURE 5.2   Computation in a DFA.

input. This combination is called a **machine configuration** and is represented by the ordered pair $[q_i, w]$, where q_i is the current state and $w \in \Sigma^*$ is the unprocessed input. The instruction cycle of a DFA transforms one machine configuration to another. The notation $[q_i, aw] \vdash_M [q_j, w]$ indicates that configuration $[q_j, w]$ is obtained from $[q_i, aw]$ by the execution of one instruction cycle of the machine M. The symbol $\vdash_M$, read "yields," defines a function from $Q \times \Sigma^+$ to $Q \times \Sigma^*$ that can be used to trace computations of the DFA. The M is omitted when there is no possible ambiguity.

Definition 5.2.3

The function $\vdash_M$ on $Q \times \Sigma^+$ is defined by

$$[q_i, aw] \vdash_M [\delta(q_i, a), w]$$

for $a \in \Sigma$ and $w \in \Sigma^*$, where δ is the transition function of the DFA M.

The notation $[q_i, u] \vdash^* [q_j, v]$ is used to indicate that configuration $[q_j, v]$ can be obtained from $[q_i, u]$ by zero or more transitions.

Computation and Reasoning

Example 5.2.1

The DFA M defined below accepts the set of strings over $\{a, b\}$ that contain the substring bb. That is, $L(M) = (a \cup b)^* bb(a \cup b)^*$. The states and alphabet of M are

$$M : Q = \{q_0, q_1, q_2\}$$
$$\Sigma = \{a, b\}$$
$$F = \{q_2\}.$$

The transition function δ is given in a tabular form called the *transition table*. The states are listed vertically and the alphabet horizontally. The action of the automaton in state q_i with input a can be determined by finding the intersection of the row corresponding to q_i and the column corresponding to a.

δ	a	b
q_0	q_0	q_1
q_1	q_0	q_2
q_2	q_2	q_2

The computations of M with input strings *abba* and *abab* are traced using the function $\vdash$.

$[q_0, abba]$	$[q_0, abab]$
$\vdash [q_0, bba]$	$\vdash [q_0, bab]$
$\vdash [q_1, ba]$	$\vdash [q_1, ab]$
$\vdash [q_2, a]$	$\vdash [q_0, b]$
$\vdash [q_2, \lambda]$	$\vdash [q_1, \lambda]$
accepts	rejects

The string *abba* is accepted since the computation halts in state q_2.   □

Example 5.2.2

The newspaper vending machine from the previous section can be represented by a DFA with the following states, alphabet, and transition function. The start state is the state *30*.

$Q = \{0, 5, 10, 15, 20, 25, 30\}$

$\Sigma = \{n, d, q\}$

$F = \{0\}$

δ	n	d	q
0	0	0	0
5	0	0	0
10	5	0	0
15	10	5	0
20	15	10	0
25	20	15	0
30	25	20	5

The language of the vending machine consists of all strings that represent a sum of 30 cents or more. Can you construct a regular expression that defines the language of this machine?

□

The transition function specifies the action of the machine for a given state and element from the alphabet. This function can be extended to a function $\hat{\delta}$ whose input consists of a state and a string over the alphabet. The function $\hat{\delta}$ is constructed by recursively extending the domain from elements of Σ to strings of arbitrary length.

Definition 5.2.4

The **extended transition function**, $\hat{\delta}$, of a DFA with transition function δ is a function from $Q \times \Sigma^*$ to Q. The values of $\hat{\delta}$ are defined by recursion on the length of the input string.

i) Basis: $length(w) = 0$. Then $w = \lambda$ and $\hat{\delta}(q_i, \lambda) = q_i$.
   $length(w) = 1$. Then $w = a$, for some $a \in \Sigma$, and $\hat{\delta}(q_i, a) = \delta(q_i, a)$.

ii) Recursive step: Let w be a string of length $n > 1$. Then $w = ua$ and $\hat{\delta}(q_i, ua) = \delta(\hat{\delta}(q_i, u), a)$.

The computation of a machine in state q_i with string w halts in state $\hat{\delta}(q_i, w)$. The evaluation of the function $\hat{\delta}(q_0, w)$ simulates the repeated applications of the transition function required to process the string w. A string w is accepted if $\hat{\delta}(q_0, w) \in F$. Using this notation, the language of a DFA M is the set $L(M) = \{w \mid \hat{\delta}(q_0, w) \in F\}$.

5.3   State Diagrams and Examples

The state diagram of a DFA is a labeled directed graph in which the nodes represent the states of the machine and the arcs are obtained from the transition function. The graph in Figure 5.1 is the state diagram for the newspaper vending machine DFA. Because of the intuitive nature of the graphic representation, we will often present the state diagram rather than the sets and transition function that constitute the formal definition of a DFA.

Definition 5.3.1

The **state diagram** of a DFA $M = (Q, \Sigma, \delta, q_0, F)$ is a labeled directed graph G defined by the following conditions:

i) The nodes of G are the elements of Q.
ii) The labels on the arcs of G are elements of Σ.
iii) q_0 is the start node, which is depicted ✗○.
iv) F is the set of accepting nodes; each accepting node is depicted ○.
v) There is an arc from node q_i to q_j labeled a, if $\delta(q_i, a) = q_j$.
vi) For every node q_i and symbol $a \in \Sigma$, there is exactly one arc labeled a leaving q_i.

Computation and Reasoning

A transition of a DFA is represented by an arc in the state diagram. Tracing the computation of a DFA in the corresponding state diagram constructs a path that begins at node q_0 and "spells" the input string. Let $\mathbf{p}_w$ be a path beginning at q_0 that spells w, and let q_w be the terminal node of $\mathbf{p}_w$. Theorem 5.3.2 proves that there is only one such path for every string $w \in \Sigma^*$. Moreover, q_w is the state of the DFA upon completion of the processing of w.

Theorem 5.3.2

Let $M = (Q, \Sigma, \delta, q_0, F)$ be a DFA and let $w \in \Sigma^*$. Then w determines a unique path $\mathbf{p}_w$ in the state diagram of M and $\hat{\delta}(q_0, w) = q_w$.

Proof. The proof is by induction on the length of the string. If the length of w is zero, then $\hat{\delta}(q_0, \lambda) = q_0$. The corresponding path is the null path that begins and terminates with q_0.

Assume that the result holds for all strings of length n or less. Let $w = ua$ be a string of length $n + 1$. By the inductive hypothesis, there is a unique path $\mathbf{p}_u$ that spells u and $\hat{\delta}(q_0, u) = q_u$. The path $\mathbf{p}_w$ is constructed by following the arc labeled a from q_u. This is the only path from q_0 that spells w since $\mathbf{p}_u$ is the unique path that spells u and there is only one arc leaving q_u labeled a. The terminal state of the path $\mathbf{p}_w$ is determined by the transition $\delta(q_u, a)$. From the definition of the extended transition function, $\hat{\delta}(q_0, w) = \delta(\hat{\delta}(q_0, u), a)$. Since $\hat{\delta}(q_0, u) = q_u$, $q_w = \delta(q_u, a) = \delta(\hat{\delta}(q_0, u), a) = \hat{\delta}(q_0, w)$ as desired.   ∎

The equivalence of computations of a DFA and paths in the state diagram gives us a heuristic method for determining the language of the DFA. The strings accepted in a state q_i are precisely those spelled by paths from q_0 to q_i. We can separate the determination of these paths into two parts:

i) First, find regular expressions $u_1, \ldots, u_n$ for strings on all paths from q_0 that reach q_i the first time.

ii) Find regular expressions $v_1, \ldots, v_m$ for all ways to leave q_i and return to q_i.

The strings accepted by q_i are $(u_1 \cup \cdots \cup u_n)(v_1 \cup \cdots \cup v_m)^*$.

Consider the DFA

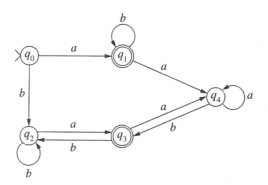

The language of M consists of all strings spelled by paths from q_0 to either q_1 or q_3. Using the heuristic described previously, the strings on the paths to each of the accepting states are

State	Paths to q_i	Simple Cycles from q_i to q_i	Accepted Strings
q_1	a	b	ab^*
q_3	ab^*aa^*b, bb^*a	bb^*a, aa^*b	$(ab^*aa \cup ba)(ab \cup ba)^*$

Consequently, $L(M) = ab^* \cup (ab^*aa^*b \cup bb^*a)(aa^*b \cup bb^*a)^*$. After we have established additional properties of finite-state computation, we will present an algorithm that automatically produces a regular expression for the language of a finite automaton.

In the remainder of this section we examine a number of DFAs to help develop the ability to design automata to check for patterns in strings. The types of conditions that we will consider include the number of occurrences and the relative positions of specified substrings. In addition, we establish the relationship between a DFA that accepts a language L and one that accepts the complement of L.

Example 5.3.1

The state diagram of the DFA in Example 5.2.1 is

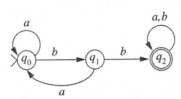

The states are used to record the number of consecutive b's processed. The state q_2 is entered when a substring bb is encountered. Once the machine enters q_2, the remainder of the input is processed, leaving the state unchanged. The computation of the DFA with input $ababb$ and the corresponding path in the state diagram are

Computation	Path
$[q_0, ababb]$	q_0,
$\vdash [q_0, babb]$	q_0,
$\vdash [q_1, abb]$	q_1,
$\vdash [q_0, bb]$	q_0,
$\vdash [q_1, b]$	q_1,
$\vdash [q_2, \lambda]$	q_2

The string $ababb$ is accepted since the halting state of the computation, which is also the terminal state of the path that spells $ababb$, is the accepting state q_2.   □

Computation and Reasoning

Example 5.3.2

The DFA

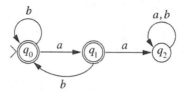

accepts $(b \cup ab)^*(a \cup \lambda)$, the set of strings over $\{a, b\}$ that do not contain the substring aa.

□

Example 5.3.3

Strings over $\{a, b\}$ that contain the substring bb or do not contain the substring aa are accepted by the DFA depicted below. This language is the union of the languages of the previous examples.

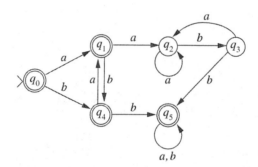

□

The state diagrams for machines that accept the strings with substring bb or without substring aa seem simple compared with the machine that accepts the union of those two languages. There does not appear to be an intuitive way to combine the state diagrams of the constituent DFAs to create the desired composite machine.

The next several examples provide a heuristic for designing DFAs. The first step is to produce an interpretation for the states of the DFA. The interpretation of a state describes properties of the string that has been processed when the machine is in the state. The pertinent properties are determined by the conditions required for a string to be accepted.

Example 5.3.4

A successful computation of a DFA that accepts the strings over $\{a, b\}$ containing the substring aaa must process three a's in a row. Four states are required to record the status of a computation checking for aaa. The interpretation of the states, along with state names, are

State	Interpretation
q_0:	No progress toward *aaa*
q_1:	Last symbol processed was an *a*
q_2:	Last two symbols processed were *aa*
q_3:	*aaa* has been found in the string

Prior to reading the first symbol, no progress has been made toward finding *aaa*. Consequently, this condition represents the start state.

Once the states are identified, it is frequently easy to determine the proper transitions. When computation in state q_1 processes an *a*, the last two symbols read are *aa* and q_2 is entered. On the other hand, if a *b* is read in q_1, the resulting string represents no progress toward *aaa* and the computation enters q_0. Following a similar strategy, the transitions can be determined for all states producing the DFA

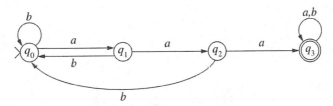

On processing *aaa*, the computation enters q_3, reads the remainder of the string, and accepts the input. □

Example 5.3.5

Building a machine that accepts strings with exactly two *a*'s and an odd number of *b*'s requires checking two conditions: the number of *a*'s and the parity of the *b*'s. Seven states are required to store the information needed about the string. The interpretation of the states describes the number of *a*'s read and the parity of the string processed when the computation is in the state.

State	Interpretation
q_0:	No *a*'s, even number of *b*'s
q_1:	No *a*'s, odd number of *b*'s
q_2:	One *a*, even number of *b*'s
q_3:	One *a*, odd number of *b*'s
q_4:	Two *a*'s, even number of *b*'s
q_5:	Two *a*'s, odd number of *b*'s
q_6:	More than two *a*'s

At the beginning of a computation, no a's and no b's have been processed and this becomes the condition of the start state. A DFA accepting this language is

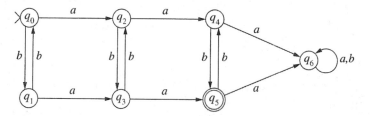

The horizontal arcs count the number of a's in the input string and the vertical pairs of arcs record the parity of the b's. The accepting state is q_5, since it represents the condition required of a string in the language.   □

Example 5.3.6

Let $\Sigma = \{0, 1, 2, 3\}$. A string in Σ^* is a sequence of integers from Σ. The DFA

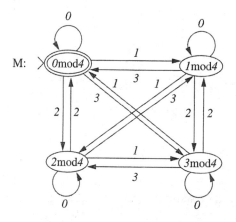

determines whether the sum of integers in an input string is divisible by four. For example, the strings *1 2 3 0 2* and *0 1 3 0* are accepted and *0 1 1 1* rejected by M. The states represent the value of the sum of the processed input modulo 4.   □

Our definition of DFA allowed only two possible outputs, accept or reject. The definition of output can be extended to have a value associated with each state. The result of a computation is the value associated with the state in which the computation terminates. A machine of this type is called a *Moore machine* after E. F. Moore, who introduced this type of finite-state computation. Associating the value i with the state $i \bmod 4$, the machine in Example 5.3.6 acts as a modulo 4 adder.

The state diagrams for machines in Examples 5.3.1, 5.3.2, and 5.3.3 showed that there is no simple method to obtain a DFA that accepts the union of two languages from DFAs that accept each of the languages. The next two examples show that this is not the case for machines that accept complementary sets of strings. The state diagram for a DFA can easily be transformed into the state diagram for another machine that accepts all, and only, the strings rejected by the original DFA.

Example 5.3.7

The DFA M accepts the language consisting of all strings over $\{a, b\}$ that contain an even number of a's and an odd number of b's.

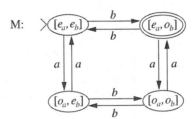

At any step of the computation, there are four possibilities for the parities of the input symbols processed: (1) even number of a's and even number of b's, (2) even number of a's and odd number of b's, (3) odd number of a's and even number of b's, (4) odd number of a's and odd number of b's. These four states are represented by ordered pairs in which the first component indicates the parity of the a's and the second component, the parity of the b's that have been processed. Processing a symbol changes one of the parities, designating the appropriate transition. □

Example 5.3.8

Let M be the DFA constructed in Example 5.3.7. A DFA M′ is constructed that accepts all strings over $\{a, b\}$ that do not contain an even number of a's and an odd number of b's. In other words, $L(M') = \{a, b\}^* - L(M)$. Any string rejected by M is accepted by M′ and vice versa. A state diagram for the machine M′ can be obtained from that of M by interchanging the accepting and nonaccepting states.

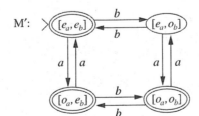

□

Computation and Reasoning

551

The preceding example shows the relationship between DFAs that accept complementary sets of strings. This relationship is formalized by the following result.

Theorem 5.3.3

Let $M = (Q, \Sigma, \delta, q_0, F)$ be a DFA. Then $M' = (Q, \Sigma, \delta, q_0, Q - F)$ is a DFA with $L(M') = \Sigma^* - L(M)$.

Proof.   Let $w \in \Sigma^*$ and $\hat{\delta}$ be the extended transition function constructed from δ. For each $w \in L(M)$, $\hat{\delta}(q_0, w) \in F$. Hence, $w \notin L(M')$. Conversely, if $w \notin L(M)$, then $\hat{\delta}(q_0, w) \in Q - F$ and $w \in L(M')$.   ▨

By definition, a DFA must process the entire input even if the result has already been established. Example 5.3.9 exhibits a type of determinism, sometimes referred to as *incomplete determinism*; each configuration has at most one action specified. The transitions of such a machine are defined by a partial function from $Q \times \Sigma$ to Q. As soon as it is possible to determine that a string is not acceptable, the computation halts. A computation that halts before processing the entire input string rejects the input.

Example 5.3.9

The state diagram below defines an incompletely specified DFA that accepts $(ab)^*c$. A computation terminates unsuccessfully as soon as the input varies from the desired pattern.

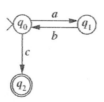

The computation with input $abcc$ is rejected since the machine is unable to process the final c from state q_2.   □

Two machines that accept the same language are called *equivalent*. An incompletely specified DFA can easily be transformed into an equivalent DFA. The transformation requires the addition of a nonaccepting "error" state. This state is entered whenever the incompletely specified machine enters a configuration for which no action is indicated. Upon entering the error state, the computation of the DFA reads the remainder of the string and halts.

Example 5.3.10

The DFA

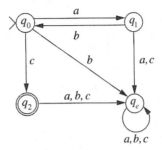

accepts the same language as the incompletely specified DFA in Example 5.3.9. The state q_e is the error state that ensures the processing of the entire string.   □

Example 5.3.11

The incompletely specified DFA defined by the state diagram

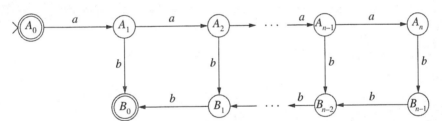

accepts the language $\{a^i b^i \mid i \leq n\}$, for a fixed integer n. The states labeled A_k count the number of a's, and then the B_k's ensure an equal number of b's. This technique cannot be extended to accept $\{a^i b^i \mid i \geq 0\}$ since an infinite number of states would be needed. In the next chapter we will show that the language $\{a^i b^i \mid i \geq 0\}$ is not accepted by any finite automaton.   □

5.4   Nondeterministic Finite Automata

We now alter our definition of machine to allow nondeterministic computations. In a nondeterministic automaton there may be several instructions that can be executed from a given machine configuration. Although this property may seem unnatural for computing machines, the flexibility of nondeterminism often facilitates the design of language acceptors.

Computation and Reasoning

553

A transition in a *nondeterministic finite automaton* (*NFA*) has the same effect as one in a DFA: to change the state of the machine based upon the current state and the symbol being scanned. The transition function must specify all possible states that the machine may enter from a given machine configuration. This is accomplished by having the value of the transition function be a set of states. The graphic representation of state diagrams is used to illustrate the alternatives that can occur in nondeterministic computation. Any finite number of transitions may be specified for a given state q_n and symbol a. The value of the nondeterministic transition function is given below the corresponding diagram.

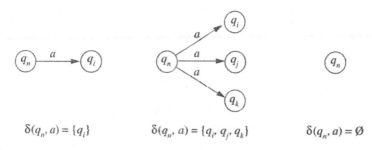

$$\delta(q_n, a) = \{q_i\} \qquad\qquad \delta(q_n, a) = \{q_i, q_j, q_k\} \qquad\qquad \delta(q_n, a) = \varnothing$$

Because nondeterministic computation differs significantly from its deterministic counterpart, we begin the presentation of nondeterministic machines with an example that demonstrates the fundamental differences between the two computational paradigms. In addition, we use the example to introduce the features of nondeterministic computation and to present an intuitive interpretation of nondeterminism.

Consider the DFA M_1

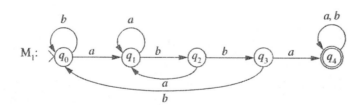

that accepts $(a \cup b)^*abba(a \cup b)^*$, the strings over $\{a, b\}$ that contain the substring $abba$. The states q_0, q_1, q_2, q_3 record the progress toward obtaining the substring $abba$. The states of the machine are

State	Interpretation
q_0:	When there is no progress toward *abba*
q_1:	When the last symbol processed was an *a*
q_2:	When the last two symbols processed were *ab*
q_3:	When the last three symbols processed were *abb*

Upon processing *abba*, state q_4 is entered, the remainder of the string is read, and the input is accepted.

The deterministic computation must "back up" in the sequence q_0, q_1, q_2, q_3 when the current substring is discovered not to have the desired form. If a *b* is scanned when the machine is in state q_3, then q_0 is entered since the last four symbols processed are *abbb* and the current configuration represents no progress toward finding *abba*.

A nondeterministic approach to accepting $(a \cup b)^*abba(a \cup b)^*$ is illustrated by the machine

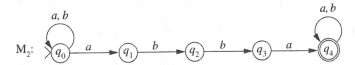

There are two possible transitions when M_2 processes an *a* in state q_0. One possibility is for M_2 to continue reading the string in state q_0. The second option enters the sequence of states q_1, q_2, q_3 to check if the next three symbols complete the substring *abba*.

The first thing to observe is that with a nondeterministic machine, there may be multiple computations for an input string. For example, M_2 has five different computations for string *aabbaa*. We will trace the computations using the $\vdash$ notation introduced in Section 5.2.

$[q_0, aabbaa]$	$[q_0, aabbaa]$	$[q_0, aabbaa]$	$[q_0, aabbaa]$	$[q_0, aabbaa]$
$\vdash [q_0, abbaa]$	$\vdash [q_0, abbaa]$	$\vdash [q_0, abbaa]$	$\vdash [q_0, abbaa]$	$\vdash [q_1, abbaa]$
$\vdash [q_0, bbaa]$	$\vdash [q_0, bbaa]$	$\vdash [q_0, bbaa]$	$\vdash [q_1, bbaa]$	
$\vdash [q_0, baa]$	$\vdash [q_0, baa]$	$\vdash [q_0, baa]$	$\vdash [q_2, baa]$	
$\vdash [q_0, aa]$	$\vdash [q_0, aa]$	$\vdash [q_0, aa]$	$\vdash [q_3, aa]$	
$\vdash [q_0, a]$	$\vdash [q_0, a]$	$\vdash [q_1, a]$	$\vdash [q_4, a]$	
$\vdash [q_0, \lambda]$	$\vdash [q_1, \lambda]$		$\vdash [q_4, \lambda]$	

What does it mean for a string to be accepted when there are some computations that halt in an accepting state and others that halt in a rejecting state? The answer lies in the use of the word *check* in the preceding paragraph. An NFA is designed to check whether a condition is satisfied, in this case, whether the input string has a substring *abba*. If one of the computations discovers the presence of the substring, the condition is satisfied and the string is accepted. As with incompletely specified DFAs, it is necessary to read the entire string to receive an affirmative answer. Summing up, a string is accepted by an NFA if there is at least one computation that

i) processes the entire string, and

ii) halts in an accepting state.

A string is in the language of a nondeterministic machine if there is a computation that accepts it; the existence of other computations that do not accept the string is irrelevant.

Nondeterministic machines are frequently designed to employ a "guess and check" strategy. The transition from q_0 to q_1 in M_2 represents the guess that the a being read is the first symbol in the substring $abba$. After the guess, the computation continues to states q_1, q_2, and q_3 to check whether the guess is correct. If symbols following the guess are bba, the string is accepted.

If an input string has the substring $abba$, one of the guesses will cause M_2 to enter state q_1 upon reading the initial a in the substring, and this computation accepts the string. Moreover, M_2 enters q_4 only upon processing $abba$. Consequently, the language of M_2 is $(a \cup b)^*abba(a \cup b)^*$. It should be noted that accepting computations are not necessarily unique; there are two distinct accepting computations for $abbabba$ in M_2.

If this is your first encounter with nondeterminism, it is reasonable to ask about the ability of a machine to perform this type of computation. DFAs can be easily implemented in either software or hardware. What is the analogous implementation for NFAs? We can intuitively imagine nondeterministic computation as a type of multiprocessing. When the computation enters a machine configuration for which there are multiple transitions, a new process is generated for each alternative. With this interpretation, a computation produces a tree of processes running in parallel with the branching generated by the multiple choices in the NFA. The tree corresponding to the computation of $aabbaa$ is

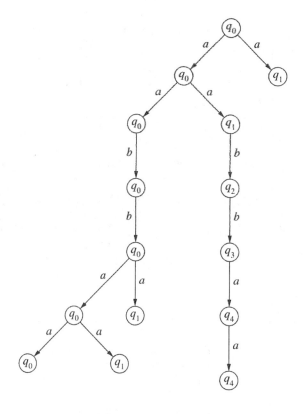

Computation and Reasoning

If one of the branches reads the entire string and halts in an accepting state, the input is accepted and the entire computation terminates. The input is rejected only when all branches terminate without accepting the string.

Having introduced the properties of nondeterministic computation in the preceding example, we now present the formal definitions of nondeterministic machines, their state diagrams, and their languages. With the exception of the transition function, the components of an NFA are identical to those of a DFA.

Definition 5.4.1

A **nondeterministic finite automaton (NFA)** is a quintuple $M = (Q, \Sigma, \delta, q_0, F)$, where Q is a finite set of states, Σ a finite set called the *alphabet*, $q_0 \in Q$ a distinguished state known as the *start state*, F a subset of Q called the *final* or *accepting states*, and δ a total function from $Q \times \Sigma$ to $\mathcal{P}(Q)$ known as the *transition function*.

Definition 5.4.2

The **language** of an NFA M, denoted L(M), is the set of strings accepted by the M. That is, $L(M) = \{w \mid \text{there is a computation } [q_0, w] \vdash^* [q_i, \lambda] \text{ with } q_i \in F\}$.

Definition 5.4.3

The **state diagram** of an NFA $M = (Q, \Sigma, \delta, q_0, F)$ is a labeled directed graph G defined by the following conditions:

   i) The nodes of G are elements of Q.
   ii) The labels on the arcs of G are elements of Σ.
  iii) q_0 is the start node.
   iv) F is the set of accepting nodes.
    v) There is an arc from node q_i to q_j labeled a, if $q_j \in \delta(q_i, a)$.

The relationship between DFAs and NFAs is clearly exhibited by comparing the properties of the corresponding state diagrams. Definition 5.4.3 is obtained from Definition 5.3.1 by omitting condition (vi), which translates the deterministic property of the DFA transition function into its graphic representation.

The relationship between DFAs and NFAs can be summarized by the seemingly paradoxical phrase, "Every deterministic finite automaton is nondeterministic." The transition function of a DFA specifies exactly one transition for each combination of state and input symbol, while an NFA allows zero, one, or more transitions. By interpreting the transition function of a DFA as a function from $Q \times \Sigma$ to singleton sets of states, the family of DFAs may be considered to be a subset of the family of NFAs.

The following example describes an NFA in terms of the components in the formal definition. We then construct the corresponding state diagram using the technique outlined in Definition 5.4.3.

Computation and Reasoning

Example 5.4.1

The NFA

$$M : Q = \{q_0, q_1, q_2\}$$
$$\Sigma = \{a, b\}$$
$$F = \{q_2\}$$

δ	a	b
q_0	$\{q_0\}$	$\{q_0, q_1\}$
q_1	$\emptyset$	$\{q_2\}$
q_2	$\emptyset$	$\emptyset$

with start state q_0 accepts the language $(a \cup b)^*bb$. The state diagram of M is

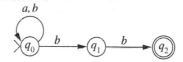

Pictorially, it is clear that a string is accepted if, and only if, it ends with the substring bb.

As noted previously, an NFA may have multiple computations for an input string. The three computations for the string $ababb$ are

$[q_0, ababb]$	$[q_0, ababb]$	$[q_0, ababb]$
$\vdash [q_0, babb]$	$\vdash [q_0, babb]$	$\vdash [q_0, babb]$
$\vdash [q_0, abb]$	$\vdash [q_1, abb]$	$\vdash [q_0, abb]$
$\vdash [q_0, bb]$		$\vdash [q_0, bb]$
$\vdash [q_0, b]$		$\vdash [q_1, b]$
$\vdash [q_0, \lambda]$		$\vdash [q_2, \lambda]$

The second computation halts after the execution of three instructions since no action is specified when the machine is in state q_1 scanning an a. The first computation processes the entire input and halts in a rejecting state while the final computation halts in an accepting state. The third computation demonstrates that $ababb$ is in the language of machine M.   □

Example 5.4.2

The state diagrams M_1 and M_2 define finite automata that accept $(a \cup b)^*bb(a \cup b)^*$.

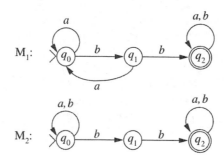

Computation and Reasoning

M_1 is the DFA from Example 5.3.1. The path exhibiting the acceptance of strings by M_1 enters q_2 when the first substring bb is encountered. M_2 can enter the accepting state upon processing any occurrence of bb.   □

Example 5.4.3

An NFA that accepts strings over $\{a, b\}$ with the substring aa or bb can be constructed by combining a machine that accepts strings with bb (Example 5.4.2) with a similar machine that accepts strings with aa.

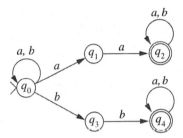

A path exhibiting the acceptance of a string reads the input in state q_0 until an occurrence of the substring aa or bb is encountered. At this point, the path branches to either q_1 or q_3, depending upon the substring. There are three distinct paths that exhibit the acceptance of the string $abaaabb$.   □

The flexibility permitted by the use of nondeterminism does not always simplify the problem of constructing a machine that accepts $L(M_1) \cup L(M_2)$ from the machines M_1 and M_2. This can be seen by attempting to construct an NFA that accepts the language of the DFA in Example 5.3.3.

5.5   λ-Transitions

The transitions from state to state in both deterministic and nondeterministic automata were initiated by processing an input symbol. The definition of NFA is now relaxed to allow state transitions without requiring input to be processed. A transition of this form is called a **λ-transition**. The class of nondeterministic machines that utilize λ-transitions is denoted NFA-λ.

The incorporation of λ-transitions into finite state machines represents another step away from the deterministic computations of a DFA. They do, however, provide a useful tool for the design of machines to accept complex languages.

Definition 5.5.1

A **nondeterministic finite automaton with λ-transitions** is a quintuple $M = (Q, \Sigma, \delta, q_0, F)$, where Q, δ, q_0, and F are the same as in an NFA. The transition function is a function from $Q \times (\Sigma \cup \{\lambda\})$ to $\mathcal{P}(Q)$.

The definition of halting must be extended to include the possibility that a computation may continue using λ-transitions after the input string has been completely processed. Employing the criteria used for acceptance in an NFA, the input is accepted if there is a computation that processes the entire string and halts in an accepting state. As before, the language of an NFA-λ is denoted L(M). The state diagram for an NFA-λ is constructed according to Definition 5.4.3 with λ-transitions represented by arcs labeled by λ.

The ability to move between states without processing an input symbol can be used to construct complex machines from simpler machines. Let M_1 and M_2 be the machines

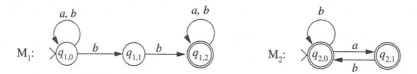

that accept $(a \cup b)^*bb(a \cup b)^*$ and $(b \cup ab)^*(a \cup \lambda)$, respectively. Composite machines are built by appropriately combining the state diagrams of M_1 and M_2.

Example 5.5.1

The language of the NFA-λ M is $L(M_1) \cup L(M_2)$.

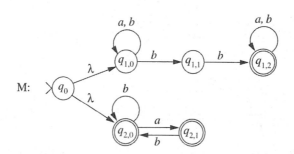

A computation in the composite machine M begins by following a λ-arc to the start state of either M_1 or M_2. If the path **p** exhibits the acceptance of a string by machine M_i, then that string is accepted by the path in M consisting of the λ-arc from q_0 to $q_{i,0}$ followed by **p** in the copy of the machine M_i. Since the initial move in each computation does not process an input symbol, the language of M is $L(M_1) \cup L(M_2)$. Compare the simplicity of the machine obtained by this construction with that of the deterministic state diagram in Example 5.3.3.

$\square$

Computation and Reasoning

Example 5.5.2

An NFA-λ that accepts $L(M_1)L(M_2)$, the concatenation of the languages of M_1 and M_2, is constructed by joining the two machines with a λ-arc.

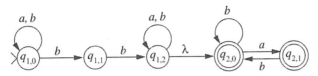

An input string is accepted only if it consists of a string from $L(M_1)$ concatenated with one from $L(M_2)$. The λ-transition allows the computation to enter M_2 whenever a prefix of the input string is accepted by M_1.   □

Example 5.5.3

We will use λ-transitions to construct an NFA-λ that accepts all strings of even length over $\{a, b\}$. We begin by building the state diagram of a machine that accepts strings of length two.

$$\xrightarrow{} q_0 \xrightarrow{a, b} q_1 \xrightarrow{a, b} q_2$$

To accept the null string, a λ-arc is added from q_0 to q_2. Strings of any positive, even length are accepted by following the λ-arc from q_2 to q_0 to repeat the sequence q_0, q_1, q_2.

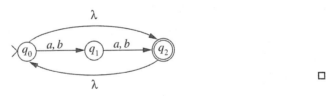

□

The constructions presented in Examples 5.5.1, 5.5.2, and 5.5.3 can be generalized to construct machines that accept the union, concatenation, and Kleene star of languages accepted by existing finite-state machines. The first step is to transform the machines into an equivalent NFA-λ whose form is amenable to these constructions.

Lemma 5.5.2

Let $M = (Q, \Sigma, \delta, q_0, F)$ be an NFA-λ. There is an equivalent NFA-λ $M' = (Q \cup \{q_0', q_f\}, \Sigma, \delta', q_0', \{q_f\})$ that satisfies the following conditions:

i) The in-degree of the start state q_0' is zero.

ii) The only accepting state of M' is q_f.

iii) The out-degree of the accepting state q_f is zero.

Proof. The transition function of M′ is constructed from that of M by adding the λ-transitions

$$\delta(q'_0, \lambda) = \{q_0\}$$

$$\delta(q_i, \lambda) = \{q_f\} \text{ for every } q_i \in F$$

for the new states q'_0 and q_f. The λ-transition from q'_0 to q_0 permits the computation to proceed to the original machine M without affecting the input. A computation of M′ that accepts an input string is identical to that of M followed by a λ-transition from the accepting state of M to the accepting state q_f of M′.   ■

If a machine satisfies the conditions of Lemma 5.5.2, the sole role of the start state is to initiate a computation, and the computation terminates as soon as q_f is entered. Such a machine can be pictured as

The diagram depicts a machine with three distinct parts: the initial state, the body of the machine, and the final state. This can be likened to a railroad car with couplers on either end. Indeed, the conditions on the start and final state are designed to allow them to act as couplers of finite-state machines.

Theorem 5.5.3

Let M_1 and M_2 be two NFA-λs. There are NFA-λs that accept $L(M_1) \cup L(M_2)$, $L(M_1)L(M_2)$, and $L(M_1)^*$.

Proof. We assume, without loss of generality, that M_1 and M_2 satisfy the conditions of Lemma 5.5.2. The machines constructed to accept the languages $L(M_1) \cup L(M_2)$, $L(M_1)L(M_2)$, and $L(M_1)^*$ will also satisfy the conditions of Lemma 5.5.2.

Because of the restrictions on the start and final states, M_1 and M_2 may be depicted

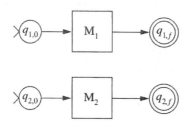

The language $L(M_1) \cup L(M_2)$ is accepted by

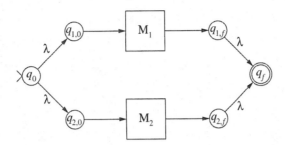

A computation begins by following a λ-arc to M_1 or M_2. If the string is accepted by either of these machines, the λ-arc can be traversed to reach the accepting state of the composite machine. This construction may be thought of as building a machine that runs M_1 and M_2 in parallel. The input is accepted if either of the machines successfully processes the string.

Concatenation can be obtained by operating the component machines sequentially. The start state of the composite machine is $q_{1,0}$ and the accepting state is $q_{2,f}$. The machines are joined by connecting the final state of M_1 to the start state of M_2.

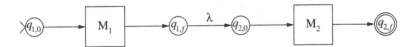

When a prefix of the input string is accepted by M_1, the computation continues with M_2. If the remainder of the string is accepted by M_2, the processing terminates in $q_{2,f}$, the accepting state of the composite machine.

A machine that accepts $L(M_1)^*$ must be able to cycle through M_1 any number of times. The λ-arc from $q_{1,f}$ to $q_{1,0}$ permits the necessary cycling. Another λ-arc is added from $q_{1,0}$ to $q_{1,f}$ to accept the null string. These arcs are added to M_1 producing

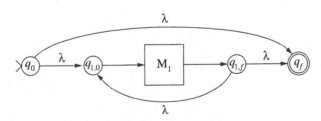

The ability to repeatedly connect machines of this form will be used in Chapter 6 to establish the equivalence of languages described by regular expressions and accepted by finite-state machines.

5.6   Removing Nondeterminism

Three classes of finite automata have been introduced in the previous sections, each class being a generalization of its predecessor. By relaxing the deterministic restriction, have we created a more powerful class of machines? More precisely, is there a language accepted by an NFA that is not accepted by any DFA? We will show that this is not the case. Moreover, an algorithm is presented that converts an NFA-λ to an equivalent DFA.

The state transitions in DFAs and NFAs accompanied the processing of an input symbol. To relate the transitions in an NFA-λ to the processing of input, we build a modified transition function t, called the *input transition function,* whose value is the set of states that can be entered by processing a single input symbol from a given state. The value of $t(q_1, a)$ for the diagram in Figure 5.3 is the set $\{q_2, q_3, q_5, q_6\}$. State q_4 is omitted since the transition from state q_1 does not process an input symbol.

Intuitively, the definition of the input transition function $t(q_i, a)$ can be broken into three parts. First, the set of states that can be reached from q_i without processing a symbol is constructed. This is followed by processing an a from all the states in that set. Finally, following λ-arcs from the resulting states yields the set $t(q_i, a)$.

The function t is defined in terms of the transition function δ and the paths in the state diagram that spell the null string. A node q_j is said to be in the λ-closure of q_i if there is a path from q_i to q_j that spells the null string.

Definition 5.6.1

The λ-**closure** of a state q_i, denoted λ-$closure(q_i)$, is defined recursively by

i) Basis: $q_i \in$ λ-$closure(q_i)$.

ii) Recursive step: Let q_j be an element of λ-$closure(q_i)$. If $q_k \in \delta(q_j, \lambda)$, then $q_k \in$ λ-$closure(q_i)$.

iii) Closure: q_j is in λ-$closure(q_i)$ only if it can be obtained from q_i by a finite number of applications of the recursive step.

The set λ-$closure(q_i)$ can be constructed following the top-down approach used in Algorithm 4.3.1, which determined the chains in a context-free grammar. The input transition function is obtained from the λ-closure of the states and the transition function of the NFA-λ.

Definition 5.6.2

The **input transition function** t of an NFA-λ M is a function from Q × Σ to $\mathcal{P}(Q)$ defined by

$$t(q_i, a) = \bigcup_{q_j \in \lambda\text{-}closure(q_i)} \lambda\text{-}closure(\delta(q_j, a)),$$

where δ is the transition function of M.

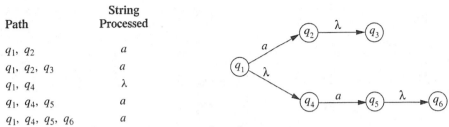

Path	String Processed
q_1, q_2	a
q_1, q_2, q_3	a
q_1, q_4	λ
q_1, q_4, q_5	a
q_1, q_4, q_5, q_6	a

FIGURE 5.3   Paths with λ-transitions.

The input transition function has the same form as the transition function of an NFA. That is, it is a function from $Q \times \Sigma$ to sets of states. For an NFA without λ-transitions, the input transition function t is identical to the transition function δ of the automaton.

Example 5.6.1

Transition tables are given for the transition function δ and the input transition function t of the NFA-λ with state diagram M. The language of M is $a^+c^*b^*$.

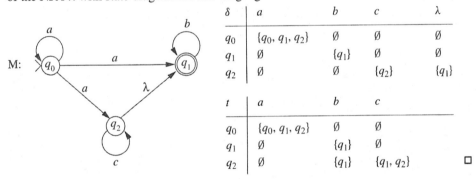

δ	a	b	c	λ
q_0	$\{q_0, q_1, q_2\}$	$\emptyset$	$\emptyset$	$\emptyset$
q_1	$\emptyset$	$\{q_1\}$	$\emptyset$	$\emptyset$
q_2	$\emptyset$	$\emptyset$	$\{q_2\}$	$\{q_1\}$

t	a	b	c
q_0	$\{q_0, q_1, q_2\}$	$\emptyset$	$\emptyset$
q_1	$\emptyset$	$\{q_1\}$	$\emptyset$
q_2	$\emptyset$	$\{q_1\}$	$\{q_1, q_2\}$	□

The input transition function of an NFA-λ is used to construct an equivalent DFA. Acceptance in a nondeterministic machine is determined by the existence of a computation that processes the entire string and halts in an accepting state. There may be several paths in the state diagram of an NFA-λ that represent the processing of an input string, while the state diagram of a DFA contains exactly one such path. To remove the nondeterminism, the DFA must simulate the simultaneous exploration of all possible computations in the NFA-λ.

Algorithm 5.6.3 iteratively builds the state diagram of a deterministic machine equivalent to an NFA-λ M. The nodes of the DFA, called DM for *deterministic equivalent of M*, are sets of nodes of M. The start node of DM is the λ-closure of the start node of M. The key to the algorithm is step 2.1.1, which generates the nodes of the deterministic machine. If X is a node in DM, the set Y is constructed that contains all the states that can be entered by processing the symbol a from any state in the set X. This relationship is represented in the state diagram of DM by an arc from X to Y labeled a. The node X is made deterministic by producing an arc from it for every symbol in the alphabet. New nodes generated in step 2.1.1 are added to the set Q' and the process continues until every node in Q' is deterministic.

Algorithm 5.6.3
Construction of DM, a DFA Equivalent to NFA-λ M

input: an NFA-λ $M = (Q, \ \Sigma, \ \delta, \ q_0, \ F)$
      input transition function t of M

1. initialize Q' to λ-*closure*(q_0)
2. **repeat**
    2.1. **if** there is a node $X \in Q'$ and a symbol $a \in \Sigma$ with no arc
           leaving X labeled a, **then**
           2.1.1. let $Y = \bigcup\limits_{q_i \in X} t(q_i, a)$
           2.1.2. **if** $Y \notin Q'$, **then** set $Q' := Q' \cup \{Y\}$
           2.1.3. add an arc from X to Y labeled a
        else done := *true*
    until done
3. the set of accepting states of DM is $F' = \{X \in Q' \mid X \text{ contains an element } q_i \in F\}$

The NFA-λ from Example 5.6.1 is used to illustrate the construction of nodes for the equivalent DFA. The start node of DM is the singleton set containing the start node of M. A transition from q_0 processing an a can terminate in q_0, q_1, or q_2. We construct a node $\{q_0, q_1, q_2\}$ for the DFA and connect it to $\{q_0\}$ by an arc labeled a. The path from $\{q_0\}$ to $\{q_0, q_1, q_2\}$ in DM represents the three possible ways of processing the symbol a from state q_0 in M.

Since DM is to be deterministic, the node $\{q_0\}$ must have arcs labeled b and c leaving it. Arcs from q_0 to $\emptyset$ labeled b and c are added to indicate that there is no action specified by the NFA-λ when the machine is in state q_0 scanning these symbols.

The node $\{q_0\}$ has the deterministic form; there is exactly one arc leaving it for every member of the alphabet. Figure 5.4(a) shows DM at this stage of its construction. Two additional nodes, $\{q_0, q_1, q_2\}$ and $\emptyset$, have been created. Both of these must be made deterministic.

An arc leaving node $\{q_0, q_1, q_2\}$ terminates in a node consisting of all the states that can be reached by processing the input symbol from the states q_0, q_1, or q_2 in M. The input transition function $t(q_i, a)$ specifies the states reachable by processing an a from q_i. The arc from $\{q_0, q_1, q_2\}$ labeled a terminates in the set consisting of the union of the $t(q_0, a)$, $t(q_1, a)$, and $t(q_2, a)$. The set obtained from this union is again $\{q_0, q_1, q_2\}$. An arc from $\{q_0, q_1, q_2\}$ to itself is added to the diagram designating this transition.

The empty set represents an error state for DM. A computation enters $\emptyset$ on reading an a in state Y only if there is no transition for a for any $q_i \in Y$. Once in $\emptyset$, the computation

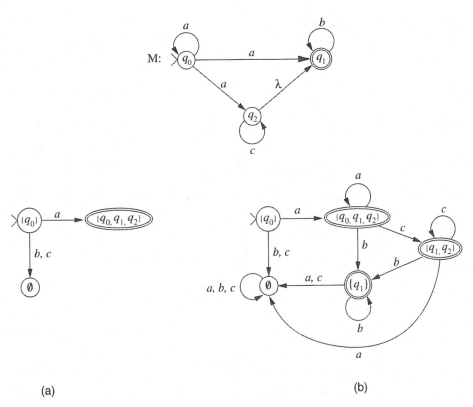

FIGURE 5.4   Construction of equivalent deterministic automaton.

processes the remainder of the input and rejects the string. This is indicated in the state diagram by the arc from Ø to itself labeled by each alphabet symbol.

Figure 5.4(b) gives the completed deterministic equivalent of the M. Computations of the nondeterministic machine with input aaa can terminate in state q_0, q_1, and q_2. The acceptance of the string is exhibited by the path that terminates in q_1. Processing aaa in DM terminates in state $\{q_0, q_1, q_2\}$. This state is accepting in DM since it contains the accepting state q_1 of M.

The algorithm for constructing the deterministic state diagram consists of repeatedly adding arcs to make the nodes in the diagram deterministic. As arcs are constructed, new nodes may be created and added to the diagram. The procedure terminates when all the nodes are deterministic. Since each node is a subset of Q, at most $card(\mathcal{P}(Q))$ nodes can be constructed. Algorithm 5.6.3 always terminates since $card(\mathcal{P}(Q))card(\Sigma)$ is an upper bound on the number of iterations of the repeat-until loop. Theorem 5.6.4 establishes the equivalence of M and DM.

Computation and Reasoning

Theorem 5.6.4

Let $w \in \Sigma^*$ and $Q_w = \{q_{w_1}, q_{w_2}, \ldots, q_{w_j}\}$ be the set of states entered upon the completion of the processing of the string w in M. Processing w in DM terminates in state Q_w.

Proof.   The proof is by induction on the length of the string w. A computation of M that processes the empty string terminates at a node in $\lambda\text{-}closure(q_0)$. This set is the start state of DM.

Assume the property holds for all strings of length n and let $w = ua$ be a string of length $n + 1$. Let $Q_u = \{q_{u_1}, q_{u_2}, \ldots, q_{u_k}\}$ be the terminal states of the paths obtained by processing the entire string u in M. By the inductive hypothesis, processing u in DM terminates in Q_u. Computations processing ua in M terminate in states that can be reached by processing an a from a state in Q_u. This set, Q_w, can be defined using the input transition function:

$$Q_w = \bigcup_{i=1}^{k} t(q_{u_i}, a).$$

This completes the proof since Q_w is the state entered by processing a from state Q_u of DM. ∎

The acceptance of a string in a nondeterministic automaton depends upon the existence of one computation that processes the entire string and terminates in an accepting state. The node Q_w contains the terminal states of all the paths generated by computations in M that process w. If w is accepted by M, then Q_w contains an accepting state of M. The presence of an accepting node makes Q_w an accepting state of DM and, by the previous theorem, w is accepted by DM.

Conversely, let w be a string accepted by DM. Then Q_w contains an accepting state of M. The construction of Q_w guarantees the existence of a computation in M that processes w and terminates in that accepting state. These observations provide the justification for Corollary 5.6.5.

Corollary 5.6.5

The finite automata M and DM are equivalent.

Example 5.6.2

The NFA

accepts the language a^+b^+. The construction of an equivalent DFA is traced in the following table.

State	Symbol	NFA Transitions	Next State
$\{q_0\}$	a	$\delta(q_0, a) = \{q_0, q_1\}$	$\{q_0, q_1\}$
$\{q_0\}$	b	$\delta(q_0, b) = \emptyset$	$\emptyset$
$\{q_0, q_1\}$	a	$\delta(q_0, a) = \{q_0, q_1\}$ $\delta(q_1, a) = \emptyset$	$\{q_0, q_1\}$
$\{q_0, q_1\}$	b	$\delta(q_0, b) = \emptyset$ $\delta(q_1, b) = \{q_1, q_2\}$	$\{q_1, q_2\}$
$\{q_1, q_2\}$	a	$\delta(q_1, a) = \emptyset$ $\delta(q_2, a) = \emptyset$	$\emptyset$
$\{q_1, q_2\}$	b	$\delta(q_1, b) = \{q_1, q_2\}$ $\delta(q_2, b) = \emptyset$	$\{q_1, q_2\}$

Since M is an NFA, the transition function δ of M serves as the input transition function and the start state of the equivalent DFA is $\{q_0\}$. The resulting DFA is

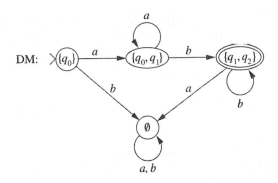

Example 5.6.3

As seen in the preceding examples, the states of the DFA constructed using Algorithm 5.6.3 are sets of states of the original nondeterministic machine. If the nondeterministic machine has n states, the DFA may have 2^n states. The transformation of the NFA

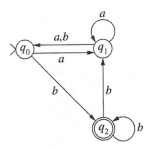

Computation and Reasoning

shows that the theoretical upper bound on the number of states may be attained. The start state of DM is $\{q_0\}$ since M does not have λ-transitions.

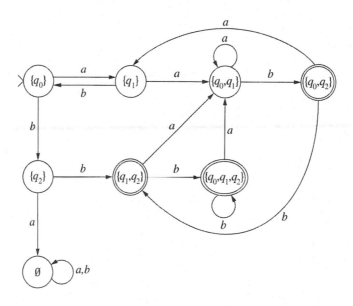

□

Example 5.6.4

The machines M_1 and M_2 accept $a(ba)^*$ and a^*, respectively.

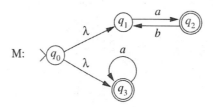

Using λ-arcs to connect a new start state to the start states of the original machines creates an NFA-λ M that accepts $a(ba)^* \cup a^*$.

M:

The input transition function for M is

t	a	b
q_0	$\{q_2, q_3\}$	$\emptyset$
q_1	$\{q_2\}$	$\emptyset$
q_2	$\emptyset$	$\{q_1\}$
q_3	$\{q_3\}$	$\emptyset$

The equivalent DFA obtained from Algorithm 5.6.3 is

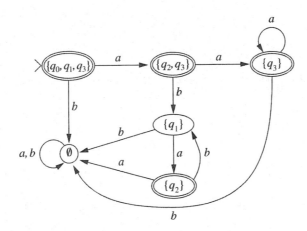

Algorithm 5.6.3 completes the following cycle describing the relationships between the classes of finite automata.

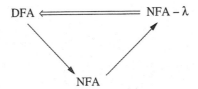

The arrows represent inclusion; every DFA can be reformulated as an NFA that is, in turn, an NFA-λ. The double arrow from NFA-λ to DFA indicates the existence of an equivalent deterministic machine.

Computation and Reasoning

5.7   DFA Minimization

The preceding sections established that the family of languages accepted by DFAs is the same as that accepted by NFAs and NFA-λs. The flexibility of nondeterminism and λ-transitions aid in the design of machines to accept complex languages. The nondeterministic machine can then be transformed into an equivalent deterministic machine using Algorithm 5.6.3. The resulting DFA, however, may not be the minimal DFA that accepts the language. This section presents a reduction algorithm that produces the minimal state DFA accepting the language L from any DFA that accepts L. To accomplish the reduction, the notion of equivalent states in a DFA is introduced.

Definition 5.7.1

Let $M = (Q, \Sigma, \delta, q_0, F)$ be a DFA. States q_i and q_j are equivalent if $\hat{\delta}(q_i, u) \in F$ if, and only if, $\hat{\delta}(q_j, u) \in F$ for every $u \in \Sigma^*$.

Two states that are equivalent are called *indistinguishable*. The binary relation over Q defined by indistinguishability of states is an equivalence relation; that is, the relation is reflexive, symmetric, and transitive. Two states that are not equivalent are said to be *distinquishable*. States q_i and q_j are distinguishable if there is a string u such that $\hat{\delta}(q_i, u) \in$ F and $\hat{\delta}(q_j, u) \notin$ F, or vice versa.

The motivation behind this definition of equivalence is illustrated by the following states and transitions:

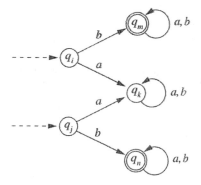

The unlabeled dotted lines entering q_i and q_j indicate that the method of reaching a state is irrelevant; equivalence depends only upon computations from the state. The states q_i and q_j are equivalent since the computation with any string beginning with b from either state halts in an accepting state and all other computations halt in the nonaccepting state q_k. States q_m and q_n are also equivalent; all computations beginning in these states end in an accepting state.

The intuition behind the transformation is that equivalent states may be merged. Applying this to the preceding example yields

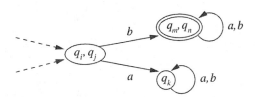

To reduce the size of a DFA M by merging states, a procedure for identifying equivalent states must be developed. In the algorithm to accomplish this, each pair of states q_i and q_j, $i < j$, has associated with it values $D[i, j]$ and $S[i, j]$. $D[i, j]$ is set to 1 when it is determined that the states q_i and q_j are distinguishable. $S[m, n]$ contains a set of indices. Index $[i, j]$ is in the set $S[m, n]$ if the distinguishability of q_i and q_j follows from that of q_m and q_n.

The algorithm begins by marking each pair of states q_i and q_j as distinguishable if one is accepting and the other is rejecting. The remainder of the algorithm systematically examines each nonmarked pair of states. When two states are shown to be distinguishable, a call to a recursive routine $DIST$ sets $D[i, j]$ to 1. The call $DIST(i, j)$ not only marks q_i and q_j as distinguishable, it also marks each pair of states q_m and q_n for which $[m, n] \in S[i, j]$ as distinguishable through a call to $DIST(m, n)$.

Algorithm 5.7.2
Determination of Equivalent States of DFA

input: DFA M $= (Q, \Sigma, \delta, q_0, F)$

1. (Initialization)
   for every pair of states q_i and q_j, $i < j$, **do**
       1.1. $D[i, j] := 0$
       1.2. $S[i, j] := \emptyset$
   end for
2. **for** every pair $i, j, i < j$, if one of q_i or q_j is an accepting state and the other is
   not an accepting state, **then** set $D[i, j] := 1$
3. **for** every pair $i, j, i < j$, with $D[i, j] = 0$, **do**
       3.1. if there exists an $a \in \Sigma$ such that $\delta(q_i, a) = q_m$, $\delta(q_j, a) = q_n$ and
           $D[m, n] = 1$ or $D[n, m] = 1$, **then** $DIST(i, j)$
       3.2. **else** for each $a \in \Sigma$, do: Let $\delta(q_i, a) = q_m$ and $\delta(q_j, a) = q_n$
           if $m < n$ and $[i, j] \neq [m, n]$, **then** add $[i, j]$ to $S[m, n]$
           else if $m > n$ and $[i, j] \neq [n, m]$, **then** add $[i, j]$ to $S[n, m]$
   end for

$DIST(i, j)$;
begin
  $D[i, j] := 1$
  for all $[m, n] \in S[i, j]$, $DIST(m, n)$
end

The motivation behind the identification of distinguishable states is illustrated by the relationships in the diagram

If q_m and q_n are already marked as distinguishable when q_i and q_j are examined in step 3, then $D[i, j]$ is set to 1 to indicate the distinguishability of q_i and q_j. If the status of q_m and q_n is not known when q_i and q_j are examined, then a later determination that q_m and q_n are distinguishable also provides the answer for q_i and q_j. The role of the array S is to record this information: $[i, j] \in S[n, m]$ indicates that the distinguishability of q_m and q_n is sufficient to establish the distinguishability of q_i and q_j. These ideas are formalized in the proof of Theorem 5.7.3.

Theorem 5.7.3

States q_i and q_j are distinguishable if, and only if, $D[i, j] = 1$ at the termination of Algorithm 5.7.2.

Proof.   First we show that every pair of states q_i and q_j for which $D[i, j] = 1$ is distinguishable. If $D[i, j]$ is assigned 1 in the step 2, then q_i and q_j are distinguishable by the null string. Step 3.1 marks q_i and q_j as distinguishable only if $\delta(q_i, a) = q_m$ and $\delta(q_j, a) = q_n$ for some input a when states q_m and q_n have already been determined to be distinguishable by the algorithm. Let u be a string that exhibits the distinguishability of q_m and q_n. Then au exhibits the distinguishability of q_i and q_j.

To complete the proof, it is necessary to show that every pair of distinguishable states is designated as such. The proof is by induction on the length of the shortest string that demonstrates the distinguishability of a pair of states. The basis consists of all pairs of states q_i, q_j that are distinguishable by a string of length 0. That is, the computations $\hat{\delta}(q_i, \lambda) = q_i$ and $\hat{\delta}(q_j, \lambda) = q_j$ distinguish q_i from q_j. In this case, exactly one of q_i or q_j is accepting and the position $D[i, j]$ is set to 1 in step 2.

Now assume that every pair of states distinguishable by a string of length k or less is marked by the algorithm. Let q_i and q_j be states for which the shortest distinguishing string u has length $k + 1$. Then u can be written av and the computations with input u have the form $\hat{\delta}(q_i, u) = \hat{\delta}(q_i, av) = \hat{\delta}(q_m, v) = q_s$ and $\hat{\delta}(q_j, u) = \hat{\delta}(q_j, av) = \hat{\delta}(q_n, v) = q_t$. Exactly one of q_s and q_t is accepting since the preceding computations distinguish q_i from q_j. Clearly, the same computations exhibit the distinguishability of q_m from q_n by a string of length k. By induction, we know that the algorithm will set $D[m, n]$ to 1.

If $D[m, n]$ is marked before the states q_i and q_j are examined in step 3, then $D[i, j]$ is set to 1 by the call $DIST(i, j)$. If q_i and q_j are examined in the loop in step 3.1 and $D[m, n] \neq 1$ at that time, then $[i, j]$ is added to the set $S[m, n]$. By the inductive hypothesis, $D[m, n]$ will eventually be set to 1. $D[i, j]$ will also be set to 1 at this time by a recursive call from $DIST(m, n)$ since $[i, j]$ is in $S[m, n]$.   ∎

A new DFA M' can be built from the original DFA M $= (Q, \Sigma, \delta, q_0, F)$ and the indistinguishability relation. The states of M' are the equivalence classes consisting of indistinguishable states of M. The start state is $[q_0]$, and $[q_i]$ is a final state if $q_i \in F$. The transition function δ' of M' is defined by $\delta'([q_i], a) = [\delta(q_i, a)]$. In Exercise 44, δ' is shown to be well defined. L(M') consists of all strings whose computations have the form $\hat{\delta}'([q_0], u) = [\hat{\delta}(q_i, \lambda)]$ with $q_i \in F$. These are precisely the strings accepted by M. If M' has states that are unreachable by computations from $[q_0]$, these states and all associated arcs are deleted.

Example 5.7.1

The minimization process is exhibited using the DFA M

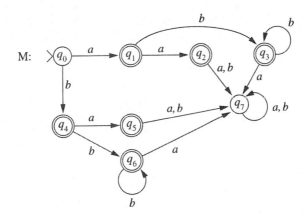

that accepts the language $(a \cup b)(a \cup b^*)$.

In step 2, $D[0, 1]$, $D[0, 2]$, $D[0, 3]$, $D[0, 4]$, $D[0, 5]$, $D[0, 6]$, $D[1, 7]$, $D[2, 7]$, $D[3, 7]$, $D[4, 7]$, $D[5, 7]$, and $D[6, 7]$ are set to 1. Each index not marked in step 2 is examined in step 3. The table shows the action taken for each such index.

Index	Action	Reason
[0, 7]	$D[0, 7] = 1$	Distinguished by a
[1, 2]	$D[1, 2] = 1$	Distinguished by a
[1, 3]	$D[1, 3] = 1$	Distinguished by a
[1, 4]	$S[2, 5] = \{[1, 4]\}$	
	$S[3, 6] = \{[1, 4]\}$	
[1, 5]	$D[1, 5] = 1$	Distinguished by a
[1, 6]	$D[1, 6] = 1$	Distinguished by a
[2, 3]	$D[2, 3] = 1$	Distinguished by b
		(Continued)

Computation and Reasoning

Index	Action	Reason
[2, 4]	$D[2, 4] = 1$	Distinguished by a
[2, 5]		No action since $\delta(q_2, x) = \delta(q_5, x)$ for every $x \in \Sigma$
[2, 6]	$D[2, 6] = 1$	Distinguished by b
[3, 4]	$D[3, 4] = 1$	Distinguished by a
[3, 5]	$D[3, 5] = 1$	Distinguished by b
[3, 6]		
[4, 5]	$D[4, 5] = 1$	Distinguished by a
[4, 6]	$D[4, 6] = 1$	Distinguished by a
[5, 6]	$D[5, 6] = 1$	Distinguished by b

After each pair of indices is examined, [1, 4], [2, 5], and [3, 6] are left as equivalent pairs of states. Merging these states produces the minimal state DFA M′ that accepts $(a \cup b)(a \cup b^*)$.

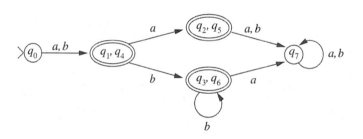

Example 5.7.2

Minimizing the DFA M illustrates the recursive marking of states by the call to *DIST*. The language of M is $a(a \cup b)^* \cup ba(a \cup b)^* \cup bba(a \cup b)^*$.

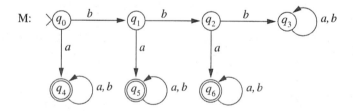

The comparison of accepting states to nonaccepting states assigns 1 to $D[0, 4]$, $D[0, 5]$, $D[0, 6]$, $D[1, 4]$, $D[1, 5]$, $D[1, 6]$, $D[2, 4]$, $D[2, 5]$, $D[2, 6]$, $D[3, 4]$, $D[3, 5]$, and $D[3, 6]$. Tracing the algorithm produces

Index	Action	Reason
[0, 1]	$S[4, 5] = \{[0, 1]\}$	
	$S[1, 2] = \{[0, 1]\}$	
[0, 2]	$S[4, 6] = \{[0, 2]\}$	
	$S[1, 3] = \{[0, 2]\}$	
[0, 3]	$D[0, 3] = 1$	Distinguished by a
[1, 2]	$S[5, 6] = \{[1, 2]\}$	
	$S[2, 3] = \{[1, 2]\}$	
[1, 3]	$D[1, 3] = 1$	Distinguished by a
	$D[0, 2] = 1$	Call to $DIST(1, 3)$
[2, 3]	$D[2, 3] = 1$	Distinguished by a
	$D[1, 2] = 1$	Call to $DIST(1, 2)$
	$D[0, 1] = 1$	Call to $DIST(0, 1)$
[4, 5]		
[4, 6]		
[5, 6]		

Merging equivalent states q_4, q_5, and q_6 yields

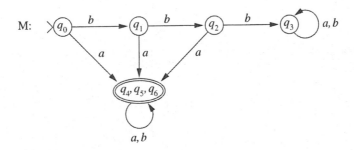

M:

The minimization algorithm completes the sequence of algorithms required for the construction of optimal DFAs. Nondeterminism and λ-transitions provide tools for designing finite automata to match complicated patterns or to accept complex languages. Algorithm 5.6.3 can then be used to transform the nondeterministic machine into a DFA, which may not be minimal. Algorithm 5.7.2 completes the process by producing the minimal state DFA.

For the moment, we have presented an algorithm for DFA reduction but have not established that it produces the minimal DFA. In Section 6.7 we prove the Myhill-Nerode Theorem, which characterizes the language accepted by a finite automaton in terms of equivalence classes of strings. This characterization will then be used to prove that the machine M′ produced by Algorithm 5.7.2 is the unique minimal state DFA that accepts L.

Computation and Reasoning

Exercises

1. Let M be the deterministic finite automaton defined by

$Q = \{q_0, q_1, q_2\}$

$\Sigma = \{a, b\}$

$F = \{q_2\}$

δ	a	b
q_0	q_0	q_1
q_1	q_2	q_1
q_2	q_2	q_0

a) Give the state diagram of M.

b) Trace the computations of M that process the strings *abaa*, *bbbabb*, *bababa*, and *bbbaa*.

c) Which of the strings from part (b) are accepted by M?

d) Give a regular expression for L(M).

2. Let M be the deterministic finite automaton

$Q = \{q_0, q_1, q_2\}$

$\Sigma = \{a, b\}$

$F = \{q_0\}$

δ	a	b
q_0	q_1	q_0
q_1	q_1	q_2
q_2	q_1	q_0

a) Give the state diagram of M.

b) Trace the computation of M that processes *babaab*.

c) Give a regular expression for L(M).

d) Give a regular expression for the language accepted if both q_0 and q_1 are accepting states.

3. Let M be the DFA with state diagram

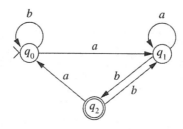

a) Construct the transition table of M.

b) Which of the strings *baba*, *baab*, *abab*, *abaaab* are accepted by M?

c) Give a regular expression for L(M).

* **4.** The recursive step in the definition of the extended transition function (Definition 5.2.4) may be replaced by $\hat{\delta}'(q_i, au) = \hat{\delta}'(\delta(q_i, a), u)$, for all $u \in \Sigma^*, a \in \Sigma$, and $q_i \in Q$. Prove that $\hat{\delta} = \hat{\delta}'$.

For Exercises 5 through 21, build a DFA that accepts the described language.

5. The set of strings over $\{a, b, c\}$ in which all the a's precede the b's, which in turn precede the c's. It is possible that there are no a's, b's, or c's.

6. The set of strings over $\{a, b\}$ in which the substring aa occurs at least twice.

7. The set of strings over $\{a, b\}$ that do not begin with the substring aaa.

8. The set of strings over $\{a, b\}$ that do not contain the substring aaa.

9. The set of strings over $\{a, b, c\}$ that begin with a, contain exactly two b's, and end with cc.

10. The set of strings over $\{a, b, c\}$ in which every b is immediately followed by at least one c.

11. The set of strings over $\{a, b\}$ in which the number of a's is divisible by three.

12. The set of strings over $\{a, b\}$ in which every a is either immediately preceded or immediately followed by b, for example, $baab$, aba, and b.

13. The set of strings of odd length over $\{a, b\}$ that contain the substring bb.

14. The set of strings over $\{a, b\}$ that have odd length or end with aaa.

15. The set of strings of even length over $\{a, b, c\}$ that contain exactly one a.

16. The set of strings over $\{a, b\}$ that have an odd number of occurrences of the substring aa. Note that aaa has two occurrences of aa.

17. The set of strings over $\{a, b\}$ that contain an even number of substrings ba.

18. The set of strings over $\{1, 2, 3\}$ the sum of whose elements is divisible by six.

19. The set of strings over $\{a, b, c\}$ in which the number of a's plus the number of b's plus twice the number of c's is divisible by six.

20. The set of strings over $\{a, b\}$ in which every substring of length four has at least one b. Note that every substring with length less than four is in this language.

* **21.** The set of strings over $\{a, b, c\}$ in which every substring of length four has exactly one b.

22. For each of the following languages, give the state diagram of a DFA that accepts the languages.

   a) $(ab)^*ba$

   b) $(ab)^*(ba)^*$

   c) $aa(a \cup b)^+bb$

   d) $((aa)^+bb)^*$

   e) $(ab^*a)^*$

Computation and Reasoning

23. Let M be the nondeterministic finite automaton

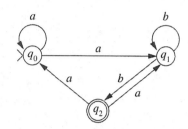

    a) Construct the transition table of M.

    b) Trace all computations of the string *aaabb* in M.

    c) Is *aaabb* in L(M)?

    d) Give a regular expression for L(M).

24. Let M be the nondeterministic finite automaton

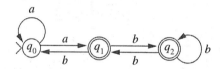

    a) Construct the transition table of M.

    b) Trace all computations of the string *aabb* in M.

    c) Is *aabb* in L(M)?

    d) Give a regular expression for L(M).

    e) Construct a DFA that accepts L(M).

    f) Give a regular expression for the language accepted if both q_0 and q_1 are accepting states.

25. For each of the following languages, give the state diagram of an NFA that accepts the languages.

    a) $(a \cup ab \cup aab)^*$

    b) $(ab)^* \cup a^*$

    c) $(abc)^* a^*$

    d) $(ba \cup bb)^* \cup (ab \cup aa)^*$

    e) $(ab^+ a)^+$

26. Give a recursive definition of the extended transition function $\hat{\delta}$ of an NFA-λ. The value $\hat{\delta}(q_i, w)$ is the set of states that can be reached by computations that begin at node q_i and completely process the string w.

Computation and Reasoning

580

For Exercises 27 through 34, give the state diagram of an NFA that accepts the given language. Remember that an NFA may be deterministic, but you should use nondeterminism whenever it is appropriate.

27. The set of strings over $\{a, b\}$ that contain either aa and bb as substrings.

28. The set of strings over $\{a, b\}$ that contain both or neither aa and bb as substrings.

* 29. The set of strings over $\{a, b\}$ whose third-to-the-last symbol is b.

30. The set of strings over $\{a, b\}$ whose third and third-to-last symbols are both b. For example, $aababaa$, $abbbbbbbb$, and $abba$ are in the language.

31. The set of strings over $\{a, b\}$ in which every a is followed by b or ab.

32. The set of strings over $\{a, b\}$ that have a substring of length four that begins and ends with the same symbol.

33. The set of strings over $\{a, b\}$ that contain substrings aaa and bbb.

34. The set of strings over $\{a, b, c\}$ that have a substring of length three containing each of the symbols exactly once.

35. Construct the state diagram of a DFA that accepts the strings over $\{a, b\}$ ending with the substring $abba$. Give the state diagram of an NFA with six arcs that accepts the same language.

36. Let M be the NFA-λ

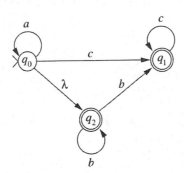

a) Compute $\lambda\text{-}closure(q_i)$ for $i = 0, 1, 2$.

b) Give the input transition function t for M.

c) Use Algorithm 5.6.3 to construct a state diagram of a DFA that is equivalent to M.

d) Give a regular expression for L(M).

Computation and Reasoning

37. Let M be the NFA-λ

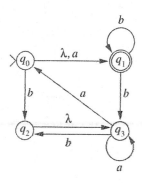

a) Compute λ-*closure*(q_i) for $i = 0, 1, 2, 3$.

b) Give the input transition function t for M.

c) Use Algorithm 5.6.3 to construct a state diagram of a DFA that is equivalent to M.

d) Give a regular expression for L(M).

38. Use Algorithm 5.6.3 to construct the state diagram of a DFA equivalent to the NFA in Example 5.5.2.

39. Use Algorithm 5.6.3 to construct the state diagram of a DFA equivalent to the NFA in Exercise 17.

40. For each of the following NFAs, use Algorithm 5.6.3 to construct the state diagram of an equivalent DFA.

a)

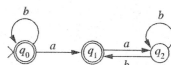

b)

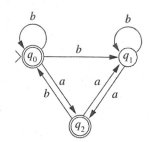

c)

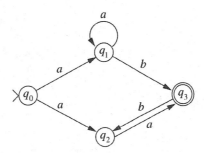

d)

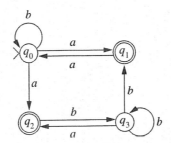

41. Build an NFA M_1 that accepts $(ab)^*$ and an NFA M_2 that accepts $(ba)^*$. Use λ-transitions to obtain a machine M that accepts $(ab)^*(ba)^*$. Give the input transition function of M. Use Algorithm 5.6.3 to construct the state diagram of a DFA that accepts L(M).

42. Build an NFA M_1 that accepts $(aba)^+$ and an NFA M_2 that accepts $(ab)^*$. Use λ-transitions to obtain a machine M that accepts $(aba)^+ \cup (ab)^*$. Give the input transition function of M. Use Algorithm 5.6.3 to construct the state diagram of a DFA that accepts L(M).

43. Assume that q_i and q_j are equivalent states of a DFA M (as in Definition 5.7.1) and $\hat\delta(q_i, u) = q_m$ and $\hat\delta(q_j, u) = q_n$ for a string $u \in \Sigma^*$. Prove that q_m and q_n are equivalent.

* 44. Show that the transition function δ' obtained in the process of merging equivalent states is well defined. That is, show that if q_i and q_j are states with $[q_i] = [q_j]$, then $\delta'([q_i], a) = \delta'([q_j], a)$ for every $a \in \Sigma$.

45. For each DFA:

    i) Trace the actions of Algorithm 5.7.2 to determine the equivalent states of M. Give the values of $D[i, j]$ and $S[i, j]$ computed by the algorithm.

    ii) Give the equivalence classes of states.

    iii) Give the state diagram of the minimal state DFA that accepts L(M).

Computation and Reasoning

583

a)

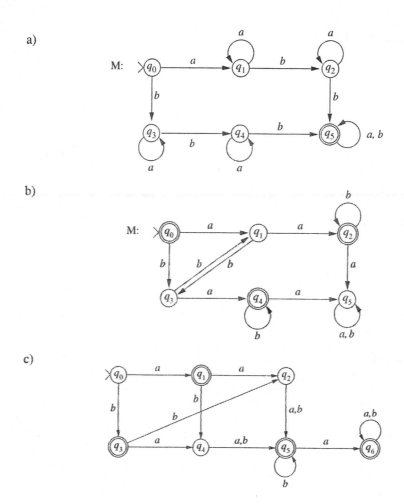

b)

c)

Bibliographic Notes

Alternative interpretations of the result of finite-state computations were studied in Mealy [1955] and Moore [1956]. Transitions in Mealy machines are accompanied by the generation of output. A two-way automaton allows the tape head to move in both directions. A proof that two-way and one-way automata accept the same languages can be found in Rabin and Scott [1959] and Sheperdson [1959]. Nondeterministic finite automata were introduced by Rabin and Scott [1959]. The algorithm for minimizing the number of states in a DFA was presented in Nerode [1958]. The algorithm of Hopcroft [1971] increases the efficiency of the minimization technique.

The theory and applications of finite automata are developed in greater depth in the books by Minsky [1967]; Salomaa [1973]; Denning, Dennis, and Qualitz [1978]; and Bavel [1983].

Backus-Naur Form Definition of Java

The programming language Java was developed under the direction of James Gosling at Sun Microsystems. Java was introduced in 1995 as a platform independent, object-oriented programming language particularly suitable for Internet and network applications. Since its introduction, Java has become one of the most commonly used languages for Internet applications.

The grammar for the language Java is derived from the BNF definition in Gosling et al. [2000]. The rules have been transformed into the standard context-free grammar notation, with the exception of retaining the designation of a terminal or a variable as optional by placing the subscript *opt* on the symbol. The use of *opt* reduces the number of rules that are needed, but rules with optional components can easily be transformed into equivalent context-free rules. A rule with a variable B_{opt} on the right-hand side can be replaced by two rules; in one, the occurrence of B_{opt} is replaced with B, and it is deleted in the other. For example, $A \rightarrow B_{opt}C$ is replaced by $A \rightarrow BC \mid C$. A rule with n occurrences of symbols subscripted with *opt* creates 2^n context-free rules. The start symbol of the grammar is the variable $\langle CompilationUnit \rangle$.

1. $\langle CompilationUnit \rangle \rightarrow \langle PackageDeclaration \rangle_{opt} \langle ImportDeclarations \rangle_{opt}$
   $\langle TypeDeclarations \rangle_{opt}$

Declarations

2. $\langle ImportDeclarations \rangle \rightarrow \langle ImportDeclarations \rangle \mid \langle ImportDeclarations \rangle$
   $\langle ImportDeclaration \rangle$

3. $\langle TypeDeclarations \rangle \rightarrow \langle TypeDeclaration \rangle \mid$
   $\langle TypeDeclarations \rangle \langle TypeDeclaration \rangle$

631

Computation and Reasoning

4. ⟨*PackageDeclaration*⟩ → **package** ⟨*PackageName*⟩ ;

5. ⟨*ImportDeclaration*⟩ → ⟨*SingleTypeImportDeclaration*⟩ | ⟨*TypeImportOnDemand*⟩

6. ⟨*SingleTypeImportDeclaration*⟩ → **import** ⟨*TypeName*⟩ ;

7. ⟨*TypeImportOnDemandDeclaration*⟩ → **import** ⟨*PackageName*⟩ . ∗ ;

8. ⟨*TypeDeclaration*⟩ → ⟨*ClassDeclaration*⟩ | ⟨*Declaration*⟩ |;

9. ⟨*Type*⟩ → ⟨*PrimitiveType*⟩⟨*ReferenceType*⟩

10. ⟨*PrimitiveType*⟩ → ⟨*NumericType*⟩ **boolean**

11. ⟨*NumericType*⟩ → ⟨*IntegralType*⟩ | ⟨*FloatingPointType*⟩

12. ⟨*IntegralType*⟩ → **byte** | **short** | **int** | **long** | **char**

13. ⟨*FloatingPointType*⟩ → **float** | **double**

Reference Types and Values

14. ⟨*ReferenceType*⟩ → ⟨*ClassOrInterfaceType*⟩ | ⟨*ArrayType*⟩

15. ⟨*ClassOrInterfaceType*⟩ → ⟨*ClassType*⟩ | ⟨*InterfaceType*⟩

16. ⟨*ClassType*⟩ → ⟨*TypeName*⟩

17. ⟨*InterfaceType*⟩ → ⟨*TypeName*⟩

18. ⟨*ArrayType*⟩ → ⟨*Type*⟩ [ ]

Class Declarations

19. ⟨*ClassDeclaration*⟩ → ⟨*ClassModifier*⟩$_{opt}$ **class** ⟨*Identifier*⟩⟨*Super*⟩$_{opt}$⟨*Interfaces*⟩$_{opt}$
       ⟨*Classbody*⟩

20. ⟨*ClassModifiers*⟩ → ⟨*ClassModifier*⟩ | ⟨*ClassModifiers*⟩⟨*ClassModifier*⟩

21. ⟨*ClassModifier*⟩ → **public** | **abstract** | **final**

22. ⟨*Super*⟩ → **extends** ⟨*ClassType*⟩

23. ⟨*Interfaces*⟩ → **implements** ⟨*InterfaceTypeList*⟩

24. ⟨*InterfaceTypeList*⟩ → ⟨*InterfaceType*⟩ | ⟨*InterfaceTypeList*⟩⟨*InterfaceType*⟩

25. ⟨*ClassBody*⟩ → { ⟨*ClassBodyDeclarations*⟩$_{opt}$ }

26. ⟨*ClassBodyDeclarations*⟩ → ⟨*ClassBodyDeclaration*⟩ |
                 ⟨*ClassBodyDeclaration*⟩⟨*ClassBodyDeclarations*⟩

27. ⟨*ClassBodyDeclaration*⟩ → ⟨*ClassMemberDeclaration*⟩ | ⟨*StaticInitializer*⟩ |
                 ⟨*ConstructorDeclarations*⟩

28. ⟨*ClassMemberDeclaration*⟩ → ⟨*FieldDeclaration*⟩ | ⟨*MethodDeclaration*⟩

Field Declarations

29. ⟨*FieldDeclaration*⟩ → ⟨*FieldModifiers*⟩$_{opt}$⟨*Type*⟩⟨*VariableDeclarators*⟩;

30. ⟨*VariableDeclarators*⟩ → ⟨*VariableDeclarator*⟩ | ⟨*VariableDeclarators*⟩ ,
                 ⟨*VariableDeclarator*⟩

31. ⟨*VariableDeclarator*⟩ → ⟨*VariableDeclaratorID*⟩ |
  ⟨*VariableDeclaratorsID*⟩ = ⟨*VariableInitializer*⟩

32. ⟨*VariableDeclaratorID*⟩ → ⟨*Identifier*⟩ | ⟨*VariableDeclaratorsID*⟩ [ ]

33. ⟨*VariableInitializer*⟩ → ⟨*Expression*⟩ | ⟨*ArrayInitializer*⟩

34. ⟨*FieldModifiers*⟩ → ⟨*FieldModifier*⟩ | ⟨*FieldModifiers*⟩⟨*FieldModifier*⟩

35. ⟨*FieldModifier*⟩ → **public** | **protected** | **private** | **final** | **static** | **transient** | **volatile**

Method Declarations

36. ⟨*MethodDeclaration*⟩ → ⟨*MethodHeader*⟩⟨*MethodBody*⟩

37. ⟨*MethodHeader*⟩ → ⟨*MethodModifiers*⟩$_{opt}$⟨*ResultType*⟩⟨*MethodDeclarator*⟩
  ⟨*Throws*⟩$_{opt}$

38. ⟨*ResultType*⟩ → ⟨*Type*⟩ | **void**

39. ⟨*MethodDeclarator*⟩ → ⟨*Identifier*⟩ (⟨*FormalParameterList*⟩$_{opt}$)
  ⟨*MethodDeclarator*⟩ [ ]

40. ⟨*FormalParameterList*⟩ → ⟨*FormalParameter*⟩ |
  ⟨*FormalParameterList*⟩⟨*FormalParameter*⟩

41. ⟨*FormalParameter*⟩ → ⟨*Type*⟩⟨*VariableDeclaratorId*⟩

42. ⟨*MethodModifiers*⟩ → ⟨*MethodModifier*⟩ | ⟨*MethodModifiers*⟩⟨*MethodModifiers*⟩

43. ⟨*MethodModifier*⟩ → **public** | **protected** | **private** | **abstract** | **final** |
  static | **synchronized** | **native**

44. ⟨*Throws*⟩ → **throws** ⟨*ClassTypeList*⟩

45. ⟨*ClassTypeList*⟩ → ⟨*ClassType*⟩ | ⟨*ClassTypeList*⟩ , ⟨*ClassType*⟩

46. ⟨*MethodBody*⟩ → ⟨*Block*⟩ | ;

Constructor Declarations

47. ⟨*ConstructorDeclaration*⟩ → ⟨*ConstructorModifiers*⟩$_{opt}$⟨*ConstructorDeclarator*⟩
  ⟨*Throws*⟩$_{opt}$⟨*ConstructorBody*⟩

48. ⟨*ConstructorDeclarator*⟩ → ⟨*SimpleTypeName*⟩ (⟨*FormalParameter List*⟩$_{opt}$)

49. ⟨*ConstructorModifiers*⟩ → ⟨*ConstructorModifier*⟩ |
  ⟨*ConstructorModifiers*⟩⟨*ConstructorModifier*⟩

50. ⟨*ConstructorModifier*⟩ → **public** | **private** | **protected**

51. ⟨*ConstructorBody*⟩ → { ⟨*ExplicitConstructorInvocation*⟩$_{opt}$⟨*BlockStatements*⟩$_{opt}$ }

52. ⟨*ExplicitConstructorInvocation*⟩ → **this** (⟨*ArgumentList*⟩$_{opt}$ } ; *mid*
  super (⟨*ArgumentList*⟩$_{opt}$ } ;

Interface Declarations

53. ⟨*InterfaceDeclaration*⟩ → ⟨*InterfaceModifiers*⟩$_{opt}$ **interface** ⟨*Identifier*⟩
  ⟨*ExtendsInterface*⟩$_{opt}$⟨*InterfaceBody*⟩

Computation and Reasoning

54. ⟨*InterfaceModifiers*⟩ → ⟨*InterfaceModifier*⟩ | ⟨*InterfaceModifiers*⟩⟨*InterfaceModifier*⟩
55. ⟨*InterfaceModifier*⟩ → **public** | **abstract**
56. ⟨*ExtendsInterfaces*⟩ → **extends** ⟨*InterfaceType*⟩ |
       ⟨*ExtendsInterfaces*⟩ , ⟨*InterfaceType*⟩
57. ⟨*InterfaceBody*⟩ → { ⟨*InterfaceMemberDeclaration*⟩$_{opt}$ }
58. ⟨*InterfaceMemberDeclarations*⟩ → ⟨*InterfaceMemberDeclaration*⟩ |
       ⟨*InterfaceMemberDeclarations*⟩⟨*InterfaceMemberDeclaration*⟩
59. ⟨*InterfaceMemberDeclaration*⟩ → ⟨*ConstantDeclaration*⟩ |
       ⟨*AbstractMethodDeclaration*⟩

Constant Declarations

60. ⟨*ConstantDeclaration*⟩ → ⟨*ConstantModifiers*⟩$_{opt}$⟨*Type*⟩⟨*VariableDeclarator*⟩
61. ⟨*ConstantModifiers*⟩ → **public** | **static** | **final**

Abstract Method Declarations

62. ⟨*AbstractMethodDeclaration*⟩ → ⟨*AbstractMethodModifiers*⟩$_{opt}$⟨*ResultType*⟩
       ⟨*MethodDeclarator*⟩⟨*Throws*⟩$_{opt}$
63. ⟨*AbstractMethodModifiers*⟩ → ⟨*AbstractMethodModifier*⟩ |
       ⟨*AbstractMethodModifiers*⟩⟨*AbstractMethodModifier*⟩
64. ⟨*AbstractMethodModifier*⟩ → **public** | **abstract**

Array Initializers

65. ⟨*ArrayInitializer*⟩ → { ⟨*VariableInitializers*⟩$_{opt}$, $_{opt}$ }
66. ⟨*VariableInitializers*⟩ → ⟨*VariableInitializer*⟩ |
       ⟨*VariableInitializers*⟩⟨*VariableInitializers*⟩

Blocks and Local Variable Declaration

67. ⟨*Block*⟩ → { ⟨*BlockStatements*⟩$_{opt}$ }
68. ⟨*BlockStatements*⟩ → ⟨*BlockStatement*⟩ | ⟨*BlockStatements*⟩⟨*BlockStatement*⟩
69. ⟨*BlockStatement*⟩ → ⟨*LocalVariableDeclarationStatement*⟩ | ⟨*Statement*⟩
70. ⟨*StaticInitializer*⟩ → **static** ⟨*Block*⟩
71. ⟨*LocalVariableDeclarationStatement*⟩ → ⟨*LocalVariableDeclaration*⟩
72. ⟨*LocalVariableDeclaration*⟩ → ⟨*Type*⟩⟨*VariableDeclarators*⟩

Statements

73. ⟨*Statement*⟩ → ⟨*StatementWithoutTrailingSubstatement*⟩ | ⟨*LabeledStatement*⟩ |
       ⟨*IfThenStatement*⟩ | ⟨*IfThenElseStatement*⟩ |
       ⟨*WhileStatement*⟩ | ⟨*ForStatement*⟩

Computation and Reasoning

74. ⟨*StatementNoShortIf*⟩ → ⟨*StatementWithoutTrailingSubstatement*⟩ |
    ⟨*LabeledStatementNoShortIf*⟩ |
    ⟨*IfThenStatementNoShortIf*⟩ |
    ⟨*IfThenElseStatementNoShortIf*⟩ |
    ⟨*ForStatementNoShortIf*⟩

75. ⟨*StatementWithoutTrailingSubstatement*⟩ → ⟨*Block*⟩
    ⟨*EmptyStatement*⟩ | ⟨*ExpressionStatement*⟩ |
    ⟨*SwitchStatement*⟩ | ⟨*DoStatement*⟩ |
    ⟨*BreakStatement*⟩ | ⟨*ContinueStatement*⟩ |
    ⟨*ReturnStatement*⟩ | ⟨*SynchronizedStatement*⟩ |
    ⟨*ThrowStatement*⟩ | ⟨*TryStatement*⟩

Empty, Labeled, and Expression Statements

76. ⟨*EmptyStatement*⟩ → ;

77. ⟨*LabeledStatement*⟩ → ⟨*Identifier*⟩ : ⟨*Statement*⟩

78. ⟨*LabeledStatementNoShortIf*⟩ → ⟨*Identifier*⟩ : ⟨*StatementNoShortIf*⟩

79. ⟨*ExpressionStatement*⟩ → ⟨*StatementExpression*⟩ ;

80. ⟨*StatementExpression*⟩ → ⟨*Assignment*⟩ | ⟨*PreincrementExpression*⟩ |
    ⟨*PredecrementExpression*⟩ | ⟨*PostincrementExpression*⟩ |
    ⟨*PostdecrementExpression*⟩ | ⟨*MethodInvocation*⟩ |
    ⟨*ClassInstanceCreationExpression*⟩

If Statements

81. ⟨*IfThenStatement*⟩ → **if** (⟨*Expression*⟩) ⟨*Statement*⟩

82. ⟨*IfThenElseStatement*⟩ → **if** (⟨*Expression*⟩) ⟨*StatementNoShortIf*⟩ **else** ⟨*Statement*⟩

83. ⟨*IfThenElseStatementNoShortIf*⟩ → **if** (⟨*Expression*⟩) ⟨*StatementNoShortIf*⟩
    else ⟨*StatementNoShortIf*⟩

Switch Statement

84. ⟨*SwitchStatement*⟩ → **switch** (⟨*Expression*⟩) ⟨*SwitchBlock*⟩

85. ⟨*SwitchBlock*⟩ → { ⟨*SwitchBlockStatementGroups*⟩$_{opt}$ ⟨*SwitchLabel*⟩$_{opt}$ }

86. ⟨*SwitchBlockStatementGroups*⟩ → ⟨*SwitchBlockStatementGroup*⟩ |
    ⟨*SwitchBlockStatementGroups*⟩⟨*SwitchBlockStatementGroups*⟩

87. ⟨*SwitchBlockStatementGroup*⟩ → ⟨*SwitchLabels*⟩⟨*BlockStatements*⟩

88. ⟨*SwitchLabels*⟩ → ⟨*SwitchLabel*⟩ | ⟨*SwitchLabels*⟩⟨*SwitchLabel*⟩

89. ⟨*SwitchLabel*⟩ → **case** ⟨*ConstantExpression*⟩ : | **default** :

While, Do, and For Statements

90. ⟨*WhileStatement*⟩ → **while** (⟨*Expression*⟩) ⟨*Statement*⟩

Computation and Reasoning

91. ⟨*WhileStatementNoShortIf*⟩ → **while** (⟨*Expression*⟩) ⟨*StatementNoShortIf*⟩

92. ⟨*DoStatement*⟩ → **do** ⟨*Statement*⟩ **while** (⟨*Expression*⟩) ;

93. ⟨*ForStatement*⟩ → **for** (⟨*ForInit*⟩$_{opt}$; ⟨*Expression*⟩$_{opt}$; ⟨*ForUpdate*⟩$_{opt}$) ⟨*Statement*⟩

94. ⟨*ForStatementNoShortIf*⟩ → **for** (⟨*ForInit*⟩$_{opt}$; ⟨*Expression*⟩$_{opt}$; ⟨*ForUpdate*⟩$_{opt}$)
    ⟨*StatementNoShortIf*⟩

95. ⟨*ForInit*⟩ → ⟨*StatementExpressionList*⟩ | ⟨*LocalVariableDeclaration*⟩

96. ⟨*ForUpdate*⟩ → ⟨*StatementExpressionList*⟩

97. ⟨*StatementExpressionList*⟩ → ⟨*StatementExpression*⟩ |
    ⟨*StatementExpressionList*⟩ , ⟨*StatementExpression*⟩

Break, Continue, Return, Throw, Synchronized, and Try Statements

98. ⟨*BreakStatement*⟩ → **break** ⟨*Identifier*⟩$_{opt}$;

99. ⟨*ContinueStatement*⟩ → **continue** ⟨*Identifier*⟩$_{opt}$;

100. ⟨*ReturnStatement*⟩ → **return** ⟨*Expression*⟩$_{opt}$;

101. ⟨*ThrowStatement*⟩ → **throw** ⟨*Expression*⟩ ;

102. ⟨*SynchronizedStatement*⟩ → **synchronized** (⟨*Expression*⟩) ⟨*Block*⟩

103. ⟨*TryStatement*⟩ → **try** ⟨*Block*⟩⟨*Catches*⟩ |
     try ⟨*Block*⟩⟨*Catches*⟩$_{opt}$⟨*Finally*⟩

104. ⟨*Catches*⟩ → ⟨*CatchClause*⟩ | ⟨*Catches*⟩⟨*CatchClause*⟩

105. ⟨*CatchClause*⟩ → **catch** (⟨*FormalParamenter*⟩) ⟨*Block*⟩

106. ⟨*Finally*⟩ → **finally** ⟨*Block*⟩

Creation and Access Expressions

107. ⟨*Primary*⟩ → ⟨*PrimaryNoNewArray*⟩ | ⟨*ArrayCreationExpression*⟩

108. ⟨*PrimaryNoNewArray*⟩ → ⟨*Literal*⟩ | **this** |
     (⟨*Expression*⟩) | ⟨*ClassInstanceCreationExpression*⟩ |
     ⟨*FieldAccess*⟩ | ⟨*MethodInvocation*⟩ |
     ⟨*ArrayAccess*⟩

109. ⟨*ClassInstanceCreationExpression*⟩ → **new** ⟨*ClassType*⟩ (⟨*ArgumentList*⟩$_{opt}$)

110. ⟨*ArgumentList*⟩ → ⟨*Expression*⟩ | ⟨*ArgumentList*⟩ , ⟨*Expression*⟩

111. ⟨*ArrayCreationExpression*⟩ → **new** ⟨*PrimitiveType*⟩⟨*DimExprs*⟩⟨*Dims*⟩$_{opt}$ |
     new ⟨*TypeName*⟩⟨*DimExprs*⟩⟨*Dims*⟩$_{opt}$

112. ⟨*DimExprs*⟩ → ⟨*DimExpr*⟩ | ⟨*DimExprs*⟩⟨*DimExpr*⟩

113. ⟨*DimExpr*⟩ → [⟨*Expression*⟩]

114. ⟨*Dims*⟩ → [ ] | ⟨*Dims*⟩ [ ]

115. ⟨*FieldAccess*⟩ → ⟨*Primary*⟩ . ⟨*Identifier*⟩ | **super** . ⟨*Identifier*⟩

116. $\langle MethodInvocation \rangle \rightarrow \langle MethodName \rangle$ ($\langle ArgumentList \rangle_{opt}$) |
$\qquad \qquad \langle Primary \rangle . \langle Identifier \rangle$ ($\langle ArgumentList \rangle_{opt}$) |
$\qquad \qquad$ **super** . $\langle Identifier \rangle$ ($\langle ArgumentList \rangle_{opt}$)

117. $\langle ArrayAccess \rangle \rightarrow \langle ExpressionName \rangle$ [$\langle Expression \rangle$] |
$\qquad \qquad \langle PrimaryNoNewArray \rangle$ [$\langle Expression \rangle$]

Expressions

118. $\langle Expression \rangle \rightarrow \langle AssignmentExpression \rangle$

119. $\langle ConstantExpression \rangle \rightarrow \langle Expression \rangle$

Assignment Operators

120. $\langle AssignmentExpression \rangle \rightarrow \langle ConditionalExpression \rangle$ | $\langle Assignment \rangle$

121. $\langle Assignment \rangle \rightarrow \langle LeftHandSide \rangle \langle AssignmentOperator \rangle \langle AssignmentExpression \rangle$

122. $\langle LeftHandSide \rangle \rightarrow \langle ExpressionName \rangle$ | $\langle FieldAccess \rangle$ | $\langle ArrayAccess \rangle$

123. $\langle AssignmentOperator \rangle \rightarrow =$ | $*=$ | $/=$ | $\%=$ | $+=$ | $-=$ | $<<=$ |
$\qquad \qquad >>=$ | $>>>=$ | $\&=$ | $=$ | $|=$

Postfix Expressions

124. $\langle PostfixExpression \rangle \rightarrow \langle Primary \rangle$ | $\langle ExpressionName \rangle$ |
$\qquad \qquad \langle PostIncrementExpression \rangle$ | $\langle PostDecrementExpression \rangle$

125. $\langle PostIncrementExpression \rangle \rightarrow \langle PostfixExpression \rangle$ $++$

126. $\langle PostDecrementExpression \rangle \rightarrow \langle PostfixExpression \rangle$ $--$

Unary Operators

127. $\langle UnaryExpression \rangle \rightarrow \langle PreIncrementExpression \rangle$ | $\langle PreDecrementExpression \rangle$ |
$\qquad \qquad + \langle UnaryExpression \rangle$ | $- \langle UnaryExpression \rangle$ |
$\qquad \qquad \langle UnaryExpressionNotPlusMinus \rangle$

128. $\langle PreIncrementExpression \rangle \rightarrow ++ \langle UnaryExpression \rangle$

129. $\langle PreDecrementExpression \rangle \rightarrow -- \langle UnaryExpression \rangle$

130. $\langle UnaryExpressionNotPlusMinus \rangle \rightarrow \langle PostfixExpression \rangle$ | $\langle UnaryExpression \rangle$ |
$\qquad \qquad ! \langle UnaryExpression \rangle$ | $\langle CastExpression \rangle$

131. $\langle CastExpression \rangle \rightarrow$ ($\langle PrimitiveType \rangle \langle Dims \rangle_{opt}$) $\langle UnaryExpression \rangle$ |
$\qquad \qquad$ ($\langle PrimitiveType \rangle$) $\langle UnaryExpressionNotPlusMinus \rangle$

Operators

132. $\langle MultiplicativeExpression \rangle \rightarrow \langle UnaryExpression \rangle$ |
$\qquad \qquad \langle MultiplicativeExpression \rangle * \langle UnaryExpression \rangle$ |
$\qquad \qquad \langle MultiplicativeExpression \rangle / \langle UnaryExpression \rangle$ |
$\qquad \qquad \langle MultiplicativeExpression \rangle \% \langle UnaryExpression \rangle$

Computation and Reasoning

591

133. ⟨AdditiveExpression⟩ → ⟨MultiplicativeExpression⟩ |
                    ⟨AdditiveExpression⟩ + ⟨MultiplicativeExpression⟩ |
                    ⟨AdditiveExpression⟩ − ⟨MultiplicativeExpression⟩

134. ⟨ShiftExpression⟩ → ⟨AdditiveExpression⟩ |
                    ⟨ShiftExpression⟩ << ⟨AdditiveExpression⟩ |
                    ⟨ShiftExpression⟩ >> ⟨AdditiveExpression⟩ |
                    ⟨ShiftExpression⟩ >>> ⟨AdditiveExpression⟩

135. ⟨RelationalExpression⟩ → ⟨ShiftExpression⟩ |
                    ⟨RelationalExpression⟩ < ⟨ShiftExpression⟩ |
                    ⟨RelationalExpression⟩ > ⟨ShiftExpression⟩ |
                    ⟨RelationalExpression⟩ <= ⟨ShiftExpression⟩ |
                    ⟨RelationalExpression⟩ >= ⟨ShiftExpression⟩ |
                    ⟨RelationalExpression⟩ **instanceof** ⟨ReferenceType⟩

136. ⟨EqualityExpression⟩ → ⟨RelationalExpression⟩ |
                    ⟨RelationalExpression⟩ == ⟨RelationalExpression⟩ |
                    ⟨RelationalExpression⟩ != ⟨RelationalExpression⟩

137. ⟨AndExpression⟩ → ⟨EqualityExpression⟩ | ⟨AndExpression⟩ & ⟨EqualiltyExpression⟩

138. ⟨ExclusiveOrExpression⟩ → ⟨EqualityExpression⟩ |
                    ⟨ExclusiveOrExpression⟩ ⟨AndExpression⟩

139. ⟨InclusiveOrExpression⟩ → ⟨ExclusiveOrExpression⟩ |
                    ⟨InclusiveOrExpression⟩ | ⟨AndExpression⟩

140. ⟨ConditionalAndExpression⟩ → ⟨InclusiveOrExpression⟩ |
                    ⟨ConditionalAndExpression⟩ &&
                    ⟨InclusiveOrExpression⟩

141. ⟨ConditionalOrExpression⟩ → ⟨ConditionalAndExpression⟩ |
                    ⟨ConditionalOrExpression⟩ ||
                    ⟨ConditionalAndExpression⟩

142. ⟨ConditionalExpression⟩ → ⟨ConditionalOrExpression⟩ |
                    ⟨ConditionalOrExpression⟩ ? ⟨Expression⟩ :
                    ⟨ConditionalExpression⟩

Literals

143. ⟨Literal⟩ → ⟨IntegerLiteral⟩ | ⟨FloatingPointLiteral⟩ | ⟨BooleanLiteral⟩ |
                    ⟨CharacterLiteral⟩ | ⟨StringLiteral⟩ | ⟨NullLiteral⟩

144. ⟨IntegerLiteral⟩ → ⟨DecimalIntegerLiteral⟩ | ⟨HexIntegerLiteral⟩ |
                    ⟨OctalIntegerLiteral⟩

145. ⟨DecimalIntegerLiteral⟩ → ⟨DecimalNumeral⟩⟨IntegerTypeSuffix⟩$_{opt}$

146. ⟨HexIntegerLiteral⟩ → ⟨HexNumeral⟩⟨IntegerTypeSuffix⟩$_{opt}$

147. ⟨HexIntegerLiteral⟩ → ⟨HexNumeral⟩⟨IntegerTypeSuffix⟩$_{opt}$

148. $\langle OctalIntegerLiteral \rangle \rightarrow \langle OctalNumeral \rangle \langle IntegerTypeSuffix \rangle_{opt}$

149. $\langle IntegerTypeSuffix \rangle \rightarrow$ l | L

150. $\langle DecimalNumeral \rangle \rightarrow$ 0 | $\langle NonZeroDigit \rangle \langle Digits \rangle_{opt}$

151. $\langle Digits \rangle \rightarrow \langle Digit \rangle \mid \langle Digits \rangle \langle Digit \rangle$

152. $\langle Digit \rangle \rightarrow$ 0 | $\langle NonZeroDigit \rangle$

153. $\langle NonZeroDigit \rangle \rightarrow$ 1 | 2 | 3 | 4 | 5 | 6 | 7 | 8 | 9

154. $\langle HexNumeral \rangle \rightarrow$ 0x$\langle HexDigit \rangle$ | 0X$\langle HexDigit \rangle$ | $\langle HexNumeral \rangle \langle HexDigit \rangle$

155. $\langle HexDigit \rangle \rightarrow$ 0 | 1 | 2 | 3 | 4 | 5 | 6 | 7 | 8 | 9 | a | b | c | d | e | A | B | C | D | E

156. $\langle OctalNumeral \rangle \rightarrow$ 0$\langle OctalDigit \rangle$ | 0$\langle OctalNumeral \rangle \langle OctalDigit \rangle$

157. $\langle OctalDigit \rangle \rightarrow$ 0 | 1 | 2 | 3 | 4 | 5 | 6 | 7

158. $\langle FloatingPointLiteral \rangle \rightarrow \langle Digits \rangle$. $\langle Digits \rangle_{opt} \langle ExponentPart \rangle_{opt}$
      $\langle FloatTypeSuffix \rangle_{opt}$ |
       . $\langle Digits \rangle \langle ExponentPart \rangle_{opt} \langle FloatTypeSuffix \rangle_{opt}$ |
      $\langle Digits \rangle \langle ExponentPart \rangle \langle FloatTypeSuffix \rangle_{opt}$ |
      $\langle Digits \rangle \langle ExponentPart \rangle_{opt} \langle FloatTypeSuffix \rangle$

159. $\langle ExponentPart \rangle \rightarrow \langle ExponentIndicator \rangle \langle SignedInteger \rangle$

160. $\langle ExponentIndicator \rangle \rightarrow$ e | E

161. $\langle SignedInteger \rangle \rightarrow \langle Sign \rangle_{opt} \langle Digits \rangle$

162. $\langle Sign \rangle \rightarrow$ + | −

163. $\langle FloatTypeSuffix \rangle \rightarrow$ f | F | d | D

164. $\langle BooleanLiteral \rangle \rightarrow$ **true** | **false**

165. $\langle CharacterLiteral \rangle \rightarrow$ '$\langle InputCharacter \rangle$' | '$\langle EscapeCharacter \rangle$'

166. $\langle StringLiteral \rangle \rightarrow$ "$\langle StringCharacters \rangle_{opt}$"

167. $\langle NullLiteral \rangle \rightarrow$ **null**

Identifier

168. $\langle Identifier \rangle \rightarrow \langle IdentifierChars \rangle$

169. $\langle IdentifierChars \rangle \rightarrow \langle JavaLetter \rangle \mid \langle IdentifierChars \rangle \langle JavaLetterOrDigit \rangle$

The variables $\langle SingleCharacter \rangle$, $\langle InputCharacter \rangle$, $\langle EscapeSequence \rangle$, and $\langle JavaLetter \rangle$ define the subsets of the 16-bit Unicode character set that can be used in input, literals, and identifiers.

Identifiers are defined by the variable $\langle Identifier \rangle$ and use characters from the Unicode alphabet so that programmers can write the source code in their own language. The first character of an identifier must be a letter, an underscore (_), or a dollar sign ($) followed by any number of Java letters or digits. Java letters and digits consist of Unicode characters for which the method Character.isJavaIdentifierPart returns true. The Java keywords are reserved and cannot be used as identifiers.

Computation and Reasoning

Input characters are Unicode characters, not including the representation of linefeed or carriage return. A ⟨*SingleCharacter*⟩ is an input character but not ' or \. An escape sequence consists of a \ followed by an ASCII symbol to signify a nongraphic character. For example, \n is the escape sequence representing linefeed. Details on both the syntax and semantics of the Java programming language can be found in Gosling et al. [2000].

Notes

Notes

Notes

Notes